Andy Warhol's mother

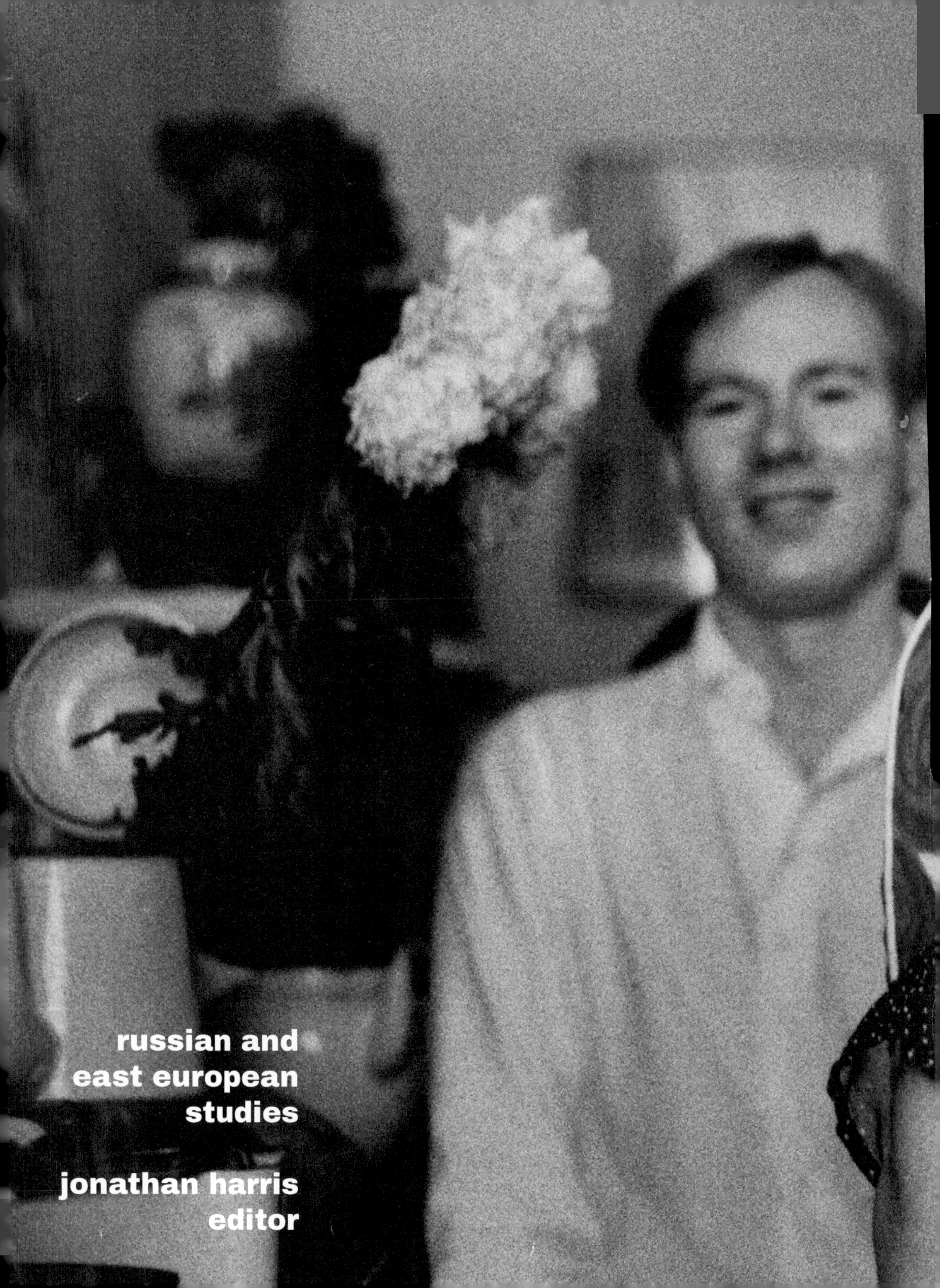
russian and
east european
studies

jonathan harris
editor

Andy Warhol's mother
the woman
behind
the artist
elaine
rusinko

A John D.S. and Aida Truxall Book

Published by the University of Pittsburgh Press, Pittsburgh, Pa., 15260

This paperback edition, Copyright © 2025, University of Pittsburgh Press

Copyright © 2024, University of Pittsburgh Press

All rights reserved

Manufactured in the United States of America

Printed on acid-free paper

10 9 8 7 6 5 4 3 2 1

Cataloging-in-Publication data is available from the Library of Congress

ISBN 13: 978-0-8229-6760-6

ISBN 10: 0-8229-6760-X

COVER PHOTOGRAPH: Portrait of Julia Warhola holding a self-portrait of Andy Warhol by Carl Fischer. © Carl Fischer / image courtesy of Ken Fischer. Within the cover photograph: Andy Warhol, *Self-Portrait*, 1966–1967. The Andy Warhol Foundation for the Visual Arts, Inc. / Licensed by Artists Rights Society (ARS), New York

COVER DESIGN: Alex Wolfe

PUBLISHER: University of Pittsburgh Press, 7500 Thomas Blvd., 4th floor, Pittsburgh, PA 15260, United States, www.upittpress.org

EU AUTHORIZED REPRESENTATIVE: Easy Access System Europe, Mustamäe tee 50, 10621 Tallinn, Estonia, gpsr.requests@easproject.com

The book should be about my mother.
She's so-o-o interesting.

—Andy Warhol

I would like someone to write a book about
Andy who knows Rusyns and Miková,
where our parents were born. Someone
who knows the kind of people our father
and mother were. Andy was like them.

—John Warhola

Contents

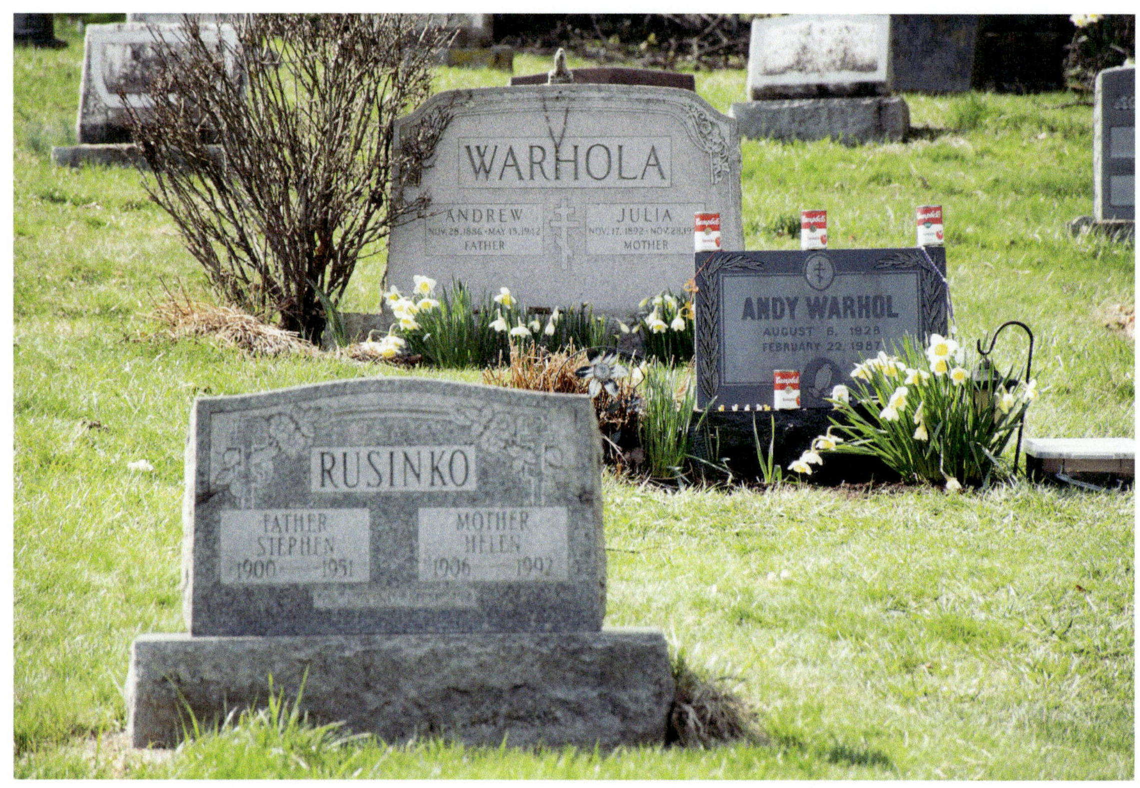

Andy Warhol gravesite, Saint John the Baptist Byzantine Catholic Cemetery, Bethel Park, PA.
Photograph by Theresa Glenn. Theresa Glenn Photography. Bethel Park, PA, 15102.

Preface

How Julia Warhola and I Found One Another

When I first visited Andy Warhol's grave at Saint John
the Baptist Byzantine Catholic Cemetery in suburban Pittsburgh, I looked up a
grassy slope to the burial site of the Warhola family. Around Andy's small but elegant polished black granite headstone, etched with the three-barred Eastern-rite
cross and an image of praying hands, fans and pilgrims had left Campbell's soup
cans, holiday ornaments, and other tokens of admiration. Further up the hill,
behind Andy's final resting place, a larger tombstone marked the grave of his parents, Andrew and Julia Warhola. But what stopped me in my tracks was the stone
just in front of Andy's, on which was carved, in large block letters, my own surname—Rusinko.

At the time, I was just beginning my work on Warhol, and the coincidence
seemed to be a sign. As a teenager, I often came across Andy Warhol in the astrological guides popular at the time—our birthdays were one day apart in August,
although separated by a generation. As I learned about the artist and my own
ancestry, I discovered that we had even more in common. Warhol's parents emigrated from Miková, a small village in Slovakia, just a few miles from Čertižne and
Vladiča, where my paternal grandparents had lived. When Warhol died in 1987,
I recognized in the broadcast newsclip of his burial the rituals of the Byzantine

Catholic religion in which I was raised. Finding the Rusinko gravesite alongside the Warholas' moved me to explore the synchronicity. Actually, the Rusinkos buried here are not related to me. But I like the idea that Rusinko is alongside Warhola in Carpatho-Rusyn eternity.

Despite all the subliminal connections, my path to Julia Warhola has been anything but direct. I began my academic career studying the modernist poetry of a Russian writer who was well known in the West, but a nonperson in the Soviet Union. When the USSR fell and archival materials were recovered by newly unfettered Russian scholars, my poet was restored to his rightful place in literary history, and my work in the field became expendable. About the same time, I was presented with an opportunity to do groundbreaking scholarship in Carpatho-Rusyn literature. This project captured my interest, since it allowed me to apply my academic skills to the culture of my ancestors. Over the next two decades, I published journal articles, translations, and a substantial book on Carpatho-Rusyn literature.

When I was asked to come up with a Rusyn-related paper for a conference where the theme was "Biography," I began a third research path, focusing on the most famous American of Carpatho-Rusyn ancestry—Andy Warhol. I immersed myself in the vast Warhol literature and studied the artist's place in American art. But what interested me about Warhol was not his art, which has been covered extensively by experts. Rather, I was intrigued by how this quintessential American artist emerged from Carpatho-Rusyn working-class roots, a background not unlike my own.

Over the next few years, I traveled to Miková and made several visits to the archives of the Andy Warhol Museum in Pittsburgh. I explored the Time Capsules, where Andy preserved various ephemera, as well as his mother's clothing, prayer books, and correspondence. I discovered that the window into "the Rusyn Warhol" is his mother. But more important, I learned that his mother has her own story that deserves telling. This book provides the first in-depth look at Julia Warhola, with an analytical focus on the sociocultural context within which she lived—the Carpatho-Rusyn immigrant experience.

There have been no major studies of Andy Warhol in the West by anyone who is familiar with Carpatho-Rusyn history, culture, and religion, or with the language that was spoken by the Warhola family in Pittsburgh and by Julia Warhola throughout her life. Observers and biographers have been, at best, bemused by Warhol's mother, and at worst, derisive. She has been described as "oddball" and "freaky." By contrast, when I became acquainted with Julia, I felt a natural connection. In the Rusyn-language videos I screened at the Andy Warhol Museum, I heard my grandmother's voice. In Julia's interviews and an English-language film, her "broken English" brings back memories of my older relatives. My father's voice resounds in her husband Andrii's admonishments to their children.

Julia's story also brought to mind recollections of the difficult life of Rusyn immigrants, especially women. When both my grandfathers died in mine accidents, one crushed in a rockfall, the other a victim of a lethal mixture of toxic mine gases called "black damp," my grandmothers suffered the tribulations that characteristically afflicted Rusyn widows—poverty and depression. In the days before government safety nets, my grandfather's dead body was carried home from the mine on a plank and left for my grandmother to deal with. My father's most vivid memory of his mother, who was also, by the way, named Julia, is an image of her clinging to the family cow for warmth as she shed tears over her hard life. (Even in an anthracite coal patch, a cow was a necessity.) Left with five children under eight, with no English and few skills, Julia Rusinko found herself in a position common to Rusyn and other immigrant women. Dependent on men for support, they often endured domestic abuse in hurried, new relationships, or became reliant on their children. Similar patterns in the lives of Julia Warhola and her sisters are familiar, and their coping techniques are admirable.

Julia's husband and brothers, like my father and grandfather, struggled for a "steady job," survived bouts of unemployment, and suffered industrial accidents in hazardous workplaces. Sustained by their Byzantine Catholic religious faith, they endured the bigotry directed at "Hunky" immigrants. Traditional family structure and supportive communities anchored the next generation in a comforting cultural space. But old-world psychology and diffidence that arose from a legacy of oppression fostered an insular attitude toward the world, placed impediments in the way of education, and hampered social mobility. No less than external obstacles, these internalized constraints hindered all but the most hardy and resolute from achieving success and self-realization.

How did Andy Warhol manage to emerge from this potentially harrowing life context, where aspirations were few and prospects were dim, into worldwide fame and unimaginable fortune? It surely had something to do with his mother, who, for most of her life, defied the limits imposed upon her by poverty, hardship, and illness. What distinguished Julia from most immigrants was the inborn artistic sense that flowed from her Carpatho-Rusyn cultural background and illuminated her life in the mountains of Eastern Europe, the slums of Pittsburgh, and the tumult of New York City. Ethnographic, historical, and sociological material sheds light on the Warhola and Zavacky families and their adaptation and self-creation in America. Conversely, their individual lives serve as an analytical window into the social and

Warhola Family Tree

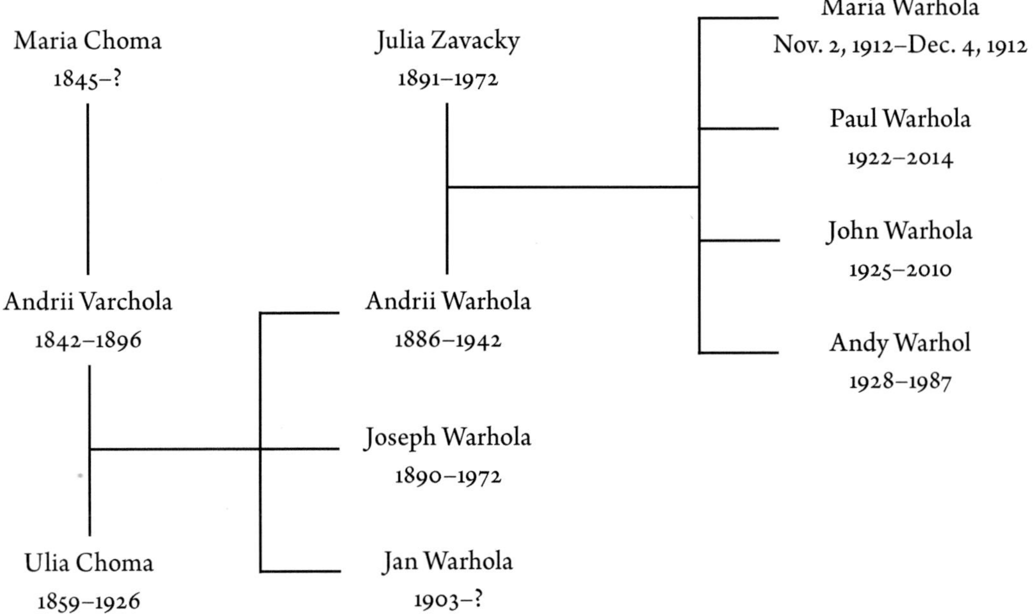

cultural context within which they survived and, to one degree or another, thrived. I tell Julia's engaging story here to bring to light the experience of the many able and resourceful Slavic immigrants who endured hardship through a lifetime of sacrifice for their children. In this case, it is the story of a simple Carpatho-Rusyn woman who had a hand in creating one of the greatest American artists of the twentieth century.

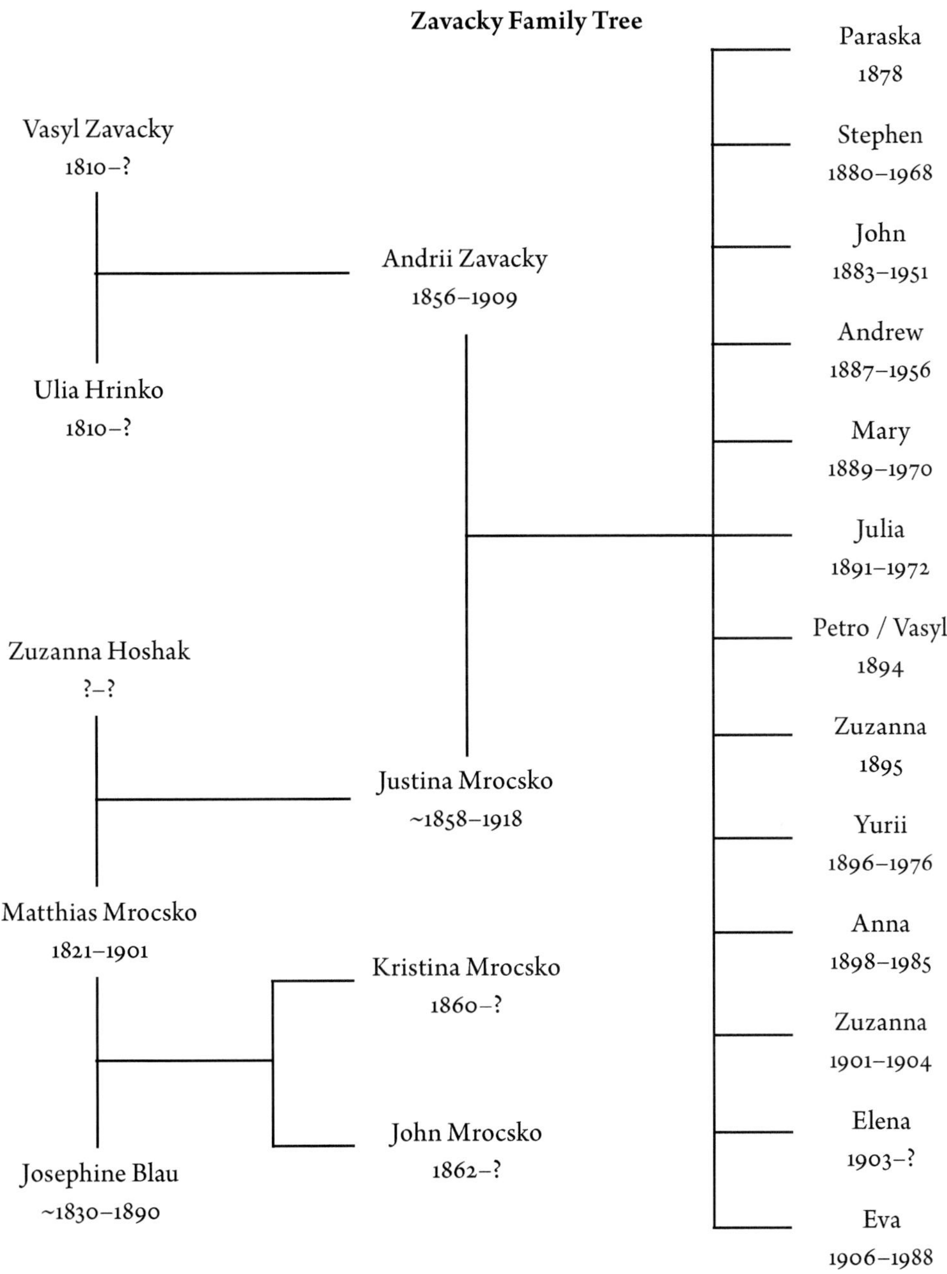

Zavacky Family Tree

- Vasyl Zavacky — 1810–?
- Ulia Hrinko — 1810–?
  - Andrii Zavacky — 1856–1909
- Zuzanna Hoshak — ?–?
- Matthias Mrocsko — 1821–1901
- Josephine Blau — ~1830–1890
  - Justina Mrocsko — ~1858–1918
  - Kristina Mrocsko — 1860–?
  - John Mrocsko — 1862–?

Children of Andrii Zavacky and Justina Mrocsko:
- Paraska — 1878
- Stephen — 1880–1968
- John — 1883–1951
- Andrew — 1887–1956
- Mary — 1889–1970
- Julia — 1891–1972
- Petro / Vasyl — 1894
- Zuzanna — 1895
- Yurii — 1896–1976
- Anna — 1898–1985
- Zuzanna — 1901–1904
- Elena — 1903–?
- Eva — 1906–1988

Warhola and Zavacky Family Trees. Family trees by Julia Rothenberg.

Note on Names, Dates, and Sources

Carpatho-Rusyns, also known as Rusyns, Rusnaks, Carpatho-Russians, and Ruthenians, are a stateless people, whose homeland today stretches across five European countries—Ukraine, Slovakia, Romania, Hungary, and Poland.[1] Rusyns have never had their own nation-state. Much of their mountainous homeland, historic Carpathian Rus', was inhospitable for agriculture and economic development, but it was strategically located. As the national borders of Eastern Europe extended and receded, Carpathian Rus' remained a peripheral region within states ruled by the major geopolitical powers. As a result, Rusyns were always among the poorest peoples of central Europe, with an uncertain ethnonational identity. At the turn of the twentieth century, about 250,000 "Ruthenians," as they were known to US immigration officials, emigrated to America, where they found work in the coal mines and steel mills of the Northeast. But their ethnic identity remained uncertain, and in many cases, became even more muddled.

Rusyns spoke East Slavic dialects that used the Cyrillic alphabet, but because they occupied an ethnolinguistic borderland, the vernacular language had admixtures of West Slavic languages (Slovak and Polish), numerous loan words from a Finno-Ugric language (Hungarian), and borrowings from German and Romanian.

Carpatho-Rusyns most often identified with their religion, Greek or Eastern-rite Catholicism, which, like their language and culture, contained elements of both East and West. The Greek (today, Byzantine) Catholic Church had a married clergy who observed the liturgy in Rusyn Church Slavonic and followed the Julian calendar, but recognized the Pope of Rome as head of their church.

In Europe, Rusyns were officially deprived of their identity after World War II, when Stalin annexed part of their homeland to Soviet Ukraine and declared that all Carpatho-Rusyns, not only in Ukraine, but in neighboring Soviet-dominated Eastern Europe, were Ukrainians. Only after the fall of the Soviet Union did a movement emerge that asserted a Carpatho-Rusyn identity. Today Rusyns are recognized as a distinct people in all the countries of Europe where they live except Ukraine, where they are considered a sub-ethnos of Ukrainian. It is only within the past few decades that Carpatho-Rusyns have become widely acknowledged throughout the world, partly because of the celebrity of their favorite son, Andy Warhol. As best as can be determined, there are approximately 1,500,000 Carpatho-Rusyns in Europe today and 600,000 to 625,000 Americans of Carpatho-Rusyn background.[2]

Names

As a result of the convoluted history of the Carpatho-Rusyn homeland, official records were kept by parish priests in Church Slavonic, Latin, Hungarian, Russian, Rusyn, or Slovak, depending on political and ecclesiastical circumstances. Consequently, because the original Cyrillic orthography was transliterated in various alphabets, there are numerous spellings for any Carpatho-Rusyn name. The reader will find several variants of given names and surnames here, with clarifications added where necessary.

The surname Warhola (Cyrillic: Вархола, pronounced Varkhola) is usually transliterated in the records as *Varchola* or *Varhola*. In America, Varchola was simplified to Warhola, although variations appeared in documents into the 1940s. Andy Warhol began to drop the *a* from his surname while still in college. His mother's surname, Zavacky (Завацкій, pronounced Zavatsky) might be spelled *Zavaczky*, *Zavaczki*, and *Zavadsky*, or feminine *Zavaczka* and *Zavadskaia* (Завадская). The various versions of Julia's family surname were simplified to Zavacky in America and usually pronounced as it appears in English, rhyming with "tacky." Traditional given names—Maria, Anna, Stefan, Andrii—recur repeatedly, making it difficult to follow a genealogical trail. Andy Warhol's father and grandfather were also named Andrew, as was Julia's father and a brother. In his birth and immigration records, Julia's husband's name appears in Hungarian spelling, András. In Rusyn, the name is Андрій (Andrii, which rhymes with "laundry.") Other spellings are found among his documents. Previous Warhol biographers have used Russian, Ukrainian, or phonetic transliterations. I will use the Rusyn "Andrii." Andy Warhol was often called Андрійко (Andriiko) by his parents, an affectionate diminutive. The elder Warhola often used "Andy" in the American context.

In her Hungarian-language birth record, Julia Zavacka's name is Julianna. She was called Ulia by her family. I use the transliterated names Ulia Zavacka and Andrii Varchola when referring to them in the Old Country or in correspondence from relatives. Ulia Varchola legally changed her name to Julia Warhola in 1942. In accordance with conventional usage, I will refer to Andy Warhol's mother as Julia in the American context. Personal names of the Warhola and Zavacky families are given in the Americanized forms they used in the immigration—Stephen, John, Joseph, Mary, and Anna. In Slovakia, female Rusyn surnames were adapted to Slovak linguistic conventions by adding the suffix -ová to the male name. Thus, Julia's sister is Eva Bezek (Rusyn) or Bezeková (Slovak).

For the genealogy of the Warhola and Zavacky families, most relevant documents can be found in the record books of the church of Saint Michael the Archangel in their ancestral village, Miková. Until 1895 the Kingdom of Hungary mandated that the Church maintain official birth, death, and marriage registers. These were subsequently transferred to regional state archives, where they became the basis for legal civil records. They have been preserved, maintained, and partially shared online by the genealogical organization FamilySearch, operated by the Church of Jesus Christ of Latter-day Saints (LDS). For Miková, only records from the last quarter of the nineteenth century are easily available, and while these registers are extremely valuable, searching them is not easy. Most are not indexed, many are incomplete, and others are illegible. Indexes, if they exist, comprise only birth records, making it necessary to browse through the original images of death and marriage records to search out details and connections.

The original images for Miková were available online until 2017, when they suddenly disappeared. FamilySearch cited privacy laws, which prohibit online images of records that are less than one hundred years old. Since the Miková parish registers include records from the past century, entire rolls of digitized film have become unavailable. Fortunately, I managed to find and download most records relevant to my research before August 2017, and later I was able to consult a few microfilms that somehow made their way into the reserve stock of local LDS FamilySearch

Centers. Information cited here from the Miková parish register refers to relevant records from "Slovakia Church and Synagogue Books, 1592–1935," which are in my possession.[3]

Dates

Lacking access to official birth certificates, few European-born Rusyns could precisely denote their birth dates. Coming from large families, where celebrations, if they occurred at all, marked name days rather than birthdays, many Rusyns had only a hazy sense of when they were born. Formal documents reveal variations and approximations, especially after immigration to the New World. Andrii's birth is registered in the church metrical books as December 7, 1886. In his 1909 marriage record, his age is given as twenty-four instead of twenty-two, and in the *1930 United States Federal Census*, his age at the time of marriage was reported as twenty-one. On an insurance policy application in 1913, he gave his birth year as 1887. Probably becoming aware of the necessity for a consistent birth date to satisfy American bureaucracy, by the time he applied for citizenship in 1924, Andrii settled on 1886 for his birth year, but perhaps attempting to reconcile the Julian and Gregorian calendars, he misidentified the month and day. His citizenship documents, draft card, and death certificate give his birth date as November 28, 1886, and this is the birth date carved on his tombstone.

The birth year on Julia Warhola's tombstone is 1892, which is a reporting error by her family. According to the parish record, she was born November 20, 1891. Such inconsistencies were typical for immigrants from east central Europe, and they persist in the records of almost all first-generation Warholas and Zavackys, making many assertions of age imprecise. Assuming the birth records in church metrical books to be most reliable, I use those dates to calculate age.

Transliteration

Villages, towns, and cities are given in the official language of the state in which they are presently located. I use Miková, the name of the Rusyn village Микова, as used in Slovakia and generally accepted in English, rather than the transliteration Mykova or the Hungarian Mikó. Names of pre–World War I Hungarian counties are given in Rusyn, with their Hungarian names added at first mention in parentheses: Zemplyn (Hung. Zemplén).

Transliteration of bibliographic sources in Russian, Rusyn, and Ukrainian follows the Library of Congress system. For ease and clarity, common Rusyn-language terms in the text, such as *holubky* (stuffed cabbage) and *pysanky* (dyed eggs), are given in a simplified version of the Library of Congress system, without diacritical marks. Terms that are already accepted in English, such as *Amerikansky Russky Viestnik* (*American Rusyn Messenger*) and *Ruska dolina* (Rusyn valley), as well as religious terminology, will be given in their established forms.

Sources

Early Warhol biographers had the advantage of knowing the artist and his mother, and they were able to interview family and associates. While working on this project, I often wished I had started it ten years earlier. I was able to meet Julia's son Paul and his wife, and I spoke with her son John by phone, but I did not know then that I would be writing a biography of their mother. Luckily, nieces and cousins, as well as numerous grandchildren, have been happy to share their memories. I am fortunate to have had access to interviews and oral histories of principals and relatives who are no longer with us: Julia Warhola, interviewed by Bernard Weinraub, John Warhola by Matt Wrbican, John and Paul Warhola and Eva Bezeková by Michal Bycko, and others.

For sources, I am most indebted to Andy Warhol. In the 610 boxes he called Time Capsules, along with his own receipts, letters, ticket stubs, and other miscellaneous items, he preserved articles of his mother's clothing, her prayer books, legal documents, medical bills, notes, letters from grandchildren, and Rusyn-language correspondence with relatives in Slovakia. Also in the Andy Warhol Museum Archives are unreleased private videos that show the Rusyn-language interaction between mother and son. These videos have not previously been screened or analyzed by anyone who understands the language. In addition, the John Warhola family preserved audio tapes from the 1950s, on which Julia recorded folk songs, hymns, prayers, and original tales she composed for her sons. These primary sources reanimate Julia and allow us to hear her story in her own voice.

Writing about Julia and her family at such a remove also has advantages. Digitized genealogical records, court files, employee records, and online newspapers, both American and Rusyn, fill in the blanks of fragile memories, amend the mistakes in family lore, and poke holes in mythological bubbles, providing information that was beyond the reach of previous Warhol biographers. Searchable newspaper archives provide access to previously unknown facts. To better understand life in the Old Country, immigration to America, and Julia's experience in Depression-era Pittsburgh, I have done extensive library and online research in English- and Rusyn-language sources. For color and detail, and to bring Julia's experience to life, I make use of Carpatho-Rusyn folklore, as well as Rusyn American literature.

Andy Warhol's mother

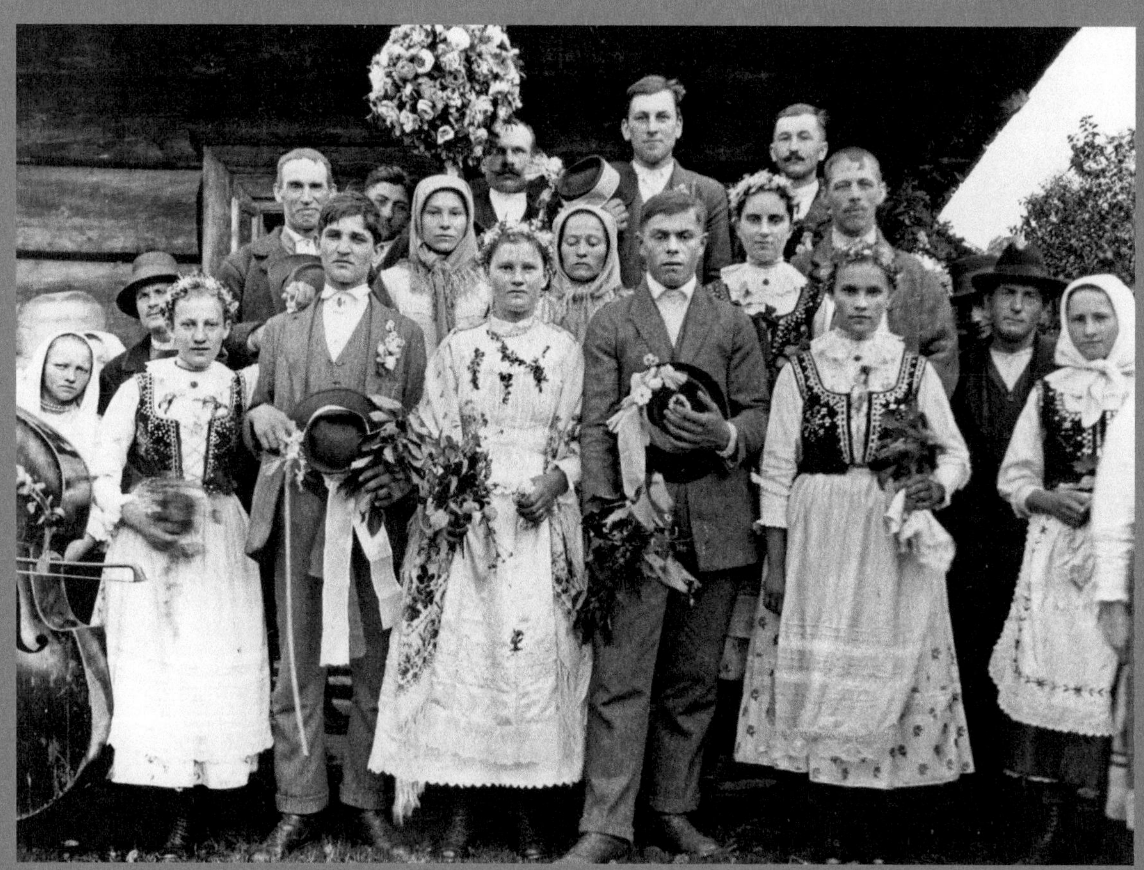

Figure 1.1. A traditional Lemko-Rusyn wedding, 1923.

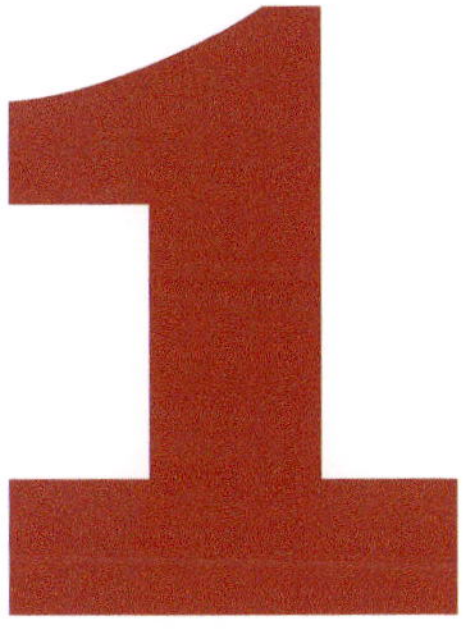

"My Town—Miková, Czechoslovakia"

Throughout her life, Julia Warhola delighted in memories of her wedding: "Wedding was beautiful, beautiful. Three-day wedding."[1] A traditional Carpatho-Rusyn wedding was literally a three-day event. In time-honored fashion, the 1909 nuptials of Ulia Zavacka and Andrii Varchola were saturated with ritualism and magical significance. Combining song, dance, music, and the spoken word, the wedding celebration was a multifaceted piece of folk theater, performed expertly by unsophisticated, barely literate peasants. Everyday Rusyn life was steeped in tradition and ritual that harked back to ancient times, but no occasion was more infused with theatrical ritual and superstition than the wedding.[2]

For Carpatho-Rusyn peasants, marriage was primarily an economic transaction.[3] As described in numerous folk songs, young women feared being married off to an elderly man out of financial considerations. Ulia was spared this anxiety. The Zavacky family was from the middle class of Miková peasant society. Her maternal grandfather, a skilled tradesman from Poland, had built a water mill in Miková, which brought in extra income for the family. Ulia's parents could offer a respectable dowry and would have been on the lookout for a moral, stable, and industrious young man. While mothers played the major role in matchmaking, courting and betrothal were the initiative of the prospective groom. With a delegation of relatives and friends, the young man went to the home of his chosen mate to present his proposal to her parents. To divert the attention of unclean spirits, his spokesman introduced the subject obliquely in formulaic speeches, with a metaphor that only a girl from an agricultural society might appreciate: "We hear that you have a young heifer to sell. We would like to buy it." When the parents and young people came to an agreement in these staged negotiations, bargaining over the bride's dowry ensued under the influence of homemade brandy.

For Ulia and Andrii, the formal matchmaking would have followed the same plot sequence, but it had a more unconventional prologue. As Julia Warhola later described it:

> My husband . . . come from my town—Miková, Czechoslovakia. I meet him when I'm seventeen, he's twenty. My husband, Andy, he go to America a year before and then come back to town.[4] He was good-looking. Blond. My husband had curly hair. Oh! He came back to village and every girl want him. Fathers would give him lots of money, lots of land to marry daughter. He no want. He want me. . . . So Andy comes into house. Oh so good-looking. I never forget. I come back from fields and I carried wheat. He sees me. "Who's this little girl?" he says. My Momma laughs. "She's gonna be your wife," she says. My mother, she jokes, for fun.

It was common for Rusyn men to emigrate to America to earn money, with the intention of returning to the homeland, buying land, and settling down. In Andrii Varchola, Ulia's mother recognized a good marriage prospect. In an unconstrained manner that would later also characterize Julia's maternal style, she set the process in motion. But while it may have been love at first sight for Andrii, Ulia was not convinced. For a Carpatho-Rusyn peasant girl, marriage meant moving in with her husband's family, where she might be looked upon as just an extra pair of hands. "I was seventeen, I know nothing. He wants me, but I no want him. I no think of no man. My mother and father say, 'Like him, like him.' I scared. My Daddy beat me, beat me to marry him. What do I know? The priest—oh, a nice priest—come. 'This Andy,' he says, 'a very nice boy. Marry him.' I cry. I no know. Andy visit again. He brings me candy. I no have candy. He brings me candy, wonderful candy. And for this candy, I marry him."[5]

The dowry was arranged, the parish priest blessed the betrothal and announced the banns, and a wedding date was set for a weekend in May, a month after the end of the Lenten season and the Easter holiday.[6] The night before the wedding, Ulia and her *druzhky* (bridesmaids) wove wreaths of periwinkle, a flowering evergreen plant that symbolized everlasting love. Andrii spent the night singing and dancing with his groomsmen, while his female relatives, led by his godmother, the senior *svashka* (matron of honor), prepared the wedding flag—a branch of spruce decorated with colorful kerchiefs, ribbons, and streamers to represent the star of Bethlehem. The next morning, the groom's party was assembled at the Varchola home by the *starosta* (master of ceremonies), who, alongside the senior *svashka*, served as director and lead actor of the play. It was their duty to ensure that all tradition was carefully observed. After prayers, rhetorical speeches, and refreshments, not sparing strong drink, Andrii received his parents' blessing. In response to his mother's tears, he sang, "Oh mother, don't cry, but be glad, for your son will bring into your home a worker for you. And a dear helpmate for my heart." Fronted by the wedding flag, the groom's party proceeded to the bride's house with shouts, whistles, songs, and lively music.

At the Zavacky home, the groom's party found the doors locked. A ritual drama ensued, again using allegorical speech to deceive evil spirits.

> —*Slava Isusu Christu!* Glory to Jesus Christ! Christ is among us![7]
> —*Slava na viki!* Glory forever. He is and will be! . . . And what do you want?
> —We know that you have in your garden a beautiful rose, which we would like to transplant to our garden so it may bear fruit. We have a young lad who would like to care for that rose.

Playing out their scripted adversarial role, the bride's family demanded to know whether the bridegroom and his representatives were wise and God-fearing people. The *starosta* responded by reciting a prayer and solving a riddle to their satisfaction. When the groom's party at last gained entrance and asked for the bride, they were presented with an old woman, a Gypsy, or a boy dressed in women's clothing. Only on the third request was Ulia brought forward, to the musical refrain: "This is the right one / A great beauty. / This one is ours / Most beautiful of all." After the *starosta* made the sign of the cross and marked the door with his ax to prevent unclean spirits from joining them, the young couple left the house, carefully stepping out on the same foot so they might live together in harmony.

Although their wedding took place near the end of May, Ulia probably wore fur and Andrii, a long linen coat, to demonstrate affluence, and according to superstition, to ensure future prosperity. "I wear white," Ulia recalled in 1966. Her homespun linen dress was embroidered with white threads in patterns that originally had magical and protective significance. "I beautiful. My husband had big white coat. Funny, funny. He had hat with lots of ribbons. Three rows of ribbons." Ulia probably wore an open tiara-like wedding headdress decorated with periwinkle and flowing with colorful beaded and embroidered streamers that fell below her knees. "I had hair like gold. Hair down shoulder, oh beautiful hair."[8] According to tradition, a maiden's headdress showed off her hair, which hung in a single braid. A married woman covered her hair with a cap or kerchief, reflecting ancient beliefs about the magic powers of women's hair. Only on her wedding day did a woman's hair flow freely in public. Ulia's joyful memory of her "hair like gold" is a poignant evocation of innocent youth.

Church bells rang as Ulia and Andrii stood before the door of Saint Michael the Archangel Greek Catholic Church, where they had both been baptized. Saint Michael's was a simple masonry building topped by a graceful baroque cupola and a three-barred cross. The nuptial ceremony of the Eastern Catholic rite of Byzantium, as developed among the East Slavs, was accompanied by a cappella congregational singing of the Carpatho-Rusyn *prostopenie*, or plainchant. Reverend Father Jan Turkiniak led Ulia and Andrii down the aisle, chanting litanies that asked God to bless them with a blameless marriage and the happiness of abundant fertility. Ulia promised to be subject in everything to her husband, and Andrii pledged to love his wife. The climax of the marriage ceremony was the "crowning" of the bride and groom. Father Turkiniak blessed the wedding wreaths prepared by the bridesmaids and placed them on the heads of Ulia and Andrii, praying, "Lord our God, crown them with glory and honor." After Ulia offered a special prayer before the icon of the Blessed Virgin Mary, the couple were showered with grain as they left the church for the bride's home.

Ulia remembered the wedding festivities: "A day and a half with my Momma. A day and a half with his Momma. Big beautiful celebration. Eating, drinking, barrels of whiskey. Wonderful food—eggs, rice with buttered sugar, chickens, noodles, prunes with sugar, bread, nice bread, cookies made at home. Beautiful. . . . And music, such music. Seven gypsies playing music." The food that Ulia tried to put into English for the interviewer was the traditional fare of Rusyn celebrations—*halushky* (dumplings or noodles sautéed with cabbage and bacon), *pirohy* (ravioli-like dumplings filled with potatoes or bryndza cheese), *holubky* (stuffed cabbage), and *kolachy* (rolled pastry filled with nuts, apricots, or poppy seed)—along with ham, sausage, and chicken. The couple ate from a common plate and drank from a single cup. They sang joyful wedding songs with the guests, and danced the polka, waltz, and czardas. The revelry continued until it was time for the saddest and most emotional ritual—the bride's farewell to her family. In a formal speech, the *starosta* thanked the bride's parents for bringing up their daughter righteously. Ulia bowed to her parents and asked forgiveness for her childhood transgressions, as her bridesmaids intoned sorrowful songs of parting and the groomsmen shouldered her feather-down quilt and other household items for the move to her new home.

In a theatrical change of scene, the wedding drama moved to the Varchola house for the second act. Andrii's mother greeted her new daughter-in-law with the ceremonial welcome of bread and salt. "What have you brought with you, daughter-in-law?" Presenting her gifts of bread and money to the women of the groom's family, Ulia said, "I bring the word of God, God's gifts, and God's blessings." Andrii's mother daubed the faces of bride and groom with honey for a sweet life together and slipped an egg down the front of Ulia's bodice, a superstition to ensure easy childbearing. Relatives and friends—the Chomas, Kacsurs, Hladoniks, Janocskos, Kalinyaks, and other villagers—gathered for more singing, dancing, feasting, and merrymaking, until it was time for another central event of the wedding, the "capping" ritual (*chepchovanie*). The *starosta* ordered that the bride's headdress be removed, asking rhetorically, "Am I to cut off your head, or just take off your wreath?" The bride twice answered, "Cut off my head!" before she finally agreed to give up her maiden's tiara. The married women from the groom's family then plaited the bride's loose hair, wrapped it in a bun, and covered it with a cap suitable for a married woman. From now on, Ulia's outward appearance told the world that she was no longer a maiden, but a wife.

The male guests lined up for the *riadovyi tanets* (dance in a row) to dance a few minutes with the bride, paying for the privilege with a monetary contribution to the couple's new life and receiving in return a shot of whiskey. All the while, like a Greek chorus, the *svashki* (matrons) sang age-old rhyming verses that narrated and commented on the action:

> Glory to Jesus Christ, / We have a beautiful bride // Our bride is like a pine tree / Where did such a girl grow? // Our girl has been capped / She is now a *baba* // Our girl has married / Leaving her friends behind // She's still ours, not yet yours / give some money and you will have her // Whoever gives for the cap / Can dance with the bride // God the Lord rejoices / The bride is dancing with her papa // May the good Lord rejoice / The bride is dancing with the groom // This lovely bride / Has grown up for you // Take her with you / And love her till death.[9]

Finally, with music and practical jokes, the young couple was led off to the bed prepared for them in the loft, while the merrymakers continued the festivities, improvising erotic jokes and bawdy songs. Many years later in Pittsburgh, Julia playfully told her granddaughter how, as a result of the revelry, Andrii clumsily navigated the ladder to their nuptial bed.[10]

Mythmakers

The Carpatho-Rusyn wedding ritual was a theatrical transformation of everyday life. Thanks to Julia Warhola's 1966 interview in *Esquire*, her wedding has become the single fixed point for the narrative of her early life. And yet, it cannot be taken as historical fact. Julia's brother Stephen was a witness to the marriage. His daughter Nora recalled her father's reaction to Julia's story, chuckling at the memory. "When she's talking about her wedding, he started to laugh . . . she said they had seven gypsies playing. He was laughing, he said that's not true."[11] Stephen's refutation was surely overstated, given the known facts from official records and the persistence of custom. But according to her niece, Julia was "a talker," who told exaggerated stories for the amusement of her audience.[12] Her story and her public image were passed down to subsequent audiences of scholars, biographers, and fans, who came to know Julia through the *Esquire* interview. In fact, the self-image she projected in her wedding narrative was not entirely natural, but rather a construction of personal identity in the context of Carpatho-Rusyn culture.

The interviewer, Bernard Weinraub, reports that he did not prompt Mrs. Warhola to talk about her wedding. Rather, Julia, who was "sort of in charge of the interview," launched into her personal narrative performance.[13] Scholars of narrative explain, "In the form a particular narrator gives to a history, we read the more or less abiding concerns and constraints of the individual and his or her community."[14] Accordingly, in Julia's narrative, we see the forces and features of her culture. Although her first reaction to Andrii was that he was "oh, so good-looking," Mrs. Warhola highlights, and probably exaggerates, her innocence, an obligatory element of Carpatho-Rusyn peasant culture. Pointing up the peasant woman's lack of agency in marital matters, she is persuaded to accept Andrii's proposal by a priest, albeit "a nice priest," and her father, who "beats" her, although this harsh phrasing may arise from Julia's limited English. In the end, it is Andrii's gift of "wonderful candy," probably a taste of America, that induces Ulia to accept him. These wistful plot features give way to the joyful narrative of the wedding, as the elderly Julia Warhola indulges in happy memories. The "barrels of whiskey," "wonderful food," the groom's ribboned hat, and the "seven gypsies playing music" are glowing details of traditional culture that brighten the gloom of her later life. The repeated exclamation "Oh!" highlights the expressive character of her performance, and the evaluative comment, "I beautiful," exposes its function. Telling the tale at almost seventy-five years of age, Julia asserts a romantic vision of her worth and vitality as a beautiful young bride in Miková.

Julia's story of her wedding was a performance in the sense that the term is used in performance studies: "a certain type of particularly involved and dramatized oral narrative," a purposeful presentation of the self.[15] From Julia's earliest performances in Miková to the stories she told her children and recorded on tape, to her relationships with her son's New York friends and her appearances in his film and video, performativity was basic to her personality and her communicative style. She passed on her proclivity for performance to her son Andy, who later made films in which self-dramatizing personalities projected a unique presence or identity in staged events and improvisations.[16] According to Weinraub, his interview with Mrs. Warhola took place in her apartment on the lower level of her son's house, where "all these weird people were wandering around. And there was this very old lady in black sitting there. She was a total fish out of water."[17] In a transformative performance for the interviewer, the "old lady in black" held on to the reality of the past, reveling in the identity she enjoyed as the innocent peasant girl with golden hair at the center of the wedding story.

The entire Carpatho-Rusyn wedding was, in fact, not real life, but ritual, "where theater and anthropology overlap."[18] In his study of Carpatho-Rusyn drama, the Russian scholar Evgenii Nedziel'skii pointed out that viewers of the wedding ritual expected not realistic role-playing on the part of the participants, but a theatrical transformation that would produce a kind of catharsis in viewers.[19] Conventional gestures, formalized expressions, and self-dramatizations were expected. One can imagine that Ulia excelled as a histrionic actress-bride. As time passed, and as she told and retold the narrative of her wedding, she reconstructed and embellished it.

Perhaps self-mythologizing on Julia's part should not surprise us. Julia's son, Andy Warhol, was known as a consummate mythmaker. He crafted his own public persona out of artistic invention (self-portraits that conceal more than they reveal), psychological defenses (his monosyllabic public nonstatements), fabrication (literary self-representations that were in fact produced by associates), appropriation (unauthorized use of photographs), and outright deception (dispatching an impersonator to substitute for him at college lectures).[20] Biographers have conceded defeat in their attempts to define his character and biography in explicit terms, resorting instead to hollow statements of ambiguity—he was "the tycoon of passivity," or "a trickster, artfully evading our attempts to pin him down," "a character without a past, who conjured himself out of his own head."[21] In the most recent biography, the art historian Blake Gopnik notes, "There had always been something theatrical about the way [Warhol] refused to be tied down to the simple facts of his own existence—about the way he'd always shaped his myth and persona to suit himself and please others."[22]

Warhol's persona was built on performance, on the presumed irrelevance of reality. He reportedly said, "Who wants the truth? That's what show business is for—to prove that it's not what you are that counts, it's what they think you are."[23]

Did Warhol learn to deflect, obfuscate, and embellish at his mother's knee? Of the numerous commentators who have mentioned Julia's tendency to embroider reality and create stories, Joseph Giordano was most explicit. An advertising art director who worked with Warhol in the late 1950s, Giordano claims that he "almost lived [with Andy and his mother] for five or six years." Archival information attests to a close relationship between Giordano and Julia, whom he called "Missy." Some of his memories strain credulity, but he admits that in Julia's stories, he could not distinguish myth from reality. "She was exactly like Andy—she was a myth-maker. . . . And I think this was the basis of [Warhol's] whole character. . . . He knows how to perpetuate the myth. . . . That is exactly what Missy was. He had the most wonderful teacher in the world."[24]

Indeed, Julia Warhola had her own flare for "show-business." Gifted with a theatrical personality, she developed her natural talent for performance and her penchant for self-mythologizing as she practiced the folkways of her native culture. Throughout her life, she created an artistic world of imagination to supplement and enhance her dull reality. The traditional culture of Carpathian-Rus', communicated across generations, encompassing attitudes, values, beliefs, norms, and behaviors, was a psychological and social construct that defined Julia Warhola's world. Her artist-son internalized his mother's creative interaction with the world, turning the focus of his own creative energy to American life and fashioning artistic images from commonplace items. Like participants in the Rusyn wedding drama, he played with different versions of reality in improvisational films, where actors role-played themselves in routine activities drawn out to marathon length. Warhol's camp artistic taste "[moved] insistently towards performance, towards the theatricalisation of everyday life."[25] Ethnographers used the same formulation to describe Carpatho-Rusyn folkways. Evgenii Nedziel'skii compared the peasants' theatricalization of everyday life to the elaborate court ceremony of English royalty: "The theatrical ceremony of the royal court pales by comparison to the traditional, ritualistic, and superstitious aspect of everyday Carpatho-Rusyn peasant life."[26] Warhol transferred his mother's old-world creative instinct to contemporary American life, employing an aesthetic that derived from a wealth of folk tradition rooted in Ulia Zavacka's lived experience—Carpatho-Rusyn life and culture in the village of Miková.

The People from Nowhere

Carpatho-Rusyns, also known as Rusyns, Rusnaks, Carpatho-Russians, Lemkos, and Ruthenians, are a stateless people whose homeland is located on the northern and southern slopes of the Carpathian Mountains in central Europe.[27] Ulia Zavacka, who would become Andy Warhol's mother, was born in 1891 in the village of Miková, in what was then the Kingdom of Hungary, a largely autonomous component of the Austro-Hungarian Dual Monarchy. Miková was located near the border with Austrian Galicia in Zemplyn (Hung. Zemplén) County, and today it is in the Prešov Region of northeastern Slovakia.

Magyars were a numerical minority in the multiethnic state they ruled, and to counteract the demographic trend, the Hungarian government carried on a rigorous campaign to assimilate national minorities. But the Carpatho-Rusyn peasants living in the villages of the kingdom were largely untouched by national movements or governmental compulsion. They went on speaking their own East Slavic dialects, practicing their Eastern Catholic religion, and performing the time-honored customs and traditions that predated states and monarchs. They viewed the nobility and government officials with suspicion and distrust, and it was typical of Rusyns to deride the gentry as lazy and pompous. "He dresses like a *pan*" (gentleman) is an insult directed at a pretentious peasant. "She thinks she's a *pani*" (lady) is a slur aimed at a woman who avoids work and puts herself above others of her own class. This way of thinking, hardwired in simple Rusyns, was unconsciously absorbed by their American children. Andy Warhol's secretary wrote, "The worst thing that Andy could think to say about someone was that he was 'the kind of person who thinks he's better than you,'" and according to his colleague from the 1970s, Bob Colacello, "his usual response to a star he had met was not 'Gee' and 'Wow' and 'Great'—it was 'Who does she think she is?'"[28]

The Hungarian government's policy of national assimilation had an impact on Rusyn peasants through the educational system. Formal education was considered a pursuit of the nobility and was little valued in Rusyn villages. As they later indicated to US census officials, none of the Zavacky or Warhola immigrants had more than a few years of elementary education.[29] By the time Ulia and Andrii began attending school in Miková, students were required to demonstrate proficiency in Hungarian, and only religion was taught in Rusyn. However, peasants never gained a real mastery of Hungarian, which was largely useless in practice, and most remained semiliterate in their own language. The Hungarian Ministry of Education replaced Cyrillic, the natural alphabet of the Rusyn language, with the Latin alphabet in a complicated

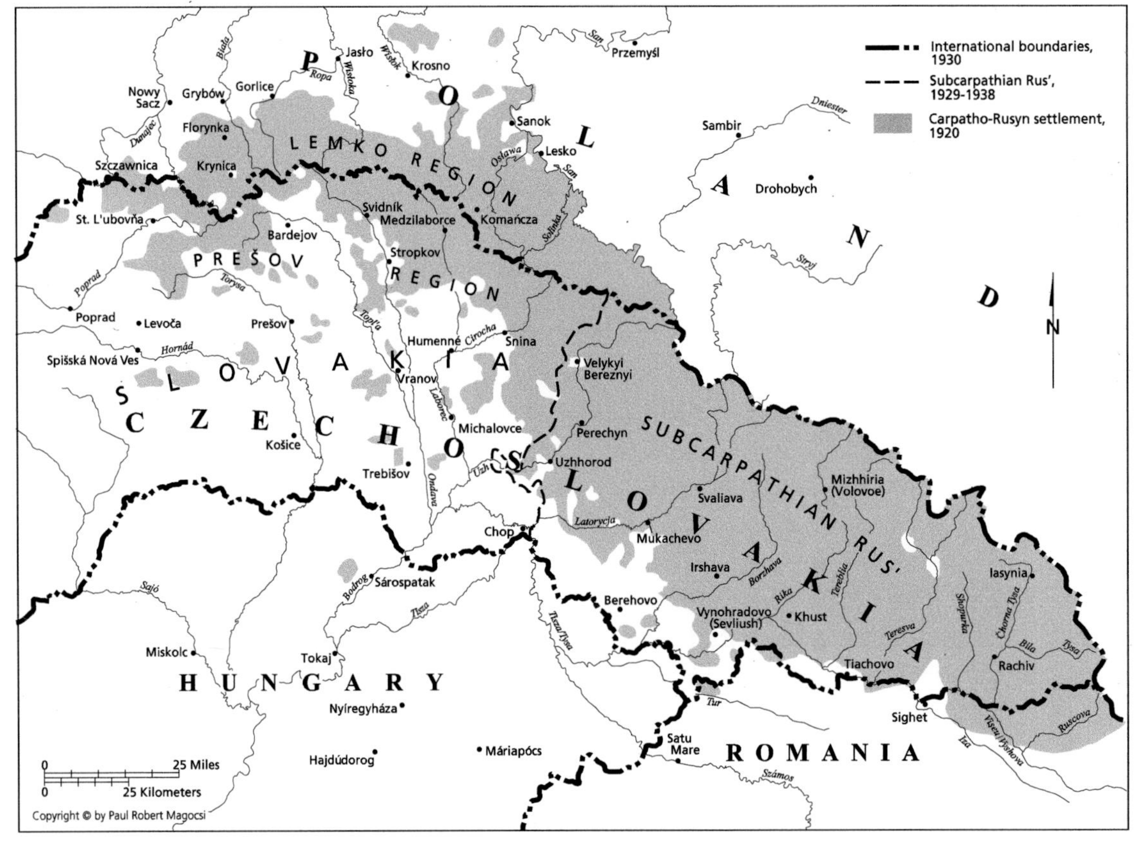

Figure 1.2. Carpathian Rus', 1919–1938. Miková is located four miles northwest of Medzilaborce.

Hungarian transcription. Throughout their adult lives, Julia and her relatives used this script, later mixed with elements of Slovak and the random misspelled English word or phrase, in a basic phonetic spelling, making their notes and letters a challenge for researchers.

Another imposition of the Hungarian government on peasant life was military conscription.[30] Every male citizen between the ages of twenty and thirty-six was subject to compulsory military service. In the infantry, recruits served one to three years, followed by nine or ten years in the active reserves, during which time they were required to participate in annual training. Even after their obligation was completed, conscripts could be called up in time of war. This was a burden for peasants, who made their living through time-intensive agricultural labor. Andrii Varchola emigrated to America first in 1905 at the age of nineteen or twenty, perhaps with the possibility of conscription in mind. By 1911, when he was back in Miková, the Austro-Hungarian army was conducting maneuvers in the region. When war broke out in the Balkans in 1912, Andrii again departed for the United States, leaving his wife in Miková.

The Carpatho-Rusyn people endured these governmental intrusions into their lives with relative equanimity, not allowing them to deflect the course of tradition. The inhabitants of Miková continued to speak, write, and pray in Rusyn, identifying themselves as Rusnaks, or simply as "our people," and referring to their language as *po-nashomu*, that is, "our way of speaking." If they were asked about their identity, Rusyn peasants might use the word *rus'kyi*, the ethnonym for "Rusyn." Since it sounded similar to "Russian" (*russkii*), it created another level of ethnic confusion for outsiders and later for Americans. Their identity as Rusyns was based primarily on their language, religion, and folklore. Rusyns in the homeland, and later immigrants in America, sang the hymn composed in 1851 by their "national awakener" Aleksander Dukhnovych, a declaration of identity and fidelity that is sung by Carpatho-Rusyns worldwide down to the present day.[31]

> I was, am, and will always be a Rusyn.
> I was born a Rusyn
> And will not forget my worthy people.
> I will remain their son.
> My father and mother were Rusyn
> As are all my family,
> Sisters and brothers,
> All the community.
> I came into the world in the Carpathians,
> Where I first breathed Rusyn air.
> I was nourished by Rusyn bread
> And rocked in a Rusyn cradle.[32]

But history was unkind to Carpatho-Rusyns, never granting them the time and stability necessary for socioeconomic progress and cultural development. Instead, they were caught in the ebb and flow of borders, as one controlling force followed another. Hungarian control came to an end with the collapse of Austria-Hungary after World War I, when boundaries were redrawn, and new states created. In May 1918, a group of Czechs and Slovaks met in the Loyal Order of Moose Building on Penn Avenue in Pittsburgh to announce their plan to establish an independent

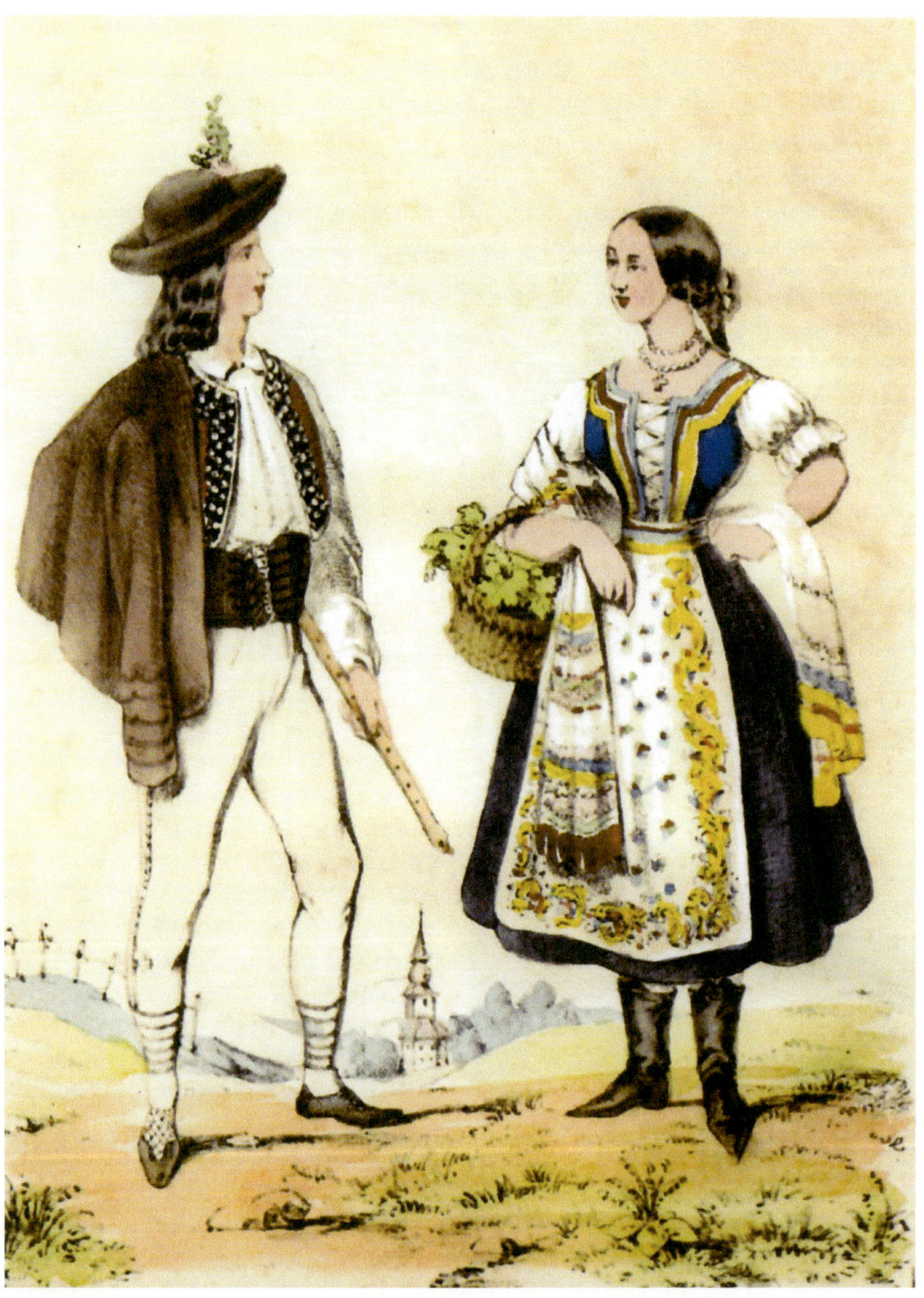

Figure 1.3. Frontispiece to the literary almanac *Greetings to the Rusyns for the Year 1851*, compiled by Aleksander Dukhnovych.

nation of Czechs and Slovaks. The document, known as the Pittsburgh Agreement, called for political and cultural autonomy for Slovakia. When the nation-state of Czechoslovakia was inaugurated after the war, Carpatho-Rusyns were included as an official nationality with their own semiautonomous province called Subcarpathian Rus'. However, the Rusyn province excluded eastern Slovakia.[33] This meant that the approximately 100,000 Rusyns living in Zemplyn, Sharysh (Hung. Sáros), and Spish (Hung. Szepes) Counties remained a minority in a state ruled by Slovaks, a related, but still alien, ethnicity. The Rusyn religious and cultural center in Slovakia was the town of Prešov, where the future bishop Pavel Goidych (Pavel Gojdič) actively promoted Carpatho-Rusyn identity and the use of the Rusyn language in schools. Theoretically, Czechoslovakia guaranteed minority rights in a liberal, democratic government, and at first, the vernacular Rusyn language was allowed in education. But through the 1920s, as Slovakia pushed for greater control over its minorities, Rusyn gave way to Slovak in schools, and Carpatho-Rusyns in eastern Slovakia once again endured assimilationist pressure.

To demonstrate loyalty to the new republic, the central government promoted a "Czechoslovak" national identity for all its citizens, blurring ethnonational distinctions. The term caught on only with Carpatho-Rusyns, who up to now had lacked a generally recognized identity, and Jews, whose identity made them subject to discrimination.[34] Although Julia Warhola had lived barely two years under the new administration, in her later life she proudly referred to "my town Miková, Czechoslovakia." To uninformed Americans, she referred to her language as Slovak. In fact, the first language in the Warhola home was Rusyn, which Julia spoke with her children all her life. But thanks to the ethnic confusion that began in Europe and often became even more muddled in America, Rusyns did not have a name for their language or even a proper term for their own ethnicity. A new label, "Slavish," was invented by outsiders as a comprehensive, but meaningless, designation for this immigrant people.

During World War II, Miková belonged to the Slovak Republic, which was then a client state of Nazi Germany. After the war, Nazi repression was replaced by Soviet domination, and the Warholas' homeland became part of the Czechoslovak Socialist Republic. For their own political and strategic purposes, the Soviets rejected the very concept of a Carpatho-Rusyn nationality and declared that Rusyns were a sub-ethnos of the Ukrainian people. Many Rusyns of Slovakia resisted the government's imposition of this alien ethnic identity and language by opting instead for Slovak. Finally, as communist governments fell throughout Eastern Europe in the late 1980s, the peaceful Velvet Revolution gave rise to the Czecho-Slovak

Federative Republic, which divided in 1993 into two sovereign states, the Czech Republic and Slovakia.

Longtime residents of Miková might have lived successively in five different countries without ever leaving their own small village. In a 1977 interview with Ira von Fürstenberg, a European socialite and actress of noble Hungarian lineage, Andy Warhol said, "Isn't it funny how they could change states. I could never understand how all that happened."[35] To be sure, given the convoluted history of their homeland, it may have been easier to say, as Warhol reportedly did, "I come from nowhere."[36] In fact, Miková was first mentioned in historical records in 1390 and has been the site of a Greek Catholic church since 1742. While it was subject to numerous political ideologies and administrative configurations, its people and their culture have always been unmistakably and indisputably Carpatho-Rusyn.

However, most Rusyn immigrants and their children could not put a precise name on their ethnic background, referring to themselves as "our people," using the meaningless term "Slavish," identifying with their Greek Catholic religion, or with the modern-day country from which they or their parents emigrated. On his application for admission to the Carnegie Institute of Technology in 1945, Andy Warhol denoted his "national descent" as "Austrian," which was incorrect.[37] His answers about his parents' origins show confusion, but in some respects, a more nuanced view of geopolitics than many Rusyns of his generation possessed. He stated that his father was born in Austria (Austria-Hungary would have been a better answer). He identified his mother's "nationality" as Slovak and her country of birth as Czechoslovakia, a country that did not exist before her twenty-seventh birthday. But then, the complex story of Carpatho-Rusyn ethnicity and nationality does not fit neatly into a college application's questionnaire.

Later when Warhol was asked about his name or ethnicity, he said he was Czechoslovakian or Czech. There is no evidence of his ever using the term Slovak, and he was never known to call himself Ukrainian. His publisher William Jovanovich, an ethnic Serb, recalls asking Andy where his mother was born. Jovanovich recounts the conversation: "'Czechoslovakia,' he said. Then I asked, 'Bohemia? Moravia?' 'No, Slovakia, I think.' 'Was she born near mountains?' It appeared so. 'Then she's from Ruthenia,' I said finally. Some weeks later Andy was being interviewed on television. He said, 'I know the most amazing man! He asks you a few questions and tells you where someone was born.'"[38] But Ruthenia, a Latin-based term for the Rusyn homeland, was not on the map, and Andy could not be more specific than to identify himself with the country from which his mother emigrated.

This confusion over ethnicity was not unique to Warhol. As late as 1997, Andy's brother John observed, "We just said we were Slovak because no one had ever heard of the Carpatho-Rusyns."[39] In a written response to a question from the Warhol biographer David Bourdon, Paul Warhola responded, "We always referred [to ourselves] as being Slavish. Mother said we were Rusnaks," a colloquial term for Rusyns.[40] Typically, Andy resorted to creative obfuscation. At various times he claimed to be from Hawaii or to have Cherokee blood. He even told his companion Charles Lisanby that he was from another planet.[41] More often than not, he told the interviewer to just "make it up." But Andy was from a time when diversity was not in fashion, information on his own ethnicity was scarce, and second-generation Americans were eager to relinquish their old-world background for a more prestigious classification as American. For Warhol, it was natural to be embarrassed and ashamed of his "Hunky" background, where Rusyns occupied the lowest rung of immigrant society, even among Slavs. At least the Poles and Slovaks knew who they were; a great many Carpatho-Rusyns had no name and no country.[42] They did, however, have a homeland.

"Ah, What a Delight It Is to Live There"

Nestled in the Lower Beskyd range of the Carpathian Mountains at 1,200 feet above sea level, the village of Miková stretches along a valley washed by three streams that flow into the Laborec River. The mountains and rolling hills, covered with beech, spruce, and pine forests, are home to deer, wolves, brown bears, and black storks. Located just off one of the highroads that stretched from the south of Hungary north to Austrian-ruled Galicia, Miková was near the site of a massive oak cross that stood at a turn in the road. Six miles to the southeast lay the fourteenth-century Krásny Brod Monastery, which housed a theological school, an icon-painting workshop, and a valuable library. Fifteen miles northwest of Miková was the Dukla Pass, the lowest point in the Carpathian Mountains, a gateway from Hungary into Austrian Galicia, which became part of Poland after World War I.

Miková would be unknown to the outside world today if not for Andy Warhol. After the fall of communism, when it became known that Warhol had connections to this obscure village, Miková became a popular destination for film crews and journalists. Documentary films, the most famous of which is Stanislaw Mucha's *Absolut Warhola*, cast a cynical light on Warhol's ancestral homeland, derisively exploiting the incongruity between the ultramodern Pop artist and the village residents, who are portrayed as backward, ignorant, clueless, and drunk.[43] Recent

Warhol biographers have taken the documentary description of Miková at face value, comparing it to the Kazakhstani village in Sacha Baron Cohen's satirical "mocku-mentary" film *Borat*. Tony Scherman and David Dalton sum it up: "Watching *Absolut Warhola*, one can understand why Andy wanted to put as much distance from his origins as possible; Miková is a warren of bigotry, . . . provincial ignorance, dim-witted literalism, grinding poverty, . . . alcoholism, and, of course, homophobia."[44] In response to *Borat*, Kazakhstan launched a campaign to repair the country's image. Unfortunately, the Rusyns of Miková had no state to protest their ethnic defamation.

Like *Borat*, *Absolut Warhola* puts comedy ahead of historicity, and for the sake of narrative effect, the film focuses on preconceived ideas about the backward-ness of the region and the degradation of the people. But *Absolut Warhola* and the biographers who cite it reveal considerable ignorance of the historical context of northeastern Slovakia. Mucha's Miková of 2001 had been shattered by two dev-astating wars, polluted by a half century of rule by a noxious sociopolitical system that corroded its citizens' culture and morality, and was now plunged into a baffling atmosphere of democracy and modernization. An effort to understand rather than deride the unwitting naiveté of the Miková Rusyns might have helped illuminate the cultural background of the American artist. The depiction of Miková presented in *Absolut Warhola* is certainly not the image that Julia portrayed in the stories she told her sons about her homeland.

For a more nuanced view, it is useful to look at the comprehensive observations of western travel writers who explored Carpathian Rus' when Ulia Zavacka and Andrii Varchola lived there. Lion Phillimore, the pseudonym of Lucy Fitzpatrick Phillimore, a wealthy British socialist who traveled through northern Hungary in the first decade of the twentieth century, recorded her observations in a 1912 book, *In the Carpathians*. Phillimore and her husband traveled from Zakopane in western Galicia into Hungary, then east to Medzilaborce and southward along the horse-shoe of the Carpathian foothills to Sighetu Marmației in present-day Romania. To bypass "the staleness of civilization," the Phillimores roved the mountains by horse cart with a Polish guide, pitching tents and setting campfires in and around Carpatho-Rusyn villages.

Writing for an audience that expected the rhetoric of romanticism, the author accordingly found clean, kind, and generous peasants who stood "primeval and erect," "unselfconscious as a child," "part of Nature herself," in valleys "flooded with pure golden radiance, dream-like and mystical." However, the author wrestles with the contradictions between romantic notions and factual observations of squa-lor and misery. Traveling east from Rus'ka volia, a Rusyn village about thirty-five kilometers southwest of Miková, she finds a wild, poverty-stricken country. "The villages were old and decayed and had fringes of one roomed filthy gipsy huts on their outskirts. The painted patterns round the house windows were rough and irregular, daubed without spirit by householders who had lost heart. . . . These people were desperately poor."[45]

Phillimore's negative tropes are similar to Mucha's cinematic images, but her presence in the narrative propitiously reveals subjective sympathies and instances of culture shock. An "evil-faced peasant," who looked like "a wild man of the woods," unexpectedly smiles with kind eyes, leaving her ashamed of her preconceptions. On the other hand, she follows picturesque peasants from church on Sunday to the village tavern, where they happily sink into intoxication. But throughout the travelogue, her European-normative moral judgment is tempered with understanding. "The villages were built of wood, and each house stood in a fenced enclosure with a few straggling trees near it. Sometimes the villages were pretty, and sometimes they were plain, but always there was a curious feeling of inertia and hopelessness about them. It was as if in them life had reached its utmost of endeavor beyond which it was useless striving. The people appeared helpless."[46]

Historic Miková was indeed poor, and its people were uneducated peasants, repressed for centuries by officials, landlords, and outside estate agents. As in most Slavic peasant communities, poverty and oppression fostered submission, fatalism, domestic violence, and alcohol abuse. Hygiene was primitive, and health was precarious. Church metrical records show frequent smallpox epidemics and occasional outbreaks of typhus. Because of its isolation, Miková was insular and provincial, and it was not immune from bigotry, corruption, and immorality. In fact, western travelers were taken aback by the deviations from conventional European moral standards that they found among the Carpathian peasantry. In 1896, H. Ellen Browning, a university-educated British woman, undertook a solo trip into eastern Hungary, where she found among the peasants "so little piety and so much religion."[47] Emily Greene Balch, an American sociologist who spent most of 1905 visiting Slavic villages in Austria-Hungary, wrote, "Anyone who knows country life anywhere is likely to be free of the widespread delusion that what is rural is necessarily more innocent than what is urban."[48] Indeed, church records show a surprising number of out-of-wedlock births. As in most European peasant communities, liturgy on Sunday morning was followed by afternoons of drinking, singing, dancing, and brawling in the tavern and the village square, the only respite from a week of hard toil. But in the church-dominated community, sins were censured, atonement was expected, and forgiveness was always available through sincere confession.

While they bewailed their poverty, Carpatho-Rusyns felt a deep love for their land and nature, while submitting to, and overcoming, the hardships it imposed. As Rusyn proverbs have it, "One's native land is heaven on earth." "Civilized" travelers like Ellen Browning delighted in the natural beauty and serenity of the Carpathians. "Imagine a stretch of the softest, finest, thickest pasture dotted over with venerable oak-trees, shut in on three sides by hills. Beeches, larches, and saplings, ruddy and golden clothe their sloping sides. Where the forest ended the valley widened. Cornfields and patches of maize stood yellow and brown against the sky, and faded away in a misty purple "distance" of forest and mountain on the horizon. . . . The grandeur and beauty of those seemingly everlasting pine-forests are utterly indescribable."[49]

Similarly, Rusyn lyric poets sang of streams, waterfalls, forests, cliffs, and soaring eagles, portraying Carpathian nature as virginal, magical, and healing, a wealth of beauty that was the birthright of the native inhabitants.[50] For them, the homeland, however poor and sordid, was a realm of beauty and spirituality, hospitality, and charity. The poet Iulyi Stavrovskyi, who lived in a village neighboring Miková, described the area as Ulia Zavacka would have seen it: "In our homeland all of nature / Blooms in eternal beauty, / There abides forever / Purity of spirit, love, and freedom. / Ah, what a delight it is to live there."[51]

Folk poets developed a mythology of the Rusyn people, transmuting characteristics judged by outsiders as negative—poverty, onerous toil, and simplicity—into national virtues, which fostered a positive Carpatho-Rusyn self-image. In folktales, they depicted themselves as pious, peace-loving, submissive, hardworking, and long-suffering, but also clever and cynical. Their lack of formal education was recompensed by common sense. Serenity and a gift of natural poetry compensated for the hardships of their life. As one writer put it, "Among our mountains there are insufficiencies, poverty, but there is also poetry, and that poetry makes us forget our grief. It enchants our souls and rewards us for our afflictions. There is not another people in the world who are as attached to their homeland as the Rusyn is to his Carpathians."[52] Indeed, Rusyn immigrants to America would yearn for the homeland, keeping the positive features alive in memories and songs, and an estimated 30 percent of Rusyn American immigrants eventually returned to their homes.[53] When asked whether Julia ever considered revisiting Miková, Paul Warhola said, "Mother used to talk about it all the time."[54] Documents and letters indicate that she contemplated a return to her native land even as late as the 1960s.

Julia was an inveterate fabulist, especially when it came to her memories of Miková. The clean water, rich soil, and pure air were imaginatively magnified in her narrative performances. One of her nieces described Julia's stories of the "beautiful Miková mansion" where she lived, the parties she hosted for "neighbors who would come in beautiful horse and buggies, and the women would dress beautiful, beautiful, all rich people." Asked if Julia was fantasizing, her niece admitted, "It had to be. I loved these stories. She was a talker, you know."[55] To be sure, the romantic image nurtured by immigrants of an earthly paradise was infused with myth and fantasy, but it captured an artistic element inherent in Rusyn nature that should not be ignored, an intrinsic sense of beauty that Ulia Zavacka carried with her to brighten life amid the smog and smokestacks of Pittsburgh.

Jews, "Gypsies," and Rusyns

In 1900, Miková was a good-sized Rusyn village with a population of 427, almost all of whom were Carpatho-Rusyns of the Greek Catholic faith.[56] Jews made up 10 percent of Zemplyn County, and a handful of Jewish families, including the Weisbergs, Grosmans, and Mellingers, had made Miková their home since the early years of the nineteenth century. The most detailed available accounting of the village comes from the 1869 Hungarian census, which counted 325 Greek Catholic Rusyns, 20 Jews, and 4 Greek Catholic Roma, a total of 349 souls in 59 households. Like the Rusyns, the Yiddish-speaking Ashkenazi Jews of Miková were small-scale agriculturalists. Some also served as merchants, tavern keepers, and moneylenders. In 1869, Jewish men were the only villagers who were literate.

Two well-to-do Jewish households stood at the head of the village. One of them, owned by Simon Grosman, housed the tavern. Each of these Jewish households had two Rusyn Greek Catholic servants and boasted numerous outbuildings with horses, cows, oxen, and the only large herd of sheep in the village. Other Jews, who were cotters or sharecroppers and owned no more livestock than their neighbors, lived side by side with Rusyns. As members of the ultraconservative Hasidic movement, their appearance—long, dark cloaks, sidelocks, and yarmulkes—and their insular way of life distinguished and isolated them from their Christian neighbors. Nonetheless, relations between Rusyns and Jews were fundamentally cooperative. In his novel about the Carpatho-Rusyn bandit Mykola Shuhai, the Czech writer Ivan Olbracht described the relationship. "Through centuries of association the Jews and Ruthenians have become used to each other's peculiarities, and religious hatred is foreign to them."[57] Paul R. Magocsi maintains that antisemitic pogroms and violence, so common elsewhere in central and eastern Europe, were absent in Subcarpathian Rus'.[58]

By the end of the nineteenth century, the Jews of Hungary were less oppressed than their coreligionists in Galicia, Poland, and Russia.[59] Until World War I, they served as economic intermediaries between the gentry, that is, the urban population, and the peasants. Jewish merchants bought peasant produce to be exported beyond the region. In return, Jewish storekeepers and peddlers provided services and sold manufactured goods from local artisans and city factories. As the sociologist Ewa Morawska writes, "Set in close proximity and a long historical tradition, this economic symbiosis bound the two groups in daily interactions and allowed for considerable familiarity."[60] Peasants assembled in Jewish-owned taverns and asked advice in matters of money and official business. Jewish midwives often attended peasant women at childbirth, and peasant girls worked as servants in Jewish homes. Gentile boys and men served as *shabbes goyim*, performing necessary tasks that were proscribed for Jews on the Sabbath, just as Julia's son, Paul Warhola, would do later in Pittsburgh.[61]

Still, the cultural divergence between Rusyn peasants and Jews resulted in what Morawska calls "simultaneous propinquity and distance," and each group viewed the other as "native" but "strange." Rusyn peasants associated Jews with money operations, which agricultural societies generally held in disdain. As Jews became business owners and moneylenders, peasants increasingly resented their economic dominance and blamed them for their own hard lot. In his 1850 temperance play, *Virtue Is More Important Than Riches*, Aleksander Dukhnovych castigated the Jewish tavern keeper for exploiting the Rusyn peasants, even as he judged harshly the villagers' failure to resist the tavern's temptation.[62] Things had not improved by the first decade of the twentieth century, when the English Phillimores visited the Rusyn village of Folyvark (Stráňany), viewing it through the prism of their own bias. "We hurried away from the inn with its crowd of peasants in their beautiful embroideries and picturesque costumes, rapidly drinking themselves blind for the profit of the sordid wide-awake Jews who owned it. The ugliness and uselessness of it all went with us."[63] A Slavic proverb advised, "The Jew sells vodka, but he doesn't drink it."[64]

Popular folk sayings repeated in various versions through the Slavic regions depict the Jew as deceitful and cunning: "As just as a Jewish scale"; "Sly as a Jew." A proverb in Aleksander Dukhnovych's list of Rusyn aphorisms touts Christian virtue, while it warns against Jewish shrewdness: "Live like a Christian, count like a Jew." However, as both Robert Rothstein and Ewa Morawska point out, peasant perceptions of Jews "contained a detectable element of at least ambivalent, if not positive and admiring, evaluation, ascribed to the initiative and resourcefulness, intellectual cleverness, and group solidarity of the Jewish traders."[65] It was a compliment to be called "as wise as a Jew," and Carpatho-Rusyns were advised "to stand for each other like one Jew for another." Peasants readily acknowledged they would rather deal with a Jewish merchant than a Christian one, a preference that continued in the immigration. They did not understand the Jewish religion, and their own Easter observances emphasized the negative role of the Jews in Christ's death, but Rothstein points to a Slavic proverb that holds up the Jews as an example of religious devotion: "The Jews pray to God most steadfastly; for this, God rewards them."[66] In their own tradition-sanctioned folk belief, Rusyns ascribed to Jews certain magical powers, both good and bad. The ethnographer Petr Bogatyrev noted the custom of the *polaznyk*, the first guest to enter the house on a holiday. "If a man is the first to enter the house on Christmas Day, it is a favorable omen; if it is a woman, it is no good at all; if it is a Jew, everything will be just fine." Failing that, a dark-haired man, perhaps closest in appearance to a Jew, was second best.[67]

In Pittsburgh, the Warholas rented part of their home for a time to Jewish lodgers. "They had the businesses, they had the money," Julia's son John recalled.[68] One of Julia's best friends in the 1930s was Bessy Zionts, a Jew from Poland, who lived with her family a few houses from the Warholas and enjoyed the services of a live-in maid. Bessy's son recalled how Julia "poured out her heart" to his mother, who had immigrated in 1900 and could give Julia advice based on her own experience.[69] Julia's familiarity with Yiddish and Jewish culture goes back to Miková. In the film *The George Hamilton Story*, Julia gives her costar a language lesson, comparing Rusyn, English, and Yiddish: "Bread. You know for Jewish people, name—*broyt* . . . English—*bread* . . . And Czechoslovak-a—*khlib*." Andy's cousin recalled Julia's wish that Andy might marry a Jewish woman, since she saw them as rich and intelligent.[70] According to Warhol's associate Bob Colacello, Andy mused about Jews often, asking, "Why are they all so smart, Bob? . . . Could it be something in their diet? Don't you wish you were Jewish sometimes?"[71] The Warhol biographer, Blake Gopnik, refers to Warhol's "important and complicated" relationship with Jews and Jewishness. "Various records of Warhol's conversation show him using language that casts Jewishness as exotic and maybe just faintly disreputable."[72] The artist's 1980 series, *Ten Portraits of Jews of the 20th Century*, reviewed by critics as exploitative, but embraced warmly by Jewish audiences, may have derived from the same mix of awe and aversion that was part of the Carpatho-Rusyn experience.

In 1869, the house on the edge of Miková was inhabited by Demeter Mihaly and his family, who are identified as Greek Catholic Roma. Mihaly was the village blacksmith. In the late nineteenth century, there were 36,000 Roma in the area that is today Slovakia, of whom only about 2,500 were nomadic. Most Roma settled on the edge of a village and interacted with the local peasant society as artisans, service workers, and traders. Some adopted the dominant religion, and numerous *tsigany* (Gypsies) can be found in the baptismal records of the Miková Greek Catholic parish. Smithery was a traditional occupation for Roma, along with basket weaving and adobe brick making. They were especially appreciated for their musicianship, and they played an essential role at every Rusyn wedding and village dance.

A symbiotic relationship existed among the diverse groups in any Rusyn village, each fulfilling a fixed function that contributed to the overall community. Julia mentioned the "seven gypsies" who performed the beautiful music for her wedding. Given her brother's recollection, perhaps there were only three or four, but Roma musicians were a vital element of any proper village wedding. The popular stereotype of thieving Roma did not apply to the sedentary population. An East Slovak villager told a researcher, "Our Gypsies did not steal. Would a villager invite a Gypsy music band to play at his son's wedding if he knew that half his poultry would disappear?"[73] Any anti-Rom antagonism was reserved for itinerant Roma, who were notorious for fortune-telling, chicanery, and thievery.

Despite the generally cooperative environment, the groups were distinct, as social and religious mores prevented them from more than everyday relationships within established social roles. Joseph Giordano's account that Julia spent "one or two seasons with a gypsy caravan" is more than dubious and smacks of Julia's mythmaking.[74] The Miková villagers put on dramas, occasionally performing for neighboring villages, and Ulia undoubtedly enjoyed and was perhaps inspired by Romani performers. Later she might well have invented fanciful stories to entertain gullible Americans, but the notion that a Rusyn girl could take off with a band of Gypsies and then return to traditional life is the stuff of romantic fiction, rather than Rusyn reality. Milena Hübschmannová, the preeminent scholar of the Roma of eastern Slovakia, writes, "To marry a Gypsy was something unimaginable among decent *gadže* [non-Roma]. In many Rom families a *gadžo* ancestor does crop up now and then. Such *gadže* were usually the poorest of the poor, themselves outcasts from the wider society."[75]

In a formula that also describes the relations between Rusyns and Jews in Miková, the scholar David Sheffel describes group interactions as "defined by accommodation of difference by means of a kind of habitual and unreflective tolerance rooted in pragmatic acceptance of, rather than activist interference in, the affairs of one's neighbors." While each group may have found the other alien and their customs distasteful, society was characterized by "a local culture of moderation" and a "live and let live" attitude, a "pragmatic tolerance that leads to a kind of grudging civility." Sheffel's assessment, that public opinion in the multiethnic communities of eastern Slovakia was "more strongly influenced by a person's ability and willingness to live up to the local standard of decency than by shrill ideology," accurately describes the pragmatic old-world judgment that Rusyn immigrants brought with them to America.[76]

Up from Feudalism

Until 1848, Carpatho-Rusyns worked as indentured peasants for Hungarian noble landowners, doing unpaid labor for the benefit of the gentry, whose manors were generally located in the empire's cities, far from Rusyn lands. Miková, along with about fifty other Zemplyn villages, was owned by the Keglević family. Keglević was a Hungarian count of Croatian origin, whose name is associated today with Keglevich vodka. In the Hungarian Urbarial Census, conducted in Miková in 1774, all the villagers are listed under the heading "Coloni Perpetua Obligationis" (Tenant farmers in perpetual bond).[77] That is, they were serfs bound to land that they farmed but could not own. Among them were six Varchola households and six Zavacky households out of a total of thirty-two.

The Urbarium was initiated by Empress Maria Theresa to clarify the subject farmers' obligations to the landowner, which were explicit and considerable. Most village households farmed a half unit of land. The actual size varied, but a half unit was the amount of land generally considered barely sufficient for a serf and his family.[78] Peasants were required to perform twenty-six days of unpaid labor on the landlord's estate if they were lucky enough to own farm animals, or double that number of days if they did not. They were also obligated to submit annually to the Jewish estate agent three-quarters of a cord of firewood, half a quart of clarified butter, one capon, one chicken, six eggs, and a portion of their crop. About half the village, including four Zavacky and two Varchola households, farmed even less land with accordingly fewer excises and obligatory days of unpaid labor. The Urbarium also stipulated the taxes to be paid to the state and the tithe required by the church. Tied to the lord's land, serfs could not migrate from the village or marry outside the estate. As time passed and restrictions eased, villages gradually attained a greater degree of autonomy, but it was not until 1848 that the feudal system was abolished in the Kingdom of Hungary. Andrii's father and Julia's grandparents were born before the 1848 emancipation. The soon-to-be American Warholas were barely a generation past harsh feudalism.

After the emancipation, the economic status of peasants in Hungary improved only marginally, as the best land, pastures, and forests went to the lords and to outsiders with money.[79] In 1851, the population of Miková was 448, with 421 Greek Catholics, 8 Roman Catholics, and 19 Jews. Its 735 arable acres had been acquired by the noble Hungarian Barkóczy family.[80] The peasants' small plots diminished with each generation, as a family's land was divided among the sons. At best, Carpatho-Rusyns were subsistence farmers, barely able to support a single family, with no surplus for profit. They cultivated oats, barley, rye, and buckwheat—hardy grains that could survive in the hilly, cloudy climate and infertile soil. Beyond the homesteads, situated along a single road, the farmland surrounding the village on the hillside slopes was divided into individually owned strips, a time-honored but inefficient system. A farmer worked a number of strips that were not necessarily adjacent. Because the nearest fields were owned by the church, peasants walked a considerable distance to reach the land they farmed. When it was inconvenient to return home at night, they slept in the field at the edge of the forest. The local priest enjoyed additional privileges at the expense of the villagers. The first calf from each cow was claimed by the priest, and a chicken or a goose was the usual compensation for a christening.

For centuries, the residents of Miková have been called "millers" for their use of sandstone, found in the forest near the village, to produce hand mills, essential tools for grinding grain. Miková peasants sold the hand mills at area markets to bring in extra income.[81] Zavacky family legends tell of one Matthias, their oldest-known ancestor, a clever man who came from Poland with his family.[82] Matthias diverted two streams and created a water mill at their confluence. The water rose overnight, peasants arrived early the next day to grind their grain, and Matthias brought in extra income. The location in Miková, known still today as the *mlyn* (mill), is located opposite the house built on the original Zavacky land by Ján Zavacky, the son of Julia's brother Yurii.

The Mikováns of Ulia's and Andrii's generation raised livestock—cows that grazed outside the village and sheep that were herded to pasture in the highland fields—to provide milk and cheese for their diet and wool and leather for winter garments. Julia told her children that she went to market with her father in the district town of Medzilaborce, about ten miles to the east by horse-drawn wagon.[83] She reportedly told Joseph Giordano that she rode "from town to town on horseback, singing."[84] As horses were owned only by families that already had a sufficient number of cows, the most essential farm animals, these seemingly authentic stories confirm the Zavackys' better-than-average economic status.

Homesteads usually included a poultry house, a pigsty, and stables for the oxen that pulled plows and carts. Garden plots supplied cabbage, potatoes, and other vegetables. Peasants ground wheat from their fields through hand-cranked grain mills to make the flour used to bake bread. Each family preserved several barrels of sauerkraut to make *keselica*, a soup from sauerkraut juice, which would be accompanied by bread with garlic and salt. Ethnic cuisine was based on bread, potatoes, cabbage, beans, and millet cereals. A pig was slaughtered in the fall to provide meat through the winter, which was saved for the most important holidays. It was rare for the land to yield enough to support most families. To augment their livelihood, peasant farmers traveled seasonally to work the harvest for six to eight weeks in the fertile Hungarian lowlands.

In winter when their fields lay fallow, men harvested timber for firewood and hewed rail ties to supply the railroad that ran through Medzilaborce. Women were occupied yearlong with the time-consuming job of producing textiles. In a tedious process requiring some twenty-three steps from start to finish, they planted and harvested flax, softened the stalks, dried, beat, and scutched them, spun yarn on an in-hand spindle, and finally wove cloth for carpets, table and bed linen, sacks, rope, and other household necessities. In spring and summer, they spread the linen on the ground by the river to bleach it in the sun. In winter, women plucked goose-down feathers for bedding—another time-consuming task, since it took sixteen geese to make a *peryna*, a down comforter, which was a household necessity on cold winter nights and brought a good price at the market. With the exception of metal products from the village blacksmith, Rusyn peasants were largely self-sufficient, and from a young age, all members of the family participated in the unremitting labor.

Agricultural work was communal. Cutting grass for hay was a social event, when meadows were filled with men, women, and children working together to the accompaniment of lively folk songs, sung in multipart harmony. Each family entrusted its sheep to the village *bacha* (shepherd), who pastured the herd in the *polonyna*, the highland meadow, and returned to each household its due portion of bryndza cheese and shorn wool. The villagers worshipped together and celebrated weddings, christenings, and religious holidays with ritualized festivities. For better or worse, everyone was known to all. As the Rusyn proverb has it, "To live in a village is to hide nothing." Along with the character of the individual, the reputation of family was firmly guarded, and each village earned its own standing among the surrounding communities. A sign of a virtuous, hardworking village was an abundance of stork nests, for according to the proverb, "Storks do not endure evil people." Miková had plenty of storks.

The Zavackys and the Varcholas

A Carpatho-Rusyn village was like a large extended clan. The families were inter-related through birth, marriage, and *kumstvo*, that is, serving as godparents for one another's children. Most families had many children, and the early deaths of wives or husbands meant that second marriages were common, ensuring that every individual had a multitude of cousins and stepsiblings. The earliest known Andrii Varchola is listed in the Hungarian census of 1715. The American Andy Warhol was the third traceable "Andrew" in the modern Varchola line.[85] His paternal grandfa-ther Andrii was a widower who, at the age of forty, married twenty-seven-year-old Julia Choma (pronounced Khoma), the sister of his first wife. It was customary among European peasants for a widower to marry the sister of a deceased wife in order to preserve the family property. Andrii Varchola and Julia Choma had three sons, Andrii (1886–1942), who would become Andy Warhol's father, Josyf (1890–1972), and Jan (b. 1893), his uncles. They were known in Miková by the "alias" or "household name," "Kost'," the name of an ancient ancestor, which had become a kind of nickname that served to distinguish this particular Varchola family from the several unrelated, or only distantly related, village families with the same sur-name.

The Varchola-Kost' family was not well-off. According to village historians, they farmed two strips of land, had two cows and two rows of beehives. The grandfather of the American Andy Warhol died of pneumonia in 1896 at age fifty-five, leaving Andy's father, who was ten, and his two brothers, who were under six. The diffi-culty of earning a livelihood and taking care of his widowed mother and younger brothers was undoubtedly the reason that Andrii left for the United States at age nineteen in 1905, when Josyf would have been old enough to take over farming duties. Andrii spent two years working in a bituminous coal mine in the Pittsburgh area, sending money home to support his family. Just months after Andrii's marriage to Ulia Zavacka in Miková, his brother Josyf (Joseph) emigrated to Pittsburgh in October 1909.[86] Jan, the youngest Varchola brother, remained in Miková to care for his mother. At the outbreak of the Great War, Jan was drafted into the Austro-Hungarian army. Although records have not been unearthed, it is believed he was wounded on the battlefield and died of his injuries after the war.[87]

Like the Varcholas, the Zavacky family had deep roots in Miková. In 1828, there were six Zavacky households in the village, and the Hungarian census of 1869 finds three generations of Zavackys living in house number 17. Like the Varcholas, they were all Greek Catholic Rusyns. Julia's maternal line is more problematic. Her mother, Justina Mrocsko, was a Greek Catholic, but recent research has confirmed Ján Zavacky's family tale that Justina's father, Mathias Mrocsko was a Roman Catholic Pole, born in Galicia.[88] Mathias's wife Josephine Blau, Julia Warhola's maternal grandmother, had roots in Bohemia. Despite family lore that claimed she was Jewish, records indicate that Josephine was an Austro-German Roman Catholic.[89]

Lingering questions about Andy Warhol's ancestry can now be answered with some specificity. Records demonstrate that the ethnic background of the Warhola and Choma families is entirely Carpatho-Rusyn, as is the Zavackys' lineage on Julia's father's side. Julia's maternal ancestry shows a more complex genetic makeup with tantalizing non-Rusyn elements. But the Mrocsko-Blau family was clearly assimilated in the Rusyn community at least a generation before Julia was born. Andy Warhol's religious and cultural heritage, going back at least three generations, is Carpatho-Rusyn and Greek Catholic.

"My Momma had fifteen children," Julia told an interviewer.[90] Fourteen, of whom five died as babies or young children, can be documented in the Miková parish records. The first documented child, a girl, Paraska, was born in 1878 and lived just three days. Four children followed at two-year intervals, and Ulia (full name Julianna) was born November 20, 1891. A set of twin boys died at birth in 1894, and the next child, a girl baptized Zushka (Zuzanna), lived just four weeks. In 1901, another daughter was given the name of the deceased baby, Zushka. It seems to have been unlucky, since the second Zushka died at age four in July 1905. The cause of death is given as "worms," a parasitic infection that was a frequent childhood malady in summer, caused usually by poor sanitation. Finally, girls were born in 1903 and 1906. When the youngest, Eva, was born, her mother Justina was forty-six years old, and Ulia, by then skilled at childcare, was fifteen. Of those who survived to adulthood, only a son, Yurii (Yurko), and two daughters, Elena and Eva, remained in Europe. Three brothers (Stephen, John, and Andrew) and three sisters (Mary, Julia, and Anna) emigrated to America.

A blurry Zavacky family photograph exists. It is difficult to match names to faces if we take into account those who would have been alive and together in the home country at one time. According to Julia's niece, the photo was taken at the wedding of her father Stephen, the oldest Zavacky son, which, according to church records, took place in February 1905. She identifies Stephen and his wife in the back row.[91] The Zavacky parents sit with the bride's father in the middle row, surrounded by six children. Julia and her sister Mary stand on either end; sources suggest that Julia is on the left in the rear. The overall appearance of the family is telling—the father wears an old-style long coat and round felt hat, while his son Stephen, who had already made more than one round trip to America, wears a

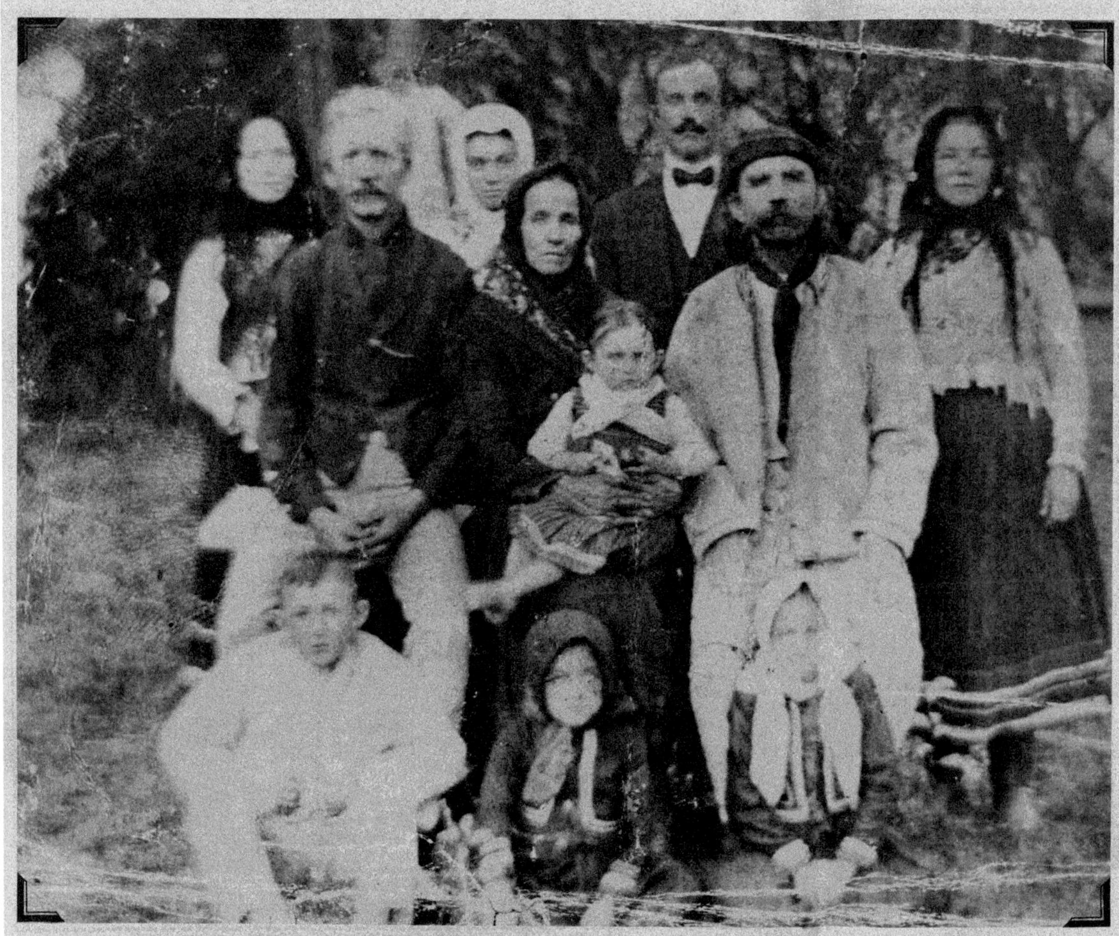

Figure 1.4. Zavacky family ca. 1905.

western-style jacket and bowtie. All the men have mustaches. Except for the baby in the mother's lap, the girls wear kerchiefs and look as though they are ready to work in the kitchen or the field.

There is a curious postscript to this photograph. In 1980 it was used in *Kentucky Monthly* magazine to illustrate an article about the decline of the traditional family in Kentucky.[92] Communication with the current editor of the magazine revealed that no photo credit was listed, and the photograph cannot be found in the magazine's photo archive.[93] No one at the magazine today is aware that it depicted a family from the Carpathian Mountains, not Appalachia, although the parallel is apt. It is unknown how the Zavacky family portrait made its way to Kentucky to illustrate a random, unrelated article, but the hoax, whether deliberate or not, seems very Warholian.[94]

"Man Must Work"

After living in house number 17, the Zavacky family lived in house number 21. The folk architecture of the Rusyn regions adapted archaic traditions to local conditions. An ethnographer describes the typical peasant home:

> The houses were most often made of split, half-round fir logs. . . . The round side of the split logs formed the exterior, the flat side the interior walls. . . . On the exterior, the timbers were rubbed with crude oil, which not only preserved the walls from rot and worms, but served as a sort of ornamentation. . . . The rounded logs were filled in or packed along the whole length with moss and clay. This "mortar" was then whitewashed, so that the resulting horizontal stripes stood out vividly against the dark oily background of the log, thereby underlining the structure of the house.[95]

The walls were freshly whitewashed every spring, inside and out, to preserve heat and provide protection from wind and rain. The roof, which had two sloping surfaces, was most often thatched with rye straw, leaving a hole in the thatch for smoke to escape. Since the homes were crowded, heated by wood-burning stoves, and lit by candlelight, Rusyn peasants had a natural fear of fire, which could spread quickly. In 1911, a fire in the nearby village of Habura destroyed the church and seventy-two homes, along with many head of livestock.[96] Rusyns brought this fear of fire with them to America and passed it on to their children. Even in New York of the 1970s, Andy Warhol harbored the peasants' dread. Finding that open cans of turpentine had sparked a blaze on the upper floor of his house, he told his diary, "I started to shake. My biggest fear had happened." Joking that the room might be "possessed," he declared, "I'm going to have a cross blessed and put it up there." On Easter Sunday 1978, he brought holy water from church and spent a "couple of hours" sprinkling it around his house, just as his ancestors had done in Miková.[97]

The typical peasant house was structured such that the family's living space and farm buildings—stables, threshing barn and storage rooms—were constructed one touching the other, all under a single roof. Entering the peasant's cottage through the unheated inner porch, which also served as a storage area for tools, buckets, and provisions, one reached the living area—a large, squarish room, about seventeen feet long and fifteen feet wide, with a seven-foot-high ceiling and an earthen floor

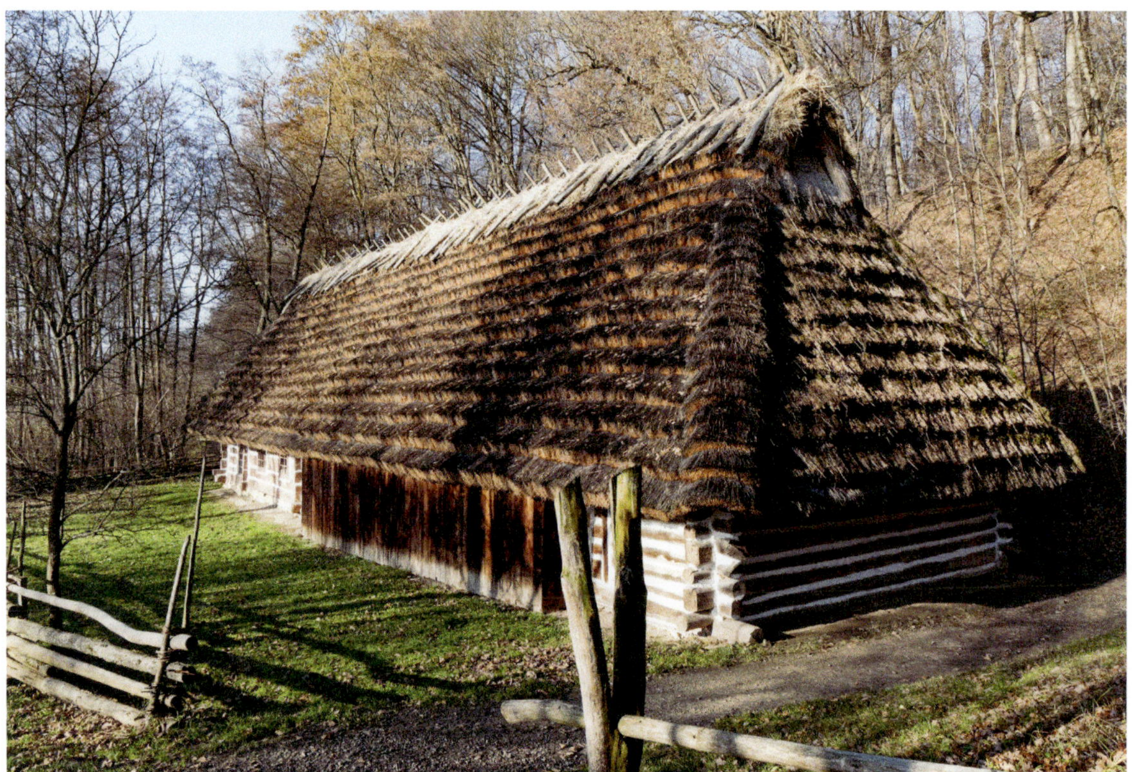

Figure 1.5. Rusyn peasant house in northeastern Slovakia.

sealed with yellowish flaxseed oil. It was here that women set up the loom and the grinder, where men fashioned footwear for their own use, and tooled woodcarvings to be sold at local fairs. It was the ceremonial space for all family rituals—christenings, weddings, and funerals. In winter, the family shared the heated living space with newborn lambs, goats, and calves to protect the animals from the bitter cold. Poultry typically nested under the benches. Visitors to an apartment where Andy lived with his mother in their first years in New York often commented on the "horrendous smell" from the many partially housebroken cats they kept. The odor was undoubtedly mild compared to Julia's first home, where, as in all peasant cottages, the atmosphere was fetid, hygiene was haphazard, and sanitation was poor.

A quarter of the total living space in the main room was taken up by the large wood-burning masonry stove, which heated the house, cooked the food, baked the bread, and provided a warm sleeping space, especially for children and the elderly. Julia's son Paul remembered his mother's stories about sleeping on the stove. Not surprisingly, he "couldn't visualize" it.[98] Around the stove hung kitchen utensils and strings of drying mushrooms. Diagonally opposite the stove was the ceremonial corner where the family's icons, sacred images used in religious devotion, were displayed, ornamented with embroidered towels. In the sleeping corner, a cradle hung from the ceiling. Four or five children huddled in a second bed, while others slept on benches along the walls or on bags filled with straw that were ranged on the floor as needed. Outbuildings attached to the house provided shelter for goats, sheep, pigs, and poultry. Oxen, horses, and cows were housed in the stable. A cold cellar was so well insulated that large blocks of ice lasted through the summer, preserving barrels of cabbage, vegetables, and fruit, as well as smoked meat and poultry.

In 1869, number 17 housed four adults and five children, one of whom was Julia's father, Andrii Zavacky. When Andrii married Justina Mrocsko in 1877 and they began their large family, they most likely shared the house with at least one set of grandparents. The Zavacky family farmed five or six hectares (twelve to fifteen acres) of land, as compared to the standard holding of two to four hectares. The minimum needed to maintain a subsistence-level existence was roughly fourteen acres. For the Rusyns of Miková, "middle class" meant having just barely enough from one harvest to the next. Ulia and her siblings grew up working in the fields and tending the cows. From sunrise to sunset, children as young as six watched over the grazing herds. Ulia told her children stories about working as a "shepherd," encountering wolves, and walking barefoot in the snow. We can assume her stories were not unlike those of the Carpatho-Rusyn memoirist Luba Fedash, who recalls:

> My job began at sunrise and ended at sunset every day of the year except for Sunday mornings, the winter months, and a brief time I attended school. Restraining the cows by a rope made from our own home-grown and home-spun flax, I led them to the pastures far from home by the forest where I watched over them while they grazed all day. . . . Many an evening I barely made it home, too tired to walk to the house. . . . Living in harmony with nature brought me satisfaction. And for the most part, I was happy and glad to be alive, except on late autumn days when patches of frost covered the ground, or early spring days when rain fell from the sky non-stop all day, and I had to walk upon the cold earth barefoot, soaked to the bone. . . . I remember clearly to this day, how soothing my warm urine felt on my freezing feet and how welcomed it was each time nature called.[99]

The peasant attitude toward work is worthy of note, because it continued to play an important role in the Rusyn immigration and in the Warhola family. As Ewa Morawska put it, "In the traditional peasant society, work had been perceived as the attribute of human existence. It was a value in and of itself. . . . Religion only strengthened the peasants' attitude toward work as an obligatory task: 'Man has to work,' stated one of the commandments most often repeated from the pulpits in village churches."[100]

Church registers denote the Varcholas as "farmers," that is, *khlieborob*, literally "grain workers," and like all Miková small landholders they employed timeworn methods, walking behind their ox-drawn plows, sowing their crops by hand, and harvesting with straight-handled scythes. They kept bees and sold honey in the market. Wild chestnut trees, found in Miková today only in the vicinity of the Varchola home, were planted by Andy's father in the belief they would increase the bees' yield. Even today, beekeepers prize honey made from the nectar of chestnut flowers. According to the reminiscences of villagers, the Varcholas were known for making agricultural tools and technical equipment to produce oil from hemp and flax seeds, beechnuts, and sunflowers.[101] Today, a covered well is all that remains of the Varchola homestead where Julia and Andrii lived.[102]

According to Ewa Morawska, while formal education was little valued, "the cultural system of East Central European peasants did not lack regard for knowledge and learning of a specific kind. Simple literacy, rather than the number of school grades completed, combined with popular wisdom, life experience, curiosity, and knowledgeability about things of the world were highly respected in all rural societies of the region."[103] The Varcholas were considered clever and knowledgeable. According to Ján Zavacky, the son of Julia's brother, they were "on a higher level" than their neighbors, literate and learned, with books in their home, which was unusual at the time.[104] They read newspapers, brochures, and technical handbooks, and expressed interest in the world beyond the village. The few letters and documents we have from Andy's father's life in Pittsburgh demonstrate a sharp mind, a sound business sense, and a feeling for family responsibility that was rooted in his life experience in Miková. His early decision to emigrate points to an adventurous, independent, ambitious character, unafraid of risk-taking. His return to Miková to find a bride indicates respect for old-world tradition and family responsibility. The Varchola practicality, combined with the Zavacky artistic sense, would shape the future artist.

"The Man Is the Head, but the Woman Is the Soul"

In Carpatho-Rusyn peasant society, the division of labor between men and women was clearly defined. Women took care of the children and the household chores of cooking, cleaning, baking, carrying water, spinning, weaving, and whitewashing the house. They also tended the poultry, the vegetable garden, the hemp and flax fields, and they fed the cows, sheep, and goats. Housewives were responsible for selling eggs, cheese, and butter at the market, and they controlled the money they earned. While men seldom took on women's chores, women participated in the fieldwork during busy agricultural periods—turning, raking, and binding the grass mowed by the men. When Andrii first saw Ulia, she was bringing in what she called "wheat" from the field. In Warhol's film, *The George Hamilton Story*, she says, "When me was little girl, and me always working *na* [*on*, Rusyn] farm . . . I always go to shepherd, grass for cow." Misunderstanding her heavy accent, her interlocutor asks, "You chopped grass for cows?" Happy to think she's been understood, Julia agrees: "Cows, yes. Yes, I chop it. . . . In Europe you want milk from cow, you have to get something for cow. You know I a farmer, ten cow my mama and *didi* [grandfather] have . . . maybe nine year old I was. I chopped wheat, *toto* [that is] grass, you know, grass? . . . Green grass, nice, grass for cow eating. . . . [*Proudly*] Czechoslovak-a. Was my Europe, long time ago." In Julia's emotional narration, pathos for her childhood burden of raking grass and tending cows contends with pride in the number of cows she had to tend. "I a farmer," she insists, and with condescension, she explains to her inexperienced American listeners the give and take involved in caring for livestock. She invokes her homeland of Czechoslovakia, in an idiosyncratic pronunciation, as a point of pride in the narrative of her life.

In her study of east central European peasant societies, Morawska notes that the highest compliment one could pay a woman was to say that she was willing and able to work hard.[105] Julia's youngest sister remembered that Julia defied the customary gender division of labor. "[Ulia] mowed, chopped wood. She knew how to do everything. Our father taught us. He wanted a son and he was sad when Ulia was born. So foolish. She wanted to be as good as a boy so father wouldn't complain. She knew how to work. She was a beekeeper, she could do anything."[106] Blake Gopnik described Andy Warhol as "a pioneer transgressor of gender roles," but challenging societal expectations was nothing new to his mother.[107]

Women were generally held in low esteem in Slavic peasant societies, and Carpatho-Rusyn folk culture was typically misogynist. The characteristically idealized mother figure was the exception to the rule, as it was generally accepted that "few people expressed such a reverent love for their mothers as did the Slavs."[108] But proverbs, which are similar across the Slavic world, express disrespectful and dismissive attitudes to women in general. "A woman's hair is long, but her mind is short"; "A dog is wiser than a woman; it does not bark at its master." Marriage is a proverbial trap sprung on men by wily women: "A robber asks for your money or your life; a wife asks for both." A few Carpatho-Rusyn proverbs acknowledge the interdependence of men's and women's roles and their necessary reliance on one another in everyday life. "The man is the head, but the woman is the soul"; "A good wife halves trouble and doubles happiness"; "A widower is not a father to his children, for he is himself an orphan."[109] Wives were expected to handle the hardships and demands of life, to cope with crises, and to make life smooth for their menfolk.

Women were not without influence in the family. They usually controlled family finances and they arranged their children's marriages, but on their own, they had little value and no agency. In the patriarchal structure of the family and the culture, women were expected to be submissive and obedient. Spousal abuse was a persistent concern. However, an oppositional feminist reading of this aspect of Carpatho-Rusyn folk culture offers the woman's point of view. As Donna Gabaccia puts it, "Evidence of virulent misogyny in European . . . folklore and religious teaching is easy to find but very hard to interpret; we cannot know if it principally reflected social reality, functioned as an ideological sop to politically powerless men, or bolstered male esteem in the face of women skilled as manipulators of kin resources."[110]

The wedding ritual described at the beginning of this chapter foregrounds the stereotypical images of women and demonstrates how they were used to condition social attitudes. The bride-to-be is metaphorically a heifer to be purchased, a rose to be transplanted and cultivated to bear fruit, and an "innocent child" to be delivered to her husband. She will be "a worker" for her mother-in-law first, and only secondarily, a "helpmate" for the groom. After the "crowning" in church, which called down "glory and honor" upon the bridal couple, the "capping" ritual stripped the bride of her girlish identity—after she twice ritually proclaimed that she would rather have her head cut off. Her new headdress imposed upon her a subordinate, matronly persona. The teachings of the church, with its emphasis on the subservience of the wife to her husband, reinforced these time-honored values.

An element of the traditional Carpatho-Rusyn peasant wedding that is usually glossed over today is its eroticism. All primitive cultures promoted the vital peasant values of fertility and fecundity, not only in the field but also in the human population. The marriage ceremony was an occasion to celebrate procreation and sex. Thus, erotic proverbs, sayings, songs, and riddles were part of the celebration. The scholar of ethnography and women's studies Christine Worobec notes that old-world peasants often concealed provocative performances from outsiders. "They sang songs and told stories that ethnographers expected to hear, leaving the bawdy versions for occasions when the village was free of busybody officials and scholars. Only an ethnographer who had earned the peasants' trust would have been introduced to the full panorama of peasant oral culture."[111] During the Soviet period in Eastern Europe, "shameful" variants were proscribed in ethnographic scholarship. Even today they are often omitted from popular collections of folk songs and tales. The ethnomusicologist Ivan Chyzhmar published Carpatho-Rusyn erotic-themed songs as a supplement to his extensive ethnographic study of the folk wedding, cautioning that it is intended "only for scholarly work."[112]

In songs and riddles, the sex act was represented allegorically in agricultural metaphors of ravens and jackdaws, cabbages and sausages, plowing and raking. But explicit terms are also used that would be shocking even today.[113] Since it expresses a man's perspective, women were most often portrayed negatively in erotic folklore, in proverbs such as, "A woman is seen best when she's standing on a ladder"; "Men love that which girls are ashamed of."[114] While the chant sung by the married women of the groom's family to accompany the "dance in a row" praised the bride's beauty and wished her well, verses that were hidden from or suppressed by ethnographers, and conveniently "forgotten" in the immigration, expressed explicit erotic motifs and vulgar images. To the same melody that praised "our beautiful bride," the *svashki* sang that the bride gave up her hair for "a piece of sausage and two eggs," called her a slut, a whore, and a seductress, and described the sex act in unambiguous terms.

These aspects of the ceremony would seem to suggest that women accepted the negative images imposed upon them, but a feminist reading points to a subversion of the male-dominated culture in its own language. The women's comic identification with negative images spotlights their understated resistance to patriarchal expectations. The exchange of a bride's hair, the symbol of her innocence, for "a piece of sausage" exposes the inequitable, oppressive nature of societal expectations. The "seductive slut" persona attributed to the bride in bawdy songs suggests a latent threat to masculinity. The ribald "capping" ceremony, performed traditionally only by married women but observed by the community at large, utilized humor and jovial irony to attack the stereotypes of women's ascribed role and status. In an expression of women's solidarity, the ceremony talked back to the otherwise male-dominated wedding ritual. The layers of meaning in the marriage ceremony initiate the new bride into the expectations of her culture, while implicitly critiquing and subverting them.

The oral art of the wedding ritual expressed the irrepressible voice of the people. By contrast, in the church and in written literature, women had no voice. Aleksander Dukhnovych elevated misogyny in Rusyn belles lettres in his classic play from 1851, *Virtue Is More Important Than Riches*. While the male protagonist is a

Rusyn "Everyman," weak and foolish, but likable and ultimately redeemed, his wife is unvarnished evil. Adhering to old superstitions, abetting her husband's alcohol abuse, and blocking her son's education, she refuses to admit her mistakes and spurns forgiveness. She is the ultimate "bad mother," whose moral defects and overindulgent child-raising practices corrupt her son and, metaphorically, the next Carpatho-Rusyn generation. In the immigration, Rusyn American writers elaborated on Dukhnovych's misogynistic theme in numerous popular plays, which were performed by amateur groups to audiences in churches and fraternal organizations. One has only to glance at the dramatis personae of these dramas to predict the conventional plot. The cast of characters will include a middle-aged *gazda* and *gazdynia* (husband and wife of the household), a daughter of about eighteen, a Vasyl or Petro who is an orphan boy or a poor neighbor, and an additional male character who may be the son of the steward, a dissolute returnee from America, or a rich man, who is also, frequently, a drunkard. The husbands are sympathetic, though weak willed and dominated by their spiteful, materialistic wives, who are determined to marry their beautiful, virtuous daughter to the rich interloper, instead of her poor soulmate. In the course of the action, the chosen fiancé is revealed to be base and immoral (and often not even rich), the mother is chastened, and the daughter and Vasyl are married. If we are to take these narratives at face value, one must wonder what happens to Rusyn women, who are uniformly modest and wise maidens at eighteen and foolish, materialistic harridans at forty. A Rusyn proverb captures the phenomenon: "A wife is dear to her husband twice—when he marries her and when he buries her."[115]

The Woman's Voice

In folk culture, women's voices were heard in the genre of the lyrical song. Women's songs present the expected theme of love, reciprocated or lost. But contrary to societal norms, in numerous songs, girls and older women expressed notably rebellious thoughts, emotions, and concerns. Contextualized in terms of the position of women in Carpatho-Rusyn peasant culture, lyrical songs provide the female perspective that is missing from men's sayings and priests' writings. Singing together in multipart harmony throughout the day, at work in the fields and especially at *prialky*, spinning parties that combined work with amusement during the long winter evenings, their songs touched on courting practices, marital relations, and self-image. The topic is far too expansive and complex for a full treatment here, but a quick look at some of the most popular songs that survived from the homeland, through the immigration, and down to the present day is revelatory.[116]

A common theme is the young girl's fear that she will be matched with an old or unfit husband, instead of her beloved village boyfriend. A girl sings to her mother: "My dearest mother / You have just one daughter, me / Look far and wide / . . . / For the one to whom you will give me." Fortunately, this particular "dear mother" concedes, "I won't give you to just anyone," and allows the girl to marry her chosen one. Numerous songs express the voice of the bride who had a less sympathetic mother and found herself married to an old *dido* (grandfather). While a lament for her fate might be expected, and probably occurred in lived experience, songs were a safe space where women could voice the tension they felt between duty and desire. "And on my wedding day my mother told me / To take good care of my old husband. // And so, I care for the *dido* well, because I must, / But please, dear God, take the old man's soul!" Another young girl who was constrained to marry a graybeard, sings: "Why, oh why, do I need that old man? / You can't kiss or lie with him, or even look at him." In folk-song performance, these outspoken women straightforwardly voice bold notions that, in real life, could only be whispered.

Perhaps the best-known and most-loved song of Rusyn women of eastern Slovakia, enjoyed today also in Carpatho-Rusyn America as an anthem of women's liberation, is "Chervena ruzha troiaka" (A red rose of three shades), one of many similar songs that Julia Warhola recorded on tape in New York. The singer bewails her fate with her husband, a drunkard who beats her, and the song celebrates women's empowerment: "Don't beat me, my husband, don't punish me / I'll leave you the kids, the kids I'll leave you / And I'll go alone far beyond the Danube." As the woman boards the ship and waves her white kerchief, the symbol of hoped-for lasting love, her husband pleads, "Come back, my wife, come home. . . . The children are crying for you." She retorts: "I will not come home . . . I would rather lose my life." The themes of independence and resistance that women expounded in these songs may not have reflected their lived experience, but they opened up an exhilarating sense of possibility and personal power within the constraints of traditional culture.

Another theme of Carpatho-Rusyn lyrical songs that mitigates against images of women's subordination and shame is the sassy attitude they take toward the conventions of courting, with thinly veiled allusions to sexuality. "At our place there is a green meadow / Boys love me, because I am young. / At our place, oh, how the meadow is raked, / I've now broken five rakes." "I was raking and raking, / and broke the rake. . . . / For I had three boyfriends. // If only I knew / where my boyfriend is mowing / I would bring him / Something from under my apron." Other attitudes toward courting and sex are more explicit. "I would like to kiss my boyfriend so deeply that my mouth would water." A young girl calls to Ivan to "come secretly to our place tonight." A piece of straw on the fence will signal that her *stary* (old folks) are at home; twigs of hay will be a sign that he can come in fearlessly. An assertive young woman sings to her fellow to warn his mother against arranging a marriage with another girl:

> Tell her that you found a girl long ago
> When you came to our place that evening,
> Stayed overnight but left early
> So you wouldn't wake my mother.
> So now tell her openly
> To prepare me a wedding "cap,"
> And tell her we'll need a cradle
> For the coming baby.

Like the bold confidence expressed here, personal responsibility, rather than victimhood, is the response of another singer: "Only I am to blame / It was me myself / Who took a liking to him. // Oh, my boy, so you think / It's all about you / When you kiss my white cheeks again and again."

These lyrical songs reveal a celebration of self that challenges men's idealistic images of women's submission. Women sing their ire when they are defamed by village busybodies for their forward behavior, and they face gossip with smug cheek: "False tales are told about me." A girl who is talked about because she "sits on boys' laps" resolves: "I'll go to my door and stand there openly / And choose a boyfriend to my liking. // Yes, I'll go to my door and stand there looking pretty. / Whoever wants to love me, let him come." A girl who is derogated as a showoff fights back: "I don't paint my face / And no, dude, I'm not interested in you." Finally, it is notable that women's affirmations of femininity and sexuality are not limited to maidens. An older woman traces her love life from her teenage years, when she had twenty admirers, to her twenties, when she was pursued by young officers, to her maturity, when she fell in love with mustached men, and her sixties, when even a stooped old man would not have her. She concludes with sardonic irony: "Now I am a *stara baba* [old grandmother] / No one kisses me, though I wish they would." Although there are also a great many songs that express women's misery and subjection, these folkloric performances, which often address males directly, affirm the legitimacy of women's emotions and desires. Shuffling the dominant discourse, they communicate a sense of power, as they transgress cultural norms. Whether or not they had any effect on the actual domestic and societal structures of peasant society, they evidence a resistant female energy that challenged and subverted the apparent dominance of men.[117]

It was within this women's folk culture that Ulia Zavacka was raised and her psyche was formed. Julia Warhola continued to sing these and similar folk songs into her sixties, when her self-representation retained traces of the sassy peasant woman persona. While some of Andy's friends saw a naive, childlike nature in his mother, others noted a coquettish demeanor that could be manipulative and defiant. One of her son's female collaborators called Mrs. Warhola "Miss Prima Donna."[118] According to the Warhol superstar Viva, the seventy-seven-year-old Julia told her stories about the suitors who had pursued her, explaining that her body was like a "magnet" that attracted any good man, a trope that could have come from the lyrics of one of her folk songs.[119] In Warhol's film, *The George Hamilton Story*, Julia, in the same folklore idiom, jokes about spurning old men who want to marry her and resisting the kisses of young men. This side of Julia Warhola's personality, along with her tendency to exaggerate and self-mythologize, had its roots in the performative features of Carpatho-Rusyn peasant culture. As scholars of narrative put it, "The culture 'speaks itself' through each individual's story."[120]

Homespun Beauty

Ulia was respected in the village not only for her hard work, but for her creativity, which was ingenious, given the conditions of poverty in which she lived. The Zavacky family homestead has not survived, but elderly residents recalled the decorative patterns Ulia drew on the whitewashed walls and the designs she painted on kitchen utensils. According to ethnographers, much attention was given to decorating the exterior walls of the peasant cottage. Decorations included various ornamental motifs, such as solar signs, chicken feet, the tree of life, braids, and flowers. The door would be ornamented with a flower that had as many stems as there were members of the family living in the house. The large and always growing Zavacky family would have required a competent artist. A cousin remembers, "Ulia Varchola, Andy's mother, was the first to paint cottages. . . . There was still no money even for whitewash, so she dug out a little reddish clay, dissolved it, and painted the walls with it. Then, when they had limewash, she 'daubed' roses on with a brush. . . . When the wall was painted red, she found some blue clay by the water and painted the plinth blue . . . painting white flowers on a blue background."[121] Painting was done yearly before important holidays, and the designs, always new, were drawn by girls and elderly women with a cloth wrapped round a stick. Ulia made stencils from wood slats and covered the interior walls with patterns of flowers, animals, sun, and stars, foreshadowing Andy Warhol's pre-Pop artwork of butterflies and flowers, which the art critic Arthur Danto described as "almost a form of folk art."[122]

Like all Rusyn women, Ulia decorated household linen and men's and women's holiday clothing with lavish cross-stitch and crewel embroidery, in geometrical patterns or in designs and colors inspired by wildflowers, trees, the moon and stars. Fertility symbols from nature, originally meant to protect the wearer from the incursion of evil spirits, were embroidered on the hems, sleeves, and openings of shirts. Each village had characteristic ornamental motifs and compositional patterns, handed down from generation to generation. The Russian ethnographer Sergei Makovsky traveled through Subcarpathian Rus' collecting objects of folk art, which were exhibited to great acclaim in Prague in 1924. He noted "the remarkable difference between the embroidery designs of Subcarpathian Rus' and those of Great or Little Russia [Ukraine]."

> The national dress, together with the embroidery with which it is decorated, is the most well-preserved element of Subcarpathian peasant culture. The persistence of the national dress may be attributed to the backwardness of the country, but also to the depth of national feeling. Whether under the rule of Hungarians, Austrians, or Poles, the Ruthenians kept to their "Rusyn" dress as to a banner. And this showed a healthy instinct. The national costume was an efficient protection against spiritual absorption by foreign elements. If, after centuries of bondage, the Subcarpathian villager still says, "I am a Rusyn," if he has not forgotten his native speech, and if he has preserved his orthodox character within the Greek Catholic faith, this is a result of his fidelity to the national dress of his ancestors.[123]

Everyday women's dress consisted of a blouse and underskirt, covered with a skirt of homespun hemp, decorated at the bottom with red and blue threads and, what Makovsky called, "a special kind of homemade lace."[124] A band of embroidery ornamented the sleeves below the shoulder, and delicate designs decorated the breast and cuffs. A *laibyk,* or sleeveless vest, made of blue or black coarse cloth or velvet, decorated with multicolored laces and embroidery, was worn buttoned up, often with a necklace of rows of glass beads. In cold weather, both men and women wore a *hunia,* a cloak made of homespun lambswool, and women wore high boots.

The most elaborate form of Rusyn folk art, *pysanky* or painted eggs, was traditionally a woman's art.[125] At Easter, girls gave *pysanky* to boys, the most beautiful egg intended for the boy a girl liked best. In an intricate and unrecorded technology, Rusyn folk artists created natural dyes, achieving various intensities in a

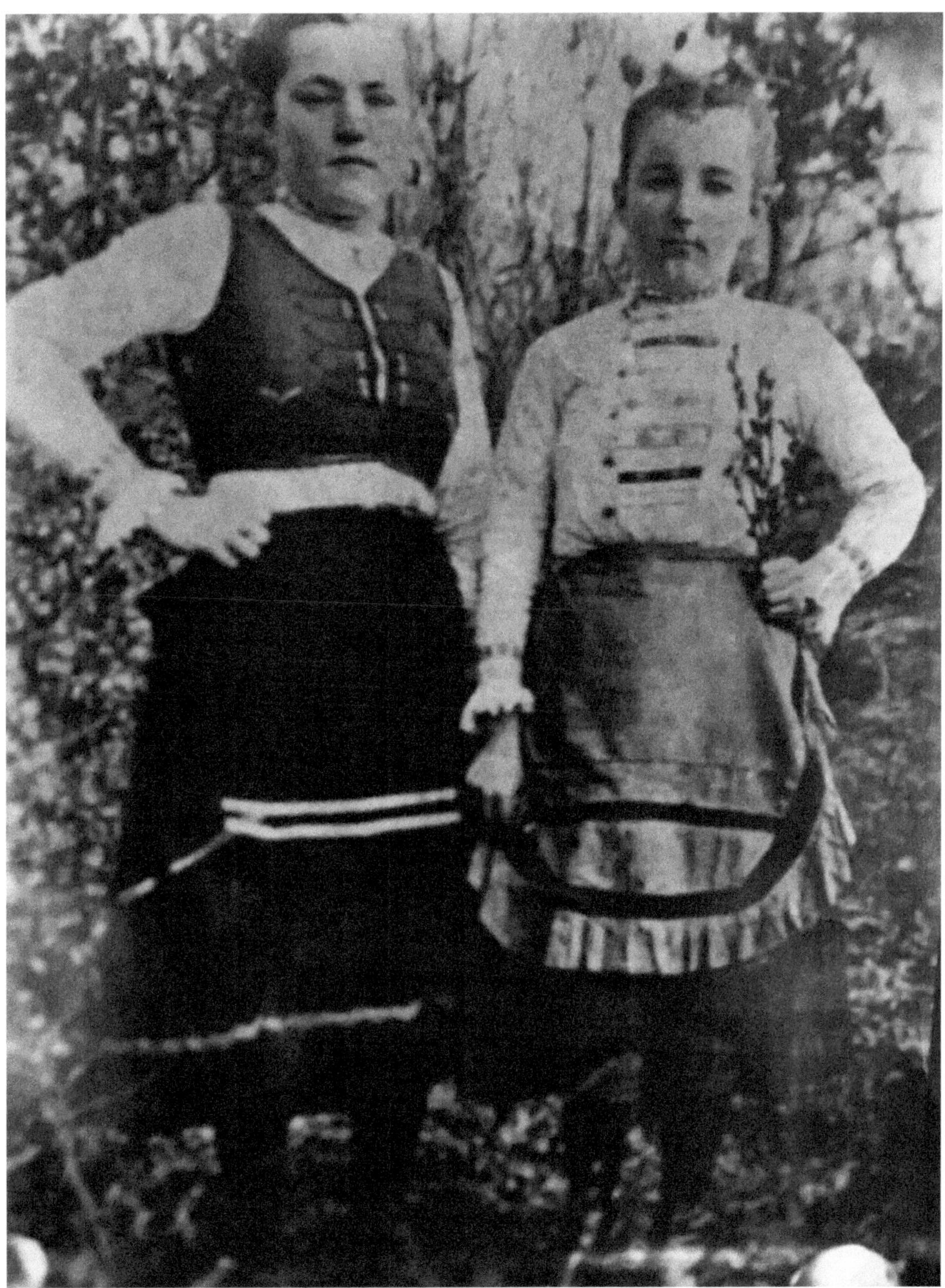

Figure 1.6. Julia's sisters Elena and Eva ca. 1920.

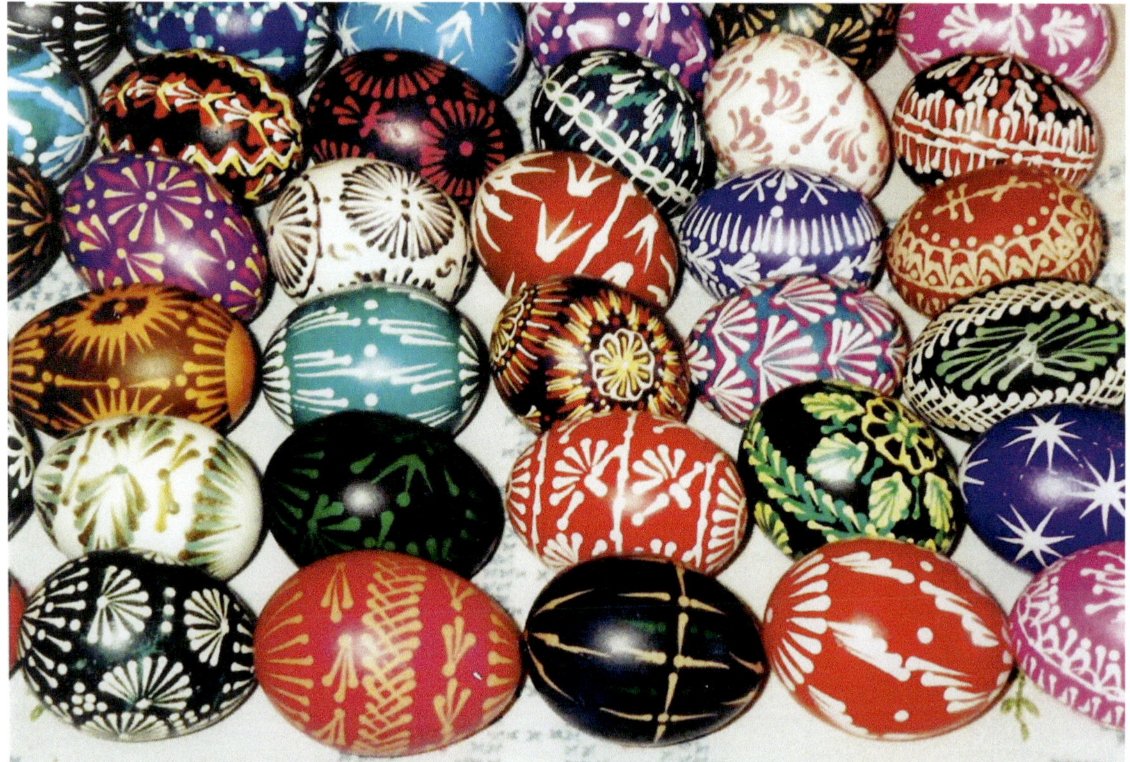

Figure 1.7. Carpatho-Rusyn pysanky by Mary Anne Mistick.

virtually infinite color scale. Throughout the year women gathered young winter rye, hemp, raspberries, walnut shells, birch branches, onion skins, and even soot to prepare the dyes. Not just at Easter but throughout the year, they decorated eggs in an atmosphere of spirituality, reciting ritual prayers before choosing symbols and motifs for what would become not just an aesthetic object, but a talisman possessed of magical powers. From time immemorial, the *pysanka* was believed to protect the house from fire and to ward off the "evil eye," to increase the yield of fruit trees and ensure a good harvest. Painted eggs were placed in coffins and on graves, and *pysanka* shells were believed to have medicinal properties. When cast on hot coals, their smoke was said to cure illness.

By the twentieth century, *pysanky* had lost their symbolic significance, and their aesthetic function became dominant. Since it was one of the few forms of decoration that did not require large financial expenditures, it was an art form accessible even to poor peasants. Styles differed from village to village, but, as the ethnographer Pavlo Markovyč writes, "All *pysanka* artists conform to certain basic principles of decoration: symmetry, alternation, rhythm, repetition, color harmony. These norms assure the aesthetic quality of the *pysanka* as a work of art. What is even more noteworthy is that these standards are observed by simple peasant women who have had no artistic training, but who exhibit a high degree of inborn aesthetic taste."[126]

Ulia decorated *pysanky* in the time-honored style native to the Carpatho-Rusyns of eastern Slovakia, which is entirely distinct from the Ukrainian cultural tradition. The Rusyn folk artist applied hot wax to the egg surface with a pin or nail, its sharp end driven into a wooden holder. Beginning with a dot, she drew a short stroke that tapered off as the wax was spent. With speed and dexterity, the artist drew an organized design of stylized motifs from nature, often bordered with ornamental geometric bands. When the ornamentation was completed, the egg was placed in the dye, the wax-coated areas impervious to the pigment. Finally, the dry egg was warmed over a flame to soften the wax, which was then wiped from the egg surface with a cloth, leaving behind a negative image of the design. This wax-resist dyeing art is similar in principle to the silkscreen technique that became Warhol's trademark.

Julia passed on the distinctive Rusyn method of ornamentation and her sense of color harmony to her son, who would later give decorated eggs as gifts to New York art directors and business contacts. One of his drawings from the 1950s of a decorated egg depicts typical Rusyn *pysanky* folk motifs of the sun and stylized flowers, with a traditional ornamental border of chicken feet. In a 1977 interview, Warhol was asked if he thought more female artists would emerge as a result of the women's liberation movement. His answer was not surprising, given that the first artist he knew was his mother: "I always thought that most artists were women—you know, the ones that did the Navajo Indian rugs, American quilts, all that great hand-painting on Forties clothes."[127] For the young Ulia Zavacka, natural and traditional bits of homespun beauty brightened and enriched the hardscrabble life that was the Rusyns' lot, and she taught her son, Andy Warhol, to appreciate the aesthetic value of ordinary objects. Today her grandchildren are consummate *pysanky* artists.[128]

Ivan Kupala and Saint John the Baptist

Prehistoric Carpatho-Rusyns were pagans who shared features of the mythology common among East Slavs. Since their livelihood depended on the success of their crops, they worshipped various gods in the forces of nature. Perun, the god of thunder, controlled the weather; Iarilo ruled fertility; Veles, the cattle god, protected shepherds and their herds; and Mokosh, the only female deity, protected women, the family, and the home. Many minor gods and goddesses governed various aspects of life and seasons of the year: Lada was the Slavic god of love; Kupala reigned over water and vegetation; and Koliada ruled the winter season. The pagan Slavs entrusted themselves to the protection of household spirits and magical charms, fearing witches and sorcerers who could manipulate the forces of nature for their own ends.

When Christianity entered the lives of the Slavs in the ninth century, it did not eliminate the old cult, but instead, supplemented it, creating a synthetic belief system in which folk rites and Christian rituals overlapped and reinforced one another. Thus, the winter festival of Koliada was merged with the feast of Christ's Nativity, and the Rusyn word for a Christmas hymn is *koliada*. The summer solstice fused fertility rites in honor of Kupala, the god of water and vegetation, with the waters of Christian baptism on the midsummer feast day of Saint John the Baptist. The feast was known to Rusyn peasants as Ioann Kupala, a conflation of the Christian Saint John and the pagan Kupala. For centuries, devout Rusyn peasants clung to the ancient rites, seeing no contradiction between magical practices and Christian beliefs, between incantations and prayers. While such practices were often prohibited by Hungarian and Slovak Roman Catholic churches, local Greek Catholic priests saw no contradiction to canon law in such play, which was viewed as an innocent reservoir of national creativity that was better than the tavern. As time went on, Carpatho-Rusyns learned to extol the tenets of church dogma, but the coexistence of pagan ideas with Christian doctrine, known as *dvoeverie* or "double belief," survived into the twentieth century and exists in various forms today.

Rusyns trace their conversion to Christianity to the Byzantine missionaries Cyril (Constantine) and Methodius, who began preaching the Christian faith to the Slavs of central Europe in 863. They devised an alphabet, the prototype for Cyrillic, to transcribe the Slavic idiom. The language they developed for liturgical use, Church Slavonic, was related to and influenced by the vernacular speech of the people. After the eleventh-century schism in the Christian church that divided the Greek East from the Latin West, Carpatho-Rusyns followed the Eastern, or Orthodox, branch of the church. However, situated as they were between East and West, feeling pressure from Orthodoxy on one side and Roman Catholicism and Protestantism on the other, the Rusyn bishops of Austria-Hungary sought a way to preserve and protect their unique religious heritage. They found it in compromise. Seeing political advantage in embracing the official religion of the country where they lived, they accepted union with the universal Catholic Church, under the condition that the Ruthenian (Rusyn) church would retain the rites and traditions of Orthodoxy. Empress Maria Theresa of Austria-Hungary later termed this compromise the "Greek Catholic Church"—"Greek" in its Byzantine ritual and "Catholic" in its union with Rome. Preservation of Orthodox customs and traditions—the Church Slavonic liturgical language, the Julian calendar, a married priesthood, distribution of the Eucharist as both bread and wine, the image-covered iconostasis (altar screen) that separated the sanctuary from the nave, *prostopenie*, a style of singing unaccompanied by musical instruments and heavily influenced by folk music—meant that the externals of the faith were essentially unchanged for the Rusyn people. By the eighteenth century, Greek Catholicism, today known as Ruthenian Byzantine Catholicism, had become decisively linked to Carpatho-Rusyns.

The appeal of Eastern Christianity to the early pagan Slavs is best captured in the legendary account of Prince Vladimir's choice of Orthodoxy as the official religion of Kievan Rus' in 988. Upon examining several world religions, Vladimir's emissaries returned from an Eastern Christian liturgy in Constantinople with the report: "We knew not whether we were in heaven or on earth and we are at a loss to describe it. We only know that God dwells there among men, and their service is fairer than the ceremonies of other nations. We cannot forget that beauty."[129] That is, Orthodox Christianity was chosen as the religion of the East Slavs not for its dogma or abstract theology, but for the aesthetic appeal of its liturgy, which has hardly changed over the millennium. According to the Carpatho-Rusyn conversion myth, the Rusyns of central Europe had adopted Christianity a century before the Kievans, but like them, they had surely been won over by the religion's splendid, symbolic allure. The primacy of the aesthetic appeal persisted in Rusyn religion through the centuries, as seen in the contrast between the simple homes of immigrant miners and millworkers and the beauty of their churches.

In twentieth-century America, Andy Warhol's approach to religion was similarly aesthetic, rather than doctrinal. More than once, he expressed thoughts along the lines of these answers in his 1977 interview with Glenn O'Brien.[130]

O'BRIEN: Do you still go to church?
WARHOL: Yeah. I just sneak in at funny hours.
O'BRIEN: Do you go to Catholic churches?

WARHOL: Yeah, they're the prettiest.
O'BRIEN: Do you believe in God?
WARHOL: I guess I do. I like church. . . . There are so many beautiful Catholic churches in New York. I used to go to some Episcopal churches, too.
O'BRIEN: Do you ever think about God?
WARHOL: No.

In the "prettiest" churches, a Carpatho-Rusyn Christian does not so much "think about" God, as feel God's presence. The Eastern Catholic liturgy appeals to the senses. The beauty of the priests' ornate vestments, stately processions, the monumental frescoes and glistening icons attract the eye. Clouds of fragrant incense from the priest's energetic swinging of the censer over icons and worshippers soothe and entrance.[131] The hypnotic resonance of the musical chant and repetitive litanies ("Hospodi pomilui, Hospodi pomilui, Hospodi pomilui" (Lord have mercy), repeated after each petition in a long series, have a mesmerizing effect. In Eastern iconography and liturgy, the value is not variety, but repetition and familiarity. In icons, as in Warhol's work, while the basic design is repeated, no two images are the same. For illiterate peasants, the iconostasis told the story of Christ and the saints in pictures, rather than texts. Models for behavior are found in Bible stories and saints' lives, rather than in dry precepts. The formulaic rituals of Sunday liturgies and holiday ceremonies provide structure and comfortable familiarity, while Lenten fasts and midnight vigils afford spiritual exhilaration. This religion was ideal for the simple, illiterate Carpatho-Rusyn people, who basked in the aesthetic delight of the liturgy and wholeheartedly accepted the sacred truth it embodied.

Ulia Zavacka found a complement to the beauty of Carpathian nature in the splendor of the church. As a young woman, she "sang like an angel," according to her sister. She knew the entire liturgy, and after World War I, when men were scarce, she led the congregational singing as a cantor.[132] Ulia's piety also found form in visual art. When the village church in Miková was being reconstructed, she assisted the painters, who were restoring frescoes that depicted scenes from the Bible. She helped mix colors and marveled at the ability of artists to make human figures come alive on the church walls.[133] Throughout her life, she drew pictures of angels that resembled the distinctive primitive style of Rusyn icons.

The rhythm of Ulia's life in Miková was regulated by the religious calendar of the church and the folk calendar of the seasons. The church prescribed ritualized holidays that were welcomed by the peasants, since work on those days was prohibited. But it also imposed eighteen weeks of strict fasts throughout the year, when meat, fish, dairy products, oil, and alcohol were forbidden. Folk proverbs indicate a spiritual appreciation of fasting ("The body fasts and the soul brightens"), as well as a grudging tolerance of the duty ("In Lent even the bed is hard"). But the laws of the church could not completely prevail over the primordial order of the seasons, in which primitive man lived at the mercy of natural forces. Instead, the Christian and the primitive merged. Christian saints took over the protective duties of ancient pagan gods, and pre-Christian rituals were endowed with religious significance.

Scholars assert that "Carpatho-Rusyns generally retained archaic elements in their folk customs more than any other Slavic people or ethnic group."[134] The Rusyn conflation of the Christian and the pagan suggests an answer to the question of Andy Warhol's religiosity, which has long perplexed biographers. At one extreme, its influence on the artist has been exaggerated, and at the other, it has been dismissed as "a mix of aesthetics and quite practical superstition."[135] In fact, a study of the "religiosity" of Warhol's Miková parents and ancestors shows that aesthetics, theatricality, and superstition were an integral part of their spirituality. Practices and beliefs that derived from pagan superstition left even devout Rusyn Greek Catholics open to alternative ways of thinking, a distrust of science, and acceptance of the paranormal. Their attachment to ritual, tradition, and the supernatural, often superseding church laws and doctrine, was part and parcel of their religious sensibility.

Ethnographers have noted more than sixty days in the Carpatho-Rusyn calendar year that were connected to various rituals and strictly formulated events, which, like the folk wedding, resulted in a theatrical transformation of everyday life.[136] The feast of the Annunciation on April 7 by the Julian calendar marked the beginning of the agricultural year. Seed grain was taken to be blessed in church, and worshipers brought home sanctified bread, which they believed to have protective powers.[137] On May 6, the feast day of Saint George, patron of peasants, cattle, and forest animals, the villagers' flocks were herded to the mountain meadows for the summer season in a ceremony that included prayers, music, songs, and jokes. The chief shepherd was a dramatic figure who enjoyed an aura of power and mystery. The haunting call of his *trembita* or alpine horn, up to thirteen feet in length, resounded six miles across the forested mountains to announce the arrival and departure of the herds or to signal the far-flung shepherds in the upland pastures. The sheep had been blessed by the priest before leaving the village, but to prevent the herd from straying and to protect it from witches and unclean spirits, the shepherd performed arcane magical acts with fire and ax. In a complex procedure, accompanied by incantations and dances, he lit a symbolic bonfire, or *vatra*, that would burn throughout the summer until the end of the grazing season.

Pentecost, celebrated on the fiftieth day after Easter to commemorate the descent of the Holy Spirit on the apostles, was a time for Rusyn farmers to pray for favorable weather and a good crop. The village priest consecrated the seedlings with holy water to protect them from lightning and natural disasters, which could destroy in a moment the hard labor of a year. But Pentecost was better known to Carpatho-Rusyn peasants as the "green holiday" or Rusalia, the name of an ancient Slavic fertility festival. The people celebrated Rusalia by decorating the church, their homes, and the horns of cattle with greenery, a symbol of vegetative power. Rusalia was a time for engagements and marriages. In a vestige of pagan ancestor worship, the Rusyns left bread, eggs, and grain on family graves, and asked their ancestors to bless the harvest.

On Saint John's Eve, the midsummer festival of the Nativity of Saint John the Baptist, young men leaped over bonfires, called *sobitky*, in what was originally a magical act of purification. Girls tossed wreaths into the stream to predict their marital prospects. Saint John's Eve, or Ioann Kupala, was a time when the community tolerated excesses in behavior and a certain range of sexual freedom. A straw effigy of a male figure with a prominent phallus was paraded around the village, as young people appealed for supplies to dress the scarecrow, and food and brandy to feed him for three planned days of merriment. Herders, both men and women, spent the night of the summer solstice in the forest, tending their cattle and passing the time in skits and games with erotic undertones. In bawdy songs and ribald tales, double-edged metaphors from agrarian life commented sardonically on marriage, sex, and seduction. As scholars of Slavic peasant life have put it, "Peasant society might have been sexually repressive, but it was rarely sexual prudish."[138] Sexual ignorance was out of the question, when a large family lived in one undivided room and in close proximity to farm animals. Sexual games were an integral part of courtship practices and folklore. The strictures of the church were counterbalanced by permissive traditional customs, which surely shaped Rusyn peasants, including Julia Warhola, in a fashion that was more complex than the naive, innocent image they may have later presented to the outside world.

Midsummer was a time for women to gather medicinal herbs before sunrise in the mountains and meadows around Miková—Saint-John's-wort or horse-heal, valerian, peppermint, and chamomile. *Kravnyk* (bloodwort) was used to staunch wounds, *kudilka* (horsetail) cured kidney disease, and *ratash* (wild chrysanthemum) eased stomach pain. But it was also the time when sorcerers and witches gathered noxious plants—swallowwort and nightshade—to bring harm to God-fearing folk. Like most primitive peoples, old-world Rusyns believed that illness was caused by supernatural forces or the "evil eye." Petr Bogatyrev, a Russian ethnographer who traveled through Subcarpathian Rus' in the interwar years of the twentieth century, reported that Carpatho-Rusyn peasants trusted folk remedies and supernatural cures, preferring to place themselves in the hands of sorcerers, rather than doctors.[139]

The feast of Saints Peter and Paul was the eve of the harvest, when the short summer was already trending toward autumn, as the proverb indicates: "Peter and Paul arrived and the first leaf dropped." Another proverb started the harvest: "On the day of Saint Procopius, cut the rye and tie the sheaf." In a practice that recognized the supernatural force abiding in the earth, harvesters rolled in the soil to derive strength for the work ahead. After prayers, the farmer swung his scythe, taking the first swath, and the long days of backbreaking labor began, in hopes of bringing in the harvest before the first frost. Women and older children followed the reapers, gathering and binding the grain in sheaves to be taken away for threshing and winnowing. Even young children helped by raking the stubble.

After the harvest came the festival, which was again a mixture of Christian prayers and pagan superstitions. Ears of grain were gathered in a sheaf, decorated with wildflowers, and ceremoniously brought to the household to be used in wedding wreaths and childbirth beds, and to be placed in the nesting boxes of hens, to increase egg production. By the end of August, the harvest was in, and it was time for pilgrimage. Villagers from Miková and the surrounding area walked in procession to the Krásny Brod monastery, stopping for prayers at roadside shrines along the way.

Preparations for winter were then in high gear, with a deadline of the feast of the Protection of the Mother of God in mid-October. Snow was already visible on the mountains, and with ritual and ceremony, the herds were brought down from the *polonyna* to the sonorant wail of the *trembita*. The last cabbages were salted for winter, potatoes were dug up for cold storage, fruit was dried, and vegetables were pickled. After the feast of the Presentation of the Virgin in the Temple in early December, it was prohibited to dig the earth, which was believed to be at rest, gathering strength for summer. The open-air festivities of young people came to an end and indoor evening spinning parties began. Women and girls spun flax into thread, while young men entertained them with music and games.

The preparation for Christmas began in late November with the beginning of Saint Phillip's fast, but on Saint Andrew's feast day, fasting restrictions were modified to allow the celebration of one of the most popular festivals, especially for girls. Andrew was the patron saint of love. On the eve of the holiday, girls visited the homes of the many boys and men named Andrew in the Rusyn village, wished them "many years," and, in Halloween style, asked for an "offering." Girls and boys then gathered for a party of feasting, fortune-telling, and magic rites to predict the girls' marriage prospects. The number of stones gathered from the stream, the first flour pellet eaten by a rooster, the condition of the ninth post from the left in a fence, the shape assumed by molten lead when dropped into a basin of cold water—all these seemingly insignificant phenomena held secret meaning and magical significance.

Mothering the Mind

Julia Warhola understood life according to the old-world Greek Catholic religious culture, supplemented by the codex of superstitions, proverbs, and instructions that guided one's actions almost every day of the yearly cycle. On Saint George's day a peasant could find out how many years he would live by counting the beats of a stork's wings. On a holiday, one could not sweep the house for fear of sweeping away happiness. While each directive may be trivial, thousands of trivialities added up to a world where every minor action or object held charmed significance, and nothing was too trifling for attention. It was a world where holy days directed daily duties, and natural phenomena exerted power over human life, a world of inspirational fantasy and destructive fear.

These attitudes, which were commonplace for the young Ulia Zavacka, became fundamental to Andy Warhol's artistic vision. When Julia left Miková for industrial Pittsburgh, she left behind agrarian precepts, which were of little value beyond her kitchen garden. But she brought with her traditions, prayers, and superstitions to pass on to her sons. Andy, her youngest, was most receptive. His cinematic collaborator Paul Morrissey said, "Andy was not a typical American. I knew both of his brothers and they are typical Americans. Andy was more like his mother. They were ... village people using their natural intuition."[140] John Richardson, the eulogist at Warhol's memorial service, attributed Andy's religious consciousness to "atavism as personified by his adored and adoring mother."[141] For Julia, as for Andy, intuition and atavism, the reversion to ancestral or primordial qualities, were integral to how they saw life and understood art.

Warhola family members insist that Julia was the most important influence on her artist son. In *Mothering the Mind*, Ruth Perry calls mothers the "necessary others" who have not been credited properly for the role they play in the creative work of their children. "And yet to a greater or lesser extent the artistic achievements were shaped by their presences."[142] Julia's presence in Andy's life was infused by the overlapping reality and fantasy of Miková. According to Perry, "Probably the most important function of 'mothering' the mind of an adult, as of an infant, is to ease the movement between inner and outer reality so as to create more usable space between the two in which to work. The 'mother's' simple accord about basic values and assumptions extends the area in which inner and outer reality overlap and, by sharing the space, protects it from threat from without." Andy Warhol's creative practice shows an easy movement between outer and inner reality, facts and fancies. For him, everyday life was worthy of artistic and cinematic attention. Minor objects were imbued with artistic power, as he painted soup cans, flowers, and the head of a cow in series that mimic the visual repetition of the iconostasis and the aural iteration of prayerful litanies. His films portray the inconsequential actions of ordinary people, who, like the actors in Rusyn weddings and Rusalia rituals, attain theatrical impact. Perry writes that the mother's influence does not need to be direct or intellectual. "She might, for instance, call forth certain qualities that are central to the work . . . or she might embody them." That is, she "speaks the culture," in this case, Carpatho-Rusyn culture, through her own personal story.

While there is little evidence of direct influence from Julia on Warhol's choice of subject, his cow wallpaper shows the kind of nebulous correlation that existed between Julia's life and Andy's art. Ivan Karp, a promoter of Pop art and director of the Castelli Gallery where Warhol's cow wallpaper was first exhibited in 1966, took credit for the idea, recalling his conversation with Andy: "'Every painter has to make cows at one time or another, right? It's one of the most important emblems in art making for five hundred years!' [Warhol] said, 'Cows! Oh, Ivan, that's wonderful! Isn't a cow like a mother?' I said, 'Yes, a cow is very much a symbol of a mother in many ways.'"[143] The source photograph for Warhol's cow image was a reproduction of a jersey cow from an agricultural industry magazine found by Andy's colleague, Gerard Malanga. According to Malanga, Warhol disliked the image, but Malanga insisted, "Oh, Andy, this is the shot! It's so maternal!"[144] For Andy, whose familiarity with cows came primarily through his mother's stories, the link must have been especially poignant. Remembering their childhood, John Warhola said, "We didn't have no radio or TV to keep you quiet and in the winter [mother] would tell us to come in the kitchen and she'd say 'Alright somebody draw a picture of a cow,'. . . and then the one who draws the best picture will get a prize. . . . Andy would always win."[145]

Warhol's Pop treatment of the pastoral image is creative and uniquely American. According to Karp, Warhol said he decided to use it as wallpaper, "something super-pastoral, too large, too big, too ridiculous," and David Bourdon comments that the vivid and abrasive color scheme of fluorescent pink against a sulfur-yellow background suggests that "the creature was on some kind of acid trip."[146] However, a European perspective opens the image to interpretation based on a way of seeing the world through Rusyn eyes. The Czech novelist Bohumil Hrabal described his visit to the Andy Warhol Museum of Modern Art in Medzilaborce, Slovakia. "We saw several hundred cows with halters, several hundred cows adorning the walls like wallpaper, and all at once I realized—that before the Campbell's Soup there had to come these cows and their meat."[147]

Warhol's images have often been intellectualized and overanalyzed. The cow may be simply a Warholian play on a common pastoral trope. But if the biographer Wayne Koestenbaum can theorize that the cow represents the "bovine aspect" of Warhol's temperament, a parody of his own public persona as "a mute who can't explain himself," Hrabal's hypothesis—that it comes from a Rusyn way of seeing that is antecedent to, and essential for, the appearance of the American Campbell's soup can—is at least as productive.[148] And of course, the link between the cows of Miková meadows and the cow in psychedelic colors is Andy's mother.

The influence subconsciously transmitted from Julia to Andy is even more apparent in his temperament and worldview, a down-to-earth practicality and superstitious mysticism that would not have been out of place in Miková. Warhol's fear of hospitals and distrust of doctors is well known. As John Richardson put it, "Like a medieval alchemist, [he] delved into mysticism and magic, and (true to his Slavic heritage) folk wisdom and folk remedies."[149] Like a Carpatho-Rusyn peasant, he rejected doctors in favor of alternative medicine. He took garlic pills to prevent illness and ate garlic sandwiches, albeit together with Reese's peanut butter cups.[150] In a practice that might have been prescribed by the village sorcerer, he let his dachshunds lie on top of him all night. "I hoped they would pick up [the illness] and take it away from me." Like the Rusyns of Miková who feared the "evil eye" and were ever watchful for the action of unclean spirits, Warhol speculated about the existence of "walk-in" souls, ghosts, and evil spirits. He was interested in Tarot cards and pyramid power. He waved crystals over vodka to render it benign and used gemstones for energy, protection, and in a futile attempt to repel roaches. Just

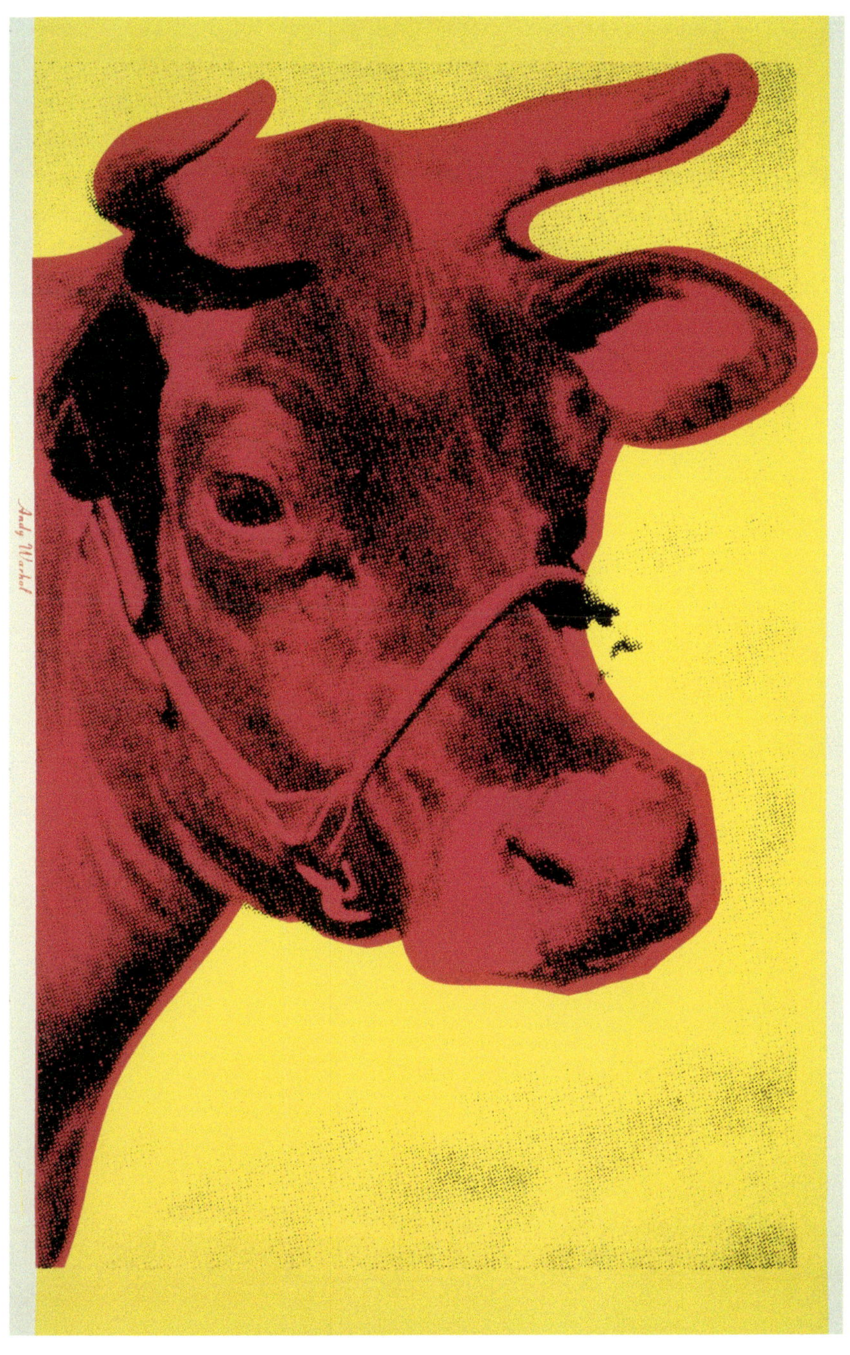

Figure 1.8. Andy Warhol, *Cow*, 1966. Screenprint on wallpaper 45½" × 29¾".

as Rusyns put themselves into the hands of sorcerers, Andy sought healing through treatment with crystals, consulting what he called a "crystal doctor."

Julia's presence in Andy's life animated Miková for him on a subconscious level. Without realizing it, he internalized and incorporated attitudes, values, and behaviors that had their source in Carpatho-Rusyn peasant culture, and he went on to reproduce them in a unique American style, both in his art and in his life. Ulia Zavacka's early experiences in Miková laid the foundation for her life in Pittsburgh and New York. Carpatho-Rusyn peasant culture both infused and circumscribed her sense of self and her understanding of the world. But before coming to America, she had to undergo the suffering of loss and war, which scarred her for life. Ulia Zavacka, the young bride with flowing golden hair, who tended cows and danced around Saint John's Eve bonfires in the Old Country, was not the same Julia Warhola who came to the New World.

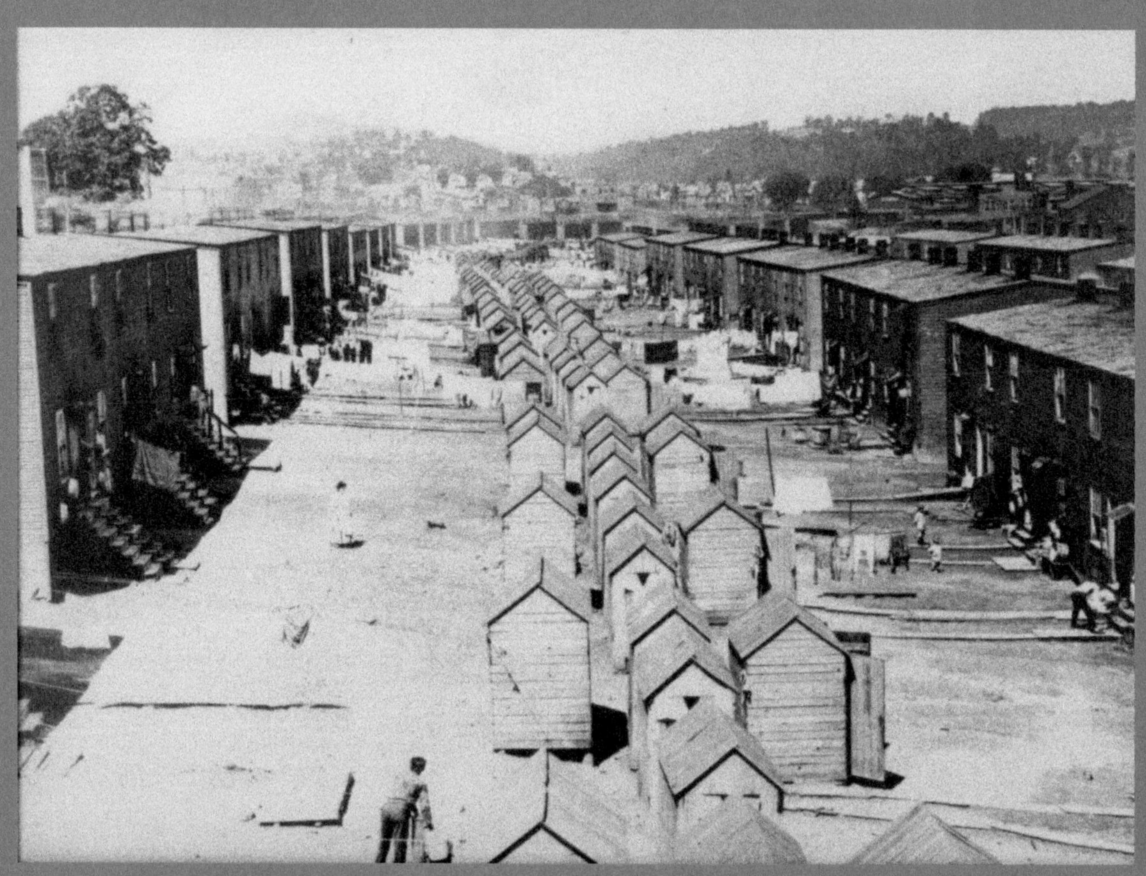

Red Row in Lyndora, PA. Communal toilets lined by frame houses.

2   "Then Everything Bad"

After the wedding, like all traditional Carpatho-Rusyn
brides, Julia lived with her husband's family, where she was subject to the authority of her mother-in-law. Relations between new brides and their mothers-in-law
were notoriously antagonistic. Andrii's mother was a widow; his father had died of
pneumonia at age fifty-five when Andrii was ten years old. After Andrii's marriage
to Julia in 1909, his brother Joseph left for America, and his brother Jan was still
a bachelor at home. As the only young woman in the household, Julia was tasked
with the domestic work at the Varchola home, but her own family also needed her
help. Just seven months after her wedding, Julia's father died of tuberculosis at
age fifty-seven. Her older sister Mary had married Vasyl Preksta in 1906 and left
in 1910 to join him in Cambridge, Ohio. Anna, seven years Julia's junior, had also
emigrated. If we can believe her reports to United States census takers in 1920 and
1930, Anna left Miková for America at age eleven in 1910. Her name is not found in
available online passenger lists. Julia's older brothers, Stephen, John, and Andrew,
had been living in Pennsylvania since the early years of the century.

As most of her siblings were in America, Julia assumed responsibility for her
mother, her fourteen-year-old brother Yurko, and her sisters Elena and Eva, six and
three years old. From an early age, she also worked for the widowed village priest,

running errands and helping to care for his four motherless children. Given the toil and hardships of daily life, having a child might not have been Julia's highest priority. But in 1912, when it became clear that the economic and military situation might force her husband to emigrate, Julia became pregnant.

In traditional Carpatho-Rusyn culture, childlessness was seen as God's punishment. Peasant society treated childless women with disdain, not allowing them the same level of participation in church or cultural affairs, and they were excluded from the circle of married *svashki* who "capped" the bride at weddings.[1] While putting off pregnancy was often recognized as desirable, the only available form of birth control was practical magic. During the wedding ceremony, the bride sat on her hand, carefully configuring her fingers such that the number of fingers she sat on conformed to the number of years she wished to defer pregnancy. Or she wore a padlock in her bodice for two, three, or four days, as many years as she hoped to wait. This primitive method of "birth control" meant that most Rusyn families were large, and the Zavacky family, with fourteen documented births and nine living children, was not atypical.

Family stories suggest that Julia was not interested in putting off pregnancy. She told her grandchildren about a traditional game of bringing water from the creek in a mug and then hanging the mug on a hook. Only after she had hung her mug on the fourth hook did she learn that this predicted the number of years before a pregnancy would occur.[2] The game was off by only a few months, as Julia became pregnant in early 1912. We have no specific information about her pregnancy, but we can assume that, according to Rusyn custom, she was respected and supported as the bearer of new life. Her workload was likely reduced, and she would have been indulged when it came to food and simple wants. She prayed and gazed at the holy icons to ensure that the child would be attractive, and she wore garlic to protect it against evil spirits. There were numerous superstitious restrictions on her behavior—baking bread might cause a fire in the child's body, eating hare meat could cause a harelip, and bathing in a stream might result in the child's death by drowning. In advanced stages of pregnancy, she could have been forbidden from going into the field for fear of triggering a hailstorm. On the other hand, she might have been asked to walk around a fruit tree, in the belief that a pregnant woman could bring about a bountiful harvest.

Childbirth took place at home, attended by a midwife or, more likely, by the old women of the village, who had some practical knowledge of folk medicine and were well-versed in the finer points of superstition. To facilitate an easy birth, all locks were released and knots were untied. The mother-to-be might be slathered with oil and bathed in a trough or the barrel that was used for making sauerkraut in winter. Sacred herbs, gathered on Saint John's Eve for this very purpose, were burned. The smoke that wafted through the air was believed to stimulate cleansing, healing, purifying, and protection from evil forces. The newborn was immediately sprinkled with holy water and laid on a sheepskin, with its feet pointing away from the door to prevent an early death. When the child received its first bath, a coin and a piece of garlic were added to the water to ensure health, strength, and prosperity. The baby would be swaddled and placed on the floor, to be picked up by the father in a symbolic demonstration of parenthood.

When relatives visited, they were expected to mock, belittle, and symbolically spit upon the child, for any praise might tempt evil spirits and bring misfortune. The christening, when babies received the sacraments of baptism and chrismation (confirmation), usually took place on the first or second Sunday after the birth. The godparents, a young man (known as *kum*) and woman (*kuma*), were chosen by the parents and became respected kin. When they returned from church with the child after baptism, the godparents sang, "We took from you a pagan, we have brought you a Christian. / That it would grow up for the joy and pleasure, / Of its parents and godparents / And especially for God, our Heavenly Father, / ... / That it would go to church, / But would not shun the tavern." If the child was a boy, the following wish was added: "So that he would not be poor in health, / Or lack money / So that he could plow and sow, / But also hold a pen." If the baby was a girl, they passed her from one person to another to ensure that she would not lack for dance partners when she grew up. They sang their wish "that she would be a good worker in the field, / A good dancer, / Able to learn, /And able to love."

After childbirth the new mother was considered unclean and vulnerable to evil forces and various maladies. She would not attend church or reenter society until she was "churched" on the fortieth day after childbirth in a rite of thanksgiving and purification that had roots in the Old Testament. As time went on, women contrived to shorten the period of their exclusion, but this custom continued to one degree or another in the American immigration into the 1960s. In Rusyn immigrant communities, a tinge of impropriety was attached to the appearance of a new mother in public before "churching." In the Old Country, the "lying in" period had practical benefits for the child, who was protected from contagion, and for the mother, who was granted a period of recuperation from childbirth and rest from heavy domestic toil. That this may have been the original purpose of the custom is supported by the ethnographer Petr Bogatyrev's report that, according to a Greek Catholic priest, the peasants took the greatest care in observing this rite, even though he told them that the church attached no great importance to it.[3]

With her first child, it is uncertain whether Julia was able to enjoy the traditional festivities surrounding childbirth or the period of recovery afterward. Her daughter Maria was born in Miková on November 2, 1912, and was baptized and confirmed the next day.[4] The following day happened to be a Sunday, the day for christenings, but the hastily scheduled ceremony may indicate that the newborn's health was uncertain. Just thirty-three days later, on December 4, baby Maria died. She was buried in Miková on December 5, without receiving last rites. Church records indicate that the cause of death was unknown, but in the *Esquire* interview, Julia gave her own account: "I have daughter. She dies after six weeks. She catch cold. No doctor. We need doctor, but no doctor in town. Oh, I cry. Oh, I go crazy when baby died. I open window and yell, 'My baby dies. . . . My baby dead. My little girl.'"[5] There were certainly no trained doctors in the peasant village. From his mother, John Warhola heard: "If anything went wrong, they would go to the priest."

The death of her daughter was all the harder because Julia had to endure it without her husband, who was by then back in the United States. Andrii sailed from Bremen on November 16, which means he must have left Miková shortly after his daughter's birth. As Julia told the interviewer, "My husband leaves and then everything bad. My husband leaves and my little daughter dies." Julia, now left on her own, took care of her siblings and her husband's family. Vasyl Bezek, the husband of her youngest sister, remembers, "Ulia did everything in the home. She even knew how to scythe. She was living here at the Zavacky place, but used to go to the Varcholas to look after the old lady."[6] Julia recalled, "My husband in America. I work like horse. His parents, old people, I live with them.[7] I carried sack of potatoes on my back. I work and work. I was very strong lady." Meanwhile, Andrii was embarking on his second trip to America.

Going to America

Carpatho-Rusyns began emigrating from the poverty-stricken northeastern districts of Hungary in the 1880s. In the Rusyn-populated counties of Spysh, Zemplyn, and Sharysh, the birth rate was high, taxation was burdensome, arable land was scarce, and productivity was low. Of the peasantry in Hungary overall, only 30 percent owned enough land to ensure self-sufficiency. In northern Hungary where Rusyns lived, peasants owned tiny parcels of land or worked as landless tenant farmers. Widespread land scarcity caused Rusyns to emigrate in numbers disproportionately higher than their percentage of the country's population. Between 1899 and 1913, 82,284 persons emigrated from Zemplyn County, the Varchola-Zavacky homeland, representing 6.9 percent of the population.[8] The exodus was so significant that the average rate of emigration exceeded natural population growth by 119 percent, resulting in a net loss of the area's inhabitants. Taking into account the fact that only half of the emigrants passed through German ports legally and were reflected in official statistics, Paul Robert Magocsi puts the total number of Rusyn migrants from Hungary before World War I at 225,000.[9] As for the Warholas' village of Miková, the historian Vasyl Choma reports that as early as 1904, at least one male from each of the ninety Miková households had migrated to the United States, constituting a loss of nearly a third of village residents.[10] Mikováns continued to leave their homeland in waves until the coming of war in 1914.

For Carpatho-Rusyns, there were abundant "push" factors motivating them to leave their economically depressed and socially repressed homeland, but even more important were what scholars of immigration call "pull" factors—the prospect of work in America that might lead to prosperity. These promises were fueled by letters from friends and relatives that told of hard work, but also extraordinary earnings. American industrial wages were five to six times higher than agricultural incomes in Hungary, and work was steady.[11] A thrifty single working man could save at least $15 a month, which meant that six months' savings could buy four cows, and a year's savings could buy a hectare of land at home. Such opportunities motivated ambitious young men to travel to America with the intention of returning to the homeland and improving their lot. Records show that in the first decade of the twentieth century, 26 percent of all immigrants from Hungary became "remigrants," that is, returnees. For Zemplyn County, the figure was 32.5 percent. A Rusyn folk song expresses the pain of leaving and the hope of return in an upbeat, czardas-like melody:

> Let's go, boys, let's go to that America.
> I'll go with you, when I sell my oxen.
> Still not enough cash, I'll sell the cow.
> We'll go stealthily. God grant that our emperor
> Will release us to another king, the Anglo-American king.
> My wife cries for me, my dear soul.
> Don't cry, dear wife, we'll be together again.
> Just let me earn a bit in America, and I'll come home.
> I'll see my homeland again.[12]

Most emigrants spent less than five years in America. Stays of three or four years were most common, since that was the minimum time required for an unskilled worker to earn and save enough to make the trip worthwhile. For Rusyn peasants, who had long accepted the necessity of itinerant labor and seasonal migration into lower Hungary to make ends meet, the idea of crossing the sea for unparalleled fortune was hardly intimidating, and many made the round-trip more than once. The English Phillimores, who roamed the Carpathian region in the first decade of the twentieth century, repeatedly came upon local peasants who addressed them in English and talked about their sojourn in the United States.

From the Hungarian perspective, large landowners and industrial capitalists watched the expansion of emigration with trepidation. The Hungarian government took measures to stem the tide, but official views on emigration were conflicted. On one hand, the government was concerned about the implications of population decline for the country's military and labor force. On the other hand, emigration was a "safety valve" to discharge internal social pressures, as well as a means of raising the proportion of the Magyar population in a nation where they were becoming outnumbered by minorities. Local officials were also conscious of the influx of American dollars and the benefits accruing to the economy. As a result, government authorities pursued contradictory principles in an unenforceable laissez-faire emigration policy, studded with numerous lapses and loopholes.

As early as 1876, a decree called on authorities to alert would-be emigrants to the difficulties of emigration and the downside of life in America. Activities of steamship company agents were restricted, and priests were ordered to read a proclamation from the pulpit to discourage their flock from fleeing to America. In 1903 and 1909, laws were passed to regulate emigration further. Men of military age could emigrate only after obtaining special permits from the proper authorities and paying an exorbitant "security deposit." Those who attempted to bypass the directive were subject to a fine and imprisonment for up to two months. Gendarmes and border guards patrolled mountain paths and railroad stations to thwart illegal migrants. In 1907 alone, about 13,000 undocumented emigrants were prevented from leaving the country. Between 1909 and 1913, 35,575 people were prosecuted and sentenced for attempting to cross the borders illicitly. And starting in 1910, rewards were offered for reporting anyone trying to emigrate without proper authorization.[13]

But even these restrictive measures could not curb the outflow. While the United States did not require incoming aliens and immigrants to present passports until 1917, obtaining an official permit to emigrate from Hungary meant struggling with a convoluted bureaucracy, paying an exorbitant fee, and enduring indefinite delays. Few were willing to take on these obstacles. As a result, many Carpatho-Rusyns, bent on leaving their homeland, relied on boldness, cunning, and resourcefulness to find alternative stratagems. Would-be emigrants crossed the border posing as peddlers with carts full of baskets or as pilgrims en route to a shrine. Those with money could purchase falsified permits. Penniless Rusyns contrived to recycle used documents, which at the time included only cursory personal descriptions, without photographs or expiration dates. As soon as emigrants reached the United States, they sent their travel permits back home for the use of relatives and friends.

Until 1914, passport authority was relegated to district offices. A favorite ruse in Miková, according to the village historian Vasyl Choma, was to acquire a cheap and easily accessible "cattle passport." Since it was scripted in Hungarian, local officials, who could not read the language, recognized only the name of the "owner" of the alleged cattle, and accepted the veterinary passport as a legal permit for passage.[14] If all else failed, emigrants set out without a permit. Heeding the counsel of zealous steamship agents, they put aside their folk costumes for city clothes and bypassed on foot the gendarme checkpoints at major railway stations Once the would-be emigrants crossed the Hungarian border, permits were no longer necessary. Police preferred to extract a crown or two as a bribe, and steamship companies were more interested in increasing the number of their passengers than enforcing local regulations.

Andrii Varchola may have used one of these sly methods when he first emigrated from his homeland, probably in 1904 or 1905. His name is not found on available ship passenger lists. We know that he was in the United States for approximately three years, because his 1912 emigration manifest includes the notation of a previous 1905–1908 sojourn in Pittsburgh. Toward the end of 1904, conditions were exceptionally favorable for impoverished Rusyns seeking an escape route. The Hungarian government had signed an agreement with the Cunard Line to channel emigrants from Hungary through the Adriatic port of Fiume (now Rijeka in Croatia), with the purpose of diverting them from the German shipping companies that carried most of Hungary's emigrants across the sea. This effort to monopolize emigration from Hungary sparked a fare war, and the German lines fought for passengers by selling tickets below cost. The customary third-class ticket price of 180 crowns ($37.50) fell to as low as 40 crowns.[15] Emigration agents advertised heavily to encourage travel and offered emigrants prepaid tickets to the seaports for 20 to 40 crowns. Recognizing a good financial deal, Andrii may well have made his way to Hamburg or Bremen in 1904. But no matter how discounted the ticket may have been, emigration was still a major expense for a peasant whose annual income from field work in Hungary was approximately 111 crowns.[16] Many emigrants traveled on prepaid tickets purchased by relatives already in the United States. Others, most of whom could not qualify for loans from financial institutions, were forced to turn to moneylenders, who charged high rates of interest. Figures of 15, 50, and even 100 percent have been reported.[17] Despite the "America fever" that swept through eastern Europe, emigration was not undertaken lightly, and in many respects, it was actively discouraged.

"What Good to Us Is This America?"

In contrast to the American cultural myth that our immigrant ancestors came to the "land of opportunity" with visions of streets paved with gold, Carpatho-Rusyns viewed emigration through dimmer glasses. It was actively discouraged not only by the Hungarian government but also by Rusyn cultural and religious authorities. At the end of the nineteenth century, the Rusyn poet-priest Aleksander Pavlovych devoted a cycle of poems to the theme, expressing the perspective not of the emigrant, but of those left behind. He deplores the hardships of migration, the cost of which often left families destitute. Even worse, a son might die in an American coal mine or forsake his old-world values and abandon his parents. For them, "America" takes on a sardonic tonality: "What will we old folks do now / When we send our son across the sea? / It will be hard, so hard on us! / What good to us is this America?" For Pavlovych and the nationally conscious intelligentsia, emigration was but another negative consequence of Hungarian oppression, causing young Carpatho-Rusyns to forsake their families and traditions in favor of higher wages and dangerous labor in America. Instead of seeing emigration as opportunity, Pavlovych feared the unknown. "People go away / To seek happiness beyond the sea, / O God, what will become of them?" While emigration might have been a strategy of survival for the individuals who left, it was a humiliation for the Carpatho-Rusyn people as a whole: "And we, Rusyn people of poor Makovytsia, / Look beyond the sea for bread in America."[18]

In 1900, the authors of a church-sponsored Carpatho-Rusyn almanac felt the need to address their audience on the issue of emigration. "In spite of all our efforts to dissuade our unfortunate Rusyn people . . . from emigrating to foreign lands, there is no help for it. And now, just as the waves of a river sometimes overflow its banks and flow in various directions, so our poor people overflow their native lands and disperse, simply so as not to die from hunger."[19] The anonymous author offered advice to naive emigrants leaving home for the first time and alerted them to the challenges ahead. He warned against underhanded agents who peddle idealistic dreams of easy riches: "All such words are nothing more than shameless and unscrupulous nonsense. Only the rich live well in today's world." He admonished his people about the proper motivation for emigration: "There are countries where there is free land and not enough people to work. This alone is what should attract you, not some good, rich, easy, and happy life." Rusyn emigrants came to America armed with cynicism.

Carpatho-Rusyns who had scarcely ventured beyond their villages needed advice in the most elemental matters, such as hygiene and dress. "You must put on clean clothing . . . in the German style, good boots. Take with you a brush and comb, soap, a towel, handkerchief. Cut your hair short and wash your body well in a steam bath or at home in warm water." He recommended the best shipping lines, warned against thieves and seasickness, and delivered half-truths and misinformation about the inspection process on Ellis Island. At the end of his pessimistic homily, he can only wish the young people well and pray for them. "And so, go where you will, dear Rusyn brothers and sisters, but do not forget the Lord God. In His infinite mercy He will help you not only to live peacefully in a foreign country, but also to earn a bit and return to your native land to remain here with your families in joy and happiness for the rest of your lives."

However, economic conditions at home and letters from relatives already in America were more persuasive than advice from conservative poet-priests, and young Carpatho-Rusyns continued to seek a better life across the sea. Aside from the economic motivation, successful emigration required a certain psychological predisposition. Those who dared to ignore the obstacles and the authorities' forecasts of doom to seek their fortunes in America were by necessity ambitious, self-confident risk-takers. If they returned with money to improve their own position and their family's well-being, they rose in status in the village, and their "American" clothes and manners set them apart, at least for a while. Before long, the constraints of field work caused them to return to the more comfortable and practical traditional dress, but psychological enhancements acquired in the New World went beyond appearance. A German journalist compared emigrants at a transit station with returnees, who "move about more purposefully and freely and feel more equal to their social superiors than they did before emigration." Indeed, the Hungarian government was wary of the individualist behaviors and democratic attitudes that might be imported from bourgeois America.[20] And Carpatho-Rusyn moral authorities decried the threat to traditional values from exposure to modern social mores and progressive American standards of education and egalitarianism. Laws in favor of prohibition and women's suffrage were particularly reviled.[21] However, most Carpatho-Rusyn emigrants spent their American years clustered within communities of their own compatriots, with relatively little exposure to broader western culture and civilization. Many did not acquire proficiency in English, and after three or four years in a coal mine or steel mill, they contentedly returned to the fields and forests of their homeland.

Mines and Mills

Little is known about Andrii Varchola's first sojourn in Pittsburgh. Presumably, he found lodging in overcrowded tenements with relatives and Carpatho-Rusyn friends, who had been flocking to the Pittsburgh area from Miková for a decade. For the unskilled, uneducated Carpatho-Rusyn immigrants, industrial Pittsburgh was a magnet. As described in the *Pittsburgh Survey*, a wide-ranging sociological study of the city and its environs compiled from 1907 to 1914, Pittsburgh was "the powerful, the iron city, the workshop of the world. Situated on the Allegheny plateau at the headwaters of the Ohio, rich in mineral resources, easily accessible to markets, such are proud claims of a district beyond all others the strategic center for the production of wealth."[22] And such were the promises of prosperity and quick riches for penniless, hardworking Rusyn migrants. The demand for unskilled labor in the steel industry made Pittsburgh "a veritable Mecca to the immigrant."[23] During the first two decades of the twentieth century, Pittsburgh's population increased by a third, and by 1914, one-quarter was foreign born, with "brawn for sale, which Pittsburgh's tonnage industries purchased cheaply."

> Take the average Lithuanian, Croatian, Ruthenian, or Slovak, and his physique compares favorably with that of any people. Most of the immigrants are from agricultural communities. Their food in the fatherland is coarse, their habits are simple, their cares few. They have an abundance of vegetable diet, pure water, pure air, and sunshine and they develop strong physical organisms. Taking them as a whole, we get the best of the agricultural population. The day has not yet come when the weak emigrate and the strong stay at home. No ship agents, however active, can reverse the natural order of the tide of immigration, and natural selection supplemented by federal scrutiny gives us a body of men physically most fit for the heaviest demands made by our industries. . . . The foreigner is nowhere more at home than here, and nowhere has he been more actively welcomed by employers.[24]

In the words of the authors of the *Pittsburgh Survey*, the Pittsburgh area was "gifted by nature" for heavy manufacturing. Three large and three smaller rivers economically carried the city's products to the south and west. Massive veins of bituminous coal in the surrounding mountains produced coke to fire the blast furnaces of the steel mills. The nearby Connellsville coal fields, a section of the Pittsburgh coal seam, produced a better coke for blast furnaces than any other grade of coal mined in the United States. As the steel industry expanded, the demand for coal increased steadily, and along with it, the demand for cheap labor. Coal companies contracted with labor agents in Europe to spread the word about the enviable wages offered in America. Mine operators were keen to hire immigrants, who were willing to work long hours and put up with inadequate and unsafe conditions in the hope that they could quickly earn enough money to return home to their farms. Slavic laborers were valued for their industry, while at the same time they were patronized and disparaged:

> The common opinion of American employers is that the newer immigrants are stupid and that the supervisory force must be much larger than that required for English-speaking help. Many employers would no doubt prefer the latter; but they cannot get them for the wages offered; they must take the Slav or run short-handed.[25] . . . On the other hand, . . . some employers of labor give the Slavs and Italians preference over English-speaking applicants because of their docility, their habit of silent submission, their amenability to discipline, and their willingness to work long hours and overtime without a murmur.[26]

A foreman in a Pittsburgh firm objectified the immigrant workers in a derisive quip: "Give them rye bread, a herring, and a beer, and they are all right."[27]

Estimating the value of money according to old-country standards, immigrants often worked for below-average wages. In fact, immigrant laborers scrimped on necessities and displayed a "mania for saving" in hopes of hastening their return trip to the homeland. A survey of Pittsburgh postal depositors by country of birth showed that on June 30, 1912, the average amount per depositor from Austria-Hungary was $124.41. That was more than those born in Russia, Italy, Germany, or England, and almost twice as much as native-born white Americans.[28] They lived in poorly constructed shack housing in coal patches or tenements in company towns, where homes, stores, and schools were managed by the company. Since more than half of the immigrants were single or had left wives in Europe, married immigrants took in boarders, men of their own nationality, who shared the crowded conditions. The lone housewife cooked, cleaned, packed lunches, and did laundry for all.

In 1907, wages for a common laborer were $1.35 to $1.65 per day.[29] The Pittsburgh mills could hire Slavs at 15¢ per hour for a ten-hour day. In mills and yards outside the city, 16.5¢ per hour was the prevailing rate. The Zavacky brothers, who emigrated in the first decade of the century, found jobs in the metal trades, subsidiary industries that used the iron and steel from the furnaces to manufacture finished products. In these plants, skilled work was done primarily by native-born Americans, while immigrants took jobs as foundry workers and machine hands. Wages for a nine-hour day were determined by what the employer assessed a man to be worth. With room and board at $10 per month, church contributions of 50¢, and a $5 drinking bill, a laborer easily saved $10 to $15 per month.

But the best wages for unskilled laborers were found in the coal mines. In union-organized mines, a Slavic immigrant could earn 50–90 percent more per hour than his fellow countryman working in the mills. Even in nonunion mines, wages were $1.00 more per day than the average mill salary for jobs that were similar in terms of the labor required. Hundreds of coal patches grew up in Allegheny, Westmoreland, and Somerset Counties around the western Pennsylvania coalfields, where company houses rented at only half of what laborers paid for comparable dwellings in the city. Miners worked eight-hour days, as opposed to the ten to twelve hours worked each day in the mills. Analysts concluded, "Taking everything into account—wages, hours, leisure, cost of living, conditions of work—it appears that common laborers employed by the steel companies in their mines were fifty to ninety per cent better off than the same grade of laborers employed at their mills and furnaces."[30] Despite the apparent dangers of underground work, perhaps it was the practical profit potential that attracted Andrii Warhola to the mines.

Andy Warhol's brother John reported that their father worked in a coal mine for two years before returning to Miková.[31] Records of that employment have not been found. It is known, however, that Andrii's brother Joseph, who followed Andrii to America in 1910, worked for the Pittsburgh Coal Company. The largest company operating in the Pittsburgh coalfield, the Pittsburgh Coal Company was a union shop that employed twenty thousand workers in numerous bituminous mines around the city. According to his 1916 Declaration of Intention and his 1917 draft registration, Joseph Warhola lived in the patch towns Treveskyn and Cuddy in what is today suburban Pittsburgh. It is not unreasonable to expect that Joseph followed Andrii's initial path and that both Warholas began life in America with jobs in the mines of the Pittsburgh Coal Company.

Lyndora

The Zavackys began to emigrate to America at the turn of the century. From available records, we can deduce that the oldest Zavacky son, Stephen, made more than one round-trip voyage to America. A notation on his 1907 ship manifest indicates that he had been in Butler, Pennsylvania, from 1901 to 1906, and he is listed as a resident in the 1906 Butler city directory. Miková parish records tell us that he was in Miková in 1905, when he married Anna Sushina there, and in 1909, when he was witness to his sister Julia's wedding. Another return trip to Butler from Miková from the port of Trieste can be documented in March 1910.[32] This was Stephen's final voyage to the United States, as listed in his naturalization documents from the early 1940s. By 1913, he and his wife had settled in the Lyndora section of west Butler, where the first of their seven children was born in 1912.

Stephen's younger brother John Zavacky immigrated through Antwerp, arriving in Philadelphia in 1902 at age eighteen with a cousin and a friend from Miková. The destination cited by all three was Butler. In 1907 in Pittsburgh, John married Anna Sluk, an immigrant from Malá Pol'ana, a village near Miková, and the first of their eleven children was born in Butler in 1909. The next link in the Zavacky migration chain was Andrew, who arrived in New York at age sixteen in 1905. His destination was noted as "Lyndora (Butler), Pennsylvania," where he was going to join his brother John. In 1911, Andrew married American-born Anna Youshock (alternate spelling: Youshaw) at Saint John the Baptist Greek Catholic church in Lyndora. Their first son was born a year later.

In 1910, Butler was a thriving city with a population of 20,728, connected to Pittsburgh and beyond by four railroads and two interurban electric lines. The Chamber of Commerce boasted seven banks, three daily and three weekly newspapers, a public library, acres of parks and playgrounds, and "the most up-to-date hotels of any city its size in [the] United States."[33] But what attracted immigrants to Butler, located thirty miles north of Pittsburgh, was the Standard Steel Car Company, a manufacturer of railroad freight cars. Established in 1902, it initially employed 2,500 men, most of whom were unskilled immigrant laborers. Many were Slavs, who were regularly derided as "Hunkies." As immigrant laborers flowed into Butler, the founder of the car works laid out a settlement to house them, naming it "Lyndora" after his wife and daughter. Between 1900 and 1905, Stephen, John, and Andrew Zavacky came to Butler to work at the Standard Car plant. Lyndora became home for the Zavacky immigrant laborers, and many of their descendants live there to this day.

Lyndora was a company town built specifically for the Standard Steel Car workforce, and nearly 70 percent of the male residents of greater Butler were employed there. Of these, 56 percent were immigrants, representing thirty-nine different ethnic groups, predominantly eastern European. The R. L. Polk and Company's *Butler Directory* for 1904 lists three currency exchange offices, two translators, and two steamship agents that catered to the needs of immigrants.[34] While apartments housed supervisory personnel, and new hotels accommodated Standard Car's businessmen, company-owned tenements were constructed for laborers. Ambitious plans were laid out for "200 modern dwelling houses." The local newspaper, the *Butler Eagle*, announced, "Plans for the settlement will make it the most modern and complete ever attempted by a large industrial establishment," and Lyndora was to be distinguished as "an ideal steel town."[35] The frame houses, painted boxcar red, were built in three rows with communal showers and toilets in between. "Red Row," as it was known, quickly became overcrowded, and deficiencies were apparent. "These houses are all constructed in a cheap manner and are scarcely fit for human beings" (August 24, 1903). Two years later, the area was described as "a striking example of regular and uniform squalor" (April 4, 1905). The *Butler Eagle* exposed "Some Pitiful Winter Scenes in Red Row."

> On a bright afternoon the streets of Butler are filled with busy shoppers, happy school children and still others who are out simply for a walk through the bright frosty afternoon air. To look at this bright picture . . . one would scarcely think at the same moment of the poverty, filth, hunger and cold that almost chills one's heart in the little suburb of Lyndora. . . . In Red Row is where some of these conditions abound, but even in the one-time pretty little houses built by the car company there is a lot of misery. (February 9, 1905.)

The writer goes on to describe drunken men sprawling on dirty steps, children in rags, barefoot women, bathtubs used as coal scuttles, doors burned for firewood, and cellars inhabited by chickens and pigs. "In fact they do everything in such an upside down way that it is simply ludicrous." From their own perspective, Lyndora immigrant-residents recall: "There were six families in each [company-owned] condominium and there were no utilities. Water had to be pumped by hand. . . . The apartments were heated by black cast iron stoves and the light was provided by kerosene lamps."[36]

Nearly three hundred families resided in Red Row and hundreds more in newly built company houses, but the immigrant-workers kept coming. Residents who were already squeezed for space took in boarders. One woman provided

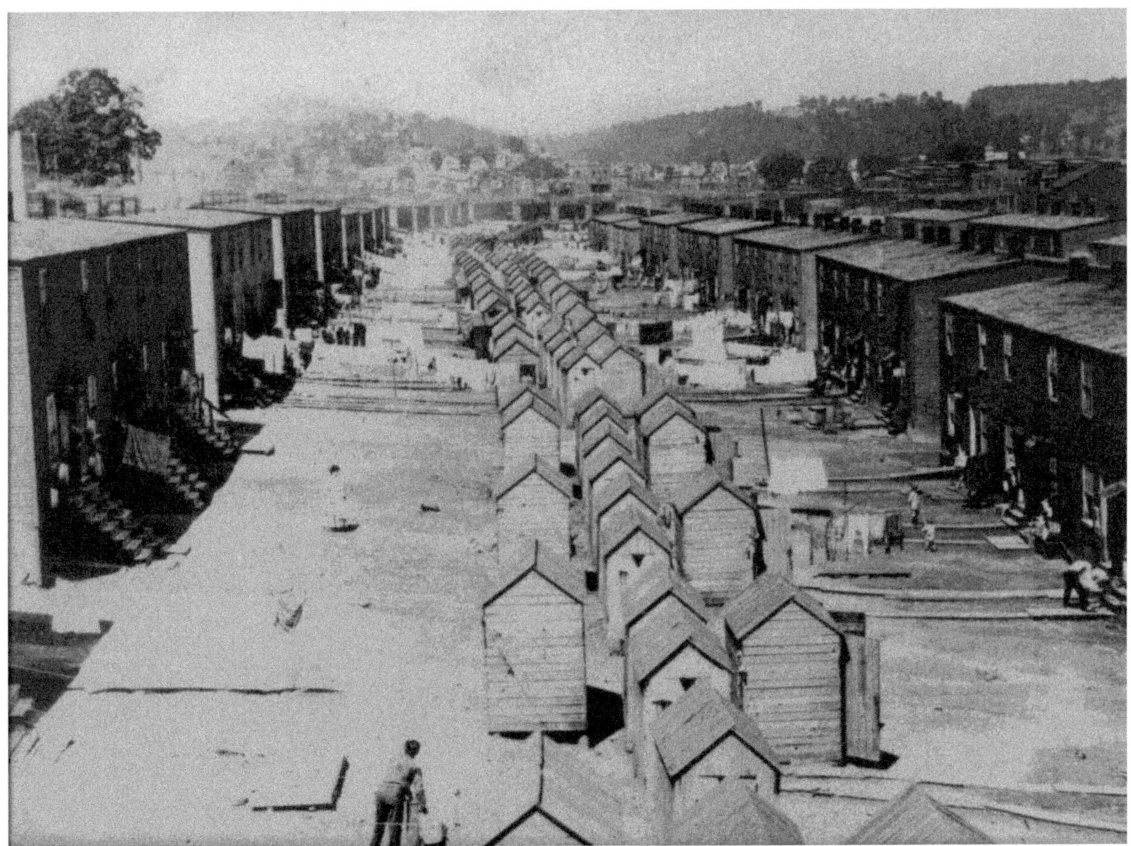

Figure 2.1. Red Row in Lyndora, PA. Communal toilets lined by frame houses.

room and board for thirty-three lodgers, where beds were shared and rotated between day-shift and night-shift workers. According to a *Butler Eagle* reporter who visited the "Hunky district," "In some of the houses there are as high as 30 or 40 men living in four and five rooms. . . . In some places there are as high as seven and eight beds in one room and each of these is occupied by several persons" (August 24, 1903). Using terminology of the biological determinism that was prevalent at the time, American-born journalists bemoaned the squalor of "a lot of people who are as ignorant as can be" in what would have been "a beauty spot if the right class of citizens had inhabited it" (April 4, 1905). A respectable observer could only "throw up his or her hands with undisguised horror when minutely inquiring into the conditions that seem popular down in those districts" (September 14, 1911).

The blatant slurs and abuse hurled by writers of the *Butler Eagle* convey the atmosphere of derision and hostility that greeted Slavic immigrants, fresh from their primitive but beautiful mountain homeland. Dismissed as "illiterate and indifferent Hunkies," their traditions were mocked, their hardships were minimized, and their faults were exaggerated in a fashion that is, by today's standards, cringeworthy. In "Brutal Murder in Lyndora Boarding House," a woman is described as "very handsome as foreigners go" (December 21, 1906), and in "Lyndora District Has a Quiet Time on Sunday," the reporter concludes, "The foreigners seem to be discovering that it is possible to do their drinking without using hatchets on each other" (May 13, 1907). "Bullets Flew at a Hunky Christening" is the headline of a 1904 article, which condescendingly describes a traditional Slavic celebration: "There was a christening at No. 34 Bessemer avenue, Lyndora, on Sunday. The name of the proprietor of the house . . . was too much for Squire Criswell, even with his experience with Hunky names. That doesn't matter so much anyway." At the close of the piece, we are informed, with feigned relief, that "the Hunky baby" took the "rumpus" as a matter of course (October 31, 1904).

The only optimism reporters expressed was for the children, the generation of Andy Warhol and his Lyndora cousins. A visiting nurse found that older immigrants refused to use the proffered medicines. "They said they knew how to take care of the babies, as only two died last summer. . . . Quite a few mothers have learned just a little, others virtually nothing. On the other hand, the children learn readily and are anxious to learn" (September 14, 1911). The immigrant children at the Lyndora school, whose attendance was "as good as that of the little Americans," were judged to be "very bright." The reporter made special note of their innate musical aptitude. "They have a natural talent for any kind of music. . . . An air they may hear on the street they can hum or whistle with more perception than most little Americans their age" (February 15, 1905). Their flair for music was perhaps the only attribute the transplanted Rusyn peasants brought from the fields of their homeland that was appreciated in the New World.

The newspaper duly, if sensationally, commented on numerous accidents and tragedies: "Russian Boy Falls into Raging Stream" (March 7, 1908); "Steel Car Worker Fatally Injured: Caught between Crane and Girder" (December 5, 1921). Pieces dealing with brawls, riotous behavior, and drunkenness are too numerous to mention. Little sympathy is expressed for the plight of the immigrant population, and even good news is given an almost comically disparaging spin: "Mysterious and Unexplained Period of Goodness in Town and Annex That Puzzles Police—But Just Wait" (August 12, 1905). In "Frenzied Red Row Mob Makes Murderous Attack on Justice and Officers," minor notice is made of the immigrants' complaints that they are "used like wild animals" by the police of the car works (August 14, 1906). However, even the most critical writers agree that "as a rule [the immigrants] are honest, few of them owe a bill at any place," and "they do not often apply for help to those above them" (August 24, 1903). It is conceded that "they are as a rule bright when they are helped in the proper manner." But the "proper manner" is thick with contempt and denigration: "In many Butler homes are efficient servant girls who can hardly speak English, and yet they are good, because the kindness that has been shown them by others, in contrast to the brutality of their homes, has made them want to become more like the people of whose country they are a part" (February 9, 1905).

The Uprooted and Transplanted

The routine deprecation of the Slavic laborers who fueled Pittsburgh's industrial success was felt not only by the Zavacky and Warhola immigrants but also by their American-born children. Andy's brother John remembers one "sad experience." When Julia sent the boys out "to dig" in the garden, John planted potatoes, and Andy planted flowers. They both submitted their produce for a school competition, and both won a prize—25¢, enough for two movie tickets and some candy. An older boy also won a prize, and a reporter from the local newspaper proposed taking a photo of the three winners together. John remembered:

> So we went with our mother to the other boy's apartment, but his mother sent us away saying she would send the photographers round to our home afterwards. We didn't much understand this but we went and waited at home. The photographers never came. She hadn't sent them round to our place. She didn't want her son to have his photo in the papers with me and Andy. The next day there was just a photo of her son in the paper.
>
> I realized why that lady didn't want us in the photograph with her son. They were people who had a fine apartment, they were better dressed than us, just people from a higher class. But those sort of people were shameless. They used to call us "Damn Hunkies."[37]

This was surely not the only such experience the young Warhola boys endured, and it could not help but have a psychological effect. In his *Diaries*, Warhol often reveals his disdain for "these rich kids" and "those rich ladies," who "still have all their energy from not having hard lives."[38]

Sensational journalism fanned contempt and intolerance toward the Slavs. The emerging field of sociology, conducted by contemporary progressive reformers in the *Pittsburgh Survey*, viewed immigrants as "others" who were detrimental to the American way of life. In "The New Pittsburghers," Peter Roberts described filthy lodgings, uncouth peasant habits, and practices that are "fatal to decency and morality." He grumbled that "the Protestant antecedents and institutions that were dear to the founders of the city are fast undermined by the customs of immigrants from southeastern Europe," who are left in ignorance of "our language, our laws, our government and our history."[39] Reformers failed to respect, or even to perceive, the newcomers' distinctive cultural features and unique social issues. In the assessment of today's academic critics, "The Survey judged the mills and the city in terms of how closely they permitted working-class families to approximate accepted American (that is, middle-class, native-born white) standards of living and patterns of behavior."[40] As a result, the Survey, like the articles that appeared in the *Butler Eagle*, was more moralistic than analytic, more judgmental than insightful.

In his 1952 Pulitzer Prize–winning book *The Uprooted*, Oscar Handlin, a trailblazer in the field of immigration history, focused on the subjective experience of the individuals, their displacement from the homeland and alienation from tradition. Handlin stressed that the "strangeness" of the American environment "exerted a deep influence upon the character of resettlement, upon the usual forms of behavior, and upon the modes of communal action that emerged as the immigrants became Americans."[41] In his chapter "The Ghettos," he expounds on images of blight like those in Lyndora, which were painted so smugly by journalists and consumed with equal self-righteousness by middle-class readers. Contrasting the American environment with conditions of life in the Old Country, Handlin validates and accounts for issues of overcrowding, sanitation, drunkenness, and ignorance. Speaking of the typical Lyndora-like mill town, Handlin described the emotional dislocation it caused.

> Into the surrounding farmland, narrow alleys were pushed, lined with three-story frame tenements or with tiny two-room cottages. The company which controlled all was hardly interested in increasing the supply of housing to an unprofitable excess over demand; nor was it anxious to go to the expense of providing gas, water, and sewerage. The results matched those of city slums. . . . These factory town immigrants, like those who went to the cities and those who settled on farms, found the physical conditions of life in America hostile. Nowhere could they recapture the terms of village life; everywhere a difficult adjustment began with the disorganization of the individual, now grown uncertain as to his own proper role.[42]

Numerous examples of such "disorganization" can be seen among Carpatho-Rusyn immigrants and within the Zavacky and Warhola families. However, Handlin's sympathy with the immigrant's plight led him to overestimate the weight of the environment and to underestimate the resilience of the individual and the power of traditional culture to recuperate the self in an adverse environment. Starting in the 1960s, young scholars, often themselves descendants of immigrants, redirected ethnic history scholarship to emphasize the durability of ethnic cultures. Shifting the perception of immigrants from the previously held image of passive, docile, damaged creatures to "fairly well-equipped, stable individuals, able to adjust successfully, intellectually, psychologically, and socially in America," scholars began to study the ethnic and social resources that allowed them to reach their goals and advance their own welfare.[43] The Zavacky men present a case study of the diverse paths, ambitions, achievements, and "disorganization" of the Miková immigrants transplanted in Lyndora.

What the immigration historian John Bodnar observed about Slavic immigrants in general was true of Stephen Zavacky. "Slavs were carefully establishing working-class worlds in America by integrating old world traditions with pragmatic innovations necessitated by the constrictions and realities of their socioeconomic status. . . . Rather than embracing the American 'dream' of personal advancement through education and a career, Slavs sought mainly secure employment. Conditions in urban and industrial America only served to strengthen the peasant view of work as an instrument of survival, not success."[44] Stephen Zavacky (1880–1968) had modest, characteristically working-class goals. He married Anna Sushina in 1905, and she joined him in Butler in 1911. Having found a secure, steady job, he spent most of his working life at the car company. On his World War I draft registration card, he noted his occupation as "shell maker" and in the 1930 census, he identified his position as "fitter," that is, machinist. By 1930 he owned a home in Lyndora and by 1934, he had a family of seven children. In 1945 at age sixty-six, he became an American citizen. In 1950, he was still working at the freight car factory as a welder. He eventually retired from the Pullman Standard Company (the outcome of a 1929 merger with Standard Steel Car), as an exemplar of the success most Slavic immigrants aspired to. He died in 1968 at age eighty-seven, leaving two sons, five daughters, and ten grandchildren.

Andrew Zavacky (1887–1956), who went by the name "Andy," had an excitable and impetuous temperament that contrasted with Stephen's sober stability. At age twenty-three, he is mentioned in an article in the *Butler Citizen* as the victim of a certain Mike Dubovick, who had "no good reason for the beating he gave Andy."

The lack of a surname here seems to indicate that "Andy" was well known to the journalists and constables of Lyndora. In an incident the same night (December 27, 1910), Zavacky was charged with assault and battery in a case that was later settled. According to the newspaper, the incidents were "occasioned by a too liberal indulgence in bottled goods" as part of holiday celebrations. At the time, Andrew was living as a boarder with a Slovak family in Butler and working as a butcher in his brother John's shop. By 1917, he was a naturalized citizen and a painter at the Standard Steel Car Company, with a wife and three sons.[45] Five years later, in 1922, his American-born wife, Anna Youshock, sued him for abandonment and nonsupport and filed for divorce. She accused Andrew of committing adultery with one woman whom she named and others, unnamed.[46]

In November 1927 at the age of forty (he cited his age as thirty-six in the records), Andy Zavacky married twenty-one-year-old Catherine Ovesney in Wellsburg, West Virginia, a nearby Gretna Green, where marriages could take place without the five-day waiting period between license and wedding that was required in Pennsylvania. After two babies were stillborn in 1928 and 1930, Catherine and Andrew had two sons. In 1930 Andrew was living with his wife's parents and their large family in Rosslyn Farms on the border with Carnegie, an industrial suburb five miles west of Pittsburgh, where he worked as an automotive painter. His World War II draft registration card describes him as slightly over six feet tall, 208 pounds, with scars on his neck, his left arm, and a finger of his right hand.

Little is known about the rest of Andrew's life. In undated photographs, he appears together with his wife Catherine and his Lyndora siblings, but it is likely that he had more problems than successes in his life, and family ties may have been strained. In a letter to Julia from November 8, 1953, he thanks her and their sisters for financial help and promises to pay them back. He tells her he is earning just $45 per month, "but that's better than nothing," and he mentions that he had no recent contact with their brothers in Lyndora. While his obituary mentions an "extended illness," his death certificate indicates that he died of a heart attack in 1956.

In addition to their full-time jobs, both Stephen and Andrew worked at times for their brother John. From childhood, John Zavacky (1883–1951) stood out as clever and more intellectual than most of his peers. Miková relatives recalled that he was always looking at the sky and knew all the stars. He was expected to become "a great man."[47] The most ambitious and resourceful of the Zavacky brothers, John was able to navigate the social structure of the New World successfully. According to his daughter, he loathed his first job in the mill and was eager to look for alternatives.[48] In 1906, four years after his arrival in Butler, the city directory shows both John and Stephen

Zavacky living as boarders in a tenement at 31 Bessemer Avenue, not far from Red Row and just a short distance from the raucous "Hunky christening" described above.

Their landlord was John Buccos, who operated a grocery on the premises, and the Zavacky brothers are listed as "clerks" in his retail store. John Buccos (originally Bakosh) was an immigrant from Poráč, a Rusyn village in the Spiš district of present-day Slovakia, about eighty miles west of Miková. He had emigrated as a child with his parents in the 1880s and received an American education. In 1893 he was a butcher in McKeesport, and by 1900, Buccos was a salesman in a general store in Fayette County. In Lyndora, he was a partner in a company that owned six grocery stores, and an investor in the Lyndora Building and Loan Association. With deeper roots in America than most Lyndora laborers, Buccos took a leading role among the community of Carpatho-Rusyn immigrants, managing the Lyndora Hall Association, a social organization for immigrants, and serving as court interpreter for his compatriots. It was most likely through his acquaintance with Buccos that John Zavacky got into the grocery business. The 1910 census tells us that Zavacky, now married with a daughter, is still living in the Bessemer tenement, but his occupation is "retail merchant" in "groceries, etc." John and his wife Anna now share their apartment with a boarder, Frank Lobert, a Polish butcher with whom John has gone into business. The 1910 Butler business directory lists, in bold type, "Lobert & Zavacky. Grocers and Meats."[49]

By 1914, John had added two daughters to his family and gone into business for himself, with his brother Stephen as clerk, and his brother Andrew as butcher. Photographs depict John and his family against the background of the Zavacky storefront. The immigration historian John Bodnar notes that immigrant entrepreneurs, like immigrant workers, closely integrated family members in their work. Lacking access to capital, they could not expand, and they served exclusively local coethnic clienteles.[50] It is likely that the Zavacky grocery could not support a larger staff, and both Stephen and Andrew were probably working part-time in the market in addition to their work at the car shop. According to his granddaughter, Zavacky was generous to his customers, extending credit to those who might never meet their obligations. Following symbols from the "hobo code," drifters from as far away as California found their way to his store, where they were given leftover cuts of meat.[51]

The census and business directory tell us that John was well on his way to the stereotypical "American dream." In 1918, he purchased property for $500 and served as team captain for the Red Cross membership drive in Lyndora. He contributed $200 to the war effort through the Pershing Limit Club War Saving Stamp campaign, and, according to an ad in the *Butler Citizen* in 1919, he was a satisfied

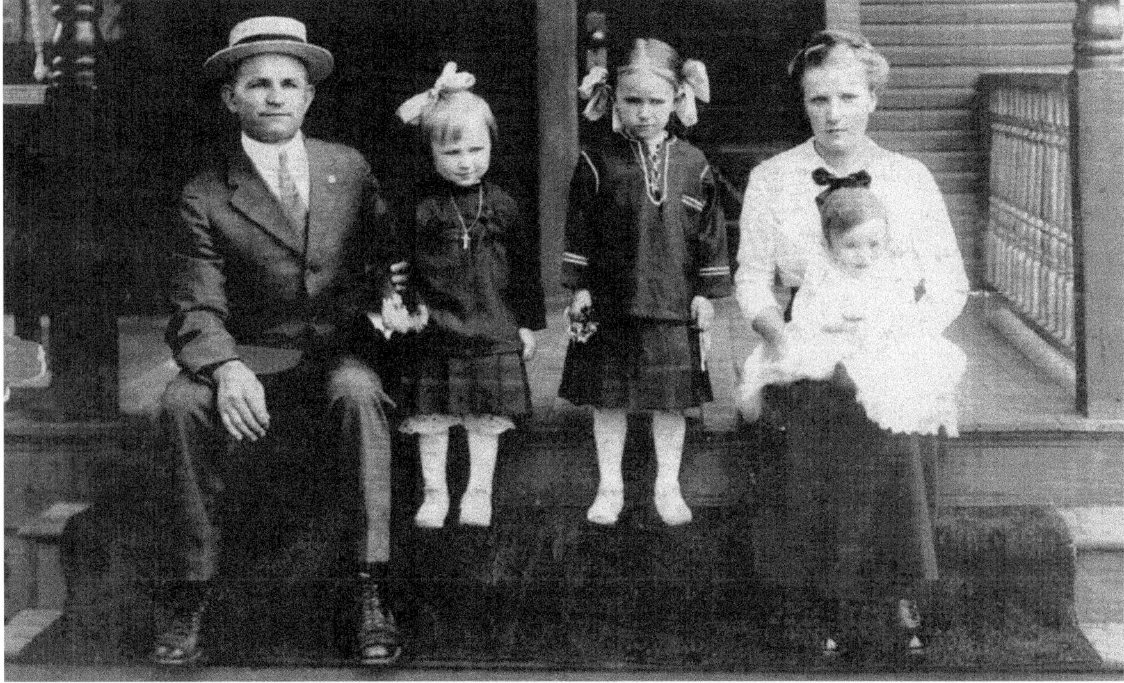

Figure 2.2. John Zavacky with his wife and daughters ca. 1915.

Buick owner.[52] His daughter and granddaughter recall that his was the first car in Lyndora, and he lent it to friends and relatives for weddings. An accomplished speaker, he was in demand for public events.

By 1920 Zavacky was a naturalized American citizen. He owned his home and grocery at 19–21 Penn Avenue free of mortgage, and employed his brother Stephen as a "meat cutter." Ten years later, he is listed as "proprietor" of the grocery and meat market, a property worth $1,500, about $23,000 in 2020 dollars. In 1939, he was working "on his own account," with income from business profits. John also had a strong Carpatho-Rusyn consciousness. He was active in the Rusyn community and instrumental in founding Saint John's Ruthenian Greek Catholic Church in Lyndora. He died of metastatic cancer of the gall bladder at the age of sixty-seven.

Even though we have limited information, the biographies of the Zavacky brothers supplement the quantitative data on Carpatho-Rusyn immigrants, giving us some insight into the lives of the otherwise marginalized masses. From sparse documentation, we can only infer which facts can be ascribed to character and disposition and which are due to the impact of social conditions. Stephen followed

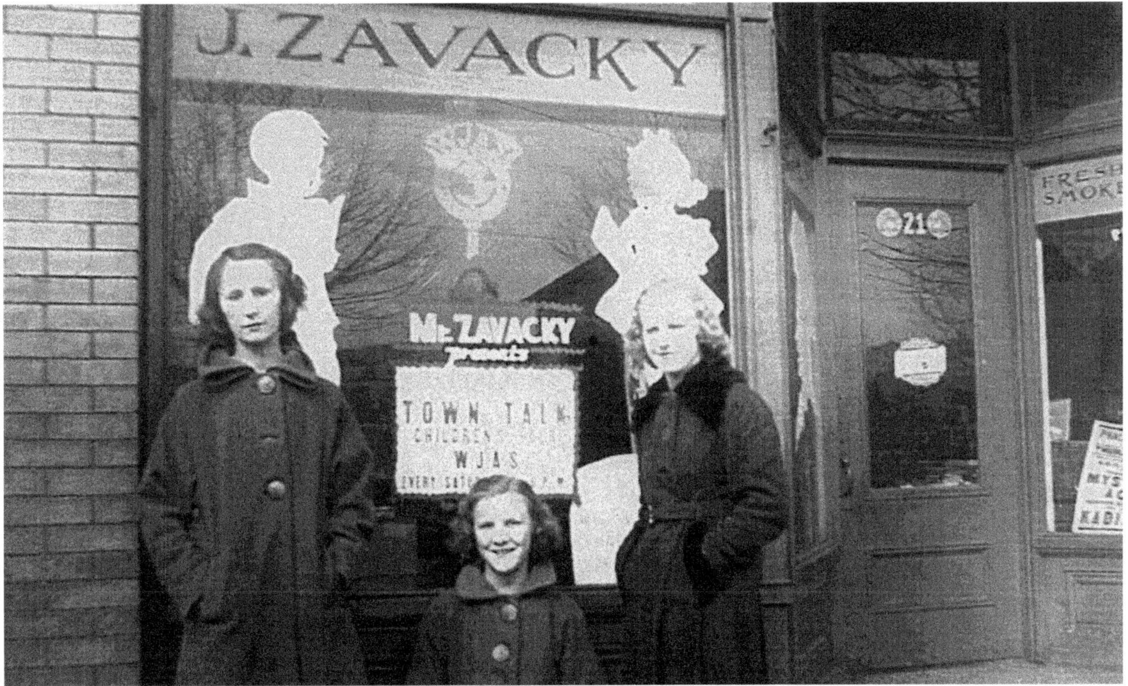

Figure 2.3. John Zavacky's daughters in front of the Zavacky store, Lyndora, PA, ca. 1920.

an old-world pattern to attenuated success in the New World, while John took advantage of new-world opportunities and became an active agent of his own advancement. While we lack a full narrative, Andy's life story seems to reflect the "disorganization of the individual" that Handlin posited was part of the adjustment of the immigrant to American societal norms and strictures. "The proper subject of biography," Handlin wrote, "is not the complete person or the complete society, but the point at which the two interact. There the situation and the individual illuminate one another."[53]

Disasters and Miracles

John Zavacky is just one example of Carpatho-Rusyn immigrants who prospered in America, achieved success, and found a new homeland. But, as folklorists note, songs of the people never mention this happy fate. Instead, folk songs created and sung by Rusyn immigrants tell of the dangerous work they perform for little recompense, while yearning for the mountains and forests of home. "Hey, chorna

Ameryka" (Hey, America is a dark place), an immigrant from Zemplyn County sings.[54] In January 1906, Standard Steel Car Company broke the world's record for the output of railroad freight cars in a single month. Running at capacity, the plant shipped a total of 2,202 cars, more than any other car factory in the world. Company officials and stockholders gathered to celebrate the event with a gala banquet. Plans were underway to improve the facilities, already the largest structure under a single roof in the United States, and double their capacity. A year later, in February 1907, the car works was the site of an explosion, "the most disastrous accident in the history of Butler."[55] In the plant, pot-shaped ladles, six feet deep and six feet across, filled with molten metal, were swung by hydraulic cranes. A span failed in a ladle filled with 9,000 pounds of molten steel, showering the workers with burning metal and sparking a fiery explosion. In all, seventeen men were killed and forty were injured. Almost all were "foreigners," as the newspaper report summarily described them, and the names of the victims indicate that many were Slavs. Horrific newspaper accounts described how workmen were "disemboweled," "literally cooked," "totally dismembered," and "burned to a crisp."[56]

The force of the explosion shook the buildings of the city like an earthquake, and "people rushed from their homes, panic-stricken." As flames shot from the car works, thousands of men and women struggled at the gate to gain admission. Many women were injured in the crush, and "their cries of pain and anguish could be heard blocks away." Pittsburgh newspapers highlighted the fact that the "the large wheel plant was totally wrecked, causing a property loss of $100,000." Press coverage went no further, but by the end of the month, the *Pittsburgh Post-Gazette* carried a terse statement to the effect that the jury inquiring into the cause of the explosion returned a verdict exonerating the Standard Steel Car Company of all responsibility.[57]

Ten months later, Pittsburgh was shocked by three major accidents in the veins of bituminous coal that underlay western Pennsylvania and West Virginia. As a result, December 1907 earned the title of "the darkest month" in US coal mining history.[58] On Sunday, December 1, 34 workers were killed at a mine in Naomi in northwestern Fayette County. Less than a week later, on December 6, the deadliest coal mine explosion in the United States occurred fifty miles south of Pittsburgh in Monongah, West Virginia, where 362 men perished. And on December 19, a gas and dust explosion killed 239 men at the Darr Mine, operated by the Pittsburgh Coal Company in Van Meter, forty miles southeast of Pittsburgh.[59] In all these cases, the actual number of deaths may have been much higher, since inadequate recordkeeping failed to account for the common practice of having more than one person, often children, work under an individual miner's name to increase his production numbers.

The Darr Mine explosion was featured on the front page of the *New York Times*. Local newspapers described the scene as "hideous in every sense of the word," with "bodies mashed almost to a pulp," "cries of half-distracted women [mingling] with shouts of rioters," and a "morbid crowd of sightseers." In other words, as the reporter John R. Ball put it, "The [Darr] disaster differs from those at Naomi and Monongah only in the number of men hurled into eternity without the least opportunity to cry for mercy." In all three cases, a large number of the victims were immigrants from central and southeastern Europe. With no rescue system in place, surviving miners became victims of poisonous gas. Recovery of the bodies was so fraught with danger that only single men were permitted to volunteer for rescue duty. An inquiry into the disaster concluded that the Pittsburgh Coal Company was not at fault and, as in the other accidents, blame was attributed to unskilled foreign workers. History has determined otherwise. In 1957, a writer in the *United Mine Workers Journal* put it bluntly: "The main thing was management neglect and in some cases brutal criminal negligence."[60]

The company ordered 250 rough wooden caskets and made arrangements to bury the bodies, many of which could not be identified. While the Pittsburgh Coal Company earned much goodwill by covering the funeral expenses, it later became known that each miner had been required to take out an insurance policy of $150 as a condition of employment. Burial costs were deducted from that amount and the remainder was given to the beneficiary.[61] With little help from the company and no governmental safety net, widows and orphans were left destitute. Unable to support themselves, many returned to their homelands. Even more bitter was the fact that, according to the Heinz History Center curator Nicholas Ciotola, the immigrant miners were three to four times more likely to die on the job in the United States than their counterparts in European mines, where safety conditions were better.

As bad as the Darr Mine disaster was for Hungarian and Italian immigrants, Carpatho-Rusyns were largely spared, and therein lies the miracle. According to the Julian calendar, which was then observed by Greek Catholic and Orthodox churches, December 19 was the feast day of Saint Nicholas of Myra. Known in the West as Santa Claus, Saint Nicholas is honored in the Eastern Church as Nicholas the Wonderworker, and he is venerated in icons, songs, and prayers. As patron of the Ruthenian Greek Catholic Church, Saint Nicholas was also deeply rooted in the folk practices and beliefs of the Carpatho-Rusyn people. Accordingly, at the beginning of the twentieth century, a Rusyn Greek Catholic or Orthodox miner would never go to work on his feast day, even if it meant giving up a day's pay.

Carpatho-Rusyns in the mining villages of Jacobs Creek, Van Meter, Whitsett, and Star Junction had no Rusyn church in the immediate vicinity, and they traveled to the Connellsville area on Sundays and Holy Days. So it was that Carpatho-Rusyns were attending Divine Liturgy at Saint Stephen's Greek Catholic Church in Leisenring when they heard a loud rumble and felt the earth shake from miles away. There were usually 400 workers in the mine, but because of the holiday, only half as many miners were at work, and most of those who were spared were Rusyns. Subsequent estimates of survivors range from 150 to 250. Newspaper headlines pointedly announced, "Majority of Victims Americans; Foreign Workers Lay Off to Go to Church and Escape Death" (*Pittsburgh Post-Gazette*, December 20, 1907), and "Many of the Victims are English-speaking Men: Foreigners Escape Owing to Religious Holiday." The author of this column stated sardonically: "Religious fervor is due to sweep through the Youghiogheny Valley as never before as a consequence of the Darr disaster. . . . Almost two hundred men, who were saved by religious devotion, will certainly be more devout than ever, after the extent of the mine's horror is fully realized."[62] Due to the language barrier, the press's indifferent attitude toward "foreigners," and the immigrants' likely reluctance to speak out against company management, there were no stories from the viewpoint of the immigrant survivors.

But within the Carpatho-Rusyn community, the miracle of Saint Nicholas was broadly disseminated. Names of victims, their families, and their native villages were shared among immigrant workers and their families, for whom the same fate was an ever-present danger. Bitter indignation erupted on the pages of the widely read Rusyn-language periodical, *Amerikansky Russky Viestnik* (*ARV*; American Rusyn Messenger).[63] Alexander Dzubai, the pastor of Saint Stephen's, penned a lengthy article titled, "There Is Justice in Heaven." In rancorous language, he excoriated the coroner's juries who investigated the Monongah and Darr explosions: "*Foreigners* [italics in the original] have no place where responsibility is being determined. Let the *foreigners* go die in the mines. . . . In twenty insensitive, meaningless words they trampled over 450 corpses."[64] The words he referred to were those of the verdict: "We find the bituminous laws of Pennsylvania were fully observed by all those having charge of the Darr mine of the Pittsburgh Coal Company."[65] Dzubai pointed out that the American press was silent on this account, simply citing the verdict without comment: "American newspapers engaged with the unhappy lot of the Monongah miners only until the last burnt corpse was brought to the surface." He rejected the notion that "rich capitalist coal barons" could not have prevented the disaster and lamented that they were not brought to justice.

It was likely small consolation for Father Dzubai when the *Annual Report of the Department of Mines* stated, in relation to the "twenty insensitive words," "We fail utterly to agree with the jury." The report pointed out the contradictions in the jury's conclusions, as had Dzubai, saying, "It would seem also that they were not quite satisfied with their own verdict." Father Dzubai concluded his article, "Given that the blame for these two horrible catastrophes has fallen for the most part on *foreigners*, and given that the rich capitalist coal barons enjoy excessive influence, we must conclude that in such affairs, only 'in heaven can one obtain justice.'" When the Darr Mine reopened under another name in 1910, Greek Catholic and Orthodox Carpatho-Rusyns built churches on both sides of the river and dedicated them to Saint Nicholas, their only advocate, in gratitude for his miraculous intervention.

The accidents at the Standard Steel Car Company and the mine disasters were but a few of many such calamities in the mills and mines around Pittsburgh, which disproportionately affected immigrant workers. From July 1, 1906, to June 30, 1907, 526 men were killed by work accidents in Allegheny County, and 509 men were seriously and permanently injured. Of the fatalities, 298 were foreign born, their deaths being attributed to ignorance of the language and unfamiliarity with modern machinery.[66] Father Dzubai's bitter denunciation of unscrupulous business owners, his gibes at the prejudiced, self-righteous press, and his defense of the much-maligned "foreigners" indicated a growing disquiet and resentment among the placid Rusyn immigrants, who had good reason to long for the open fields of their homeland. Immigration to America reached a peak in 1907, but at the same time, changes in the American economy reinforced the anxiety felt by immigrant workers. Since most of them had planned only a temporary stay in America, many did their accounts, calculated profits and losses, and, foreseeing an economic downturn, they bought tickets for the return journey home. This was very likely the reasoning behind Andrii Varchola's return to Miková.

Remigrants

At the end of October 1907, the Knickerbocker Trust Company, the third largest bank in New York, closed its doors and declared bankruptcy, sparking what became known as the Panic of 1907. The New York Stock Exchange fell almost 50 percent from its peak the previous year, and waves of bank failures rippled across the country. It was only thanks to the intervention of J. P. Morgan, who propped up the banking system with his own money and spurred John D. Rockefeller and other Wall Street titans to do the same, that a deeper recession was averted. Still, the downturn in economic activity was substantial, and Pittsburgh was seriously affected by the panic and its aftermath. The *Pittsburgh Survey* maintained that "hardly another city in the country was hit as hard or stunned as long by the panic as Pittsburgh."[67]

Between 1907 and 1908, steel production decreased by 40 percent and the number of locomotives manufactured fell by almost 70 percent.[68] Blast furnaces ceased their roar, plants were shuttered or took up deferred maintenance, and workers were laid off en masse. In 1908, the labor force was slashed by almost a third, and in Pittsburgh, where by 1910 almost 40 percent of the workforce was foreign born, the first to be cut were unskilled immigrant laborers. For many, this was a signal that it was time to cash in their earnings, gather their hoarded savings, leave behind the dirt and smoke of "the iron city," and return to the fresh air of their European homeland. According to the *New York Times*, "In the single month following the financial panic 15,000 foreigners departed the city . . . and by August 1908 many thousands of foreigners had returned to Europe." Trainloads of anxious aliens converged on New York City, and the traffic was "noticeably heavy from the Pittsburgh district and territory adjacent."[69] The *Butler Times* reported on March 6, 1908, that "nearly 100 foreigners have gone from Butler to their homes in the old country during the present week."[70] From November 1907 through July 1908, eastbound ocean crossings (normally about 40 percent of westbound crossings) soared to 190 percent.[71] For the first time ever, the outflow of migrants from the United States was greater than the inflow. This proved advantageous for the American economy, since large-scale emigration reduced the pressure on the American workforce. "It has been a decidedly favourable development that so considerable a portion of the alien element has been so well circumstanced as to be able to make a temporary sojourn abroad."[72]

Whether "the alien element" was thankfully "well circumstanced" or desperately counting their pennies, many found the means to finance a return trip. There is no evidence that the Zavacky brothers left Lyndora at this time. Perhaps John's entry into the grocery business provided a backstop against layoffs at the car shop, and later, a safety valve during the violent strike of July 1909 against the Standard Steel Car Company. For Andrii Varchola, the timing of the depression was fortuitous. He had been mining coal for two or three years, saving money, and was probably ready to return home with his earnings. By 1909, Andrii was back in Miková, where he was introduced to Ulia Zavacka, whom he married in May.

Folk and popular arts provide insight into the process of immigrant acculturation, as well as the limits of assimilation. A workers' song expresses the prevailing atmosphere and pragmatic attitude of Carpatho-Rusyn immigrants.

> In America it's very good
> For a man who has a job.
> But he who hasn't any work,
> He'll fall into ruin.
>
> It will be good, yes it will,
> Good to be back home.
> Help me God, oh help me God,
> Earn money for the trip.
>
> For when I'm back in my own country
> I will pray to God
> That He will somehow give me help
> To live well on the land.[73]

While Rusyn immigrants trusted in God, they also believed that God helps those who help themselves. Records show that the dollars Slavic immigrants earned in America had been regularly returning to the homeland in money orders, letters, and eventually with returning travelers, and we can assume that Andrii returned to Miková as a relatively prosperous man, by Rusyn standards. From 1900 to 1906, the total amount sent in money orders to villages in Hungary was approximately $23 million. Ewa Morawska gives the example of two unnamed villages in Zemplyn County, where Miková was located, that received about $15,000 annually, approximately $200 per emigrant, not including funds sent in personal letters or the money, about $400–$800, with which individuals often returned to their villages. These remigrants soon undertook improvements to their homes and farm equipment. As American money began to flow into the country, many landowners offered portions of their estates for sale, and since ownership of property was the primary measure of status in the village, Carpatho-Rusyns were quick to seize the opportunity. After three to five years in the New World, many "Americans," as remigrants were called in the homeland, could afford to purchase up to five hectares (twelve acres) of land.[74] In Zemplyn County, even more than elsewhere in Hungary, peasant-farmers were able to join the ranks of small landowners, thanks to money earned in the mines and mills of America.

With his earnings from the Pittsburgh coal mines, Andrii purchased land in his native village. Unfortunately, land records from Miková are not available, but from documents preserved by her Miková relatives, we know that in 1946, four years after Andrii's death, Julia Warhola filed a document with the Czechoslovak Consulate in Pittsburgh that officially granted her sister Eva power of attorney to administer her husband's property.[75] "I, Julia Varcholova neė Zavacky, coming from the village Miková . . . empower my sister Eva Bezeková neė Zavacka . . . to take under her administration all the properties that are in my husband's name, Andrej Varkhola, who died May 15, 1942 in Pittsburgh, Pennsylvania, registered in the land record of the village Miková, to use these properties and to pay tax and other charges connected with them until the time when I am back in the homeland and can administer the properties myself." A year later, Julia's sons Paul and John relinquished the right of inheritance to their father's property in favor of their Aunt Eva, and Andy, who was still underage, certified that "the content of this document was read to me and explained and it was signed for me by my mother as my natural guardian at my request, and that I will never under any circumstances claim my inheritance share, as I am well looked after here by my mother."

We cannot know how much land Andrii Varchola owned or when precisely he acquired it. When Andrii returned to Miková in 1908, ownership of property would have increased his status and made him an attractive marriage prospect. After their 1909 wedding, Andrii worked the land and Julia took charge of the Varchola household, while continuing to care for her mother and younger siblings. But just when she was expecting her first child, her husband was forced to think about leaving once again for America.

Miková to Bremen

The actual journey to the New World has hardly been mentioned in Carpatho-Rusyn immigrant memoirs or in the belletristic literature of Rusyn American authors.[76] In none of the literature of the first generation of Rusyn immigrant authors is there a full description of the journey. There are a few references to borrowing money from the Jewish moneylender or receiving a ticket from an uncle already in America, but the most detailed description takes up all of two sentences, as a young man plans his trip: "I have a ticket in my pocket and clothes packed in my trunk. Today I leave for Levoča, and in three days I'll be on a ship in Hamburg."[77] In another emigration narrative, we are told that a young man must cross into Galicia to evade the Hungarian gendarmes and that he will be met there by numerous agents from shipping companies. But about the overland trip to the port and the sea passage, we learn nothing at all. Since most Rusyn immigrants came to America with the intention of returning to their homeland, the voyage itself may have been of minor importance. Research is required to fill this blank spot in the narrative, and Andrii's story is a relevant case study of the Rusyn emigrant's path in the first decades of the twentieth century.

In September 1911, extensive military exercises were already being conducted around the Dukla Pass, just fifteen miles northwest of Miková. Attended by Archduke Franz Ferdinand, heir to the Austro-Hungarian throne, the Dukla exercises fueled the growing rumors of war.[78] The First Balkan War of 1912, in which the combined forces of the Balkan states defeated the Ottoman Empire, made conscription a vivid reality. One would like to think that Andrii was able to wait until Julia gave birth to their daughter on November 2, 1912, before he felt the need to make his way to the seaport. Julia told the *Esquire* interviewer, "Andy leaves in 1912. He no want to go to Army, to war. He had $160. I stayed in Europe. He go to America. He runs in the night to Poland, only one mile away. He runs to Poland, then America. I stay in Europe."[79]

Despite Julia's suggestion of a frenzied midnight flight, evidence shows a well-thought-out departure. As military preparations began, Habsburg emigration policy explicitly targeted men who were subject to the draft. Starting in December 1912, the government prohibited for a year the emigration of men liable to conscription.[80] Andrii may have recognized that he could better provide for his family from the distant shore of America than from the emperor's army. Therefore, leaving his wife and baby, he made plans to sail in November, when the farming was done, and just before the ban on men subject to conscription went into effect. The ship's passenger manifest shows that he did not flee alone. He departed with two companions from Miková, young men who were also probably evading conscription. Jan Zavadzki, not of the Zavacky family of which Julia was a part, was Andrii's cousin. Both Andrii and Jan noted as their contact in America a relative, Andy Janocsko, brother-in-law to Andrii and uncle to Jan, living at 2350 Forbes Street in Pittsburgh. Ilko Tkacek, the third member of the group, like Andrii, left a wife behind in Miková. Traveling on the same ship were two seventeen-year-old girls from Miková. Maria Rudavsky was going to join her brother John at 2436 Forbes Street in Pittsburgh, and Maria Choma Dudich, a Varchola cousin, was joining her husband Peter at 2501 Forbes Street. (As we will see, this section of Forbes Street was a block of slums populated largely by Carpatho-Rusyn immigrants.) Peter Dudich would later be the chief of Andrii's work crew at the Eichleay Construction Company. As kinship networks worked, Dudich may have offered Andrii a job in return for shepherding his young wife through the hazards of the journey. Women traveling alone were often forced to defend themselves against the advances of fellow travelers and the crew.[81] As a return migrant, Andrii would have been aware of the dangers of swindlers, thieves, and would-be assailants.

Between 1871 and 1914, almost three million emigrants from Austria-Hungary left from the German ports of Hamburg and Bremen. Much has been written about the processing of immigrants at Ellis Island, but the inland trek from the Carpathian Mountains to the port city has received little attention. Andrii and his companions might have made travel arrangements even before they left Miková. Agents and subagents, teachers, priests, and innkeepers, sent weekly lists of their sales to the shipping company, which returned "interim papers," or *Schiffskarte*, to the agents or local government officials to be distributed to migrants. Travelers were informed of the port of embarkation and a timetable of departures, from which they could reserve a departure date. For migrants who had relatives in the United States, as did Andrii and his companions, much of this business was taken care of and prepaid through local agents in American cities. Julia's description of Andrii's departure suggests that the Miková emigrants probably followed hidden mountain trails to cross a loosely patrolled state border into what was then Austrian Galicia. As Carpatho-Rusyns lived on both sides of the national border, Hungarian and Galician Rusyns routinely did business and conducted religious pilgrimages together, traveled to markets, or pursued lost livestock across the indistinct frontier. Passports and permits were unnecessary for such transient purposes, and cross-border communication networks provided counsel on emigration regulations and strategies.[82] In Galician towns, Andrii and his companions would have encountered shipping company agents. Several thousand subagents of the largest Bremen emigration agent, the Friedrich Missler agency, are said to have been active in Galicia.[83] With their help, the Miková party likely made their way to Mysłowice, a border city in the German province of Prussia. Mysłowice, one of the busiest emigration stations, was the main western gateway for migrants from Galicia and northern Hungary.

The waves of Russian and East European transmigrants flowing through Prussia to the German North Sea ports since 1880 alarmed government officials and motivated a restrictive policy toward foreign migrants. The fear of social disorder and a general distrust of foreigners who might carry disease or become a public charge prompted medical inspections and cash requirements. A cholera outbreak in 1892, attributed inaccurately to Russian emigrants, led to further governmental regulations that checked the flow of migrant traffic to German ports. These restrictions were countered by private steamship companies, unwilling to lose the lucrative trade in migration. As Nicole Ingrid Kvale indicates in her study of immigrant trains, the two principal German shipping lines, North German Lloyd (NDL) and the Hamburg-America Line (HAPAG) proposed a compromise that addressed the Prussian state's need to protect its population, while allowing shipping companies to maximize their business. Accordingly, a complex system of regulations and inspections was contrived.[84] Since steamship companies had to cover the cost of the return journey for immigrants turned away at Ellis Island, they were keen to rebuff unfit travelers before they entered Germany. Consequently, HAPAG and NDL erected control stations along the long Prussian land border with Russia and Austria-Hungary, where migrants were given medical inspections and were checked for sufficient funds. The border station controls were also advantageous for migrants, since a valid health certificate would facilitate their progress through the system. To satisfy Prussia's concerns about transmigrants passing through their country, the shipping lines ran special closed trains to the ports for emigrants, which isolated them from the general population. NDL and HAPAG bore the cost of establishing and maintaining control stations, emigrant trains, and emigrant lodging houses in port cities, but those costs were offset by the greater control the companies gained over migrant traffic.

Especially strict control stations were established along the border with Russia, where Jewish migrants were subjected to intrusive financial and medical inspections, as well as sanitation and disinfection procedures. At the Mysłowice and Racibórz stations along the Austro-Hungarian border, inspections were less stringent, and health examinations were often perfunctory. Considered "less threatening," migrants from Galicia and Hungary were registered at the border by the shipping companies. If they did not already have prepaid passage sent by American relatives, at the border station Andrii and his companions would have been able to procure *shifkarty,* or "interim papers," which would later be exchanged for steamship tickets at the port city. The Friedrich Missler company offered package tickets that covered inland-rail, overseas passage, and railway tickets to the traveler's final destination in the United States. The Miková companions may have stayed as little as one day in the Mysłowice station, or they may have waited several days until there was a sufficient number of emigrants to fill a train or an emigrant car that would be attached to a regular train.[85]

The transmigrants boarded closed emigrant trains at Mysłowice for transport through Wrocław to Ruhleben, a secondary transit and control station on the western outskirts of Berlin. Here the emigrants' papers were examined, Russian passengers were again inspected and disinfected, and any travelers who had evaded the border controls were processed. To the exhausted migrants, Ruhleben was all chaos and confusion in an unknown tongue. Rushed roughly from shower to inspector to doctor, children cried as families struggled to stay together in the crush. For emigrants fresh from a quiet village, the noise and bustle must have been overwhelming. A German reporter described the scene with undisguised disdain: "The Russian and Polish Jews with their long, greasy Kaftans; the Ruthenian farmer with his long inexpressively dirty sheepskin turned inside out with the wool on the inside, the women with long boots covering their naked legs, and country folk and workers from all over the far east, and children everywhere."[86] If the Miková party had received health clearances in Mysłowice, they would have been able to avoid the worst trials of Ruhleben. After their train cars were washed and disinfected, the emigrants were again loaded into the locked cars for transport to Bremen.

Advocates for emigrants promoted the segregated emigrant trains as low-cost transportation and a means of protecting naive newcomers from the swindlers and flimflam artists who overran train stations and seaports. But travel was hardly comfortable. Confined in an overcrowded, locked car with dim lighting and poor ventilation, seated (if they were lucky) on wooden benches, diverse groups of emigrants from dissimilar cultures shared close personal space for extended periods of time. The din of multiple languages assaulted the ear, and unpleasant odors of all kinds filled the heavy air. Each car had a toilet and radiator, but the facilities were surely inadequate. Responsible for their own provisions, travelers often lacked sufficient food and water. At some stations, charitable organizations passed bottles of milk, tea, fruit, and food to the captive passengers. Emigrants slept crowded together wherever they could find space, in their seats or on the floor. Often side-tracked in favor of regular trains, emigrant transport was slow and uncertain. Assuming all went according to schedule, and not counting the stopover in Ruhleben, Andrii and his companions spent at least twenty-four hours on the train from the border to Bremen.

In Bremen, passengers were taken to one of the emigrant hotels operated by Friedrich Missler, the exclusive agent for the North German Lloyd steamship line. Missler's Bremen dormitories had facilities for up to six thousand emigrants in what became known as the "Russian Quarters," because of the predominant East European clientele. Separate halls for various East European ethnic groups offered "sufficient food of decent quality, prepared according to cultural preferences," and conditions were generally satisfactory.[87] After another cholera epidemic in Russia, regulations were tightened. Arriving emigrants were led to their quarters in closed ranks and confined until medical inspection. They were vaccinated against smallpox, and if there were signs of any contagious disease, they were detained.

The Miková party may have spent a few hours or a few nights at Missler's hall before they boarded the boat-train for the thirty-mile two-hour trip to the port at Bremerhaven, where the steamers were docked. The emigrants presented their tickets and health certificates, and their baggage was inspected and tagged. Finally, undoubtedly with trepidation, but also relief at having completed the inland journey, they boarded the SS *George Washington* of the North German Lloyd line on Friday, November 16, 1912.

Andrii very likely found conditions on board the ship improved from his first voyage in 1905, when as many as three hundred people slept in rows of narrow double-deck berths and, in bad weather, were compelled to remain below deck. Edward Alfred Steiner, who emigrated from Austria in 1886 in steerage class, tells the story from the immigrant's point of view in his book, *On the Trail of the Immigrant*.[88] Writing in 1905, Steiner says, "The steerage ought to be and could be abolished by law. . . . Every cabin passenger who has seen and smelt the steerage from afar knows that it is often indecent and inhuman; and I, who have lived in it, know that it is both of these and cruel besides." The United States Immigration Commission, a bipartisan committee established in 1907, investigated. Agents of the commission, traveling in the guise of immigrants in steerage class on transatlantic ships, issued a critical report that detailed closely packed bunkbeds in open dormitories, foul air, lack of privacy, food that was insufficient in quantity, inferior in quality, and served crudely, inadequate deck space, and an atmosphere of "general lawlessness and disrespect for women."[89]

As a result of follow-on legislation and competition between the major North Atlantic passenger lines, as well as the heightened discernment of repeat migrants, onboard passenger comfort and safety became higher priorities, and conditions improved for steerage passengers. The "new steerage," or "third-class," accommodations were advertised as considerably better quality, with improvements in ventilation, sanitation, food preparation, dining arrangements, and privacy. As a newspaper article put it in 1909: "The third class passenger in his twentieth century surroundings is an aristocrat compared to his cousin who crossed a decade or less ago. He travels in the privacy of a two berth, four berth or six berth room, eats three excellent meals a day . . . [can take] shower baths . . . with hot and cold water [and] tiled floors . . . [and] . . . like every other globe trotter . . . has his own deck corridor for exercise, open in fair weather and covered when the ocean rages."[90] Real life may not have lived up to advertising hype. A German passenger from Romania, who kept a diary of his 1911 voyage on North German Lloyd's *Friedrich der Grosse*, complained about the cost of food on board. Migrants faced another problem in crossing the north Atlantic in winter. The German diarist wrote, "The first and second days were fine, but the other ten days we had very stormy weather so that not a single person remained healthy or found any joy or pleasure on the ship. The ship flew up, then down, and made us completely dizzy.... To travel over the water in winter is gruesome. The weather was so stormy that we could only see 80 [or] 100 meters at the most, and the water flew about."[91]

The Miková party's ship, the SS *George Washington*, launched in 1908, was the largest German-built steamship and the third-largest ship in the world at the time, with a sumptuous first-class cabin that attracted celebrities and aristocrats. According to the ship's passenger list, traveling on board with Andrii and his companions were Ambassador Henry Percival Dodge, the celebrated socialite Edyth Deacon, Princess Carolyn Salome Stickney, the banker J. P. Morgan, and Count Ernst Hans Christoph Roger Hermann von Scherr-Thoss of Rozkochów, Silesia, whose occupation is noted as "Lord of the Manor."

Andrii's emigration record gives physical details that help fill the dearth of photographs. In 1912 Andrii was twenty-six years old, a farm laborer, five feet, eight inches tall, with blond hair, a fair complexion, and gray eyes. He gave his ethnicity as "Ruthenian." His last permanent residence was Miková, Hungary, and his closest relative in the country from which he came was his wife, Julia Varchola. A notation indicates that he had previously been in Pittsburgh 1905–1908. He is going to join his brother-in-law Andy Janocsko in Pittsburgh, and he has a ticket to his destination. In the column under "Whether in possession of $50 and if less, how much?" the illegible number seems to be substantially less than the $160 that Julia later said he had. After a nine-day voyage, the SS *George Washington* docked in New York on November 25, 1912. After going through a medical inspection and other processing, Andrii would have had an all-night ride on another closed train to Pittsburgh.

"You Don't Know How Bad"

In her interview with *Esquire*, Julia interrupts the joyful memory of her wedding with a painful recollection: "Now everything gone. I had big, beautiful pictures of my wedding. Gone. War, war, war. War start. Oh, you don't know how bad. Soldiers come." Julia is speaking of the Great War of 1914–1918, specifically the fighting in the Carpathians from October 1914 until May 1915, when Russian and Austro-Hungarian armies crisscrossed the Rusyn homeland. This traumatic experience was another of Julia's favorite narrative topics, and she shared gory stories with her children and their friends. Her son John was convinced that Julia's war experience was partially responsible for Andy's personal and artistic obsession with death. We have only fragments of Julia's tales but enough facts and historical data to reconstruct the experience of a young woman caught up in the sad swirl of Carpatho-Rusyn history.

When Andrii began working in Pittsburgh in 1912, he sent money regularly to his wife in Miková and began saving to fund her voyage across the ocean as soon as it was practical for her to leave the family members she was supporting. In the summer of 1914, as fears of a general European war swelled and armies began to mobilize, Andrii undoubtedly watched with trepidation. German passenger lines withdrew their ships from foreign waters, and a speedy reunion with his wife would now be impossible. Since German ships carried the mail between America and the European homeland, international communication became unreliable. Anticipating imminent difficulties, Andrii did his best to provide for his wife. A receipt from a foreign exchange remittance order purchased at the Union Savings Bank of Pittsburgh shows that on July 13, 1914, just two weeks before Austria-Hungary declared war on Serbia, Andrii sent Julia what might have been his most recent paycheck. His hard-earned $12.30, exchanged for 60 Hungarian kronen, must have eased Julia's troubles somewhat as war loomed. Another preserved receipt shows that Andrii was able to wire money to Julia even during the war, although with less confidence. A receipt from November 18, 1916, is stamped, "Subject to delay on account of the war."

Russian Cossacks were already seen in the southern foothills of the Carpathians in September 1914, and from the beginning of October, villages on the southern slopes were barraged with troops and refugees fleeing the fighting in Galicia. The Eighth Russian Army planned an offensive through the mountain passes to penetrate the Hungarian plains and open the road to Budapest. The nearby Dukla Pass was of primary interest to the tsarist army, and more than once it became the site of particularly fierce fighting. South of the Carpathians and about four miles east of Miková lay Medzilaborce, a major communications center and railroad hub. In the words of the historian Graydon Tunstall, "Mezőlaborcz [Hungarian spelling] became the brass ring both sides fought fiercely to possess."[92] Unfortunately for the inhabitants of Miková and other Rusyn villages, as the front shifted forward and back, their homes lay in the path of the military advances and retreats. A constant ebb and flow of battles and bombardments pounded the Rusyn-occupied territory of northern Hungary.

By the end of November, Russian forces had cut through the Dukla Pass from the north, occupying 18 towns and 125 villages in Sharysh County and several dozen villages in Zemplyn. This occupation was short-lived, and by mid-December, the Russians were pushed back beyond the Carpathians, leaving the area to the

Austro-Hungarian armies. In January, the Russians attacked the Dukla Pass a second time and again penetrated Hungary, occupying 79 Rusyn villages.[93] The Habsburg army retreated to Krásny Brod, the site of a historic fourteenth-century Basilian monastery. In the ensuing battle, the monastery with its valuable library was destroyed.

In mid-January, the Habsburg army launched a counteroffensive, which became known as the Carpathian Winter War. A cycle of attacks and counterattacks followed. Skirmishes with Russian soldiers raged throughout the border districts, destroying towns and villages and displacing millions. By February 3, the Russians were in Miková, and the next day they occupied Medzilaborce. According to the historian Martin Drobňák, a historian of military history in the Beskyd region, the territory of today's Prešov Region of Slovakia was the scene of bloody fighting that was fully comparable to the world-famous battlefields on the western front.[94]

The Carpathian battlefield was an "icy hell," for which the Austro-Hungarian army was woefully unprepared. Heavy autumn rains left seas of mud, which gave way to deep snow and icy mountain roads, making transport and troop movements difficult. A Habsburg colonel recalled the horrors.

> Every day hundreds froze to death. The wounded that were unable to drag themselves forward were left behind to die. Entire ranks were reduced to tears in the face of the terrible agony. Each night, the 21st Infantry Regiment dug in until the last man was found frozen to death at daybreak. Pack animals could not advance through the deep snow. The men had to carry their own supplies on foot. They went without food for days. At –25°C, food rations froze solid. For seven days straight, the 43rd Infantry Division battled overpowering Russian troops with no warm food to sustain them. For a full 30 days, not one single man had any shelter.[95]

The Habsburg army lacked boots and winter uniforms. Supply lines were difficult to maintain, and provisions often did not reach the front. Nighttime battles in the densely wooded highlands and mountain passes were fierce. Combatants skirmished at close range in bayonet charges, often up to their waists in snow. Dysentery and typhus spread through the troops, and hastily buried bodies gave rise to outbreaks of cholera. By April 1915, when the Austro-Hungarian and German forces drove the tsarist army out of Carpathian Rus', the Russians had lost no fewer than a million men, and Habsburg losses were around 800,000.[96]

The suffering was no less harrowing for civilians, although their story has scarcely been documented. In Warhol's film, *The George Hamilton Story,* Julia tries

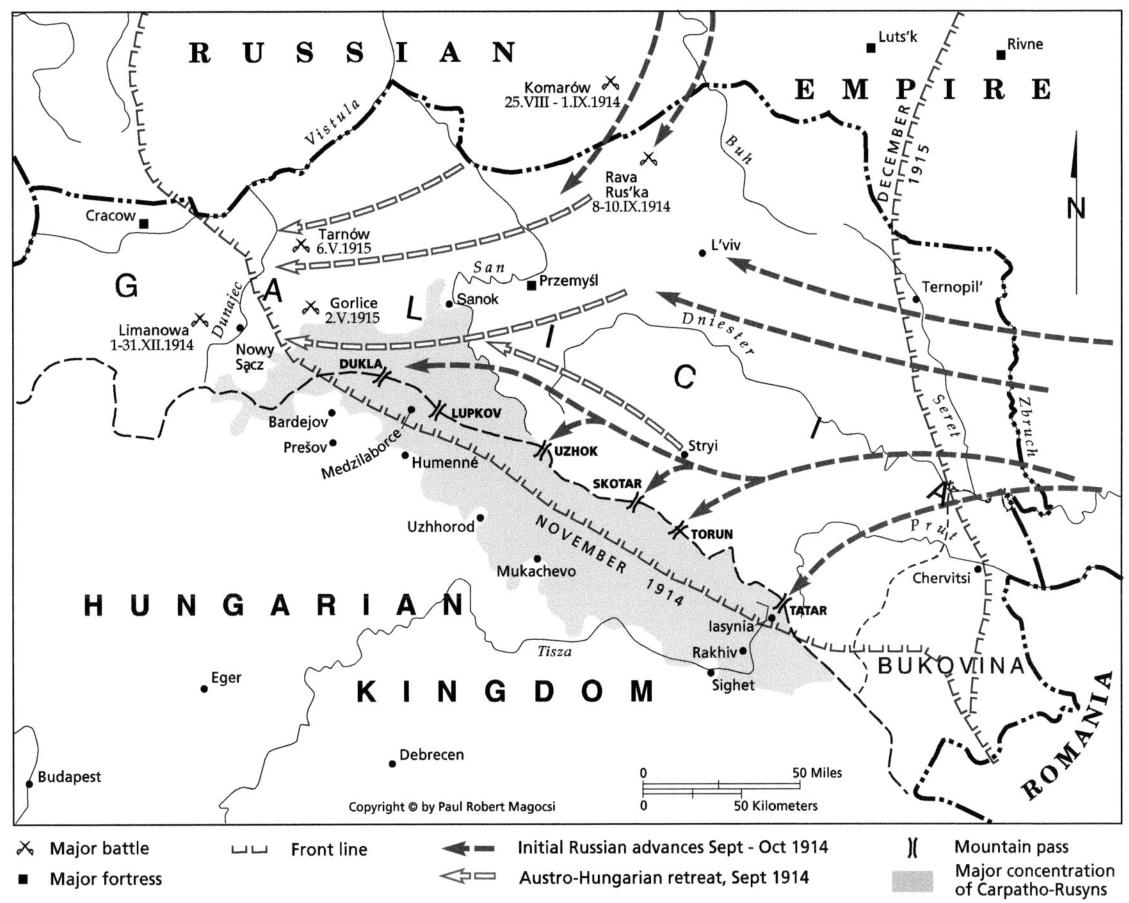

Figure 2.4. World War I in the Carpathians.

to tell her own war story, but she is put off by a quip from her interlocuter. The loss of what might have been a recorded version of her personal wartime experience is regrettable. Memories from Warhola relatives, uncertain as to historical facts, were later garbled by biographers, leaving only a few vague facts about Julia's hiding from soldiers in the forest with her mother and sisters. Victor Bockris reports, "Every time she was warned of the approach of soldiers she would bundle her little sisters and the old widow into a horse-drawn cart and take off for the forest, where they would hide for days. These trips were often made in the middle of the night in snow or rain. By the time she reached her destination Julia's skirt was sometimes frozen stiff."[97] While this impressionistic account captures the tone of Julia's terrible experience, it actually diminishes the realistic horror that civilians suffered.

Unfortunately, we have no surviving wartime letters from Julia to her husband in America. However, there do exist published letters of civilians from the region that offer eyewitness accounts and emotional outpourings. When the first delivery of newspapers and letters arrived in America from Europe, the *Amerikansky Russky Viestnik* invited readers to submit for publication letters they received from relatives in the Old Country.[98] These firsthand accounts, written between October 1914 and May 1915, were published under the rubric "Pys'mo yz staroho kraia" (Letter from the old country). Deriding the compulsory optimism of official Hungarian press reports, the *ARV* editor told his readers that the letters described conditions in the homeland "in all their unvarnished terror." We can be confident that the horrors they describe coincide closely with Julia's experiences.

What stands out in these letters is the writers' fear—fear of the sights and sounds of battle, fear of the loss of family and property, fear of the unknown. Writers describe their suffering in vivid detail, with emotional fervor and grim wit, in surprisingly poetic folk imagery. In a letter written August 2, 1914, a mother cries, "My dear sweet son left today for the war, and I remain here like a sad turtle dove in the dark forest, whose nest is empty without her son, whom she so lovingly nurtured. My dear son has flown away." A woman from Sačurov, forty miles south of Miková, tells her husband on December 14, "I am terribly frightened. The Russian troops are not far away. We can hear their cannons roar.[99] People are running around helter-skelter. The troops take our cattle and fodder, and we can't say a thing about it. Since autumn, the troops have been marching through the region day and night. There are so many soldiers in the village, you would expect the ground to cave in." The Russian historian Igor Slepcov confirms that from the beginning of October, villages south of the Carpathians resembled a military camp. "Day and night, endless convoys of troops and caravans of Galician refugees trudged along." He cites the Zborov village chronicle: "The clamor of military convoys, along with the *Lord have mercy's* of the refugees, merged in the wet, dark October nights with the neighing of horses and the clip-clop of their hooves in a terrible, unbroken melody."[100]

A father compares the sounds of war in the homeland with his immigrant son's work in America: "The thunder of the cannon was terrific and terrible, the earth shook. You won't hear that kind of rumbling even in the mines!" A seventy-year-old father writing on December 30 in Nižná Jablonka, twenty miles southeast of Miková, compares the current war to his own military service: "I was in the war in Italy in 1866, but that was a game compared to this. Bullets fall on the village like rain.[101] The troops took everything we had—cattle, fodder, and our stores of food. They gave us nothing for it, not even a kreuzer. When we ask them to pay so we won't die of hunger, they tell us to be quiet or they will burn down the house." His closing signature is forthright and painful: "We have hardly anything to eat. We will probably die from hunger. We send you greetings, dear son, and we remain, your parents." Most writers can think of no comparison at all for the distress they suffer. They can only feel glad that their relatives in America are spared: "Now only those who have gone to America are lucky" (February 18, 1915).

The writers describe villages empty of men, ravaged fields, and the glut of the dead and wounded. Already in December 1914, a villager wrote, "Now they're taking everyone to the army, even those who were rejected three times before." Troops confiscated the oxen. People dug holes in the earth to hide their grain. Fields became graveyards. "So many have died that behind the houses and stables, the ground is full of graves. They take the wounded away by the cartful, but they bury the dead wherever they fall. There are as many wounded as there are stars in the sky. One is missing an arm, another a leg, another was shot through the head. There will be many beggars." An elderly woman laments hopelessly, "What will become of us? We only have God. As God gives, so it will be. May His will be done."

Andrii could not have been happy to read a report in the November 2, 1916, issue relating to the wives of émigrės. "If a woman whose husband is in the United States goes to a notary on business, she is told to eat dirt. 'Your husband is earning money in the United States and not fighting for the homeland.'" A woman in Čukalovce, twenty miles southwest of Miková, expressed her despair in a letter to her husband in South Chicago:

> I write to you, my dear husband, to say that we have absolutely nothing left. We still have one cow, but it's no use because there is nothing to feed her. We have nothing to eat ourselves. The troops took everything—cattle, fodder, grain, potatoes. Now we can only sit in the cold cellar, because the rooms, the stables, and the cowsheds are full of soldiers. The fences have all been burnt. I don't know where to go with the children. We have already suffered so much that we don't care if we are shot, just so as not to suffer any longer. We have absolutely nothing. Everything has been burnt down to the ground.

From what we know of Julia's experience, this could have been her letter to Andrii.

According to Vasyl Bezek, the husband of Julia's youngest sister, he was evacuated from Miková with Julia and her sister "as far as Budapest."[102] Several letter writers comment that anyone with money flees the frontline regions, and with Andrii's financial support, Julia may have had more options than some. Becoming a refugee, however, was not a pleasant prospect. Leaving one's home meant abandoning it to looting and pillaging by soldiers of both armies. Even as late as the end of May in 1915, a man named Andrei in Sharysh County writes to his brothers and sisters in America:

> Yesterday I packed my belongings in a sack, as did my wife and children. You can imagine what I feel in my heart thinking about all the hard work that went into building my household property, and now I must leave it all behind. We were sheltering refugees from Polianka, and now we must flee together with them. I'm afraid to write everything, but the black earth has been laid bare by hot-stone-hail from the shooting. My dear brothers and sisters, you left home for America in tears, but at least you knew where and to whom you were going. We know nothing.

By mid-1915, 1.1 million people had sought refuge in the interior of Hungary. Evacuations were carried out in just a few hours, very often in situations of open violence and pillaging.[103] Endless files of refugees left most everything behind, taking only what they could pile on cattle wagons and carry on their backs as they plodded to unknown destinations in sad parades. Some were taken to camps, where living conditions were barely tolerable and mortality rates were high. Others were moved to small villages, where they felt rising resentment from the host communities. Most refugees preferred to return to their home villages as soon as possible, no matter what devastation they might find there. Julia's experience as a refugee was probably short, most likely in early 1915.

Between Hungary and Russia

The Carpatho-Rusyn populace on both sides of the Carpathians came in for especially brutal treatment from the Austro-Hungarian army. Historically, Rusyns had found themselves "in between" their maternal Slavic ancestry and their political Habsburg fatherland. Based on their related language, religion, and the self-identity of Rusyns, whose ethnonym was easily confused with the term *russkii* (Russian), Carpatho-Rusyns were suspected of sympathy with the Russian enemy from the very start of the war. The Australian journalist J. F. Archibald, a war correspondent traveling with the Austro-Hungarian army, related the Hungarian notion of conspiracy to Americans in an article for *Scribner's Magazine*: "It has been suspected that the priests of the Greek [Catholic] Church have organized the peasants of their various districts into corps of spies, and, in consequence of the perfection of that organization, there is scarcely a move of the Austro-Hungarian army made that is not immediately communicated to the enemy."[104]

The Carpatho-Rusyns certainly had reason to resent the Habsburg government. By the early days of the war, Hungarian oppression of Rusyns had stiffened. Cyrillic orthography was no longer being taught in schools of the Prešov eparchy. The Julian calendar of the Greek Catholic Church was dictatorially revoked, and Rusyn priests could no longer conduct services on traditional feast days. Cyrillic books were confiscated and burned by Austro-Hungarian troops, and Carpatho-Rusyns buried their prayer books in the earth to preserve them. But while the Carpatho-Rusyns had reason for resistance, the notion of "corps of peasant spies" is surely overblown. In any case, the inhumane retaliation of the Austro-Hungarians against civilians was unwarranted. The assessment of modern scholarship is unequivocal.

> Even before 1914, widespread hysteria [in the Austro-Hungarian government] concerning espionage and treason now escalated into a conduct of war that was racist and radical; the patriotism now on show with its attendant rejection of anyone or anything different meant that civilians were now increasingly targeted. As a result of this the Austro-Hungarian battle forces made "extensive use" of the "right for self-defence" against "Russophiles" right from the start, which meant that they shot anyone suspicious on the spot, took hostages who were executed at will, accused entire villages of treason and as a consequence "flattened them to the ground."[105]

Most of the letters published in *ARV* express fear of the Russian invaders, rather than sympathy for them, and writers clearly differentiate the "Moskal," a pejorative term for Russian, from *nashy* (our side). But Austro-Hungarian propaganda fanned the people's natural fear of invasion into panic at the coming of the Russians. One woman implored her American relatives, "Pray to the dear Lord to help us defeat the enemy, for when the Moskal moves in, it will be the end of us." Meanwhile, the Austro-Hungarian army's presumption of sedition among Carpatho-Rusyn civilians fueled the peasants' fear of their own troops. A letter from a Zemplyn Rusyn from November 1914 cautiously described the atmosphere of terror that ensued. "Panic and anxiety are all the greater since it is strictly forbidden to speak of things that are happening around us and hanging over us. If three women are found having a private conversation together, they will be arrested. The region is full of spies; it seems that the trees have ears, and the stones understand not only our words but our thoughts." And several letters include qualifications such as the following: "I can't write everything I want because it is prohibited. There is a very strict order against writing about the war. If God helps me get to America, I'll tell you what's going on here. I can't write more now." On December 14, a woman from a village forty miles south of Miková wrote that it was forbidden to say "even one little word" about the Russian troops without being arrested, which explains the letter writers' self-censorship on the subject.

Russian historians insist that their soldiers behaved "completely correctly" toward the civilian population, although "not without some looting," especially in the homes of refugees who had fled. Citing local historians and village chronicles, Igor Slepcov describes many examples of positive interactions between civilians and Russian soldiers.[106] While Carpatho-Rusyn civilians may have been more comfortable under Russian than Austro-Hungarian occupation, the horror of war was not diminished. Village chronicles describe the efforts of the Jewish population to pass themselves off as Rusyns to evade Russian mistreatment, even displaying icons to feign religious solidarity. After the Russian forces were driven out of Carpathian Rus', the Austro-Hungarian military intensified their punitive reprisals against Carpatho-Rusyn civilians. Arrests and summary executions, especially of Greek Catholic priests, were common. Father Petrasovich, who had been pastor of both Saint John the Baptist Greek Catholic Church in Lyndora, which John Zavacky helped to establish, and Saint John Chrysostom Greek Catholic Church in Pittsburgh, which would become the Warhola family's parish, was one of those arrested. The historian Paul Robert Magocsi notes that in March 1915, a Hungarian military tribunal found eight hundred Carpatho-Rusyn peasants guilty of "cooperation" with the Russian army. He comments, "Hungarian troops, in particular, amused themselves by beating up men, women, and children in Carpatho-Rusyn villages 'liberated' after Russian troops retreated."[107] Such an incident has been immortalized in Jaroslav Hašek's novel of the Great War, *The Good Soldier Švejk*. "On the platform surrounded by Hungarian gendarmes stood a group of arrested Ruthenians from Hungary. It included priests, teachers and peasants from far and wide in the region. All of them had their hands tied behind their backs with cord and were fastened to each other in pairs. Most of them had broken noses and bumps on their head, since immediately after their arrest they had been beaten up by the gendarmes." The author goes on to describe a Hungarian gendarme's vicious, mocking assault of a priest and the subsequent removal of the prisoners to a location where "they were to be beaten and pounded without anyone being able to see it." Hašek concludes sardonically, "This episode was a topic of conversation in the staff carriage and, generally speaking, most of the officers condemned it."[108]

Back Home in Miková

As the hostilities were coming to an end in Carpathian Rus', the *Amerikansky Russky Viestnik* published an editorial titled, "The Situation of Subcarpathian Rusyns in the Homeland." The column opened with a fatalistic judgment: "Such is our fate. Of all the bitter things in this world, we have been dealt the largest part." After reviewing the notorious catastrophes to date in western Europe, the editor concluded:

> But most unfortunate is our Carpatho-Rusyn people. They suffered the longest and most terrible fighting. Their own troops and then enemy troops perished in our highlands. Through the fields of green winter wheat, trenches were dug for soldiers and cannons; there will be no harvest this year. There is no milk, because the one cow the soldiers left behind perished from cold and hunger; her fodder was confiscated for the war horses that stand in the stables. And since supply trains often could not reach troops in the hinterland, the soldiers in some mountain villages ate the residents' last potato. By order of the government, only cornbread is available anywhere in the country, but in our highlands, there is not even corn. Our people are living on water and roots steeped in the blood of their brothers. Hunger, hunger, hunger reigns in our homeland![109]

Throughout the war, the newspaper repeatedly requested donations to aid fellow Rusyns in the homeland and published the names of contributors.

Four months after the cessation of hostilities in the region, on September 23, 1915, *ARV* published "An Interesting Letter from the Old Country." The unnamed author describes a bicycle trip through a dozen towns and villages in Sharysh County, all within thirty-five miles of Miková. His descriptions are sad and shocking. "Everywhere I went, everything is destroyed down to the foundations. The Russians and our own troops demolished and burnt everything. People are living in huts in the forest. Lord, how horrid and sad it was to walk through these villages and small towns. My heart beat fast and I could barely breathe. Tears came to my eyes, and I cried like a child."

In Zborov, people were sleeping under the open sky, with no protection from the elements. "But sleep they do, because the poor things are exhausted from the work of repairing and re-plastering their demolished cottages. The entire village was obliterated down to the bare earth. Not a single cottage has a roof or a window. Nothing remains but the walls and the shrapnel-splattered chimney." The writer is dismayed that under these circumstances, Jews were selling alcohol and asking for Austro-Hungarian currency. "Our poor Rusyns have nothing, not even oat-bread, but they are so simple, timid, and honorable, that they don't know where to go to take advantage of the goods that are being distributed free of charge. Our people and their children are so tattered that they are almost naked, without even scarves—everything was burnt. In a word, they have nothing, just barely their health. Nevertheless, they work hard rebuilding their houses; after all, the walls are still standing."

Some villages were so totally destroyed that only bricks and powder remained, overgrown with weeds. "People ramble through the weeds with heads bowed, trying to salvage some small thing—maybe some coins or hinges from the door. Children run around wearing only shirts, with fingers in their mouths, pale and thin from hunger, so scruffy that they look like wild people. Where a stove still stands, women light a fire and bake bread, but without paddles or pokers. Lord what will happen to them in winter?" When the bicyclist tried to talk with the people, he found them uncommunicative. "They say that they have a constant din in their ears, clamor, and moaning, the thunder of guns, and the neighing of horses. The silence of the grave prevails." This description accurately describes the situation in and around Miková in January 1915. According to the village website, peasants hid in cellars or fled as refugees. Nearly all the houses were looted and damaged. Many were burned to the ground, the Zavacky home among them.

About forty-five men from Miková fought with the Austro-Hungarian army. Eight were killed and six were injured.[110] Andrii's youngest brother Jan was among the injured. Although military records have not been discovered and no death notice has been found in the accessible parish registers, it is believed that Jan was wounded in battle and died of his injuries soon after the war.[111] The third Varchola brother, Joseph, who followed Andrii to America in 1910, served in the United States army from May 1918 until July 1919, arriving in France just one month before the armistice. If Joe Warhola had signed on earlier, he might have found himself at war with his brother Jan.

Julia's brother Yurko also fought in the Austro-Hungarian army. A family story has it that when Julia went to the Red Cross to inquire about her brother, she was told he had perished in battle. When her mother heard this news, the shock brought on her death. After the war, it became known that Yurko had exchanged uniforms and identification with a mortally wounded comrade. The notice of his death was inaccurate, and he returned home unscathed. This romantic story is redolent of Julia's starry-eyed mythmaking, but it is not implausible. Church metrical records show that Julia's mother, Justina Mrocsko, died November 22, 1918, just days after the end of the war. The cause of death is given as Spanish flu, which claimed four to five times more lives than the Great War itself and was, in many ways, interwoven with it.[112] We do not know when Yurko returned home, but he was Justina's only son remaining in the homeland, and news of his death was surely a blow. His surprise return is a fitting denouement to the family legend. If this was a case of Julia's mythmaking, it shows novelistic and theatrical flair.

Dozens of soldiers, both Austro-Hungarian and Russian, died on the fields of Miková. Julia's son John remembered his mother's description: "Dead bodies were scattered in the forest and on meadows. Skulls of soldiers shined like large white mushrooms long after the war was over."[113] John attributed Andy's *Skulls* series to his mother's memory. In July 1922, after Julia's departure for America, the scattered remains of the war dead were exhumed from the village and buried in two military cemeteries in Miková. The burial grounds have recently been mapped and restored by the Beskyd Military History Club, an association that promotes the study of military history in northeastern Slovakia.[114] One cemetery, located on the grounds of the Greek Catholic church, is home to five soldiers of the Austro-Hungarian army and two Russian soldiers. Their names, as well as the dates and causes of their deaths, are unknown. The second cemetery was laid out on the property of the local farmer Jan Kaliniak, who released his land for the purpose. It became the burial place for soldiers whose bodies were found in graves scattered on five plots in the village, belonging to Jan Varchola and Stephen Zavacky. It is unknown whether they were from Andrii's and Julia's families. Eight Russian and six Austro-Hungarian victims are buried here, under a large wooden cross.

The troubles of civilians did not end with the fighting. The war began just before the fall harvest of 1914. When the Russians were finally pushed to the east at the end of April 1915, spring planting had already been disrupted, causing a second season of shortages. On March 4, 1915, a man from a village near Bardejov wrote in a letter published in the *Amerikansky Russky Viestnik*: "It's now spring, time to work the fields, but there's nothing to work with. The horses were taken to the war and the oxen were taken for meat for the soldiers. Inflation is terrible and there is nothing to buy anywhere. We are living on roots." Since there were few able-bodied men in the villages, the burden of rebuilding and replanting fell on women, the elderly, and children. In summer 1915, the Hungarian government set up the War Produce Corporation, which monopolized the acquisition and sale of grain. Hungarian gendarmes traversed the countryside to requisition grain, potatoes, and cattle. Price ceilings for agrarian products were set well below market value, while consumer goods were selling at inflated prices. Peasants responded by withholding and hoarding produce, and a black market sprang up. The government retaliated with military raids, inspections, confiscations, and searches for hidden reserves, taking punitive action against the peasants. Living conditions in the countryside, already bleak, deteriorated further, and fears of famine intensified.[115]

After the fighting in the Carpathians ended in 1915, Julia managed to maintain the farm and care for her family for another six years before she was finally able to emigrate to America to join her husband. It is unfortunate that details about her experience during the war and in the recovery period are missing from Julia's personal story, but there are hints that her sufferings were harrowing, and she may have suffered stress that lasted into her old age. In a Rusyn-language video of Julia taken by her son when she was almost seventy-nine years old, she is eating lunch when crumbs fall on her shirt. Her mind wanders for a moment, and she mumbles, "Then the Germans will come and they will eat all this ... no one will eat ... Germans will come."[116] We know that she talked about the war frequently, but because of faulty memories and lack of interest on the part of interlocuters, what was a horrendous trial for Julia has been reduced to facile anecdotes that minimize her ordeal and downplay her pain. This reconstruction of her nightmarish experience, based on historical facts and parallel narratives, elaborates Julia's own modest summary of those years: "War, war, war. You don't know how bad." And, "I was very strong lady."

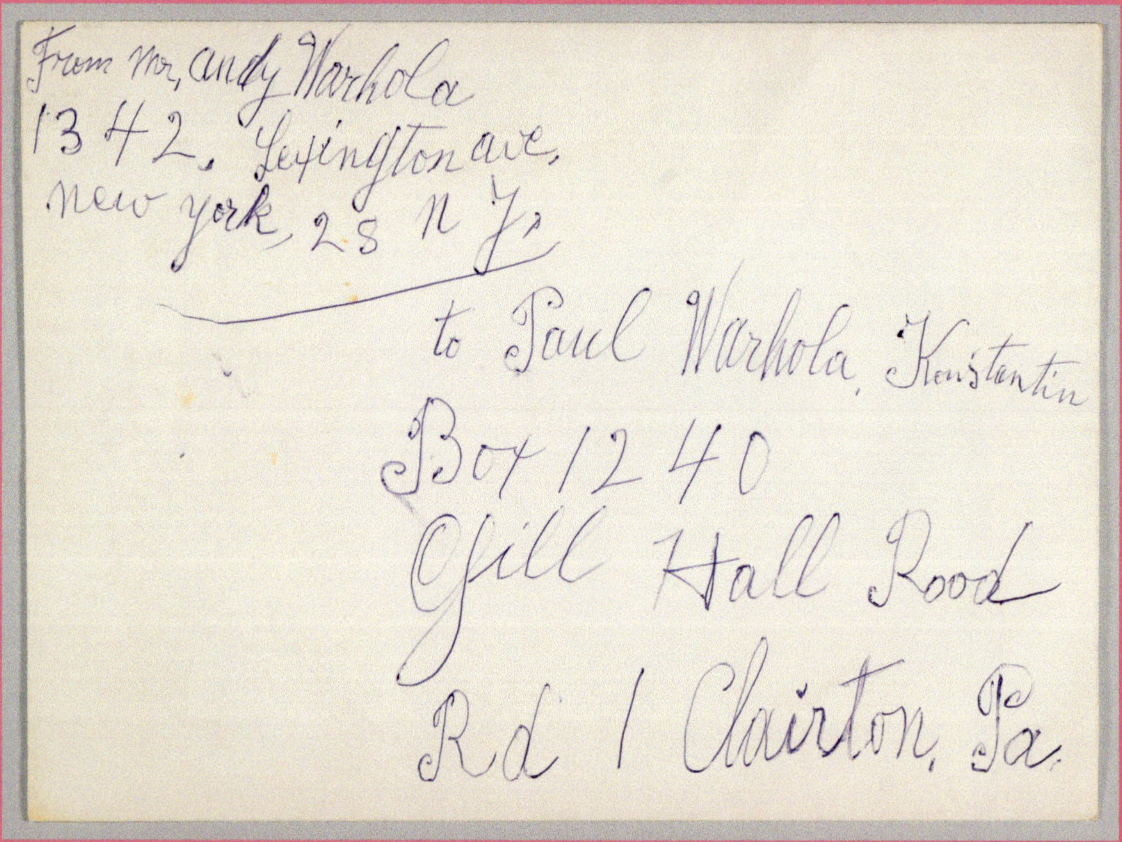

Figure 3.1. Envelope addressed to Paul Warhola (Konstantin) by Julia Warhola, 1960s.

3

Pittsburgh, Pennsylvania

The Warhola family myth about Julia's emigration deals not with the facts of her voyage, but how it was financed. According to Victor Bockris's interviews with family, Andrii sent Julia the fare for her passage five times beginning in 1919, but letters containing the money never reached her. So, in 1921, "Julia Warhola borrowed $160 from her priest and made her way by horse and cart, train and ship to look for her husband in Pittsburgh."[1] David Bourdon reports family memories: "She placed her sisters in the care of relatives, borrowed about one hundred eighty dollars from her priest, and sailed for America to rejoin her husband."[2] In both accounts, the dollar amount is suspiciously reminiscent of the $160 that, according to Julia's *Esquire* interview, Andrii took with him when he left for America.[3] This suggests a conflation of facts based on previous interviews and publications that is typical of the reminiscences of Warhol associates, which are often accepted without question by biographers.

According to Julia's daughter-in-law Ann, the wife of her son Paul, a local Miková priest helped Julia to emigrate by lending her money.[4] When Julia demurred, saying she could not repay him, the priest asked her to name a son after him. The priest's name was Constantine, (Konstantin in Rusyn). Church records show that from 1919 to 1923, Reverend Konstantin Turkiniak was pastor in Driečna, a village neighboring Miková. Almost the same age as Julia, Father Konstantin had grown up in Čertižne, a few miles away, where his father was cantor-teacher in the Greek Catholic church. His uncle Jan had been parish priest in Miková since 1902. It was he who married Julia and Andrii in 1909 and baptized and buried their baby Maria in 1912. Young Father Konstantin filled in at the Miková church after the death of his uncle in 1920, and he served there until a new priest took over in November 1922.[5] The fact that his service can be substantiated in Miková, when Julia was planning her emigration, lends credence to her story and to these particular family memories.

When Julia's sons were born in America, her husband rejected "Constantine," in American spelling, as a given name, and middle names were not customary for children of Rusyn American immigrants. But Julia did not forget her promise to Father Konstantin. When her first grandson was born, she asked her daughter-in-law Ann to use the name. Ann and Paul Warhola named their first son Paul after his father but gave the child the middle name of Constantine. Julia objected quietly that it should be spelled with a *K*.

Father Konstantin died in 1964, probably never knowing how well his "loan" to Julia worked out. Paul Constantine Warhola would go on to attend Saints Cyril and Methodius Byzantine Ruthenian Catholic Seminary in Pittsburgh, where his education was largely financed by his Uncle Andy. In 1969 he was ordained to the Byzantine Catholic priesthood. "Bubba" Julia and grandson "Pauly" would later conduct a long correspondence, as he studied in Pittsburgh and Washington, DC. Julia continued to emphasize the name "Konstantin," with a *K*.

Julia's mother died of Spanish flu in Miková in November 1918. After the war, her twenty-two-year-old brother Yurko took over the Zavacky farm. Her sisters— Elena, fifteen, and Eva, twelve—were now old enough to help with household duties and field work. Julia lived with and took care of Andrii's mother, who was left alone after her son Jan's death from war injuries. Andrii had been helping his mother financially from abroad. A niece recalled, "Andy's father, Andrii, wrote letters from America, he sent her dollars. She had money. I know, because she couldn't have survived otherwise. She had two red cows."[6]

Still primarily responsible for two households, Julia put off her trip to America until her brother's marriage, but on both sides of the ocean, she and Andrii began planning for their reunion. In April 1920, Andrii filed a notary certificate to guarantee his ability to support his immigrant wife. In September of that year, Yurko married Maria Gramata, and together they took charge of Elena and Eva. One month later, Julia traveled to Prague and acquired a passport. Perhaps anticipating

Julia's departure from his mother's home in Miková, Andrii's brother Joseph applied for a passport in Pittsburgh in January 1921, with the stated intention of visiting his mother in Czechoslovakia for three months. If, in fact, he made this trip, for which no records can be found, he might have made new arrangements for the care of his mother. However, the absence of records and references suggests that Joseph's planned trip never took place. Julia Choma Varchola, the mother of Joseph and Andrii, died in Miková of typhus at age seventy in 1926.

Another impetus for Julia's emigration was the Emergency Immigration Act of 1921. The act, which went into effect June 3, 1921, restricted the number of immigrants into the United States by imposing annual quotas for each country. The number of Czechoslovak citizens who could be admitted to the United States in fiscal year 1921–1922 was limited to 14,282. In 1924, a subsequent Immigration Act further reduced the quota for Czechoslovakia to 3,078.[7] The American press and the *Amerikansky Russky Viestnik* (*ARV*) had been reporting since 1915 on the US Senate's deliberations to restrict immigration, and Andrii would have been aware of the coming changes. Emigration from Europe had practically halted at the onset of war. Between 1913 and 1915, voyages from Europe to the United States fell by more than 70 percent, and steerage passenger arrivals dropped by 91 percent.[8] Emigration did not begin to pick up until 1920. Julia made plans to depart as soon as travel was safe and her family was settled, and before the limitations would constrain her. Her ship, the *Celtic* of the White Star Line, sailed from Liverpool on June 11, 1921.

Emigration for Julia in 1921 was a longer and considerably more difficult process than it had been for Andrii in 1912. The new state of Czechoslovakia had complex passport and visa regulations that were more strictly enforced than Hungary's laws in the laissez-faire prewar atmosphere. After 1918, valid passports were necessary, as well as other bureaucratic approvals and authorizations. Julia's passport material includes a "Traveler Report," filed on June 26, 1920, in Michalovce, a district seat of Zemplyn County, which certified her photograph and signature. It was attested that she had no tax debt, and the purpose of her travel was to reunite with her husband. Having received approval from local authorities, Julia had to make a long and costly rail trip from Miková to Prague to submit her documents. Issued by the American consulate on October 12, 1920, the passport and visa documents authorized her to depart for the United States anytime during the following year. Her photograph shows a fresh-faced young woman with a pleasant expression, but a serious gaze. Dressed in a white blouse with lace-trimmed sleeves and a dark skirt, she wears a neatly folded dark kerchief to cover her hair.[9]

Back in 1912, Andrii most likely traveled on a closed emigrant train directly from the Prussian border to his point of departure in Bremen. He may have had a hurried stop in Ruhleben near Berlin for a perfunctory inspection. The total travel time from Miková to Bremen was probably no more than a day or two, and emigrant service at Bremen was fast and efficient.[10] In 1921, Julia's journey was much longer. As a result of the war, German shipping lines had lost virtually their entire fleets, as passenger ships were repurposed for military use or appropriated by the allies.[11] By contrast, British lines had benefited from the transfer or purchase of German vessels and were able to restore regular passenger services by 1919.[12] But for residents of eastern Czechoslovakia, the inland journey to British ports was much more difficult than the trek to Hamburg or Bremen.

Julia was accompanied on the voyage to America by Miková neighbors Ilona Kalinak (Kalinyak) and her eight-year-old son Jan. According to the ship's passenger list, both Julia and Ilona reported that passage had been paid to their final destination by their husbands. Andrii Warhola and Stephen Kalinyak, who were neighbors and coworkers in Pittsburgh, planned their wives' travel with the help of steamship and railway agents. The White Star Line had an office in Pittsburgh and regularly advertised in local newspapers. A package ticket purchased in America covered rail transportation in Europe, passage across the English Channel, the cost of food and lodging at emigrant halls along the route, a ticket for the ocean liner to New York, and a railway ticket to Pittsburgh. After receiving a blessing from the parish priest and farewell greetings from a procession of villagers, Julia and her traveling companions would have made their way by horse and cart to Medzilaborce or Bardejov, where they could board a train to Prague. They probably spent several days there in early May acquiring visas and documents for the journey forward.

The visa stamps in Julia's passport indicate that the overland journey from Prague to Liverpool took at least four weeks. A transit visa through Germany was valid for three weeks. A stamp of the American consulate in Prague, dated May 11, indicates that she was scheduled to depart from Le Havre, but that notation is crossed out. By the beginning of June, the Miková travelers were in Belgium, where they transferred to the Belgian State Railway and proceeded to the port at Ostend to wait for a boat of the Belgian State Railway and Mail Packet Service. A cramped packet boat carried them across the English Channel on a three-hour journey to Dover.

From Ostend, Julia and Ilona were included in a party of twenty-four passengers, whose trips began in Romania and Czechoslovakia.[13] They traveled to London, changed trains, and probably stations, to London Euston, where they boarded a boat train to Liverpool. Boat trains represented a collaboration between railway

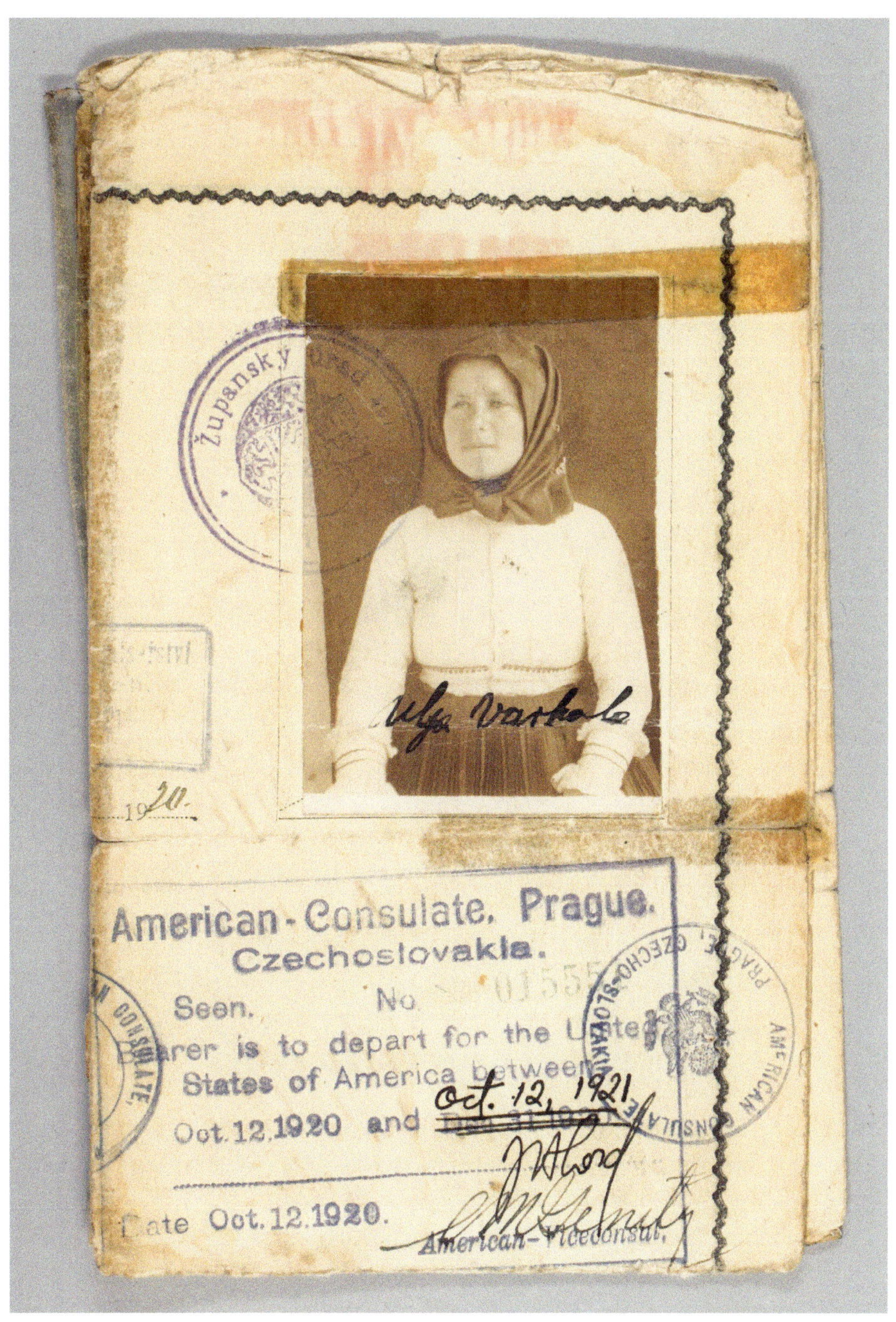

Figure 3.2. Julia Warhola's passport, 1920.

companies, port authority, and travel agencies to deliver passengers directly to special quayside stations so they could be transferred seamlessly to the waiting ships, unencumbered by their luggage. According to the railway historian Martyn Pring, "The boat train has a special place in the complex story of railway travel, combining as it does high romance and drama with an efficient and integrated transport system." But he cautions,

> In many ways the boat train was a miniature version of society demonstrating the shocking divisions between rich and poor at the turn of the twentieth century. Whilst some services undeniably conveyed the world's elite, at the other end of the scale dedicated third-class boats [*sic*] trains always departed far earlier than their first and second-class combinations to arrive first at port destinations and awaiting liners, so these passengers could embark on vessels before the elite passengers arrived. . . . Emigrant passengers were squashed in boat trains with hard-seated carriages providing only the most basic of amenities. Squalor was ever present on special third-class boat trains.[14]

This characterization of the emigrant's four- or five-hour journey undoubtedly describes most of Julia's trip to the port. Narratives of European immigrant passengers tell of long delays at every stage of the journey, communication difficulties, and ineffective consular service. Julia must have marveled at the gigantic liners moored alongside the new Liverpool Riverside landing stage, and it must have been with exhilaration and relief that she and her traveling companions boarded the ship and embarked on the transatlantic segment of their voyage. They departed on the White Star Line steamer RMS *Celtic* on Saturday, June 11, 1921. The next day, the ship docked in Queenstown (Cobh) on the south coast of County Cork, to embark mail and additional passengers from Ireland. The passage across the Atlantic from Queenstown to New York took eight days.

RMS *Celtic* of the White Star Line

In 1921, the White Star Line was one of the most prominent shipping companies in the world, operating ocean liners on the North Atlantic service between Liverpool and New York. Rather than speed, White Star focused on providing comfortable passage for both upper-class passengers and immigrants, and during the years of mass migration, the line played a leading role in improving steerage-class accommodations. The *Celtic* was one of the White Star Line's "Big Four," the largest ocean liners then sailing regularly across the Atlantic. A company brochure boasts: "They are of robust and sturdy build, with graceful, stately lines, and if there is one comment about them heard more often than another, it is that these vessels are 'so very steady.'"[15] A brochure from 1907 shows off the first-class lounge, smoking room, and spacious staterooms. The caption to a photograph of the *Celtic*'s dining saloon reads, "The ceiling is done in white and gold lincrusta [wallpaper], and the walls are superbly paneled with elaborate figures, and rich carvings and moldings. In the center is a beautiful domed skylight, through the stained glass of which a beautiful soft light falls." In sum, "The White Star Line . . . has always made it a point to be satisfied with nothing less than the highest standard of excellence as regards its arrangements for the comfort of travelers."

Of course, Julia and her companions did not travel first-class, but after their long and arduous overland journey, they probably welcomed the *Celtic*'s upgraded third-class accommodations. According to the company's promotions, "The democratic age we live in demands strenuous efforts on the part of steamship companies to provide nothing short of the best for Third Class patrons; and it is well known that the White Star Line has from its inception been the forerunner of many improvements, with the result that for years past it has carried the largest number of Third Class passengers from these shores to New York." Photographs depict a spare but spacious dining room, where, as in first class, third-class passengers were waited on by stewards. Passengers were housed in two-, four-, and six-berth semi private, "airy" cabins, and during the voyage, immigrants had access to "ample, open deck space" on the Promenade Deck. A 1919 dinner menu from the *Celtic*, presumed to be from third class, offered potage brunoise, boiled salmon with cucumber Hollandaise, sweetbreads à la Saint-Cloud, Surrey capon with supreme sauce, baked Cumberland ham, braised Bermuda onions, plum pudding with brandy and hard sauce, and coffee.[16] One can only wonder about Julia's reaction to cuisine and service that must have seemed luxurious, if alien. Unlike immigrants in steerage at the turn of the century, by 1921, most third-class passengers thoroughly enjoyed their time at sea.

On Monday, June 20, the *Celtic* arrived in New York with 1,080 passengers. Whereas in 1912, Andrii traveled amid crowds of Slavic immigrants, Julia's fellow travelers were primarily English, Irish, and Scandinavian, with a smaller number of Poles and Jews from east central Europe. Passengers from Czechoslovakia were not distinguished as to race or people on the passenger list, so it is not possible to count the number of Carpatho-Rusyns aboard. They were likely very few, as most residents of Czechoslovakia on the manifest identified home villages in the western part of the country. New York newspapers announced the arrival of the *Celtic* in articles with droll headlines such as, "200 Irish Girls Land Here to Be Movie Stars, Not Servants," stressing that the "colleens" had come to America "to seek employment as stenographers, typists, models, and motion picture actresses. Housework? Nothing like that!"[17]

Among the first-class passengers were several well-known theatrical lights: the English actor, director, playwright, and songwriter George Grossmith Jr.; Daisy Hancox and Heather Thatcher, actresses of the London Gaiety Theater; and a future film star, thirteen-year-old Douglas Fairbanks Jr. of Hollywood, California, who was traveling with his mother and stepfather. Another American celebrity aboard was Francis Ouimet, known today as the "father of amateur golf," who had traveled with the American team to the British Open Golf Championship. According to reporters meeting the ship, passengers had participated in a golf tournament on deck during the voyage, with Ouimet as referee. Ship musicians provided entertainment. The atmosphere aboard ship was lively in all classes, and Julia must have had some fun.

The ship's passenger lists were filled out by immigration officers of the steamship line at the point of departure, based on information provided by the immigrants. The forms were then delivered to officials at the receiving station, in this case, Ellis Island, where follow-up inspections were made and additional notations were inserted to correct or clarify details. Julia gave her name as it was written on her passport, Ula Varhola.[18] When asked about her occupation, she called herself a farmer. Having fended for herself and her family for the past nine years, Julia likely considered herself worthy of the title. But on review at the receiving station, the inspector crossed out "farmer" and wrote in "wife."

As of 1917, it was required that immigrants coming to the United States must be literate in their native language. When Julia and Ilona were asked whether they could read and write, they responded in the affirmative. Since they did not have a recognized name for their language, they referred to it by the name of their country, and it was abbreviated on the list as "Czecho-Sl." Instructions to steamship officials on the reverse side of the passenger list directed officers to distinguish between nationality and "race or people," and it provided an "accepted list of races," which included "Ruthenian/Russniak," the US immigration bureau's term for Carpatho-Rusyn. Perhaps because Czechoslovakia was a new country, peopled by numerous unfamiliar minorities, immigrants from Czechoslovakia on this predominantly English-speaking ship were almost all classified meaninglessly as "Czechoslovakian" in categories for nationality, "race or people," and language.

Inspectors and interpreters at Ellis Island were somewhat more discriminating. Notations show that Julia and Ilona were suspected of being illiterate and were subjected to a reading test. The language test was complex.

The government initially tested the immigrants by having them read selected passages from the Bible, but it became clear this system could be controversial. So the Immigration Service soon developed a rather complicated system to perform the testing. First, each known language was issued a number. Then, a number of phrases and passages in each language were printed on slips of paper (one phrase per slip), and each phrase received a serial number. So each slip had one number for the language, and another for the phrase (i.e., #-####). A second set of slips were printed in English, and numbered with the exact corresponding numbers. The phrases usually contained simple instructions, such as "Get up, open the door, and return to your chair," or "Shake the hand of the person next to you." The literacy test involved first determining what language the immigrant spoke/read, locating a slip for that language, and giving the immigrant the test language slip and the testing official the corresponding English language slip. By reading the corresponding instructions in English and observing the immigrant's actions, even an inspector who spoke only English could discern whether the person before him could read.[19]

Julia and Ilona were given different phrases to read in language number three, presumably Rusyn, but perhaps Slovak, and both passed the test.

Under "Name and complete address of nearest relative or friend in country whence alien came," Julia gave her brother's name, Yurko Zavacky, the spelling of which was mangled on the form. She claimed to have $25 in her possession; Ilona had $37. Immigrants were frequently less than truthful about the money they carried, but the checkmark next to the item on the manifest indicates that an inspector had verified the amount. In answer to the question whether she was going to join a relative or friend, Julia responded that she was going to her husband, Andrej Varhola at 2425 Forbes Street in Pittsburgh. Ilona and her son planned to join her husband Stefan Kalinak at 2430 Forbes Street. Both women said they intended to remain in the United States and become citizens. Julia described her health as good. She was twenty-nine years old, five feet tall, with a fresh complexion, fair hair, and gray eyes.

Officially, the *Celtic* arrived in port on Sunday, June 20. But arriving late in the day, the ship was forced to take anchorage off the Statue of Liberty because there was no room at the White Star piers. First- and second-class passengers underwent quick inspections on board and were ferried to the pier. Third-class passengers spent an additional night on the ship.[20] Although they undoubtedly enjoyed being almost close enough to touch the Statue of Liberty and must have marveled at the New York skyline, they were surely impatient to set foot on American soil. The next day, packed onto barges, with tags pinned to their clothing to indicate their manifest numbers and destination, the immigrants finally disembarked and were shepherded through the immigration process at Ellis Island.

Numerous accounts of the inspection procedure at Ellis Island are available. All stress the shock, anxiety, and exhaustion of even the hardiest immigrants. A medical exam and the inspectors' verification of the passenger manifest took three to five hours. When the inspector was satisfied, the immigrants received a landing card and proceeded to collect their baggage and continue their journey. For immigrants traveling to western Pennsylvania, the Pennsylvania Railroad (PRR) was the preferred means of transportation. Since the 1890s, the PRR had chartered entire immigrant trains, or, depending on demand, coupled separate wagons to regularly scheduled trains.[21] Met by an agent of the PRR in New York, who identified the travelers by the tags affixed to their clothing, Julia and the Kalinyaks boarded a ferry to Jersey City. Handling the immigrant business in Jersey City meant that immigrants could be transported directly from Ellis Island to the PRR depot without entering New York City. The temperature in New York on that partly cloudy June day reached 88 degrees Fahrenheit with almost 50 percent humidity. One can imagine the discomfort Julia and Ilona felt in their ever-present cotton kerchiefs, as they lugged their heavy bundles. Memoirs of Carpatho-Rusyn immigrants describe the important items they carried with them: "Women began to follow men, with one difference. Woman-wise, each brought with her a huge peasant bag from which she was never parted—not until she reached her final destination. Each bag, made of sturdy homespun, was stuffed with basics: towels, bed sheets, an embroidered tablecloth, at least one, specially embroidered blouse and apron, and last but not least, a downy feather tick, the proud result of long winter nights of diligent plucking. It also represented the sum and total of her girlhood dreams."[22]

After a spell in an immigrant waiting room, they boarded the No. 3 train, the Pacific Express. In the United States, immigrant cars ranged from converted boxcars to outdated passenger wagons that had been downgraded from first class, but in general, they were not comfortable for long-distance or overnight travel. Described as the counterpart of ordinary PRR cars on the exterior, the interior was devoid of upholstery "for entomological reasons." Timetables indicate a roundabout route from Jersey City through Philadelphia to Harrisburg, where passengers transferred to a train that traveled through Altoona, Johnstown, and Greensburg, finally arriving in Pittsburgh fourteen hours later. If all went according to schedule, it very likely took a day or two after the *Celtic* arrived in New York before Julia and her companions reached "Pittsburgh, Pennsylvania," as Julia always referred to her new home. We can only hope that Andrii and Stephen were at Penn Station to meet their stoic, but exhausted, wives.

Julia Warhola arrived in the United States at the dawn of the Roaring Twenties. Shortly after her arrival, President Warren G. Harding signed a resolution declaring an end to America's war with her native state, Austria-Hungary. In her new homeland, women had won the right to vote in the 1920 presidential election. Prohibition was in effect, but in Pittsburgh, the law was broadly flouted. Bootlegging was rampant, speakeasies flourished, organized crime and political corruption boomed. In the crowded and dirty city, where rivers ran orange from industrial waste, immigrants herded together in tenements that backed to noisy steel mills and freight yards. The Ku Klux Klan staged public demonstrations and burned crosses to intimidate Catholic immigrants.[23] Americans and immigrants alike escaped to the moving pictures, where *The Kid*, a sentimental drama-comedy starring Charlie Chaplin as "The Little Tramp," was a box-office hit, and *The Sheik* propelled Rudolph Valentino to stardom. In Pittsburgh, radio station KDKA, billed as the "Pioneer Broadcasting Station of the World," began to offer popular programming, featuring live musical performances and religious broadcasts. A few months after Julia's June 1921 arrival, the first baseball game was broadcast on radio, as the Pittsburgh Pirates took on the Philadelphia Phillies at Forbes Field. Having left behind the fresh air of Miková, Julia faced the sooty haze of industrial Pittsburgh and traded the simplicity of folklife for the bustle of modernity. She stood on the threshold of a new life in the world of Rusyn American immigrants.

Soho

Abraham Oseroff began his 1914 master's thesis, "Survey of Workingmen's Homes in the Soho District of Pittsburgh: A Study of Civic Neglect in the Heart of a Great City," with this striking contrast:

> Within five minutes street-car ride of that imposing monument of Architect Henry Hobson Richardson's skill and artistry—the Allegheny County Courthouse; within ten minutes walk of the beautiful Schenley Farms District, in the other direction, where are grouped some of Pittsburgh's finest and richest homes; within view of the University of Pittsburgh and the Carnegie Institute of Technology; and as a next-door neighbor to the several rich and influential churches, lies an example of housing conditions which, in its absolute disregard of the most urgent and essential sanitary requisites for human habitation, is thoroughly revolting to every sense of civic decency.[24]

Within this district of dilapidated tenements, open sewers, and privy vaults, 126 families, counting 619 people, lived in 65 dwellings on Maurice, Lawn, and Cornet Streets, and in Rock Alley. The author goes on to make an unequivocal assessment: "The worst housing conditions of the district, however, are to be found on Forbes Street," and he pinpoints for special attention four blocks of Forbes Street from Cornet Street to the Brady Street Bridge, houses numbered 2300 to 2600. It was precisely here that Andrii Warhola lived from 1912 to 1921, along with relatives and friends from Miková and nearby villages.

Andrii's 1912 passenger manifest has him joining his brother-in-law at 2350 Forbes Street. A remittance receipt from 1914 indicates that he then lived at number 2415. Another receipt from 1919 gives his address as 2425 Forbes Street, which is the address Julia gave as her destination in 1921. For the immigrant Carpatho-Rusyn laborers, the boardinghouses, as crowded and uncomfortable as they were, replicated to a degree the extended kinship housing pattern of the Old Country. But while housing in Miková was primitive, the Forbes Street tenements presented a new kind of squalor.

Known today as Uptown or the Bluff, the Pittsburgh district where the Miková immigrants settled in the early twentieth century was called Soho, named by an early settler after the district in Birmingham, England, where he learned his trade. Pittsburgh's Soho was located on the bluff overhanging the Monongahela River and the Brady Street Bridge, replaced in 1976 by the Birmingham Bridge. Along the riverbank below, the Jones and Laughlin steelworks stretched three and a half miles in length. The National Tube Company plant and Hussey and Company's copper works filled the remaining flat area along the river. Above the industrial plants, hastily constructed ramshackle houses perched on the vertical hillside to provide residential housing for workers who could not afford carfare and needed to walk to work. Long staircases stretching up the steep grade provided pathways through the neighborhood and down to the mills. Ranged along a garbage-strewn hill, backing to the rails of the Baltimore and Ohio Railroad, blackened, wood-frame tenements lined the south side of Forbes Street. On a roadway paved with Ligonier blocks, trolley cars connected Soho with Pittsburgh's central business district. Oseroff described the street in 1914:

> Here we have a long row of houses and tenements, almost every one of which is in utter dilapidation. Those houses designated as the rear of Forbes Street are, if anything, even worse than those in the front. There is a total neglect of most of the essentials of sanitation. The houses are breeding places of filth and disease and some are veritable fire

traps. Underground rooms abound, totally dark rooms used for sleeping purposes are plentiful. One tenement, two stories in front and four stories in the rear, sixty-eight percent of whose rooms are underground, houses eleven families and boarders in dark, damp, poorly ventilated, overcrowded quarters, besides providing stable quarters for a huckster's horse.[25]

Andrii's first home at 2350 Forbes Street housed nineteen people. According to Oseroff's statistics, its water supply was a hydrant in the yard shared by eight families, and it had "but one privy vault with four compartments in very bad condition." Four tenements from 2350 to 2356 Forbes Street, front and rear, shared a single privy vault with four compartments "in very bad condition." Authors of the *Pittsburgh Survey* had criticized the pervasive primitive arrangement for the disposal of waste in privy vaults since 1907, and the Bureau of Health mounted a campaign against them. Yet in 1914, eight thousand to ten thousand were still in use in the city, particularly in Soho. According to Oseroff, "The privy-vault nuisance in this section is pernicious in the highest degree. Every house has its vault arranged usually in battery style and sending its sewage down the hillside. Back of Forbes Street in most cases the ground to the very houses and often even under the houses is thoroughly permeated with sewage foulness and dampness. Wherever one turns the odor of the foul, unsanitary, privy-vault pervades the atmosphere." For a tenement that had two stories in front and five stories in the rear, "one unsewered vault represented the sole closet accommodations for the nineteen families living in this group of houses (including boarders, a total of 151 persons)."[26] It goes without saying that any existing safety or sanitary regulations were not enforced.

In order to meet the rent, which was $6.00 to $8.50 per month for a two-bedroom apartment and $9.50 to $11.00 for three bedrooms, occupants sublet space to as many boarders as they could crowd into a room. In the same tenement described above, "One room was occupied by 10 boarders, two of whom were on a night shift and slept during the day, and there were two rooms each occupied by nine boarders, one room with eight occupants, two with seven each, three with six each, two with five each, one with four, one with three, and one 'star boarder' had a room entirely to himself, while the family of six slept in the kitchen."[27] Men like Andrii, transient immigrants marking time until they could return to their homeland or pay for a wife's passage to America, were willing to sacrifice all comfort in order to grow their savings. Crowded together with compatriots from the Old Country, single men depended on the lone housewife for cooking, cleaning, laundry, mending, and packing lunches. Keeping

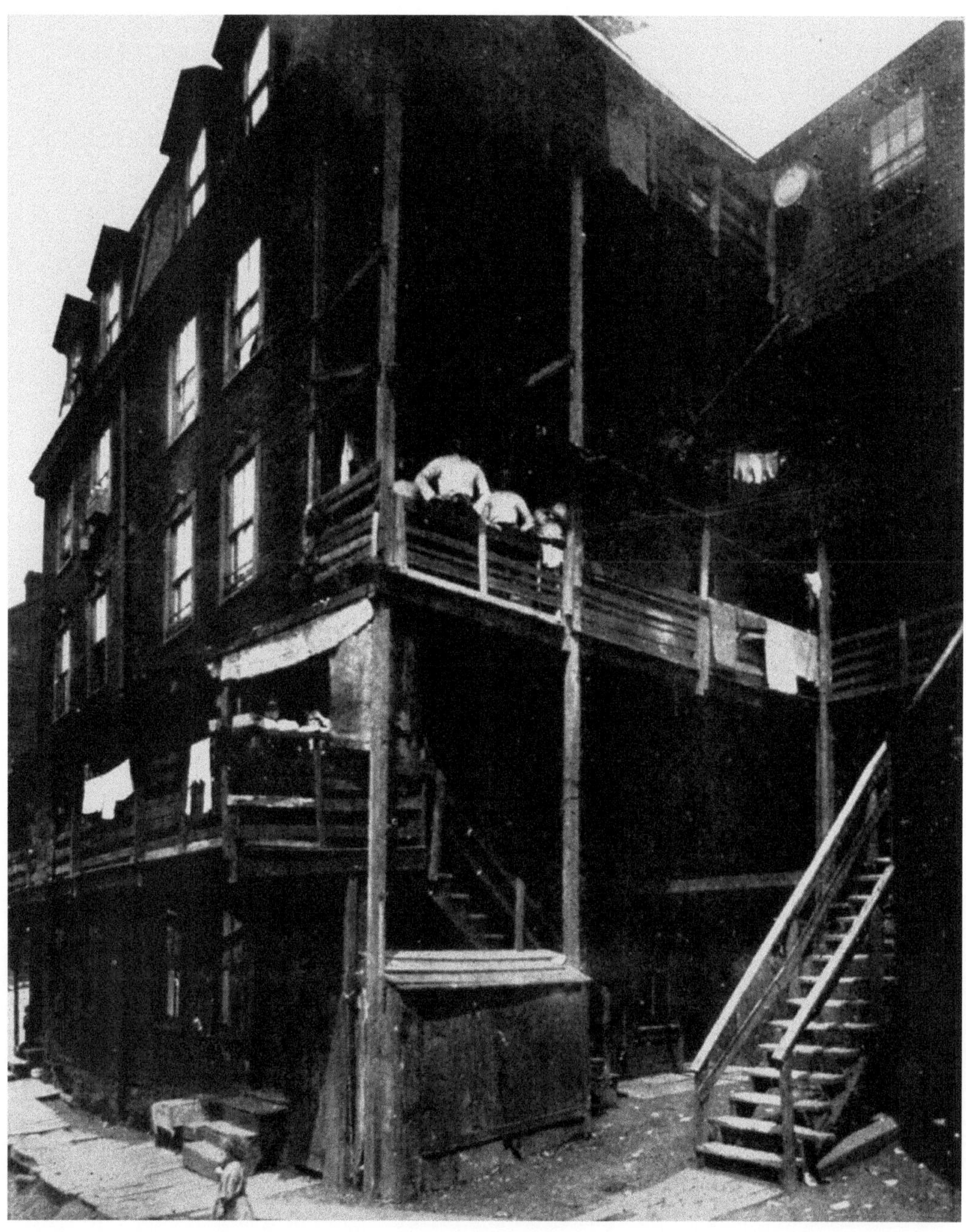

Figure 3.3. Wing of a tenement housing twenty families, two stories on Forbes Street and five stories in the rear.

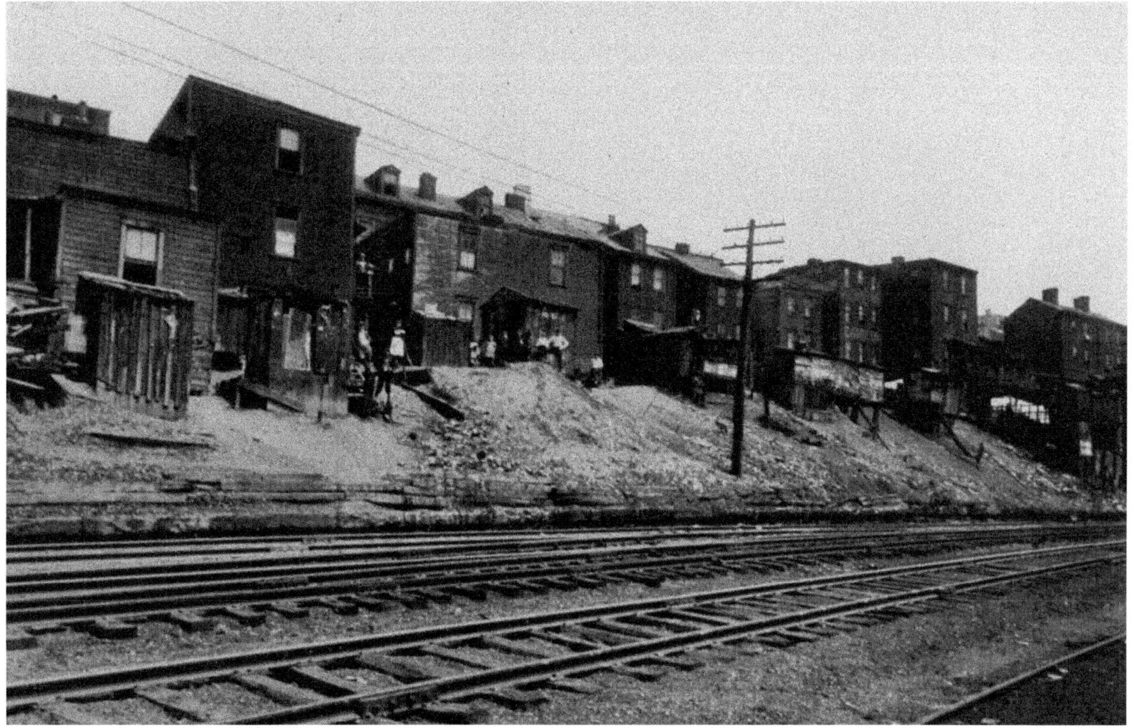

Figure 3.4. Unsewered privy vaults lining the rear of Forbes Street tenements.

lodgers allowed the occupant's family to make ends meet, but it was at the expense of the wife, whose housework was hardly less demanding than her husband's millwork.

The *1910 US Federal Census* shows ethnic clusters in the Soho district, with pockets of Irish, Jewish, Polish, Lithuanian, and Croatian immigrants on Forbes Street. Rusyn names begin at number 2300 and continue in the four blocks of decrepit tenements described by Oseroff. In house number 2354, Andrew Yanochko (Janocsko) lived with his wife, four children, and two boarders.[28] Janocsko was the brother-in-law whom Andrii named as his destination contact in 1912. In 2408, John Zapcara (alternate spellings: Subsara, Cepcera) from Miková shared an apartment with his wife, three children, and three boarders. In the same building lived one Croatian and four additional Rusyn families, with seventeen children and nine boarders among them. Andrii spent the nine years from his return to Pittsburgh in 1912 until Julia's arrival in 1921 as a lodger here with the family of one or another of his Miková relatives.

By 1920, construction of the Boulevard of the Allies caused the demolition of many of the Forbes Street tenements. The census shows fewer Rusyns (now called

"Slavish") amid a more diverse population, which included an influx of southern Black people. Although the address Julia gave as her destination in 1921 was 2425 Forbes Street, she probably did not live in the Forbes tenements. In anticipation of her arrival, Andrii must have endeavored to improve his living conditions, even though Pittsburgh was then experiencing the most serious housing crisis in the nation's history. A postwar shortage of affordable housing and rising construction costs caused rents to spiral upward. From 1917 to 1926, rent for the scarce workers' dwellings in Pittsburgh rose 75 percent, the sharpest increase occurring between 1917 and 1921.[29] During the war, prices on everything had risen, making it more difficult to economize. However, by scrimping and saving and tightening their belts, many Rusyns and other Slavs were able to move out of the worst districts, if not yet out of Soho.

A remittance receipt for funds sent by Andrii to Julia's sister in Miková on September 12, 1921, just three months after Julia's arrival, gives his address as 3 Orr Street. Six years later, his petition for naturalization shows the couple living at 73 Orr Street. On the G. M. Hopkins maps from 1923, Orr is a short street in a neighborhood that straddled the border between Soho and the Hill District.[30] Six rows of small, boxlike houses were squeezed between Orr and Soho streets. At the north end of Orr stood the Lithuanian Community Hall, a large brick building built in 1916. The neighborhood had a predominantly Lithuanian population, with no recognizable Rusyn names in the census.[31] To the south on Fifth Avenue was the large F. S. Delp warehouse of furniture, appliances, and building materials.

The two-story frame houses on Orr Street, each of which accommodated two or three families, were typical of the housing available to unskilled immigrant workers. In *Out of This Furnace*, a 1941 documentary-style novel about Rusyn and Slovak millworkers in the industrial towns around Pittsburgh, Thomas Bell writes, "Real-estate speculators put up the houses that became so characteristic of the steel towns, long, ugly rows like cell blocks, two rooms high and two deep, without water, gas or conveniences of any kind."[32] Closely built back to back, with no concern for light or ventilation, they were still an improvement over the worst Forbes tenements. While city maps show they had an indoor water supply, outdoor privies stood in the muddy alleys between the blocks of boxes.

"They Always Cry"

What was the reunion of Julia and Andrii like? After nine years of separation—years of hard work for Andrii, struggle, loss, and war for Julia, anxiety and loneliness for both—it was surely emotional. Married just three years before their prolonged separation, euphoria was undoubtedly accompanied by trepidation. For almost a decade, their personal lives had been vastly different, and each must have felt remote from the experience of the other. Their communication had been limited to written correspondence that was subject to censorship and interruption. Maintaining an emotional connection under those circumstances would be difficult even for experienced letter writers, let alone correspondents with elementary writing skills. The prospect that the separation might be permanent would have generated grief and despair.

Unfortunately, there are no witnesses or diaries to give firsthand testimony about the Warholas' reunion, but accounts of other such reconnections are telling. When the wife of Kracha, the protagonist of *Out of This Furnace*, arrives from the Old Country to join her husband, she immediately begins to weep. "What are you crying about? It's all over," he tells her. An observer comments, "They always cry. No matter what happens, they cry."[33]

After what must have been tears of joy, mixed with anxiety and exhaustion, Julia enjoyed a reunion not only with her husband, but with the three brothers and two sisters she had not seen for ten to twenty years. So much news from the homeland to share, new spouses and children to meet, stories of the war in Miková and life in Lyndora and Pittsburgh—one can imagine Julia's exhilaration. If, as research suggests, a strong social support system aids the resiliency of separated spouses, Julia was well equipped to weather the adjustments she would face. Her history and personality recall Dorta from Bell's book: "There was an air of competence and dependability about her; of her easy self-assurance there could be no doubt. Unlike most of the wives and sweethearts who came from the old country she neither simpered nor became a dumb image in the presence of strangers. Half an hour after her arrival she was perfectly at home."[34]

One might hope that the process of adjustment was as easy for Julia, but common sense would suggest otherwise. Having left behind the primitive but pristine environment of Miková, Julia encountered a congested atmosphere suffused with sulfuric smoke, where steel mills lit up the night sky with balls of flame, emitting mechanical booming noises around the clock. A Polish immigrant woman recalled her initial reaction to a working-class neighborhood in Pittsburgh: "The streets, dirty, unpaved, made a very unpleasant impression . . . bad smells beyond endurance."[35] Julia's new house on Orr Street—a four-room smoke-blackened lodging shared with at least one other family, with an outside privy in a dirty alley—was this what Julia was expecting in the New World? In *Out of This Furnace*, Kracha sheepishly tells his newly arrived wife, "It is the best I could do."[36] Andrii, who had recently left the even more appalling Forbes Street tenements, might have said the same.

It is worth recalling, however, that Carpatho-Rusyn immigrants never expected American streets to be paved with gold. Their preparation for America, as well as the information they gleaned from those who had gone before, stressed hard work and passive endurance. From a middle-class American perspective, social workers and authors of the *Pittsburgh Survey* were appalled at the immigrants' squalid living conditions, explaining them as a result of the evils of American industrial society and the immigrants' own uncivilized backwardness. But immigrants saw their situation quite differently. A Slavic woman who immigrated when she was ten years old remembered her mother's reaction to her new life in an industrial town near Pittsburgh.

> My mother didn't have to go to work when she came here. She cleaned the house, but that was no problem for her, because she was a hard-working woman. There was dirt, because we lived right by the mill. There was our house, and there was an alley, and there was the mill. It didn't seem bad to us. My mother said that she went through so much in Europe that life here was a little bit easier for her, and she felt good because she knew what she left behind. She enjoyed life here. She enjoyed every bit of it.[37]

To abusive bosses, workers may have appeared "docile and willing," happy with just "rye bread, a herring, and beer," but they had a very different perception of themselves. "The immigrants' apparently passive acceptance of exploitative work and abusive treatment masked a determined ambition to better themselves." Their purpose was not to join middle-class America, but to attain status and prosperity as they knew it in the homeland. "The (comparative) abundance of food and an opportunity to dress in what the immigrants perceived as an upper-class style . . . were seen as the rewards of coming to America."[38] A Rusyn American folk song depicts the positive side of American life.

> It's good in America
> When there's work.
> When Saturday comes,
> You get dressed up.
> You get dressed up,
> And wash up well,
> If it's going bad in the field

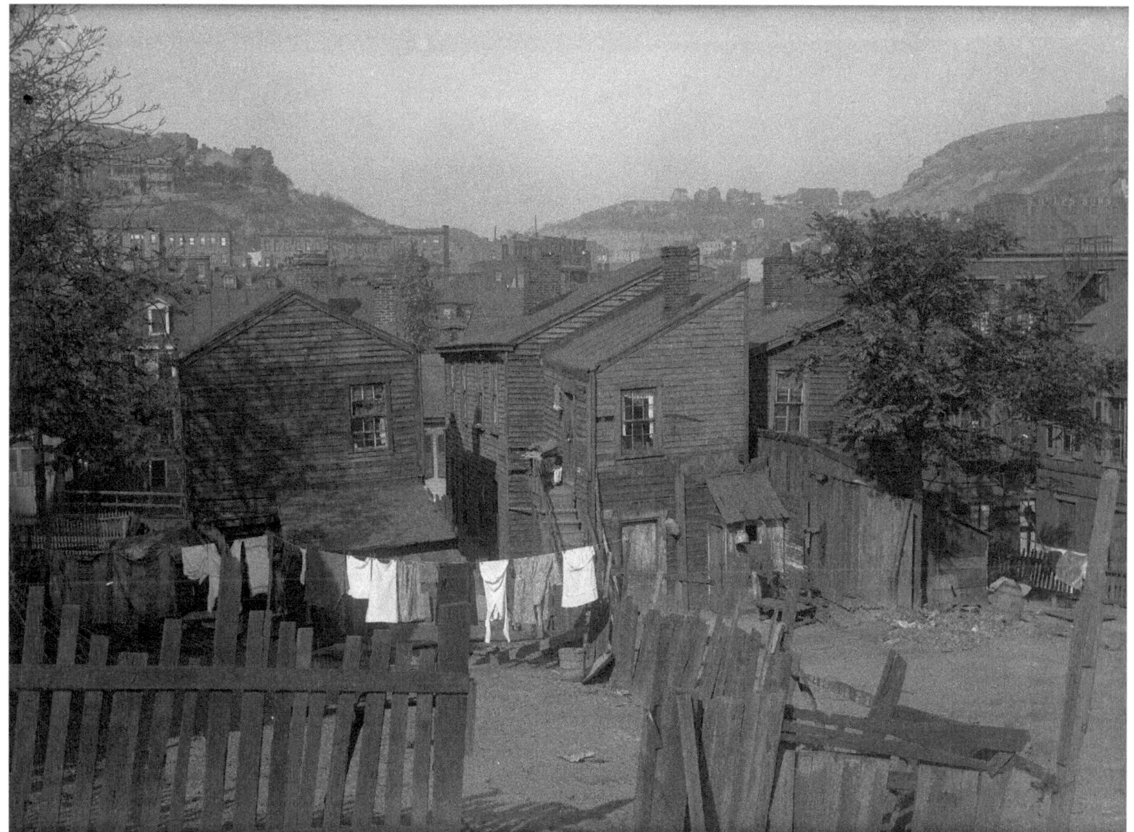

Figure 3.5. Homes on Tustin Street in the Warholas' Soho neighborhood, 1921.

You don't worry,
No rotting in the field,
No carrying water,
Farmers bring everything
Right to your house.[39]

As unpleasant as they may have been, smokestacks belching gritty clouds meant work and prosperity; clear air indicated that workers were on strike, or a plant had closed. Squalid housing was often an improvement over what had been left behind, and it was a situation that was expected to be temporary. Immigrants did not resent the millionaires in Pittsburgh's East End. The business historian Quentin Skrabec points out, "The eight-hour day was actually opposed by most Pittsburgh unions because they wanted to earn as much as they could. Pittsburgh workers wanted mobility more than protection. For many, the East End was not an example of unfair accumulation of wealth but a goal of what could be obtained through hard work."[40] Julia's motivation for immigration was the desire to help her family in Europe financially, and eventually, to bring her sisters to join her. Given what we know of her determination and resourcefulness, it is likely she embraced the hardships she encountered, looked forward to the possibilities ahead, and resolved to make the best of her new life.

Records show that the Warhola family lived on Orr Street until 1929, and all three sons were born there. Today the neighborhood's block configuration is still evident, although most of the houses have been demolished. According to Paul Warhola, the family moved to Kirkpatrick Street, just a block away, where they lived for three months in a similar two-story frame house. The 1930 census, recorded April 9, finds them living at 55 Beelen Street. Beelen Street stretched west from Soho Street along the side of a steep hill. Today, only foundations of the houses remain. On November 24, 1925, a classified ad in the "For Rent" section of the *Pittsburgh Press* announced a four-room house for rent at "55 Beelen Street near Fifth Avenue and Brady Street, with gas, water, and modern conveniences." As Paul Warhola remembered it, the Warholas' Beelen Street house was heated by a potbellied stove. There was no bathroom, but it boasted the convenience of an indoor toilet.[41] The Warholas lived here from 1929 to 1932, paying, in 1930, $19 rent per month. In the 1925 ad, the monthly rent was listed as $25, but the Great Depression undoubtedly affected rents, as well as, perhaps, the availability of "modern conveniences."

From Beelen Street, seventy-seven stairsteps led down the incline to Fifth Avenue, and an even longer cement staircase scaled upward to Mohawk Street. The house where the Warholas rented space, valued at $7,000, according to the census, was owned by Alexander Stanek, a Polish immigrant who lived on the premises with his wife and five children. John Zabolotny, a Russian, his wife, an immigrant from Czechoslovakia, and their two children were the third family in the house.[42] Many of the Warholas' immediate neighbors were native-born American mill and railroad workers, with a smattering of Poles, a few Jews, and several Rusyns, who, like the Warholas, were mislabeled here "Czechoslovakian." Two large families of African Americans from Alabama lived down the street, and a few blocks away, at 12 Beelen Street, lived Julia's older sister Mary Zavacka Preksta with her five children, ranging in age from five to sixteen.

Andrii's unstable employment during the Depression may have been the reason for the Warholas' frequent moves around Soho during these years. The move to

Beelen Street and another move in 1932 to Moultrie Street, just across Orr from their first home, probably reflected a drop in income. The Moultrie Street house was a two-story brick dwelling, a step down from the house on Beelen Street. Paul remembered, "We lived on the first floor. People rented the second floor. The bathtub was just a steel tub. We heated water on the stove. The two rooms were the kitchen and the bedroom. Three of us slept on one bed."[43]

Life in Soho

Life in Soho was grubby and turbulent. Julia and Andrii probably took up residence at 3 Orr Street in late June 1921. On June 24, the *Pittsburgh Press* described unsanitary conditions in Soho due to laxity in the removal of garbage. "A resident of the district said garbage collectors had called about two months ago, for the first time in nearly a year." In November, the *Pittsburgh Post-Gazette* reported a murder-suicide at 61 Orr Street, and the *Daily Post* described an attack on a female resident that resulted in a charge of attempted murder. Through the 1920s and into the 1930s, there were stories of shootings and holdups on Beelen and Moultrie Streets, frequent fatal automobile crashes at the intersection of Moultrie and Fifth Avenue, and numerous raids on distilleries in the area and a speakeasy at the Lithuanian Hall.[44]

Social workers of the settlement movement made efforts "to improve the tenements and hygienic conditions in the district, to awaken the highest ideals of culture and character, and to furnish a neighborhood house where Jew, Protestant and Catholic meet on friendly ground as neighbors."[45] The Soho Baths Settlement House was established on Fifth Avenue in 1907. Public baths were a necessity for laborers who came home from work to tenements with no plumbing, and the Soho facility was known as one of the best-equipped institutions of its kind in the country. The large swimming pool provided recreational and instructional swimming and summer programs for children. The community center offered medical and dental services, classes in sewing, cooking, and housekeeping, as well as art and music lessons, reading rooms, and story hours for children. Social events, holiday celebrations, and patriotic parades were sponsored in the spirit of middle-class Americana. However, such agencies reached relatively few Slavic immigrants with poor English, who were wary of outsiders and tended to socialize exclusively with family and coethnics. American Slavs of the second generation were more likely to participate in "American" activities. One young second-generation Carpatho-Rusyn woman, who lived in a cluster of Rusyn families on Lawn Street, worked as a secretary in the settlement office in the 1930s and recalled that she volunteered to work on Sundays after church "for the good meals they served there."[46] In 1930, seven hundred local children patronized the Soho community house, which was then lobbying for the removal of commercial billboards in order to build a playground. The only existing play area in the neighborhood on Moultrie Street was described as "one big mudpie playground," with a pool that had not been filled all season, sandless sandboxes, and a field half covered with tin cans and broken bottles. This was the Warholas' neighborhood play space until 1934, when Paul was twelve and Andy was six years old.

On June 26, 1922, a year after Julia's arrival in America, she gave birth to her son Paul. John was born three years later on May 31, 1925. Her youngest, Andy, was born August 6, 1928, when Julia was four months shy of her thirty-seventh birthday. They were all born in the murky gloom of Soho. Given Andy's birth in the dark, dismal, dingy surroundings, some biographers have readily accepted the notion that his first words were "Look at the sunlight! Look at the sun! Look at the light!"[47] But this account, allegedly coming from Julia Warhola, is actually from David Bailey's "documentary" film, in which an actress portrayed Mrs. Warhola and made comments that were totally inconsistent with the real Julia Warhola.[48]

At home, the Warhola family spoke Rusyn. In Pittsburgh, most immigrant children picked up some English in the neighborhood, but entered school with only a rudimentary knowledge of the language. According to Paul's recollections, his "inability to speak English and his hunkie [*sic*] name made him an object of derision and abuse."[49] Paul's memory may be sensitive. The Soho School, which included kindergarten to eighth grade, had a very diverse student population. A 1917 report showed that 12.8 percent were American students, 30.7 percent were "African," and 44 percent represented various eastern European ethnicities, including 9 percent known as "Slavish." Even a decade later, Paul could hardly have been singled out for ethnic abuse. According to the principal, the fundamental subject of the school was English, since "many of our children hear no English in their homes and they come to school with a meager vocabulary of words and ideas." Ninety-three percent of the parents were industrial workers with large families living in "small unsanitary quarters in many cases." But, the principal adds, "It is surprising how neat and clean most of the children come to school."[50]

Paul Warhola recounted a story of Andy's first day at the Soho School. Paul, who was just ten years old himself in 1932, decided that Andy, age four, should start school. According to Paul, "At first he didn't want to go to school but I forced him. He was all right the first day when I took him along and registered him." But Andy's first day at Soho was his last, at least for that year. "The first day he was in school some little Black girl slapped him and he come home crying and says he's not going back no more. . . . So mother says, 'Don't push him. He's just too young yet.' So we didn't force him."[51] As Paul Warhola, not always a reliable witness, repeated this story to several biographers, the reference to the little girl's race came and went, perhaps in a nod to societal norms.

It is uncertain whether this incident took place as Paul related it, or whether it was conflated with another later occurrence, but there is evidence that something of the sort did indeed take place, and perhaps more than once. The source is Julia Warhola herself. In 1970, Andy Warhol began experimenting with a Sony Portapak reel-to-reel video system. With his assistants, he documented the goings-on in his studio on tapes that became known as *Factory Diaries*, uninterrupted and unedited footage of people talking or performing everyday activities. But before he focused his camera on friends and visitors, Warhol performed test runs, with his elderly mother as subject. In these "home movies," the camera focuses on Julia, who speaks with Andy and others almost entirely in Rusyn. Until now they have been incomprehensible and inaccessible to scholars. The video film labeled by the Warhol Museum, "Julia Warhola in T-Shirt Sick," fills in details of Warhol's childhood biography and the Warholas' life in the rough Soho neighborhood.

The camera focuses on Julia, as she greets a caregiver who has come to make chicken soup. Julia asks about her grandchildren, and Mrs. T (as I will call her), responds that she will not bring her granddaughter to visit Julia because the child dislikes the African Americans in the neighborhood. Just then Andy returns from the store with carrots for the soup, and Mrs. T tells him in English, using a racial slur, "My little granddaughter, she don't like n- - - - -s." Andy responds with faux innocence, "Oh really?" But Julia reacts emotionally, with her arms outstretched, "Oh, Mrs. T," then energetically in Rusyn: "Listen. I'll tell you a story. When Andriiko was little, there were Black people walking around the yard. He yelled 'n- - - - -.' They caught my son Paul [in reprisal] for his brother. They punched him in the ribs. For a month he was home sick." Julia goes on to lecture Mrs. T in Rusyn. "You tell your kids not to use that word, or they will beat them up. They are very offended. Teach the kids, so they will know. You should just use the words 'colored man.'"

But Julia's confidence dissolves when Mrs. T asks why she had not done anything to protect Paul. "What can you do?" she asks. "They might kill you at night." This sad, unmediated and uncensored outburst from Julia reveals what went on beneath the surface in her first years in Pittsburgh. Living in the diverse and often dangerous neighborhood of Soho was strange and frightening. The incident can be dated to the years between 1932 and 1934, when the family lived on Moultrie

Street, when Andy was five or six years old and Paul was eleven or twelve. Moultrie Street was located on the edge of the Hill District, the center of a thriving Black sub-culture in the 1930s, but also a site of overcrowded poverty that engendered crime, corruption, and gangs of juvenile delinquents. The overflowing disorder prompted a reactive racism in new immigrants, that was picked up by their children. Julia tells Andy, "You heard what we said, so you shouted that word."[52]

Black people were the only group below "Hunkies" on Pittsburgh's working-class social ladder. Like many immigrant groups from eastern and southeastern Europe, newly arrived Slavs were seen as "not-quite-white" by native-born Americans. "Hunkies" became "white" by conforming to current American racial attitudes and treating their dark-skinned neighbors to the same discrimination they had endured themselves. Near the end of the story of Rusyn immigrants in Thomas Bell's *Out of This Furnace*, the protagonists look back on the changes in the mill town and regret the loss of the "good times." "It's too bad the n- - - - -s had to come," says an old-timer, who denounces their fighting, drunkenness, squalor, and dirt. Dobie, the positive protagonist, responds: "I know. But I was just thinking that once it was the Irish looking down on the Hunkies and now it's the Hunkies looking down on the n- - - - -s. The very things the Irish used to say about the Hunkies the Hunkies now say about the n- - - - -s. And for no better reason."[53] In blunt language, articles on lynching and race riots in Slovak and Rusyn newspapers presented a portrait of Black otherness. "While somewhat sympathetic, these arti-cles nevertheless enabled immigrants to distance themselves from the 'blackness' of victims and became part of the strategy of asserting newcomers' tentative claims to 'whiteness.'"[54]

Julia and Andy might be partly excused for their use of offensive language by the fact that the neutral term in Rusyn is very similar to the English slur. But as a child steeped in immigrant culture, and smart enough to pick up both its abasement and its prejudices, Andy may have been testing his American tough "whiteness." Warhol was known to donate to liberal causes and to support civil rights.[55] But in the 1970 video, he made no response to his mother's narrative. It is not certain whether Paul's story about Andy's confrontation with an African American classmate and Julia's story, about his provocation of Black neighbors refer to the same incident. But Andy, the victim of the story told by Paul to biographers, is the culprit in Julia's private narrative. Whatever the facts of this particular incident, it suggests that in the early 1930s, Andrii Warhola would have felt the need to move his family from Soho to a stable neighborhood with good schools. For this to happen, he needed to make money.

Eichleay

Instead of sending agents to Europe to recruit immigrants, many companies relied on foremen to hire laborers, usually coethnics, who would, in turn, vouch for newly arrived friends and relatives. Or in the general term used by Rusyns to apply to such relations—they brought along a *kum*, which might be loosely translated as "cousin" or "buddy." The abundance of entry-level jobs in all areas of Pittsburgh industry encouraged these informal kinship networks, which, in turn, furthered chain migration and resulted in clusters of particular ethnicities in certain locales and occupations. "Once an occupational beachhead was established, it tended to be maintained by a flow of brothers, cousins, and childhood friends. At the Jones and Laughlin steel mill, for example, Poles dominated the hammer shop; Germans, the carpentry shop; and Serbs the blooming mill."[56]

For Carpatho-Rusyn immigrants, more important than what a job paid was its stability. As the Chicago social worker Mary McDowell learned from her work with immigrants, "It is the word first learned by the immigrant, the children lisp it, and the aged cling to it to the end. A 'steady job' or 'please get me a job' is ever at the front of their minds and on the tips of their tongues."[57] Writing in Rusyn, an immigrant author says, "We all know how much a 'стеди джяб' (*stedy dzhiab*) means. One 'stedy' is better, even if the pay is lower, than five not 'stedy' but well-paid jobs."[58] The immediate goal of Rusyn immigrants was to ensure their own survival and to earn money as quickly as possible to return to the Old Country. As time passed, circumstances changed, and the desire to return home faded, they became fixated on economic security. Blocked from promotions and career advancement, and not open to risk-taking, their aims were modest—a steady job that would allow them to accumulate savings and enjoy some of the consumer goods of the American working-class lifestyle.

When Andrii returned to Pittsburgh in 1912, he probably knew he did not want to go back to the mines, and his previous experience in Pennsylvania had likely taught him the perils of work at the open-hearth furnaces in the Jones and Laughlin mill.[59] Instead, he responded to recruitment offers from friends and relatives and it is likely he returned to Pittsburgh with a position in hand as a house mover. Andrii's traveling companions to America in 1912 included a Warhola cousin Maria (Mary) Dudich from Miková, who, according to her immigration records, was joining her husband Peter in the Forbes Street tenements. Peter Dudich was one of the relatively rare Carpatho-Rusyn immigrants, like John Zavacky in Lyndora, who had an entrepreneurial spirit and opened a business on the side, even as he maintained a laboring job. In the 1920 census, he was identified as proprietor of a grocery store and meat market at his residence on Fifth Avenue in the Soho district. The same year, the store was destroyed in a two-alarm fire. Another of Dudich's business ventures also had negative consequences. A newspaper article from 1925 reports the raid of a saloon, which Mr. and Mrs. Peter Dudich had taken charge of just the previous day, a chancy undertaking in the era of Prohibition. The newspaper quotes Dudich, "I'm through with saloons hereafter."[60]

By the 1930 census, Dudich had traded the risks of business ownership for full-time manual labor, winning a managerial position in the house-moving industry. He was the main link in a chain of Zemplyn County Rusyns who became Pittsburgh house movers. By 1920, Dudich already owned his own home and housed four lodgers, two of whom were from Miková and also worked as house movers, doubling as butchers in Dudich's store. One of these was a Warhola cousin and the other was Stephen Kalinyak, the husband of Julia's travel companion. It was through these kinds of interconnections that Rusyn immigrants carved out a niche for themselves and their compatriots in particular industries, creating a web of mutual aid and support in the American industrial workplace.

Along with Dudich and other Rusyns, Andrii Warhola became a house mover and construction worker at the John Eichleay Jr. Company. In 1912, when Andrii was preparing to leave Miková once again for America, the Eichleay Company began a major construction project in Pittsburgh—grading the Grant Street hill, popularly known as the "Hump." With a grade of 20 percent, the "Hump" was difficult for horse-drawn wagons and pedestrians, and two efforts had been made in the early nineteenth century to lower it. In 1912, an additional seventeen feet were cut from the hill, transforming the previously below-ground basements of the Frick Building and the County Courthouse into entrance-level lobbies. The project was executed by the John Eichleay Company and completed in 1914.[61] Peter Dudich would have reached out to friends and cousins in Miková to take advantage of the new job opportunities the project offered.

In the 1920s, the Eichleay Company, located on Pittsburgh's South Side, was famous for its seemingly impossible feats of structural moving. In 1875, John Eichleay, a city building inspector, recognized that the growth of industry and technology in Pittsburgh would require massive changes in the urban landscape. Believing that houses and commercial structures could be moved for a fraction of the cost of razing and rebuilding them, he founded a family business that became a leader in rigging, shoring, underpinning, and moving structures and heavy objects. From 1915 to 1925, the company was moving two hundred to three hundred structures every year. In its heyday, Eichleay relocated or shored up over ten thousand houses, bridges, buildings, statues, naval guns, grounded ships, and in 1926, a dead pachyderm.[62] But what attracted attention nationwide and was celebrated in a Ripley's *Believe It or Not* newspaper panel was the fact that huge department stores were moved without disturbing shoppers, displacing merchandise, or disrupting business; bridges were relocated while pedestrians walked across the span; and houses were repositioned with furniture and household items intact.

The complicated moving process entailed elaborate planning, sophisticated engineering expertise, and brute strength. In his memoir, John W. Eichleay, who took over the family business in 1933, describes fifteen sequential steps necessary for a successful move, but to understand the work done by Andrii Warhola and his coworkers, a quick sketch is sufficient. After bracing the structure, a frame of heavy timbers or steel beams was constructed under the load-bearing elements, and a lattice work or "cribbing" of wooden blocks was placed underneath it. The weight of the structure was then transferred to acme threaded screw jacks, operated by the workmen, who would lift and move the building laterally. Eichleay explains: "Hydraulic jacks were generally unavailable before the second quarter of the 20th century. Most Eichleay raisings and lowerings relied on the simple mechanics of turning an acme threaded screw. Raising a structure with such screw jacks required a crew of brawny men. All had to simultaneously pull a lever bar inserted into the head of each jack. To keep the load level, each pull had to advance the screw one quarter turn. The physical strain inherent in making repeated 90-degree horizontal pulls gave rise to the joke that one could identify a house mover by his long uneven arms."[63] At the foreman's whistle, the workers pulled the lever bars in unison to raise or lower the structure, repeating the process as often as necessary to reach the required level. Steel rollers were positioned under the structure. Using lateral force, the team of workers pulled or pushed the structure on its rollers. As the mass moved off one roller, workers place a roller ahead to allow for continual movement.

Eichleay's "crew of brawny men" consisted largely of immigrant workers who had no choice but to accept labor-intensive jobs that were dangerous to life and limb. He comments on the strength and skill required: "A house mover had to have exceptional balance as well as upper body strength. Often the structure had to be raised several feet. Eventually the house mover would be standing on a parapet or nothing more than a high lattice of cribbing as he pulled the quarter turn. Early in the 20th century safety was less of a concern. Unlike today, there were no man nets nor safety line tie-off requirements." Indeed, photographs reveal that there were no requirements even for protective clothing or hard hats. Workers dressed in street clothes, and fedoras seemed to be the preferred headgear.

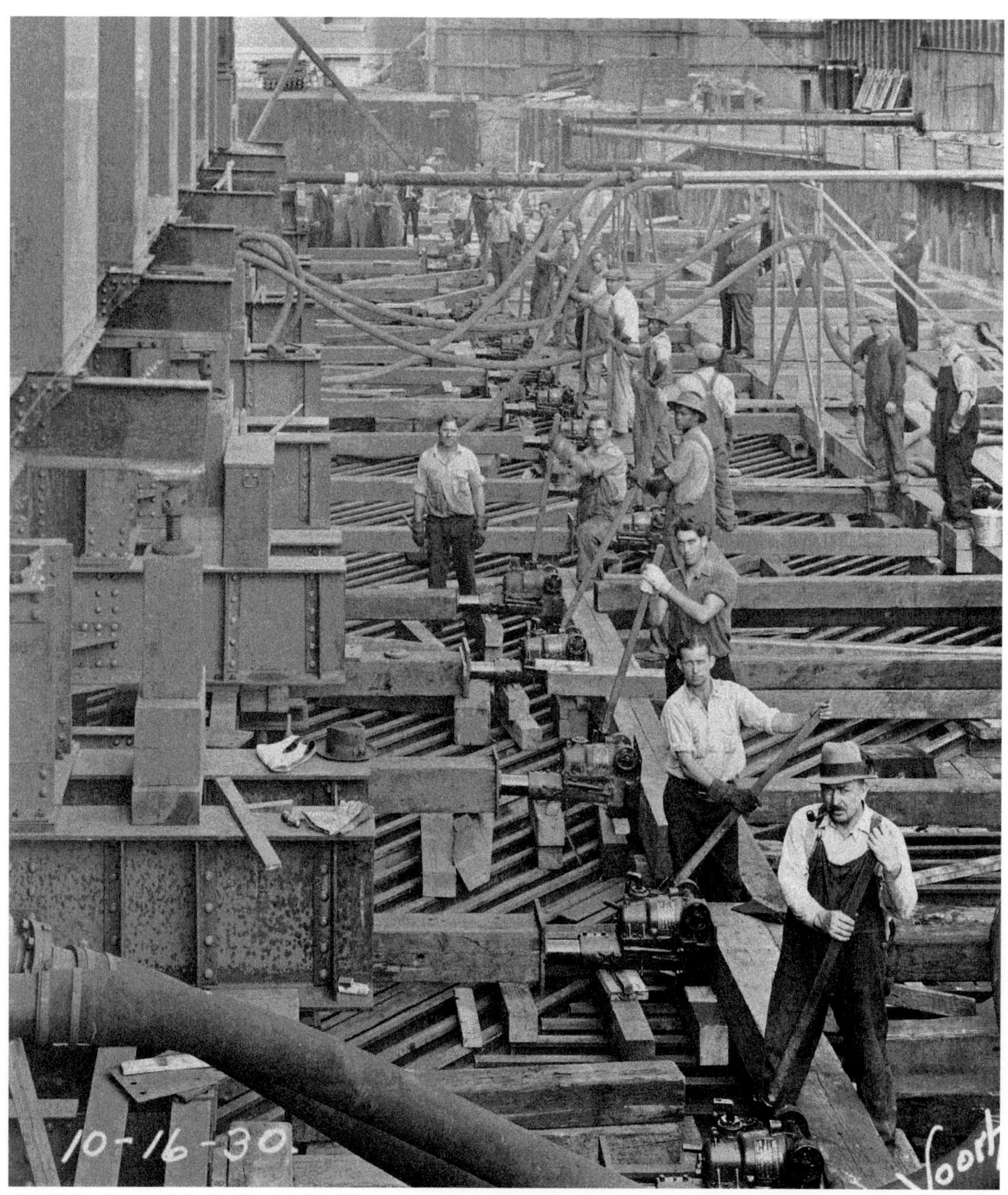

Figure 3.6. Eichleay workers move the Indiana Bell Telephone Company Building, 1930.

House moving was generally considered a more desirable and less dangerous job than millwork or mining, but it was no less demanding of physical strength. Few photographs of Andrii Warhola have been preserved, but according to the information on his passenger list, Andrii was five feet, eight inches tall when he came to Pittsburgh at age twenty-six. At age thirty-seven, his petition for naturalization described him as five feet eight, 175 pounds, with a scar on his right cheek. His son John later insisted that his father was a hefty man. "I'd say he was about 5'10" but when he couldn't speak the language when he came here, on one paper they put down his weight at 165 and I know he was closer to 200 pounds but he was built, he was real solid, and they had 5'6" and he was no 5'6". That's short. Because his brother was like 6'1" or 6'2"."[64] Andrii's scar, "from the ear down to his mouth," matched one on his brother's face, both acquired in a razor fight at a raucous wedding. "When you're a kid and you see a scar like that, it's real intimidating. Neighborhood kids thought they were real tough guys. They couldn't get over how they both had a scar in the same place." John recalled how his father frightened some "tough Irish kids" who were bullying him. "My dad wouldn't do anything to harm them, but if he had grabbed one of them, he could have broken them in half. When my dad died, a buddy of mine said, like in the summer [when] he used to wear a T-shirt—just to see the arms on him! I thought he'd live to be 100 years old."

According to John, his father would have preferred a construction job at the mill, "because it was cold working outside," and millwork was steady, "but he couldn't get in." He implies that Andrii's brother Joe, who worked at Jones and Laughlin, owed the job to his status as a veteran, which Andrii lacked. Not only was work at Eichleay intermittent, but it demanded travel and stints away from home. John recalled how his father would walk from Oakland over to the South Side. "If they didn't have work, he would come home . . . I remember when he had a job close by, he used to come home, and he would have like a cut on his head or something. He's lucky he didn't get killed."

Many Eichleay projects were in Pennsylvania and other mid-Atlantic states, but in the 1920s, jobs ranged from Wisconsin to Arkansas to West Virginia and Florida. Biographers have stated that Andrii worked on the Hoover Dam, but that is unlikely. Recovering from bankruptcy in the early 1930s, Eichleay procured a contract to move massive penstock pipe sections through tunnels within the dam from 1934 to 1936, and three Eichleay employees were killed in the operation. The Hoover Dam project was featured in company brochures for more than thirty years, but there is no evidence that the Miková workers were part of it. John Warhola reported that the longest period his father was away from home was six months when he worked in Connecticut, probably in 1941. Besides this Connecticut project—moving two large airport hangars in an expansion of the Pratt & Whitney facilities in East Hartford, and the move of the Allegheny County morgue in 1929—the only job we can be sure Andrii worked was one of Eichleay's biggest and heaviest moves—the Indiana Bell Telephone Company building in Indianapolis.

Indiana Telephone News, a publication of the Indiana Bell Telephone Company, ran an article about the project in the October 1930 issue, with photographs of the planning and moving process. John W. Eichleay described the move:

> The Indiana Bell Telephone building was a 9-story, steel and brick structure weighing 11,000 tons. It was the workplace of 600 switch board operators. Rather than demolish the 25-year-old structure or replicate its switching gear, its owner economically contracted for its movement. Every steel column was fitted with an elaborate rail shoe and jacked up. The structure then moved over 4,000 steel rollers 52 feet in a straight line to the far corner of the block and back 241 feet through a 90-degree arc to face a perpendicular street. Except for its basements, the structure was fully occupied and all business conducted as usual. Telephone service pulsed through cables whose slack allowed them, and all other utility connections, to follow the moving building.[65]

A crew of eighteen men operated one-hundred-ton ratchet screw jacks. "At the blast of a whistle the workmen manning the jacks took six strokes and then rested. Each six strokes of the jacks moved the building three-eighths of an inch—an almost imperceptible movement."[66] The average speed of the rolling building was about fifteen inches per hour, approximately eight feet each day, which means the workers pulled the heavy levers in unison about thirty-five times every hour, or 240 times a day, from Tuesday, October 14 at 10:30 a.m. to Wednesday, November 12 at 3:05 p.m. The author of the article in *Indiana Telephone News* casually concluded, "Believe it or not, eighteen men, working with ease the handles of the jacks, moved with ease the eight-story structure weighing more than 11,000 tons."

One of those eighteen men was Andrii Warhola. A photograph included in the article is one of the few pictures we have of him. Forty-four years old at the time, dressed in bib overalls, he appears older and shorter than his coworkers, although he has a stocky build. Judging from their surnames and based on family and church records, in addition to Warhola, nine members of the twelve-man crew were Carpatho-Rusyns, and another photo in the article includes a few others. They had roots in Rusyn villages, and most now lived in Soho. Fathers and sons, brothers and cousins worked together, and others were related through marriage. The

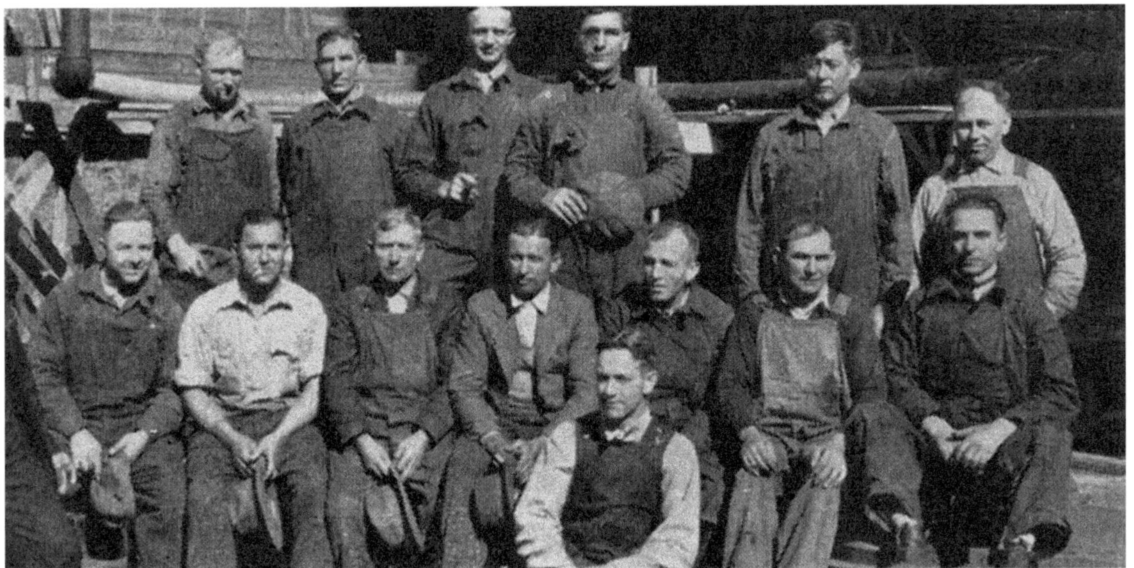

Figure 3.7. Eichleay work crew, 1930. Andrii Warhola is in the rear on the right.

interconnectedness provided a measure of security, and the language of the crew must have been Rusyn. But it is unlikely the workers would agree with the editor of *Indiana Telephone News* that "there is romance, imagination and adventure in the moving of a 22,000,000 pound mass of iron and brick." Sketchy company records show that labor costs were figured at the rate of $10 per man per day, plus $3 a day for room and board, and $40 for railroad transportation to the job site.[67] Grandchildren remember hearing that Andrii had moved a racetrack in Florida. Eichleay records indicate that racetrack stands in Coral Gables, Florida, were moved for the opening of Tropical Park Race Track in December 1931. By then the Eichleay company was in dire straits, and workers were sometimes not paid at all.

Dawson Street

When the Great Depression hit Pittsburgh in 1929, the Eichleay company experienced an acute drop in business. In a letter from June 1934, President John P. Eichleay wrote that he could not meet the current week's payroll and still owed wages from the previous week. "I am trying to figure some way, whereby I can give each of the men possibly $5.00 or $10.00 tomorrow." He was "so stretched financially that between 1931 and 1934 he failed to pay taxes on his home." In 1936 the company was forced into bankruptcy.[68] Reorganizing as the Eichleay Engineering Corporation of Delaware, the company subcontracted with the Babcock and Wilcox Corporation to install piping at Hoover Dam, a job that buoyed the company. In the second half of the 1930s, Eichleay's jobs included moving the iron Calvert Streetcar bridge and the General Thomas equestrian statue in Washington, DC, the Allegheny County airport hangar in Pittsburgh, and the Brown Thomson Building and department store in Hartford. By the 1940s, with the increase in overhead power lines and other obstructions, as well as building codes and the rise of unions, moving large structures became more complicated and prohibitively expensive, and the business of moving buildings tapered off.[69]

As Eichleay was failing, the Carpatho-Rusyns who made up a considerable percentage of Eichleay's house movers attempted to continue the business on their own. According to the son of one of the workers, a group, headed by foreman Peter Dudich and including Joseph Mulick, John and Wasyl Shack, John Zavacky, and Andrii Warhola, established the short-lived Pittsburgh House Moving Corporation.[70] Rusyns also made up the bulk of laborers at the Kress-Oravetz company, the result of a 1922 merger between a Slovak-owned company and the well-established Kress Brothers Construction Company. According to family memories, Andrii was involved in the company's 1929 move of the Allegheny County morgue, a six-thousand-ton building. During the three months it took to move the morgue, the coroner and his staff continued to conduct autopsies and inquests. Gas, water, and sewer lines were maintained. Pittsburgh preservationists recall the feat: "They manned screw jacks that they gave a quarter turn every time a whistle sounded, until the three-story building was 27 feet in the air. It then was moved onto a system of beams designed by the Kress-Oravetz Company and slowly, laboriously pulled by cable to the foundation at 542 Fourth Ave. Once there . . . they had to 'shoehorn' the building between two structures."[71] A curious and comic feature of the retrospective coverage of this move is the description of the Kress-Oravetz laborers, which probably came from reports by early, clueless journalists. According to one author, they "hailed from the Baltic region and apparently had generations of experience in moving houses." Another described them as "100 men from a Balkan tribe—specialists in moving buildings from the 'old country.'" The notion that a "tribe" of Carpatho-Rusyn peasants from the fields of central Europe, performing this punishing and perilous job in the New World for their own economic survival, had "generations of experience" in the craft of moving heavy buildings is absurdly funny.

Andrii probably also worked with the Kress-Oravetz company to move the old structure of the Warhola family's church, Saint John Chrysostom in the *Ruska dolina*

(Rusyn valley) neighborhood of Greenfield in 1932–1933. But there were numerous house-moving companies in Pittsburgh, and little work during the 1930s. Andrii bounced from job to job as a laborer. Unemployment in Pittsburgh in the early 1930s ranged from 18 percent to 25 percent, and both Paul and John Warhola mention that their father was periodically unemployed.[72]

However, for immigrant workers who had carefully put aside their earnings, the Depression had a silver lining. As years passed and plans to return to the Old Country faded, immigrant Carpatho-Rusyns set their sights on buying homes of their own. Coming from agricultural areas where status was based on landownership, former peasants, now industrial laborers, translated their dream in American terms and made every effort to become homeowners. The scholar of Slavic immigration John Bodnar explains, "Denied opportunities for significant occupational mobility, particularly since earlier arrivals such as the Irish and Germans already held skilled industrial jobs, Slavs turned intensely to home ownership as a means of solidifying their precarious economic status. . . . Slavs exceeded nearly every ethnic group in urban America in purchasing homes."[73] In 1930, 40.2 percent of Pittsburgh's households owned their homes. Breaking the figures down by ethnic group shows that 52.2 percent of foreign-born white people owned homes, as compared to 38.1 percent of native white people.[74] In addition to status, homeownership furnished independence and control to families who had been sharing cramped, rented living space. It also provided an additional source of income from lodgers and built equity as a hedge against old age, an important consideration for manual workers in jobs that did not offer pensions. Decades later, the artist Andy Warhol cited a favorite quote from Margaret Thatcher: "Property brings with it security and independence."[75] Usually interpreted as an indication of his obsession with consumerism and the valorization of capitalism, it may simply have been an echo of his father's voice.

At the beginning of 1927, the *Pittsburgh Gazette-Times* announced in a subheadline, "General Prosperity along with Broad Program of Public Improvements Had Helpful Effect on Real Estate Values."[76] The "Big Sales List" in the same article noted the sale of five brick double houses at 3248–3266 Dawson Street from L. J. Stein to Abraham Berger for $70,000.[77] A few years later, real estate values collapsed. During the Depression, foreclosures in Pittsburgh increased from 406 in 1926 to 2,310 in 1932. The value of residential property plummeted, causing mortgage defaults and wiping out real estate investors. In 1931 and 1932, the Berger properties on Dawson Street appeared in the long lists of sheriff's sales.[78] Widespread foreclosures meant misfortune for owners, but a bit of luck for would-be buyers, as real estate investors, eager to unload their negative-equity properties, sold off their holdings. For Rusyns looking to get out of Soho, Dawson Street in the South Oakland district—just over a mile to the east, but remote in terms of ambience—was a promising destination.

By 1930, Warhola relatives and coworkers Peter Dudich and Stephen Kalinyak already owned homes on nearby Orpwood Street, and the census shows other Carpatho-Rusyn names in the neighborhood. On April 30, 1934, Andrii's brother Joseph and his wife Mary purchased a six-room brick residence at 3250 Dawson Street "in consideration of ONE ($1.00) DOLLAR, and other good and valuable considerations."[79] In 1930, Joe and Mary Warhola had been lodging with the family of a Miková relative, John Rudavsky, on Lawn Street, and Joe was working as a laborer at Jones and Laughlin. In February 1934, Joe applied for payment under the Veteran's Compensation Act passed in Pennsylvania the previous month. He was granted $10 per month for every month he served on active duty, a total of $140, which may have facilitated his purchase of the Dawson Street house in May. Three months later, on August 15, Andrew and Julia Warhola purchased a "two-story and attic brick building known as No. 3252 Dawson Street . . . for and in consideration of the sum of One Dollar."[80] According to John Warhola, his father paid $3,200 in cash for the house, which was just half of what Berger had paid for it seven years earlier.[81] Other Rusyn families were able to benefit from similar Depression-era bargains. The duplex neighbors of Andrii and Julia were Alexander and Katrena Elachko, Carpatho-Rusyns from villages near Miková.

The Andrii Warhola family's new home was a semidetached, two-story brick house, built in 1915, with a full basement, an attic, approximately 1,100 square feet of living space, and a good-sized back yard.[82] John remembered, "Andy asked me 'Is there a yard?' because we didn't have no yard where we lived before. . . . Then he says 'Is there a bathtub in our house?' I said, 'Yeah, we've got a whole bathroom.' He was real happy about it."[83] Their father dug out a root cellar under the porch next to the coal bin to preserve the vegetables and food supplies that he and Julia would grow in their kitchen garden. Andrii was unemployed at the time, and John helped him renovate the new house, scraping wallpaper, painting, and restoring the wood floors. "Dad would scrape, sand, and varnish. It looked like new." John wondered, "Where did he learn it all?"[84] Holmes Elementary school was half a block up the street, and it was just a short walk to Schenley High School. John Warhola said, "It was just like going into a different world."[85]

The root cellar and the vegetable garden in the backyard were almost the only aspects of the house that resembled the Warhola homes in the Old Country. A coal-burning furnace fueled the hot-water heating system, and radiators provided constant heat in winter. Brick fireplaces in the front living room and an upstairs bedroom may have been used for additional cozy warmth. The house was solidly built, with high ceilings, wood floors, and wood trim around windows and doorways. Pocket doors could close off the kitchen and dining room from the living room. All other rooms had heavy, paneled wood doors with glass doorknobs. There were two sizable bedrooms on the second floor, each with a view of the street, and a small bathroom. The attic was more spacious than might be expected, with a window facing a wall of the neighboring house, and a dormer window facing the street, from which one could see the tall buildings of downtown Pittsburgh in the distance. Julia had a tiny kitchen, with a large sink and stove. The back door opened from the kitchen to a small porch leading to the backyard, where the boys kept rabbits and dogs. The pole from the clothesline, where Julia hung the family's laundry out to dry, still stands.[86] Photographs from the 1940s show that the front porch was shaded by greenery and screened by climbing vines of Morning Glory. The house was, in both practical and aesthetic terms, a Rusyn immigrant's dream.

In order to make ends meet, however, the Warholas acquired boarders almost as soon as they moved in. The days when unmarried immigrant men flowed into the area, requiring a housewife's backbreaking services, had long passed. The Warholas' lodgers in 1935 were a young newly married Jewish couple, Harry and Helen Shlakman. According to the 1940 census, Harry, age thirty, was a naturalized immigrant from Poland, a dealer in produce, who had worked twenty-six weeks the previous year, earning $400. His wife Helen, age twenty-seven, was a native-born American, a saleslady in a department store. She had worked fifty weeks the previous year, earning $500. They reported that they paid $25 rent monthly.[87] The Shlakmans were given a bedroom on the second floor. It may have had a sink, but they would have shared the bathroom with the family.[88] The three boys slept in the attic in a single bed. Julia and Andrii had their own bedroom, although they may have sometimes slept in the attic or the dining room, depending on the needs of children and boarders. The Shlakman couple did not lodge with the Warholas long after the 1940 census was taken. On October 8, 1941, a notice was published in the *Pittsburgh Press* that Harry Shlakman, residing then on Boulevard of the Allies, would no longer be responsible for Helen's debts. According to John Warhola, the Shlakmans were followed by other married couples, who rented the space for $10–$20 per month. Lodgers were students attending the university on the GI Bill, or Jewish merchants, because, as John put it, "they had the businesses; they were the ones that had the money."[89]

The Warholas' home was in the center of a small Rusyn-Slovak cluster on Dawson Street. Their immediate neighbors, the Elachkos, were Greek Catholic

Rusyns from Sucha and Driečna, villages near Miková. The Girmans were Greek Catholics with Slovak roots, and the Kish family were Roman Catholic Hungarians from eastern Slovakia. The couples were all in their late thirties or early forties. The men had immigrated around 1912, and most of them worked at the Jones and Laughlin plant. All the families had moved to Oakland from Soho. John Warhola recalled, "It was about a block from the park and the homes were very nice. They were mostly like Jewish people, Polish, Greeks, and we all got along good."[90] Further up and down Dawson, there were numerous Jewish families, who had roots in Russia and Lithuania. Bernard Baer, an immigrant from Minsk, owned the corner store. At Holmes Elementary School, where the Warhola boys attended, 41 percent of the students were Jews, followed by Italians and Slavs.[91]

From the Warhola home, the family could walk to the Museums of Art and Natural History, the Music Hall and the Library of the Carnegie Institute, all of which offered free admission. Just down the hill was Schenley Park with its acres of parkland, ponds, and pavilions. Trolleys traversed the city and beyond, making it easy to explore other Pittsburgh neighborhoods and suburban towns. H. L. Mencken's 1926 essay, "The Libido for the Ugly," famously condemned Pittsburgh's "dreadfully hideous," "intolerably bleak and forlorn" aspect. "Here was wealth beyond computation, almost beyond imagination—and here were human habitations so abominable that they would have disgraced a race of alley cats."[92] Andy Warhol later recalled Pittsburgh as "the worst place I have ever been," but he might not have realized how lucky he was. Andrew Carnegie and the Pittsburgh magnates believed that those who acquired wealth had the responsibility to further civilization's progress by helping people to improve themselves.[93] Therefore, they established libraries and educational institutions. In Bell's *Out of This Furnace*, workers, who hoped Carnegie would be beaten by the union, sarcastically commented, "Well, I suppose Carnegie will give them a library. And much good may it do them."[94] For first-generation immigrants, libraries were of little use, but for their children and grandchildren, they were precious. Few Carpatho-Rusyn immigrant communities in America were so favorably located to enable the education and cultivation of their members. Mencken and Warhol probably never visited the Rusyn-inhabited anthracite coal patches of eastern Pennsylvania for comparison. Descriptions in the biographical literature of Warhol's origins in "a Slavic ghetto" or "a cloistered Eastern European ghetto community" are shortsighted.[95]

There was tension between the two Warhola families on Dawson Street, which Paul attributed to Joe's envy and resentment of Andrii's frugality and to the influence of Joe's wife, "a domineering, bossy person" who was "not very intelligent."[96]

Joseph Warhola, age thirty-two, married twenty-two-year-old Mary Bezek, an immigrant from Miková, in 1922, a year after Julia's arrival in Pittsburgh. Mary affixed her mark, rather than a signature, to the marriage license. Joe's address on the license is 3 Orr Street, which was the first home of the Andrii Warholas. He and Mary may have lived with Andrii and Julia in the first years of their marriage, which would surely have been a source of tension. Paul recalled *stryko* and *stryna*, Rusyn terms for paternal uncle and aunt: "We liked my uncle, he was terrific, but he was being dominated by her. My mother could never get along with her."

Just as in the old-country village, status in the immigrant community depended on a family's reputation, which was earned by hard work, thriftiness, and self-restraint. As Ewa Morawska found in her study of the Johnstown immigrant community, "These basic 'reputational requirements' applied to all members of the immigrant communities and served for upward and downward adjustments of their overall status in the group social hierarchy. The positions at the top of the ladder carried with them a set of additional moral obligations of a social nature: charity, compassion, readiness to provide assistance, public identification with one's group and its people."[97]

Both Andrii and Julia conformed well to these high criteria. "My husband was good man—not a drunk man," Julia told the *Esquire* interviewer.[98] Her trenchant description of Andrii is all-encompassing for Carpatho-Rusyn immigrants, among whom alcohol abuse was not uncommon. Abstemiousness was a prime virtue, especially for a man who was often away from home. John said, "I talked with one of the men who worked with him. . . . He said, your dad would just have one drink and then go up to his room. He was so loyal to the kids, to the family."[99] Sobriety also implied gravity, constancy, industry, integrity, and frugality. Neighbor Ann Elachko recalled, "We all liked [Andy's] father. He was a wonderful man. He was totally different than his brother Joe. Andy's father was a little bit of a step above. He seemed to be self-educated and there was nothing brash about him. He was a very nice gentleman."[100] According to his son John, Andrii read newspapers and listened to the radio, with John's translation assistance. "He picked up the language by himself. He never went to school, but picked it up on his own."[101]

Andrii's long years in America before Julia's arrival testify to his self-sacrifice and foresight. In February 1913, just a few months after his arrival in Pittsburgh, Andrii joined the Russian Brotherhood Organization, a fraternal benefit society established in 1900 by and for Rusyn immigrants in the United States. The organization provided insurance for members, whose dangerous jobs made them too great a risk for American insurance companies. Through their lodges, based in

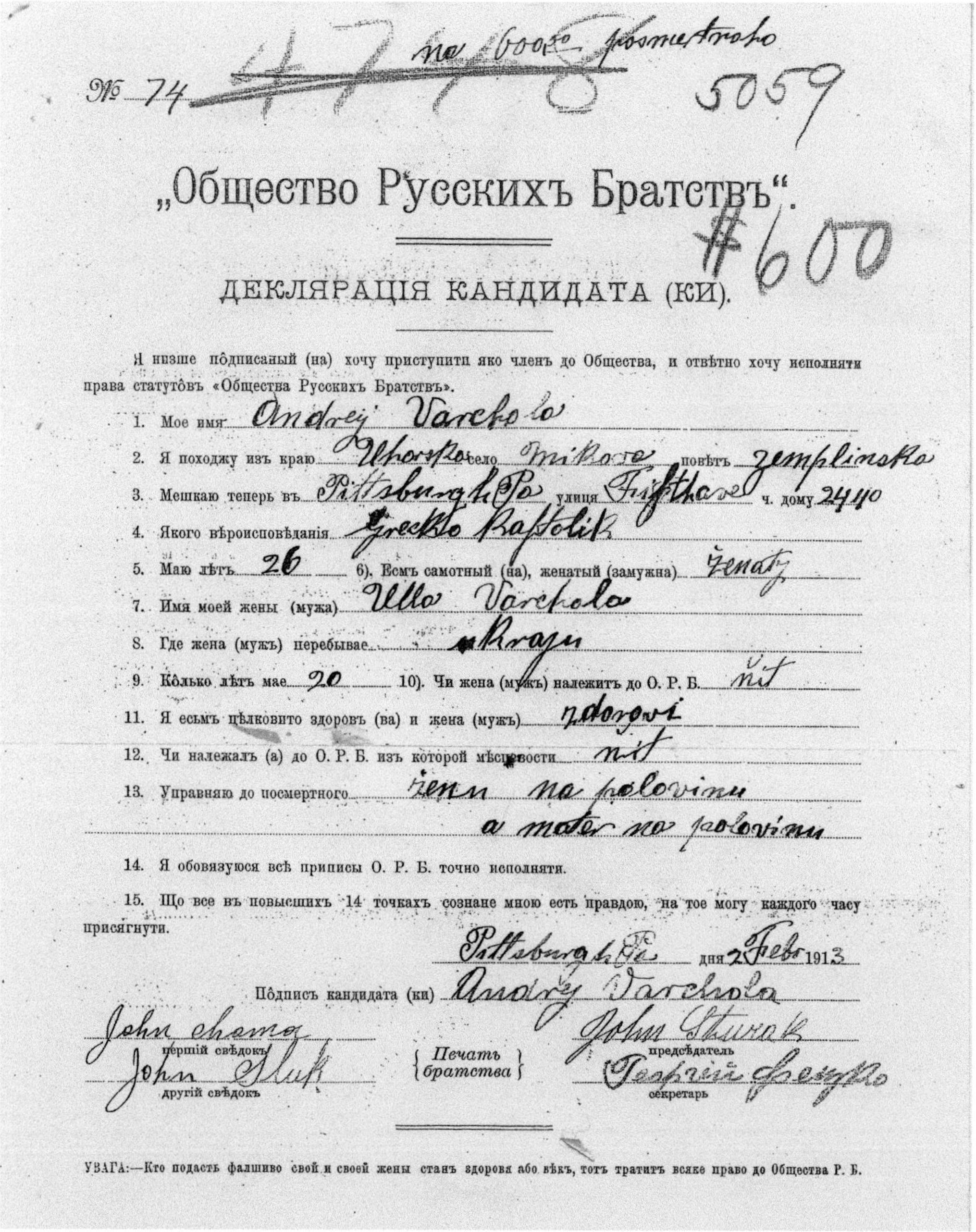

№ 74   5059

„Общество Русскихъ Братствъ“.

ДЕКЛЯРАЦIЯ КАНДИДАТА (КИ).

Я низше пôдписаный (на) хочу приступити яко членъ до Общества, и отвѣтно хочу исполняти права статутôвъ «Общества Русскихъ Братствъ».

1. Мое имя *Andrej Varchola*
2. Я походжу изъ краю *Uhorsko* село *Mikova* повѣтъ *Zemplinsko*
3. Мешкаю теперь въ *Pittsburgh Pa* улиця *Fifth ave* ч. дому *2440*
4. Якого вѣроисповѣданiя *Grecko Kastolik*
5. Маю лѣтъ **26**   6). Есмъ самотный (на), женатый (замужна) *ženaty*
7. Имя моей жены (мужа) *Ulla Varchola*
8. Гдѣ жена (мужъ) перебывае *u kraju*
9. Кôлько лѣтъ мае **20**   10). Чи жена (мужъ) належить до О. Р. Б. *nit*
11. Я есмъ цѣлковито здоровъ (ва) и жена (мужъ) *zdorovi*
12. Чи належалъ (а) до О. Р. Б. изъ которой мѣстовости *nit*
13. Управняю до посмертного *ženu na polovinu a mater na polovinu*

14. Я обовязуюся всѣ приписы О. Р. Б. точно исполняти.

15. Що все въ повысшихъ 14 точкахъ сознане мною есть правдою, на тое могу каждого часу присягнути.

Pittsburgh Pa дня *2 Febr* 1913

Пôдписъ кандидата (ки) *Andrij Varchola*

John Chama
першій свѣдокъ

John Bluk
другій свѣдокъ

{ Печать братства }

John Sturak
предсѣдатель

Georgij Feyko
секретарь

УВАГА:—Кто подастъ фалшиво свой и своей жены станъ здоровя або вѣкъ, тотъ тратитъ всяке право до Общества Р. Б.

Figure 3.8. Andrii Warhola's application for life insurance with the Russian Brotherhood Organization, 1913.

Greek Catholic and Orthodox parishes, brotherhood organizations provided death benefits and trust funds for dependents, even for beneficiaries who lived in Europe. Andrii purchased a policy to provide a onetime death benefit of $600 to be shared equally by his mother and his wife, both of whom lived *u kraju* at the time, that is, in the Old Country. His monthly contribution was 95¢. In 1924, he altered the policy to leave the entire amount to his wife, "due to my mother's illness." His mother, Julia Choma Varchola died of typhus in 1926. Andrii also put aside money in the United States Postal Savings System, a safe and convenient way for immigrants who lacked bank accounts to save money. In 1916, 80 percent of depositors were persons of foreign birth. Given the low interest rate of 2 percent, their motive was not investment, but security.[102] The *Amerikansky Russky Viestnik* assured "our people" of the safety of the system and encouraged its readers to deposit their money in the postal bank, instead of stuffing it in mattresses.

Ann Elachko, thirteen years old when they moved to Dawson Street, remembered Julia. "She was delightful. She had a sense of humour and she saw a little beyond what an ethnic group of people could understand. Even her insight into religion was a little beyond what most of our people discussed."[103] Ann told Bob Colacello, "Mary [Warhola, Joe's wife] was very gabby. Julia wasn't like that. She didn't stop and talk to everybody on the street. She wasn't cozy or intimate friends with anyone on the block."[104] One woman who claimed a close friendship with Julia was Bessie Ziontz, a Jewish immigrant from Poland, who lived at 3276 Dawson Street. Close to Julia in age, Bessie lived with her husband, who worked as a fruit vendor, their three children, and a household maid. Her son remembers Julia confiding in Bessie on the front porch, while the young Andy sat nearby listening. "[Julia] would bemoan the fact of how poor they were. And we would load her up with vegetables and fruit, and home-baked bread."[105] Carmen and Elizabeth Marino, grandparents of the future NFL quarterback Dan Marino, lived around the corner on Frazier Street, and family stories have it that Julia was friendly with Elizabeth, an immigrant from Italy. Ever since Orr Street, when they lived in a largely Lithuanian neighborhood rather than a segregated Rusyn block, Andrii and Julia demonstrated openness to others outside their ethnic circle and an interest in the broader world. But much of their life focused on the church.

"My Religion Greek . . . No Rome Catholic"

With these words, Julia Warhola tried to explain her religious background in Warhol's 1966 film *The George Hamilton Story*. The term "Greek Catholic" refers to the fact that the Slavs of east central Europe received Christianity not from the Latin West, but from the Orthodox East, that is, from the Byzantine Empire, with its Greek language, culture, and Eastern Orthodox religion. To avoid ethnic ambiguity and to more accurately denote the church's derivation, "Greek" was officially replaced by "Byzantine" in the United States in the 1950s. Today the Warholas' church is properly termed the Byzantine Ruthenian Catholic Church, the label "Ruthenian" being the Latin-based equivalent of "Rusyn."

Julia, like most of the Greek Catholic faithful, would not have been aware of the history and evolution of her church, but she surely distinguished it from Roman Catholic on one side, and Orthodox on the other. The Ruthenian Byzantine rite of the Catholic Church stems from a seventeenth-century compromise by which the Carpatho-Rusyn people in central Europe preserved the rites and traditions of Orthodoxy, but accepted the authority of the Pope of Rome. That is, they used the Church Slavonic language instead of Latin, the Julian instead of the Gregorian calendar, and they had a married priesthood. They received the Eucharist in the form of leavened bread and wine, rather than an unleavened wafer, and whereas Roman Catholics are confirmed by bishops as adolescents, Greek Catholic priests administer chrismation (confirmation) to infants together with baptism. Immigrants and second-generation American Greek Catholics often found it difficult to explain their Byzantine Catholic identification, and they could be uncomfortable with its distinction from mainstream Christian churches. Paul Warhola recalls that the Warhola boys "were a bit ashamed" of celebrating Christmas on January 7 and "had to make up all kinds of excuses to get us out of attending [school] on that day."[106]

The Byzantine Catholic religion, situated as it was, between western Roman Catholicism and eastern Orthodoxy, was a cause of discomfiture for Andy Warhol even as an adult. In his diary entry for Easter 1984, which he spent with Roman Catholic friends, Warhol says, "On Easter services, they got up at 4:30 to go, but I couldn't go. . . . I would feel too peculiar in a church where they might see me praying and kneeling and crossing myself because I cross the wrong way. I cross the Orthodox way."[107] Warhol's description of the right-to-left Eastern Christian sign of the cross as "the wrong way" speaks volumes about his ethnic insecurity, but it also demonstrates the firmness of his religious allegiance. Although it made him feel awkward in a Roman Catholic setting, he persisted in making the Greek Catholic sign of the cross as he had learned it in childhood, and as an adult, he continued to pray with his mother in Church Slavonic. Like most American Greek Catholics, he was not equipped to understand the complex historical background of Byzantine Catholicism or to explain it to his Roman Catholic companions, but he never completely abandoned it. When a Greek Catholic church was inconvenient, Greek Catholics attended Roman Catholic churches, and in the last decades of his life, Warhol often visited Saint Vincent Ferrer Roman Catholic Church. In the documentary film, *Vies et morts d'Andy Warhol*, Father Damian McCarthy points out the pew in the back of the church where Warhol would sit, "very modest" and "out of the way," where he likely felt free to cross himself "the wrong way."

Not surprisingly, the first Greek Catholic parishes in the United States, established by immigrants in the 1880s, were an anomaly and anathema to Roman Catholics. Latin-rite bishops met their nonconformity with a lack of comprehension and outright hostility. In response, twenty-five thousand Greek Catholics broke with Catholicism entirely in 1891 and joined what is today the Russian Orthodox Church in America. As their own culture became overlaid with Russian liturgical forms and artistic styles, many of these converts adopted a Russian ethnonational identity. Carpatho-Rusyn Greek Catholics in America then found themselves in danger of assimilation by the Roman Catholic Church on one side and the Russian Orthodox Church on the other.

Just as destructive as the friction with the Roman Catholic hierarchy was the internal factionalism that arose within the Greek Catholic Church. Variations in language, culture, and politics between Rusyns from Galicia on the northern slopes of the Carpathian Mountains and those from the Kingdom of Hungary to the south resulted in contrary notions of national identity. Galician Rusyns increasingly distinguished themselves as Russians or Ukrainians, while Rusyns from Hungary retained their ancestral identity, denoted as "Rusyn," "Uhro-Rusyn," or "Ruthenian."[108] Lay fraternal benefit organizations, designed to provide insurance and promote social interaction among Greek Catholics, became advocates for specific national and religious positions within the Rusyn immigrant community. For Rusyns from Hungary, "The Greek Catholic Union of Rusyn Brotherhoods in the USA" (GCU) was created to assist its less fortunate members, but also to provide "a super-structure for the promulgation of a national identity for the Rusin people."[109] In their newspaper, the *Amerikansky Russky Viestnik*, the GCU advocated for Greek Catholics in their struggle with the Latin clergy, supported a distinct Rusyn cultural identity, and virulently opposed efforts to convince the Carpatho-Rusyn people that they were Ukrainian.[110]

Ewa Morawska, a scholar of Slavic immigration, points out that the conflicts and internal disputes "strengthened the collective identities of the members" and "sharpened group ethnic boundaries."[111] As a result, each Carpatho-Rusyn was compelled to decide—sometimes independently, sometimes influenced or imposed by clergy—to identify as Rusyn, Russian, or Ukrainian.

> Throughout the country among most East European groups every Slavic Catholic was forced to recognize at hand the internal argument over the nature of his origin. He had to distinguish and judge his ethnicity contemporaneously. . . . In a quest perhaps deeper and more pervasive than that of other American nationalities, every church-going Slav had to endure this soul-searching. Ethnic loyalty was not an abstract issue discussed only by the more patriotic. Its realization was the experience of every man, woman, and child in the community. The immigrant saloonkeeper, banker, grocer, even the factory hand and his family had sacrificed much to organize the parish, pay for the property, and continue to contribute to their institution.[112]

The Warhola and Zavacky immigrants faced the same questions and acted accordingly. Their children, usually subconsciously, followed their lead.

Most of the Rusyns living in Oakland, including many Miková natives and Andrii Warhola's brother and his family, attended Holy Spirit Greek Catholic Church at the corner of Atwood and Bates Streets, just a few blocks from their homes. In distinction from their countrymen, Andrii and Julia and their children worshipped regularly at Saint John Chrysostom "down the run" in *Ruska dolina*, to which they walked more than a mile up and down hills and steps and across railroad tracks from their homes, first in Soho and later in Oakland. The historian Richard Custer's examination of church records shows that members of Holy Spirit were primarily from Miková and surrounding small villages, whereas parishioners of Saint John Chrysostom came from the district center Medzilaborce, the monastery site Krásny Brod, and villages farther west in the prewar counties of Sharysh and Spysh.[113] Some of the few Oakland neighbors who attended Saint John Chrysostom with the Warholas were the Slovak Greek Catholic Girmans from Dawson Street—Margie Girman was Andy Warhol's childhood friend—and the Stephen Kalinyak family from Miková—Stephen was Andy's godfather, and his wife had been Julia's travel companion from Miková in 1921. Aside from its less insular character, the only discernible difference between the Oakland and the *Ruska dolina* churches was the autonomous character of Saint John Chrysostom, which allowed the parishioners to assert their Subcarpathian Rusyn culture and traditions with less interference from the hierarchy, western or eastern.

However, they could not avoid the intrusion of the 1929 papal decree *Cum Data Fuerit*, which directed that newly ordained Greek Catholic priests in the United States must be celibate. The bishop's efforts to enforce the Vatican's decree met with powerful resistance from priests and laity in many parishes, leading to a large-scale schism that gave rise to an independent entity, the American Carpatho-Russian

Orthodox Diocese, centered in Johnstown, Pennsylvania. Despite its name, the parishioners were Carpatho-Rusyn, not Russian. Over the next decade, as the battle over celibacy consumed much of the oxygen in Carpatho-Rusyn churches and homes, families were divided, and numerous legal battles over control of church property ensued. The parish at Saint John Chrysostom saw *Cum Data Fuerit* as an attack on Eastern-rite traditions, and the church became a hotbed of the anticelibacy movement. Some of the most outspoken critics of the Vatican policy had connections to Saint John Chrysostom and the Warhola family. Peter Korpos, the teacher-cantor from 1926 until 1960, who taught the Warhola children in religious classes, was an officer of the Committee for the Defense of the Eastern Rite. Peter Zeedick, the author of numerous articles and pamphlets condemning the Latinization of the Eastern rite, was the Warholas' family physician. And Michael Hahalyak, Julia Warhola's personal attorney, brought suit against the bishop, defending the autonomic status of Saint John Chrysostom Church as far as the Pennsylvania Supreme Court, in defiance of the Vatican. Finally, by the end of the 1930s, the GCU, weakened by the Depression and a decrease in membership, made peace with the reigning bishop. Most parishes followed suit, and the battle against celibacy was lost.

Julia Warhola most likely did not fully comprehend the intricacies of the ecclesiastical arguments. But surrounded as she was by the controversies whirling through the community, it is not surprising that she had opinions on the celibacy issue. The first half of Warhol's 1966 film *The George Hamilton Story*, often referred to as "Mrs. Warhol," features a colloquy between Julia and Richard Rheem, a young boyfriend of Andy's, with whom she had become close. After telling him about her childhood work helping the village priest in Miková with his children, she explains, "You know, long time ago my *priest-y* [Rusyn plural ending] married. Now no 'lowed [allowed]." Asked why, she responds, "From *poperome* [the Pope of Rome]. Everybody bow to *poperome*, my religion. Not 'lowed married." With incredulity in her voice, Julia explains how this came about: "Some *bishoop* [Rusyn pronunciation of bishop] come to, from Europe. I don't know what year was, but he made the *priest-y* be not married. . . . *Priest-y*, young *priest-y* still no get married . . . [with disbelief] still, no can get . . . lots of *priest-y* want to get married, you know." The issue was personal for the Warhola family, as Julia's grandson Paul Constantine had recently completed Saints Cyril and Methodius Byzantine Catholic Seminary and was then pursuing studies in moral theology at Catholic University in Washington, DC. "Already six year, in Washington he teaching self for priest. Maybe he gonna get married too someday."[114] Paul Warhola recalls, "She couldn't understand why I couldn't be married."[115]

Julia's comments on the celibacy movement may appear charmingly naive, but they reveal an independent streak and a spark of cynicism. The intonation of her comment, "Everybody bow to *poperome*, my religion," suggests a halfhearted acquiescence to ecclesiastical technicalities. "Lots of *priest-y* want to get married, you know" reveals a predilection for old truths over new edicts. Into the mid-1960s, Saint John Chrysostom continued to fight the battle over the introduction of Roman Catholic practices into the Greek Catholic Church. For Julia Warhola and her family, their religious faith was inextricably interwoven with their Carpatho-Rusyn traditional culture.

In Lyndora, the Zavacky family's church became the site of a colossal battle between Rusyns and Ukrainians, in which Julia's brother John Zavacky played an active role. In the early years, Subcarpathian Rusyns like the Zavackys joined forces with Galician Rusyns from north of the mountains: "Since our people were still too small in number to organize their own parish they joined in with their Greek Catholic brethren from Galicia, to organize St. Michael's Greek Catholic Church of Lyndora. At first things went well with the congregation but in time differences arose. These differences led to dissension and to bitter feelings."[116] This anodyne description masks a turbulent history that involved threats, arrests, litigation, and violence. For several weeks in August 1910, the Butler County sheriff and his deputy attended weekly services to provide security.

On May 19, 1910, John Zavacky was one of a small group of Uhro-Rusyns from Hungary that met to organize a new parish, named in honor of Saint John the Baptist, where they could have their own priest, their own cantor, and could better preserve their Rusyn customs and traditions. John Zavacky was elected secretary. Father Alexis Petrasovich, the pastor of the newly founded Saint John Chrysostom Church in Pittsburgh, became an itinerant pastor, ministering also to Saint John the Baptist in Lyndora. The congregation erected a new church building, which was dedicated on March 9, 1913. In their letter to *Amerikansky Russky Viestnik* from September 25, 1910, the trustees wrote: "We've had liturgy four Sundays now, and it was joyful. Delight was visible on every face. The Pittsburgh cantor-teacher sang our old melodies, which we never heard in the Butler church. The entire congregation sang until the windows shook. Petrasovich gives beautiful sermons, the likes of which we haven't heard before. He doesn't preach politics, but explains the word of God."

Was Andy Warhol Ukrainian?

As bizarre as they may sound, the stories of dissension and schism in Pittsburgh and Lyndora were commonplace among Carpatho-Rusyn religious communities in the first decades of the twentieth century, but they acquire a special significance in regard to Andy Warhol. The Ukrainian-Rusyn antagonism that roiled early twentieth-century Greek Catholic churches continues to the present day, mutatis mutandis, in religious, political, and scholarly settings. Carpatho-Rusyns have been recognized as a distinct ethnic group in every European country where they live except Ukraine, where they are considered a sub-ethnos of Ukrainians.[117] In North America today, conscious Ukrainian Americans consider "Rusyn" to be an archaic term for "Ukrainian," and are certain that those who call themselves Rusyn are, in fact, Ukrainian. When attention is focused on Andy Warhol, discussions often become firestorms. Carpatho-Rusyns cling tenaciously to their famous favorite son, while Ukrainians blithely and imperiously claim Warhol as a political naïf, who would have eventually "become Ukrainian" if he had only lived long enough to understand prevailing truths.

In 2018, the historian Alexander Motyl curated an exhibit of Warhol's *Endangered Species* series at the Ukrainian Museum in New York, billed as the "First-ever exhibition of Warhol works at a Ukrainian American institution." Informational wall texts explained Warhol's roots and ethnic identity from the Ukrainian perspective:

> When Warhol lived in Pittsburgh, few Ruthenians possessed a modern national identity. It was only in the period from the beginning of World War I to the end of World War II that Ruthenians, in the United States and in their homeland in Eastern Europe, divided into three national groups. Most opted for a Ukrainian identity; many reimagined themselves as Rusyns or Carpatho-Rusyns; some chose a Russian identity. . . . Unsurprisingly, both Carpatho-Rusyns and Ukrainians today claim Andy Warhol as their own. And both have good grounds for doing so: after all, Warhol was born and raised a Ruthenian.[118]

Following Motyl's logic, Warhol was both Ruthenian and Ukrainian. And since, as he believes, all Ruthenians are Ukrainian, this makes Warhol Ukrainian. The historian Paul Robert Magocsi refuted Motyl's claim and accused him and Ukrainian activists of cultural imperialism. "How else can one explain claims by Ukrainian patriots in Ukraine and abroad that Warhol's ethnicity is Ukrainian?"[119] While Motyl and Magocsi agree that Andy Warhol's national identity was American and his ethnic roots were Carpatho-Rusyn, they adamantly disagree on what that means for his ethnic identity and which group is justified in claiming him as their own. The exhibit sparked a fervid dispute, as Ukrainians protested Magocsi's judgment that Warhol cannot be said to be Ukrainian—not nationally, ethnically, or culturally.

The story of Warhol's uncle John Zavacky's activity in the rebellion against the imposition of Ukrainian identity and culture at the Lyndora church strongly indicates that, contrary to Motyl's opinion of *most* Ruthenians/Rusyns, the Zavacky family did indeed possess a national identity before World War I. They did not "reimagine themselves as Rusyns." They were, originally and persistently, obdurate Subcarpathian (Uhro-) Rusyns and they obstinately resisted a Ukrainian identity. In 1911, John Zavacky penned a letter over his own signature in the *Amerikansky Russky Viestnik* to relate the progress made by the new church in the first year of its existence.[120] "Our Rusyn parish, thank God, is so far going well. We have a cantor who very nicely teaches our children to read and write in our language, as well as the catechism and the Bible. We also have a priest, Father Aleksei Petrasovich. . . . He comes to us every Sunday, conducts liturgy, and gives beautiful sermons. It is now calmer and more pleasant when we can hear sermons from our own Rusyn priest. When we were together with the Ukrainians, we heard nothing but envy, agitation, and nasty imprecations." In vituperative language, Zavacky refers to the corruption and legal squabbles at the church: "We were compelled to leave our work of many years, the church and its property, which passed fraudulently into Ukrainian hands, and to separate ourselves completely in order to save ourselves from Ukrainian politics." In flowery rhetoric, he thanks "God in Heaven, the Blessed Virgin Mary, Saint Nicholas and all the saints" for their preservation from "the Ukrainian abyss." He denounces those renegade Rusyn priests who manipulate the "spiritual weakness, gullibility—and even worse—the piety of the Rusyn people." Zavacky's strident tone manifests the bitterness felt by the Rusyns in their struggle to preserve their time-honored identity and culture.

Zavacky's active choice of *Rusyn* in opposition to *Ukrainian* was surely shared by his sister's family. The position Andrii Warhola took in the ethnonational squabbles can be inferred from his membership since 1913 in the Russian Brotherhood Organization, lodge number 74, which was affiliated with Holy Spirit Greek Catholic Church and strongly opposed to the imposition of Ukrainian nationality on Carpatho-Rusyns. The Warhola children were also associated with the Greek Catholic Union, the primary guardian of Rusyns against encroaching Ukrainianism. Records show that in 1944–1945, when he was sixteen years old, Andy Warhol was a member of the Gymnastic Branch of the GCU, an organization for young people ages fourteen to twenty-one. Membership included insurance, a death benefit, and a subscription to the *ARV*. Members were taught "to spread the

Rusyn spirit" and to uphold, strengthen, and protect their Rusyn nationality.[121] Subsequent record books show that Andy Warhol was a dues-paying member of the GCU as late as 1964, fifteen years after he had left Pittsburgh for New York. The Warhola brothers' membership may have been initiated by Julia primarily for its insurance benefits after her husband's death in 1942, and Andy's membership may have been maintained by his brother John, in whose papers the records were found. But whether or not Andy Warhol developed a conscious Carpatho-Rusyn identity in the GCU, he could not have escaped the ecclesiastic controversies and battles over identity that permeated everyday life in the Rusyn community into the 1930s.

In New York of the 1960s and 1970s, the Rusyn–Ukrainian antagonism of Andy's parents' generation was no longer an immediate and pervasive provocation. Still, it is clear that Andy Warhol was highly attuned to ethnicity, regularly commenting or speculating in his *Diaries* about the ethnicity of people he met.[122] "I asked if he was Italian and he said no, that he was French and Irish" (240); "The girl was Irish marrying a guy from South America" (383); "The mother is, I think, Polish" (417); "She has a Polish last name" (500); "I couldn't tell if they were Italian or Jewish" (482); "She was Jewish" (555); "He was Indian" (745). For ease, he identified himself as Czech, until he met the Czech model Paulina Porizkova (Pavlína Pořízková) and her mother. He commented in his diary, "I guess maybe I'm not really Czech, because I didn't understand it when they were talking" (744). Like most Rusyn Americans of his generation, Warhol could not put a name to his own ethnic background, but he knew what he was *not*. He resisted the efforts of a certain Dr. Warchol to convince him that he was Polish (178–79). And he distinguished between someone who was "half Russian and half Ukrainian" (165) and "a good-looking Czechoslovakian boy" (578), using for the latter the faux ethnonym that he applied to himself. He recognized that those who, like himself, claimed a fuzzy "Czechoslovakian" identity were not Russians, Poles, or Ukrainians.

There is also evidence that Warhol had an embryonic Carpatho-Rusyn consciousness and even a muted sense of pride in his ethnic background. There is a positive identification with Rusyns in a diary entry for November 29, 1978, where Warhol recalls attending a screening of *The Deer Hunter*, Michael Cimino's film about three Pennsylvania boys who are physically and psychologically ravaged by the Vietnam War. He says: "The Deer Hunter was the new kind of movie—three hours of watching torture. [The opening scene] took place in Clairton, Pennsylvania, where all my cousins are from, and in the movie they said it was Russian-Polish, but that was just to make it more something, because it was really Czechoslovakian.

. . . For a whole hour it's the Polish wedding, and they could have cut it, but it was fun—so real and beautiful. It shows a new kind of people in the movies that haven't been shown before, so it's really good" (185). In fact, Warhol recognized his own people. The wedding scene of *The Deer Hunter* was filmed at Saint Theodosius Russian Orthodox Cathedral in Cleveland. Established by a group of Carpatho-Rusyn Byzantine Catholics in 1896, the church became Russianized in language and culture after accepting Orthodoxy, and its Rusyn character was diluted and overlaid with features of Russian culture. The extras in the *The Deer Hunter* wedding scene are locals, who are heard to speak Rusyn during the wedding reception. Warhol undoubtedly identified with this peculiar difficult-to-identify mixed culture, and his sense of a vague, nameless "people from nowhere" is apparent in his comment that the filmmaker presented them as Russian-Polish "just to make it more something." Andy's Rusyn identity can be said to be blurry and imprecise, but not totally lacking.

Warhol was part of an "in-between" generation of American Rusyns who were left without a name for their ethnic identity. In a country of immigrants, all striving to become Americans, it was not easy, especially for a small, uneducated ethnic group, to pass on their ethnonational consciousness. The *Amerikansky Russky Viestnik* regularly railed about the necessity of preserving Rusyn language, culture, and nationality against the pressure of assimilation. However, belonging to a people that had numerous names, but had never had their own country was beyond the capacity of hardworking miners and steel mill workers to comprehend and explain to their American-born children, especially in terms, such as "Uhro-Rusyn" that would have been meaningless to them. According to Julia's oldest son Paul, who practiced Rusyn cultural traditions all his life, he did not know how to name his ethnicity until the American Carpatho-Rusyn Research Center, established in 1978 by a small group of scholars, began to share information about Rusyn history and culture with Americans of Carpatho-Rusyn descent. Zavacky cousins from Warhol's generation referred to themselves as "Russian," although they knew they were not, "because it was a big country everyone knew."[123] The sociocultural-religious history of their parents' generation demonstrates why "Ukrainian" was not an option.

Social Life in *Ruska dolina*

The original Saint John Chrysostom Church on Forward (later Saline) Avenue in *Ruska dolina* was a small wooden structure, dedicated in 1917. It was there that Andy

Warhol was baptized and confirmed.[124] In 1933, a large, steel-and-stone structure was completed at the Depression-era bargain price of $85,000, and the old church building was moved to the adjacent lot by the Kress-Oravetz house-moving company and was used as a social hall. As an aid to the large number of unemployed workers, labor and materials were procured locally.[125] The third largest Greek Catholic parish in the United States at the time, with 450 families and a seating capacity of 850, Saint John Chrysostom nestled into the hillside among trees and shrubbery. Built in the baroque style of Austria-Hungary, the church was patterned on the Rusyn Greek Catholic Cathedral of the Exaltation of the Holy Cross in Subcarpathian Uzhhorod, its twin towers topped by graceful cupolas and the three-barred Eastern-rite cross. The steep outside staircase leading to the second-floor portal, and yet another interior flight of stairs to the entry hall and nave, suggest that the builders believed parishioners would never grow old or infirm. Today, stairlifts convey worshipers to the vestibule.

The large icons in the original iconostasis were created by the Hungarian American artist Stephen Hegedus, originally from Košice, a city about sixty-five miles from Miková. Hegedus specialized in painting Greek Catholic churches throughout Pennsylvania. Smaller icons were done by the Polish-immigrant artist Peter Niemczynski from Galicia. Characterized by naturalism and realism, with perspective and chiaroscuro, the work of these artists bore the influence of western art, which, over the decades, had gained popularity over Carpatho-Rusyn and Byzantine traditions. The original iconostasis has since been renovated, and today, Byzantine-style icons and frescoes adorn the church. While Andy Warhol may have kissed traditional Byzantine-style icons in processions and reverenced gold-backed feast-day icons on the tetrapod before the Royal Doors to the sanctuary, it was the Renaissance-style paintings of Hegedus in the iconostasis that he gazed upon in his childhood. His own portrait work represents a confluence of both. Biographers often exaggerate the number of hours Andy Warhol spent in church as a child. Liturgy was obligatory on Sundays and holy days, with perhaps Wednesday or Friday services during Lent. However, all liturgies were lengthy, and liturgy required the utmost endurance of high-spirited children. Many a young worshiper bore the experience by becoming immersed in the pictorial lessons offered in the paintings of saints and events from biblical history.

For immigrants, life revolved around religion and the church. In Magocsi's words, "The role of religion is so great that in the mind of most immigrants and their descendants, Carpatho-Rusyn culture is virtually synonymous with the Eastern-rite liturgy (originally sung in Church Slavonic) and the attendant

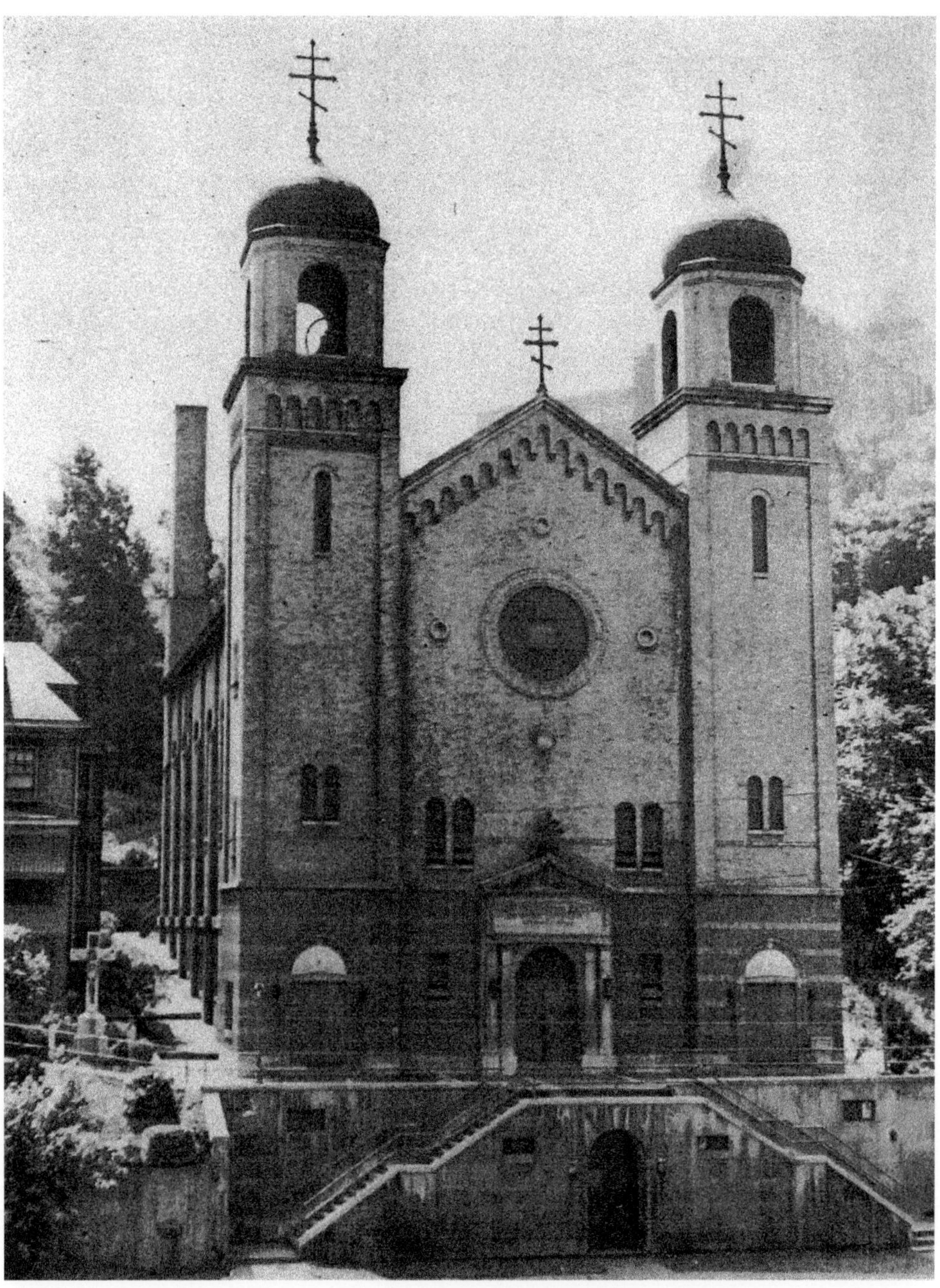

Figure 3.9. Saint John Chrysostom Church in *Ruska dolina*, 1935. The original wooden church was moved to the left and served as a social hall.

rituals and family celebrations (births, marriages, funerals) associated with the church."[126] The Warholas were not movers and shakers at Saint John's. Their names do not appear in the *Amerikansky Russky Viestnik*'s accounts of church activities or in the jubilee books of the parish. Neither do they show up in the *ARV*'s lists of major donors to social causes, delegates to church congresses, officers of clubs, or members of event committees and athletic teams. What Ewa Morawska noted about Johnstown was true as well in Pittsburgh: leadership positions in influential ethnic organizations and church associations circulated among a limited number of people, and "the 'personnel core' of ethnic leadership remained virtually unchanged during the whole interwar period."[127] Leadership was contingent on occupation, education, American political connections, and length of time spent in the United States. As a result, the vast majority of Carpatho-Rusyn immigrants in America were followers, rather than leaders. Still, beyond spiritual guidance, Julia Warhola surely found much that was of interest in the activities of the church.

All the Pittsburgh Greek Catholic churches had excellent choirs. In addition to singing the liturgy at their own church, choirs performed concerts of religious and folk music at other churches in town. Saint John Chrysostom had a well-respected fifty-five-member choir, directed by the cantor-teacher Peter Korpos. In 1935, the *Pittsburgh Sun-Telegraph* sponsored a "huge festival of song" at Forbes Field. For a 25¢ grandstand admission fee, 35,000 music lovers thrilled to performances by 4,000 voices in diverse groups and choirs from all over western Pennsylvania. Governor George Earle attended the event, which was emceed by the radio celebrity Floyd Gibbons and featured the famous American baritone John Charles Thomas as guest star. Choirs from Rusyn, Polish, Russian, Serbian, and Ukrainian churches performed at the jubilee, along with Scottish groups, a 500-voice Negro choir, and the Syria Temple Oriental Band. The front page of the metropolitan section of the June 25 issue of the newspaper announcing the concert featured a photograph of the Saint John Chrysostom Greek Catholic Church choir. Unfortunately, neither here nor in the church jubilee books are we given names of the pictured choir members. It is unknown whether Julia was able to employ her musical talent in an organized choral group at the church, but she undoubtedly sang together informally with family and friends at weddings, picnics, and festivals.

During the 1930s, numerous special interest groups were established under church auspices, primarily for the American-born generation. The Sokol (Rusyn for *falcon*) movement sponsored athletic teams in each GCU lodge, and its members, both men and women, participated in basketball, softball, golf, and bowling competitions with teams from other Greek Catholic churches in western Pennsylvania and beyond. In the late 1930s, *American Russian Sokol*, a regular insert in the *ARV*, reported in English on tournament results. The interests and lifestyles of the first American-born generation of Carpatho-Rusyns took center stage in the newsletter for youth, demonstrating the rapid pace of its American acculturation, but also the tenacity of old religious precepts. At Saint John Chrysostom, a social club for young ladies was called "The Saline Starlets," named for the Saline Street address of the church. A "Sokolette" (Americanized feminine of *sokol*) dubbed "Snoopy Sue" targeted news to young people in her column. "Now that Lent is here and the basketball season is over the Sokolki [Rusyn feminine plural] and Sokols of Ruska Dolina are wondering what to do with themselves.... I guess they crave action; like dancing for instance. No more dancing until after Lent."[128] Written in typical 1930s American teenage argot, columnists indulged in comments on fashion and even local gossip: "It seems to be getting serious with a certain couple seen in church together for two consecutive Fridays. Is the love bug biting Ann D. and Joe H.?"[129] But the young people's publication also included serious articles to reinforce the GCU's ethnonational position, such as "Don't Call a Carpatho-Russian a Slovak or Ukrainian!" and "Carpatho-Russians may be listed as Slavs, but they cannot be classified as Ukrainians, Slovaks, or what have you."[130] News of "grab-bag parties," masquerade dances, and baby showers were set next to columns about "Christian discipline" and the Greek Catholic Union. Bus trips to Scranton and Youngstown for sporting and social events alternated with pilgrimages to the GCU's orphanage, which carried a plenary indulgence from the bishop. Advertisements for local and national products in mixed English and Rusyn, were transliterated in the Latin alphabet, since the younger generation had largely lost Cyrillic: "Iron City Lager—Najlučšoe pivo za 80 rokov" (Iron City Lager—the best beer for 80 years), and "Pepsi-Cola—Bol'sha fl'aska—lučšij vkus" (Pepsi-Cola—Big bottle, best taste).

While the pace of acculturation is notable, the church also sponsored programs to reinforce the Carpatho-Rusyn identity of the American-born generation. Theatrical performances and musical entertainments, acted primarily by young people, opened with singing "The Star-Spangled Banner" and "I Was, Am, and Will Be a Rusyn." At Saint John Chrysostom, the presentations tended to serious, didactic melodramas. In 1934, Aleksander Dukhnovych's classic drama from 1850, *Virtue Is More Important than Riches*, was presented in two showings, a matinee for children and an evening performance for adults. In the play, set in a Rusyn village, the righteous teacher and upright young people manage to prevail over

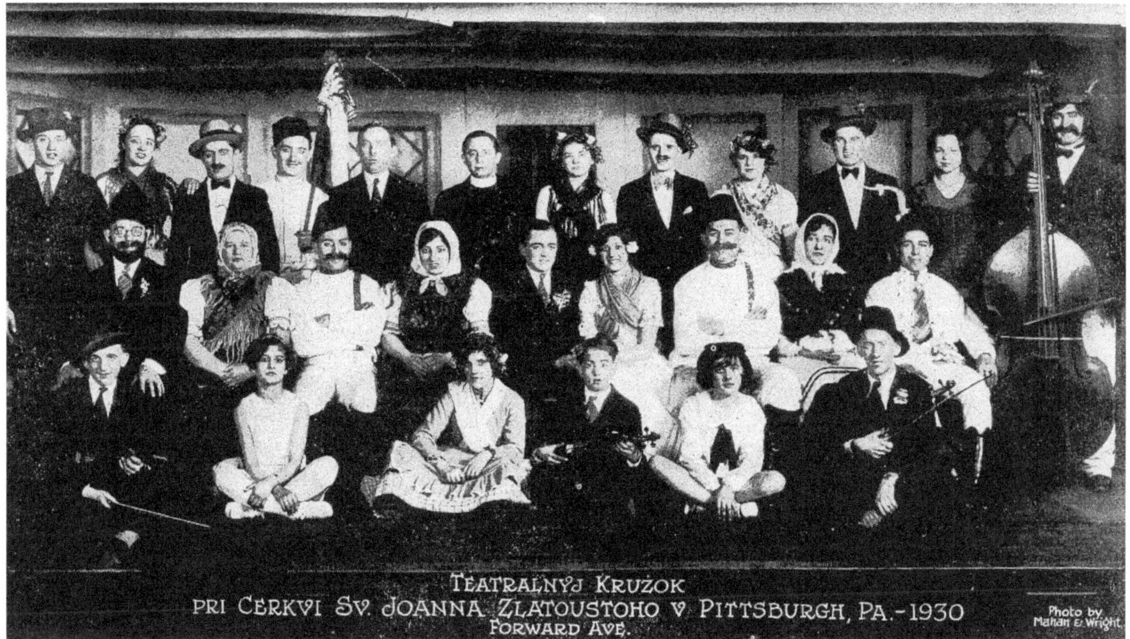

Figure 3.10. Theater circle at Saint John Chrysostom, 1930.

the village villains—the exploitative Jewish tavern keeper, the manipulative sorcerer, and a corrupt mayor—bringing the weak and foolish, but likable, Rusyn "Everyman" to redemption, while his superstitious wife sinks into sin.[131] Despite his nineteenth-century prejudices, the author praises the youth of the play, a new generation of Rusyns, who are open to education and the outside world. Proud to assert their Rusyn identity and unafraid to apply traditional values in the modern world, they are able to attain justice and achieve success in an unjust and intolerant society. Dukhnovych's didactic message was just as relevant for Rusyn Americans in the 1930s as it was in 1850. A reviewer of another of Saint John Chrysostom's dramas wrote: "One must take note that the Forward Avenue [Saline Street] church has been a nest of Rusynness for many years and continues so today. . . . It seems to me that of all our parishes, only the Forward parish can boast of this. Although almost all the actors were born and raised here in America, they spoke their native language as beautifully and purely as though they had only yesterday arrived from the Subcarpathian homeland."[132]

The common image of Carpatho-Rusyns, along with other Slavs, Hungarians, and Lithuanians in industrial America, was that of "hunky," a term that had entirely derogatory implications.[133] Hunkies were stereotyped as hard-drinking, polka-dancing, wife-beating, unskilled laborers, possessed of physical strength, but suffering from mental insufficiency. The term was used as an adjective as well as a noun; "hunky jobs," "hunky bars," and "hunky food" were derided by Americans, as well as by Irish and German immigrants who had preceded the Slavs by just a few decades. As in the Butler newspapers from the first decade of the twentieth century, the distinctly negative stereotype was reinforced by journalists, and by social workers, government officials, law enforcement, and Protestant clergymen. Carpatho-Rusyns, deprived of education and subjected to centuries of linguistic and cultural imperialism, tolerated the insults, which for many, negatively affected their own self-image. The damaging "hunky" image, which was built on the opinions and analysis of outsiders, is contradicted by the congregation of Saint John Chrysostom, with its respect for church art and architecture, its talent for musical performance, its acknowledgment and promotion of classical Carpatho-Rusyn culture, and its young people's adaptation to the American lifestyle, while respecting native traditions. Even more impressive, but little known outside the ethnic community, were the folk dramas and traditions that accompanied religious holidays, which were passed down from the Old Country to the New World and the American generation of Rusyns.

Jaslichkari and *Paska*

The calendar feasts that regulated the agricultural seasons in the Old Country did not have the same salience in industrial Pittsburgh, but the most-significant religious holidays, accompanied by dramatic rituals, continued to punctuate the year.[134] Following pagan rituals of ancestor worship, Christmas Eve was considered a magical time on Carpathian farms, when ordinary acts were considered to have miraculous power. In twentieth-century Pittsburgh, Christian symbolism replaced pagan superstitions, and prayers took the place of incantations in a spiritual celebration of Christ's birth. Children had received gifts—perhaps an apple or an orange—on Saint Nicholas Day, December 19 by the Julian calendar. Christmas Eve on January 6 was celebrated with a traditional meal known as "Sviatyi vechur" or "Holy Supper," which was full of religious symbolism. Straw was placed under a white tablecloth to recall the manger where the infant Jesus was born and the swaddling clothes in which he was wrapped. In the center of the table, a round loaf of bread, once used to divine the success of the harvest and to cure cattle, now symbolized Christ as the Bread of Life. The candle it held represented the star of Bethlehem. Greeting one another with *Christos razhdaetsia!* (Christ is born), "Slavite Yeho!" (Glorify Him!), the family gathered around the table in chairs that were often linked by a chain to ensure family togetherness through the new year. After a whiskey toast, the housewife dipped garlic in honey and made the sign of the cross on the foreheads of all present to ensure health and happiness for the coming year, and to acknowledge that they will experience not only sweetness but also bitterness.

Pittsburgh Rusyns prepared a vegetarian meal of twelve dishes, varying slightly depending on the family's village of origin, composed of what was available to peasants in the Carpathian Mountains in midwinter—sauerkraut, peas from the summer's garden and mushrooms picked in the fall, both dried by the stove. According to Paul Warhola, relatives in Miková sent Julia dried mushrooms from the surrounding forest so she could make an authentic, thick soup known as *machanka*.[135] The main course of the meal consisted of *pirohy*, dumplings stuffed with potatoes or sauerkraut and sautéed in oil, or *bobalky*, balls of dough sweetened with honey, or savory with onion and sauerkraut. Stewed fruit, dried produce from the family's fruit trees, may have been supplemented by home-baked pastry for dessert. No one could leave the table until the candle was snuffed out. In superstitious suspense, everyone watched the smoke. If it swirled toward a young woman, it might foretell a marriage; wafting toward the door meant departure or death; spiraling upward portended well-being for the coming year.

After dinner, the family awaited the arrival of the *jaslichkary*, performers of the "Bethlehem Play," who trudged from hut to hut in the Old Country, and house to house in Pittsburgh's Carpatho-Rusyn neighborhoods, reenacting the story of the birth of Jesus. Dressed in white garments and high cylindrical hats decorated with stars, the men represented angels and shepherds, their staffs bedecked with bells. The miniature Carpatho-Rusyn wooden church they carried symbolized the manger where Christ was born. Entering each neighbor's house, the group proclaimed, "S nami Boh!" (God is with us), and sang the Nativity Troparion: "Your nativity, O Christ our God, / Has shed upon the world the light of knowledge. / For by Your birth those who worshipped the stars / were taught by a star / to worship You, the Sun of Justice, / and to know You as the Orient from on high. / Glory be to You, O Lord."

The European Bethlehem Play derived from western miracle plays, but in eastern Europe, it was popularized in folk culture. To the biblical story were added comedic and parodic characters from everyday peasant life—musicians, Gypsies, Jews, and caricatures of the nobility.[136] Like the wedding drama, it was

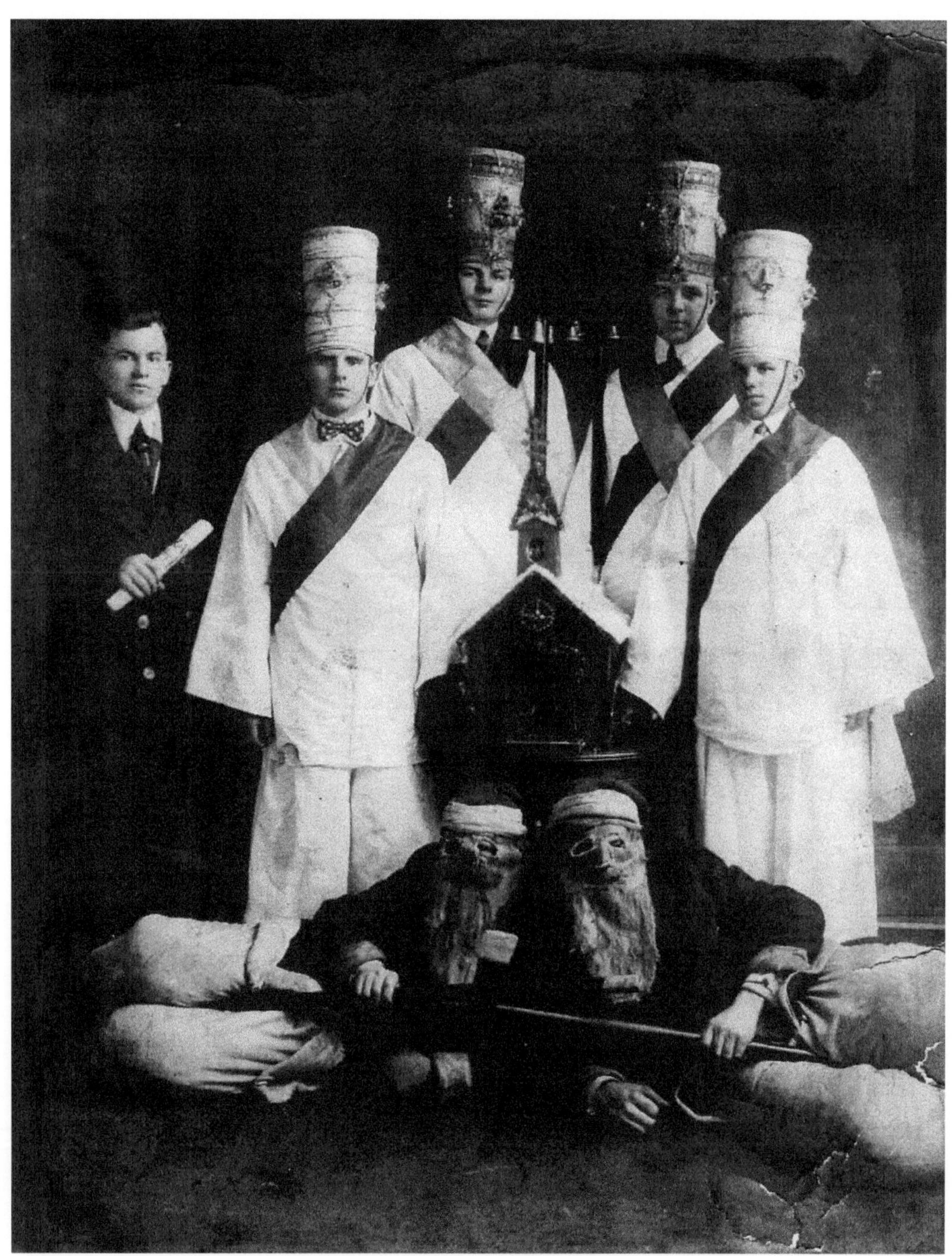

Figure 3.11. *Jaslichkari*. Bethlehem players and carolers.

a theatrical presentation consisting of song, dance, and formulaic speeches, this time performed by men. In twentieth-century America, where the *jaslichkari* were sponsored by the church, the original didactic mien prevailed, as young men told the story of the Nativity, sang traditional Christmas hymns, and offered good wishes to the host in exchange for sweets or drinks. Elements of comedy were retained in a milder form, as the unruly and irrepressible Guba character, named for his sheepskin cloak, cavorted, misbehaved, and threatened the children with his long-handled Carpathian axe, before he was converted to Christ's truth. However, as the men moved through the neighborhood, as libations flowed and spirits rose, the *Vifleemshchiki* (Bethlehemers) became more uninhibited and spontaneous, entertaining their neighbors and satisfying their natural theatrical instinct.

The Christmas season continued until the feast of Theophany on January 19, which commemorated the baptism of Christ in the River Jordan. Churchgoers were given water blessed by the priest to protect their homes throughout the year. Soon after Theophany, the parish priest and cantor made the rounds of parishioners' homes to bless them for the New Year.

Before winter ended, Rusyns celebrated *Fashengy*, a time of exuberant entertainment and indulgence in rich food and excessive drink. Masks and costumes allowed for uninhibited merrymaking, as men dressed as women and vice versa in a ritual suspension of rules and restrictions. Eastern Christians were then eased into Lenten austerity. A week before the beginning of Lent came meatfare Sunday—the last day when eating meat was allowed. Seven days later was cheesefare Sunday—the last day when Byzantine Catholics could eat eggs and dairy products. Lent commenced for Greek Catholics not on Ash Wednesday (ashes are not part of Eastern-rite tradition), but on Monday, the day after cheesefare Sunday, beginning a long forty days of fasting from meat and dairy products until Holy Week, which had even stricter fast requirements. The memoirist Ann Walko recalled: "Eating during Lent was a ritual in itself. Soup every day: lentil, or bean, or potato, thickened with *zaprashka* [a roux of butter and flour]; or *halushki* (dumplings), rolled out the size of a bread board, then torn, cut, crimped, or spooned into boiling water, drained, then mixed with either sautéed cabbage or sauerkraut, and if you were still hungry, in the pantry, always a crock of pickled herrings."[137] During the cold days of Lent, in Pittsburgh as in the Old Country, Sunday liturgies were longer, and enforced abstinence from amusements made the days drearier. Women scrubbed and washed to put the house in order, and in the evening, they designed, waxed, and dyed *pysanky*, using the eggs they could not eat. On Palm Sunday, called "Willow

Sunday" in the Eastern church, branches of pussy willow, the first plant to bud as the weather warmed, were distributed to parishioners in place of palms. The willows were preserved through the year to be burned in the stove for protection when thunderstorms raged.

Solemn and dramatic services during Holy Week focused the worshipper's soul on repentance, redemption, and the forgiveness of sins through the Crucifixion. At Good Friday vespers, the priest and the congregation intoned the story of Christ's suffering and death, as the burial shroud, a life-sized icon of the body of Christ, was processed around the church and laid in a symbolic tomb. Throughout the ceremony, a rhythmic drumbeat or the clack of a clapper, representing Christ's scourging, evoked an eerie, otherworldly atmosphere. The parishioners, young and old, reverenced the Holy Shroud in silent prostration, approaching it on their knees from the back of the church. For children, the dark church, the icons illuminated by candles, the clouds of incense, the hypnotic, incomprehensible, soaring chant, and the atmosphere of mysterious solemnity created incomparable, indelible memories.

After the long fast, Greek Catholics looked forward to *Velykden'*, the Great Day, and the Easter basket, which offered all the delicacies so long forbidden— an egg-rich, cylindrical bread called *paska*, about six inches tall and six inches in diameter, decorated with a cross and braided trim, eggs, ham, *kolbasa* (sausage), a soft cheese called *hrudka*, butter, salt, and horseradish root—a bitter reminder of the Passion of Christ, even on the joyful day of Resurrection. According to Paul Warhola, his parents made and smoked their own *kolbasa*. Julia used a goose feather to coat her *paska* with egg yolk before making the sign of the cross over it. She added a bit of colored crayon to the wax to create resplendent patterns on *pysanky*. Placing the Easter foods in a traditional basket set aside exclusively for this purpose, she covered it with a cloth of embroidered linen, and took it to church to be blessed. Women proudly exhibited their own *pysanky*, and jealously peeked into the baskets of their neighbors, while the priest intoned: "As we partake of them, may we be filled with Your generous gifts and unspeakable goodness."

On Easter morning, liturgy began with a procession three times around the church, ending at the closed front doors. The priest knocked on the door, children rang bells, and all sang the Paschal Troparion: "Christ is risen from the dead, by death He trampled death, and to those in the graves He granted life." Now, instead of "hello" or the Carpatho-Rusyn "Slava Isusu Christu!" (Glory to Jesus Christ), the standard greeting was "Christos voskrese!" (Christ is risen), and the response was "Voistinu voskrese!" (Indeed He is risen). Having prepared themselves during the Great Fast, and after making their Easter confessions, Byzantine Catholics received Holy Communion, which, in the 1930s and 1940s, was customarily a once-a-year event. Julia told the *Esquire* journalist, "Every year before Easter [Andy] go to confession."[138] After the solemnity of Easter, the first day of Bright Week, Easter Monday, was a day of frivolity, when boys in the village doused the girls with water. The next day, roles were reversed. This happy custom survived in the immigration, where no one recalled its original meanings—a tribute to the pagan goddess of fertility, or alternately, a memory of the Jews throwing water on believers to prevent them from spreading the news of the Resurrection of Christ.[139]

Julia Warhola continued these Christmas and Easter traditions in Pittsburgh and later in New York, and she passed them on to her children. Andy sprinkled his house with blessed holy water from Saint Vincent Ferrer Church.[140] In a Time Capsule, he preserved a branch of Palm Sunday pussy willow together with his mother's clothing. John Warhola recalled that in New York, Julia and Andy transported their Easter basket to Saint Mary's Church by taxi. Julia taught her sons to make *pysanky*, and Andy presented them as gifts to agents and art directors in New York. Julia's grandchildren today continue the traditions, creating beautiful works of *pysanky* art. As a matter of course, other traditions of the Old Country were attenuated in the immigration. Holidays that originated in boosting the fecundity of crops, for example, lost their meaning in industrial Pittsburgh. But on Pentecost, known in the Old Country as *Rusalia*, originally a pagan feast to nurture the crops, Carpatho-Rusyns in Oakland decorated their houses with greenery, although few remembered the origin of the custom.

The conventional image of Slavic immigrant workers, established by early sociologists as poor, unskilled, naive, passive, and psychologically downtrodden in industrial America, is today considered inaccurate. Since about 1960, American social and labor historians have found that the immigrants' social and psychological conditions altered in the New World but not significantly. "The immigrants possessed, accumulated, and utilized considerable ethnic resources to advance their welfare. They essentially survived the transfer relatively undisturbed. Old World peasants kept much of their peasant heritage in America's mines, mills, and factories."[141] Rather than viewing the immigrants through the prism of native-born Americans, as "self-sufficient, atomized individuals who simply sought great material success," scholars who take into consideration their goals, their ethnic traditions, and their social resources have seen immigrants as active, energetic, and stable figures in their communities. This is true of the Carpatho-Rusyns, for whom elements of old-world tradition were reinforced by working-class pragmatism within the basic foundational family unit. It is in this context that the Warhola immigrant family struggled, survived and, in relative terms, flourished in early twentieth-century Pittsburgh.

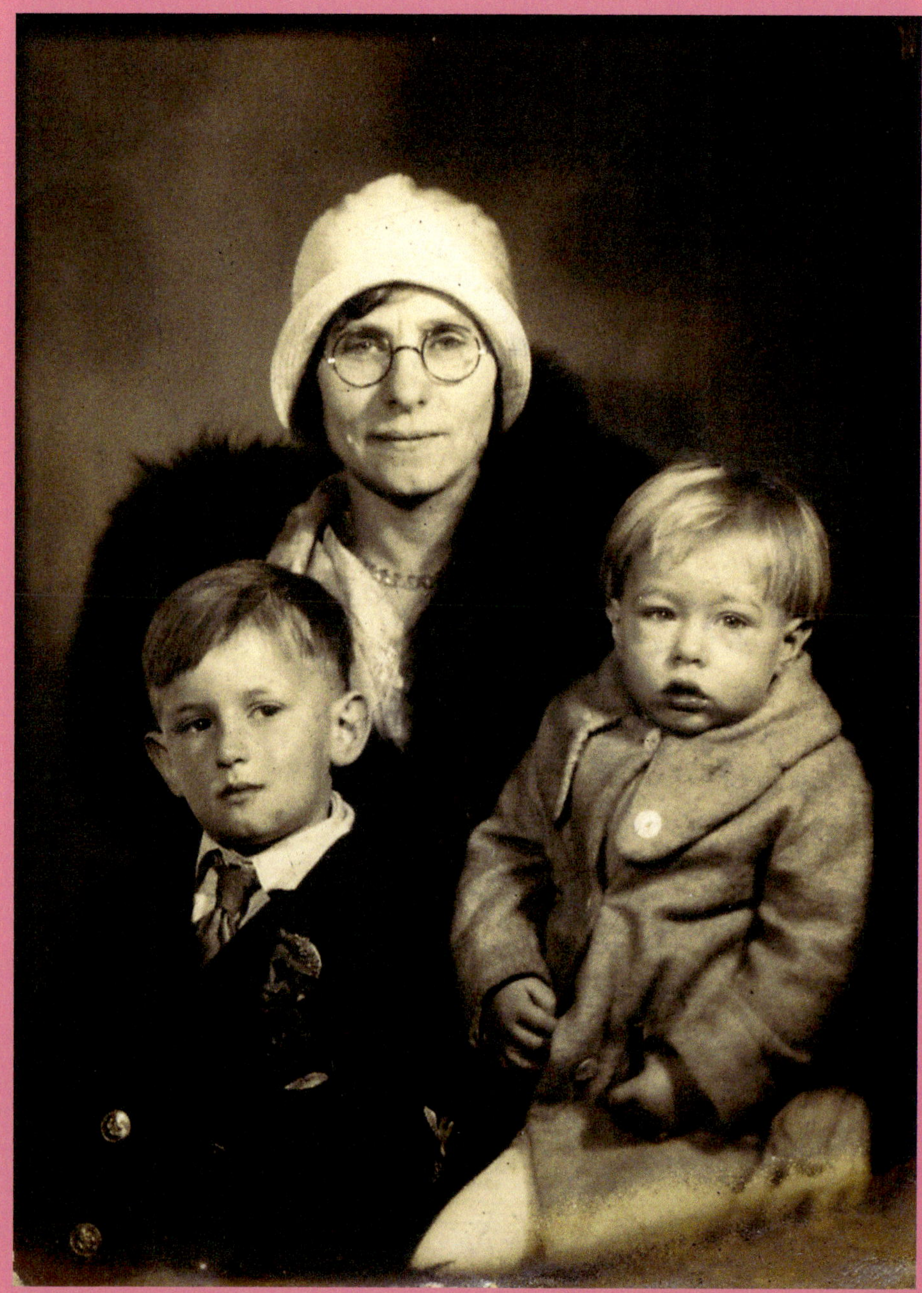

Figure 4.1. Julia, John, and Andy Warhola, 1932.

4

"I Raise My Children Okay"

The *Esquire* interview from November 1966, in which
Julia told the story of her wedding, was part of a larger article by the journalist
Bernard Weinraub, which featured interviews with the mothers of four prominent
names in the news: the White House press secretary Bill Moyers, the Green Bay
Packers running back Paul Hornung, the comedian Jonathan Winters, and the
artist and filmmaker Andy Warhol.[1] The article, titled "Mothers," featured full-
page photographs of the women, each holding a framed picture of her famous son.
The women tell their own stories, revealing diverse backgrounds and distinctive
personalities. Mrs. Moyers, a "sedate, impeccably coiffed" working woman, shares
her parenting philosophy and shows the interviewer complimentary letters about
her son from President Lyndon Johnson. Jonathan Winters's mother is a natural
comedienne, who, during the interview, smokes cigarettes, and quaffs bourbon.
Mrs. Hornung, "her reddish hair . . . piled high atop her head," is a government
worker who shows off her spacious, "spotless" apartment and the color television
that was a gift from her son. Mrs. Warhola is last in the sequence and, in her photograph as well as her story, she stands out markedly from the others. The interviewer
describes her as "a slight grey-haired woman who speaks with animation, throws
her hands excitedly in the air, weeps easily." Her photograph shows a stolid elderly

woman in what must be her Sunday-best hat and flowered dress, her veined, gnarled hand resting on her chin in a pose similar to that of her son in the portrait she holds in her lap.

The interviewer asked each of the mothers the same basic questions, encouraged them to talk freely, and then presented their words as a free-flowing discourse in their own idiosyncratic speech styles. Each woman talks about herself and her background, her parenting philosophy, her son's childhood, achievements, relationships, and their own mother–son bond. In contrast to the interviews with the "elegantly coiffed" and "impeccably dressed" mothers, Julia's account contains no political views, cultural critique, or explicit parenting philosophy—concepts she would not have understood and could not articulate. Whereas the other women compare indulgent and authoritative parenting styles, Julia says simply, "I raise my children okay. . . . Oh, Andy a good boy."[2]

At the beginning of the 1920s, the sociologists William Thomas and Florian Znaniecki traced the subjective experience of Polish immigrants in a groundbreaking study. Their book, *The Polish Peasant in Europe and America*, has been called "the first American work to study ethnicity systematically and to value it positively."[3] Rather than theory and statistics, they based their research on empirical data found in letters, diaries, newspaper accounts, and court documents. Analyzing immigrants' adaptation to social change, Thomas and Znaniecki concluded that "social disorganization" of the individual was inevitable when the social rules of peasant society were weakened in a new environment. But they also saw the promise of social reorganization: "The fundamental process which has been going on during this period is *the formation of a new Polish-American society* out of those fragments separated from Polish society and embedded in American society."[4] That is, in America, immigrants formed new communities, not American, but Polish American, or Rusyn American—novel ethnicities that mixed old-world traditions with American social values. "The new community would perpetuate the family centeredness, the personal solidarity and stress upon conformity of the old village community, but it could never have the same totalizing influence upon life; outside contacts were too numerous, participation too voluntary."[5] This was the effective trajectory of the Warhola family.

Carpatho-Rusyn immigrants interpreted American life through the prism of their preexisting values and convictions. Accordingly, they replicated the conservative, patriarchal family structures they knew in the Old Country, where tradition and local folkways limited choice and constrained everyday life. Their history of oppression in Europe and the discrimination they met in

America left Carpatho-Rusyns with a narrow vision of one's prospects, and most had few aspirations to wealth or success. They valued hard work over education, and religious values over materialist ambitions. At the same time, deep piety was tempered by folk beliefs and cynicism, born of their lived experience. Familial love and parental affection were masked by premodern child-rearing practices. Traditional attitudes toward sexuality and gender roles prevailed, but a matter-of-fact approach to life and the intimacy of peasant existence prevented sanctimonious prudery.

The importance of family solidarity and the cohesion of the group in the Old Country meant that the social psychology of Slavic immigrants was "conformist, routinized, and prescribed," and personality was "stereotyped and rigid."[6] As a result, the first American-born generation's individuation could be difficult. But despite changes of setting and shifts in circumstances, traditional culture adapted slowly, and long-established familial standards persisted. From old-world Miková to modern Pittsburgh and cutting-edge New York, cultural norms, thought patterns, and values proved resilient from one generation to the next. According to Andy's nephew James Warhola, "Andy Warhol had a thoroughly Eastern European childhood immersed in a culture that was less American than most people realize."[7] Even the ultramodern Andy Warhol retained elements of the traditional worldview he absorbed in the Carpatho-Rusyn Warhola family. In a 1975 interview with Warhol, the singer Diana Ross refers to "the president and doctors and people like that" who "think they are God. . . . But they're all just men, they're all just people—same hang-ups, same everything." Warhol responds, "Oh, I know. But it takes a while to learn that. When you learn that about your mother and father then you've really learned everything. They're just people. There's nobody that great. But you do learn from them."[8]

Andrii

"Andy was afraid of Dad. We all were," his brothers recalled. John said, "He was so strict that when you were a kid you'd think that he was a mean father. . . . He'd discipline me and Paul. . . . He'd warn us once and then if we did it again he would pull off his belt, but we ran and hid under the bed. He never hit us but the threat was just like a beating."[9] It would be unusual, however, if there was no corporal punishment in the household. John later told his sons about being cracked on the head with one of his father's wooden household utensils, and he described how Andrii's facial scar turned crimson when he was angry.[10] Julia advocated a modified form of corporal punishment. "Mother was very critical of anybody that would even hit a child in the head or the back. She always thought if you had to punish somebody whack them in the ass."[11] Thomas and Znaniecki explain, "In all the relations between parents and children the familial organization leaves no place for merely personal affection. Certainly this affection exists, but it cannot express itself in socially sanctioned acts. The behavior of the parents toward the children and the contrary must be determined exclusively by their situations as family members, not by individual merits or preferences."[12] In the immigration, affection was expressed by the father through his work and protection, and by children, through their respect and obedience.

The Carpatho-Rusyn family, in Pittsburgh as in Miková, was authoritarian and father-centered. Looking back as adults, John and Paul understood: "Dad didn't like us starting a commotion, because he was so exhausted and he would get emotionally upset. Mother used to say he worked hard."[13] In every immigrant family, the father was respected for the backbreaking manual labor he performed to support his wife and children, who showed him special deference. Immigrant fathers were typically even more distant from their children than American working-class fathers of the time, who hardly practiced intimate parenting styles. "If sons had any image of their father it included manual work as an inevitable aspect of life," an exigency for survival.[14] The ever-present fear of unemployment or incapacitating injury flooded the consciousness of the entire family. In addition, Andrii's arduous and unsteady work as a house mover for Eichleay required regular stints away from the family. While the children dreaded his ire at home, they sympathized with him and missed him when he was away. His longest stay at a work site, according to John, was six months. "When you're a kid, six months felt like six years." When the entire Warhola family slept in the attic of the Dawson Street house to provide space and comfort for their lodgers, Andrii lay on a mattress on the floor. After a night in the sweltering attic, John remembered, "I felt sorry for Dad when he had to get up early to go to work."

When work was slow during the Depression, Andrii busied himself with household tasks at their new house. He showed John how to paint the gutters and seal the joints with tar, and he taught him to putty the windows. He scraped, sanded, and varnished the floors to make them look like new. He was also a barber to his sons and neighbors. "I remember they didn't have electric clippers, just the hand clippers, and when he put that on my neck, I start crying because it was real cold," said John. Andrii's tools included cobbler's cast-iron forms in various sizes that he used to repair the family's shoes. "Sometimes he'd buy a piece of leather to replace soles on our good shoes, the ones that we'd wear to church," remembered John Warhola.[15] For everyday footwear, cut-up rubber tires were good enough. Early photographs show thick rubber soles on the young boys' shoes. The Andy Warhol Museum exhibits the wooden household utensils Andrii fashioned for Julia's use. A potato masher and spoon, a cabbage shredder, a heavy wooden bread board, and a large mixing bowl were Andrii's contributions to family meals.

Andrii was frugal to a fault. John remembered how, on the way home from the store with a quart of milk that cost "six or seven cents," he dropped the glass bottle. "My mother just told me to be more careful next time. But I was glad my dad wasn't home." Even Julia's sister Mary, who was no better off financially than the Warholas, told her, "Don't be so tight. Put on the lights!"[16] According to Paul, Joseph Warhola resented his brother for his frugality. "They used to ridicule him because he had the money to fall back on. His brother always brought it up. He said, 'You're loaded and you're cheap!'"[17] Desserts were uncommon in the Warhola house, which was as much a matter of discipline as an act of frugality. "If you're still hungry, rye bread with butter is better for you," Andrii told his sons. "But," said John, "he made sure that we had enough to eat and that it was good."

Andrii had become head of his Miková family at the age of ten, and Julia cared for her younger siblings and tended cows from the age of seven. They incorporated their own old-country experience in their expectations for their American children, counting on them to contribute to the support of the family collective. The mark of successful progeny was their work ethic and their respect and care for parents. This idea was reinforced in time-honored folk songs and Rusyn-American immigrant literature, where the keys to success were hard work, modesty, and temperance.[18] For immigrant parents, their children's collaboration in supporting the family was a matter of pride, "because, in peasant thinking, judgments upon the group as a whole are constantly made on the basis of the behavior of members of the family, and vice versa."[19]

In Pittsburgh, the Warhola children peddled papers, sold cardboard for scrap, shoveled snow, and carried ashes to the dump to earn a few pennies, which were most often turned over to the family funds.[20] Poverty prompted industry, and business acumen ran in the family. The boys collected old bottles, prized by moonshiners during Prohibition. Just as his mother had assisted her Jewish neighbors in Miková, Paul played Shabbos goy for observant Jews on Dawson Street, for whom certain activities were prohibited on the Sabbath. When he was thirteen, John sold papers at Forbes Field, the Oakland home of the Pittsburgh Pirates.[21] Before Saturday football games, John and Paul bought a ten-pound bag of peanuts for 90¢, repackaged the nuts in small bags, and sold them at a profit. Paul, a natural entrepreneur, had his own regular customers and a group of kids working for him. He paid $200 to use a resident's front porch as a salesroom for the season. "We sold peanuts, pennants, pins, these beautiful gold mums. And of course, I'd scalp tickets and high school coaches always had extra tickets. I'd give 'em $1, sell for $2."[22] Paul's luck ran out at the first football game of the 1943 season, when Pitt was crushed by Notre Dame, 41–0. "Tickets selling at $3.30 went begging for practically any price. . . . Some speculators offered such tickets for as low as 75 cents." Oakland police arrested four alleged scalpers, including Paul Warhola, age twenty-one, of 3252 Dawson Street. They were released on a $15 forfeit for a hearing in Oakland Police Court.[23]

John undertook a less hazardous venture. In the late 1930s, Andrii converted the root cellar he had dug out under the porch to a darkroom, where John and his cousin, Johnny Preksta, ran a photography business. Preksta worked in the darkroom, his sisters were colorists and assistants, and John joined them after school. John believed that this primitive photo business inspired Andy's use of the automatic photobooth for his portraits of the 1960s.

When the boys were growing up and money was tight, their father's frugality meant that they had to depend on themselves, or sometimes their mother, for things their father considered inessential. Even routine medical and dental expenses were not an option for most Slavic immigrant families. John used some of the money he saved for dental work, "because [my father] couldn't afford to send me to the dentist."[24] Even toothbrushes were unfamiliar to peasants from Miková who grew up in Pittsburgh and Lyndora with outhouses instead of bathrooms. According to Andy's cousin Nora Zavacky, Andy Warhol had dentures from a young age.[25] Zavacky's statement has not been verified, but Warhol showed a significant creative interest in false teeth and amassed a substantial collection of dental models.[26]

"We never got toys for Christmas," remembered Paul. "Mostly it was something to eat, fruit or nuts, and some small change."[27] John was a saver from an early age, squirreling away his earnings behind the family radio. At fourteen he spent $27, a fortune for a young boy at the time, for a red bike, keeping it shiny and clean in the front room of the house. He later sold it for $14, recouping some of his extravagance.[28] Andy had roller skates, but what he really wanted for Christmas was a projector. The most wished-for, cutting-edge Christmas gift of the early 1930s, according to advertisements, was a Kodatoy movie projector. "He's a lucky lad who gets Kodatoy for Christmas!" announced an ad in *Boy's Life*. "What a whale of a time you'd have with Kodatoy—the movie projector made for boys!" Another projector made by Keystone Manufacturing Company had the same target audience: "Big

Fun for Boys—Real Enjoyment for Everybody." To fulfill Andy's wish, Julia found part-time work doing housecleaning and laundry. According to John, she saved $9 and bought, without Andrii's knowledge, the projector that sparked her son's lifelong interest in film.[29]

Carpatho-Rusyns were unstinting in support of their Greek Catholic churches. In addition to adding to the collection basket, families paid yearly dues. Impressive brick houses of worship topped with gilded domes, their interiors adorned with brightly muraled walls and stained-glass windows, stood amid dingy clubs, seedy bars, and the shoddy homes of workers. The splendor of their churches compensated for numerous deficiencies in their own homes, and a beautiful church was a point of pride for parishioners. In *Ruska dolina*, a new building for Saint John Chrysostom Church was going up in 1933. The chairman of the building committee attributed construction to the sensible and progressive parishioners, who had long been supporting the church and wisely husbanding its funds. "There are not many such churches in America where the treasury is full and there is money in the bank."[30] Saint John's was flush with more than $60,000, almost enough to cover the cost of the building. Today, the stained-glass windows bear the names of individual contributors and supporting organizations.

A more direct form of charity for the Warholas was Julia's support of her family in Europe. She saved spare pennies, nickels, and dimes to purchase necessities and send them to Miková. Paul Warhola: "I remember how as a boy of six and seven I used to sell newspapers on the tram. Sometimes I came home with twenty-five, thirty cents in my pocket and mother would put it away and then ask me, 'Paul, what are you going to do with this money? You'd better send it over the ocean to my sisters. They need it very much.' . . . Everything I earned mother would send to the sisters."[31] Letters from Julia's sisters express gratitude for the gift of a single dollar, but Andrii was reportedly unhappy about Julia's beneficence to her family. "One day when a letter was returned in the mail and he found a dollar in it he got furious."[32] In the 1920s, Andrii had sent Julia's sisters and her brother remittances, which are documented by receipts, but in the middle of the Depression, he may not have felt so generous. Julia continued sending donations, clothing, and household items to her sisters through the 1960s.

Andrii was not without a sense of charity, but it was guarded and circumspect. John's wife Marge recalled a telling incident:

> He says they didn't have loan companies back then and when they came from Europe
> they used to borrow from one countryman to the other to buy a house. So they come

up to Andy's father and they would ask him to borrow some money and he would say, "What did you do with yours?" He knew this man drank. He says, "Well, I spent mine." He says "Oh, you spent yours. Now you want to spend mine," and he wouldn't give it to him. But, he said, if it was a person who he really knew was watching his money he would lend them money.[33]

Another story, or perhaps a different version of the same occurrence, is told by Paul Warhola:

He was thrifty, but he wasn't ungenerous and could even be gullible. I remember how one day in the days of the economic crisis a strange man spoke to us in the city. He had a handlebar mustache and ragged clothes. He claimed he was a miner who had lost his job. He was weeping and asking for help. Father gave him his coat, but later we saw the same man selling the donated coat in the market under the bridge. Dad was terribly angry. He had a fight with the man and took the coat back. It upset him to know he could have been conned so easily.[34]

"Z Bohom" (Go with God)

Four preserved letters written by Andrii to Julia in 1941, not previously translated, give us a rare firsthand look at the man and his feelings for family.[35] By 1941, wartime expansion had increased Eichleay's business, and Andrii was working on a project to move two United Aircraft Corporation hangars to accommodate a new Pratt & Whitney plant in Hartford, Connecticut. Andrii's first two letters are written on letterhead stationery of New Dom, a "modern and up to date" downtown hotel that was popular with "commercial travelers." The hotel may have seemed welcoming to Andrii and his Slavic coworkers, since "dom" is the Slavic word for "house" and "home."[36] But on March 15, Andrii wrote to his wife, "I cannot get used to anything in the restaurant here," and he hoped to move with his coworkers to more independent and less expensive housing. A week later, he notified Julia of his new address, apparently an apartment or lodging house.

The letters are written in a neat, refined penmanship, using an adapted Slovak-Latin transliteration of Cyrillic that featured a confused blend of alphabets. Like all the correspondence to and from Julia Warhola, they testify to the low level of their authors' schooling, and they are difficult to decipher. Andrii writes phonetically, not recognizing lexical segments or sentence boundaries, interspersing English words, and forgoing capitalization and punctuation entirely.[37] For example, he writes *nakari*, using and misspelling the English word for "car" and combining it with a Rusyn preposition and case ending to mean "in a car." *Taustinemam sto take pišati* is "and I have nothing more to write you" (*ta už ti ne mam što take pisati*). But formal matters aside, his thoughts and feelings come through clearly.

Much of the content refers to money matters. In the March 15 letter, he references an enclosed money order for $15, promises more money to come, and grumbles about a $35 expense incurred in Hartford. He asks Julia whether "those people" have given her the rent money. Aware that she will need money for household necessities, he gives her detailed instructions: "I will write what you need to do. Go to Farmer [*sic*] bank, withdraw one hundred dollars, and in two weeks you can take out another hundred. The books are in the little trunk. Put a padlock on it so no one gets into it." He tells her to buy herself some fabric before the price goes up, as well as shoes for the family. "It will be expensive, but buy yourself shoes [*shusi*, English], and also for John and Andy, but buy one size larger." Frugality demanded that the children "grow into" their shoes.

These letters give us important information about the Warholas' finances. The family was not destitute, at least not in the late 1930s. According to the 1940 census, their income from 1939 was $1,200 for forty weeks of work. This put them among the better-off households on Dawson Street. The annual income of most steel mill laborers, including Andrii's brother, was $1,200; a few skilled mill workers earned $1,500 to $2,300. But most respondents on Dawson Street worked fewer hours and earned less in wages, and in many cases, considerably less. Among the relatively few who cited higher earnings were a carpenter ($1,500), a grocery store manager ($1,800), a tailor who owned his shop ($2,080), an insurance agent ($2,700), and a railroad conductor ($5,000). For context, according to the United States Bureau of Labor Statistics, in 1939 the median salary of Pittsburgh elementary school teachers was $2,243.[38] As for purchasing power, the Warholas' electric bill from Duquesne Light Company for November–December 1938 was $3.04.[39] The Warholas were not wealthy, but it surely was not every working-class family that could withdraw $200 from their savings account within two weeks' time, as Andrii instructed Julia to do. Their relatively comfortable economic status, by standards of time and place, must be attributed to their frugality and abstemious lifestyle. The family lived within their means, doing without conveniences and luxuries they might have stretched to afford. Instead, Andrii put his hard-earned money aside in anticipation of a rainy day, or in hope of a better future.

Another repeated subject in the letters is health, with many thanks to God for continued well-being. Andrii reports that he has a tooth that needs to be extracted.

He had a bad cold and fever, but thank God, it passed and he recovered. There is no hint in the letters of the illness that will result in Andrii's death just one year later. He expresses concern and affection for the children, who were then eighteen, fifteen, and twelve years old, relaxing his customary frugality to accommodate a child's winter cold. "You wrote that Johnny was very sick and had a fever. Let him go to school in a [street]car, because the weather is very bad now." Paul, who had by then left high school, was a cause for parental concern. "You write that again Paul is not going to work." Andrii hopes that he "will behave better." He expresses anxiety about whether the family will have enough coal to last the winter. Finally, he closes his letter with greetings and wishes for the family's health, using a folksy Rusyn formula that defies exact translation. "I send greetings to you, my dear wife Ulia, to Paul, John, and Andy, *bars krasno na mnohokrat raz*" (very sincerely and many, many times). He tells them to take care of their health, ending with the Rusyn farewell, *Z Bohom* (Go with God) and four *x*'s, symbols for kisses, presumably one for Julia and each of the boys. The final preserved letter from May 29 ends with a pseudo-English greeting, "Gud by *xxxx*."

A note of tenderness and deep affection resonates through the mundane concerns about weather, work, and money. In a short letter from March 22, the purpose of which was to notify Julia of his new address, Andrii repeats the phrase, "my dear wife Ulia," five times, in the common, respectful style of Rusyn-language correspondence. The following is a loose translation of the note in its entirety, with punctuation added for easier comprehension.

> My dear wife Ulia, I got your letter and I understood everything well. I thank God, my dear wife Ulia, that I am healthy. The work here will be long. Today, Saturday, is a sunny day. I hope you got the check, as I had to move. I have nothing more to write you except to say watch the children and help with their affairs. I'm sending you a money order, my dear wife Ulia, for thirty dollars. I have nothing more to write, my dear wife Ulia, except to send many sincere and heartfelt greetings to all of you there—my dear wife Ulia, Paul, John, Andy.

"My father was not a very emotional or talkative man," said John Warhola, who could not remember him speaking with the children very much when they were young.[40] Slavic men were characteristically taciturn and gruff with their children, a behavior that, on top of the strict parenting conventions of the time, was attributed to overwork and exhaustion. But Andrii's affectionate style here and his involvement in the everyday affairs of his wife and children, even from a distance, shows a sensitive side of his character.

Andrii and Andy

Andy Warhol talked very little about his father. According to Joseph Giordano, who spent a good deal of time with Andy and Julia in the 1960s, "His father was never mentioned at all," and Nathan Gluck, another early assistant of Warhol's and a confidante of Julia's, echoed that remark.[41] In his writings and interviews, Warhol's rare comments about Andrii are highly unreliable. In a few pages of the partly ghostwritten *Philosophy of Andy Warhol*, which is packed with deliberate untruths, he says, "My father was away a lot on business trips to the coal mines, so I never saw him much."[42] Spurious statements about his father dot a pseudo-interview with his associate Gerard Malanga, in which Andy capriciously describes how he would change his film *Chelsea Girls* if he set it in the South. "As the fat pill pusher and dope addict I would probably use my father. . . . If it weren't for the colored people in the South, my father's refrigerator factory would close down."[43] It is unclear whether this fabrication was generated by Warhol or Malanga, but it had no basis in reality.

John Warhola noted, "If there was any outstanding thing that affected Andy during his childhood more than anything else I think it was when my dad passed away."[44] Indeed, for Andy, his father evoked associations with death, stemming from the trauma he felt at almost fourteen years of age, when Andrii's dead body was laid out in the family home, as was customary at the time. In his eight-hundred-page *Diaries*, Warhol mentions his father only twice—first, in an irritated reference to an interviewer who inaccurately reported, "Father died in coal mines" (389), and second, in reference to an unwelcome reminder of the anniversary of his father's death (500). Warhol's refusal to engage with the memory and image of his father has evoked idiosyncratic analysis. Biographers describe Andrii as a distant parent and a strict disciplinarian, who, in death, left a painful legacy for his youngest son. Wayne Koestenbaum suggests that in Warhol's film *Sleep*, five hours of footage of his then boyfriend sleeping, Andy reenacts the encounter with his father's corpse as erotic play.[45] Kelly Cresap, another scholar from the gay community, views Andy's attraction to Jed Johnson, "a straight-looking man," as "a sign of longing for his father—or at least *a* father, if not the remote disciplinarian he grew up with and came to fear from an early age. What [Andrii] left behind to his youngest son was a composite legacy—thirteen years of strict behavior and physical intimidation, followed by the three-day trauma of a corpse in the house, and then permanent absence, except in the form of financial provision."[46] Commentators have filled in the previously sketchy portrait of Andrii Warhola with questionable psychologizing, suspect interpretations, and ignorance of Carpatho-Rusyn customs and immigrant life. The New Dom letters, along with Andrii's forethought and provision for Andy's education, are the only empirical facts we have about his family feelings, and in the Carpatho-Rusyn context, they tell a much more positive story.

There is no question about the influence Andrii had on his youngest son, who, whether intentionally or not, echoed his father's words and emulated his actions. Andy Warhol's attitude toward work is legendary: "I like working better than relaxing"; "I like work and work is what I do—a lot."[47] His associates corroborated his statements. The Factory photographer Stephen Shore said, "Warhol worked as hard as anyone I have ever encountered," and Christopher Makos recognized the origin of his work ethic: "Warhol worked seven days a week. It was part of his working class Eastern European background. . . . Andy used to paint even on Christmas Eve."[48] In his *Philosophy*, Warhol expressed respect for manual labor, extolling "the people who do the wonderful job of keeping the toilets clean," and he voiced his own embarrassment at the service of maids: "It really has to do with how you're raised. . . . I'm truly embarrassed at the idea of somebody cleaning up after me."[49] His diarist, Pat Hackett, recalls Andy's meeting with Joan Crawford at the Rainbow Room atop Rockefeller Center. "Andy loved Joan because she was a big star who still believed in working hard and not becoming spoiled. She was never above getting down on her hands and knees and scrubbing the floor herself. Andy loved stars who were hands-on."[50] In his *Diaries*, Warhol recalled a conversation with the president of US Steel, in which he suggested, "What you should do is put one of the unused buildings to use and make it into a Disney World and give tours and charge people $10 to get a little coal on their faces and see the hot lava being poured."[51] Warhol's years growing up around the mines and steelworks had instilled in him something of the working man's mentality. According to Sterling Morrison of the Velvet Underground, Andy knew a lot about iron and heavy engineering. And he saw his own work as no different from that of the common laborer. "Why do people think artists are special? It's just another job."[52] He objected to Bianca Jagger's depiction of his Pittsburgh upbringing in a book she was doing on great men. "She went on and on about how I broke the system, broke the system, broke the system, and I felt like saying, 'Look, Bianca, I'm just here. I'm just a working person. How did I break the system?' God, she's dumb."[53]

But as much as Warhol "liked" work, he accepted it as a fact of life with a kind of fatalism inherited from his peasant ancestors. In Warhol's constant refrains, "Life isn't easy" and "I've got a lot of mouths to feed, I've gotta bring home the bacon," one can hear the voice of his father.[54] Playing the parent role to his Factory followers, Andy complained, "I can never stop painting because I have to pay all the kids' bills."[55] Warhol worried about "paying the bills, paying the IRS, paying the kids at the office."[56] Complaining about the cost of his boyfriend Jed Johnson's decorating of his new home, he said, "All I do is pay the bills around here." From an adult perspective, he recognized emotional implications that he may have missed as a child: "That's what I call love, when someone pays the bill for you now and then."[57]

Andy learned both frugality and firmness from his father. John accompanied his brother in New York to pick up some promotional material he had ordered.

> He told the printer, "This isn't what I told you to do." And he says, "Well, I thought you wanted it this way," and Andy says, "Well, no, you didn't listen to me." The way Andy stood up to him just reminded me of my father. . . . And the guy says, "Jeez, I'm going to lose money on this." Andy says, "Well, next time you'll listen. You didn't do what I told you. Now I'm going to have to wait and have that all done over again." My father was that way. Even though he wasn't built like Dad, Andy was tough.[58]

Warhol's fastidiousness was backed by economy to the point of parsimony. In his *Philosophy*, he said, "My conscience won't let me throw anything out, even when I don't want it for myself."[59] The result was a house crammed with goods he had purchased at antique stores and flea markets, ranging from furniture, fine art, and jewelry to cookie jars, plastic Fred Flintstone wristwatches, and wooden toilet seats. Much of it was unwrapped, still in shopping bags, indicating a compulsion to accumulate items that had little value or actual appeal. After his death, the evidence of more than thirty years of obsessive collecting shocked "even the most jaded Sotheby's employees," and the ten-day auction generated $25.3 million.[60] Although Andy's collecting was on a higher artistic level, his Carpatho-Rusyn ancestors, who would never discard a spare nail or piece of string, would have identified with his obsession for property and the security it signified.

Andy's relationship with money was rooted in old-country habits. He dodged mortgages, paying $310,000 outright in 1974 for his East 66th Street town house. Bob Colacello says he did not use credit cards.[61] According to Warhol's business partner Vincent Fremont, "He didn't want his name on his checks. He felt someone could take one of his checks, run to the bank and steal his money."[62] His cautionary suspicion recalls Andrii's instruction to Julia about padlocking their money box. Joseph Giordano said, "Andy could see through people. . . . He was very, very chary about certain things. . . . He could pick up checks, but I've seen people trying to take advantage of Andy, and he cut them off immediately. No matter who they were, what they did or what their desires were. Just like that . . . if he felt that he was being taken advantage of."[63] Like Andrii, Warhol was accused of being cheap. He dickered with antique dealers, and around the Factory at holiday season, his nickname was "Scrooge."[64] On the other hand, he was often generous, but like his father's charity, his benevolence was practical. "Andy ran a tab at Max's Kansas City [restaurant]. He would pay for any artist or person that he thought needed to eat. But he wouldn't give them cash—he gave them food."[65]

It must be noted, however, that despite all his talk about "bringing home the bacon" and his put-on "workingman's sensibility," Andy learned quickly to enjoy his newfound wealth. Blake Gopnik's extensive research into Warhol's spending in the 1950s shows striking extravagance on furnishings, antiques, and clothing as soon as he started making money. Even so, while he bought his clothes at Brooks Brothers, "he always looked bedraggled; always had his tie lopsided, as if he didn't have time to tie it, and he never tied his shoe laces, and he even wore different colored socks. . . . He bought the stereotypical Brooks Brothers business suit, but when he wore it, it was all askew." While it may have made people think he dressed "like a hick from Pennsylvania," "it was calculated, and charming."[66] He bought expensive shoes, "but before wearing them, he would spill paint on them, soak them in water, let the cat pee on them. He wanted to appear shabby, like a prince who could afford expensive shoes but couldn't care less and treated them as worthless."[67]

In fact, Warhol played down and hid many extravagances throughout his life. He shopped for expensive jewelry with his friend Suzie Frankfurt, who recalled after his death, "I never saw him wear a single jewel until one night at Studio 54. I saw a slight bulge under his Brooks Brothers shirt which turned out to be a rather grand emerald necklace, so I suppose he occasionally wore them in secret."[68] Gopnik attributes Warhol's affectations of poverty to his faith in the bohemian habits of the artistic vanguard.[69] From another perspective, one might presume that as much as Warhol enjoyed flying the Concorde, dining at the Palm Court, and buying expensive art, he may have retained a vestige of the mindset that characterized his impoverished background. He confided to Frankfurt that he felt guilty about his distinction from his brothers. "I make more in two minutes than they make in a year."[70] And in an unpublished diary entry, he said it was "so sick" that rich people could spend $5,000 on sheets.[71] Given his Gatsby-like self-mythologizing, this conflict rarely came to the surface in public, but as for so many children of poverty who come into wealth, it must have occasionally pricked his conscience.

"He's Going to College"

When Andrii's illness worsened in 1942, he took his son John aside. "'I'm going into hospital tomorrow and I'm not coming out.' He felt bad. It wasn't that he was crying or nothing, he just talked real sad." Andrii told John that he had saved enough in postal bonds to pay for Andy's first two years of college. "'You're going to be real proud of him, he's going to be highly educated, he's going to college. . . . Make sure you do that. Make sure the money isn't spent in any other way.'"[72] While this may seem a commonplace concern of a dying parent, in the context of Rusyn immigrant life, it points up the singularity of Andrii's directive.

Slavic immigrants typically attached little importance to formal education. Work, a value in and of itself, led to property ownership and family security, which were considered more precious than schooling. Ewa Morawska's study of Slavic immigrants in Johnstown found: "The fulfillment of the primary, and realizable, goal of the immigrant families—to accumulate the maximum possible amount of financial and material resources—required . . . a combined effort of all employable members. Keeping children at school for a prolonged period of time not only did not bring visible rewards in terms of economic success; in fact, it significantly decreased, if not annihilated, the family's choice to accomplish this dominant purpose."[73] In 1930s Pittsburgh, school attendance of Black Americans exceeded that of foreign-born and second-generation children.[74] In the didactic and melodramatic Rusyn-American immigrant literature, where characters thrive on moral virtue alone, one cannot help but notice the lack of attention given to education as a practical means of getting ahead, especially in comparison with the American Horatio Alger stories from the popular dime novels of the time.[75] Even reading books was discouraged in many Rusyn immigrant homes. The memoirist Ann Walko recalls that her mother threw a book she had forgotten to hide into the fire, because "only a lazy girl reads books."[76] "The Child Who Reads Too Much," an article in *Svit ditej* (Children's world), a publication of the Greek Catholic Union for families and children, points to the putative health risks of reading for fun and offers suggestions for outdoor occupations to "cure" children's attraction to fairy tales and adventure stories.[77]

Most children of Slavic immigrants expected no more than to follow their fathers into the mills, perhaps in a more stable position. A study of intergenerational mobility among Slavic Americans found that between 1920 and 1940, fewer than one in four sons was able to attain an occupational status above his father's.[78] In many families, it was only the youngest child who might achieve a practical skill or trade, as a result of the work and concentrated financial resources of the rest of the family. Paul had left high school for a job at the Homestead works of US Steel before his father's death, bringing home a salary that enabled his mother to buy dining room furniture and a refrigerator.[79] In May 1943, he married Anna Lemak, and then served in the US Navy from July 1944 to December 1945. After a summer huckstering produce, Paul bought and sold scrap metal. "It turned out you could make a nice living with it," and he went into the scrap metal business full time.[80] John Warhola attended Connelley Trade School and became a machinist and then a parts clerk for Sears appliances.[81] He married Margaret Dancisin in 1952. Both sons modestly exceeded their father's occupational station, and they achieved tolerable success in the lifeworld of second-generation Rusyn-Americans.

When asked if he knew that his brother Andy was a genius, Paul answered, "Jeez, we were just glad he didn't end up laboring in the steel mills."[82] How did Andrii Warhola, who could have had little familiarity with higher education, even envision the possibility of his then thirteen-year-old son going to college? "That surprised us. Dad never talked about school," said John.[83] The $1,500 he had saved in postal bonds was a fortune, especially given an annual income of $1,200 at best. Many conveniences that would have made life easier for the family, not to mention luxuries and indulgences, must have been neglected in favor of an abstract future benefit for his youngest son. Biographers who stress the mockery Warhol allegedly received from his family fail to appreciate the enormous significance of Andrii's bequest and the pride and affection it represented.

In the literature, Julia gets all the credit for encouraging Andy's art, but perhaps Andrii also recognized art as a viable career for his youngest son. In a throwaway comment in *Warhol: The Biography*, Victor Bockris enigmatically relates Julia's reaction to Andy's decision to go to New York. "Julia warned him that if he went to New York, he would end up dead in the gutter without a penny in his pocket like Bogdansky, a Ruthenian artist whom his father had once tried to help. She repeated the name Bogdansky as if it were a religious portent every time Andy brought up the subject."[84] A bit of research reveals that Zygmunt Bogdański (1877–1968) was from a large family of Polish artists, who were famous for painting churches on the northern and southern slopes of the Carpathian Mountains since the mid-nineteenth century. In 1911, Bogdańksi, his wife Zofia, and his cousin Feliks came to America and opened a studio in Newark, New Jersey. A photograph shows the artists working at their easels, with an American flag and a Cornell University pennant in the background. According to a Polish biography, "They achieved considerable success, not only financially, but also artistically, creating numerous paintings in American churches."[85] No American church paintings by the Bogdańskis are easily identifiable, but Zygmunt's draft-registration card from 1918 shows him living with his wife in a new apartment building in the Yorkville area of New York City, which suggests at least some level of success.

At some point, the Bogdański artists made their way to Pittsburgh. In 1919, Feliks painted an allegorical feminine personification of "Poland Reborn" for what was then the Polish House of Culture. The artists' other activities in Pittsburgh are unknown, but they included Zygmunt's meeting with the young Warhola family. Among archived materials at the Andy Warhol Museum is a dark photograph of a young Julia from the early 1920s. Beneath the photo she wrote, in a mixture of languages and alphabets: "Mr. Bogdansky mene spikčeruval yak moy szin ~~Pol~~ Paul bil maly chlopec" (Mr. Bogdański took my picture when my son Paul was a little boy). As it turns out, the Warhola and Bogdański families had ties going back to Miková. Jozef, Pawel, Antoni, and Zygmunt Bogdański renovated eighteen Greek Catholic churches south of the Carpathians, including the church in Miková.[86] According to village stories, the young Julia Zavacka observed and assisted the artists, learning skills she eventually passed on to her son. Unfortunately, there is no evidence of how Andrii tried to help Bogdański in Pittsburgh.

According to the *1920 US Federal Census*, Zygmunt was living in New York, working as a self-employed artist. He maintained a correspondence with his Pittsburgh friends. In October 1923, Julia, living then at 3 Orr Street, received a postcard photograph of the artist. Forty-six years old at the time, he was dapper in a suit and wing-collar dress shirt and tie, with a carefully trimmed beard and piercing light eyes. The handwritten message opens with "Dear Mrs. Julia," but unfortunately the card is damaged, and the message is illegible. In another photo postcard dated July 23, 1924, Zygmunt asks Julia to pass on condolences to her sister Mary. Mary Zavacka Preksta's husband had died three months earlier, and Julia apparently related her family news to the Polish artist. Bogdański ends his message with "kind greetings to you, your husband, and your son."

Bockris does not identify his source for Julia's alleged denigrating remarks about Bogdański, but her correspondence with him does not support such a harsh assessment. And even if his attempt to make it in the world of American religious art was unsuccessful, there is no evidence Bogdański ended up "dead in the gutter without a penny in his pocket." In the 1930 census, Bogdański's occupation is no longer "artist," but clerical worker at the Polish Consulate. Still, if Andrii wished to promote Bogdański's work, he was not wrong about the artist's potential. In 1938, Zygmunt returned to Poland and devoted himself to easel painting. As of 1946, he was living in the village Domaradz, still corresponding with Julia and sending photographs of his family, some of whom lived in Brooklyn. He continued painting until his death in 1968, primarily doing portraits on commission, like Warhol in the last two decades of his life. Today the Bogdański artists are experiencing a renaissance in the Polish Borderlands. Their work is collected and exhibited in a reproduction of their house and studio at the open-air Museum of Folk Architecture in Sanok, Poland.[87]

Unfortunately, there are more questions than answers to the Warholas' tantalizing connection with the Bogdańskis. What was the reason for Andrii's effort to help the Polish artist, and what was the nature of his assistance? We do not have enough information to conclude that Andrii was a promoter of the arts, but there are coincidental parallels between Bogdański and Andy Warhol, not the least of which is that both artists were assisted in their careers by Andrii Warhola.

The Slavic Immigrant Woman

"There is no lonelier person in American life than the Slavic immigrant woman." This was the stereotypical image of female Slavic immigrants put forward by reformers of the Americanization movement in the 1920s. "In making the transition from the old country to America, the Slavic immigrant woman is thrown into a maze of problems. She comes meagerly equipped physically, spiritually, economically, and educationally. . . . It is the mother who makes the greatest sacrifice. In most cases she is lost entirely to American life and remains a lonely stranger in a foreign land."[88] Men held jobs in industry, where they learned English and American ways. Immigrant children were exposed to American values in school. But the mother was isolated in the home and "ignorant of the true American spirit." But, for better or worse, "She nonetheless exerts more influence over the lives of others than does anyone else."[89] Accordingly, social workers focused on immigrant mothers and, in a rhetorical question that smacks of xenophobia, they asked, "Can we permit thousands of foreign mothers to hold their old country ideals unchanged and expect their homes to be truly American?"[90]

Creating "truly American" homes and families was the goal of early twentieth-century sociologists. Since mothers were responsible for the kind of citizens their children would become, immigrant women were urged to aspire to a "higher, more 'American' quality of motherhood."[91] Social and governmental institutions, women's clubs, and Protestant church groups sponsored classes and promoted social workers to inform and "educate" immigrant women to adopt modern "American" ways and to foster the "unlearning" of cultural practices deemed primitive or "unhealthful." On issues from housekeeping to procuring food, swaddling and breastfeeding babies, to health care, discipline, and education, reformers encouraged immigrant women to abandon the customs of their own culture in favor of modern "scientific" methods. The federal Bureau of Naturalization issued a pamphlet titled *Suggestions for Americanization Work among Foreign-Born Women.* Suggested topics included teaching immigrant women about "suitable play clothes for children," and giving them instructions on "good taste in home furnishing." The General Federation of Women's Clubs even campaigned for the elimination of cabbage in immigrant homes, which would not have been popular among Carpatho-Rusyn cooks. Reflecting the gender bias of the time, little attention was paid to civics lessons, current events, or naturalization.[92]

Americanizers had little success among Slavic immigrants. Oral history studies of immigrant women in Pittsburgh show that most were able to adapt to America, find a niche for themselves, and achieve a level of self-esteem without sacrificing their own ethnic and cultural identity. A sociologist who studied three generations of immigrant women in Pittsburgh found that, "given the culture shock and alienation faced by all immigrant women and the special nature of Pittsburgh, a city devoted to heavy manufacturing, immigrant women were surprisingly successful in the transition from European peasant small town life to industrial, urban Pittsburgh."[93] Networks of friends and relatives eased the adjustment, and ethnic churches provided religious and cultural bonds between old and new societies. For Julia, the reunion with her husband and siblings surely eased the pain of separation from her Miková family, and the familiar rituals of the Greek Catholic Church furnished spiritual support, continuity, and a sense of community. The sociologists' concern about whether immigrant women could raise "truly American" children is challenged by the success of the second generation of Rusyn-American Zavackys and Warholas, and completely controverted by Julia's son, Andy Warhol.

Julia

One can imagine that Julia must have been overwhelmed initially by the city of Pittsburgh, clouded in black smoke and teeming with people of all nationalities speaking incomprehensible languages. During her first decade in America, primitive living conditions in poor neighborhoods, coupled with concern for her family in Europe, surely caused distress. But unlike the sociologists' theoretical immigrant mother for whom "a trip to the central shopping district is a strange and terrifying adventure," she successfully negotiated the transition and began to feel comfortable, and even at home, in Pittsburgh.[94]

Unfortunately, we know little about Julia's life during the 1920s, as the Warholas settled and resettled in Soho. On June 26, 1922, one year after her arrival in America, she gave birth to her son, Paul. Paul remembers going with his father to fetch a doctor when John was born on May 31, 1925, but since he was barely three years old at the time, his memory is not reliable. A bit more certain is his recall of Andy's birth three years later, when Julia was almost thirty-seven: "I heard somebody screaming and then somebody said, 'It's half past five.'"[95] Well into the 1930s, most babies in Pittsburgh were delivered by friends, relatives, and midwives, especially in immigrant neighborhoods, but it seems that Andy Warhol was delivered by a doctor. In 1934, an affidavit signed by B. B. Wood was submitted to the Pennsylvania Bureau of Vital Statistics, attesting that Andrew Warhola was born at home on August 6, 1928. Dr. Benjamin B. Wood, listed in numerous newspaper articles as B. B. Wood, was a staff doctor at Mercy Hospital in Pittsburgh. Attendants to home births, even doctors, were lackadaisical about filing an official birth certificate. The reason Dr. Wood gave for failing to file information within ten days of the date of birth was "oversight." The 1934 affidavit was probably needed to register then six-year-old Andy in school.[96]

Few memories of the Warhola family can be unearthed from the time they lived in Soho. Colacello quotes one Beelen Street neighbor, Mary Bradenton, who cannot be found in the census: "[Julia] had a very, very sad look. She never looked happy. There wasn't a lot of chuckling, just a real slow smile. A wry smile."[97] When the Warholas lived on Beelen Street from about 1929 to 1932, Julia's older sister Mary Zavacka Preksta lived nearby with her five children. Mary had relocated to Pittsburgh from Ohio after her husband's death in 1924. John Warhola remembered, "[Mary] and my mother were very close, in fact, if you closed your eyes you wouldn't know which one was talking—both personalities were the same." Mary's daughter Justine, known as Tinka, was Andy's playmate. When their mothers got together, they spoke Rusyn and read letters from Europe. "It was always so sad," Tinka recalled, "because they didn't have the money to send Ella and Eva and they would always talk about the sadness of Europe and cry." A Dawson Street neighbor, Ann Elachko, recalled Julia as "very anxious." John Elachko remembered, "She and my mother used to sing these songs from the Old Country. Most of them were sad songs. Honest to truth, our people were always sad. They were negative thinkers."[98] The women in the Zavacky family had much to be negative about.

We have more information about Julia's life and personality after the family's move to Dawson Street, when she had at least partly assimilated to American life. If Andrii could be intimidating and distant, Julia was affectionate, gentle, and warm. Nora Zavacky, the daughter of Julia's brother Stephen, said, "My parents weren't very close or huggy, but she was. Always hugging, always holding your hand. That's why I loved Andy's mother. If you sat beside her, her arm would come around you. Every

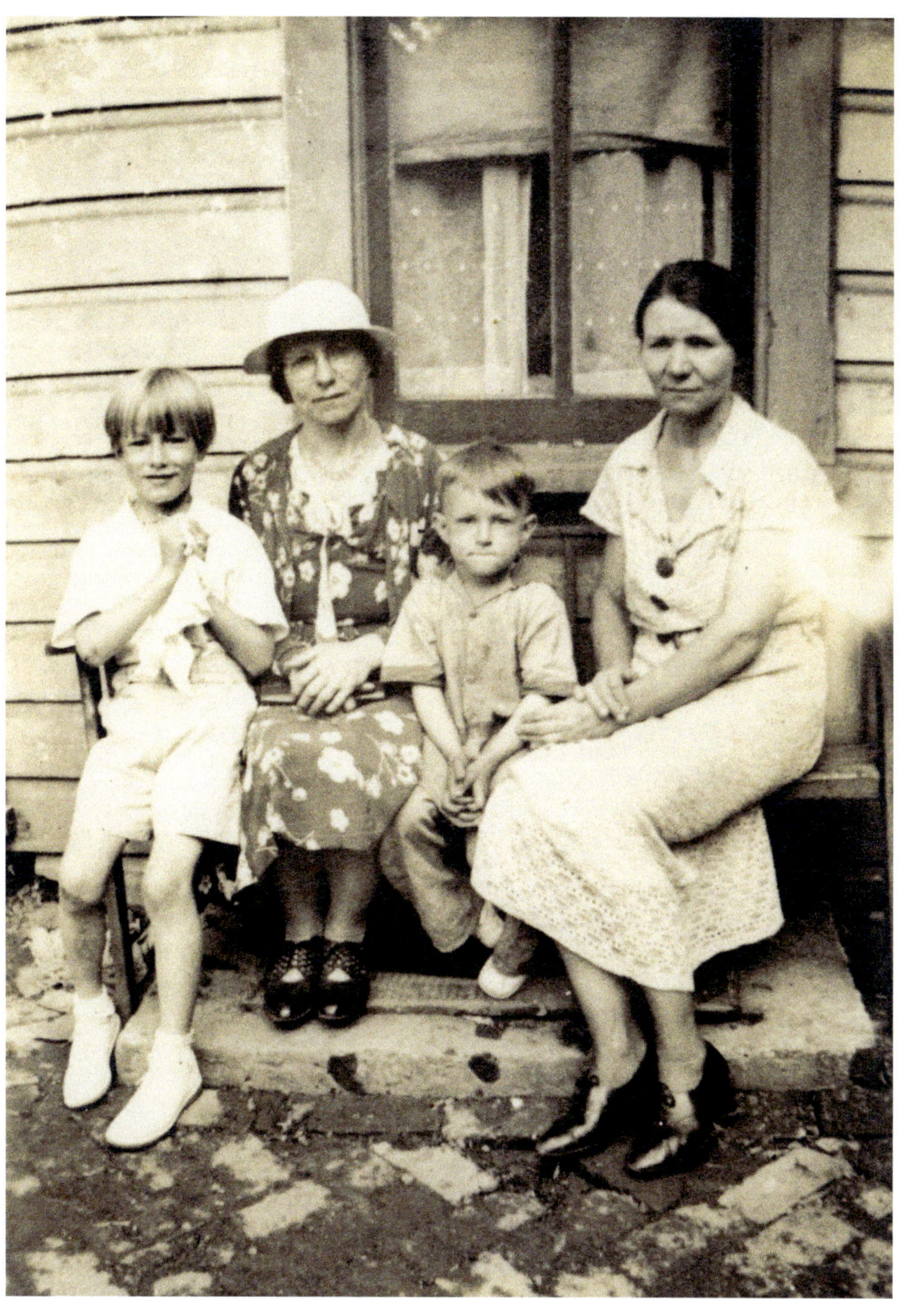

Figure 4.2. Andy Warhol, Julia Warhola, her sister Mary Zavacky Preksta and Mary's son George Guke, 1937.

time you walked down the street she'd be holding [your] hand."[99] John Elachko concurred: "If you were going to kill something, a bug or a fly, she'd say, 'Loving one, don't do that.' She was a very gentle, flowery-speech-type person. She wouldn't call you whatever your name was, she would say, 'My heart, my dear, lovely one.'"[100] Young people were especially attracted to Julia. Neighborhood boys going off to World War II stopped by to say good-bye to Mrs. Warhola, whose traumatic experience of World War I made her a sympathetic adviser. "She told them to 'take care of themselves,' and not to be reckless, not to volunteer for dangerous duty."[101] Her grandchildren highlight the loving, caring, and nurturing aspect of her personality. "She was very patient. I don't think I ever saw her get upset about anything," recalls her oldest grandson.[102]

Women's work in Depression-era Pittsburgh revolved around the home. The time when male immigrants were pouring into Pittsburgh was long over, and on Dawson Street, Julia did not have to care for teams of male boarders, as did early immigrant housewives. It is unlikely that she needed to wait actively on the Shlackman couple or other lodgers to whom the Warholas rented space over the next decade. The house had indoor plumbing and electricity, and it was heated by a coal-burning furnace. Coal was delivered by horse-drawn wagon or truck; hauling away the messy ashes was a job for the growing boys. Andrii's cold cellar under the porch preserved root vegetables from Julia's garden, and fruits would be pressure-canned for winter consumption. By 1930, trucks delivered ice for the icebox, "the best and most economical medium of refrigeration for the home," according to contemporary advertising. In winter, refrigeration was freely available on the back porch. Meat was sold from trucks, hucksters peddled produce, and milk was delivered to the doorstep. Clothes were washed on a corrugated washboard, boiled in a copper kettle, wound through a hand wringer, and finally hung on wire clotheslines. An iron would be heated on the kitchen stove to finish the time-consuming laundry job.

Julia used Andrii's wooden utensils to make her own bread, *holubky* (stuffed cabbage), and *pirohy* (dumplings stuffed with potatoes and cheese or cabbage). Soup was a mainstay for traditional midday dinners, and Carpatho-Rusyn cuisine includes a great variety. Nora Zavacky remembered that Andy especially liked Julia's chicken soup. "She had a special place in Squirrel Hill where she would buy Jewish [kosher] chicken." With a chuckle, she added, "She always called every [merchant] a Jew."[103] For Slavic transplants from Europe, "storekeeper" meant "Jew." The "Jewish chicken," a stewing hen, boiled with carrots, celery, onions, and garlic for soup, would be the first course for Sunday dinner.[104] When poultry was beyond the family's finances, vegetables from the garden—cabbage, tomatoes, peas, and beets—simmered on the back of the stove. The Warhola boys especially liked a soup made from caraway seeds.[105] Cultivated widely in northern Europe, caraway plays a major role in Hungarian, Slovak, and Jewish cooking. The Warhola boys called it "cahmin" soup, probably from the Hungarian *kömény*. A light soup served often by Rusyns to children and pregnant women, it was especially good with dumplings. Although Andy later frequented upscale restaurants and is said to have prepared a Thanksgiving dinner of pheasant under glass, he never lost his taste for simple food.[106] Pat Hackett recalled, "Andy liked uncomplicated fare where he could easily determine exactly what it was." In his *Diary* entry for Easter, April 16, 1981, Warhol said he cooked himself an early Easter dinner, "And it smelled like the old days when [Pat Hackett] used to come up and cook me cabbage with caraway seeds and onions."[107]

Although Warhol remarked repeatedly that he painted Campbell's soup cans because he had the soup every day, and his brothers endorsed that statement, it is simply not the case, at least as far as his early childhood is concerned. Gopnik agrees that in Depression-era Pittsburgh, no one was flush enough to buy tinned products for the table.[108] But Warhol's story that they ate soup "made from water, salt, pepper and ketchup—Heinz brand, of course," is also fictitious.[109] It is more likely that Julia used ketchup to flavor bland broth made from subprime cuts of chuck (9¢ per pound in 1933), with boiled cabbage and potatoes. In the early 1930s, a three-pound stewing chicken for 59¢ at the A&P went farther to feed the family than Campbell's soups, three cans for 25¢. Not to mention the fact that Slavic women were convinced of the superior quality of homemade meals from scratch over processed foods in tins, even after Campbell's became affordable. In the 1950s when Nora Zavacky visited New York, Julia told her, "Come round to our place. I'll make chicken soup."[110]

Julia occupied herself with traditional handiwork. "She was always doing something. When she came to America she sewed curtains, knitted and embroidered."[111] Andrii's comments in the New Dom letter about purchasing fabric corroborate Julia's granddaughter's memories that she sewed many of her own clothes, and probably, clothing for the family.[112] An American niece said, "Aunt Julia made the most beautiful crochet things you ever saw."[113] A niece in Slovakia remembered, "Once when I was about thirteen Julia crocheted me a wonderful pink dress with a square neckline. There was a bolero to go with it."[114] Handmade crocheted lace was an art developed in early twentieth-century northern Hungary as a cottage industry. During the long winter evenings in Miková, Julia and her friends crocheted lace that was used as decoration for clothing and household linens. The items were sold at the market or to traveling peddlers to contribute to the household economy. She continued the craft, which was hard on the eyes and stiffening for the fingers, in Pittsburgh.[115]

In 1947, Andy Warhol's teacher of pictorial design, Robert Lepper, engaged his students in what was known as the Oakland Project, a visual and ethnographic study of the Oakland neighborhood. "We were to become sociologists and anthropologists," remembered Andy's classmate Bennard Perlman. The students were to search the streets for a house with "individual identity." Lepper instructed, "Now I want you to take one single room in this house based on what you think the people would be like who live in it."[116] In preparation for their work, Lepper had assigned Ruth Benedict's book *Patterns of Culture*, which stressed the diversity of cultures, the role that custom plays in experience and belief, and the fact that culture is learned, not biologically transmitted. Given his own experience, straddling the culture of his parents and the American world he was entering as a homosexual, these ideas must have been stimulating for the young Andy Warhol.

According to Perlman, Andy was the only member of the class who actually lived in Oakland. Perhaps inspired by Benedict's views on culture, Andy chose to depict his own family's living room. Instead of speculating on what the people would be like who lived in an unfamiliar house, Warhol figuratively personified his own family. An upholstered sofa with sunken, well-worn cushions and a matching overstuffed chair are sloppily covered with mismatched throw covers. Roller shades hang unevenly at the curtainless windows, and lampshades perch crookedly on their bases. The walls are bare, covered with what seems to be mottled, stained paint. Newspapers are scattered on the sofa and the Oriental rug, which is partly protected from scuffling feet by a rumpled carpet. An old-world-style wooden rocking chair, made more comfortable by a floppy throw pillow and a knitted or crocheted afghan, stands next to a straight-backed chair painted an otherworldly white, which seem to personify the warm, affectionate mother and the strict, strait-laced, deceased father.

The art critic Jerry Saltz described the watercolor as "a startlingly condensed, rich, incredibly well-observed and precociously complicated and bewitching picture that pulls us into its world."[117] David Bourdon called the image of the room "comfortable, if rather dowdy," but a less erudite viewer might see it as a working-class ideal of cozy well-being.[118] No longer fashionable among middle-class consumers, Victorian-style plush, upholstered furniture, draped fabric, doilies, and carpets were the material values that, for immigrant workers, represented acculturation to

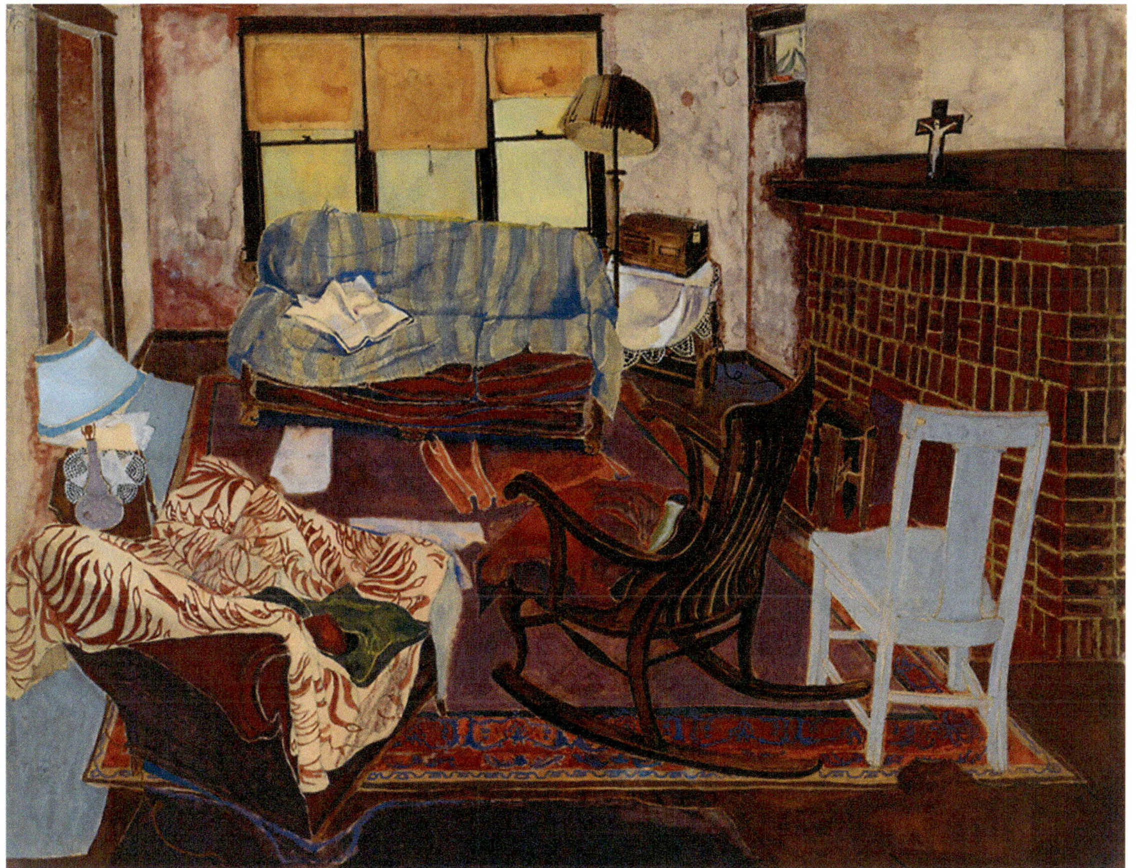

Figure 4.3. Andy Warhol, *Living Room*, 1948.

industrial America. Aware of the working-class market, furniture companies produced inexpensive lines of faux-Victorian furniture. Scholars of American studies affirm that "working-class culture indeed had an integrity of its own."[119]

Presiding over the living room from the fireplace mantel was the cross from Andrii's casket, which had stood there since his death in 1942. Paul told his son James that the painting was "identical to their old living room right down to the doily."[120] He told Colacello, "[Andy] only left out mother's holy pictures."[121] But Julia is not absent from the painting. In the doilies on the side tables, under a lamp and under the radio, Andy captured the intricate patterns of his mother's crocheted lacework. A scholar of design history sees *Living Room* in the context of Benedict's *Patterns of Culture*. "Every item in that room and the arrangement of them was the result of long-standing cultural patterns established in the peasant villages of the Warhola family's Ruthe-nian heritage and transferred to their working-class Pittsburgh home."[122] Julia's objects of beauty were essential elements of the family space, and together with the crucifix from Andy's father's coffin, they symbolically evince the pervasive presence of his parents in the family's transition from rural folk life to industrial Pittsburgh. Recognizing the connection between the Old World he had never seen and the city where he was born, in this early, personal painting, Warhol captured both the cultural and class attributes of his family.

Mothering Rusyn Style

As one would expect, many of the child-rearing techniques practiced by Carpatho-Rusyn and other Slavic immigrants were transposed from the peasant culture in which they had been raised. Before Dr. Benjamin Spock revolutionized the matter with his 1946 *Common Sense Book of Baby and Child Care*, traditional American beliefs about parenting were not essentially different from those of immigrants. Rigid feeding schedules and early toilet training, warnings against excessive affection and "spoiling" the child, gender stereotyping and benign neglect of the emotional needs of the growing child were norms. Studies of eastern European practices add detail. Ruth Benedict studied "the way in which the child's experi-ences within a culture mould his character."[123] Howard F. Stein's ethnography of the processes of socialization and individuation among Slovak- and Rusyn-Amer-icans complements Benedict's work.[124]

Benedict focused on east central Europe, where babies were swaddled tightly for the first months of their life to protect their fragile limbs.[125] In peasant fam-ilies like the Zavackys, where up to ten children were cared for by mothers who worked in the field, swaddling protected the baby from harm. For the same reason, it was not possible in peasant life to respond immediately to a child's cry. Immi-grants, like most pre-Spock parents, believed that crying exercised a baby's lungs. Weaning was sudden and uncompromising, and toilet training was enforced by punishment and shaming. Any pain felt by the baby as a result of these practices was considered a step in "hardening" the child's character. Benedict noted that in Slavic child-rearing, "hardening is valued . . . and since one is hardened by suffer-ing, suffering is also valued."[126] Misbehavior might be corrected by evoking fear or threat. Scolding, shaming, and comparing the child with others were typical child-rearing techniques, and the withdrawal of love and approval pressed a child to conform.

It has become a commonplace in the literature to attribute Warhol's habit of fostering conflict among his Factory followers and "playing rivals off against one another" to his mother's practice of playing favorites among her children.[127] According to Bockris, "Just like any movie mogul Andy pitched everybody in competition with everybody else for his attention. . . . In his manipulation of people Andy was being a lot like his mother, who had kept her three sons in such constant competition for her affection that in their fifties the Warhola brothers were still each insisting that he was her favourite."[128] Sibling rivalry, found frequently in immigrant Carpatho-Rusyn families, was the natural outcome of peasant conditions and cultural patterns. It is also to be expected that low socioeconomic status would decrease the available parental time and attention, thereby exacerbating the problem.

The topic of sexuality did not come up in traditional Slavic immigrant families. Erogenous zones were "repulsive, bad, or nonexistent."[129] Andy Warhol recalled that his first exposure to sex was in "Northside Pittsburgh, under the stairs" when he was five years old, although he "never understood what it meant."[130] Gopnik conjectures that Warhol first came out, "at least to himself and other gay men," in his late teens, when he worked on window displays at the Joseph Horne Company department store. He describes in detail the rampant homophobia in Pittsburgh and the abuse of gays by the corrupt Morals Squad in the late 1940s.[131]

In his ethnography of Slovak and Rusyn immigrants in McKeesport, Stein focused on the mother. "From the child's earliest experience, the mother constitutes a paradox and a contradiction." The "entire meaning of her life lies in giving—though on her terms. . . . On the one hand she can be extremely warm and gentle, and infinitely compassionate. On the other hand she can be icily cold and cruelly rejecting." In an effort to prevent the child's insecurity, the mother "over-gives," and becomes dependent on the child's dependence. In turn, the child is eternally indebted to the mother's overwhelming self-sacrifice, simultaneously craving dependency and refusing it.[132] The result is often a pattern of codependence, like that which characterizes the Warhola mother–son relationship.

Although she made a more successful transition to America than many immigrant women, Julia's character was formed in Miková. She could not divest herself of inbred ethnocultural and psychological predispositions, which to some extent, were passed on to her closest child. According to psychiatrists, "[Ethnicity] patterns our thinking, feeling, and behavior in both obvious and subtle ways, although generally we are not aware of it. It plays a major role in determining how we eat, work, celebrate, make love, and die." And in groups where heritage remains strong even in American assimilationist culture, these patterns are transmitted to the second and even the third generation.[133]

Family and Fun in Pittsburgh

For the Warholas, social life centered around the family. "There was nobody closer than my mother and her brothers and sisters," remembered Paul.[134] Julia often took the boys to visit her brothers' families, riding the train forty miles from Pittsburgh north to Lyndora. "We enjoyed it up there because it was like farmland." According to Nora Zavacky, "Julia wanted Andy to see the cows and the hills. My brother used to take him down to the chicken coops to see the pee-pees, we used to call them. . . . We had a big sheep and goats, cows . . . We had a creek and a little bridge. They would always tell me, 'Take Andy for a walk up the hill. We don't have any hills in Pittsburgh.'"[135] At least, not grass-covered hills, conducive to climbing up or rolling down. Andy's cousin, the daughter of Julia's brother John, wrote to him in 1972, "I have such sweet memories of your mother and dad. When they came to Lyndora to visit, my father would get his brothers together and then the violins would come out and that was to me the sweetest music this side of heaven. They were all so emotional that they all shed tears of joy just to be together. . . . Not one of them ever had a lesson but they were musically inclined."[136] In almost every Carpatho-Rusyn family were self-taught violinists, who brought the folk songs they had grown up with to America. Julia and Mary sang in harmony at family get-togethers, church picnics, and weddings, where music-making was always accompanied by bitter-sweet tears. After Julia's sister Eva visited from Miková in 1967, she was asked about the Carpatho-Rusyns in America: "Oh dear God . . . there are a lot of them, as many as poppy seeds. They have it good, but they yearn for home, the Old Country."[137] As comfortable as they may have become in the New World, the longing for what had been left behind was an ever-present sorrow.

Ethnic Pittsburghers enjoyed cultural entertainments fostered by American institutions. The Works Progress Administration's recreation department sponsored a "nationality parade and amateur show" at the Holmes School playground on Dawson Street, with prizes for costumes from foreign lands. The anniversary of the founding of the Republic of Czechoslovakia was celebrated annually by Czechs, Slovaks, and Carpatho-Rusyns with speeches and performances by a "prize winning group of Carpatho-Russian singers." The Pittsburgh Carpatho-Rusyn community was represented at such events by Dr. Peter I. Zeedick, a Carpatho-Rusyn cultural activist who was also the Warhola family doctor. Zeedick received his medical degree at the

University of Pittsburgh in 1916 and served as medical adviser for the Greek Catholic Union for fifty years. Born in America, Zeedick had spent seven years as a student in northeastern Slovakia, traveling around Carpatho-Rusyn villages and studying customs, songs, and history. As a Pittsburgh physician, he was sophisticated and cosmopolitan, yet fluent in Rusyn and comfortable with his immigrant patients. Moreover, he was committed to preserving and promoting Carpatho-Rusyn culture and the Greek Catholic Church in America.[138] He wrote, "In America it is impossible to preserve everything that our people brought with them from the Old Country. We cannot preserve the language, but . . . it is possible to successfully preserve our religion and other treasures of our national culture."[139]

At least once a year the Zavacky and Warhola families went to Kennywood, the popular amusement park on the bluff above the Monongahela River, about eight miles from downtown Pittsburgh. "That was our vacation," remembered Christine Soley, the daughter of Julia's brother, John Zavacky.[140] Another John Zavacky, the son of Andrii's cousin, connects one of his first memories of Julia with Kennywood: "We'd take dinner in a basket and take a streetcar out. We'd put the baskets on the table, then the kids would go play and come back to eat." He remembers getting lost as a child and running to Julia for comfort. She called him "John-ee-ko," refashioning the American "John" as a Rusyn diminutive. "As soon as she came to me, I stopped crying."[141] Zavacky also remembers how Andrii joked with him, asking, "John-ee-ko, does your father have a *fliash-ee-ku* [bottle, or flask]?" Andrii had traveled to America with John's father, and they shared boyhood memories.

With a roller coaster, tilt-a-whirl, swimming pool, and picnic facilities, Kennywood drew crowds of working-class revelers on summer weekends. In 1921, Dr. Zeedick organized the first annual "Carpatho-Russian Day" at Kennywood Park. By 1940, 25,000 Carpatho-Rusyns from Greek Catholic parishes from as far away as Minnesota and Massachusetts gathered at Kennywood to celebrate. Rusyn speech and song resounded from the streetcars that provided free transportation from Pittsburgh and its suburbs. The day began with remarks from state senators, local American officials, and representatives of the Consulate of Czechoslovakia. The singing of "My Country 'Tis of Thee" was followed by "Ya Rusyn byl, esm' i budu" (I was, am, and will be a Rusyn), the Carpatho-Rusyn anthem. Young and old participated in field sports. Separate races were designated for thin and "fat ladies." In a representative mix of traditional and modern American culture, there were old-country costume contests, a potato-picking competition, softball games, and of course, music and folk-dancing. The *Amerikansky Russky Viestnik* (*ARV*) crowed that the Carpatho-Rusyn people turned out at Kennywood "to bear witness that they are true to their ancestral traditions, that they love their people and are proud of their ethnicity, and, if necessary, they will fight for everything sacred and dear to our people."[142] The event ended with the singing of "Mnohaia lit'," a classic Rusyn song wishing "many blessed years" of health and happiness to the entire assembly.

One of Julia's favorite everyday activities was playing the numbers. Bockris quotes her son Paul, "My mother used to always say, 'You know, you're never gonna have nothing!' She says, 'All you like to do is gamble'"[143] But Paul's son told me, with a smile in his voice, "My grandmother was a gambler. She used to send my father to play the numbers for her."[144] In Pittsburgh, the illegal numbers racket was widespread, especially in working-class neighborhoods. Bets on a sequence of three digits drawn at random the following day could be placed at the local tavern or candy store for as little as a penny. Julia's niece Nora Zavacky recalled, "Every night we went to play numbers. She would have her little list."[145] Jacob Sharnin's grocery store at 3274 Dawson Street, a block away from the Warholas' home, was a convenient betting shop. It made the newspapers in 1935 when it became known that children from Holmes School, where the Warhola boys attended, were spending their pennies on the numbers at Sharnin's store.[146] Since they were minors, their names were not released, but one cannot help wonder whether Warholas were among them.

Though the odds of winning were one in a thousand, playing the numbers provided "a chance outside of a world within which there was little chance," a gamble to escape a difficult life, just as immigration to America had been a gamble.[147] And for Julia Warhola, it was culturally sanctioned. In his *Philosophy*, Andy recalled, "When I was little Mom used to play the numbers and I remember she used to have a dream book and she'd look up her dream and the book would tell her whether it was a good dream or not, and there were numbers after it which she played."[148] In Carpatho-Rusyn tradition, the interpretation of dreams goes back to pre-Christian lore. Popular "dream books" made their way into seventeenth-century religious anthologies and found a place within the broad, though not clerically authorized, frame of church doctrine.[149] Like her ancestors, Julia conflated folklore with faith, and now she conflated traditional folkways with American gaming culture.

Having shared her home with farm animals in Miková, Julia welcomed pets—a white cat that would stray for three or four days, but always came back home, a blonde dog named Lucy, after Lucille Ball, and a Chow and Dalmatian mix named Brownie that snapped at everyone but Julia. Brownie was ultimately banished to the Allegheny County Workhouse, where neighbor Pete Elachko worked, to serve as a guard dog. John and Andy kept two rabbits in the backyard, planning to market their bunnies, until they learned that they had been given two males by relatives who feared the breeding competition. Sledding, roller-skating, and street hockey were outdoor amusements after school.[150] Saturday mornings when they had a dime for a ticket, the boys went to the movies. The Strand Theater in Oakland, renovated in 1936 with the latest sound and projection equipment, offered three double-bill changes of program weekly. On one occasion, John and Andy stole into the Strand through an alley door left open to ease the heat, but they felt so guilty and scared, they couldn't enjoy the show.[151]

At age fifty, Andy remembered frequent childhood visits to the Heinz Factory on the North Shore of the Allegheny River. The "factory tour," initiated by H. J. Heinz himself, showed visitors the can-making process, soup and ketchup preparation, and the bottling of pickles. At the end of the tour, visitors received a souvenir—the famous "pickle pin," a Heinz advertising bauble introduced at the 1893 Chicago World's Fair that became "one of the most famous giveaways in merchandising history." According to his assistant Nathan Gluck, Warhol's initial concept for the 1964 World's Fair was a Heinz pickle. "Andy had evidently seen these or heard about it or something and thought, 'Wouldn't that be great. For this year's World's Fair to do a Heinz pickle,'" Warhol told Gluck. Instead, he created his notorious mural *Thirteen Most Wanted Men*, which was promptly removed following a public protest.[152]

"I No Speak English So Good"

In 1921, the sociologist Sophonisba Breckinridge saw the prototypical immigrant woman as "a Ukrainian mother, who admits being afraid to go beyond her own neighborhood" and who "would do nothing but sit at home and cry."[153] In reality, many Carpatho-Rusyn women were unable to adjust to the new world, and given the hard life most of them lived, the image of the *baba* (grandmother) sitting in tears is one that many Rusyn-Americans retain. Julia Warhola cried her share of tears, but she was by no means incapacitated. Having survived the rigors of peasant life, war, and emigration, she would not be intimidated by Pittsburgh, or later, by New York.

It is true that many Slavic immigrant women did not venture far beyond their small ethnic enclaves. By those standards, Julia Warhola was exceptional. Prompted perhaps by her experience of dealing with peddlers and going to market in Medzilaborce, she recognized the monetary value of her handiwork in Depression-era

Pittsburgh. Moving from traditional women's work to inventive and resourceful plastic arts, and using free, expendable materials, Julia created flower sculptures from tin cans and crepe paper, cutting and shaping the metal to form leaves and petals. Confident in the value of her work, she was not afraid to market her product in the affluent public space. She called on her son Paul to accompany her: "You gotta go with me, you gotta do the talking."[154] As Julia told Bernard Weinraub as late as 1966, "I no speak English so good."[155] According to Paul, he was too embarrassed to "do the talking." "We'd walk a mile and a half into the better sections of town, and while she sold door to door, I'd hide behind the tree, embarrassed. Fifty cents she sold 'em for. It was a lot of work for 50 cents. She did it because we needed the money." Four-year-old Andy trudged along and learned from his mother the technique of what he later called "business art." Despite her limited English, Julia's theatrical personality made her a skilled salesperson and a model for her artist son.

In a 1985 interview for London's *The Face* magazine, Warhol was asked about his mother's tin-can flowers. He answered, "Oh God, yes, it's true, the tin flowers were made out of those fruit cans, that's the reason why I did my first tin-can paintings. … You take a tin-can, the bigger the tin-can the better, like the family size ones that peach halves come in, and I think you cut them with scissors. It's very easy and you just make flowers out of them. My mother always had lots of cans around, including the soup cans."[156] The parallel use of cans by Julia and Andy made an apt story, but it is just one variant in a complex matrix of clarifications and obfuscations that Warhol promulgated to explain his Campbell's soup cans. It is significant, however, as Gopnik says, that Warhol wanted "to credit his mother as the source of his first blockbuster work."[157]

Julia called on Paul to "do the talking" as she sold her wares in neighborhoods where English was the predominant language. According to Paul, "Our mother didn't speak English. We boys learned English at school. With our mother—you know how it is—when someone is older it's hard for them. She just spoke what they called broken English and the children just laughed at her. With us she spoke just our way and they laughed at that too."[158] In his *Philosophy*, which was largely ghostwritten by associates, Warhol claims he didn't understand a word of his mother's "thick Czechoslovakian accent."[159] John Warhola firmly debunks this notion, which is absurd on its face.[160] Bernard Weinraub, who interviewed Julia for the *Esquire* article "Mothers" in 1966, found her English difficult to understand and her stream-of-consciousness conversational style disjointed.[161] Still, he managed to elicit factual, detailed information about her courtship, her wedding, and her husband's emigration and death. To the end of her life, Julia's English was accented and idiosyncratic, but for patient listeners who became accustomed to it, like Warhol's assistant Nathan Gluck, it was "adequate and quaint," even if it sometimes aroused humor. "Well, Mrs. Warhol was quite a character too because . . . she didn't know English too well and . . . she once started to tell me a Bible story about Moses that was hysterical because everything was confused."[162] As in most immigrant families, the men, who had been in the country already for several years and had to communicate at the worksite, picked up a good bit of English. Their wives were slower to learn and could be timid about using English among Americans, but there is no indication that Julia "refused" to learn English, as some have suggested.[163]

John Warhola related a story of Julia's purchase of the family's first radio in 1936:

> She brought it home and it played for a while, then it went bad. She took it back and they didn't want to give her a radio. . . . She was paying like fifty cents a week on it. . . . She only had this for one month. She said, "You know what I'm gonna do. I'm gonna take this radio"—it was right near the 6th Street bridge—she said, "I'm gonna go by the bridge and I'm gonna throw it in the river." The guy called the manager. They probably thought she was gonna jump in the river, and they didn't want that to happen. But she come [*sic*] out with a new radio.

John laughed as he told the story, but he remembered that his mother was serious. "They didn't want to give her a new radio, and they gave her a hard time."[164] But Julia persisted, undoubtedly embellishing her faulty English with theatrical flourishes until she won her point.

Paul remembered earlier childhood Sundays, when all work was prohibited. "Mother wouldn't do anything. No sewing, nothing. . . . And we didn't have a radio or nothing so whatdya do? Mother used to tell us stories."[165] In the Old Country, talented storytellers were highly prized and widely praised. The practiced storyteller knew how to use direct speech in many voices to enhance the suspension of disbelief, heighten drama, and build suspense. Telling tales was a performance, a onetime unrepeatable event. Julia continued the art throughout her life, telling tales that were not written down, but improvised, different at each telling. Traditional Carpatho-Rusyn folktales taught a moral lesson. Like fairy tales worldwide, they featured repetition (especially the number three), an unlikely hero, travel from home to a new, frightening land, a physical or moral test, and a magical reward. The conclusion elevated the lowly hero and brought the ultimate restoration of justice. Tales might include talking animals or mysterious agents who bestow a magical charm upon the hero. Hyperbole was expected. This is not to suggest that Julia was aware of the conventions and intentionally replicated them. Rather, immersed in Rusyn narrative folk culture, she naturally reproduced them.

Julia's niece Nora remembered, "Andy's mother and I were real close, I really liked her funny stories, like about her wedding, and how rich we were in [Miková], how rich our relatives were, like they lived in big houses. But those were exaggerations. She talked about the Old Country a lot, her early life." Asked whether the stories were sad, Nora responded, "No, it was fun, lots of funny stories."[166] Julia's grandson Paul recalls, "She was a terrific storyteller. In Pittsburgh and even in New York, she would gather us around and tell us these stories about the wolves and all different things. . . . She'd always mention the gypsies . . . I'm sure she had a way of embellishing. But we loved listening to her."[167] However, when asked to recount Julia's stories, none of her sons, grandsons, or nieces could comply, probably because the art of the tale was in the telling.

In the 1950s, Andy procured a reel-to-reel tape recorder for his mother. His assistants have described how Julia recorded Rusyn songs, singing over the original recording in harmony to create the impression of a duet.[168] Most observers were dismissive of her pastime, and no one took any interest in the fate of the tapes. Jerry Jumba, a Carpatho-Rusyn church cantor and musicologist in Pittsburgh, was close to the Warhola family and served as cantor for Andy Warhol's funeral in 1987. In the first half of the 2000s, Jumba worked with the Education Resource Department of the Warhol Museum in Pittsburgh to mount an annual Carpatho-Rusyn event. In 2005, he asked John Warhola if there were any songs or hymns favored by the Warhola family that he might include in his next presentation. Warhola answered, "You know, I have tapes of Mom singing, but they're somewhere in the attic." When Jumba expressed interest, Warhola said, "Yah, OK, we'll look for them and find them."

The attic shoe box held a treasure trove of reel-to-reel tapes, which Julia made "for the family," according to John Warhola, who agreed to share the family legacy. At the annual Warhol Museum Carpatho-Rusyn event in 2006, Jerry Jumba presented a "sonic exhibit" titled *Selections from Julia's Tapes: Carpatho-Rusyn Songs, Chants, Prayers and Stories Recorded by Julia Zavacky Warhola*. Jumba wrote, "The Julia Warhola material sheds light on the traditional living culture and the world at large. Julia is charming and imaginative when she tells stories, spiritually nurturing when she chants the Carpatho-Rusyn Eastern Christian hymns, and entertaining when she sings the Rusyn folk art song."[169] Jumba has studied and cataloged the ninety-seven entries that Julia Warhola recorded on tape at her kitchen table while she lived with her son in New York. The list includes Carpatho-Rusyn folk songs, religious chant, prayer recitations, a Rusyn-language moral parable, and an original story in English.[170] Julia's tale, which John Warhola said she told her children on boring Sunday afternoons, gives us a sense of her imagination, her creativity, and performativity, not to mention her charmingly imperfect command of English.[171]

The Hobo and the Magic Pocketbook

Julia's hero is a down-and-out hobo, or, as she calls him, a "hobo-bum," and her wonder tale is set not in some fairyland, but in her contemporary Pittsburgh. Like an epic hero who enters a new, frightening world, the hobo crosses the Homestead High Level Bridge into Pittsburgh. Built in 1936, the bridge, a marvel of modern engineering that brought jobs to Depression-weary workers, spanned the Monongahela River to connect Homestead with Pittsburgh. Homestead is famous in labor history for the violent 1892 strike against the Carnegie Steel Company that resulted in a major defeat for workers. None of this is expressed explicitly in Julia's story, but implicitly the reference suggests the hobo's escape from an experience of poverty, strife, and injustice in search of opportunity in a new world.[172]

The hobo enters the land of Pittsburgh with just four pennies to his name. "He no can buy everything what he want," Julia explains with compassion in her voice. He encounters a gray-haired man, who entreats him, "Hallo, meester. Please meester, gimme some help, gimme some one penny." Julia's voice and intonation are plaintive. The hobo objects that he is in need himself, but he gives the gray-haired man a penny. This episode is repeated three times, with three gray-haired men and the repeated singsong refrains of "Hallo, meester" and "Thank you very much." With just one penny left, the hobo "go far away some more, no can walk, too weak. He even no can count money. He say, no can buy nothing, just something drink, maybe cuppa tea." (Julia seems to have forgotten that the hobo has no money to count.) He gives his last penny to a fourth gray-haired man. As evening approaches, "already little bit dark," the four gray-haired men seem to materialize as one. Breathlessly, Julia clarifies, "And this one man was like God."

The hobo asks the God-like gray-haired man for help. With animation, Julia recounts his response: "He say, yes sir, I goin' help you. I goin' help you good. I give you for you something, good one. I give you for you good pocketbook, wallet, you will have plenty money. This pocketbook never no be empty. Always you gonna have money. Just you gonna say like this: Pocketbook, open self. Give me money." He also gives the hobo a pipe with a never-ending supply of *tabak*: "You be happy. You never no have pipe empty." Finally, the hobo receives a magical leather sack that will entrap any would-be assailants, and a hammer to punish them. "I give you some more something. I give you, for you, hammer, very good hammer. This hammer help you. Somebody be fight you, you say: Hammer, beating, beating him, beating him. Hammer goin' help you, beating from you. Everybody be no can touch you, no can fight you, no can do nothing for you. No steal, no nothing. He say, 'Thank you very much. Oh, I'm-a get happy. I have these things good for me.'" Their encounter concludes with a repetition of Julia's essential, though understated, explication: "The gray-haired man was like God." As he parts from the hobo, "He say 'Good-bye, good-bye,' gray-haired man say. 'Good-bye, God bless you. Take it easy.'"

It is impossible to capture in written form Julia's dramatic intonation and her sweet accent, which lend poignancy to the tale. Typical of Slavic accents, the /th/ sound becomes /d/ or /t/ and /w/ becomes /v/. "He go derr far avay. He no 'fraid notting." The short /i/, as in "mister," becomes /ee/, /h/ is a deeper /kh/, and /r/ is trilled. Articles (a, an, the) are dropped, and Julia often substitutes Rusyn prepositions and conjunctions for English. Her performance features other typical aspects of the Slavic accent that were embarrassing to the children of immigrants but appreciated in storytelling today as authentic and charming. Adding to the authenticity of Julia's performance is the occasional "meow" from the cats prowling the kitchen where she recorded her story. Her use of the 1930s-style idiomatic English phrase in a not entirely appropriate context ("Take it easy") is an ingenuous attempt to sound modishly American.[173]

Having passed the moral test by demonstrating his generosity, the hobo-bum moves on to a little town called *Mickeyshport*, that is McKeesport, the town Andy often claimed as his birthplace. Julia's mangled pronunciation here is actually a direct articulation of the Cyrillic spelling of McKeesport as used in the *Amerikansky Russky Viestnik*, but the mispronunciation contributes to the otherworldly aspect of the wonder tale. In Mickeyshport, the hobo finds a *restoorant*, where he orders breakfast. "How much I owe you?" "Ten cents soft-boil eggs, fifteen cents toast-bread, *a* [Rusyn: and] twenty cents coffee." The hobo commands, "Pocketbook, open self." He takes out $10, pays the bill, and leaves the change. The hobo rents a room from the restaurant owner, who later attempts to steal the pocketbook while his guest sleeps. But the hobo calls on his magic sack and hammer to halt the theft, and the "boss," having learned his lesson, becomes "goodest man," serving the hobo food to eat and wine to drink. Later, two men ignore the boss's warning and attempt another theft. They "slow open door." Julia's soft voice heightens suspense. But the hobo wakes up, and Julia cries out with spirit, "Hey, wait, wait, wait, I see you, big stealer!" The sack swallows up the two men. "These two men in sack, hammer beating, beating, almost kill him." One thief "was *na* [at] hospital half a year sick." In the third hyperbolic repetition of the would-be theft, a gang of ten men enter the sack and are beaten by the hammer, "all the men crying like, like dog," and Julia yelps like a dog with a stepped-on tail. "This hobo-bum, he no 'fraid nothing . . . he eat, he smoke, he sing, he happy."

At this point, Julia seems to notice that the feed reel on the recorder is running out, and her leisurely recitation quickens as the tale moves to its conclusion. The hobo continues his epic journey to a new town, where he rents a room in a hotel. A boy sent to make his bed sees the pocketbook and asks for money. "Okay, he fix for me bed good," thinks the hobo, and he gives the boy $20. With the money, the boy's mother buys him a suit and shoes. "He dress up nice." The hobo exclaims, "Hey, are you sport!" He then gives the boy $20 for his mother. "Mother was widow. She happy, she buy for self clothes, buy for self eat, she come back, tell him thanks." But the hobo is nowhere to be found. "He go way far away *do* [to] someplace, Europe, *na* [on] aeroplane. He just go far away, nobody no can find him no more. He go, I think," and Julia slows down to think, "*na* Czechoslovak-a," where the people "take him for king." "He was very good king . . . he was big, big king for this . . ." And the tape runs out.

In the end of Julia's story, the down-and-out hobo is recognized for his virtue and recompensed for his hardships. Just as in traditional folklore and Carpatho-Rusyn immigrant literature, the tale of the hobo and his magic pocketbook teaches traditional moral lessons and faith in God, but now they are transposed to contemporary Pittsburgh. The story's concern with money and security, personalized in the persona of the boy's widowed mother, reflects Julia's reality, the only solution to which is divine intervention. The hobo's benevolence to the widow and her response of innocent happiness, is a touching personal disclosure. His surprising royal return to Czechoslovakia, a metaphorical heaven, exposes Julia's nostalgic yearning for the recovery of a romantic past as the solution to present difficulties.

Julia's Religion

The narrative of the hobo and his magic pocketbook is an allegorical illustration of Julia Warhola's deep and pervasive religiosity. Her husband's awareness of the clerical controversies in the Byzantine Catholic Church indicate that he must have had a relatively sophisticated understanding of religious tenets and church doctrine. Julia, on the other hand, practiced an intrinsic religious faith that was internalized as part of her personality. As her grandson, Father Paul Warhola put it, "It was part of her mindset, an understanding that God will always be there, He will always take care and He will lead and guide in the best possible way."[174] Simply put, she trusted in God, loved Jesus, and especially revered the All-pure Virgin Mary, a popular intercessor for Slavic women. "Precsista diva Maria" is a prayer-doodle she scribbled, in her idiosyncratic spelling, in the margins of notes, envelopes, and newspaper articles. Letters between Julia and her sisters open and close with sincere pleas for God's blessings. Julia's beliefs reflect the basic conditions to obtain eternal salvation as set forth in the preface to *Heavenly Manna: A Practical Prayer Book of Devotions for Greek Rite Catholics*: "It is necessary that we possess the true faith, have a childlike confidence in God, keep His commandments, receive the sacraments worthily, pray frequently, war against our evil inclinations, conform to the Will of God in our regard and persevere in doing good."[175]

In a corner of her apartment in Warhol's New York town house, Julia set up an altar, where she kept holy cards and images, a crucifix, and candles. Her prayerbook, which she brought with her from the Old Country, was worn from heavy use. She lined the book with heavyweight professional drawing paper and bound the yellowed, brittle pages with embossed silver cardboard, cut from a Chivas Regal box, stitching it all together with black thread. Published by the Prešov Greek Catholic eparchy in 1897, the *Molitvennik dlia vostochnyia tserkvi kafolicheskykh pravoslavnykh khristiian* (Prayer Book for the Eastern Church of Catholic Orthodox Christians) was printed entirely in the early Rusyn Church Slavonic script, in which many letters retained a similarity to the Greek forms on which they were based. The hefty book contained the liturgy and a calendar of holy days and the feast days of saints. It included devotions for confession and Holy Communion, morning and evening prayers, psalms, and songs, prayers for children, prayers during a time of war, and for almost any conceivable circumstance.

In a study of the cultural dimensions of mental health, Corinne Azen Krause interviewed three generations of Italian, Jewish, and Slavic women in Pittsburgh. "Regardless of the denomination professed . . . religion was part of the very fiber and texture of their lives, providing a comprehensive framework encompassing every aspect of life." Krause found that the deeply internalized religious commitment of Slavic women was "sharply distinguished from that which merely follows the forms of institutionalized religion." In fact, the rules of churches and denominations paled against the women's understanding of the individual's religious responsibility. "Even when the church itself was intolerant and quite doctrinaire, many Slavic-American women lived according to their own principles. They were committed to religion, but they were quite critical of hypocrisy and arbitrary authority."[176] It was this kind of

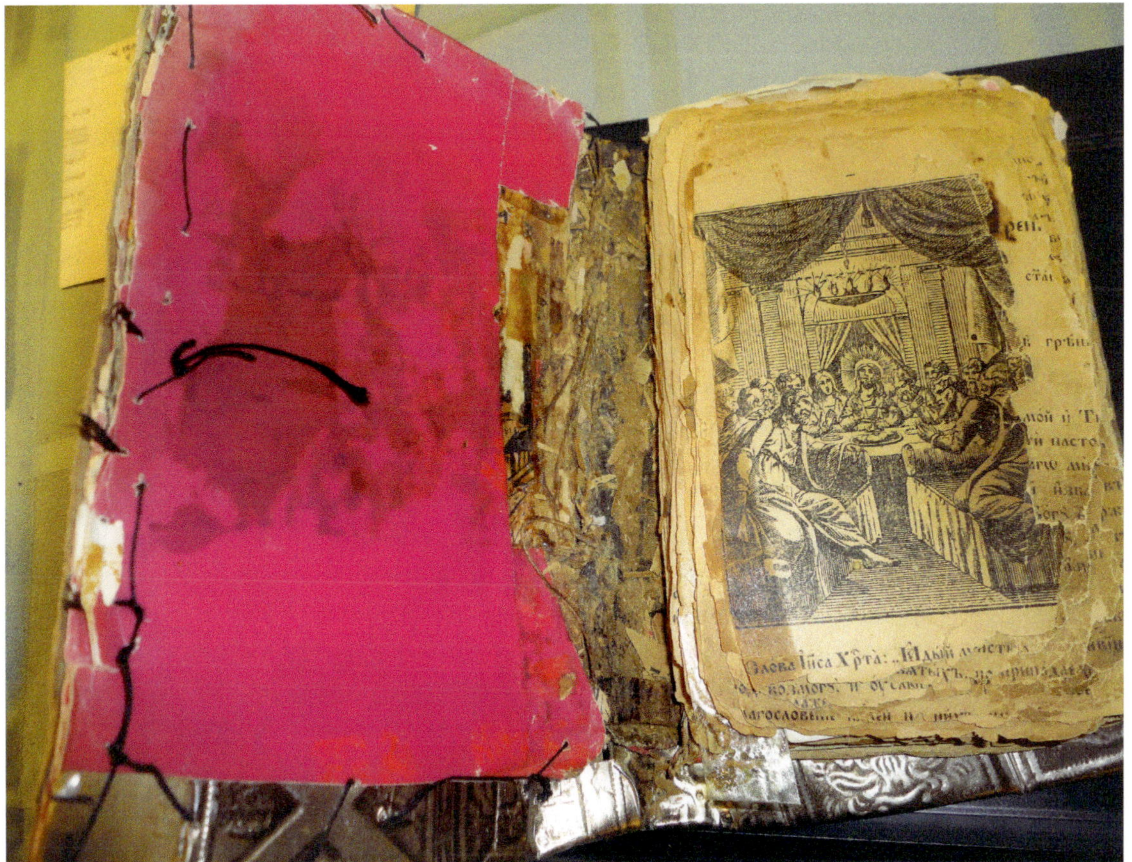

Figure 4.4. Julia's prayer book, *Prayer Book for the Eastern Church of Catholic Orthodox Christians.* Repair improvised with the cover of a Chivas Regal box.

religiosity we saw in the church splits in Lyndora and among the Greek Catholics of Pittsburgh, where their understanding of God's will trumped ecclesiastical law, and it was this tolerant faith that Julia's generation passed on to their children. Julia's son Paul Warhola recalled, "We were Byzantine Catholics, but Mom said, 'If it's a long way to a Greek-Catholic church, go and pray wherever you want. God is everywhere.'"[177]

Julia's grandson Paul recalls that she enjoyed listening to the evangelist Kathryn Kuhlman's radio programs. Kuhlman, who hosted healing services around the country, began her ministry in Pittsburgh in 1948. In 1953, six thousand followers attended a communion service led by Kuhlman in Oakland.[178] According to Father Paul, "Bubba would put Kathryn Kuhlman on the radio, blasting. I could see she was listening, she understood, and I can remember my mother specifically saying, 'Now you kids, don't listen to this lady, she's not Catholic, don't listen to her.' You couldn't help but hear her, she was preaching, blasting, over the radio."[179] Julia was either unaware of, or unconcerned with, denominational designations. Father Paul elaborates, "Just think about this, it had nothing to do with the Byzantine Catholic Church, with the prayers, the services that she was familiar with, but she knew that Kathryn Kuhlman was talking about the Lord, and she enjoyed it, I can tell you this. And this happened several times."

Kuhlman preached a Christian message of love and forgiveness, and Julia responded to it, with little or no consideration for the many controversies surrounding the faith healer. A newspaper clipping about a Kuhlman baptismal service in Beaver County near Pittsburgh is found among Julia's belongings. It may have been sent her by a niece, Mary (Sally) Zymboly, who proselytized for Kuhlman. In 1977, Sally tried to convert Andy. She urged her cousin to "[take] God seriously" and told him, "Your mother and I discussed this when I visited her in the hospital shortly before she died."[180] In several letters, Sally grumbled about not receiving a response to her previous correspondence, so it is unlikely Warhol replied. He also resented reminders about observing holy days of obligation from his sister-in-law Ann, who had stringently cautioned her children not to listen to Kuhlman. Warhol called Ann a "religious fanatic."[181] But grandchildren attest that he regularly prayed with his mother in Church Slavonic before he left the house for work or a social event.

Julia's moral lessons were universal in spirit. According to her sons, her most important religious teaching was simply to "be a good person." She raised her children not with the Baltimore Catechism or a Byzantine version thereof, but with simple lessons and instructive stories. John Warhola said, "The way we were brought up was never to hurt anybody, to try to do everything right, to believe that you're just here for a short time and to build up your treasures and your spiritual things because you are going to leave the material things behind."[182] She pinned medals of the Virgin Mary inside the boys' shirts, and according to Ultra Violet, who claimed to have gone shopping with her, she had three gold medals of Christ and the Virgin Mary pinned to the strap of her homemade camisole.[183] Her faith in their protective power was not unlike the old-world belief in a magic talisman.

Alexander Motyl accurately points out that the kind of Greek Rite Catholicism practiced by many Rusyns, especially among first-generation Americans, allowed for an existential religious meaning, rather than one based on dogma and strict moral codes. "The Vatican—together with its dogmas, pomp, and circumstance— is as far from the Carpathian Mountains as it is from Pittsburgh's Slavic slums."[184]

First-generation immigrants maintained the peasants' earthy amalgamation of church teachings with pre-Christian superstitious magic. In the New World, this predisposed them to mysticism, nonconventional religious appeals, and alternative medical claims.[185] Warhol told an interviewer that his mother believed in flying saucers, and Andy himself put faith in tarot cards.[186] This matter-of-fact, peasant-like approach to life and faith, with its roots in Rusyn folklore, produced a broad-based spiritual belief system that prioritized the individual's private and personal relationship with God, rather than a narrow, rule-defined dogmatic creed. It was within this spiritual belief system that Andy Warhol grew up.

"The Way the World Thanks You"

However deep Julia's religiosity, life had taught her that while faith in God was all-important, one needed a healthy dose of pragmatism to survive. Her confidence in divine mercy and justice was balanced by traditional peasant cynicism toward the world and her fellow man, which, along with her piety, she communicated to her youngest son. A Carpatho-Rusyn folktale, "How the World Thanks You for Doing Good," demonstrates a more jaundiced sensibility than the lesson preached by the story of the hobo. It describes the travails of a Rusyn Everyman, Ivan, who starts from the moral presumption that "every person has an obligation to help another in times of need."[187] But when he frees a snake caught in a rockslide, instead of thanking him, the snake tries to strangle him. "Well," explains Snake, "that's fair and just. This is the way the world thanks you for doing good." Ivan protests and appeals to a series of animal judges for redress. Horse describes his hard life of toilsome burden, only to be tied up and left to perish. "This is how I am thanked for my work. Therefore, it is fair and just that Snake should strangle you—just like my master has left me to die here." Dog gives a similar response: "This is how people treat each other. Never expect something good for doing good." Finally, Fox, "the wisest of animals," tricks Snake into reenacting the initial encounter, and she goads Ivan not to rescue the snake, but to leave him to perish. The snake dies, and Fox extracts the promise of a chicken from Ivan to be given her the next morning.

When Ivan returns home, his hard-hearted wife berates him for his promise to Fox, even as Ivan repeats that he is morally obligated to repay Fox's help. "Ivan couldn't sleep all night, so tormented was he with doubts. But what is a man to do? He couldn't go against his wife." The next day, Ivan's wife recites the Lord's Prayer, not once, but twice amid her housewifely duties. Then she calls to her husband, "Mother of God! Go husband, bring out the dog … and if Fox comes, don't allow her to take a chicken." When Fox arrives, Ivan lets the dog loose, and the dog catches Fox by the tail. The conclusion of the story is swift and brutal: "Fox tugged in one direction. The dog tugged in another, pulling off half of Fox's tail. Fox took off toward the woods, while the dog choked on her tail. At the edge of the forest, Fox stopped and shouted: "So this is how the world thanks you for doing good!"

This extraordinary tale violates all expectations. Instead of justice and mercy, it foregrounds distrust, resentment, and vindictiveness. While the church taught moral fables that highlighted ideal visions, folktales emerged from the life of the people, revealing the practicalities of survival in a harsh and brutish world. Interesting here is the coupling of religious faith and unpitying ruthlessness. Ivan's initial conviction that everyone has an obligation to help others is deflated by his encounters with reality. As is often the case in Slavic folklore and in misogynistic Carpatho-Rusyn literature, men's compassion is no match for women's callousness. The incongruity between extrinsic religious piety and practical expediency becomes explicit when Ivan's wife invokes the Lord's Prayer, with its plea for forgiveness "as we forgive others," while she plans the attack on Fox. She then calls on the Mother of God in her battle cry. The final message to this piece of folk wisdom is that there are no winners in this "dog-eat-fox" world. There are only survivors.

Julia Warhola understood both the world of the virtuous hobo and the folktale of the duplicitous snake. There was room for both in the Slavic *dvoeverie* (double-belief), that merged Christian faith with folk belief in the life of Carpatho-Rusyn peasant immigrants. For all her warmth and affection, Julia could also be spirited, feisty, and harsh. In a Rusyn-language video from 1970, she reveals a tough and fiery personality that contrasts with the naive and childlike image often attributed to her.[188] "Everybody looks out for themselves," she complains. Speaking about an acquaintance, she carps, "For the whole world, she won't buy anything for herself. That's how [tightly] she holds onto money. She thinks she can eat it. And then she comes here and she's hungry." Warhol's boyfriend from around the same time described the duality and likened it to Andy's personality: "Like Andy, she could say devastating things to put people down; but she could also be sweet and very funny."[189]

In the same video, Julia goes off on a seriocomic riff in Rusyn about a beauty salon on Lexington Avenue where she got a perm. As she performs this narrative, she lies in bed on her side, fixed in the frame of the camera that her son is testing.

> I don't know why I have a scab on my head. I don't know why I have peeled skin on my head. I don't know who gave that to me. And it's hurting me a lot. Is it because they burned my scalp when they were curling my hair? That damn medicine burned my skin.

> That old lady [pejorative]. It's the fault of that old *boss woman*, she burned my hair. For
> my *twenty-five dollars*, she burned my head with that strong evil stuff. I could have her
> arrested for what she did to my head. . . . The old devil, she burned my head herself. *With*
> *poison*. . . . If it were just my hair, it would be nothing, but it's my skin. She boiled it.[190]

The story Julia tells of her mishap at the beauty salon is another example of her
flare for performance. The repeated phrase "I don't know why . . ." serves to position her as a character as well as a narrator in her story and emphasizes its poetic
and expressive features. Code-switching from Rusyn to English, she sets apart
the terms "boss woman," "twenty-five dollars," and "poison" to emphasize their
import. The phrases "old lady" (*starulia*) and "old devil" (*staryi fras*) that she applies
to the "boss woman" are relatively mild, folksy terms of insult. And with her final
formulation of the damage to her hair and her skin—"she boiled it"—Julia reaches a
dramatic catharsis. After the energetic monologue, delivered in a lively intonation,
she becomes silent and pensive. A lengthy pause follows before she changes the subject. Behind the camera, Andy listens to her tirade in silence, offering no response.

The image of Julia in this video, shot when she was almost eighty years old and ill,
contrasts with the fond memories of sons and nieces and with the storyteller of "The
Hobo and the Magic Pocketbook." But they are not incompatible. The feisty persona
Julia "performs" was part of her intrinsic makeup. She passed on her worldly cynicism
to her youngest son along with her ingenuous faith in a worldview that combined the
paradoxical values of power and piety, gall and grace, guile and naivete.

Andy

In their childhood, the older boys were charged with looking after Andy—for better
or worse. Paul told the Czech and Slovak writers, Rudo Prekop and Michal Cihlář
about a time when Andy ran after him to the bus stop, tripped on a curb, and broke
his arm. "Since Mom didn't have enough money for a doctor, we didn't take him to
the hospital. The arm healed, but wrong. So then when the family came to us on a
visit and saw Andy's arm was crooked, he had to go to the hospital where they broke
his arm again and then put it in plaster properly. It was the wrist of his right hand,
the one Andy painted with all his life."[191] Given his parents' unfamiliarity with the
American medical and educational systems, Andy was dependent on his older brothers, and despite the accident at the curb, their intervention was providential. While
their mother encouraged drawing at home, it was Paul who carried through Andy's
teacher's recommendation and facilitated his entrance into the Tam o'Shanters pro-

gram, the Saturday morning art classes at the Carnegie Institute.[192] More than once, Paul told a story that "predicted" Andy's future artistic success. Around the time of the Great Saint Patrick's Day flood of 1936, Julia sent the boys to visit their Aunt Mary, who lived across the Allegheny on the North Side. "Well, the streetcars weren't running and that meant we had to walk. We had to use a different bridge than we would have normally." Eight-year-old Andy complained that he was tired of walking, and Paul refused to carry him. "[Andy] says, kind of irritated, 'Well, I'm going to sit and rest.'" He sat on the front steps of a 1911 industrial warehouse owned by the Volkwein Music & Instruments Company. In 1990 the Volkwein building became the property of the Carnegie Institute, and in 1994, the building opened as the Andy Warhol Museum.[193] As unlikely as it may seem, the coincidence fits in the Warhola family's album of myths that may be too good to be true, but impossible to refute.

As a small child, Andy clung to his mother's skirt. In family photos, he is often the only child at gatherings of adult relatives. "He was her baby," said neighbor Ann Elachko, "the daughter she never had."[194] His cousin Tinka Preksta recalled that Andy went shopping with his mother and helped pick out her hats. "He liked to do that. His mother loved hats. I remember her buying a black felt hat and as a very young boy he painted it gold around the edges."[195] For Julia, a hat was an important symbol of modernization and a sign of refinement, a chic advancement over the traditional kerchief (*khustya*), disparaged in America as a *babushka*, that was worn by east European women.

As the youngest son, Andy was coddled and spoiled. Bob Colacello made famous the appellation "holy terror," which is how the son of the Warholas' landlord on Beelen Street remembered the three- or four-year-old Andy. Chester Stanek, who was just three years older than Andy, told Colacello, "I'll never forget the time we were standing on the front porch and he urinated on me." Another Beelen Street neighbor, who sometimes babysat for Andy, told Colacello, "He was really a handful to watch, a sprightly, rambunctious, high-strung nervous type."[196] According to Zavacky cousins, Andy was so mischievous that they had to tie him to the bedpost when they were babysitting.[197] According to Paul, things only got worse when they moved to Moultrie Street. "Andy picked up some bad language when he was about three and this wasn't allowed in our house. He heard some of the kids swear and he was just a youngster. . . . And the more you smacked him the more he did it, the worse he got. He was real bad. Just because we didn't want him to say it he said it. Nobody swore in our house. We weren't allowed to say 'hell.'"[198] Paul's broad comments support Julia's story about Andy's use of the n-word, which resulted in the attack on Paul by Black people living in the neighborhood.

In a letter from 1965, a Zavacky cousin writes to Andy, "You know Andy, I remember an amusing thing about you when you were about 4 years old. Your mother asked you what you're going to be when you grow up and you answered, 'Ya budu bom, ya vas zastreliu.' Oh how we all laughed."[199] That is, at around four years of age, Andy told his family, "I'm going to be a bum, and I'll shoot you all."[200] In Carpatho-Rusyn immigrant culture, the term "bum" had a sinister meaning that was stronger than the standard American connotation of vagrant or beggar. Akin to a menacing bogeyman, a "bum" was an ominous malefactor, a rogue scoundrel, an ever-present specter, used to induce good behavior in children. We see Julia use the term in Warhol's film *The George Hamilton Story*, as she locks the kitchen door to deter a possible burglar, and as a moniker for one of her least favorite cats, the "black bum."

It would be interesting to know what was behind Warhol's hyperbolic power-grab and how he reacted emotionally to the family's well-intentioned but ultimately derisive laughter. Warhol's recorded comments indicate a continuing frustration learned in childhood. In his *Philosophy* he recalled, "Mom always said, 'Don't be pushy, but let everybody know you're around.' I wanted to command more space than I was commanding, but then I knew I was too shy to know what to do with the attention if I did manage to get it."[201] This is corroborated in the ghostwritten *POPism* from the 1960s: "I don't think of myself as evil—just realistic. I learned when I was little that whenever I got aggressive and tried to tell someone what to do nothing happened—I just couldn't carry it off. I learned that you actually have more power when you shut up, because at least some people will start to maybe doubt themselves."[202] Although he was known as sweet and humble with his girlfriends, Andy's accrual of passive power made him act "like an arrogant little prince at home."[203]

Just after his sixth birthday, Andy started school at Holmes Elementary School, up the block on Dawson Street, where he did well in class. When he became ill with rheumatic fever two years later, Julia's overweening concern and indulgence amplified his sense of entitlement. Andy described his episodes of illness as "nervous breakdowns." "I had three nervous breakdowns when I was a child, spaced a year apart. Once when I was eight, one at nine, and one at ten. The attacks—St. Vitus Dance—always started on the first day of summer vacation. I don't know what this meant. I would spend all summer listening to the radio and lying in bed with my Charlie McCarthy doll and my un-cut-out cut-out paper dolls all over the spread and under the pillow."[204] Rheumatic fever, an infectious inflammatory disease, which had disastrous implications for the heart, sometimes, as in Warhol's case, attacked the nervous system.[205] In the 1920s, rheumatic fever was the leading cause of death in individuals between five and twenty years of age, and it continued to be one of the chief causes of death in school-age children into the 1950s, usually as a result of cardiac complications. When Andy was afflicted in the 1930s, Pittsburgh newspapers carried numerous stories about children's deaths from rheumatic fever, and fewer accounts of high school basketball stars or cheerleaders who had recovered from the illness, which was endemic in overcrowded neighborhoods with poor hygiene and limited access to health care. By 1930, it was known that the disease typically developed following a streptococcal throat infection, but before the advent of penicillin in the 1940s, the only treatment was rest and aspirin. The disease was protracted; the average duration of a single attack was about six months. In children, four of five afflicted patients had recurrent attacks with intervening periods of apparent well-being. Hence, Andy's "three nervous breakdowns."[206]

Andy was among almost half of children with rheumatic fever who developed chorea or Saint Vitus's dance, which was characterized by involuntary, irregular, jerking movements, especially of the face and upper extremities. According to Bockris's interviews with family, Andy, who had been doing well at Holmes Elementary School, now found it difficult to write or draw, and schoolmates laughed at his shaking hands. As the illness progressed, he started slurring his speech, fumbling, and fidgeting. Afraid of going to school, he became emotionally irritable.[207] A chorea specialist wrote, "Personality changes are always present; the child is hypersensitive and irritable. Fidgetiness or restlessness may be the first sign."[208] Gopnik suggests a connection to an illness that today is known as PANDAS, pediatric autoimmune neuropsychiatric disorders associated with streptococcal infections, which relates strep infections and rheumatic fever in children to adult psychiatric problems, such as obsessive-compulsive disorder and body-image issues, both of which are relevant to the adult Andy Warhol.[209]

In the 1930s, the regular treatment for rheumatic fever was bed rest in a quiet environment. Most cases of chorea appeared in the spring, which explains Andy's summers spent in bed. Julia was disturbed enough to call Dr. Zeedick, although his fee of $2 was an extravagance the family could ill afford.[210] The doctor came from his office on the North Side to make a house call and confined Andy to bed. School records show that Andy was absent forty-eight days in the spring of 1937, twenty-two days in the following fall term, and thirty-seven days in the spring of 1938.[211] Medical journals of the time recommended a long period of physician's care, but stressed, "In most instances, the mother carries the biggest burden."[212] At 3252 Dawson Street, Andrii slept in the attic with the older boys, to allow Julia to share a bed in the dining room with Andy. Julia sometimes sat up all night watching him sleep. Since the jerking movements ceased during sleep, she was probably consoled by the image of a peacefully sleeping child.

Physicians advised, "Although the infection may remain active, the patient need not necessarily feel 'ill.' . . . Oftentimes, it is very difficult to keep the child amused and occupied while he is in bed, but it is essential to keep him content and optimistic. Games and story-telling may be extremely helpful."[213] Julia was a perfect caregiver and companion. She listened to children's radio programs with Andy—"Little Orphan Annie," the adventure series "Jack Armstrong, the All American Boy," and "Let's Pretend," with its whimsical tales of fantasy—while he played with his paper dolls. Every time he finished a page in his coloring book, she gave him a Hershey bar, probably following advice from physicians, who advised a high caloric diet.[214] She was a collaborator and an appreciative audience, conferring unconditional approval on his creative work and mirroring his behavior. Her interaction with him could not have been based on theories of art education. Rather it was an instinctive outgrowth of her own creative talent. "Andy always wanted pictures. Comic books I buy him. Cut, cut, cut nice. Cut out pictures. Oh, he liked pictures from comic books."[215] In a house where the language was not English and books were rare, images, everything from icons to comics, were precious, instructive, and inspirational. When Andy was nine, his interest in images extended from comic books to the stars of Hollywood. He sent away for a photo of his idol, Shirley Temple, and he received a large glossy signed "To Andrew Worhola [*sic*] from Shirley Temple." He carefully kept it in a photo album.

Julia also entertained her son with stories. "My mother would read to me in her thick Czechoslovakian accent as best she could and I would always say 'Thanks, Mom,' after she finished with Dick Tracy, even if I hadn't understood a word."[216] Julia may well have had difficulty reading Dick Tracy comics in English, but her conversation and stories were surely delivered *po nashomu*, rather than in English. She told Andy about life in Miková and narrated edifying tales of her own invention, like "The Hobo and the Magic Pocketbook." From the studio of his sickroom, she passed on to him her gift of mythologizing the stuff of everyday life and interacting with the world creatively. In the Ric Burns documentary on Andy Warhol, the art critic Dave Hickey, speaks of Julia's "secret kitchen workshop" as more crucial in Warhol's artistic training than, say, his understanding of Duchamp.[217] Wayne Koestenbaum echoes that judgment, saying it is easy to imagine that Andy learned more about how to be an artist from Shirley Temple, Lana Turner, and Julia Warhola than Duchamp, Jackson Pollock, or Picasso. "His art has the maternal inscription in it."[218]

In *Mothering the Mind*, Ruth Perry describes the vital role of mutual, creative play between artists and their mothers. "It is a way of trying on solutions in the mind, of experimenting with what is and what ought to be . . . a duet with reality, patterned in the sheltered space first established by the mother . . . for the child, its terrain covering ever-shifting proportions of self and world." In his sickbed studio, his mother allowed Andy to "slip back and forth from fantasy to reality, constructing, demolishing, and reconstructing [his world]."[219] Julia had a lifetime of experience shifting between reality and fantasy—from folk drama in Miková to the fanciful memories she invented. Even more than her practical encouragement of Andy's artwork, it was the creative vision that she communicated to him throughout his childhood that inspired and enabled his career.

Julia recognized her son's talent and his eccentricity, which was not unlike her own. "Andy, he look like me. Funny nose."[220] She had survived life in Miková by flouting gender conventions, and now she gave Andy permission to be original, as he left the outfield in the middle of a softball game to draw pictures on the porch. The willful, childlike nature she encouraged in him persisted into his college years and beyond. As Ruth Perry said, it was customary for the "silent partners" of artists to "[grant] permission to the figures they 'mothered' to be infantile."[221] This was certainly true of Julia and her relationship with Andy, whom she addressed with childish diminutives into his late forties and to the end of her life.

The childlike aspect that Julia encouraged in Andy became part of Warhol's artistic vision. Jack Wilson, a college classmate, said, "Andy was the damndest mixture of the six-year-old child and, yet, all the skills of a well-trained artist. . . . And I think that's part of his success. It's my feeling that he sees the world through the mind of a six-year-old child." The top literary agent Andrew Wylie, who spent the late 1960s in Warhol's circle, described the artist's influence in words that capture Andy's easy movement between childhood and maturity, between inner and outer reality. "He expanded and adjusted my notion of what and how an educated person could think; he had a playful, unconventional approach to reality."[222] When he was considering a career in art education at Carnegie Tech, a classmate asked him about his life's ambition. "Andy replied that he wanted to teach children how to play."[223]

According to testimony from his brothers, Andy's illness was not considered critical in the family, since "he only came down with it seriously once, and was really too young to worry about it." Unaware of the danger of potential cardiac and possible neuropsychiatric complications, John said, "It was like having chickenpox or a sore throat."[224] As the brothers recalled, Andy spent only one month in bed after his first attack, which is much less than what the medical literature of the time recommended. While Andrii was away from home, Julia acceded to the uninformed opinions of her sons, who encouraged her to send Andy back to school. As Andy threw a tantrum, Paul and the Warholas' neighbor, John Elachko, physically held him down. "Andy tried

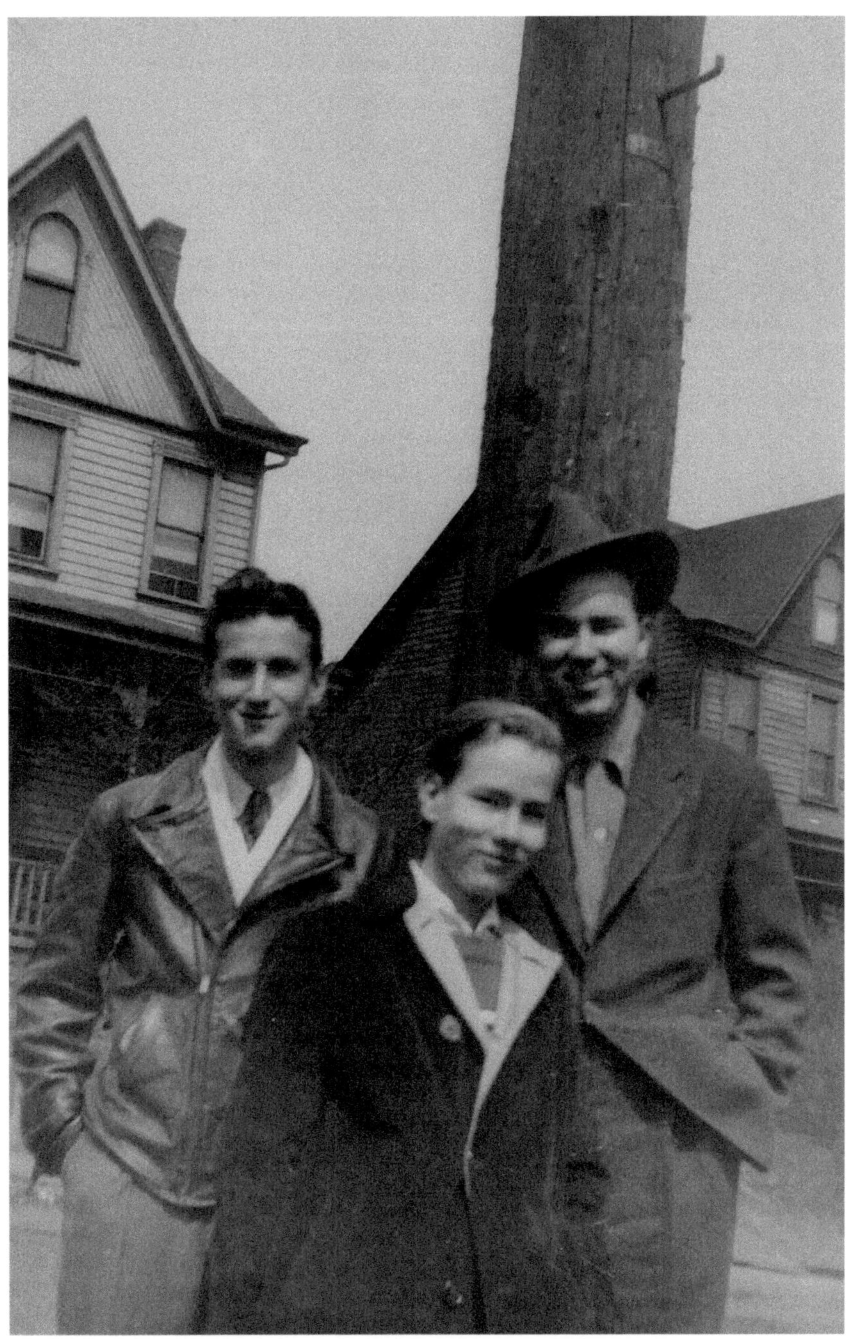

Figure 4.5. John, Paul, and Andy Warhola, ca. 1940.

to kick him," said Paul. "He fought us not to go and we did force him to go to school. Now that was the worst thing to do because after that he developed a worse nervous twitch." John recalled, "We didn't know he wasn't completely cured. . . . I remember the doctor says he got it all over again."[225] Medical journals advised, "It is hard to tell at times when the disease is over in children. It frequently lasts for many months."[226]

Andy settled into the role of the sickly child, who happily took advantage of his infirmity. "When I was little and I was sick a lot, those sick times were like little intermissions. Innermissions. Playing with dolls."[227] Ultra Violet, whose take on Andy was highly cynical, wrote: "How did he acquire his astonishing entrepreneurial spirit? I think back over his life and decided he learned to maneuver in his cradle. Still a baby, he put his mother to work around the clock, nursing him, singing him lullabies, showing him picture books, coloring for him, telling him stories. Thus was the twig bent."[228] If Andy was manipulating his mother, she also played a role in the developing partnership. With her husband putting in long hours at work or away at distant sites, she was left to manage challenges on her own. Ill-equipped to deal with educational matters and regulations, she let her older sons, who were themselves only nine and twelve years old, take the lead. She certainly felt the anxiety that comes from lack of control and the frightening experience of witnessing her child's struggle with illness.

It is probably not unreasonable to describe most immigrant Slavic families in early twentieth-century America as dysfunctional by today's standards. Parenting styles based on authoritarian old-world patterns, coupled with a lack of coping strategies to deal with a new culture and changing times, set the stage for maladaptive family dynamics even under the best of circumstances. Despite deep familial love and the best of intentions, parents experiencing the stress of poverty and unemployment, not to mention a child's illness, were ill-equipped to adopt healthy parenting strategies. Although we have no reminiscences from Julia about those creative "innermissions," as Andy called them, we can assume they left an indelible impact not only on the future artist but also on the overgiving, self-sacrificing mother, who devoted herself to his care.

"Eternal Memory"

In 1919, seven years after his arrival in America, Andrii Warhola started the process to become a United States citizen. Living then as a boarder in the Forbes Street tenements, Andrii cited his age as thirty-three and listed his place of birth as "Mikowa, Austria (now Czechoslovakia)." He was described as fair-complexioned, five feet, six inches tall and 165 pounds, with brown hair, gray eyes and a "long scar on his right cheek." On April 29, 1924, he submitted a formal Declaration of Intention, with a $1.00 fee to the District Court, under his American name, Andrew Warhola. His height is now five feet, seven inches, and his weight is 175 pounds, perhaps a result of better living conditions at 3 Orr Street and Julia's care and cooking over the previous three years. He gave his date of birth as November 28, 1886. Miková church records show that he was born on December 6. Uncertain, as most Carpatho-Rusyn immigrants were, of their actual birth dates, Andrii adopted November 28, the approximate date on the Gregorian calendar, for American legal and bureaucratic purposes. He swore that he was not an anarchist or polygamist and he renounced all allegiance to the "Czecho Slovakia Republic."

Three years later he repeated this information on a Petition for Naturalization, changing his address to 73 Orr Street, adding two children, and attesting "I am able to speak the English language." Witnesses were the naturalized citizens John Galayda and John Sturak. Both were immigrants from Slovakia, and both were neighbors on Beelen Street in 1930. Galayda, a craneman at the J&L steel plant in Soho, would meet his death in 1939 in an explosion of molten metal that covered his body in burns. Sturak, an Eichleay coworker, was chairman of the branch of the Organization of Russian Brotherhoods to which Andrii belonged. Andrew Warhola's final Certificate of Naturalization was dated March 26, 1928.[229]

After the worst of the Depression receded, Andrii went back to work with Eichleay, performing strenuous labor six days a week, with frequent travel for out-of-town projects. His health had been declining for several years. According to his sons, his gallbladder had been surgically removed sometime previously. "He had been sick with yellow jaundice for a couple of years earlier on, after he was operated on to have his gallbladder removed, and then for so many years it was OK."[230] An invoice from Mercy Hospital dated January 28, 1930, "For Mr. Andrew Varhola," may refer to this operation. It itemizes two weeks of hospitalization ($35), X-rays ($20), operating room fee ($10), gas ($4), and laboratory fee ($10). An addendum to the invoice states, "We must have a payment on the above account by return mail," suggesting that the bill was overdue. While the date of the surgery is uncertain and may have been a year earlier, we know that Andrii was doing hard physical labor again for Eichleay by October 1930, when he participated in the move of the Indiana Bell Telephone Company building. By the mid-1930s when work at Eichleay had slowed, Julia urged him to cut back, but he picked up odd jobs at other house-moving companies. In 1938 he was working for Standard Hide Company, a business that skinned, cleaned, and salted fresh animal skins in preparation for tanning.[231] In 1939, brawny and muscled from

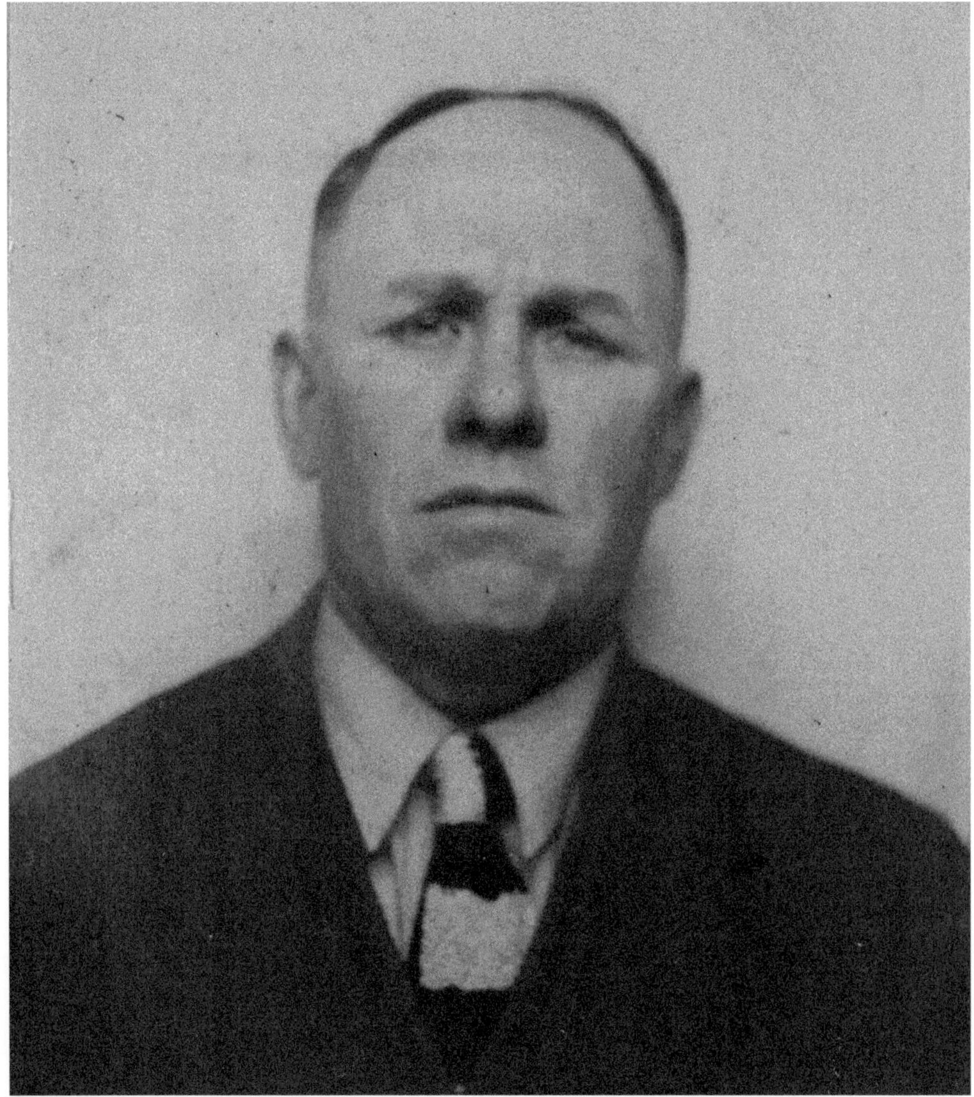

Figure 4.6. Andrii Warhola, identification photograph for Selective Service Registration, 1942.

physical exertion, Andrii was just fifty-three years old. According to his son John, he seemed the picture of health. "I thought he would live to a hundred."[232]

The 1940 census showed that Andrii had worked only forty weeks the previous year. During and following World War II, the Eichleay Engineering Corporation transitioned from house moving to industrial construction and mechanical installation. In spring and summer 1941, Andrii was at work in Hartford, Connecticut, moving two multiton United Aircraft Corporation hangars for Eichleay, but in the year starting September 1941, he was out of work fourteen weeks and claimed unemployment benefits, according to his Pennsylvania State Employment ID Card.[233]

According to family lore, Andrii was sickened when he drank contaminated water on a job in West Virginia. As Julia put it, "He go to West Virginia to work, he go to mine and drink water. The water was poison. He was sick for three years. He got stomach poisoning. Doctors, doctors, no help."[234] The facts of Andrii's final illness are uncertain, and family memories are unreliable. John recalled, "Dad was ill and housebound from 1939 to 1942," confirming Julia's estimate of three years of illness. John said, "He was up and about, he just couldn't work."[235] His statements conflict with verifiable facts. Andrii may have been employed intermittently during those years. The Pittsburgh City Directory shows him as being employed by the Kress-Oravetz house moving company and the Standard Hide Company. The New Dom letters show him working in Hartford from March through May in 1941, and perhaps longer. The work in Hartford began in early March and was slated to be completed in three months, although newspaper reports indicate that the hangars were not finally moved until the end of July.[236] Andrii's father had died of pneumonia in Miková, according to church records, in February 1896 at the age of fifty-five, and Andrii would not live much longer than his father. Paul remembered that "all at once he was getting yellow. Apparently, his liver was failing him."[237]

According to John Warhola, Andrii went to German doctors, who gave him "some kind of tea to drink."[238] The doctor who signed Andrii's official death certificate and the certification for his Russian Brotherhood Organization's life insurance policy was Morris Hershenson, an American-educated Russian Jewish immigrant. On the insurance certificate, Hershenson, a specialist in digestive diseases and gallbladder removal, stated that the duration of Warhola's final illness was six months, and that he was treated at Montefiore Hospital from May 6 until his death on May 15, 1942. Paul Warhola also mentions six months of illness. "All the workers who went out from our area to work in West Virginia ended up with serious health problems, you know. There was badly polluted water there, which everyone drank and everyone got sick from it. We were told that Dad died of liver problems. He had never been ill before, never taken any medicines and then he was suffering for six months and slowly dying, until he passed away."[239] An autopsy determined the cause of death as tuberculous peritonitis, a tubercular infection of the abdomen, which may occur via reactivation of a latent TB infection or by ingestion of tuberculous mycobacteria. Difficult to diagnose, tuberculous peritonitis manifested as abdominal pain, fever, weight loss, nausea, and vomiting. In the pre-antibiotic era, the mortality rate was around 49 percent.[240]

There may be a kernel of truth in the family's story of poisoning by tainted water on a job in West Virginia. Eichleay records show work in 1942, exact date uncertain, for the Koppers Coke Company in Follansbee, West Virginia.[241] Follansbee was home to the Koppers Follansbee Plant, a tar refining and naphthalene production facility on the Ohio River. Today, the Environmental Protection Agency website notes, "The site is contaminated from a century of coal tar processing operations." The plant was cited for contaminating the soil and groundwater with coal tar constituents, and the nearby Ohio River has been contaminated with numerous toxic agents. Repeating Paul Warhola's comment, Donald Warhola, John's son, claims that other men in the work crew were sickened but recovered, and he suggests that Andrii's previous gastro-enterological issues may have predisposed him to infection, although it may not have been the direct cause of death. Andrii's cousin John Zavacky remembers that Andrii was working out of town when he came down with his fatal illness.[242] We do not know whether Andrii was on the job at Follansbee, but like most anecdotal Warhola family stories, when set against observable facts, it has a ring of truth.

According to John Warhola, in May 1942, Andrii predicted that he would not be coming out of the hospital and gave him instructions about financing Andy's college education. The family visited Andrii during his stay at Montefiore Hospital. Paul remembered: "The day before he died, Dad had an awful fever and he was in a lot of pain and he asked me to get him a drink of water, and the head nurse grabbed me and said, 'Don't you dare give him no water! We're running tests on him!' Dad looked at me so pitiful and he says, 'Just give me some water to wipe my lips.' And I felt so bad because I couldn't even give him a little bit of water."[243] Just a month before his hospitalization, Andrii was pursuing a relatively normal life. On April 2, 1942, he had a "reinterview" for unemployment compensation. And just one week before his hospitalization, Andrii registered for the draft. Known today as the "Old Man's Draft," the registration officially took place on April 27 at draft boards around the country. In the "Old Man's Draft," the Selective Service targeted men from forty-five to sixty-four years of age to assemble an inventory of manpower resources that could be useful for service on the home front.[244] On April 28, the *Pittsburgh Post-Gazette* reported, "Local and county draft registration centers were jam-packed with long lines of registrants almost continuously from 7 o'clock yesterday morning to 9 o'clock last night."[245] Andrii's draft registration indicates his height now as five feet, five inches and his weight as 180 pounds.

Andrii's death has been given much attention by Warhol biographers because of the effect it had on his youngest son. According to John, the morning after his father died, Andy asked his mother, "'How come you tickled my nose with a feather?' And my mother says, 'I wasn't even in the room.' And he says, well, somebody tickled his nose and when he woke up he looked up and he says he just seen like a body going out the door into the hall. About eight hours later, my dad passed away and my mother said, 'That must have been an angel or God leaving, you know.'"[246] Andrii's death certificate states the time of death as 7:45 p.m. and his insurance certificate gives it as 9:00 p.m., but the story of the overnight nose-tickling and Julia's explanation for it suggests her own and Andy's tendency to the otherworldly. On Monday, May 18, 1942, an announcement in the *Pittsburgh Press* read, "WARHOLA—On Friday, May 15. Andrew, husband of Julia and father of Paul, John and Andrew, Jr. Friends received at his late residence, 3252 Dawson St., Oakland. Requiem high mass at St. John's G. C. Church, Saline St., Tuesday at 9 a.m." Andrii's death was handled by Albert A. Novak, whose funeral home on the North Side catered to the Roman Catholic Slovak community. The Warholas' Rusyn neighbor, John Elachko, assisted at Andrii's funeral. A year later, Elachko would operate his own mortuary business out of his home on Dawson Street.

The elaborate, grim funeral customs of the Carpatho-Rusyn folk tradition were moderated in the immigration, but it was still customary to hold viewing and visitation in the family home, where mirrors were covered but caskets were open, candles and flowers were positioned around the deceased, and visitors knelt at the side of the casket to pray. The priest and cantor chanted mournful prayers in protracted, lugubrious ceremonies, accompanied by the wailing (*holosynia*) of women. Relatives and friends recited speeches of fixed formulae, which highlighted the good deeds of the deceased and his loving relationship with family. John Elachko recalled, "The old country people had a singsong wailing kind of thing they did, telling a story about the dead person's life with their arms across their chests, hopping from foot to foot. Julia Warhola was one of those wailers."[247] Members of the deceased's fraternal society turned their ribbon badges to the back and sat up with their brother overnight, praying, reminiscing, and not infrequently, drinking. A prayer card, stamped with Warhola's name and date of death, bore a prayer and a lachrymose image of a suffering Jesus crowned with thorns.

Anyone who has experienced the traditional Carpatho-Rusyn funeral of a loved one, especially at a young age, is forever haunted by the doleful chant of *Vichnaia pamiat'* (Eternal memory), the powerful scent of flowers and clouds of incense, the tears and wailing of relatives, and the visual image of the loved one lying in a casket

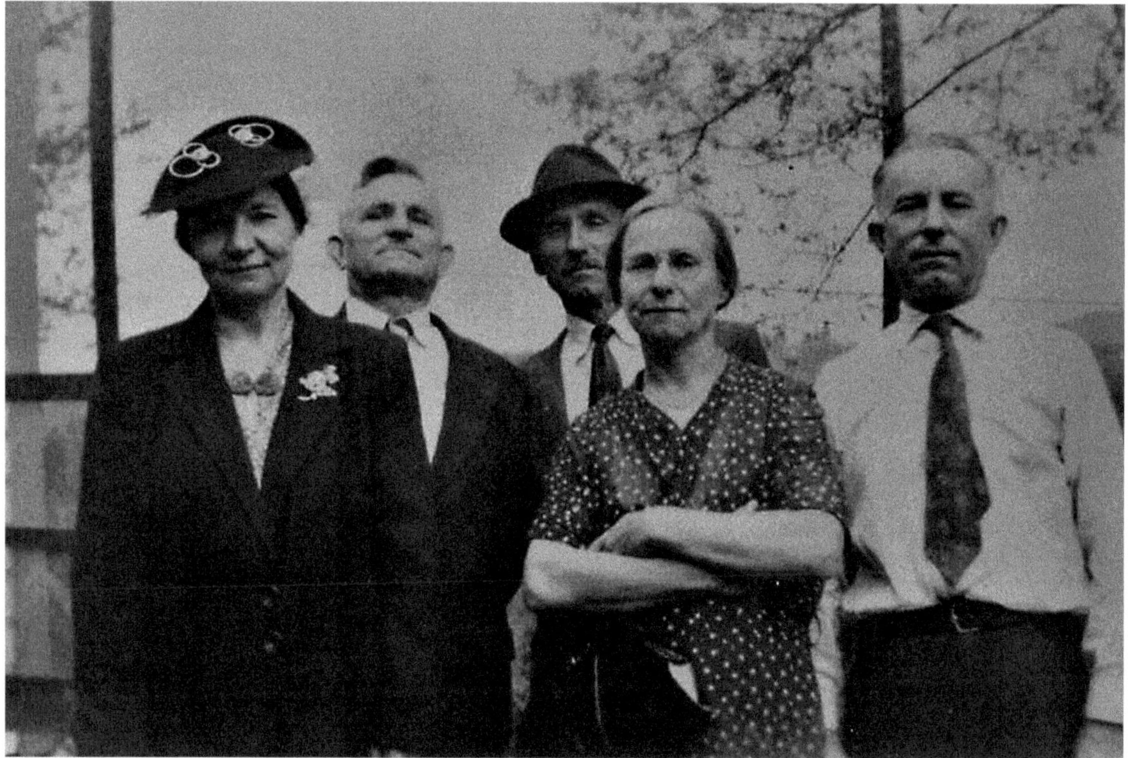

Figure 4.7. Mary Zavacky Preksta, John Zavacky, Stephen Zavacky, Julia Zavacky Warhola, Andrew Zavacky, ca. 1942. Of Julia's "American" siblings, only Anna is missing.

in the family living room. Thirteen-year-old Andy was particularly disturbed. Paul recalled, "He just didn't wanna see Dad. When they brought the body into the house Andy was so scared he ran and hid under the bed." But it is unlikely that he stayed under his bed all three days of the viewing, as Paul implied. John explained, "He was just frightened to sleep in the house with the body, so he stayed with my aunt for a couple of nights." Six years after his attack of rheumatic fever, Paul's statement that Andy did not attend his father's funeral because his mother was afraid it might cause another attack of his "nervous condition" is also improbable. Photographs taken after the funeral show Andy in a jacket and tie with his cousins, evidently coming from church.

In the Old Country, young people passed the time of the funeral vigil playing archaic folk games, which were completely inconsistent with the sad atmosphere. "On the contrary, they were marked by youthful mirth, high spirits, and eroticism."[248] In the immigration, young people were usually exempted from the most dolorous parts of the ritual, often escaping to unoccupied space, where they enjoyed soda pop and snacks that were not commonly available and took advantage of freedom from adult supervision. In family photos taken after the funeral, the almost fourteen-year-old Andy is surrounded by his older brothers and women cousins, who hold him by his arms. It is uncertain whether they are embracing him within the family group or preventing him from running away. Another family photograph has not been dated, but internal evidence—Julia wears the same dress that she wore for the photo on her naturalization certificate dated a month earlier—relates it to spring 1942. It shows Julia with her three "American" brothers and her sister Mary. The posed photograph indicates a solemn occasion, and it is likely that the gathering was for the funeral of Julia's husband. Julia looks weary and somber, but resolute and determined. Just as she told the *Esquire* interviewer about Andrii's departure for America, she might now have repeated, "My husband gone and then everything bad."[249] She now faced another difficult time, and she took charge after Andrii's death, just as she had after his emigration, bowing to God's will. Twenty years later, her advice to a recently widowed niece hints at what her response to her own fate must have been: "It is very sad for you. But on the contrary, I ask you not to think about him. Let his soul rest there with God. Just pray for the deceased and that will be better. . . . It was Jesus Christ God's will. He wanted to take him, and we have nothing to say about it."[250]

Julia in Charge

On May 19, Andrii's funeral was celebrated at Saint John Chrysostom Greek Catholic Church, officiated by Reverend Stephen Kozak. Julia had reported her husband's death to his branch of the Russian Brotherhood Organization on May 18, and on May 20, she received $600 from the insurance policy that Andrii had purchased in 1913.[251] Andrii was interred on a green hillside at Saint John the Baptist Cemetery in Castle Shannon, then a rural area south of the city. The gravesite was newly purchased. A receipt dated June 13, 1942, for $187, from Saint John the Baptist Church to the undertaker for Lot #134 Section 2, was found among the papers of John Warhola.

Andrii and Julia had made out wills in 1931, probably around the time of Andrii's first gallbladder surgery. Just as John Buccos assisted the Zavacky brothers to become established in Lyndora, Stephen Fechosko, an American-born son of Lemko-Rusyn immigrants, shepherded the Warholas through their financial planning. Fechosko, who eventually rose to the position of supervisor of postal savings, had a reputation for helping immigrants prepare for naturalization.[252] With an American education and a native command of his parents' Lemko dialect, he was a valuable resource.

It has not previously been noted that Andrii wrote a second will, dated December 4, 1939, "hereby revoking any will or wills heretofore made by me."[253] Just as in 1931, he named Julia his executrix and bequeathed his estate to her and her heirs. Andrii may have been counseled to revise his will to ensure that his wife and children would be eligible for Social Security survivors' benefits, which were instituted only in 1940. The 1939 date also suggests that Andrii must have been aware that his illness was worsening. Stephen Fechosko again witnessed the will. The 1931 wills had been witnessed by his clerk but, in a significant change in 1939, the second witness was Julia's sister, Mary Preksta. John Warhola recalled that Mary visited Andrii in the hospital before his death, and he told her "not to listen to nobody but Johnny" about how he wished the money he was leaving to be used, that is, for Andy's education.[254] He may have feared that Julia would be pressured to use the funds for other purposes, and he very likely wanted a trusted family member named on the will as a safeguard. Andrii's will was filed in November 1943 and submitted for probate. An appraisal by Fechosko was notarized in January 1944, showing three $500 United States postal saving bonds bearing 2.5 percent interest, for a total value of $1,514.07.[255]

In March 1946, Julia navigated the Czechoslovak Consulate in Pittsburgh to transfer her husband's property in Miková to her sister Eva, "to use these properties and to pay tax and other charges connected with them until the time when I am back in the homeland and can administer the properties myself." According to Paul Warhola, his mother used to talk about revisiting Miková "all the time," but it is significant that as late as 1946, Julia referred to a potential return to the homeland.[256] In documents signed a year later by Julia and her sons, the possibility of return is omitted, and the relinquishment of inheritance rights is termed "irrevocable." This may have been prompted by changes in the political climate in the postwar years, in particular the impending communist takeover of Czechoslovakia.

On May 25, 1942, just ten days after her husband's death, Julia submitted a claim for Social Security survivors' benefits. A letter from the Social Security Board to Julia from June 20, 1942, informs her that her monthly benefit would be $17.48. This probably does not include coverage for her two underage children, which might have brought the monthly check up to $35.00.[257] When Andy turned eighteen in 1946, the checks stopped coming until Julia could reapply for Social Security at age sixty-five on November 20, 1956. A letter from July 15, 1957, when she was already living with her son in New York, informed her that she would receive $40.10 per month.[258]

Citizenship was not required to receive Social Security benefits, but it was necessary to qualify for welfare under the Pennsylvania state public assistance law. Paul Warhola insisted that his father had never taken public assistance, but it may have been something Andrii thought could be a resource for Julia after his death. Through the 1930s, with the benefits of the New Deal and unsettled conditions in Europe, applications for naturalization in the Western Pennsylvania district climbed. They reached record numbers in 1939, the bulk of the applications coming from Italians, Poles, and "Czechoslovakians."[259] Julia's preliminary documents are not available, but we can assume that Andrii convinced her of the advantages of citizenship and Fechosko helped her through the process. In 1941, with the help of her sister and brother-in-law in Miková, she managed to procure copies of her birth and marriage certificates, and on April 9, 1942, just a month before Andrii's death, Julia became a United States citizen. She officially changed her name from Ula Varhola to Julia Warhola, and in July 1943, she registered to vote as a Democrat.[260] She may have contributed to FDR's fourth-term landslide victory in Allegheny County in 1944. It is difficult to imagine the peasant shepherdess from Miková managing all the details involved in becoming a widow and citizen in America. Andrii, in his frugal, businesslike manner, had prepared the way. Now, Julia took upon herself the business of surviving in wartime Pittsburgh.

Western Pennsylvania played an important role in World War II, both on the battlefield and the home front. An estimated 175,000 people from the Pittsburgh area served in the armed forces in Europe and the Pacific, and local industries turned to military production. Heinz, Westinghouse, and Pittsburgh Plate Glass developed weapons, radar systems, and new technologies. The region's steel mills broke production records, pouring ninety-five million tons of steel into the effort. When the War Department needed a lightweight motor vehicle, the American Bantam Car Company in Butler invented the prototype of the Jeep. By 1943, more than thirty thousand women were playing the role of "Rosie the Riveter" at US Steel. In fact, the famous "Rosie the Riveter" image was designed by a Pittsburgh artist for a Westinghouse poster.[261] Pittsburgh was proud of General George Marshal, who hailed from nearby Uniontown. Butler County's Lieutenant Carl J. Woods was a member of the Tuskegee Airmen, the first group of African Americans to serve as bomber and fighter pilots. A third local war hero, Michael Strank, was identified in American newspapers as "a native of Czechoslovakia," but like Andy Warhol, he was Carpatho-Rusyn.

Michael J. Strank (Mychal Strenk) was one of the five marines and a navy corpsman who raised the American flag on Iwo Jima on February 23, 1945.[262] The AP photographer Joe Rosenthal's iconic photo of this event was the model for the Marine Corps War Memorial that stands just outside Washington, DC. Strank was born in 1919 in Jarabina, a Rusyn village about seventy-five miles from Miková, and came to the United States in 1922. Settling in the mining and steel-working town of Franklin

THE UNITED STATES OF AMERICA

ORIGINAL
TO BE GIVEN TO
THE PERSON NATURALIZED

No. 5545545

CERTIFICATE OF NATURALIZATION

Petition No. 133481

Personal description of holder as of date of naturalization. Age 49 years; sex Female; color White; complexion Medium; color of eyes Grey; color of hair Brown; height 5 feet 2 inches; weight 120 pounds; visible distinctive marks Mole on right side of face.
Marital status Married former nationality Czechoslovakia
I certify that the description above given is true, and that the photograph affixed hereto is a likeness of me.

Julia Warhola
(Complete and true signature of holder)

UNITED STATES OF AMERICA
WESTERN DIST. OF PENNSYLVANIA } ss:

Be it known, that at a term of the District Court of The United States held pursuant to law at Pittsburgh on April 9th, 1942 the Court having found that MRS. JULIA WARHOLA then residing at 3252 Dawson Street, Pittsburgh, Pennsylvania intends to reside permanently in the United States (when so required by the Naturalization Laws of the United States), had in all other respects complied with the applicable provisions of such naturalization laws, and was entitled to be admitted to citizenship, thereupon ordered that such person be and (s)he was admitted as a citizen of the United States of America.

In testimony whereof the seal of the court is hereunto affixed this 9th day of April in the year of our Lord nineteen hundred and forty-two and of our Independence the one hundred and sixty-sixth.

G. H. BERGER,
Clerk of the U. S. District Court.
By H. I. Collins Deputy Clerk.

It is a violation of the U. S. Code (and punishable as such) to copy, print, photograph, or otherwise illegally use this certificate.

DEPARTMENT OF JUSTICE

Figure 4.8. Naturalization certificate of Julia Warhola, 1942.

Borough in Cambria County, the Strenk family attended Holy Trinity Rusyn Greek Catholic Church in Conemaugh. Strank was struck by a mortar and died on Iwo Jima just two weeks after the flag-raising. He is buried in Arlington National Cemetery, and like Andy Warhol, he is honored by a bridge in his hometown that bears his name.[263]

The Home Front

On the home front, ration books were distributed with coupons for scarce items like sugar, meat, and canned goods, as well as tires, gasoline, and clothing. The civilian population pitched in to support the war effort through scrap metal drives and victory gardens. Poster and media campaigns urged citizens to purchase war bonds. It is not surprising to find that in Pittsburgh, these campaigns took on an ethnic motivational character. On October 3, 1942, the *Pittsburgh Press* ran an article titled, "Plan Initiated Here May Help to Sell Bonds." The plan was to establish nationality-based booths to sell war bonds and stamps, organized and run by female volunteers.[264] The first group to organize was Czech, the second was Polish, and Slovaks were thirteenth. By December 1942, there were fifteen nationality booths, ranging from Lithuanian and Serbian to Greek and Chinese. The chair of the program, Mrs. Francis Tarnapowicz, got the idea from speaking to women's ethnic groups in Allegheny County. "These women appreciate the freedom of America more than many of us do. . . . They aren't 'foreigners,' as they are so often called. They are Americans, citizens of this country."

Each booth was set up with great fanfare—speeches, concerts, and entertainment in native costume. Rallies were held, and amounts raised by various groups were publicized in local and ethnic newspapers. On November 14, the *Amerikansky Russky Viestnik* reported that a Carpatho-Russian-American Booth was dedicated at Diamond and Market Streets in downtown Pittsburgh. John P. Sekerak, the supreme president of the Greek Catholic Union, delivered the main address and urged his audience to buy Victory Bonds. "By purchasing bonds at this booth, Americans of Carpatho-Russian [read Carpatho-Rusyn] extraction will achieve the recognition that they really deserve." On November 19, the *ARV* announced that the Greek Catholic Union had purchased bonds worth $100,000 during the dedication rally and pledged the same amount for the following year. A Rusyn columnist reported, "Our American Carpatho-Russian Booth began by leading all other nationality booths in the city of Pittsburgh." It is unknown how much the average Rusyn-American citizen contributed at the booth, then located in Kresge's on Fifth Avenue, but overall, the program was tremendously successful. By April 1944, the nationality booths had raised $100 million in bonds and stamps.

When Paul Warhola filed his draft registration on June 30, 1942, about a month after his father's death, he was working at the Carnegie-Illinois Steel Corporation's Homestead plant. Not quite a year later, he married Anna Lemak. Their marriage license, filed April 26, 1943, was accompanied by a waiver signed by Anna's mother to approve the marriage of her underaged eighteen-year-old daughter. Paul and Anna, who later went by Ann, were married on May 1, 1943, in West Virginia. Their son Paul Constantine, named after Julia's benefactor in Miková, was born later that year. Paul and his wife moved in with Julia and her other two sons, renting a room on the second floor of the Dawson Street house. On July 14, 1944, Paul reported for duty with the

US Navy, and served eight months on the USS *Stockton*, a destroyer that saw action in the Pacific theater during the 1944–1945 Iwo Jima operation.[265]

While Paul was away, the situation on Dawson Street became tense. In the Old Country, where a new bride traditionally supported the groom's family and was accountable to his mother, it was not uncommon for mothers-in-law to treat daughters-in-law as harshly as they had themselves been treated. Julia's experience as a daughter-in-law in the Warhola family in Miková, where she kept house for Andrii's mother and brothers for over ten years, might have created unreasonable expectations that a young American bride could not satisfy. Ann was a feisty and independent woman, not unlike Julia herself. Resourceful and entrepreneurial, she eventually became one of the first female trolley drivers in Pittsburgh.[266] The same family situation in Thomas Bell's novel of Rusyn working-class life, *Out of This Furnace*, prompted the comment, "No house is big enough for a wife and her mother-in-law."[267] Ann moved back to her parents' house in the Greenfield section of Pittsburgh, and when Paul returned in December 1945, the family continued to live with the Lemaks. Julia's relationship with her youngest son became even closer. According to John, "Mother says she didn't think she would have made it without Andy. Andy really kept her company because he would stay home and paint and study more than I would stay with her. I'd go up to the corner and play ball, but Andy spent most of his time with my mother."[268]

After the war, production slowed in the mills, jobs were scarce, prices sky-rocketed, and money was tight. In 1946, a wave of strikes affected steel, coal, and electrical industry workers. The city's power supply was cut to 45 percent when Duquesne Light Company employees failed to report for work. Mills in the district were shut down for 27 days, and steel production hit a 50-year low. Autumn saw a 53-day shutdown of city hotels, due to a staff walkout. A nationwide strike of miners caused a "brown-out" in November, idling 120,000 steel workers and railroad work-ers.[269] Wartime price controls were lifted in stages through 1946. Inflation for the year was 14 percent, and the Bureau of Labor Statistics cost-of-living index was 46 percent higher than before the war began.[270] The 59¢ three-pound stewing chicken that made Julia's Sunday soup in the early 1930s now cost $2.25 at A&P.

The Warhola family tightened their belts. On April 7, 1946, the *Pittsburgh Press* classified ads listed a 120-bass Castelli mother-of-pearl accordion for sale at 3252 Dawson Street in Oakland. It is unknown who, if anyone, played the accordion in the Warhola family, so it may have been an easy item to part with to earn some extra income. On September 4, the same newspaper advertised a "PHOTO booth. camera and showcase" at the Warhola's home address, which meant the end of

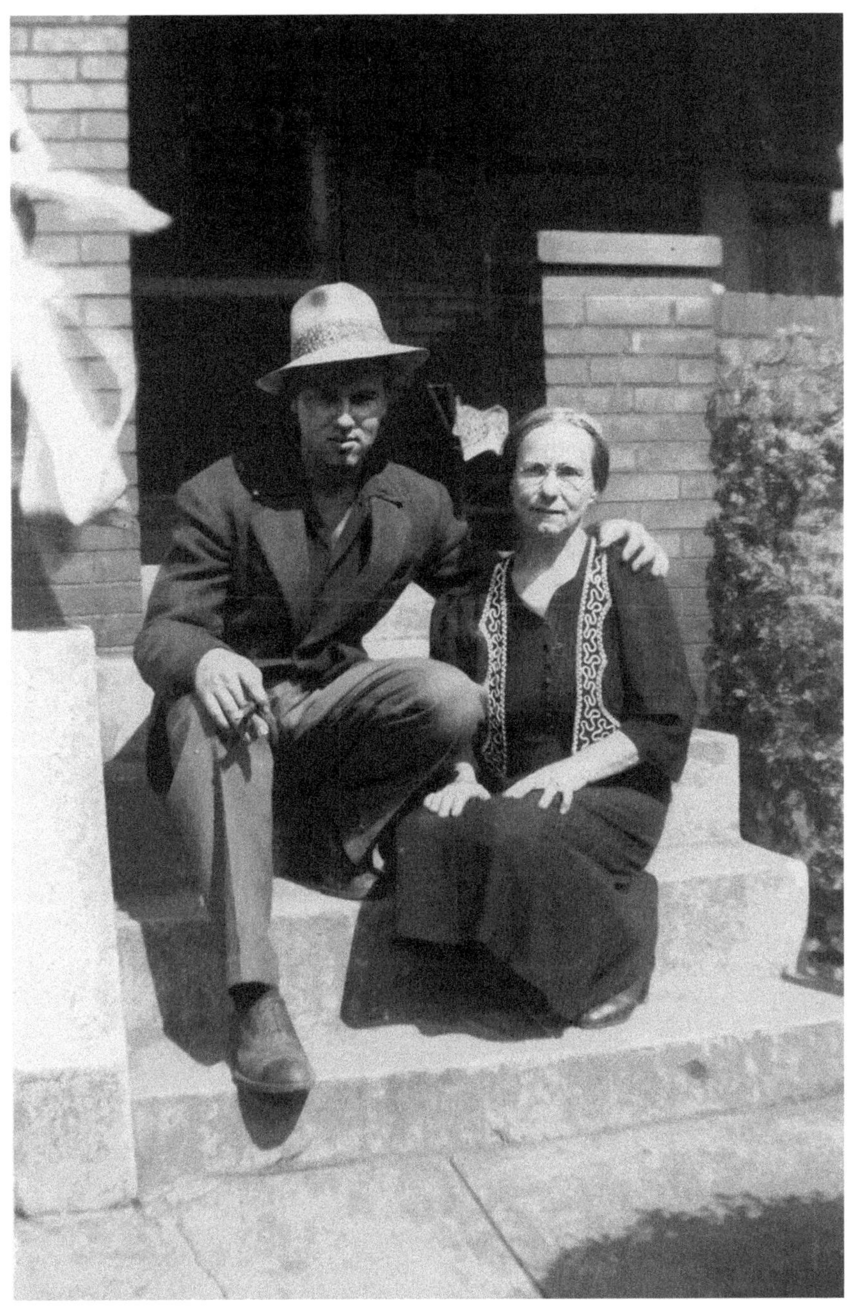

Figure 4.9. Julia with her son Paul on steps of the Dawson Street house, ca. 1945.

John's photo business and Andy's dabbling in photography at home. In November 1946, an ad under "Furnished Rooms" offered a "furnished sleeping room" in a private home at 3252 Dawson Street to a "business gentleman," references requested. On April 6 and 7, 1947, at the same address, a more elliptical ad reads "3252 Dawson St.: room, businessman, 2 schoolboys, private home, bath." Dollar amounts are not listed in any "For Rent" ads, but according to John Warhola, returning soldiers taking advantage of the GI bill rented a room in the Warhola home, which was convenient to the university, for $5 a month.[271] Julia may have resumed her housecleaning and laundry work to the extent possible, given her age and her health.

In 1944, just two years after Andrii's death, Julia developed rectal bleeding that she attributed to hemorrhoids. Tests and doctors diagnosed colon cancer. She was told that her chance of survival was 50/50, but only if she agreed to a colostomy, an operation that, as John and Paul have stated, was in the experimental stage. In fact, colostomies go back to the late nineteenth century, but it is true that there was little mention of the operation in medical journals or in the popular press until after 1945. The operation had become more common during the war to handle abdominal wounds. Details of Julia's condition and surgery are unknown, but John Warhola recalled the effect it had on the boys.

> My mother had so much faith in religion, she told me not to worry. . . . Don't worry, she says, she'll be all right. I don't think the doctors knew that much. I'll never forget the first day Andy come down there after she was operated on. The first thing he asked me was, he says, "Did Mumma die?" It was a sad situation to lose your father, then two years later . . . It was too close . . . We tried to listen to my mother and we just prayed, we prayed a lot. We visited mother in the hospital every day. She was in there for about three weeks.[272]

No documents relating to the colostomy have been found, but an $86 bill for hospital care for Julia Warhola at Elizabeth Steel Magee Hospital, from February 4 to February 25, 1940, includes a $10.00 operating room charge. Three payments of $25, $5, and $10 brought the balance down to $46 by March 28, 1940. Assuming that this was the bill for Julia's colostomy, Blake Gopnik suggests that it puts the date of the operation in doubt.[273] However, Elizabeth Steel Magee hospital focused on obstetrics, gynecology, and "women's diseases." It is unlikely that a relatively new, risky operation in the field of gastroenterology would be performed there. Moreover, John Warhola's memory that the experience was so difficult for the boys because it came shortly after their father's death is not liable to confusion. All this suggests that Julia had undergone a previous surgery in 1940, two years before Andrii's death. If it involved "women's diseases," it may not have been known to the boys, which would explain why it is not mentioned in the biographical literature. Whatever the case, it multiplies the difficulties that Julia faced from 1939 through the 1940s.

John has said that Julia was not prepared for what the operation entailed and was shocked at the results. For the rest of her life, she insisted that she never had cancer and the operation was unnecessary. She told her granddaughter that as a child, she had been run over by a wagon wheel, which "hurt her insides."[274] Now, in her early fifties, she was left to deal with primitive ostomy belts and irrigation procedures. Paul recalled that the operation was "pretty successful." "It was just that you get into a very bad depression with an operation like that. You kind of feel, do you want to live?"[275] An optimistic 1946 article on colostomy management maintains that the operation's "ominous significance for the patient" and his ensuing doubt and depression gives way to increasing confidence and finally personal pride in being able to manage the condition successfully.[276] Julia was just such an optimistic patient. Her yearlong recovery was so successful that she was asked to share her experience with patients who were facing the operation. Her granddaughter remembered, "She accepted it. I remember when we'd go to New York, mother would come around and say, if you need to use the bathroom, use it right now. [Bubba's] gonna be in there a while." She made her own dirndl-style skirts with gathering at the waist that hid the colostomy bag she wore for the rest of her life, and she rejected Andy's efforts to have the procedure reversed in New York.

Andy Becomes an Artist

Starting with the kitchen-table drawing competitions and sickbed entertainment, Julia created the conditions for Andy's creativity. In addition to acquiring art supplies and an expensive projector through her own hard labor, she nurtured his imagination with stories and games. For Julia, art was not a lofty concept but an activity that had practical implications, like her folk-art decoration of kitchen utensils in Miková and the tin-can flowers she sold for pennies and dimes. In school, Andy drew portraits of classmates and neighbors and sold them for movie money.[277] In 1966, Julia reported with some incredulity: "'My Andy draw for fun neighbor boy's face. Andy was nine year old. Boy, now big man, come here and say someone wanted to give him $300 for picture.' (She laughs)."[278] Andy also sketched family members and relatives. While his mother and Julia spoke *po nashomu* in the dining room, Andy drew cousin John Zavacky's portrait. Andy reportedly told Zavacky that a coethnic could see what the camera missed. However, Gopnik describes a sketch Warhol did of his cousin Joe around the same time as only "middling good."[279]

Andy's second-grade teacher recalled, "As he went through school, all of his teachers seemed to recognize his art ability, and they would get him to come in and maybe make a border for the room or something."[280] His fourth-grade teacher recommended him for Saturday-morning art classes at the Carnegie Institute. Blake Gopnik writes, "Given the modest culture of the Warhola home, the immersion Warhol would have needed in the language of art could only have begun in [the Carnegie Institute]." According to the account of the superstar Ultra Violet, a witness prone to hyperbole, the Tam o'Shanter program, as it was known, also introduced Warhol to other social worlds. "Several times he mentioned two youngsters who arrived in limousines, one in a long maroon Packard and the other in a Pierce-Arrow. . . . The art classes opened a peephole for Andy to the world of the rich and successful. He never forgot what he saw."[281]

In high school, his tenth-grade teacher considered Andy Warhol an outstanding student, but noted that "he was too thin," and wondered if there was enough food at home.[282] This would have been around the time when Julia was ill or recovering from her colostomy, and John and Andy were fending for themselves. They had both held summer and part-time jobs through high school; John drove an ice-cream truck and operated a photo booth with Zavacky cousins, and Andy worked at a soda fountain, washing dishes until 3:00 a.m.[283] While Julia was convalescing, John took a job at night and the brothers shared nursing duty in split shifts. They were probably assisted by Julia's sisters and nieces. Even if it could be afforded, hiring outside professional help would have been out of the question for traditional Rusyn immigrant families.

Despite the disruptions to his schedule, Andy received good grades at Schenley High School, graduating in June 1945 in the top 20 percent of his class.[284] Julia was probably not closely involved with Andy's schooling, the practice and procedures of which would have been incomprehensible to her. Like most children of immigrants, the boys were forced to grow up quickly and learn to handle administrative matters on their own. But Julia must have made an effort to engage. She later said, "Oh, Andy a good boy. He's smart. His schoolteacher, a lady tells me he teaches himself good."[285] The phrase "teaches himself" here probably has a literal meaning.

Andy passed stringent entrance exams and was accepted into the art education program at the Carnegie Institute of Technology for the term beginning October 1945.[286] But his enrollment was still uncertain. Tuition and incidentals for two semesters was estimated at about $800, which would quickly exhaust the $1,500 in postal savings bonds that Andrii had allocated.[287] John Warhola recalled, "They weren't going to accept him because he was going to just go in the evenings to save money, but my mother told him to go back and tell them that he'll go in the daytime and she gave him the money. I think it was $200 a semester. I remember before he went to talk to the people at the office he had to kneel down and say some special prayers with my mother."[288] Aside from prayer, it is hard to imagine what resources Julia could have been counting on. Warhol may have received a partial scholarship.[289]

Andy had to overcome other obstacles to his college dream. According to Bockris's interviews, his brothers made fun of him for wanting to be an artist, which is not hard to believe. What working-class teenager, raised in a Carpatho-Rusyn immigrant neighborhood of factory workers, could envision such a pie-in-the-sky career? In his first days at Carnegie Tech, Andy reached out for support, not to esteemed professors, but to a woman he considered more approachable, the art department secretary. He confided in her about his mother's illness, "in clinical detail with no embarrassment," and complained about the family's poverty. Mrs. Twiggs later interceded for him when Andy was suspended after his first year. His brother John remembered that Andy came home that day in tears. "Then Mother said, 'We'll say some prayers and everything will be all right.'"[290] Once again, Julia's prayers had the desired effect. The faculty decided to put Andy on probation, pending summer makeup work.

That summer, the always resourceful Paul Warhola, who had returned home from the navy just a few months earlier, acquired a truck and went into business huckstering fresh produce through city neighborhoods and surrounding towns. In the wee hours of the morning, he showed up at the Pittsburgh Produce Terminal, a building that stretched a quarter mile alongside the tracks of the Pennsylvania Railroad in the Strip District. When the railroad cars were unloaded, grocers and buyers for restaurants and institutions eyed the displays of fruits and vegetables to assess their shelf-life. Paul Warhola probably looked for overripe peaches and other "distressed" produce that he could sell the same day in Greenfield and Munhall from the back of his truck to turn a profit. A longtime wholesale merchant called huckstering "a con game." "It's like gambling. Gambling on the weather. Gambling on market conditions. Gambling on what you can sell."[291] Called "a handshake kind of business," huckstering was a good fit for the gregarious Paul Warhola. His son Paul Constantine recalled, "I would go with him to the market where he would load up. By mid-day we would be in West Homestead. Women would stick their heads out and yell, 'Hey Paul, give me such and such,' and he would put it on their doorsteps. We'd stop at Luke's bar. Dad would give me pop and chips. When I looked in the backroom, I'd see men playing cards. One man had a visor on his head." Paul advised his son, "Don't tell your mother."[292] According to John Warhola, "People told him he should run for mayor. Everyone knew him. He had the personality."[293]

Huckstering was labor-intensive, sorting out the "bad stuff," packaging and repackaging apples, peppers, and potatoes, hawking the daily offerings to customers, and dickering over prices. Paul paid Andy to help load, sell, and deliver the produce, as well as to wheel and deal with the clientele. Recognizing an opportunity for creativity in the downscale world of produce sales, Andy took along his sketchbook and drew pen-and-ink sketches of customers, selling many of them for 25¢. He used the proceeds to buy art supplies. When he returned to Carnegie Tech in the fall, he had a portfolio of drawings that won him readmission.

On his return to Tech, Warhol was one of three recipients of the $40 Martin B. Leisser Prize for "unsupervised artwork" during the summer vacation.[294] On page 2 of the Sunday, November 24, 1946, edition of the *Pittsburgh Press*, he was featured in an article titled, "Artist-Huckster Sketches Customers and Wins Prize." A posed photograph depicts eighteen-year-old Andy Warhola showing his drawings to a girl in his class. Andy must have been pleased with the publicity, but he could not have been happy that his name was misspelled as "Warhols" in the first paragraph. Perhaps this first brush with fame spurred him to drop the final vowel.

The short, unsigned newspaper article said next to nothing about Warhol's art. Instead, based on the artist's comments, it offered a sociological take on its satire. Focusing on the huckstering experience, rather than the sketches, the subhead of the column reads, "Series of Drawings Shows Everything from Idle Rich to Scrambling Poor." The writer explained:

> [Warhola's] biggest headache, and favorite subject, was the "new rich," who would ask him to carry a pound of tomatoes to a sixth-floor apartment just to impress their friends. Another was the people "who have so many children, they didn't know what to do." They solved their problem by bringing them all to the wagon, where they committed assorted indignities on the vegetables while their mothers chatted. The tomato-squeezers were a class in themselves. They refused to buy any vegetable until they'd mangled two or three others.... Another of his classes was the "truck-horse," a woman approximately twice his size who was unable to summon the strength to carry a ripe cantaloupe across the street.

Andy distinguished the "new rich," who felt entitled to have tomatoes carried up to the sixth floor, from the "real rich," the "most gracious class" he served. "The silver-spoon families, Andy says, asked less in the way of service than even the poor." According to the author, "[Andy's] favorite subject" was not the artwork that prompted the publicity, but the customers and the social scene that motivated the art. As Gopnik points out, Warhol may have learned the lesson that "art built around the public's own culture can grab that public's attention."[295] We are told that Andy is not sure he will be back in the huckstering business the following summer, but it was "a wonderful experience." "People," he says, "are funny."

The following summer, Warhol landed a job that was more to his liking—painting backdrops for window displays at the Joseph Horne Company in downtown Pittsburgh. A department store that catered to upper-class customers, Horne's was known for its elaborate windows and annual Christmas tree. The experience was transformative for Warhol. Not only did it offer an entrée into the world of commercial and avant-garde art, it provided him with his first major exposure to gay sexuality.[296] Warhol began to develop a new flamboyant image and experimented with bending gender norms. He painted his fingernails a different color every day, dyed his shoes, and let his tie dip into cans of paint. He showed up at a student party with his hair dyed chartreuse.[297] "The skinny young man wore such raggedy clothes that some Horne's employees asked their wives to assemble care packages of spare shirts, pants and shoes to give to Warhol. . . . He would be very appreciative and grateful." Then he would cut the sleeves off the shirts and paint the shoes silver before wearing them to work at the department store.[298] While he acknowledged the sympathy that his down-at-heel self-presentation elicited, he dressed it up, anticipating one of the classic lines from his 1970s *Philosophy*: "Think rich, look poor." As Bockris described it, he had turned his hunky heritage into a style.[299]

Gopnik describes in detail the perils of coming out gay in the virulently homophobic Pittsburgh of the 1950s. He also cites an apt metaphor to describe flickers of public indulgence: "A certain condescending tolerance existed for the most outrageous gay men—the Horne's window dressers, for example—to whom 1940s straights 'afforded a liberty not unlike that granted by peasants to the village idiot.'"[300] Ann Warhola reportedly derided her brother-in-law's effeminacy: "It came to me whenever he would wave his hand, that he was from another world—you know what I mean?"[301] How Julia reacted to her son's eccentricities is unknown, but it is likely that she would have felt the same benign tolerance that was extended to the village idiot in folktales or to the hobo in her own narrative, as an ingenuous, unique individual who occupied an acceptable, and often a constructive, social role.[302] She might have been amused by Andy's resourceful, if peculiar attire, given their continued difficulty to finance his education. And when Andy depicted himself as a girl for a self-portrait assignment, it is unlikely she would have objected.[303] One cannot help but think she would have enjoyed the depiction of the daughter she never had.

On June 16, 1949, Warhol was awarded a degree in pictorial design by Carnegie Tech at the Syria Mosque, a large performance venue in Oakland. An invitation to the Baccalaureate Service and Commencement Exercises on June 15 and 16, 1949, is found among the items in a Time Capsule that holds Julia's possessions. It is hard to say how Julia understood or reacted to Andy's educational achievements. She later told Bernard Weinraub, "Andy, my son, he likes college. I say, stay in college. He goes ahead. If I was smart, all my children would go to college. Like Andy." But it is likely that she did not, and could not, appreciate Andy's academic and intellectual accomplishments, which would have been frustrating both for the immigrant mother and her assimilated son. When Weinraub asked her to comment on Andy's art, Julia could only speak of his practical hands-on work. "[Andy] sells peaches and pears from truck. Later he works for big store in Pittsburgh, Joseph Horne." Weinraub recalled, "She talked about Andy with a kind of puzzlement."[304] Julia "kept bringing up the store," saying that "Andy liked to decorate store windows." As a perceptible job that paid 50¢ an hour, window dressing was something she could understand, and her modest aspirations probably envisioned no more. Even in this 1966 interview, after Warhol had launched Pop and was recognized in the press, when he had begun to dabble in film and music, Julia's intellectual appreciation of her son's success was minimal, not out of neglect or indifference, but because her son's world had widened beyond her comprehension.

According to his brother John, Andy had unsuccessfully sought a teaching position at a school in Indiana and "was really disappointed when they sent everything back and says they can't use him. He was very upset and that's when he said, 'Well, I'm going to New York.'" Paul recalled the immigrant mother's dilemma: "Mother didn't want him to go but she didn't want to stand in his way."[305] Julia resisted Andy's insistence on going to New York until she was assured that Warhol's classmate Philip Pearlstein would accompany and protect him. "They knew my father, who, like them, made a living as a huckster. . . . So Andy's brothers and I had a meeting, and they decided that as I was several years older, and an army veteran as well, that I would be able to look after him, but they would let him go only on the condition that he and I would live together."[306] Still, even Pearlstein was uncertain that one could survive in New York as an artist. It was not long before Julia decided that Andy needed maternal guidance, and her New York experience began.

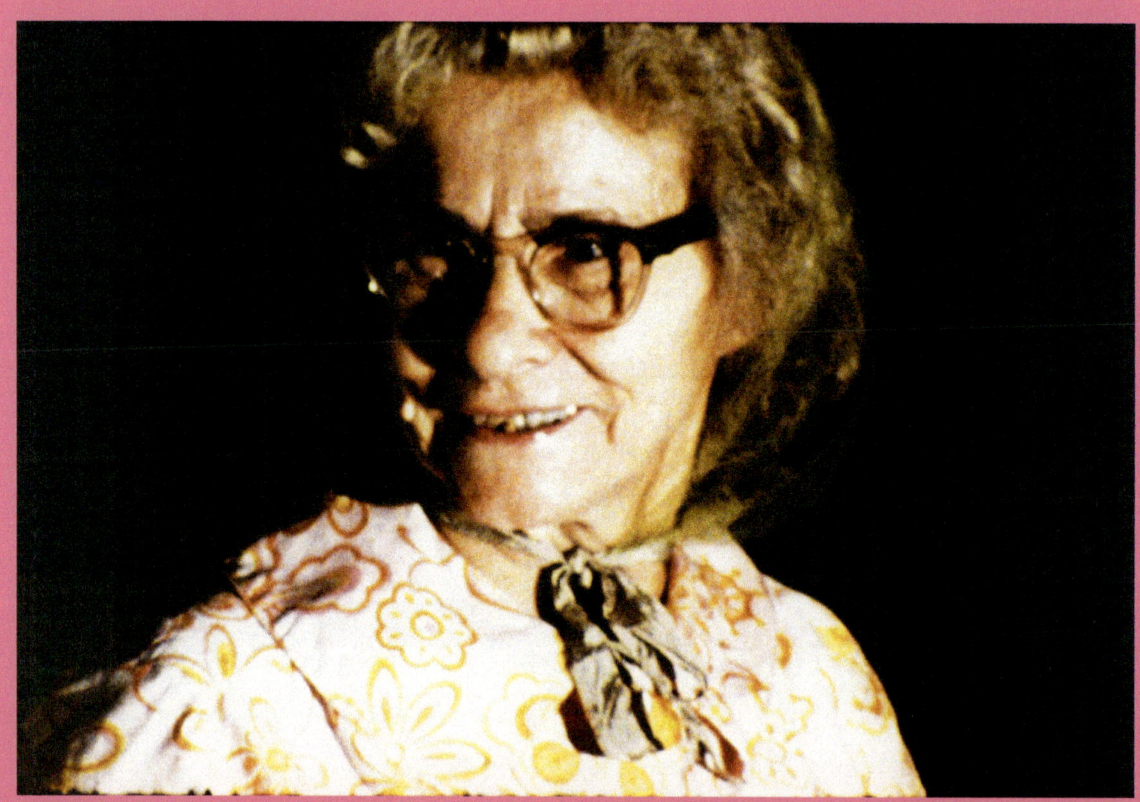

Film still of Julia Warhola, from Andy Warhol, *The George Hamilton Story*, 1966

5

"To Come Live with My Andy"

Warhol recalled, "My mother had shown up one night at the apartment where I was living with a few suitcases and shopping bags, and she announced that she'd left Pennsylvania for good 'to come live with my Andy.' I told her okay, she could stay, but just until I got a burglar alarm."[1] Julia saw her role differently: "Andy go to New York by himself. I prayed, God, oh God, help my boy Andy. He no get job. I help him with a little bit of money. Later I visit him. One time, two time, third time. I stay."[2] Julia Warhola then lived in New York with her youngest son for nearly two decades.

When Andy said good-bye to his mother and brothers and left for New York with Philip Pearlstein, he entered what he would later call his "Cockroach Period."[3] Together with Pearlstein, he sublet a sixth-floor walk-up on the Lower East Side. For the next several months, he bounced around from one roach-infested tenement to another, living with diverse sets of artsy roommates. In March 1951, after eighteen months of sharing overcrowded flats, Andy signed a lease for his first private apartment. A one-room semibasement at 216 East Seventy-Fifth Street, it boasted a kitchen and bath. Now living alone, he could play host to family, even if conditions were less than ideal. When his mother and brother visited Andy's new digs, Paul complained that he and his kids returned to Pittsburgh with lice.[4]

More commonly than not in Slavic working-class families of that era, sons lived in the parental home until they married. Especially when the mother was a widow, bachelor-sons contributed to household finances, while benefiting from maternal care. Meals appeared on the dinner table like manna from heaven, laundry scrubbed itself on a washboard, and dust bunnies evaporated as if by magic. Like so many Carpatho-Rusyn men of his generation, Warhol had not learned basic housekeeping skills. Now on his own, he dismissed the details of self-management as inessential. Friends remember that he subsisted on cake and candy and "sometimes smelled as if he had not taken a bath in days."[5] When he came into money, he simply bought new shirts to replace those too dirty to be reused. In what was surely a hyperbolic statement, Julia claimed to find ninety-seven unwashed shirts in her son's closet.[6] On her visits, she pitched in to help, undoubtedly leaving her son with pots of chicken soup and *holubky* (stuffed cabbage). On her return to Pittsburgh, she worried about him and prayed.

John Warhola later told an interviewer, "Everybody talks about how important his mother was to Andy but he was equally important to her."[7] In a postcard dated January 13, 1952, barely a week after Rusyn Christmas, Julia expressed concern about Andy's absence and chafed at his neglect. In an idiosyncratic mix of Rusyn and English, she opens with a formulaic blessing: "I greet you wholeheartedly, my dearest Andy, with God's blessing." Then she moves to the purpose of her note: "For some reason, I haven't heard any news from you," and with a mild rebuke she reminds him, "but you have our new telephone number." She shares good but dull news from home: "Johnny is working, Paul is working too," and closes with another prayerful wish, "May God keep you healthy. Bye. Mum."[8] In fact, Andy had plenty of news, but not such that he would share with his family. Warhol was leading a lively social life in New York, frequenting trendy restaurants and gay bars.

Around this time, Julia was reconsidering her own life plans. Paul had moved his family out to Clairton, a suburb about fifteen miles south of Pittsburgh, dubbed on road signs, "City of Prayer."[9] According to Paul, Julia had agreed to leave Oakland, and they purchased a house for her in Clairton. But like many Carpatho-Rusyn women of her generation, Julia considered it her responsibility to care for the menfolk of the family until she could hand them over to a wife. John Warhola married Margaret Dancisin on September 13, 1952, and they moved into the Warhola family home on Dawson Street. Just as Julia had waited to leave Miková until her brother Yurko got married, she could now leave John to Marge and focus on her youngest son. "Well, the only thing I can see, I guess, is I'd like to be with Andy in New York." Her plan was to take care of him until he found a nice girl and got married.[10]

In the early spring of 1952, John drove Julia in his ice-cream van to visit Andy, and she discovered just how much he needed her help. "Andy had a hole in the sole of his shoe as big as a silver dollar, so I left him my best pair of shoes. I think when mother saw that, she decided to move up there at once to look after Andy."[11] According to a niece, Julia worried, "'Oh, my Andy doesn't know how to live, how to buy food, how to eat, he know nothing. He doesn't know how to take care of money.'"[12] Julia's grandson James remembered, "She provided a foundation, an anchor. It was like it was before. He had a good feeling of security at home."[13] And Warhol's associate Gerard Malanga said, "Andy welcomed the opportunity. It relieved him of any domestic situations which he wasn't capable of dealing with. When Julia came to New York she basically took care of [Andy]."[14]

John and his family lived in the Warhola family house through the 1950s, and Julia stayed with John and Marge when Andy traveled. In summer 1956, he sent postcards to his mother at the Dawson Street address from a trip to Asia and Europe. His postcards are at once dismissive in their semi-dyslexic carelessness, and touching in their desire to allay parental concern: "Dear Mum, i got your letter im OK everything is real nice here"; "im OK im in Japan."[15] The Warhola house, Andrii's hard-earned $3,200 Depression-era bargain, was sold in December 1960 for $10,500.[16] Although the deed identifies the seller as "Julia Warhola, widow, of New York City, New York," the sale was undoubtedly handled by her son John. Julia's signature was notarized in New York, and the deed was registered in Pittsburgh by her personal lawyer and coparishioner, Michael Hahalyak. According to Paul, "When mother went to live with Andy, she did not want to have a large savings account. Just enough money for her funeral. She told me she came to USA with no money and wanted to die the same way, as long as she had Andy who gave her everything she wanted."[17]

Andy's prospects were not quite as poor as Julia's prayers might have suggested. According to Blake Gopnik, he arrived in New York at an especially auspicious moment for commercial artists, when the industry was seeking "a new breed of illustrator" whose images alone could sell a product.[18] Warhol fit the bill. Through his first hot summer in the city, he scoured New York offices in a rumpled corduroy suit, pitching his paper-bag "portfolio" to art directors. His persistence won him an interview with Tina Fredericks, the art director of *Glamour* magazine, who asked him to draw shoes for an advertisement. When his first attempt did not suit, Warhol worked all night and returned the following day with more effective illustrations. Fredericks included them in a special insert of the September 1949 issue of the magazine, titled "Success Is a Job in New York." According to Pearlstein, Warhol fortuitously "snagged a major job . . . people in New York had been knocking themselves out trying to get that kind of job for years."[19] Warhol very likely lived on the well-paid *Glamour* assignment for some time, supplemented by money from his mother and his brother. In the Ric Burns documentary, John Warhola mentions sending Andy to New York with a gift of $150. In an interview from 2014, John says that when he left Julia in New York with Andy in 1952, he gave Andy a check for $600. "I was flush with money at the time."[20]

Assignments for magazine covers, album and book jackets, and other newspaper ads followed, but Warhol's freelance work was irregular and low-paid, far from the standard "steady job" that immigrants like Julia understood. But Andy had an American-born confidence that supplemented the inventiveness and industriousness he had learned from his immigrant ancestors. Joseph Groell, a former Carnegie Tech classmate and a New York roommate, recalled Warhol's "bizarre" cold calls in search of work: "'I planted some bird seed in the park yesterday. And would you like to order a bird. And do you have any work for me?' . . . That kind of childlike or apparently childlike quality seemed to appeal to them. So, they would give him some work."[21] Gopnik recounts a Tech classmate's memory of visiting the Metropolitan Museum of Modern Art with Warhol, who approached a random staff member, offering to do Christmas cards for the museum, "and, amazingly, getting a gig to do just that." The pay was minimal, but Gopnik speculates that Warhol's motive was more ambitious. "Through sheer force of chutzpah he got his work into the museum by the back door, you could say, long before he made anything worthy of hanging on its walls."[22]

The coy tactics Warhol used to get work in New York are reminiscent of the "chutzpah" Julia demonstrated by selling tin-can flowers door-to-door in affluent neighborhoods of Pittsburgh. Warhol also demonstrated the business savvy his father had used in the Miková immigrant network to move from the coal mines to a job at Eichleay. By spring 1951, after just eighteen months in New York, Warhol was recognized in the business as an "upcoming artist."[23] Still, Andy's income was irregular, and he spent what came in lavishly, eating at pricey restaurants and buying sweets at expensive bakeries, which disturbed the ever-frugal Julia. According to one story, they shared their first Thanksgiving dinner at a Woolworth's counter.[24] Victor Bockris suggests it may have reflected a low cash flow, or Andy's embarrassment about taking his mother anywhere else. Another reason, which might occur only to others from Julia's background, is that for her, Woolworth's counter was a comfortable model of fine dining. Second-generation Carpatho-Rusyn Americans in Pittsburgh remember receiving coupons in school to enjoy a Thanksgiving dinner at the Salvation Army.[25]

Rusyns in New York

Carpatho-Rusyns began to emigrate to New York City in the late nineteenth century, where they joined Czech, Slovak, Syrian, Polish, and Yiddish-speaking Jewish immigrants on the southern tip of Manhattan. According to historians, "The short ferry ride from Ellis Island landed the new arrivals at Battery Park, often with family and friends anxiously waiting."[26] Before the Brooklyn Battery Tunnel and the World Trade Center, peasants from the Old Country figuratively reconsolidated their villages in tenements alongside the elevated trains and beneath the early twentieth-century skyscrapers. In five-story walk-ups, families of eight lived in two or three small rooms heated by coal stoves, sharing a toilet and sink with neighbors in the hall or sometimes in the yard. The tenement buildings along Greenwich Street, home to many Rusyns, were dark and noisy. The Ninth Avenue El ran along the street, and former residents recalled, "While sitting on the fire escape, one could almost touch the train tracks."[27] In her documentary film of New York's Carpatho-Rusyn immigrants, Joanne Medvecky interviewed an old-time tenement resident. "Downtown Manhattan was a poorer neighborhood than you could associate with Harlem, say. Later on, when I went to Harlem and compared it to what we had in Downtown Manhattan, I thought Harlem was the lap of luxury."[28]

Rusyn immigrants found jobs in urban businesses as elevator operators, porters, and window washers. Some worked in stores and restaurants that served Wall Street. Women cleaned office buildings in the financial district, working at night in banks and brokerage houses. As time passed, many immigrants opened small businesses—grocery and liquor stores, butcher shops, and restaurants. Peter Herko rose from a butcher's helper to owner of his own meat market, which sold to banks, law offices, and shipping companies on Wall Street. The Slezak family expanded their grocery store on Greenwich Street in 1931 to include a restaurant that hosted various community functions.[29] On warm Sunday afternoons, downtown residents gathered in Battery Park, arranging the benches in clusters corresponding to their native villages. Young people gathered for dances in community centers and churches, with music supplied by Slovak and Rusyn musicians. In the 1920s and 1930s, bands from outside the community were hired to perform in the ethnically diverse neighborhood. According to resident John Petrick, "[African American groups] played our songs better than the Gypsies in Europe."[30] The Wall Street Crash of 1929 and the Great Depression affected the community to a lesser degree than it did many other New York neighborhoods, since, as Petrick said, "We were poor before the Depression."

The close-knit neighborhood was demolished in the 1940s to build the Brooklyn Battery Tunnel, and the last vestiges of the community disappeared with the construction of the World Trade Center in the late 1950s. According to historians, "Unlike many residents of tenement neighborhoods, these people did not want to leave the place they called their 'village.'"[31] But eventually, they followed Czech and Slovak immigrants, who had for several years already been moving north to the Upper East Side area of Yorkville, known as "Little Bohemia." Edward Kasinec, the son of Carpatho-Rusyn immigrants who settled in Yorkville, described the atmosphere "as that of a village writ large," or "a kind of Eastern European village transposed to Manhattan," where Czechs, Rusyns, Slovaks, and Hungarians mixed with some Irish and Germans.[32] The neighborhood was home to Czech and Slovak churches, Czech restaurants and butcher shops, and Karel Pan's "Little Slovakia" bar. Three local travel agencies arranged trips to and from the Old Country, and export–import agencies mailed parcels to the homeland. Czechoslovak Day parades, reminiscent of Pittsburgh's ethnic celebrations, featured folk music and national costumes. One Yorkville resident recalled, "When I came here in '48, even the cops in the street spoke Czech. There were bakeries, food stores, little places to eat where they cook like home."[33] In the 1930s, the Rusyn newspaper *Lemko* ran numerous ads and announcements for Carpatho-Rusyn events being held at the Bohemian National Hall on 73rd Street and in the Sokol Hall, a community social and athletic club, on East 71st Street. In 1967, Warhol rented the Sokol Hall for a month, calling it "the gymnasium," as a venue for his rock band, the Velvet Underground. He may have noticed the large medallions in the hall's pub representing the five administrative divisions of Czechoslovakia, including one bearing the familiar coat of arms of Subcarpathian Rus'.[34] As late as 1976, Mr. Sereda's "Czechoslovak Store" sold newspapers published in the United States in Czech and Slovak, and perhaps Rusyn.[35]

As always, the center of Carpatho-Rusyn life was the church. The first Greek Catholic churches in New York were established in the 1890s in Yonkers and Brooklyn. Greek Catholics who settled in Lower Manhattan took the 14th Street ferry across the East River to Saint Elias Greek Catholic Church in the Greenpoint neighborhood of Brooklyn.[36] As immigrants continued to arrive, the need for services in Manhattan became apparent, and Rusyns from Hungary cooperated with Galician Rusyns to celebrate liturgy in the basement of a nearby Roman Catholic church. But just as in Lyndora, cultural differences between Rusyns from north and south of the Carpathian Mountains were irreconcilable. Galician Rusyns adopted a Ukrainian identity, and in 1905, they established what is today called Saint George Ukrainian Catholic Church on 7th Street in the East Village.

Uhro-Rusyns continued to ferry to the Brooklyn Greek Catholic church until 1912, when they purchased a building at 225 East 13th Street and established Saint Mary's Greek Catholic Church. In 1920, Father Alexis Vislocky became the pastor of Saint Mary's and served there for thirty-two years. In old-country style, he celebrated the Divine Liturgy in Rusyn Church Slavonic, and into the early 1950s, he gave the homily in Rusyn. Vislocky, from the older generation of married priests, was remembered as a caring and self-sacrificing pastor. Under his guidance, the congregation grew to 2,500, making it one of the largest Greek Catholic parishes in the United States.

In 1925, parishioners who wished to return to Orthodoxy split from Saint Mary's to form what is today Saint Nicholas of Myra Carpatho-Russian Orthodox Church on 10th Street and Avenue A. The parishioners at each church were the same Carpatho-Rusyn people, many from the villages of Jarabina, Litmanova, and Kamienka, about seventy-five miles west of Miková. They shared the same liturgy, language, and plainchant, but Saint Mary's pledged allegiance to the pope of Rome, while Saint Nicholas claimed independence, not affiliating with any diocese until 1938, when they joined the newly founded American Carpatho-Russian Orthodox Diocese. Both churches had outstanding choirs, educational programs, and social organizations. In 1941, a Grand Concert and Dance was held by the Carpatho-Russian Choir of Saint Mary's Greek Catholic Church. Reflecting the cosmopolitan nature of New York, in addition to folk songs and devotional hymns, the program included works by the first professional musician of Galicia, Denis Sichinsky, the Ukrainian Mykola Leontovych, the Russian Nikolai Rimsky-Korsakov, and the French Romantic composer, Jacques Offenbach.[37]

In a letter to the *Amerikansky Russky Viestnik* (*ARV*), Father Vislocky wrote, "We live in the largest city in the world, where it is difficult to sustain our Greek Catholic church, since our people are widely dispersed. It is not possible here to maintain constant contact as is done in other parishes to promote progress." The annual church picnic, a profitable fundraising event, was an opportunity to gather Greek Catholics from across the metropolitan area. The 1949 fest netted $1,522.10, around $16,000 in 2020 dollars.[38] The 1950 picnic, held in Woodside, Queens, included liturgies at 8:30 a.m. and 1:00 p.m. An orchestra and a Gypsy band provided continuous music and dancing in the afternoon and evening, and sports events were scheduled for children. The mortgage was paid off and the church was able to contribute to the Eparchial Fund and several American charities.[39]

As the Seventy-Fifth Anniversary booklet of Saint Mary's Byzantine Catholic Church declared in an understatement, "The 1930s were not a glorious period in the history of America's Eastern Catholic churches." In addition to the financial difficulties brought on by the Depression, the battles over celibacy, Latinization, Americanization, and church control made the latter years of Father Vislocky's pastorate difficult. In 1952, he was summarily transferred to New Jersey, to the dismay of loyal parishioners. In his early New York years, Andy Warhol might have known this old-world Greek Catholic traditionalist. Pearlstein recalled that Warhol got up early and went to church several mornings a week, most likely to nearby Saint Mary's.[40] With liturgies offered in Church Slavonic, it might have been a welcome familiarity for him in his new surroundings.

After Father Vislocky's departure, the church began to move in a new, modern, "American" direction. After 1929, when celibacy was enforced on the Greek Catholic priesthood, the formation of American-born priests became problematic. Until World War II, candidates for the American priesthood received two years of training at Latin-rite institutions in the United States, followed by two years in Greek Catholic seminaries in Slovakia or Subcarpathian Rus'. With the outbreak of World War II, this became impossible, and a program for Greek Catholic seminarians was established at Saint Procopius College and Seminary in Lisle, Illinois, run by Roman Catholic Czech monks of the Order of Saint Benedict. An entire generation of Greek Catholic priests was educated under the influence of the Latin-rite Benedictines, which diluted and altered Byzantine traditions.[41] In 1948, Holy Trinity Priory, the first and only Benedictine monastery that followed the Byzantine Rite, was established in Butler, Pennsylvania. According to the *Amerikansky Russky Viestnik*, the duty of the Benedictine monks of the Byzantine Rite should consist exclusively "in working and praying that in all things God may be glorified."[42] However, churches were badly in need of priests, and bishops withdrew monks from monastic life to assist with pastoral duties. The next pastor of New York's Saint Mary's came from Holy Trinity Priory. Julia Warhola was familiar with the monastery, as it was located near her Lyndora relatives, and she continued to receive solicitations from the monastery over the next two decades.

The "Benedictine interlude" at Saint Mary's lasted only four years, but these years saw major changes in the development of the parish. A chapel was opened in Brooklyn for the convenience of parishioners there, and an "American sense of parish organization" was introduced. The 13th Street church was renovated and dedicated by the Pittsburgh bishop Daniel Ivancho in 1952 in an elaborate ceremony, which the *New York Times* described as the "ancient ceremonial splendor of Christian Byzantium."[43] The dedication was followed by a large banquet, at which Vincent R. Impellitteri, the mayor of New York City, gave the keynote address.

Julia's "Brand New Church"

By the 1950s, the Greek Catholic Church in America was no longer a church of immigrants. In 1955, at age forty-six, Nicholas Elko became the first American-born bishop, and he immediately effected changes to appeal to the younger generation of Greek Catholics. He rebranded the church as "Byzantine Catholic" and introduced English into the liturgy to replace Church Slavonic. Violating traditional cultural and architectural norms, three-dimensional statues appeared in some churches, and icon screens were removed. The bishop's dissociation of the church from ethnic, cultural, and religious traditions antagonized many parishioners. The Warhola family's church in *Ruska dolina*, clinging to Ruthenian Greek Catholic ritual and Carpatho-Rusyn tradition, resisted the bishop's reforms to the point of suing for independent status.

In 1956, Father Paul Dano was appointed pastor of New York's Saint Mary's. Father Dano had grown up in Saint John the Baptist Greek Catholic Church in Lyndora, which was established by John Zavacky and other Carpatho-Rusyn immigrants. Reverend Dano had ambitious ideas for Saint Mary's, initiating plans to relocate the church in a new building at a prominent location. In 1957, it was decided to build on a lot on 15th Street, and a fundraising goal of $200,000 was set. The finance committee visited every parishioner in teams of two, explaining the project and soliciting a pledge. On April 10, 1960, Father Dano notified the parish that within two years of beginning the campaign, pledges exceeded $200,000.

A number of church bulletins, mostly from the 1960s, are found in Warhol's Time Capsules. In addition to schedules and parish news, they contain accounts of the weekly income, with lists of contributors and the dollar amounts of their donations. On an ordinary, nonholiday Sunday, the church's intake was around $800. Julia's weekly contribution, when noted, was usually $1. In her notebook and in miscellaneous scribbles on letters and envelopes, she kept track of the amount she contributed for weekly and holiday offerings, flowers, and candles. Her donation to the building fund was especially generous, placing her among the top 10 percent of the seven hundred member-families. According to Gerard Malanga, it was Julia's son Andy who made the contribution, for which Julia got credit. A letter from Father Dano dated December 12, 1961, acknowledged the receipt of $1,000, which represented payment in full of her pledge to the Saint Mary's Church Building Fund. Julia was granted a certificate naming her a Memorial Donor: "It is recorded that the sacrificial support of Mrs. Julia Warhola has helped make possible St. Mary's New Church."[44]

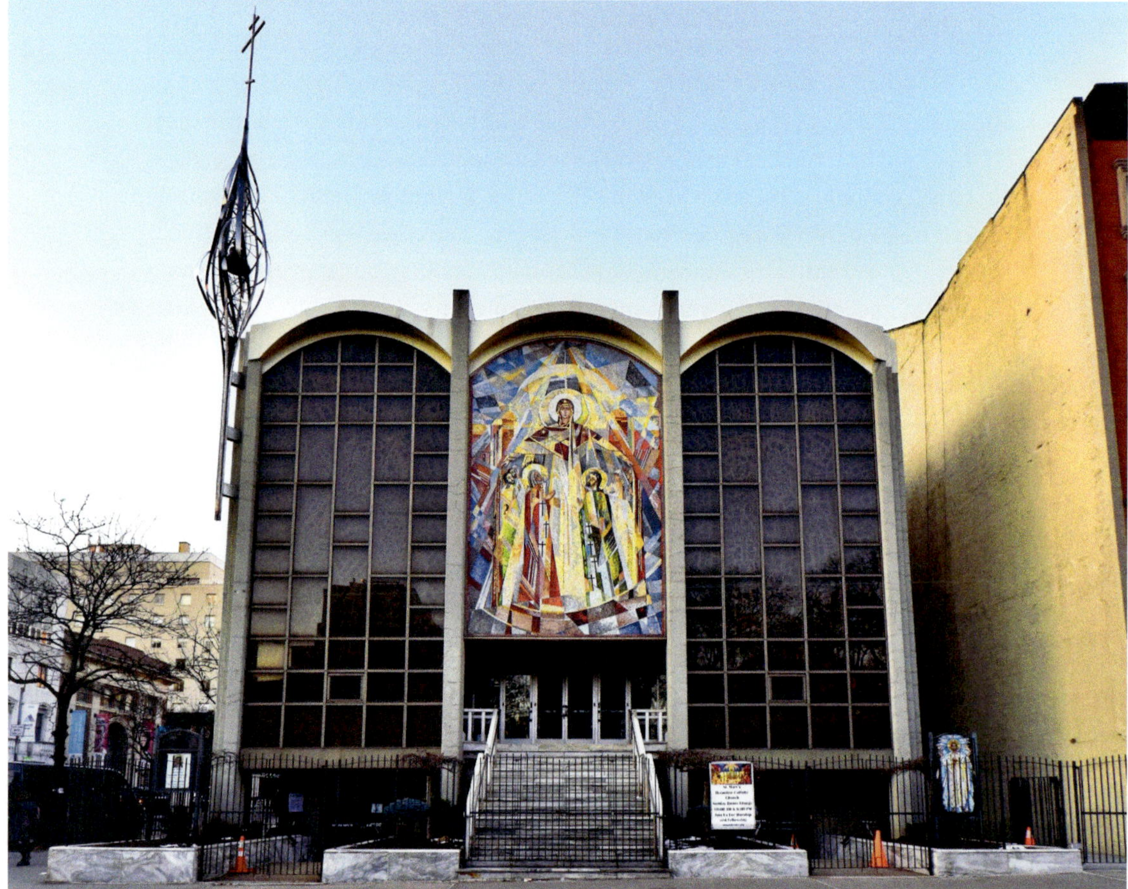

Figure 5.1. Saint Mary's Byzantine Catholic Church, the principal façade, on 15th Street and 2nd Avenue, New York City.

The new church building was unlike anything Julia could have imagined in the Old Country.[45] The architect, Cajetan J. B. Bauman, a fellow of the American Institute of Architects, and Felix Senger, the designer of the faceted stained-glass window walls, the interior and exterior mosaics, and the iconostasis, worked with Father Dano to blend traditional Slavic and Byzantine aesthetics with contemporary art forms. The fleche, or spire, on the northeast corner of the church, is a modern adaptation of the distinctive Eastern Christian onion dome, and it houses the original bell from the old Saint Mary's Church. The church was dedicated on Sunday, June 30, 1963, by Bishop Elko, who ceremoniously carried the

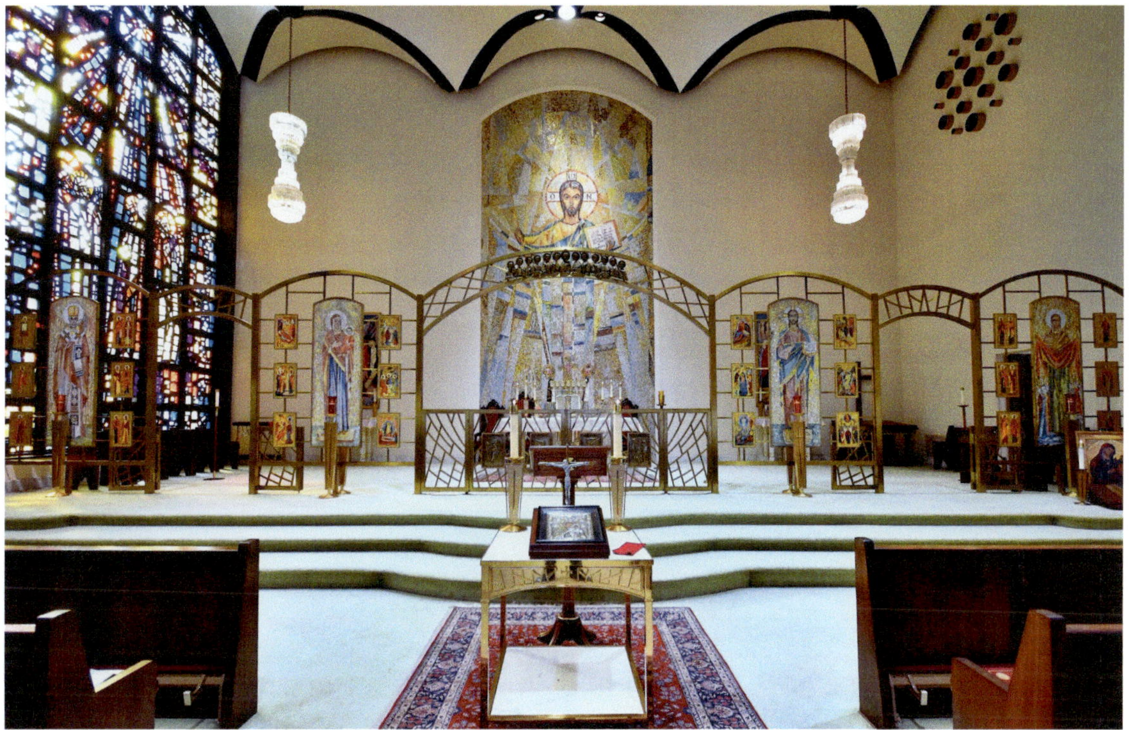

Figure 5.2. Saint Mary's Byzantine Catholic Church, iconostasis and tetrapod.

Blessed Sacrament in procession from the old church on 13th Street to the new place of worship.

In 1966, Julia proudly told the *Esquire* interviewer, "Here I have my church, big nice church on Fifteenth Street and Second Avenue. I go to ten-thirty Mass. Brand new church."[46] While Andy may have made a major contribution to the construction of Saint Mary's and must have been intrigued by "the meeting of tradition and the avant-garde" in its design, how frequently he attended the new church is uncertain.[47] In 1960, Julia and Andy moved to Lexington Avenue and 89th Street, seventy-five blocks away from Saint Mary's. John Warhola recalls taking his mother to church by taxi to have her Easter basket blessed. Another Easter story has her son Paul taking the paschal foods to church with Julia in a suitcase on the subway.[48] Andy's first boyfriend, Carlton Willers, was among those recruited to accompany Julia to the joyful traditional Easter basket blessing.[49]

Saint Mary's continued Rusyn religious customs even as it fostered American-style social gatherings. The Ladies Guild served coffee and rolls in the social hall after Sunday liturgy, and women gathered to make and sell *pirohy* to benefit the church. Mother's Day banquets and Father's Day breakfasts were held. Dances, dinners, holiday celebrations, and picnics brought the parishioners together. Unfortunately, Julia's generation of fellow parishioners is no more, and the extent of her participation in such activities cannot be determined. A ticket to a 1956 concert and dance to benefit the building fund is found among her possessions. She is seen in a photograph of a Sunday post-liturgy picnic, where the older women sang together and reminisced about the Old Country. Adolf Benca, a Slovak American artist, claims to have met Julia at one of these picnics. "It was kitsch," he said, "but it had a really interesting dimension. It reminded me of my childhood in Slovakia when my grandmothers sang so much it scared me."[50]

The "Junk House"

Andy and Julia lived in the 75th Street apartment for about a year. When the lease expired and the rent increased, Warhol sublet an apartment from the illustrator Leonard Kessler at 242 Lexington Avenue, between 34th and 35th Streets. Julia would later refer to this as her "junk house."[51] In the early years, the fourth-floor walk-up apartment was almost devoid of furniture, and the decor consisted of a church calendar and a picture of Jesus pointing to his Sacred Heart. Julia and Andy shared a bedroom behind the kitchen. Vito Giallo, one of Warhol's early assistants, recalled, "It was like a railroad flat. In the back room at the very end where the bathroom was there was a bedroom and I noticed that there were no beds but two mattresses next to each other on the floor."[52] For Julia, it might have brought back memories of family life in Miková, except for the fact that the apartment was located above a "girlie bar" called "Florence's Pin-Up Room." Julia's granddaughter remembered how the music from the bar resonated through the walls.[53]

Julia was a prodigious letter writer throughout her time in New York, writing to relatives and friends in Pittsburgh and Europe and preserving their letters in what would eventually become Warhol's Time Capsules. Unfortunately, her correspondents were not so forward-thinking, and few of the letters Julia wrote to them have survived. But one of Julia's letters from her time on lower Lexington Avenue was returned for insufficient postage and found its way into one of Warhol's Time Capsules. Addressed to Mrs. Anna Lasky, Julia's youngest sister in America, and postmarked January 3, 1954, it gives us a sad description of Julia's life at the apartment above the Pin-Up Room.

After the customary greetings that characterize traditional Rusyn letters, Julia apologizes for not responding earlier to Anna's Christmas card.

Dear sister Anna, I'm writing you a few words late, because sometimes I am too tired to do anything. . . . Dear sister Anna, we are already old and have nothing good to look forward to, just old age. I'm here in New York with my Andy. He works a little now and then, painting, but he hasn't had any work for a month now. He earns just enough to get by. He pays $100 a month rent for the apartment, which is very high—up four flights of stairs. It is hard for me to carry things from the store and hard for me to go up the steps. It is a lot of work for me to clean up the apartment. I don't like to do the work, but I must.[54]

Nathan Gluck, another assistant during this period, described Julia's role: "She was like the housekeeper and everything else, and she'd do his laundry and Andy would be like 'Mom where'd you put my necktie?' and 'Mom where are my shoes?'"[55] Vito Giallo remembered that Julia did all the shopping. "One time I said to Andy, 'You know your mother has to go down these five flights to go to the A&P and come up the steps all by herself with all these shopping bags. Don't you think that's too much for her?' He said, 'Oh no, she loves it.' She'd be floating in and out of the rooms cooking, cleaning, picking up. He depended on her completely, which always kind of shocked me, but I think she really enjoyed it."[56]

In Julia's behavior, Gluck and Giallo discerned a typical Carpatho-Rusyn cultural pattern. While Julia complained privately to her sister, she continued to play the role of the self-sacrificing, overgiving mother, which was established in the time of her son's childhood illness. Now, to wrest appreciation from her insensitive adult son and to maintain her complaisant self-image, she put her own needs last. She cleans the apartment, she says, "because I must," and boasts of her self-sacrifice. She was left feeling depleted, depressed, and resentful, a prescription for codependence and passive aggression. Julia's eagerness to please and the Rusyn parental tradition of self-sacrifice induced her son's obliviousness to any distress on her part. In 1985, not long after Andy had turned fifty-seven and was bemoaning the "aging factor," he told his *Diaries*, "My mother was the age I am now, when she came to New York. And at that time I thought she was really old. But then she didn't die until she was eighty. And she had a lot of energy."[57] In 1954, when she complained to Anna about climbing the stairs and her son expressed indifference, Julia was sixty-five. Fifteen years of life with Andy lay ahead of her.

By the mid-1950s, Warhol was in demand as a commercial artist. Known for working quickly and meeting deadlines, he followed directions to do the job "right." "I was getting paid for it, and did anything they told me to do. If they told me to draw a shoe, I'd do it, and if they told me to correct it, I would—I'd do anything they told me to do, correct it and do it right."[58] He designed greeting cards for Tiffany's, stationery for Bergdorf Goodman, and windows for Bonwit Teller. He published illustrations in *Mademoiselle*, *Glamour*, *Vogue*, and *Harper's Bazaar*. He even drew raindrops, sun, and clouds for an early morning television weather report.[59] Warhol's big break came in 1955, when he became the exclusive illustrator for an advertising campaign for I. Miller Shoes. His weekly ads in the *New York Times* brought him commercial acclaim and a minimum annual income of $12,000. In July 1957, on the advice of his accountant, Warhol set up a corporate entity called Andy Warhol Enterprises. According to Paul Warhola, the family did not trust the financial arrangements, and since Warhol had been sending money to support his brothers, it was a matter of concern to all. Paul said the accountant took advantage of Andy. "I think that was a scam. . . . But Mother, she had a sense of discernment. As soon as this guy walked through the door, she said, 'Andy, watch out!'" Whether Andy deferred to her judgment or devised his own stratagem to ward off the IRS, of which he was always cautious, the undated "Certification of Officers," which lists Andy Warhol as president, is ostensibly signed by the secretary of the corporation, "Julia Warhol."[60]

Now with something resembling a "steady job" and numerous prestigious clients, in November 1957, Warhol rented a second, lighter, more spacious, and more expensive apartment on the main floor of the same building above the bar.[61] Relying on artsy acquaintances for advice, he spent lavishly on furniture, antiques, and collectibles, creating a showplace to entertain friends. Tiffany lamps and a Japanese-themed folding screen, a teak table with Danish modern silver flatware and other finely crafted furniture stood alongside folk art, a cigar-store wooden figure, and carousel ponies.[62] He also began buying and collecting art.

The description of Warhol's parlor floor contrasts dramatically with the modest family living room he painted in college. Andy's new taste for home decor reflected his evolution in the campy, gay world of New York. How this unsophisticated "hunky" transformed himself and adapted to ultramodern New York society recalls the typical Slavic folktale, in which the third son, thought to be a witless dunce, manages to conquer the kingdom. Associates still complained about his poor hygiene. A roach crawled out of his portfolio at a job interview, and when he was hired by Amy Vanderbilt to illustrate her cookbook, he did not know on which side of the plate to draw the fork.[63] He would not have learned proper table-setting etiquette from Julia, who was at a loss to understand his extravagant spending or his fanciful decor. Vito Giallo recalled that when Warhol put a carton of exotic antiques near a trash bin, "Mrs. Warhola threw out the antiques and kept the trash."[64] Her experience with Andy in the early New York years did not inspire confidence. She warned her two older sons, "Andy's going to be broke someday. You better be ready to take him in and treat him like one of your own kids."[65]

Having two apartments provided more space, but since they were separated by at least one floor occupied by other tenants, the new arrangement did not make Julia's life easier. She and Andy had to use a communal stairway to get from one level to the other, which meant more navigation of steps. Consequently, Julia settled in the small workspace on the upper floor, which rapidly filled with piles of papers, photographs, sketches, and art supplies, earning it the name "junk house." Warhol's friend Ted Carey said, "I mean, I just can't describe it. It was piled from floor to ceiling with magazines, old tracing papers, old drawings, a lot of canvases. . . . It was a terrible mess." According to Bockris, "Every surface was covered, and Andy was confined to doing his work on a portable desk on his lap. The shoes, gloves, scarves, hats, handbags, belts and jewelry he was assigned to draw added to the clutter."[66]

A Professional Collaboration

A Warhol friend from the late 1950s, tells a story that might be apocryphal, but rings true. "[Warhol] was rushing to do a job which had lettering, script involved. He was late and he was hurried, so he thought, well, his mother could help him. But his mother could not read or write English. So . . . he would print it, and then she would sit down and copy what he had written, not, I think, knowing very much what she was writing. . . . He was so pleased, and apparently the client was so pleased with the result, that from then on, she did all the writing."[67] Thereafter, Julia Warhola was an important asset to her son's commercial art business.

Warhol made his name in New York with his signature "blotted line technique," developed while he was a student at Carnegie Tech. It involved drawing a sketch on a sheet of nonabsorbent tracing paper that was hinged with tape to a piece of absorbent paper. He then inked the outline of the drawing bit by bit and pressed the wet drawing on a third piece of paper. The result was a delicate, broken line, with which Warhol could make several prints from one drawing.[68] According to Blake Gopnik, Warhol's signature "blotted line" was "his secret weapon on New York's commercial scene in the 1950's."[69] The method was not unlike the primitive printing technique Julia used in Miková to impress patterns on clothing by repeatedly painting an etched wood plate and blotting it on fabric.

After he discovered his mother's talent for calligraphy, Julia's handwriting became another "signature" of Warhol's work. Her distinctive, playful, curli-cued script stemmed from the old-world cursive penmanship style taught in

Austro-Hungarian schools in the late nineteenth century. Warhol's assistant Nathan Gluck said, "[Warhol] always liked his mother's 'Middle Europa' penmanship, so whenever he was finished with a drawing, he would give it to her and indicate where she was to sign it."[70] When he needed text, Julia wrote out captions or entire sentences. Since her English was fragmentary, spelling and punctuation errors were common, but Warhol, who always embraced mistakes, relished the effect. Graphic designers described Julia's handwriting as combining "a genuinely naïve awkwardness with the traditional associations of cursive script," which appealed to the advertising industry's taste for both decoration and spontaneity.[71] Andy and his assistants learned to replicate Julia's penmanship and Warhol had it made into Letraset dry-transfer sheets for easy reproduction.

Julia's artistic calligraphy, as utilized by her son, was not her natural, everyday penmanship. While she might address envelopes in elegant script, most of her notes and letters were written in a slapdash, cacographical scribble. By contrast, the writing Julia did for Warhol's ads was distinctive. For her, transfiguring English-language block letters into a harmonious, flowing form was art, and she approached it as such. Since she was most often transcribing texts she did not understand, it was almost like replicating an unfamiliar, foreign-language document, letter by letter. "When Andy wanted a sentence written, we would write out the words, and then his mother . . . would copy it letter for letter. If you wrote, 'the,' and the 'h' looked like a 'b,' she would make a 'b.'"[72] Entire paragraphs, sentences and even individual words might hold no meaning for her, except as visual art. An illustrative example is her 1960 collaboration with her son and his friend Suzie Frankfurt on *Wild Raspberries*, a takeoff on the popular gourmet cookbooks of the day. A related drawing not included in the book was *Tranches de Truite à la Jeanne d'Arc*, for which Julia transcribed a fifteen-line text entirely in French.

Frankfurt said of Julia, "She was gifted and untutored, and we left all the spelling mistakes."[73] But examination shows that Julia was not as careless as she has been described. Nina Schleif argues that extant writing samples "show that the spelling mistakes were often not so unintentional as they seemed, having been copied and varied across the repetitions."[74] Susan Rossi-Wilcox, who examined Frankfurt's typed sheets, concludes that "Mrs. Warhola faithfully copied the text. The typos, corrections, hyphenations, and duplications are in the original."[75] Although there are some spelling errors and crossed-out words, indicative of errors stemming from a faulty text rather than a careless transcriber are lexical items like "Marashino," "kirsh," "lizzard," "Dorothy Killgallen," and "unetable," all words Julia could not have known, but might be commonly misspelled by native English speakers.

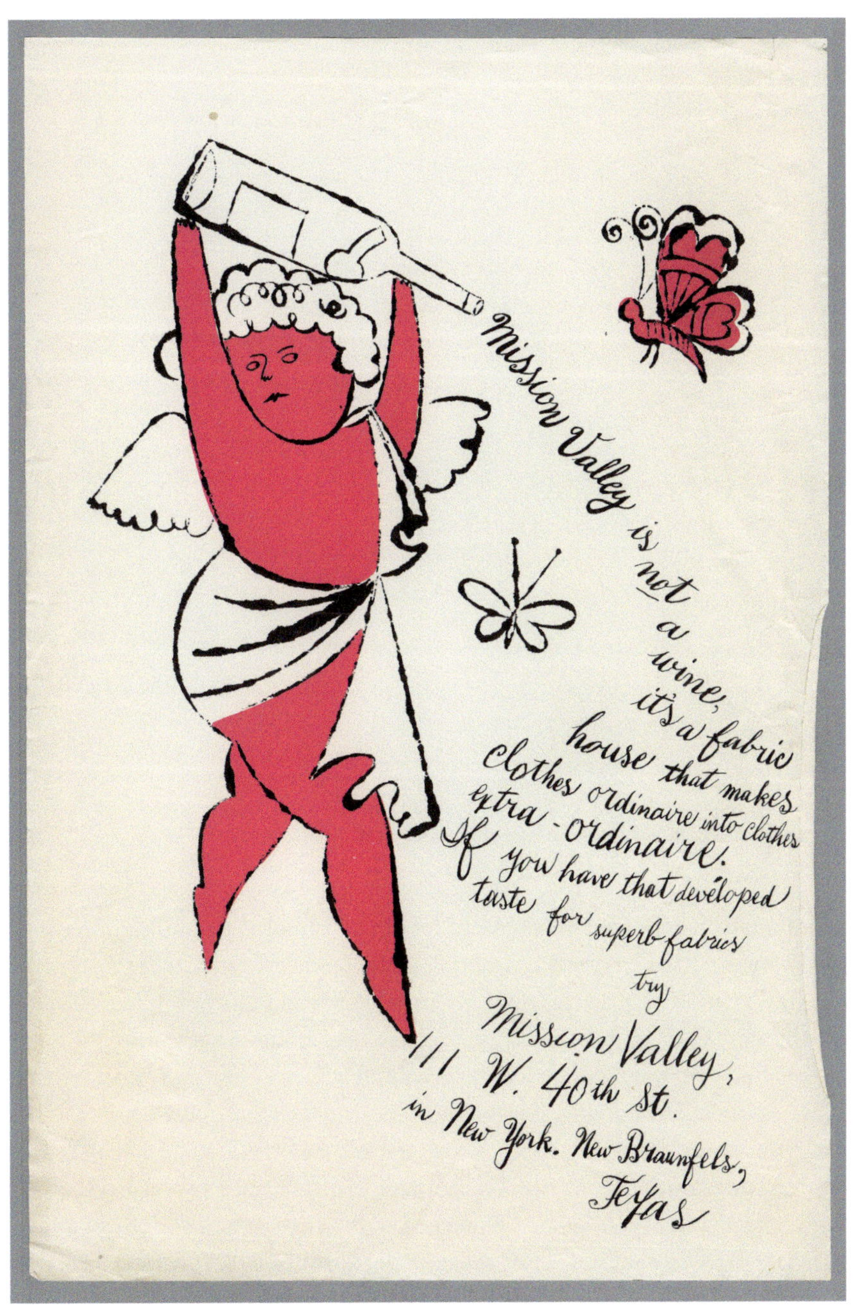

Figure 5.3. Ad for Mission Valley Mills, 1950s. Drawing by Andy Warhol, lettering by Julia Warhola.

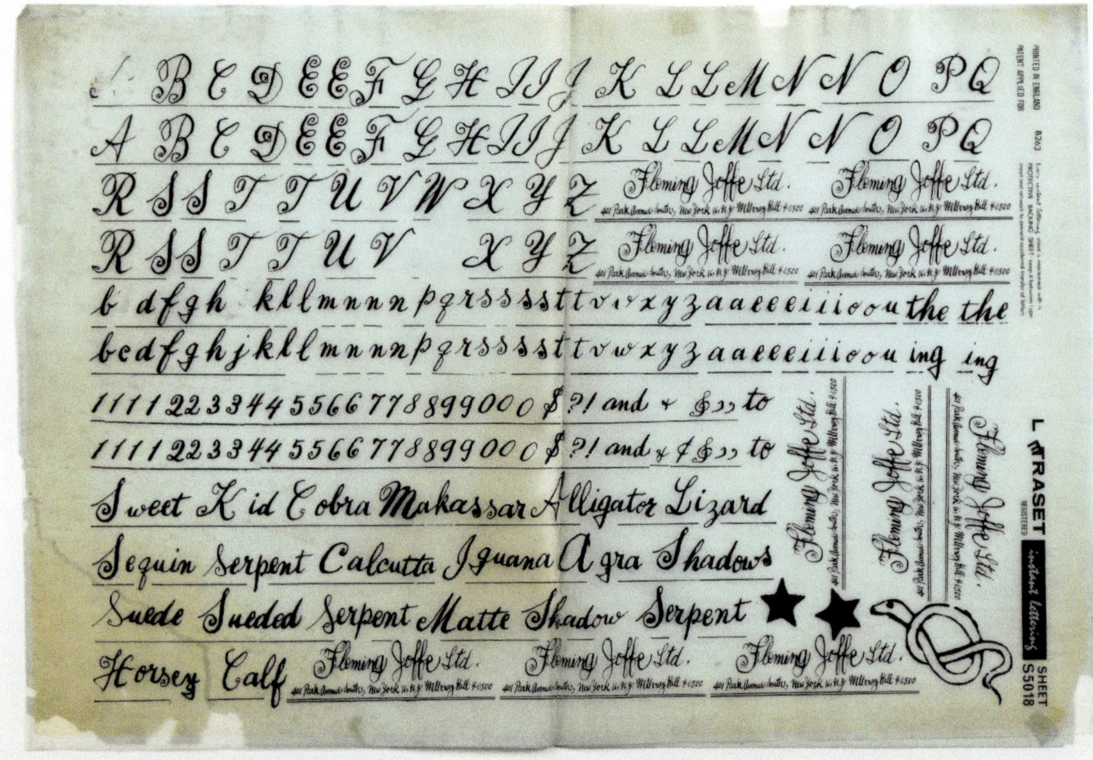

Figure 5.4. Letraset of Julia Warhola's handwriting, ca. 1963.

Semiliterate in her own language and totally unschooled in English, Julia could hardly be expected to edit the material. Instead, she focused on her calligraphy, carefully reproducing the original, errors and all. Her grandson James Warhola, who became a professional illustrator, remembers watching her work. "She'd have her dipping pen, and she'd be looking over and jabbering at me. And all the time, her hands would be moving. It was almost like a maestro performing."[76]

In the 1950s, Julia collaborated with her son on several handmade, limited-edition promotional books that Warhol gave as gifts to clients and art directors. Between 1952 and 1960, Warhol published eight of these artist's books, and Julia's lettering is prominent in four of them.[77] Most of Warhol's drawings were done with the blotted-line technique. Julia's text was copied as a negative photostat, arranged on the page, then made as a positive photostat, and the portfolio was sent to a bookbinder to be reproduced in offset printing.[78] Some or all the images would

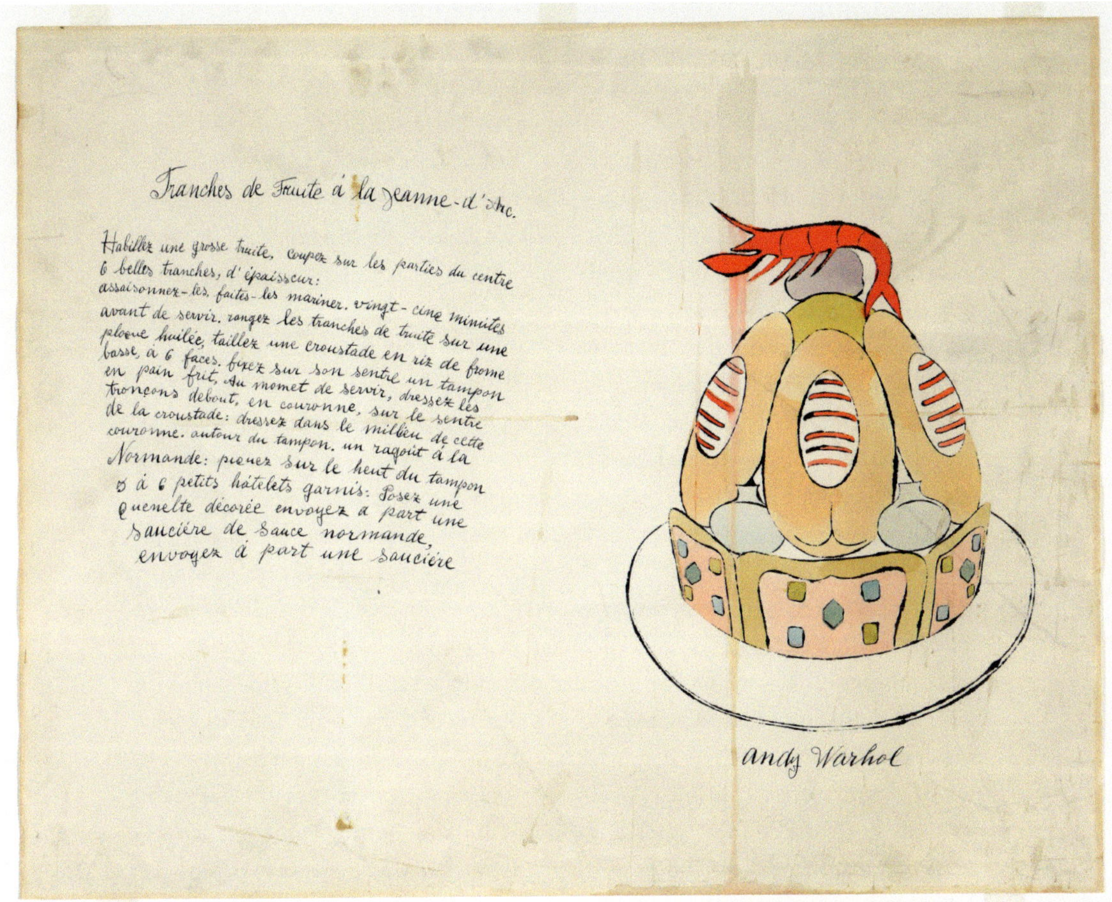

Figure 5.5. *Tranches de Truite à la Jeanne d'Arc*, ca. 1959. Drawing by Andy Warhol, lettering by Julia Warhola.

then be colored by Warhol's acquaintances at what became known as "coloring parties," where Warhol set a few guidelines, but encouraged improvisation.[79] He also enlisted his visiting nieces, telling them to "try to stay between the lines." He paid them a quarter an hour, and "at the end of the week, he would take us shopping at Bloomingdale's."[80]

The first book that used substantial lettering by Julia was *A la Recherche du Shoe Perdue* (1955), which was produced for the clients of I. Miller as a portfolio of loose pages. On each sheet, Andy drew a stylized shoe, accompanied by a witty phrase or cultural reference written by Ralph Pomeroy, a poet-friend. The text captions, written out by Julia, range from the Proustian reference in the title to Shakespeare ("To shoe or not to shoe"), to song lyrics ("I dream of Jeannie with the light brown shoe"), to slogans and catch phrases from popular culture ("Uncle Sam wants Shoe"). It is likely that Julia would have failed to catch the puns. In December 1956, Warhol returned to shoe drawings, this time, flamboyant designs decorated with imitation gold leaf. Warhol named the different shoe styles for celebrities—a polished gold boot was tagged for Elvis Presley, a jeweled stiletto for Zsa Zsa Gabor, and a classic high heel for Julie Andrews. Julia Warhola added the name tags to the drawings, with her own "corrections." Zsa Zsa was simplified to Za Za, and Julie Andrews was renamed "Julia." Andrews, who attended the show, did not appreciate the modification, and did not purchase the drawing.[81]

In the Bottom of My Garden (1958), also known as "The Fairy Book," was Warhol's fifth self-published artist's book The titles alluded to a song familiar to New York's gay community and the colloquial term for gay men. It has been called "one of the sprightliest and 'naughtiest' of Warhol's publications," and "one of the most louche of Warhol's products."[82] The water-colored plates depict chubby, impish, winged cherubs in suggestive positions. While one set of readers understood the veiled meaning of the text, "everyone else saw a book full of fat little putti and plants of the sort known to every reader versed in art history."[83] Other than the cover and "the End," texted on the rear of a chubby cherub on the final page, only one drawing in the book has text, which looks to have been written by Julia. The drawing, with its text caption, expresses the ambiguous eroticism of what seems at first sight to be a children's book. It shows a demure-looking young girl, angel's wings sprouting from her shoulders, with her hands in what appears to be a pocket in the low middle-front of her dress, where a cat's head peeks out. The text reads "Do you see my little Pussy." Matt Wrbican discovered the source of the image in a risqué vaudeville act from the 1890s, the Barrison Sisters, who were known as "The Wickedest Girls in the World."[84] In their act, the actresses lifted their skirts to reveal real kittens. This drawing is unlike others in the book, where fat fairy figures cavort mischievously. Here the erotic message is in the wordplay rather than the image, and Julia very likely missed the double entendre.[85]

Julia did the lettering for exhibit announcements and invitations. When they were still living in the Murray Hill section of lower Lexington Avenue, Warhol had his mother design his letterhead. Her loopy handwriting took up half the page, and he did not correct the address when she spelled it "Murry Hill." Julia also did letterhead for Warhol's agent, Fritzie Miller and his assistant, Joseph Giordano. Work and preparation went into these projects. Doodles of "Joe Giordano" can be found

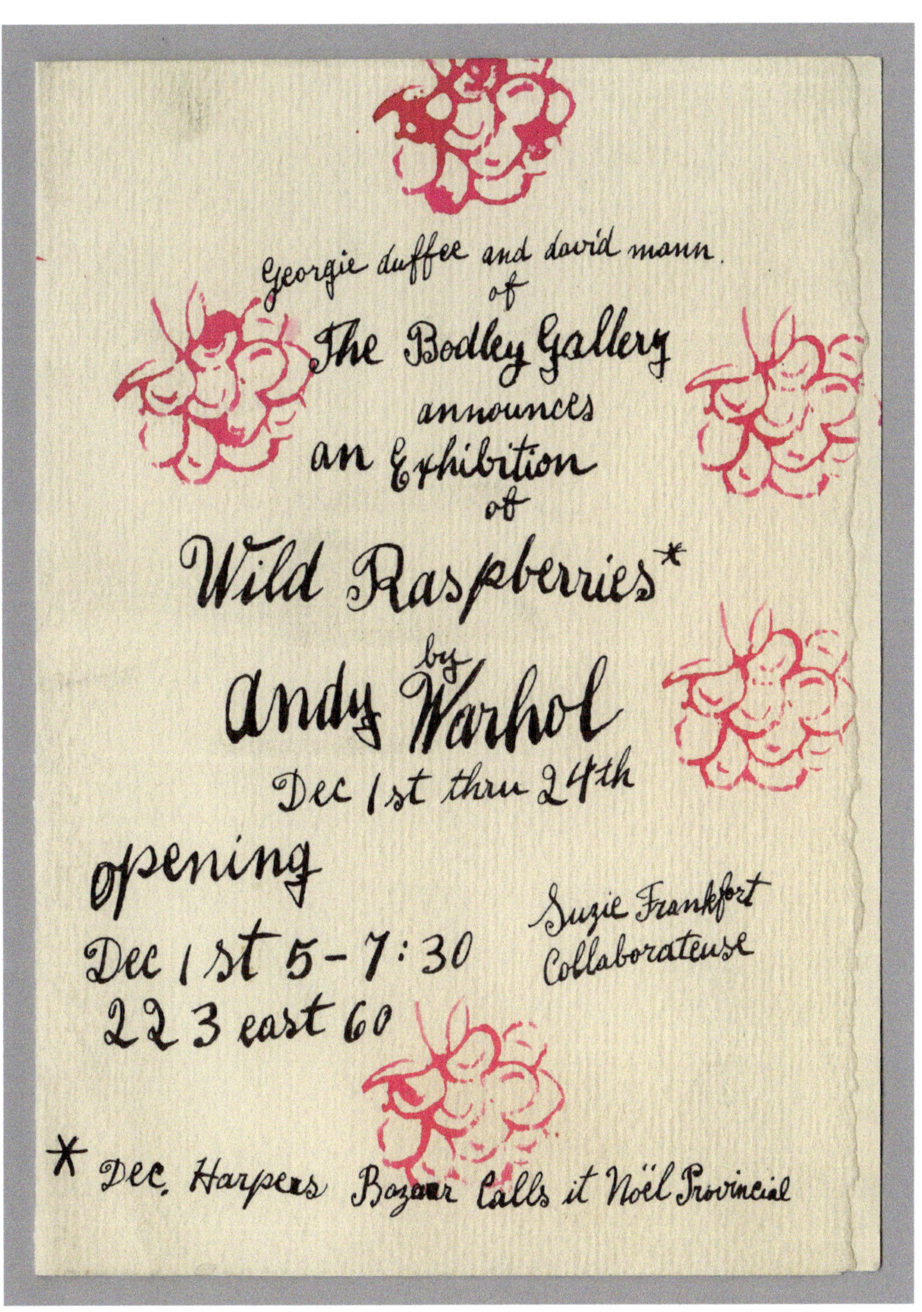

Figure 5.6. Exhibition announcement for *Wild Raspberries*. Drawing by Andy Warhol, lettering by Julia Warhola.

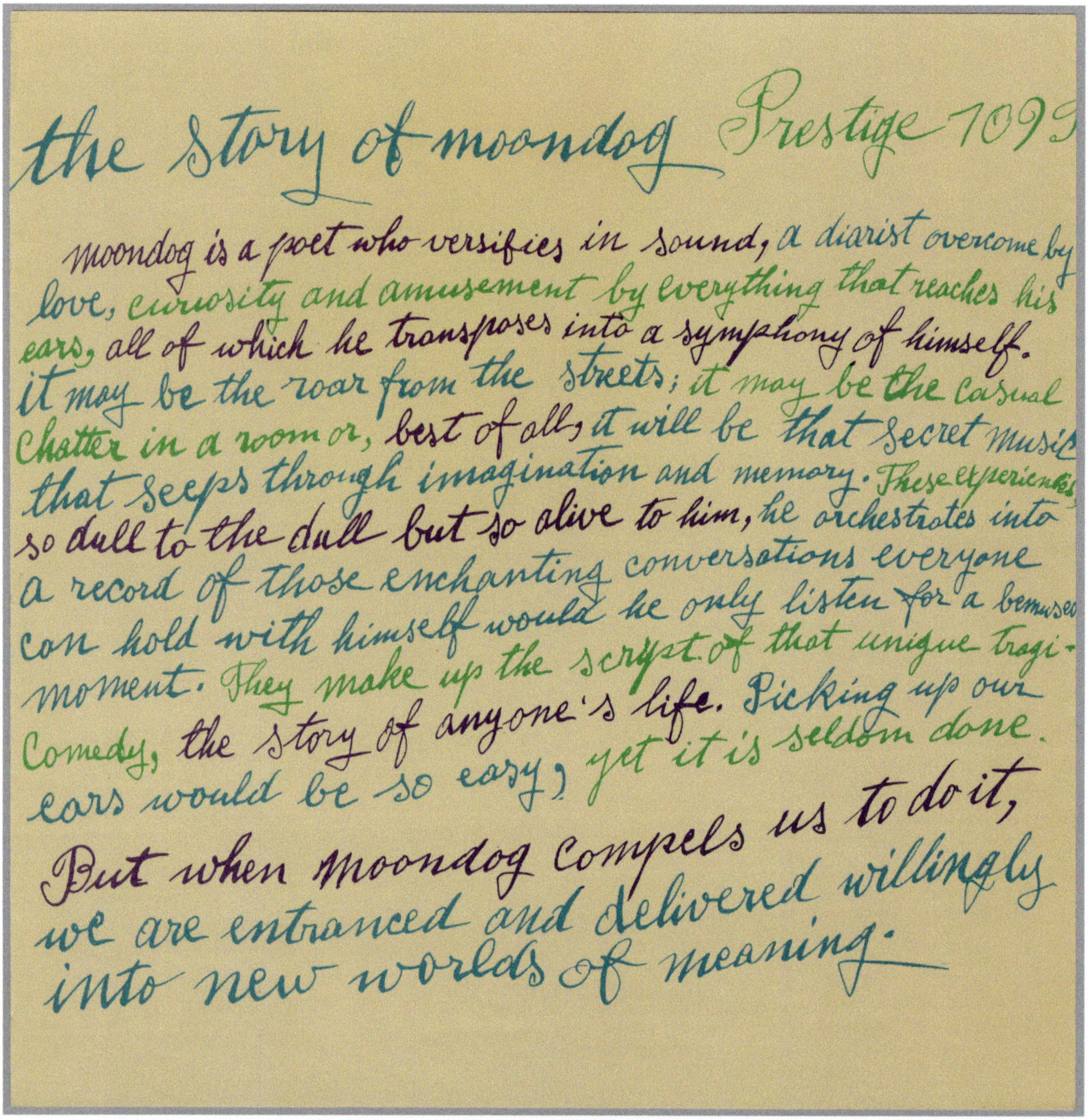

Figure 5.7. *The Story of Moondog*, record cover proof. Lettering by Julia Warhola, ca. 1957.

on used envelopes and on the cover of a Greek Catholic Union almanac—evidence
that Julia was working out the design and practicing the lettering. In 1957, Warhol
used Julia's script for the cover of *The Story of Moondog*, a record album by the street
musician Louis Thomas Hardin. A long, complex paragraph of sixteen lines, the

sense of which Julia could not have followed, has no spelling errors.[86] For her work, Julia Warhola won a Certificate of Merit from the Art Directors Club, inscribed to Andy Warhol's Mother.[87]

Scholars have interpreted the "Andy Warhol's Mother" epithet as a marketing ploy and a means of self-promotion on Warhol's part. The up-and-coming artist's use of his mother's calligraphy both "plays up his identity as a mama's boy and sissy, while exploiting the script's spontaneous and decorative qualities to charm his clients, develop his distinctive brand, and succeed in business."[88] According to Gopnik, the "Andy Warhol's Mother" figure to whom the certificate was awarded was "treated more as an alternate Warholian persona" than a fully independent person.[89] Other commentators posit that "Warhol turned [Julia's] ornate European handwriting into a trademark—his trademark," using her uncompensated work for his profit. "It also underscored his dawning ambition to be perceived as an artist. The artist's mother—Dürer's or Whistler's mother, say—is an art-historical topos that even those unversed in art would recognize, and it was useful in helping Warhol to develop an identity as a fine artist."[90]

These may have been Warhol's motivations, but they could not have been Julia's. Warhol's exploitation of his mother's talent was little different from his taking advantage of her housekeeping, which Julia accepted as the normal course of things, even as she discreetly grumbled about it. Julia, who came from Miková with a strong ego, a confident personality, and an assertive sense of self, surely found aesthetic pleasure in the work and fulfillment in the title. If it helped Warhol to develop an identity as a fine artist, it granted Julia Warhola an identifying hallmark and a professional brand. But the collaboration intensified their codependent relationship, in which the identity of each was contingent on the other. In the mid-1950s, Warhol began to sell his unpublished shoe drawings at the Serendipity 3 café. The café's owner, Stephen Bruce, thought it odd that Warhol refused to put his signature on the drawings. "Warhol would back away nervously and murmur, 'No, my mother signs them for me.' He took the unsigned drawings away with him, bringing them back the next day with the florid lettering added."[91] Bruce interpreted Warhol's deference to his mother as "his own P.R.," based on the evocation of mystery. But Warhol's sharp refusal to sign his own early drawings and his "nervousness" imply a crippling codependence. Julia's purpose in life was her extreme dedication to her son. His satisfaction from having his needs met by his mother led him to rely excessively on her neediness. Ellen Lupton described the relationship: "The persistence of Julia Warhola in the life of her famous son added to the mystique of the eccentric young artist.... She garnered some mystique herself.... Julia made a lasting and

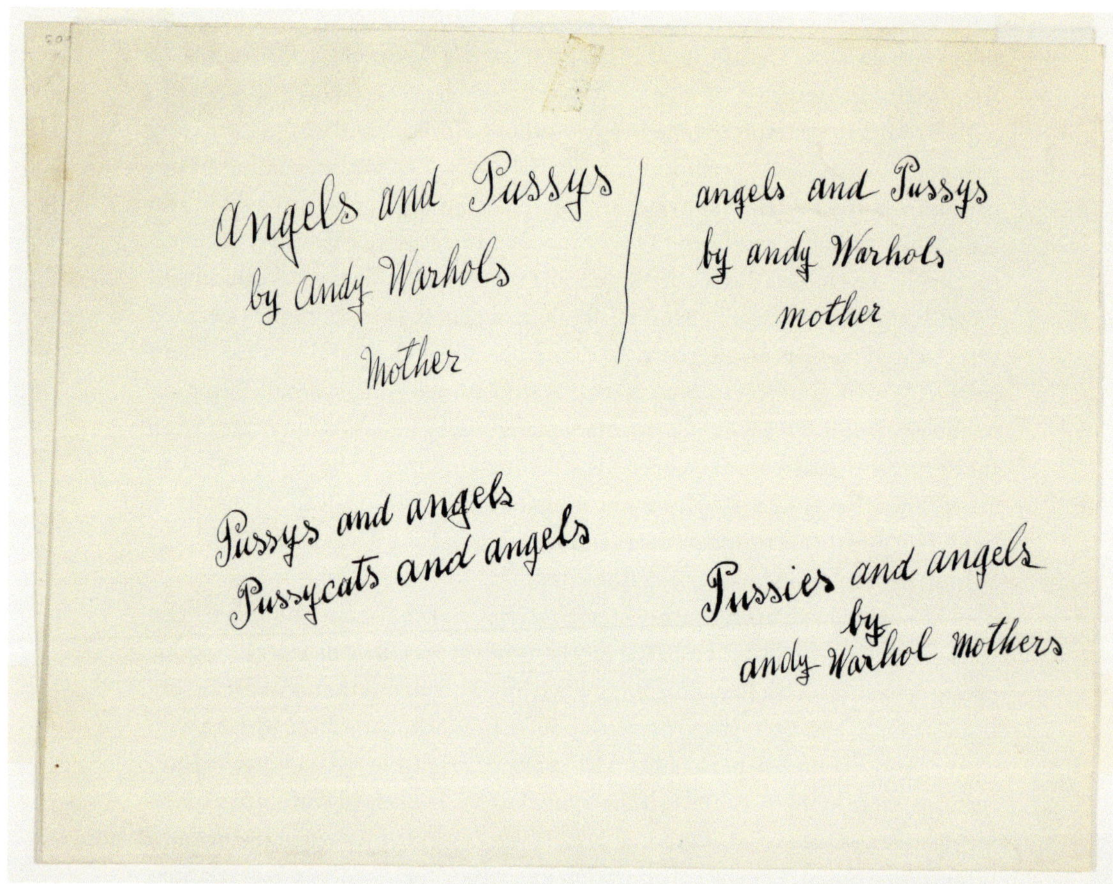

Figure 5.8. *Angels and Pussys* **by Andy Warhol's Mother. Lettering by Julia Warhola, ca. 1960.**

visible contribution. Her flawed yet decorative handwriting amplifies the childlike quality of Warhol's illustrations. Mother and son are locked together in a perpetual conversation on the page. They talk awkwardly in a language of strained innocence in which neither part seems quite at home."[92]

What evolved into a professional collaboration in New York began with cultural patterns of attachment established in early childhood. While Warhol exploited his mother, Julia took advantage of her son to express her personal creative vision and satisfy her long stifled talent. The Warhol archives hold what seems to be an advertising leaflet, a writing sample of the alphabet, penned by Julia, over the caption, "Lettering by Andy Warhol [*sic*] Mother." A phone number was listed along with a note: "Contact her son." Warhol may have been behind the initiative, if that's what it was, but just as Julia had taught her son the basics of "business art," selling crepe paper flowers door to door in Pittsburgh, Julia proudly promoted it. Another item in the archives is a draft of titles in several variations, meant to market what became her trademark subject: "Pussys and angels by Andy Warhol's mother."

Mrs. Warhola's Cats

"Uncle Andy said it all started with a little blue pussycat named Hester." So begins James Warhola's illustrated children's book, *Uncle Andy's Cats*.[93] Depending on which story you believe, Warhol got Hester from "a fabulous movie star called Gloria," or from Gloria Swanson's housekeeper.[94] Or perhaps Gloria Swanson had nothing to do with it. Andy gave Vito Giallo a Siamese, said to be the offspring of Gloria Swanson's cats, who lived to be twenty-two years old. But Giallo expounded, "It was important to remember, when considering Andy's version of a story, that he lived by the rule that you should always lie a little if it made the story better," a practice he may have learned from his mother.[95] According to Paul Warhola, who shared a family tendency to exaggeration, "[Hester] must have had twenty litters in her lifetime. . . . Someone brought another cat, this time a tom. That's the reason for the twenty litters. Together that makes sixty, seventy cats."[96] The tom, Sam, was allegedly cross-eyed and neurotic, thanks to the sirens from a nearby fire station. Soon there were multiple Sams in the small apartment. Anywhere from two to twenty-five are mentioned by Warhol or visitors at various times. According to Patrick S. Smith, who interviewed Warhol's associates, "The exaggerated effect of having dozens of loose cats in his apartment was part of Warhol's notoriety during this period. In fact, in more than fifty of my interviews, Warhol's many cats were vividly remembered by his friends and professional associates."[97] "The cats left messes everywhere, from the drafting table to the bathtub and soiled Andy's drawings and his mail. His mother kept a mop and a bucket of water in the kitchen and was always rushing into action, cleaning up the felines' 'accidents' as well as the spilled ink." "The cats went everywhere. No one had time to train them. . . . The beds had to be covered with plastic. And the smell!"[98]

Andy and Julia acquired their first cats, Hester and Sam, to catch mice when they lived in the 75th Street semibasement. It is unlikely that Julia came up with the uncommon name Hester, which perhaps lends credit to the cat's beginnings with "a fabulous movie star." Unless, as some have suggested, the name was Andy's idea.[99] Sam, a classic American moniker, was sufficiently adaptable in Rusyn to apply to an entire litter. Sam, Samko, Sama, Samka, Big and Little Sam, Smart and Dumb

Sam, they all became part of the family. In the next few years, Sam and Hester would become Warhol stars.

Gopnik is surely correct in saying, "There were almost certainly not twenty-five Warholian felines, ever, since there are only seventeen on view even in Warhol's famous *25 Cats Name Sam and One Blue Pussy*, the chapbook whose title gave rise to that now-mythic number. The feline overpopulation on Lexington lasted a few years at most, and was only sometimes as insane as people have said."[100] But even after Andy and Julia moved to a larger space in 1960, stories about Julia's cats abound. Like the fierce dog the family owned in Pittsburgh that could be calmed and fed only by Julia, her cats owed allegiance almost exclusively to her. Inbred and erratic, they were skittish, unsocial, and vicious. Julia's granddaughter Madalen remembers opening the cupboard to get her breakfast cornflakes, only to have two or three Siamese dart out at her. One went up the chimney and her father Paul "got cut up real bad" when he tried to rescue it. Paul's wife Ann, appalled by the mess, covered the kitchen table and counters overnight with newspapers to catch the cat hair. "The cats hid themselves all day. Bubba played with them at night, and they often slept on Uncle Andy's bed. He would tell us 'Don't be afraid, the cats won't hurt you.' Uncle Andy wanted us to pet them, but they wouldn't let us get near them. They didn't like us. We liked to play in the attic, where Uncle Andy kept lots of interesting things, but the floor was covered in cat excrement. Once we tried on a pair of big leather boots we found, and there was cat poop in one of them."[101] Madalen's sister Mary Lou has similar memories. "Bubba loved her cats. But they were scary to us. They didn't want to be around us, just her. I remember sleeping in that room with the Campbell's soup boxes and looking up. And one time I opened my eyes, and there's a cat looking at me! But Bubba took care of them. It was good company for her."[102]

According to Vito Giallo, Julia was once badly bitten by Hester, and she and Andy realized they had to get rid of some of the brood.[103] They gave away many cats and kittens to friends and associates and sold others. In 1975, Warhol recalled, "I used to have a lot of cats, and I gave them away so the people didn't care about them and they let them run out in the street and get killed. So then I started to charge 30 cents for each cat and then they kept them. They lived to be thirteen. . . . It made a difference. For 30 cents they lived."[104] Even Julia was not in love with all her cats. In Warhol's 1966 film *The George Hamilton Story*, her costar Richard Rheem asks whether she likes one of the cats then living in her house. "No, I don't like him, bum, terrible. He make noise in the night. He make a meow, meow, meow. . . . Sometimes I kill *toto* [that, Rusyn] blackie, he a big noise. He wake me up." "The black bum?" asks Rheem, repeating a term that he had already heard from Julia. "Bad, bad, bad bum. Andy no want him be killed, and I want kill him but I can't." "Why not? Why don't you?" Julia responds, laughing, "You can kill a pussycat? Oh, no . . . No, I can't." In the next interchange, however, Julia says, "And you have to kill it. What else?" It is uncertain whether Julia was speaking literally. However, she had surely killed many chickens in her day, so it is not out of the question that she may have ruthlessly reduced the feline horde.[105] Andy, on the other hand, repeatedly expressed his empathy for animal life and his unwillingness to kill even waterbugs and roaches. "I corner this one bug every night and then I can't bring myself to kill it. He's been eating my food for the past three years."[106]

Hester was the favorite of both Julia and Andy. Julia's emotion for the "mother pussycat" can be felt in her voice in the filmed conversation: "She die. I always think about this cat, I like this Hester. She was really good, she was smart." Julia's voice trails off and she shakes her head regretfully. Andy cried at the news of Hester's death, and as late as 1980, he was still mourning her.[107] "I once gave [Bettie Barnes] a kitten and the kitten was crying and I thought it wanted its mother so I gave him the mother. We had two cats left, my mother and I had given away twenty-five already. This was the early sixties. And after I gave him the mother he took her to be spayed and she died under the knife. My darling Hester. She went to pussy heaven. And I've felt guilty ever since." Scholars relate Warhol's regret at the loss of Hester to his "aesthetic of emotional indifference" or "homoerotic wish fulfilment."[108] But it is revelatory also on a personal level. Hester's death came about because Warhol tried unsuccessfully to reunite a kitten with its mother. And he felt guilty ever after.

In the mid-1950s, Warhol collaborated with Charles Lisanby, a onetime would-be boyfriend, on a "cat book," which appeared as *25 Cats Name Sam and One Blue Pussy*. Lisanby recalls preparing a text, expecting it to be transcribed by Julia and illustrated by Warhol. However, when the book came out, there was no narrative. "Whatever happened to my story, I don't know."[109] The book depicts seventeen, not twenty-five, cats named Sam. Julia's calligraphy is seen in the ungrammatical title, where she left off the *d* in "named," and in the tags, all "Sam," that went with each drawing except for the last one, which is labeled "One Blue Pussy." Warhol's cats, most of them depicted at their cat's-eye level, are posed in various natural postures, and most direct their gaze at the viewer.[110] Their expressions suggest surprise, wistfulness, haughtiness, innocence, or wide-eyed wonder. A chubby Sam looks naughty, and a mother-Sam nestles her baby-Sam in her protective embrace, with pride and affection in her eyes. Finally, One Blue Pussy sits calmly, head uplifted and eyes looking skyward. The viewer familiar with the story of Hester may even see in them a hint of sublime perception. But for all the natural postures and expressions, it is up to the viewer to contrive an interpretative narrative. The only clue to the communicative act between artist and viewer is in the distinction between the Sams and the Blue Pussy.[111] By contrast, in Julia's cat book, *Holy Cats by Andy Warhol's Mother*, she starts with the story of Hester and takes the viewer and the cats into an entirely unexpected dimension of her own visionary imagination.

Holy Cats and Angels

The archives of the Andy Warhol Museum hold approximately 300 drawings attributed to Julia Warhola. About 112 of her drawings feature cats, around 85 depict angels, and in several additional images, cats appear together with angels. In a few sketches, Julia draws hippos, birds, and dogs. In others, she depicts heads and torsos of unidentified individuals. Much of Julia's work might be described as casual drawings or even doodles. Rather than conscious and purposeful artwork, most of her pieces are quick, loosely drawn sketches, exuding experimentation, personal expression, and whimsy. Violating rules of perspective and defying reality, her cats and angels float in empty space, scatter across the page, or cluster together in a corner in no planned composition. Many are fragmentary, unfinished, incomplete figures. Further contributing to the haphazard effect is her drawing surface. Julia does most of her work in pen and ink or graphite on Strathmore paper, but the paper is often an irregular shape that appears to be a leftover, torn from another drawing. Occasionally, her images fill the blank space on remnants of Warhol's commercial art projects. One of her sketchy flying angels appears above Warhol's drawing of a shoe; another floats in the blank space of his "Three skirt lengths." Overall, her angels are smaller and less aesthetically executed than her cats, many of which were preparatory sketches for a book.

In 1960, three years after *25 Cats Name Sam*, Warhol published *Holy Cats by Andy Warhol's Mother*. "Holy cats," an exclamation of amazement, surprise, or bewilderment, captures both the fantastic aspect of Julia's hat-wearing felines and her suggestion of sanctity, as they frolic with angels in "pussy heaven."[112] The book is similar in volume to *25 Cats Name Sam*, and the title suggests that it is a companion to Warhol's cat book from 1957, but its concept is quite different. It opens with a dedication in Julia's words: "This little book is for my little Hester who left for pussy heaven."[113] On the dedication page, the contour of Hester, in a hat with decorative flowers extending from the top as if on wires, is sketched in dots and dashes, suggesting an ethereal being. But her dark eyes, looking coyly upward, and a hint of a smile exhibit vitality. In contrast to Warhol's book of Sams, where there

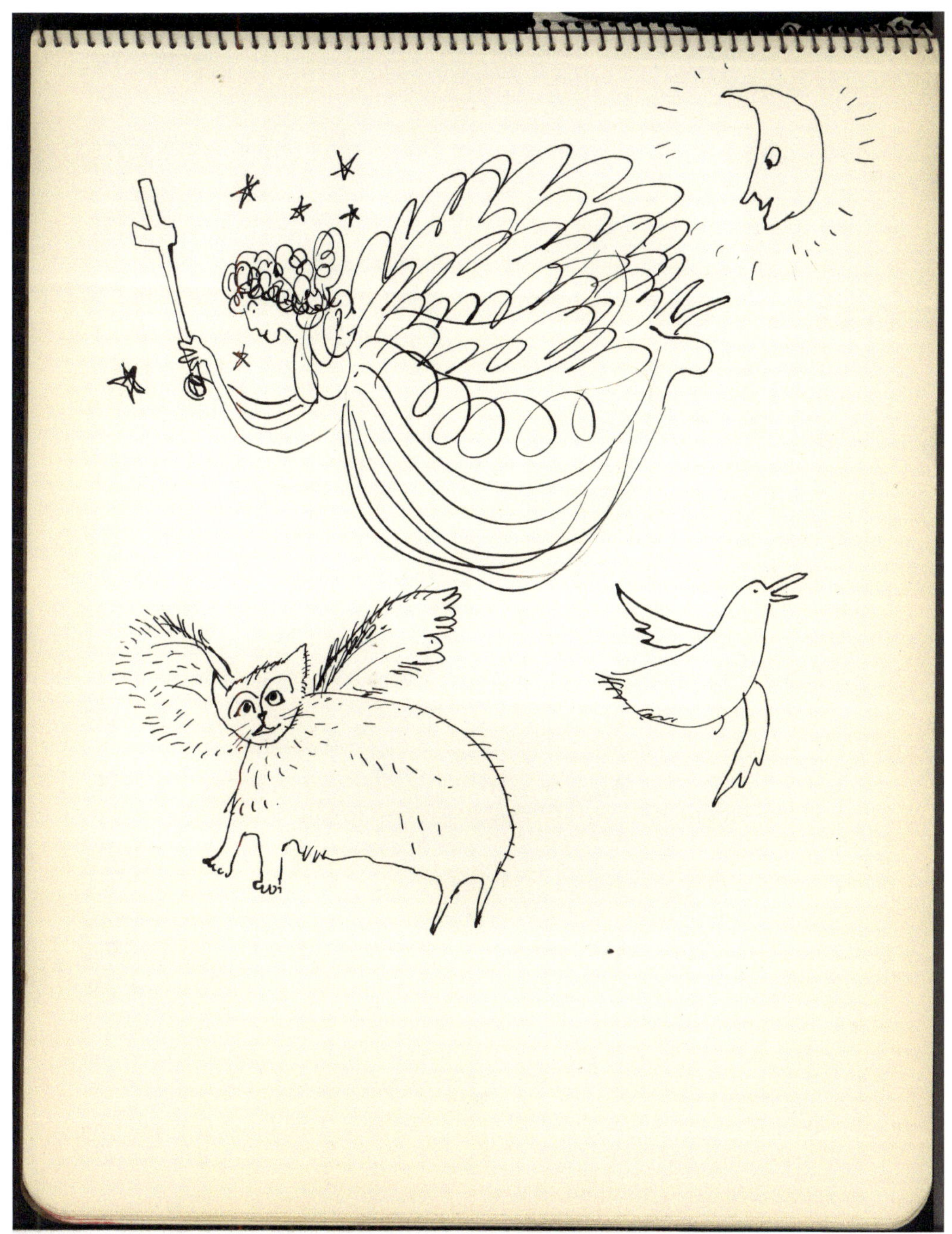

Figure 5.9. Drawings by Julia Warhola.

is no narrative, or at best, a hidden message, Julia's twenty drawings follow Hester in a story about her afterlife. While the tale is simple, the overarching narrative is provocative, unfolding in a zigzag pattern to a curious conclusion. Holy cats and earthbound angels sometimes lead to the devil.

While the drawings are Julia's, she very likely had help with the concept and the text. Nathan Gluck claimed that Warhol's art assistant Joe Giordano worked with her on the book and was responsible for the final text.[114] Julia had a close, affectionate relationship with Giordano, who was fond of her and indulged her, listening patiently to her fantastical stories. Archival information shows that they shared a sense of fun. On letterhead, for which she did the calligraphy, Giordano writes to Julia in an undated letter, "Say hello to God for me. I love you and I always will. Your sweetest sweetheart, Joe Giordano." This is followed by seven x's (kisses), "and one x for Andy." On the envelope, Julia wrote a note, as she often did, to identify the correspondent in her own terms: "Jow holupki." The phonetic spelling of "Joe" and the Rusyn word for stuffed cabbage may have been a nickname, or perhaps an indication of Giordano's favorite dish from Julia's ethnic cuisine.[115] Also consistent with the notion that Julia worked with Joe Giordano on *Holy Cats* is an original copy of the book in the Morgan Library and Museum, which bears an inscription in Julia Warhola's handwriting, "To Joe's mother from Andy Warhol's mother." Joe Giordano's home address on East 61st Street is in Julia's address book.

Hester explores pussy heaven in a story structured by contrasts. The final text is whimsical and charming, with just a hint of the suggestive innuendo of Warhol's other artist's books. On the first of the variously colored pages, we are told, "Some pussys up there love her." Seven stylized cats, most in outlandish feathered hats, smile or grimace at the viewer. The text on the following page reads, "Some don't," and one large cat frowns in wide-eyed consternation. "Some angels up there love her" labels a drawing of three cheeky, chubby cherubs who might have come from Warhol's *In the Bottom of My Garden*, frolicking in the air above a confused large bird. "Some don't" describes the expression of a full-page angel with a severe look in her eyes, her hair sketched in tight circular squiggles and her wings textured by tangled swirls. "Some like it day" and "Some like it night," the latter in silver ink on black paper, call to mind motifs of Carpatho-Rusyn folk art, as images of the sun, moon, stars, butterflies, flowers, and birds surround fanciful winged cats. The contour drawings embellished with hatching and cross-hatching recall the *pysanky* art Julia practiced, with its dot-and-dash patterns and short curved designs. Next, in an existential snit, a small, obstinate cat in a hat sits amid a page of open space over the caption, "Some don't like it at all."

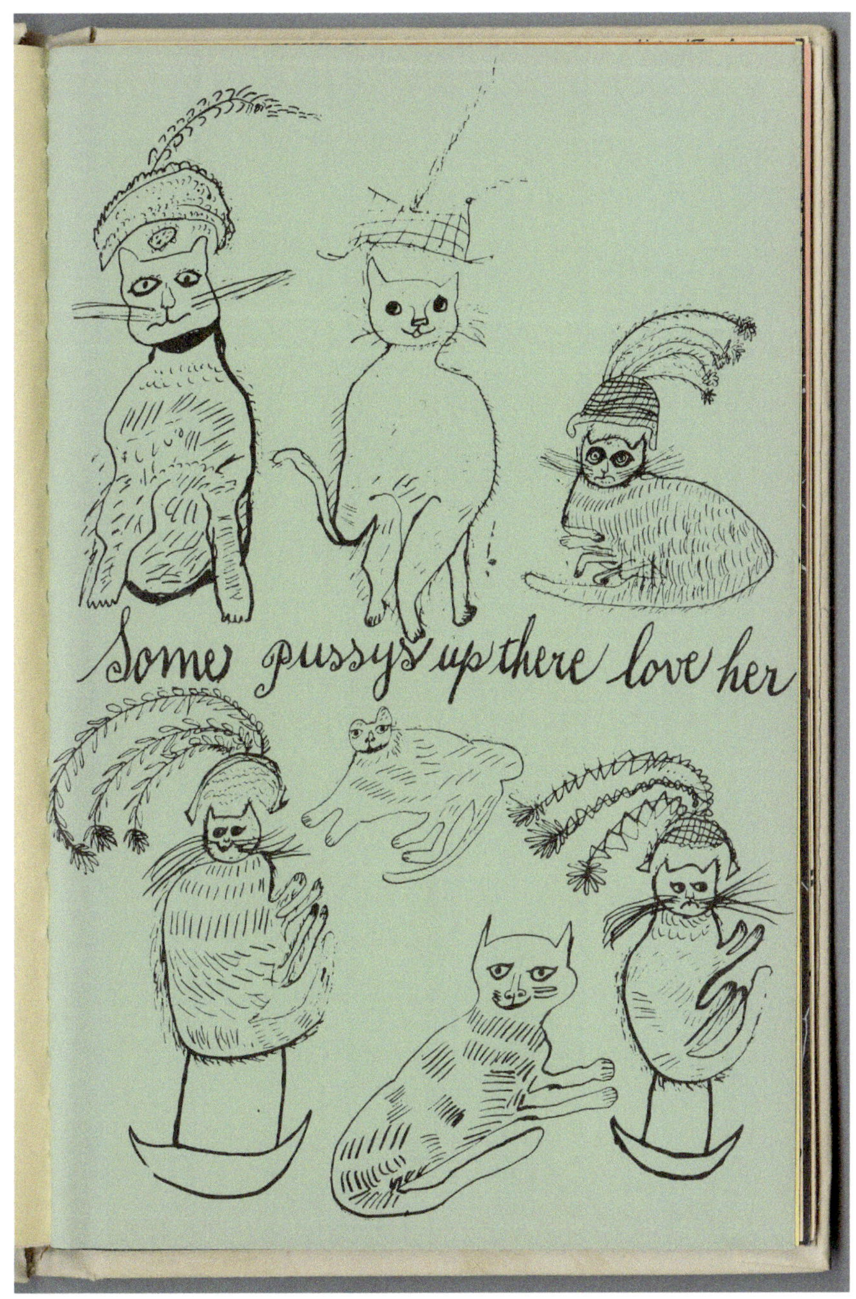

Figure 5.10. "Some pussys up there love her." *Holy Cats*, 1960. Drawing and lettering by Julia Warhola.

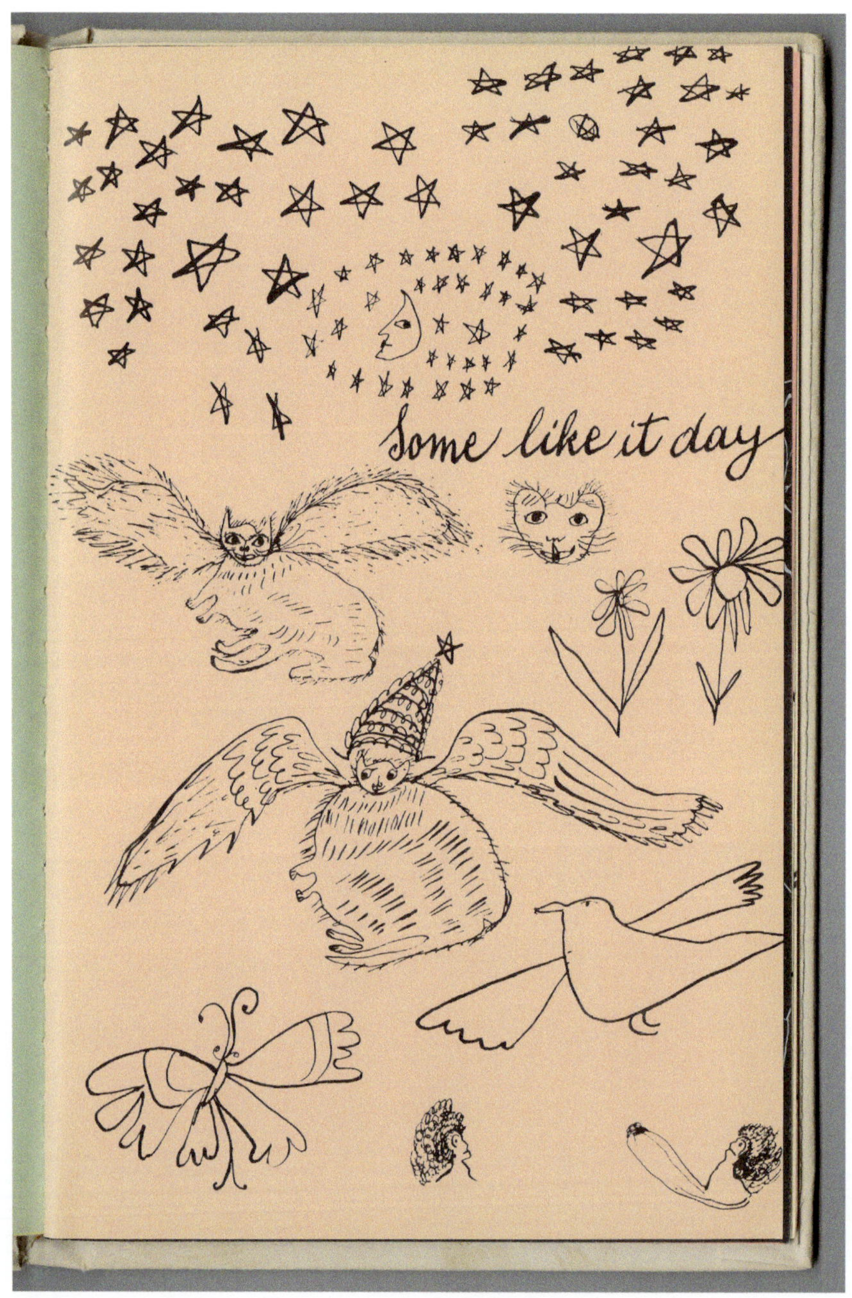

Figure 5.11. "Some like it day." *Holy Cats.* Drawing and lettering by Julia Warhola.

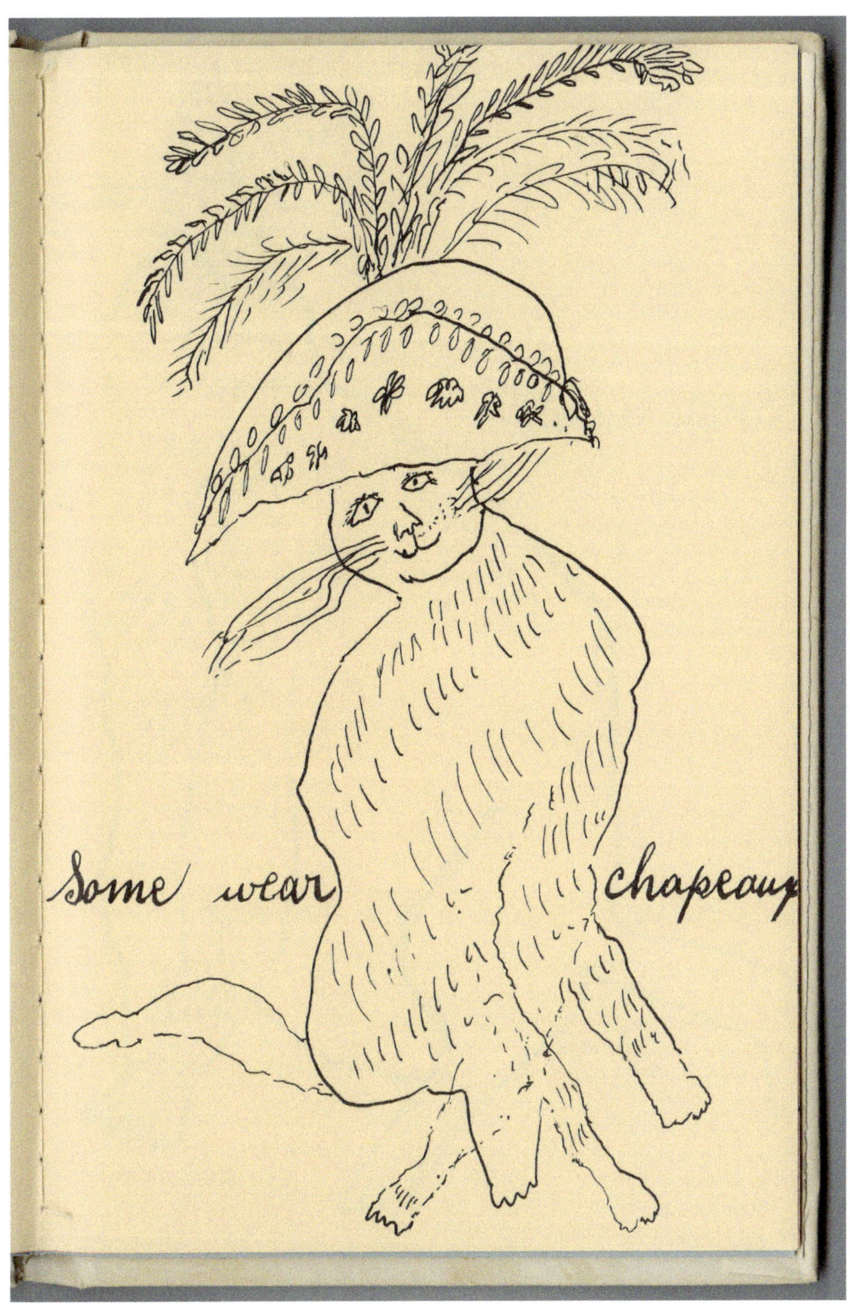

Figure 5.12. "Some wear chapeaux." *Holy Cats.* Drawing and lettering by Julia Warhola.

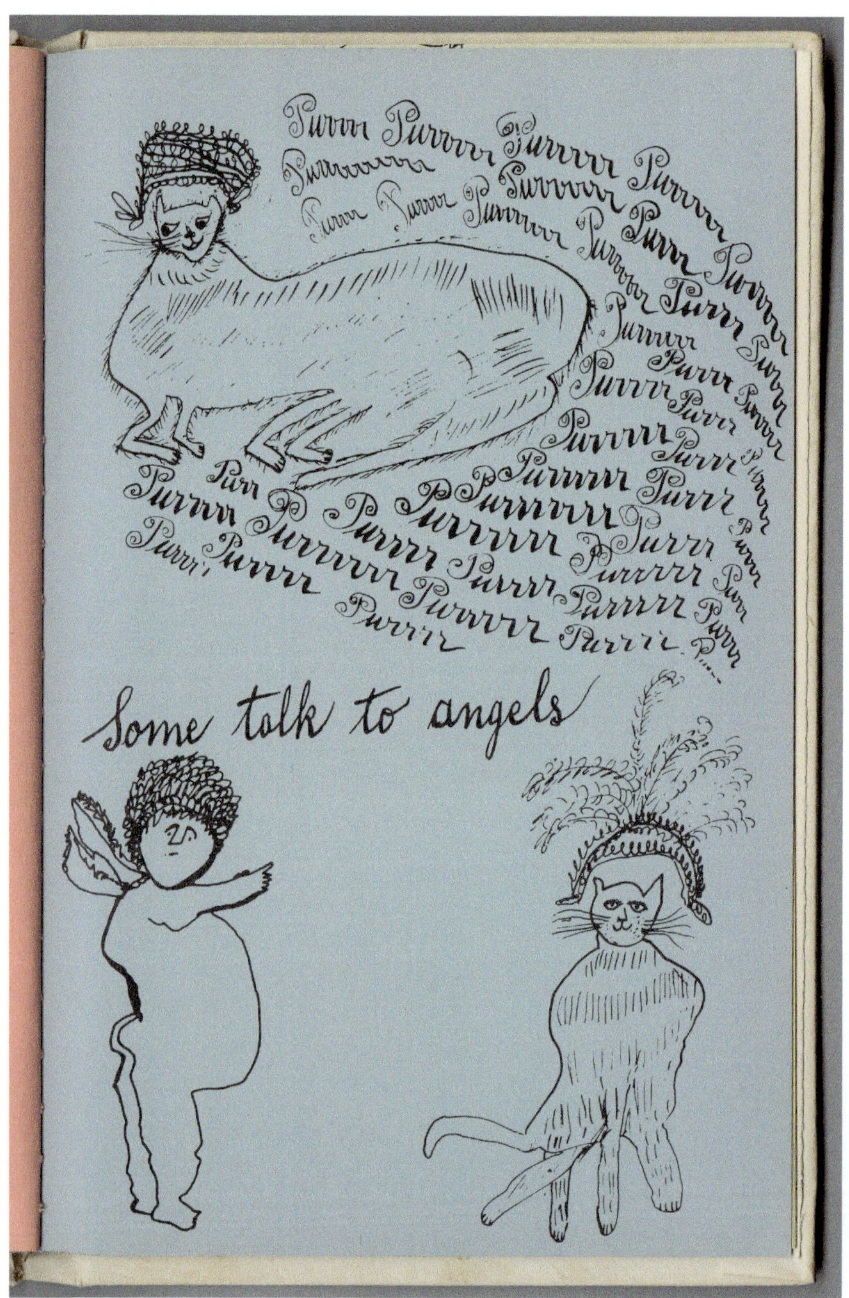

Figure 5.13. "Some talk to angels." *Holy Cats.* Drawing and lettering by Julia Warhola.

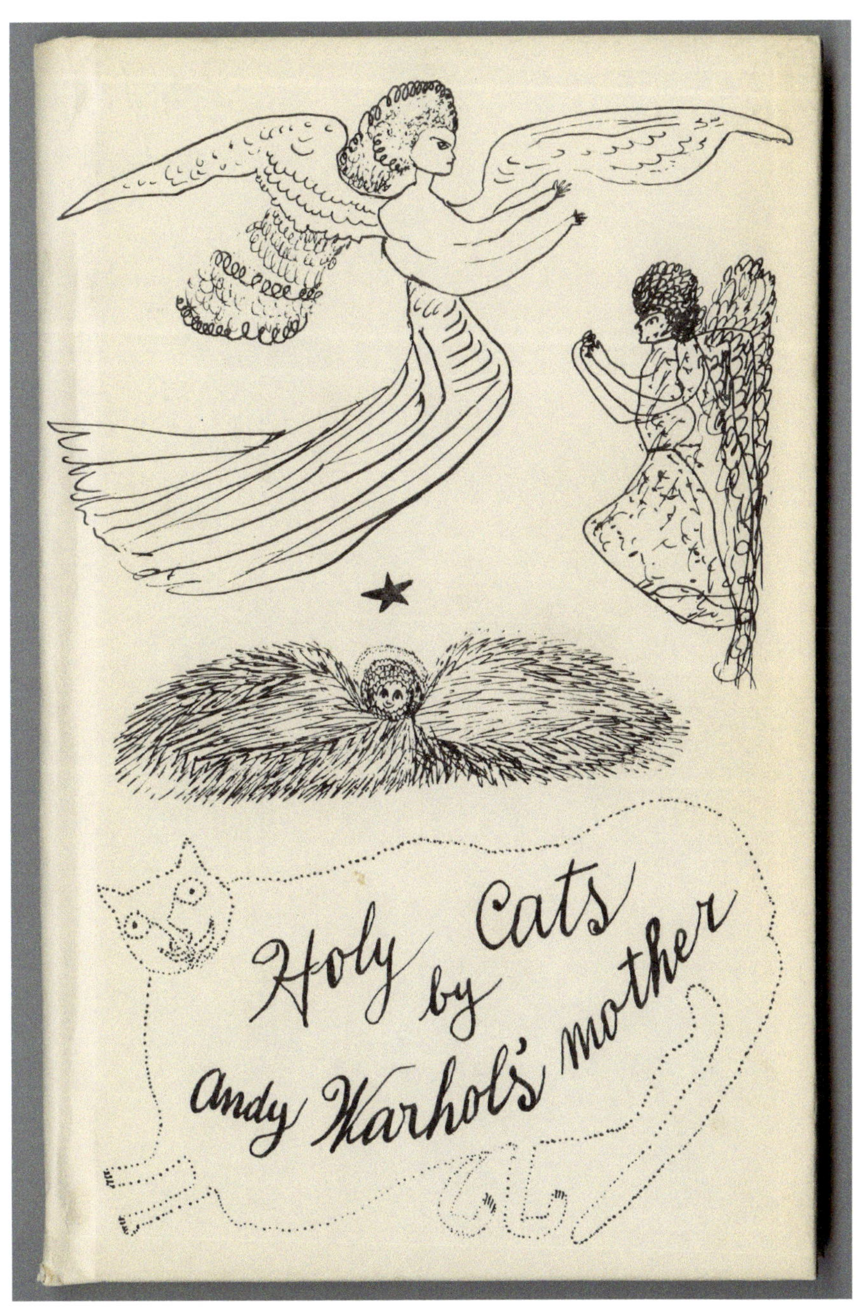

Figure 5.14. *Holy Cats by Andy Warhol's Mother*, cover drawing. Drawing and lettering by Julia Warhola.

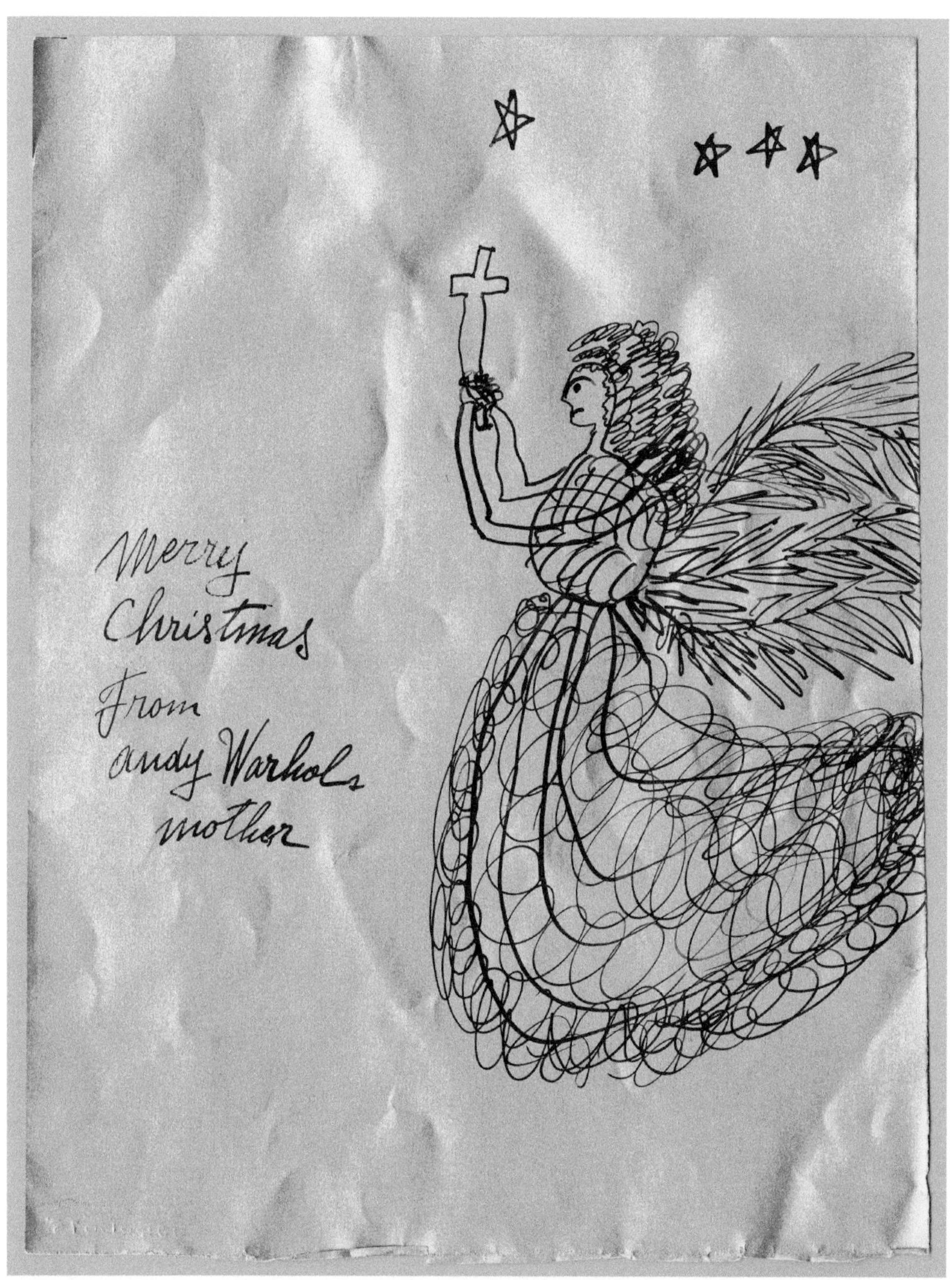

Figure 5.15. *Merry Christmas from Andy Warhols Mother.* **Drawing and lettering by Julia Warhola.**

On the next three pages of pussy cats, we are told, "Some wear hats," "Some wear chapeaux," and "Some don't." Julia surely did not come up with "chapeaux" on her own, but the illustration of a sophisticated pussy in an elaborate bonnet is apt. "Some talk to angels" depicts a contented cat encircled by "purrs," spelled with up to eight *r*'s. Beneath the purring pussy, a comical cherub points to a smug cat in disbelief. Then in a dose of reality, we are told, "Some know they are pussycats so they don't talk at all." Four cats in hats look on as one feline is shown with an obstinately closed mouth. "Some play with angels" depicts three angels in flight, with stars and holy images; "Some play with boys" tags a youngster pulling a cat on a chain; and "Some play with themselves" labels a sly-looking cat in a close-up. Finally, "Some don't play with nobody" ends this "play" series in Julia's own speech style.

The final page, however, is unexpected. A cat's face with a roguish expression fills the entire page. The caption tells us, "And once in a while one of them goes to the devil." The language here, "once in a while," does not sound like Julia's limited English, and the drawing, distinctly different in style, may have been the work of a collaborator. But the story that begins with beloved Hester's departure for pussy heaven ends with Julia's characteristic peasant cynicism. Exactly how much of the content came directly from Julia and how much was suggested by a collaborator is uncertain. While the text injects subtlety into Julia's simplicity, her artwork adeptly captures the nuanced implications of the narrative.

In contrast to Warhol's twenty-five lifelike Sams, Julia's cats are impractical, individual, and fantastical. Rendered with naivete, their legs and tails are posed in improbable positions. Some have angel wings. All seem to levitate with birds and butterflies. They have distinct personalities, as indicated by the opinions attributed to them in the text and the facial expressions that affirm those convictions. From knowing smiles to impertinent grins and self-satisfied smirks, they fill out the simple story of contrasts with commentary and evaluation.

The only cat on the book's cover is a large, smiling, big-eyed creature, her outline sketched in dots, and her feet turned in an awkward, unrealistic position. The dotted outline gives the cat an airy quality, perhaps meant to depict Hester in pussy heaven. But the cover art of *Holy Cats* is dominated not by cats, but by a large angel, with widespread wings, in what appears to be a depiction of the announcement of the Nativity to Carpathian shepherds. The angel's arms are outstretched to a smaller, kneeling figure, as though in visitation. Contour lines in the angel's robe convey a sense of movement, and delicate curved lines in the wings suggest flight. Her long hair surrounds her head in squiggly circles. The smaller figure kneels with hands folded in prayer and looks up to the angel. In distinction from the smooth swirls of the

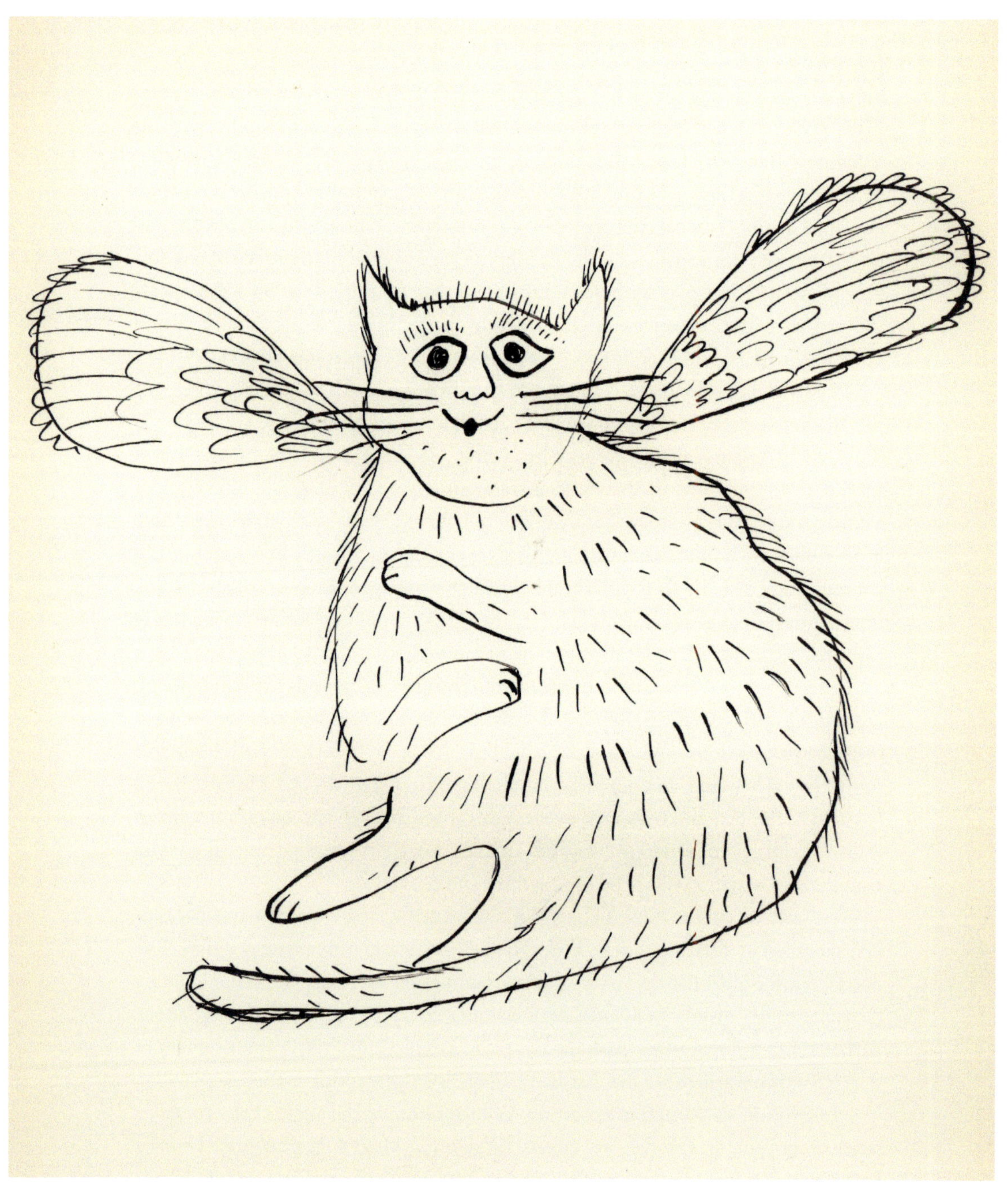

Figure 5.16. Julia Warhola, *Cat with Wings.*

angel's gown, the stippling on the clothing of the kneeling figure marks it as a coarse garment, likely a *hunia*, the Carpatho-Rusyn shepherd's long sheepskin cloak. In the center of the composition is a baby's face, with circles of wavy lines to suggest soft hair, peaking out of a winglike mass that is hatched to look like straw. Above the child's sweetly smiling face is a star, and he is crowned with a halo, which distinguishes him from the angels. The details of the scene evoke the story of the nativity of Christ as told in numerous Rusyn Christmas carols and the Divine Liturgy for the feast of the Nativity: "The Angels sing His glory with the shepherds . . . the manger has become an honorable place in which lies Christ God . . . let us praise and extol Him."[116]

While Julia was surrounded by cats in her daily life, angels populated her spiritual world as guardians and intermediaries with God. The daily devotions in her prayerbook *Heavenly Manna* address the heavenly hosts: "All ye heavenly powers, holy Angels and Archangels, beseech God for us sinners." Cherubim and Seraphim are invoked repeatedly in the Divine Liturgy. A prayer recited after the consecration of the body and blood of Christ reads, "O holy Angels of the sanctuary, Angels of light, adore, praise, love and thank my Jesus for me!"[117] This is the image that Julia depicted in numerous drawings of angels in gowns of swirling, curved lines that suggest translucence. In ink on gold paper, they float to the heavens or pray to the baby face in a manger of straw, and this became her signature Christmas card, signed "from Andy Warhol's Mother."

Outsider Art

There is no easy way to characterize Julia Warhola's drawings in terms of style or genre. Nathan Gluck said of *Holy Cats*, "[Julia] did it with complete naivete, a real primitive, almost like Grandma Moses."[118] But Julia's work does not exhibit the nostalgic and lyrical qualities of rural life for which Grandma Moses and other practitioners of folk art are known. Her *pysanky*, embroidery, cottage painting, and perhaps the artwork she practiced with her young sons might qualify as Rusyn folk art, but none of these survive, and except for a few minor ethnographic touches, her drawings do not evoke the community traditions of folk art. Warhol described his mother as "a really good artist, in the style of the primitives," by which term, he was most likely referring to the simplicity, sincerity, and childlike imagery of her work.[119] Many of her drawings portray an imaginative world, where cats with wings commune with snub-nosed angels, which might qualify as visionary art. However, rather than conjuring up a fantastic world, her angels and cats-in-hats seem to maintain a foothold in her personal reality.

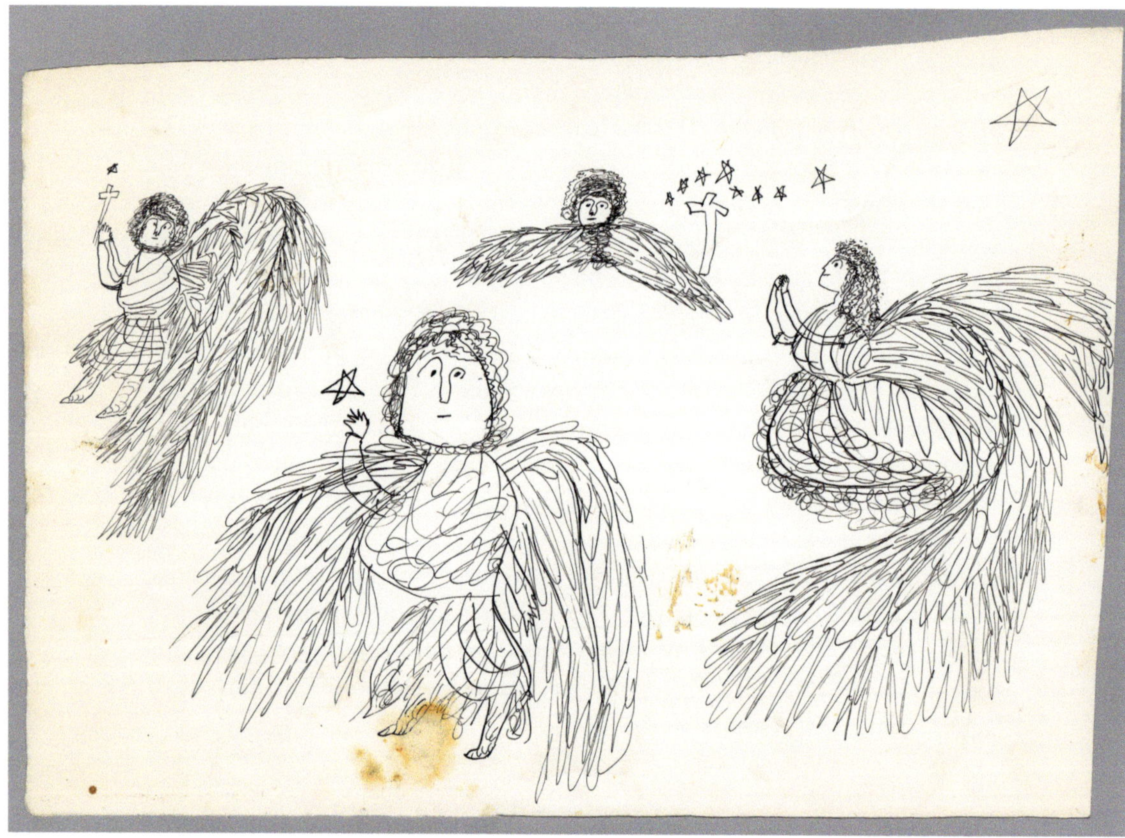

Figure 5.17. Julia Warhola, *Four Angels*.

Julia's flying angels with crosses raised aloft resemble the Archangels Michael and Gabriel on the icon of Our Lady of Perpetual Help, which Julia knew from reproductions in her prayer book and a large color photograph featured on the wall calendar that was distributed by Saint Mary's Church and preserved by her son in a Time Capsule. But for the most part, Julia's favorite angel images do not mimic existing icons but are her own imaginative interpretations of prayer texts. In religious belief, angels are genderless, but unlike the comedic putti-like cherubs who play with cats in pussy heaven, Julia's praying angels have a distinctly feminine appearance. However, some are more farcical than beatific, wearing less-than-angelic, plebian facial expressions.[120] Others are posed awkwardly, their wings arching upward and curving in large crescents to the ground. Angels raise crosses in elastic-like elongated arms. The meaning and message of some of her drawings are inexplicable. Angels pray to

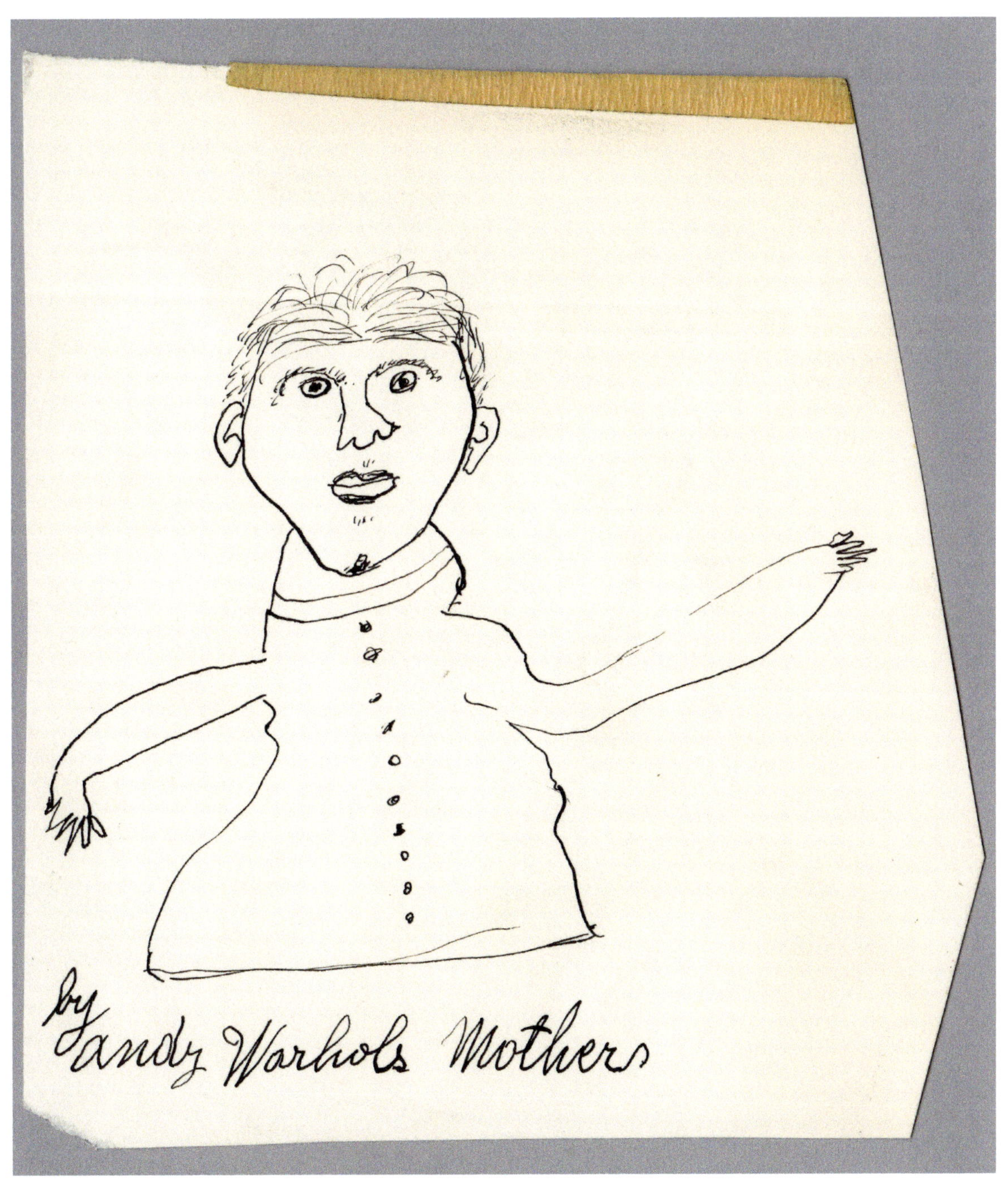

Figure 5.18. Julia Warhola, *Male Torso*.

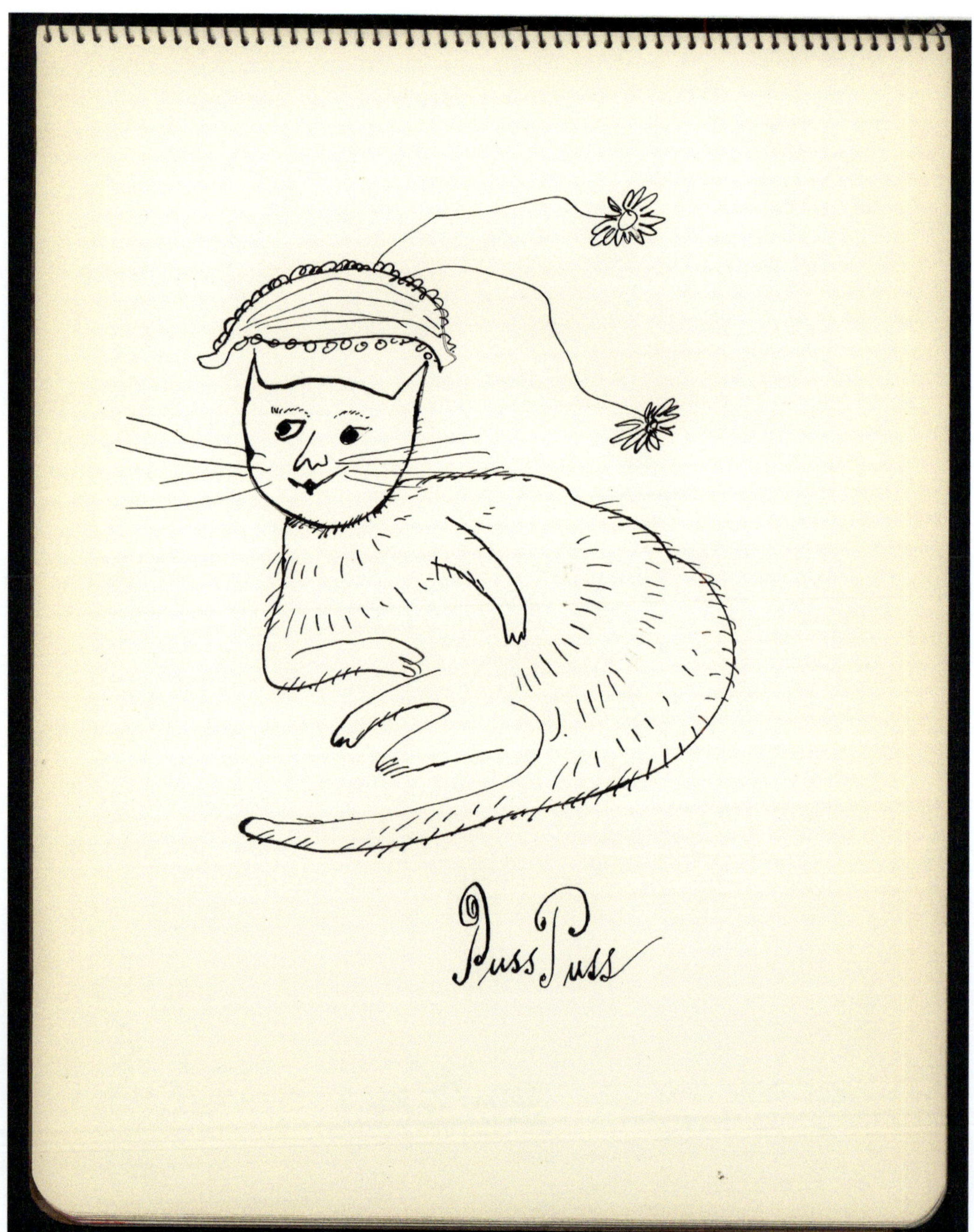

Figure 5.19. Julia Warhola, *Puss Puss.*

the baby Jesus before what seems to be a palm tree; one angel with flowing wings and coiled robe wears a bodice studded with buttons; two kneeling angels look up prayerfully to a floating cat's head; pussycats balance on rocking pedestals. Characterized by simple forms—circles, crosses, stars—most of her work is childlike and idiosyncratic. A male figure with arms emerging almost from his neck might have been drawn by a six-year-old, whose attention focused on what was perceived as the most important details—eyes, nose, and the ten buttons on the figure's shirt.

The term "outsider art," which has been applied to the work of self-taught or untrained artists, is especially apt for Julia Warhola. Most often quirky and idiosyncratic, outsider art expresses a personal, often obsessive, vision. Outside the realm of academic and mainstream art, these artists "derive everything from their own depths, not from the conventions of classical or fashionable art."[121] The therapeutic creative process and the expressive content take precedence over technical precision, and the artist's biographical narrative contributes to its meaning and value. Taking a sociological, rather than aesthetic, approach to self-taught art, the scholar Gary Alan Fine submits that in no other field more than in self-taught art is it truer that "the authenticity of the artist justifies the authenticity of the artwork. . . . Ultimately self-taught art is a form of identity art in which the characteristics of the creators matter as much as the characteristics of the work."[122] That is, the art is "as much about the story of the artists behind it as what's on the canvas."[123] Julia Warhola's art granted her the freedom to express herself and to confront the ennui of daily life. Although she may at one time have hoped to display or even sell her work, she does not communicate a message to an audience. Instead, viewers are given the chance to live, at least momentarily, in her world of pussies and angels.

Despite his college degree, Andy Warhol often described himself as "self-taught," and in his early years in Pittsburgh, he showed a serious interest in folk and naive art. According to Gopnik, he was "bathing in outsiderism," and consequently, the signature style he developed at Carnegie Tech mixed naiveté with modernism. "Part of the appeal of Warhol's 1950s illustrations came from their simulation . . . of a childlike directness." Warhol's outsiderism, according to Gopnik, was something he came by honestly in Pittsburgh, the city of immigrants. "Julia Warhola, the artist's devout mother, most clearly represented that eccentric outsider culture in his life."[124]

"I Am Andy Warhol"

Warhol was well known for inveigling friends into contributing to his commercial work and promotional books without compensation, and he expected no less from his mother. He was a harsh taskmaster. "She would complain later that she was 'so tired,' but he'd insist 'you have to get up and do another pussycat.'"[125] Suzie Frankfurt, who worked with Warhol and Julia on *Wild Raspberries*, confirmed the arduous work, but cast blame on Julia. "She was very talented in some mad way, but she was so manipulative. When we were doing *Wild Raspberries* Andy had to chain her to the lightbox to get all the calligraphy done. She said she'd copy it over and she didn't. He gave her too much bloody credit. I mean, she was like Miss Prima Donna."[126] According to Frankfurt, they worked through September, and by the middle of October had finished just one copy. "Our progress was very slow, and in the end we only made thirty-four full-color books."[127] A sensitive viewer of Julia's transcribed recipes in *Wild Raspberries* might perceive her fatigue, as her cursive script, which faithfully reproduced Frankfurt's errors and misspellings, becomes irregular and cramped.

There is evidence that the codependent, self-sacrificing artist-mother at times harbored resentment at her son's impatience and insensitivity. Joseph Giordano claimed Julia was bitter that Andy was not "shelling out" enough financial support for his brothers and was upset that he "made her move" to New York.

> So, she packed her bag and returned to Pittsburgh. Andy was very, very upset because he just couldn't function. . . . It was too much of a house, a household to run. And so, he finally called her back. . . . She insisted that I be there that night. She wouldn't come home unless I was there. So, she came in and slammed the suitcase on the ground and she turned around. She looked at him and she said, "I am Andy Warhol." And there was a big discussion about why she was Andy Warhol. But, I guess she convinced him that he was.[128]

Although Giordano was sympathetic to Mrs. Warhola, he alone among commentators expresses a negative opinion about her mothering style. "I knew she was doing something wrong. I just knew it. It was untoward. I just knew she made [Andy] feel so insignificant. She made him feel that he was the ugliest creature that God put on this earth."[129] Giordano reports that Julia told him a story about a man in Czechoslovakia who was so ugly that no one in the world would possibly want to marry him. "But if they do want to marry you, it's for your money. It was for the money. And she was telling this story, looking Andy directly in the eye."[130] This cynical outlook on love and money, which comes from the peasant worldview, where marriage was primarily an economic transaction, became entrenched in Warhol. Bob Colacello reported: "When you told him any two people were getting married, he'd say, 'Which one has the money?'"[131]

Some of Giordano's statements and judgments are questionable, and he admits he "could never separate myth from reality."[132] Julia's reported comment that she had a house in Pittsburgh "that looked like a church" sounds like one of her fabulations. But in reporting that Andy insisted she move to the city, which she "resented very much," Giordano contradicts all the family stories about her move to New York. His assessment of her attitude toward Andy has been disputed by others who knew Julia well. When asked specifically whether he agreed with Giordano's opinion that Julia made Andy feel insignificant and ugly, Gerard Malanga said, "Not at all, not at all."[133] It is worth noting, however, the Carpatho-Rusyn folk superstition against complimenting children. Even at a christening, the custom was to symbolically "spit upon" the newborn.

The curious interaction described by Giordano, which begins with Julia claiming Andy's identity and ends with her convincing him of the same, is puzzling. It is likely that after Julia's belittling comment, she softened and reassured her son of his distinction, restoring harmony to their relationship. Insult, followed by remorse and conciliation, is a common cultural pattern. Howard Stein, who has extensively studied the psychology of Slovak and Rusyn Americans, points to the prevalence of jealousy in the culture, which manifests in sibling rivalry and paternal narcissism. "[The parent's] impetus for the American ethos of success, achievement, mobility, and independence induces a narcissistic identification with the potential success of their offspring, thus enabling them vicariously to succeed through their children, even as they envy and resent that very success they were unable or unwilling to try for."[134] Julia Warhola, a would-be artist, may have neurotically, if not naturally, identified with her son, resenting the relative ease of his success, the futility of her own artistic aspirations, and his lack of appreciation for her self-sacrifice, even as she appreciated his talent. It is consistent with the dysfunctional family dynamic that emerged from expectations of peasant family life, where "the attitudes of social pride are primarily familial and only secondarily individual."[135] The artist Ara Osterweil, adds personal insights to Giordano's narrative:

> Like many of Warhol's other collaborators who later claimed responsibility for his creative work, Julia may have recognized that her Andy couldn't be "Andy Warhol" without her help behind the scenes. After all, she frequently signed her name for him. Stumbling on such telling moments of identity crisis in Warhol's biography, I cannot help but recall a painting I made of my own mother, which she admired and which she persisted in referring to as her "self-portrait" until her death. Is it possible that in the space between unintentional malapropism and deliberate misidentification

there is a deeper truth about the inextricability of the child's creativity from the mother's idiosyncrasies?[136]

"I Like New York. You Never Lonesome"

Suzie Frankfurt, a prominent high-priced interior decorator for celebrities and businesses, formed a negative opinion of Julia. "She wasn't really a very nice person. I never liked her. . . . She was too weird for me, too ill-kempt, too much of a Czechoslovakian peasant."[137] Fritzie Wood, who lived in a neighboring apartment at 242 Lexington Avenue, assessed Julia's simplicity more positively. "She was very childlike—and that's not a patronizing statement. She was childlike and a great joy, a great joy to be alive, a great joy to be with Andy."[138] Among Andy's friends, followers, critics, and commentators, there was a major fascination with Julia, and their descriptions range from admiration to vilification. She was either "a very naïve woman" or "complex, manipulative, and powerful."[139] She was "a really lovely lady," or "one of the strangest creatures I've ever seen."[140] The fascination with Mrs. Warhola was so great that in 1971, the London photographer David Bailey had an actress impersonate her in his controversial documentary of Warhol.[141]

Bailey claimed to have had tea with Andy's mother in the decade of his acquaintance with Warhol, but the tongue-in-cheek narration of the film calls that into question. In one exchange, Bailey asks when they can get together with Mrs. Warhola. Warhol asks him, "Do you know my mother?" Bailey responds, "No, but I'd like to know your mother," to which Warhol retorts, "I don't think she'd like you."[142] The impersonation of Julia by the actress Lil Picard in Bailey's documentary was far from convincing. Trying unsuccessfully to approximate Rusyn speech patterns, Lil Picard's "Mrs. Warhola" makes some insightful and some outrageous statements, which have often been taken at face value and quoted as fact, though often noted as "bizarre."[143] The faux-Julia wishes that Andy would marry "one of the boys" and have "all these little Andys . . . Andys, Andys, Andys, Andys, like the pictures you know, what he paints." Another comment that is often quoted both in the West and by the Rusyns of Slovakia expresses an idea that is appealing, but completely inconsistent with the unsophisticated Julia Warhola: "He represents the . . . American and the European . . . fuse[d] together, and he's very very keen and sensitive to everything that goes on every day and he registered it like . . . a photographic plate."[144] In 1980, Warhol told his diary, "[An acquaintance] told me he saw 'my mother' on TV in England, that stupid David Bailey 'documentary' about me where Lil Piccard [sic] made believe she was my mother . . . and I just didn't have the heart to tell him that wasn't my mother."[145] Unfortunately, many others have also been fooled.

Everyone in Andy's entourage seemed to be intrigued by the notion that Julia lived with her son. Many simply did not know what to make of her, and few really got to know her well. Still, she formed close attachments with some of Andy's associates. According to Ted Carey, "Andy was very timid about people coming to his house, unless he knew you very well. And even more timid about letting you meet his mother. If you got to meet Andy's mother, then you knew that Andy liked you very much."[146] Carey was one of Julia's favorites. She spent so much time talking with him that Andy rebuked her for distracting him from his work. "But as soon as Andy would go out she would come up to the upper level apartment, and we would just talk. And she loved television, and she loved programs like *I Love Lucy*. And she would laugh. She was like a child. She had a wonderful sense of humor."[147] Others recalled her playfulness and sense of fun. Vito Giallo described how she would stand holding a shoe while Warhol drew it. "And then she'd put it on, and then she'd get into both shoes and they'd laugh because she looked so funny in those shoes. She couldn't really walk in them at all, she had very wide feet, she always was barefoot. Andy laughed a lot."[148] Carlton Willers, an early Warhol boyfriend, described Julia as extremely funny and kind. "She was innocent and spoke this broken English and was always taking care of Andy. . . . She was as funny as Andy and she loved to laugh at funny things."[149]

Like all Rusyn grandmothers, Julia urged her visitors to eat. Ultra Violet describes being offered what must have been the popular Rusyn dessert, *kolache*, or nut roll. "She urged me to eat, eat, it's a roll."[150] When Andy's first live-in boyfriend taught him to bake a cake, Julia played judge of a bake-off.[151] She served lunch to many of Warhol's assistants. Nathan Gluck remembers mushroom and barley soup, stuffed cabbage, and baloney or cheese sandwiches. Gerard Malanga was served "a Czechoslovakian hamburger with raw chopped-up onion on a roll with 7 Up."[152] When Warhol worked with Leonard Kessler, Julia encouraged the men to "verk, verk, verk," and she cooked sauerkraut for lunch. Kessler recalled, "She used to make *kapusta*, which is cabbage, with short ribs of beef. It's marvelous if you live in Alaska or the Yukon. On the hottest day of the summer, she'd say, '*Kapusta* will keep you warm.' 'Mrs. Warhola,' I'd say, 'I am warm.' 'You can be warmer,' she would reply."[153] The overgiving Rusyn mother brooked no refusal when it came to food.

Gerard Malanga, Andy's 1960's silk-screen assistant, was introduced to Julia in June 1963, on his first day of work with Warhol. Malanga remembers Julia as old, with silvery gray hair, wearing dresses down to her ankles. "She was spry, she was lively, it was just that she had this old-lady look about her."[154] Malanga recalled their introduction: "After work we walked to his house which is when I met Julia. She looked at me. Then she looked at Andy and back to me. She said, 'You are Andy's younger brother' and embraced me. It was like being blessed by the Pope."[155] Like Warhol, Malanga was the son of working-class immigrants. "Julia and my mother were very similar in their immediate concerns for their sons. The first instance of that was when Andy and I did the road trip to Los Angeles in December of 1963. My mother and Julia were on the phone all the time worrying about their sons" (laughs).[156] Malanga understood the worries of immigrant mothers. In several post-cards from his travels with Andy, he assures Julia, "Don't worry. I am taking care of him." The actor Taylor Mead was part of the motley crew that set off for Califor-nia from Lexington Avenue. "I had the feeling he was hiding his mother from his friends. . . . But this time when we were leaving she came to say goodbye to us. In a sense it was an honor to meet his mother, a mark of his trust."[157]

In 1966, Julia told the *Esquire* interviewer, "I like New York. You never lone-some. People nice."[158] Andy introduced the photographer Duane Michals to Julia in the 1950s. Michals, from McKeesport, near Pittsburgh, was the great-grandson of immigrants from Červenica in the Prešov Region of Slovakia, about fifty miles from Miková. "As a matter of fact, I spoke Slovak with Andy's mother. She was overjoyed, because I was the only one of Andy's friends who spoke a language similar to hers."[159] In 1958, Michals traveled to Slovakia and visited his ancestral village. Andy did not share his interest in their common roots, but Julia must have been intrigued. William Milié, a dancer from the Pittsburgh area who gained world acclaim, was a recipient of two of Hester's Siamese progeny. A note from Milié's mother to Julia with the gift of an apron reads, "Just a little note to thank you for all you did for my son Bill." In 1968, Bill visited Julia in New York and she gave him a copy of *Holy Cats*. His sister wrote to thank Julia and to express her condolences about the loss of Hester.[160] Freddy Herko, a dancer with the experimental Judson Dance Theater and star in a few of Warhol's films, was of Carpatho-Rusyn ancestry, but there is no evidence that Julia met him. In *POPism*, Andy recounted a visit to Herko's Aunt Harriet, who, in Rusyn-immigrant style, pressed a dollar bill into the hands of each of his friends, which Warhol, perhaps touched by a familiar gesture, described as "the really sad part."[161]

Julia's grandson Paul, who was then studying at Catholic University in Washing-ton, DC, often took his classmates to New York, where they stayed at Andy's home. "We were always treated very well, he was very gracious. And my grandmother, of course, she was a wonderful hostess."[162] An undated letter to Warhol from Paul's wife Ann tells him that Pauly decided not to go to New York as planned, but to get a summer job in Pittsburgh. "These boys who he was suppose [*sic*] to go to N.Y. [with] will stop by to visit your mother. There gone [*sic*] to the Russian Church this week end somewhere near 86th st. so if your mother wants to or feels like talking let them in and if she doesn't feel good don't open the door. Pauly told them to visit her for him since he couldn't make it." Warhol himself was conflicted about his mother's popularity with his friends and other young people. In David Bourdon's notes covering a college lecture tour on which he accompanied Warhol, he cites Andy's response to what was probably a question from the audience: "I'm not really that close to my mother. A lot of other people like her better, get along with her better, enjoy talking to her more."[163] This conflict is felt by many children of immigrants, whose fascinating stories and open personalities often appeal to typical Americans, while they embarrass or bore the children who have grown up with them.

By 1960, Andy was one of the most successful commercial artists in New York. He bought a town house at 1342 Lexington Avenue near the corner of 89th Street for $60,000, paying half in cash. Four stories tall, three thousand square feet of space with eleven-foot ceilings, two rooms on each floor, and five wood-burning fireplaces, it was forty-eight feet deep and just sixteen feet wide.[164] Julia's grandchildren called the brick town house the "skinny house." From the street level, the black and white tiled foyer opened to a short staircase that led up to the parlor level. From there another wooden staircase wound down in a spiral to the garden floor, which was Julia's apartment. The garden or English-basement lower floor was partially above and partially below ground level, with windows facing the Finast grocery store across Lexington Avenue. When Andy's brothers visited, their children enjoyed watching people's feet pass by. A kitchen in the rear opened to a small garden patio. Julia's bedroom area was in the middle of the floor-through apartment, where her bed stood parallel to an exposed-brick wall. Barn doors could be closed to screen the kitchen. The subway rumbled beneath the full basement, shaking the house, and just around the corner was the Roman Catholic church of Saint Thomas More, which Julia and Andy would occasionally visit. When Gerard Malanga began working for Warhol, he was surprised when Andy said after lunch, "'Let's go to the church around the corner.' He'd sit quietly and after about ten minutes, we'd leave."[165]

As Warhol initiated his Pop period, Julia was less involved with his day-to-day work and his colleagues. Most new assistants and collaborators knew her only slightly. One associate said, "Her presence was ectoplasmic. She would float through, Andy would sort of guide her away."[166] Although he stated that in the lower

Lexington flat, "Andy's friends doted on Mrs. Warhola," David Bourdon claimed later, "She's very old, and although she could navigate the stairs, she won't."[167] Similar comments from other visitors to 1342 Lexington gave rise to the legend that Andy kept his mother hidden, or even "confined," in the basement.[168] When the art dealer Ivan Karp visited in 1961, "There was a noise down below, and Andy looked at me. 'Oh,' he said, that's my mother, she lives down there, she cooks for me, she does all kinds of things.' I said 'Don't you want to introduce her?' He said, 'Oh, she doesn't want to be bothered.'"[169] Warhol continued to be selective about introducing associates to his mother. Two Los Angeles gallery owners, with whom he was negotiating his first Pop solo exhibition in 1961, may have been so honored. "Andy took us down to the lower floor of the building, where we met an old woman he introduced as his mother. And he gave me one of his little books, '25 Cats Name Sam and One Blue Pussy,' which he autographed."[170] At some point, it became rather prestigious to have been introduced to Mrs. Warhola, and stories changed to claim that honor. In an earlier version, Andy gave Walter Hopps and Irving Blum copies of *Holy Cats*, his mother's book, which she autographed as "Andy Warhol's Mother."[171]

When asked whether Andy kept his mother hidden, Gerard Malanga said, "That was not my experience. At the time we didn't have the Factory yet, so any business or socializing took place at the townhouse. And I was present also when Andy was, I would say, entertaining people . . . and Julia once in a while would sit in on those gatherings. Not the entire time—she had things to do, so eventually she would depart and head down to the kitchen. But there was no sign of anything that Andy was ashamed of his mother."[172] However, it was around this time that, according to some biographers, Julia became "a potential embarrassment" for Andy, even as others perceive the growing intensity of her influence on his creative outlook.[173]

It is when Julia's direct involvement exits and Andy turns Pop in the early 1960s that his mother's presence is reintroduced in his art in a more insidious way. . . . Paradoxically, it was by abandoning the American aristocracy of the Vanderbilts and Manhattan socialites with whom he lunched, and turning to his immigrant mother's kitchen that Warhol found America's most authentic images of itself—the Campbell's Soup cans, the Coke bottles, the *Daily News*, the dollar bills, the Brillo boxes. Warhol stumbled across "the real America" in the pantry of a woman who never adapted to the American way of life, or mastered the English language, or altered a peasant lifestyle which revolved around daily visits to the local food store.[174]

"Leave Me Alone, Ma!"

Comments from Warhol's friends and associates on the relationship between mother and son are as disparate as their descriptions of Julia. Andy is described as treating his mother respectfully and formally or cringing in embarrassment and whining, "Oh Ma! Leave me alone, Ma!"[175] According to Gerard Malanga, "I saw situations between them that were typical of a mother-son relationship. He would do something that would make her irritated with him. Andy would start whining like a little boy, 'Oh Ma.' . . . The dynamic of the interaction was very interesting."[176] According to the gallery owner Leo Castelli, one of the chosen few to be introduced to Julia, "[Andy] loved her very dearly." Vito Giallo said, "His mom absolutely worshipped him," but he thought Andy did not respect her.[177] Suzie Frankfurt felt that Julia was "too much of a force in Andy's life. He adored her too much."[178] Joseph Giordano's atypical opinion was the singular contradiction: "The crux of Andy Warhol is that he felt so, so unloved. It just makes me want to cry. I know it comes from his mother."[179]

Warhol's nephews highlight Julia's overindulgence. "[My grandmother] would take care of him as though he was a baby"; "She coddled him, there's no question about it, from his sickly childhood through adulthood"; "We would ask our Bubba when is Uncle Andy going to wake up? 'Oh, let him sleep,' she would say. 'He was out all night.' Then she would squeeze fresh orange juice and carry it up three or four flights of stairs to him."[180] She cooked his meals and cleaned his house, some said obsessively, while others claimed she was an indifferent housekeeper. But many agreed there was a bizarre emotional undercurrent in the mother–son relationship. Vito Giallo: "Sometimes [Mrs. Warhola] would say strange things like, 'Oh, Vito, I didn't get any sleep last night. All I did was stay up all night and watch Andy sleep.'"[181] This recalls Julia's care for her son in childhood when he suffered from Saint Vitus's Dance and she stayed up to watch him, consoled by the cessation of jerking movements in sleep. The parallel to Warhol's 1963 film, almost six hours of footage of his then-boyfriend sleeping, has often been noted. "It was, predictably, deemed unwatchable. Who could possibly endure watching someone sleep for so long? Well, a besotted lover, for one, pillow-gazing at this slumbering Adonis, or a mother admiring her children. . . . Perhaps *Sleep* reproduces not just the mechanical gaze of the camera as it has been uniformly interpreted, but also its very opposite: an unflinching, loving gaze."[182] In one of Warhol's *Factory Diary* videotapes, Andy focuses his camera on Julia, asleep in her kerchief and eyeglasses, for twenty-two minutes.[183]

Herbert Muschamp, a onetime regular at Warhol's Factory, relates the following experience:

> When I was a freshman at college in 1966, I used to crash at Warhol's place on weekends. His mother lived downstairs. . . . What dreams Warhol must have had, even after many of them came true! Sometimes I would hear him cry out for his mother in the middle of the night: "Ma! Ma!" Minutes later, with a rustle of skirt, a shadowy presence would darken the doorway . . . an apparition somewhat resembling a cross between Old Mother Hubbard and Mrs. Bates. An antiphonal exchange would ensue, a call-and-response duet that hinted at dark, primitive histories of tribal uprootedness and separation.
>
> "Andy . . . Andy . . ."
>
> "Ma! Ma!"
>
> "Andy . . ."
>
> "Ma!
>
> Some might call this the primal interview.[184]

Muschamp's reference is to the psychologist Arthur Janov's primal therapy, as popularized in the 1970 book *The Primal Scream*. Janov believed that neurosis is caused by the pain of repressed childhood trauma, resulting from unmet physical, emotional, or intellectual needs. To resolve the trauma, he advocated reliving the pain and expressing the emotions that were initially suppressed. The meaning of Muschamp's reference to "dark, primitive histories of tribal uprootedness and separation" is unclear, but if his account is to be believed, the incident does seem to re-create an experience of childhood insecurity.

Andy and Julia were both extremely emotional. According to Carlton Willers, Warhol's first boyfriend, sometimes when they were cuddling Andy would begin to cry. "This would usually come unexpectedly or spontaneously about something in his past that was sad. And he did have a somewhat sad past. They were very poor. His mother was always kind to him though. He was her favorite."[185] Giordano saw Warhol "burst into tears" when another sketch was chosen over his for a magazine. "Every time I met him he cried. I don't know why. He was always crying."[186] Bernard Weinraub, who interviewed Julia for *Esquire*, said, "I tried to ask questions that were very basic. . . . She didn't really answer, she just began talking, and then began crying. I didn't understand what was going on. I asked, 'What do you remember about Andy as a kid,' and she began to cry. . . . She was always on the edge of tears, always emotional. I don't know what she was emotional about."[187] It was in this interview that Julia recalled the happy memories of her youthful courtship and long-ago wedding and the sad memories of war, emigration, and the death of her daughter. Emotionalism accompanying explorations of the past, whether negative or positive, has been observed by many children and grandchildren of

Carpatho-Rusyn immigrants. Deep-seated, untreated depression, especially in women with limited ability to express it in English, often found release in tears.

In an oral-history study of three generations of Jewish, Italian, and Slavic American women in Pittsburgh, Corinne Krause found that Slavic women were least likely to report emotional problems and least likely to seek mental-health care. "They place great value on working things out themselves."[188] Julia and Andy had their own private, mutually accommodating emotional rapport. The photographer Stephen Shore tells of a conversation with Warhol about a 1930s film he had watched on television the previous night. Andy wanted to know how the tearjerker ended, because, he told Shore, he had started crying and fallen asleep.

> Then he said, "And the television was off in the morning, so I guess my mother must have come in and turned it off." He never talked about his mother. She was just mentioned as a part of his life. . . . He never said anything reflective about her. But I remember, at the time, finding it stunning and poignant that he's Andy Warhol, who's just come from some all night party or several of them, and has turned on the television and cried himself to sleep to a Priscilla Lane film, and his mother had come in and turned it off.[189]

Was Andy embarrassed by his immigrant mother? As Gerard Malanga, the son of immigrants himself, put it, the notion of Andy's embarrassment was partly true, but partly a myth. "There was nothing any different from other children of immigrants."[190] Ted Carey said, "[Julia] had a very strong accent, and Andy, I think, would have liked to have thought of his mother as very glamorous. And Mrs. Warhola was not glamorous, and I think he felt a little ashamed of her." If so, it did not prevent Andy from introducing Julia to Ted and even to Ted's affluent, upscale parents. Carey's father was a prominent businessman and his mother, a society woman. In a letter to Julia, dated November 1, 1961, Carey's mother writes, "We are so happy that we had the opportunity to meet you last Sunday afternoon. We enjoyed ourselves so much and want to thank you for your kind hospitality and also the many kindnesses you have extended to Teddy over the last few years. He has spoken of you often, so we really felt we know you." A Christmas card from Ted Carey, postmarked December 20, 1965, is addressed to "Mrs. Julia Warhol and her son Andy." Before putting it away, Julia wrote on the outside of the envelope, "From Dear Ted." Ted Carey's New York address is in her address book.

Carey met Andy at an exhibition of "drawings he had done" called "Cats with Hats" at the Serendipity 3 café.[191] "I can remember Andy taking his mother to the show at Serendipity. And I remember that he was so nervous. He was afraid to take her. Should he take her? She wanted to go. And, finally, I think she did go to the show, and Andy was, I think, very uncomfortable about it."[192] Many of Warhol's promotional books were coupled with exhibits at the Serendipity 3 café. The title "Cats with Hats" relates more closely to Julia's *Holy Cats* than to any of Warhol's artist's books. If the drawings were hers, or based on her book, it would have made sense for Julia to be present, however uncomfortable it made Andy.[193] Bockris points to the "disdain [the Warhola family] would show to Andy's work throughout his life, never once, for example, going to one of his shows even when Andy asked [them]."[194] Biographers who take this tack seem to lack an appreciation for the inherent complexities on both sides when one member of a working-class family "makes it big." When Michal Bycko, founder of the Warhol Museum in Slovakia, asked John Warhola why the brothers never attended Andy's exhibitions, John responded, "There were famous celebrities there, and we're modest, simple people."[195] Still, Julia understood her son's fame and was proud of his celebrity. A photograph published in *Mademoiselle* in 1962 of Warhol standing against the backdrop of his *200 Campbell's Soup Cans* was one of Warhol's first appearances in the national media.[196] Julia carried the clipping in a purse with her personal belongings. It was wrinkled, torn, and taped, probably from being taken out and shown off.

In 1960, Warhol's gross income from his commercial art was $70,000, equivalent to more than $600,000 in 2021 purchasing power. But after his contract with I. Miller ended and photography began to replace drawn images in advertising, he turned to what he had always wanted to do—fine art. Blake Gopnik writes, "That hardly makes sense: Who goes into fine art as a business move?"[197] But Warhol's timing of the art market and his feel for popular culture were right. In 1961 his Pop paintings were shown as the background of a Bonwit Teller department store window, and in 1962, his first solo show of *32 Campbell's Soup Cans* at the Ferus Gallery in Los Angeles launched his Pop career and identity. Later that year his first solo show in New York featured silk-screened portraits of *Marilyn* and *Elvis* to positive reviews and notable sales. In early 1964, Warhol moved his studio out of his home to an industrial space on East 47th Street that would become the famous Silver Factory, where he produced silk screens and attracted artists, musicians, drag queens, and various hangers-on. In the early 1960s, Warhol began shooting films in which amateur actors played themselves in routine activities drawn out to marathon length or engaged in more provocative activities. His eight-hour slow-motion footage of the stationary Empire State Building defied the very concept of cinema, and his Brillo boxes challenged the definition of art. Dubbed "the Peter Pan of the current art scene" and "Saint Andrew" in *Newsweek*, he became a household name.[198] By 1965, Judy Garland, Tennessee Williams, and Rudolph

Nureyev attended a Factory party. Warhol's photo was in the *New York Times, Esquire, Time,* and *Newsweek,* and he appeared with his "superstar" Edie Sedgwick on the *Merv Griffin Show.*[199] In 1966 he became an impresario, organizing a raucous multimedia show called *The Exploding Plastic Inevitable,* which featured the radical rock band, the Velvet Underground. In the same year, his film, *The Chelsea Girls,* was the first underground movie to be shown in a commercial theater, and despite harsh reviews from mainstream critics, it was an exceptional moneymaker for Warhol. Julia's reaction to all of this, according to her son John, was that her son Andy was just doing a job like any other.[200]

In the first half of the frenetic 1960s, fueled by sex, drugs, and rock and roll, Andy Warhol broke norms and shattered conventions. His groundbreaking achievements, briefly summarized here, met with ardent acclaim and vehement blame. His greatest creation may have been his public persona. His monosyllabic interviews bemused television audiences, and his trademark silver-gray wig was universally recognized. Blake Gopnik provides an explanation of what was behind Warhol's self-creation: "If the avant-garde's interest in self-creation added prestige to Warhol's constructed persona, it had deeper roots in who and how he had always been: There was no way to be homosexual in postwar America without self-consciously playing a role, because the culture didn't leave you feeling that there was any 'natural' self you could inhabit. You were either playing at being straight to hide being gay, or you were figuring out how to be gay by adopting one of the models that had worked for others before you."[201]

"Andy, Why Don't You Get Married to Her?"

New research has put the lie to previous speculations that Andy Warhol was an innocent, a voyeur, or asexual. Gopnik documents Warhol's active sex life and numerous partners in detail. But from the early days in New York, Andy's mother doggedly sought a wife for him. According to his first boyfriend Carlton Willers, "Andy thought this was hilarious. Sometimes people would come to the studio and she'd … point out a girl and say, 'Andy, why don't you get married to her?'"[202] In 1963, she told Sarah Dalton, "I wish my Endy [*sic*] find a nice girl like you."[203] According to Nathan Gluck, "She was truly very naïve about homosexuality, and I guess she just assumed that Andy *had* to get married at some point."[204] Carlton Willers said, "I don't think she understood the gay thing at all."[205]

In their caricature of post-socialist Miková presented in the 2004 film *Absolut Warhola,* Tony Scherman and David Dalton emphasize the bluster of one alcohol-besotted resident, "No homosexual has ever come from Miková!"[206] His statement smacks of the ludicrous claim from the final years of the Soviet Union, "There is no sex in the USSR."[207] To be sure, under communism, homosexuality, along with prostitution and other divergent forms of sexual activity, was seen as a sign of Western degeneracy, and its existence was simply denied in Soviet-dominated countries. Even in postcommunist states like Slovakia, acceptance or even recognition of homosexuality has been slow in coming, especially among the older generation of churchgoers.[208] If we extrapolate these universal attitudes to a small, provincial, religious village isolated in the Carpathian Mountains, the Mikováns' reactions to Warhol's homosexuality in 2004 was predictable.

Did Julia understand "the gay thing?" Anthropologists maintain that east European peasant society might have been sexually repressive, but it was rarely sexually prudish. Ignorance was out of the question when "a large three-generation family lived in a single, undivided room with close proximity to animals."[209] Courtship practices allowed for sexual openness, and celebrations like Saint John's Eve festivities and off-color wedding rituals were hardly puritanical. But homosexuality was another matter. The early twentieth-century sociological study by William Thomas and Florian Znaniecki includes the account of a Galician priest, who ministered to Polish peasants and their Lemko-Rusyn neighbors.

> As far as my personal experience in the confessional has taught me, masturbation is a very rare kind of sexual deviation among peasants. . . . There is a greater tendency to a normal satisfaction of the sexual instinct, particularly among boys, or to bestialism. . . . Pederasty is very rare among our peasants; it happens almost only among young people of small towns and only in the form of experiments. At least I have never observed it as a habitual vice. Relatively more frequent is Lesbian love among girls, but also only in towns and between servants living together.[210]

Perhaps, then, the Miková drunk's claim that there were no homosexuals in Miková was not far off the mark. When I asked a sophisticated Miková contemporary what a member of Julia's generation might have known, I was told that "her mind just wouldn't go there."

Carlton Willers entered Warhol's life when he and Julia were living in the lower Lexington flat. He said, "[Julia] was always very nice to me but the only time Andy and me had any time together was late at night after she had gone to bed and fallen asleep in the bedroom in the back. She also called me Andy's boyfriend. To her a boyfriend was just a chum. I was just staying over because I was helping him with his work."[211] From the same period, Nathan Gluck described Andy's passion for drawing the lower regions of his male friends. "They're drawings of the penis, the balls and everything, and there'd be a little heart on them or tied with a little ribbon. And they're . . . in pads just sitting around. I used to wonder what his mother would do if she saw them. But I guess, she never saw them or didn't recognize them."[212] At 1342 Lexington, Julia's bedroom was on the lower level, where she was distanced from her son's life on the third and fourth stories of the house. In 2007, to an interviewer who asked Malanga whether Julia understood that these were Andy's boyfriends, he responded, "I think she did."[213] But asked in 2016 whether Julia knew about Andy's boyfriends, Malanga responded, "I don't know, I never thought about it. I don't have a clue. It could have been that she just accepted these people as his close friends, that's all."[214] Charles Lisanby, a friend from the early 1950s "felt sure that she knew what the score was."[215]

When Andy moved his studio out of the house in 1964, Julia was less involved with his work and his friends. Andy sheltered his family from the Factory and discouraged them from seeing his films. But by 1966, news of Warhol's career began to appear in the press, even in Pittsburgh, in connection with his controversial film *The Chelsea Girls*. In the *Pittsburgh Press*, the syndicated author and film critic Stanley Kauffmann categorized it among recent films that express "an anarchic viewpoint . . . one of absolute divorce, isolation, loneliness, with no sense of being in the hands of some larger force. . . . When I think of the future of art and morality dominated by the Warhols, it helps to reconcile me to my advancing years."[216] In March 1968, Warhol made a rare visit to his hometown and, with the film director Paul Morrissey and the actress Viva, he spoke before a standing-room-only audience on the University of Pittsburgh campus. A local reporter sardonically covered the event, at which Warhol showed "one of his double-exposure adult home movies with a presumably (but not clearly) nude co-ed on what passed for an LSD 'trip.'"[217] "Rapid-fire exchanges about sex" at the event could not be reported, since "this is a family newspaper." Paul Morrissey explained that Warhol's recently released *Lonesome Cowboys* started out as a boy-gets-girl movie, but "they ran out of girls so the boy wound up with a cowboy." According to Warhol's nephew Paul, "All my mother had to do was read something in the newspaper about his exploits, especially some of the movies, and she didn't hesitate to lower the boom on him. I think these interactions—not often—kind of created a little tension, but he got over it and we moved on."[218] Even Julia could not have been completely unaware of Andy's more notorious activities. In the wake of the *Chelsea Girls* controversy, she is said to have admonished him, "Don't you make no dirty movies!"[219]

What Julia knew about homosexuality and the gay lifestyle is uncertain. She knew that Andy was "different," although, given translation difficulties, "different" should not necessarily be interpreted to mean "gay." Warhol's second cousin, John Zavacky, four years younger than Andy, recalls a letter written by Julia to his father, in which Julia referred to Andy as a "*velykyi pan*," a term of respect applied to a priest or a dignitary. "That stuck in my mind," said Zavacky. It was in this sense that he understood Julia's conception of Andy's "difference."[220] Another Warhol cousin also reported Julia's comment that Andy was "different," but she did not interpret it to mean homosexual. "[Julia] never said anything like Andy had too many boyfriends. She was always saying, oh, they're good looking, oh nice, so handsome. She was very flirty. She liked young people."[221]

Andy was "different" in many ways, and Julia encouraged his eccentricities without necessarily connecting them with his sexual identity. In the *Esquire* interview, she described her almost forty-year-old son as though she were talking about a teenager: "I have two older sons. Paul . . . he has seven children. And John . . . he has three boys. Andy no marry. He always go out with company. He go out with boys and girls. Two girls, three boys, like that. Always like that. He no go steady."[222] Pat Hackett recalled, "She may have decided—or just as likely, he may have told her—that he was working so hard he had no time to find a wife to take care of him, because when I met Julia Warhola one afternoon in 1969 she said hello, thought for a second, then concluded, 'You'd be nice for my Andy—but he's too busy.'"[223] His brothers and old-country cousins understood him similarly—he did not have time for women, he was devoted to his mother, are all bachelors homosexual? Warhol's homosexuality did not affect family relations or, apparently, the mother–son relationship. It is important to note also that Julia died fifteen years before Andy, that is, before his international renown, Studio 54, and AIDS. Whether Julia knew or whether she did not want to know cannot be determined. It is entirely possible that she was completely unaware, that "her mind just didn't go there."

Andy's Religion

"When Andy was a boy, we thought he was going to be a priest," said John Warhola. This may, as Blake Gopnik says, be "more like a general comment on the boy's demeanor than a real assertion of his religiosity."[224] It is more difficult to dismiss the sentiment behind the plaster statue of Jesus that Warhol painted between the ages of ten and thirteen, which, according to his brother John, he kept in his room until he left Pittsburgh for New York at age twenty.[225] Like the religious images in the Warhola house and the flea-market plaster sculpture Warhol chose as a model for his *Last Supper* paintings, it is decidedly kitsch, but his careful coloring of the Sacred Heart and the bloody wounds of Jesus expresses an innocent sincerity.[226]

The Greek Catholic (later Byzantine Catholic) religion practiced by the Warhola family has a complicated history that is difficult for Americans of any religious denomination to understand.[227] Gopnik offers a broader explanation of church history than what is available in most biographies, but he is largely dismissive of Warhol's faith and unfamiliar with Byzantine Catholic religious practice in the Carpatho-Rusyn community. His glib comment that Andy "never even took the lessons in Church Slavonic that his brothers endured" is probably based on Paul Warhola's exaggerated description of the classes attended by Byzantine Catholic children. Bockris referred to the lessons as an "arduous course" in "Old High Church Slavonic."[228] But parish schools did not teach Old Church Slavonic, high or otherwise. Rusyn American children had been praying in Rusyn Church Slavonic with their parents since they could talk. They went to after-school classes attached to their church, popularly known as *Ruska shkola*, translated as "Rusyn school" or sometimes "Russian school." Paul Robert Magocsi describes the language taught in these schools as "a corrupted form of Russian intermixed with Carpatho-Rusyn vernacular." This was not a foreign tongue, but the children's first language. Andy's childhood friend Margie Girman remembered that she and Andy attended these religion classes together.[229] It is inconceivable that Andy would not have undergone a serious preparation for the sacrament of Penance (confession) and the Eucharist as a seven-year-old. Paul Warhola's complaint about the difficulty of learning Rusyn in the Cyrillic alphabet was preceded by the comment, "It was a must to go [to Rusyn religious classes] because they prepared us for our first communion."[230]

After his death, Andy Warhol's religiosity became the subject of rampant curiosity and intellectual inquiry. After John Richardson "outed" Warhol in his memorial eulogy as a "saintly simpleton," a proselytizer of prayer, and a doer of good works, art scholars searched out religious qualities in his soup cans and flowers.[231] The exhibition *Andy Warhol: Revelation* (2020–2022) ramped up interest in the subject once again. Reviewers responded enthusiastically, astonishing many Warhol aficionados who had never thought to include Warhol and religion in the same sentence. The exhibition presented more than one hundred objects "that show how Warhol's relationship to religion served as both a muse and a methodology for his art, and a guiding force in his personal life."[232] Reviewers essentially agreed that after viewing *Andy Warhol: Revelation*, "It's hard to argue with the idea that Catholicism mattered

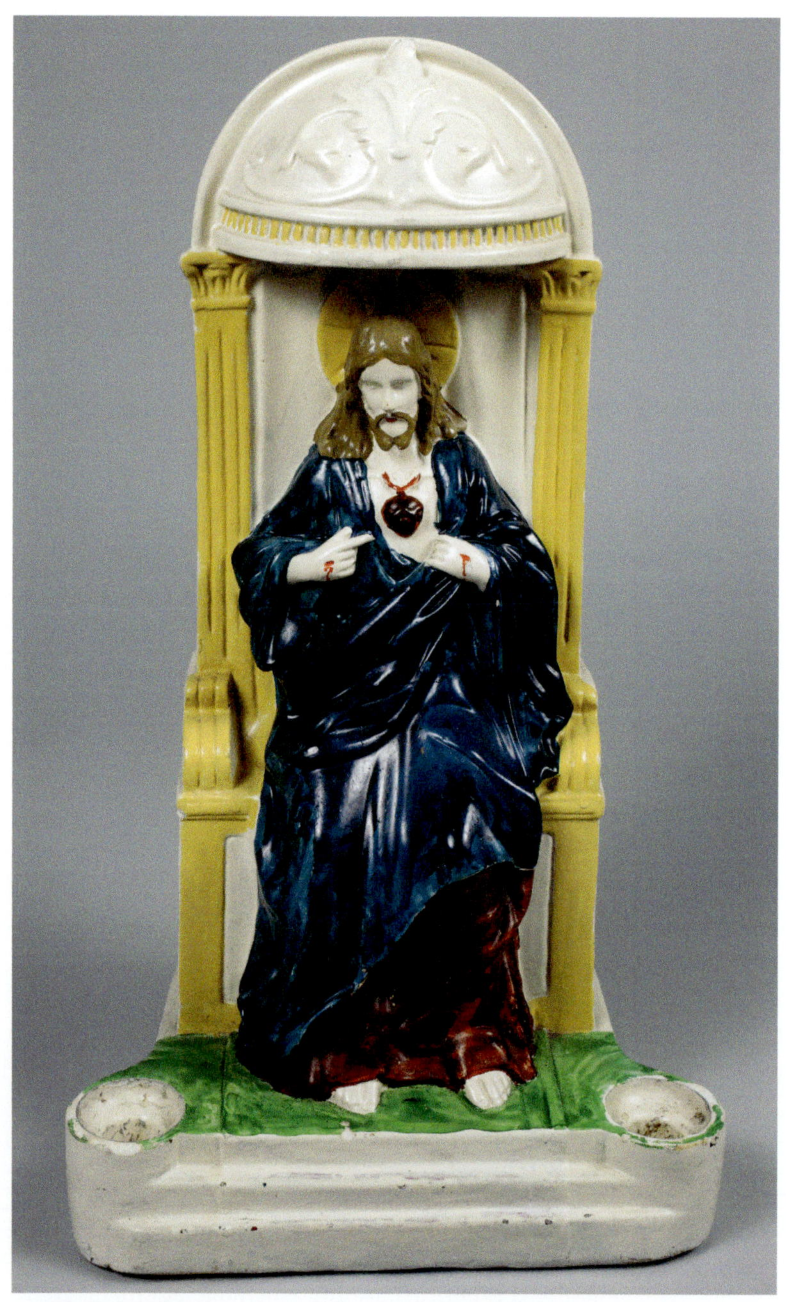

Figure 5.20. Plaster statue of Jesus painted by Andy Warhol between 1938 and 1941.

to Warhol. Its rituals, structures, and even some of its beliefs seeped into his art, and complicate our understanding of it—and of him."[233]

The matter of Warhol's religiosity is thornier than most Warholian paradoxes and inconsistencies. While previously questioned facts about his sexuality can be resolved by newly discovered medical bills, the truth hidden in his contradictory comments about God, faith, and religion can be illuminated only by looking into his soul, which is not accessible to researchers. His religious art reflects the tension that lay between his gay lifestyle and the moral norms of his religious background, within the larger context of Carpatho-Rusyn ethnic folk belief. His mother holds a key to his negotiation of the conflict.

The faith of Carpatho-Rusyn immigrants was deeply felt and almost entirely instinctive, with a strong streak of down-to-earth practicality. For them and their children, this meant an artless, guilt-free, trusting relationship with God, which distinguished them from many American Roman Catholics and other Christians. Numerous observers have commented on the predominance of Catholics in Warhol's New York circle. The photographer Christopher Makos observed that Andy "may have related better to us Catholics because we all had the same background: mass, priests, nuns, Catholic school, a sense of guilt." The superstar Viva held that what the Catholics in Warhol's circle had in common was guilt and the need to purge themselves of "Catholic repression."[234] This stereotypical vision of 1950s Roman Catholic life was foreign to a Carpatho-Rusyn raised in a Greek Catholic environment, where religious education came from peasant-like parents and a church that was headed by a married priest, and where ritual may have overshadowed doctrine. In the January 1983 issue of *Interview*, Warhol and Bianca Jagger interviewed Sting (the English musician Gordon Sumner).[235] Sting comments that he was brought up Roman Catholic, attended "a school that was run by priests," and recalls "the reactionary regime that was down on us." Asked about feelings of guilt, Sting responded, "Yes. I mean there are demons inside me but I manage to use them for my furtherance." Warhol's reaction is telling:

> WARHOL: I grew up a Catholic and I don't feel any demons.
> JAGGER: Andy, do you feel any guilt?
> WARHOL: No. About what? I go to church, it's so pretty. I never understood it because everything was always in Latin.

The three Catholics agreed that they preferred the Latin Mass to English, for "the mystery in it." Of course, in Warhol's childhood, the language was Rusyn

Church Slavonic, but the effect was the same, and "mystery" was part of the appeal. Warhol's nephew Paul, the Byzantine Catholic priest, reiterated the religious sensitivity Andy expressed to Jagger and Sting. "To me there was no indication that he was scared of hell. I don't think he had a burden. I didn't detect that at all. I never sensed any kind of guilt or fear."[236] In 1978, Warhol gave his own definition of Catholicism: "I'm Catholic. Being Catholic is just being honest and serious and nice. Isn't everyone?"[237] His comment echoes his mother's notion of religiosity as being "a good person." No one would claim that Andy Warhol was a theologically sophisticated, rule-observing "good Catholic" (although in a 1980 interview he volunteered, "I'm a good Catholic").[238] But Warhol followed a different standard. Like his mother, he saw religion, broadly understood, as comforting, not judgmental. As for most Carpatho-Rusyn peasants and many Rusyn American immigrants, it provided protection in an uncertain world and aesthetic satisfaction in a bleak life.[239]

There is conflicting information about Warhol's church attendance in his early years in New York, but after his brush with death in 1968, he visited church often. Although he did not sit through Sunday Mass, he popped in frequently for a few minutes of quiet prayer, a practice that was more customary in Eastern Rite liturgies than in Roman Catholic Masses. While some who knew him well "couldn't imagine him having any religion at all," others were convinced of his piety.[240] Bob Colacello recalls a visit with Warhol to the Shrine of the Virgin of Guadalupe in Mexico, "not knowing quite how to behave, like tourists or believers. Then Andy said in a hushed voice, 'I think we should kneel.' It was the first time I had been in a church with Andy, and I realized then that his religion wasn't an act, something that sounded good in a cover story." All agree that Warhol did not go to confession or take communion regularly, which, in fact, became customary only in the post–Vatican II era of relaxed regulations. For Byzantine Catholics of Warhol's generation, Holy Communion required preparation and fasting, as well as confession, which he avoided for fear of being recognized. Many devoted Greek Catholics took the sacraments just once a year in the Easter season. In the *Esquire* interview, Julia says, "Every year before Easter [Andy] go to confession. He was a little boy. Now he grown up. He go to confession more."[241] Lacking the audio, it is uncertain whether her unsupported comment reflects approbation or admonition.

Evidence exists of at least one time that Warhol went to confession and received Holy Communion in the New York years. When Andy was recuperating at home after being shot in 1968, he was attended by his nephew Paul, whose seminary education Andy was then financing at Saints Cyril and Methodius Byzantine Catholic Seminary in Pittsburgh. Father Paul recounts the story.

I said, "Uncle Andy, would you like to go to confession and communion?" He thought about it and said, "Yeah, yeah, Pauly, I'd like to . . . I'd like that." There were many things we had discussed, you know—heaven, hell, you name it, we ran the gamut. So, I made the phone call [to Father Paul Dano, pastor of Saint Mary's Byzantine Catholic Church]. Within a couple of days, we set up a time. Father Alexander Papp came, a married priest, a very gentle, kind man. They probably talked for ten or fifteen minutes, and Uncle Andy made his confession. Then Father Papp brought him communion. I could see it was really important for my uncle.[242]

After Warhol's death, it became known that on his bedside table stood a crucifix, a santo carving, a statuette of the risen Christ, and a Byzantine Catholic prayer book, *Heavenly Manna: A Practical Prayer Book of Devotion for Greek Catholics*.[243] Gopnik writes that "Warhol certainly wasn't 'religious' in the sense of knowing or caring about the details of his faith's actual precepts and theology." The 1960 edition of *Heavenly Manna* includes the precepts and theology of the Byzantine Catholic Church in a schematic list form. Whether or not he cared about the precepts or abided by them, Warhol was certainly familiar with them. And Father Paul's comment that he discussed theological concepts with his uncle—"heaven, hell, you name it, we ran the gamut"—counters the notion that he had no awareness or interest in the theology of his faith.

However, Warhol was frustratingly evasive about what he believed, obscuring his truth behind a screen of irony. A 1977 interview with Glenn O'Brien went as follows:

GO: Do you believe in God?
AW: I guess I do. I like church. It's empty when I go. I walk around. There are so many beautiful Catholic churches in New York. I used to go to some Episcopal churches, too.
GO: Do you ever think about God?
AW: No.
GO: Do you believe in the devil?
AW: No.
GO: Do you believe in the end of the world?
AW: No. I believe in As the World Turns.[244]

It was typical of Warhol to evade a serious question with a comic quip. Ronnie Cutrone, Warhol's assistant during the 1970s, tells a story about another interview that elicited an unexpected admission from Andy:

> What impressed me most about Andy was his belief in God. . . . I remember one time,
> Andy and I were doing an interview with a French journalist. . . . She said to him, "You
> were once quoted as saying you don't believe in anything. Is that true? Do you not believe
> in anything?" Andy was the coolest man on earth, at least during interviews; he would
> never, ever lose his temper. But he took this as a threat. . . . And he turned totally red in
> the face. I was shocked. Andy said, "I never said that." . . . And then she asked, "Well,
> what do you believe in?" He knew he was hemmed in. But he just straightforwardly
> said, "I believe in God." And then he realized what he had said, and it was almost like,
> "Man he just shattered the whole image." So he added, "And I also believe in Ronnie."
> . . . I'll never forget that day. It was the first time he ever in public just rolled out of his
> shell and took a stand.[245]

Gopnik disputes Warhol's religiosity, citing Andy's answer to "a point-blank question" about whether he was Catholic, or in any way religious. "He answered . . . with a clear-cut 'no.'"[246] It should be noted that this exchange came from David Bailey's film, which Warhol referred to as "that stupid David Bailey 'documentary' about me."[247] The transcript of the film indicates that Bailey followed up Warhol's "clear-cut 'no'" with the question, "Why not?" Warhol retorted, "Because it's too expensive," prompting laughter from observers. With its tongue-in-cheek narrative style, the Bailey film was not a serious discussion about religion.

It is a similar simplification that "Warhol actively denied the existence of an afterlife, which is just about the most basic belief of any Christian faith."[248] "'I believe in death after death,' he once said. And, 'When it's over, it's over.'"[249] These were also examples of Warhol's flip responses to what may or may not have been earnest questions. As for life after death, Warhol must have had some interest in the subject. His library included the 1975 best seller *Life After Life and Reflections on Life After Life* by Raymond Moody Jr., which explored near-death experiences and documented cases of reincarnation and life after physical death.[250] Like crystals and Kathryn Kuhlman, Moody's research and published conclusions did not have the imprimatur of the Catholic Church, but it is the kind of esoteric spiritualism that appealed to those who were raised as much on peasant superstition as on sacred tradition.

First-generation immigrants maintained the peasants' earthy amalgamation of church teachings with pre-Christian superstitious magic and passed it down to their children. Some rejected it out of hand, some, like Ann Warhola, became doctrinaire, and others, like Warhol, found it agreeable. From his mother, he inherited a down-to-earth practicality and superstitious mysticism that would not have been out of place in

Miková. But just as Rusyn peasants blended pagan and Christian rituals and imposed religious meaning on ancient practices, Warhol tried to reconcile his belief systems, transferring from a Jewish to an Episcopalian "crystal doctor," because, said Warhol, "Knowing he believes in Christ I don't have to worry that crystals might be somehow against Christ."[251] The seriousness of Warhol's faith is derided: "The way he sprinkled holy water around the house, as a kind of heavenly disinfectant, seems more pagan than Vatican II."[252] Exactly. The mix of faith, aestheticism, and superstition cloaked in spirituality, as Warhol practiced it in the twentieth century, was the Greek Catholic religion as it had persisted in his mother's life in Miková and was still observed to a considerable extent in immigrant Pittsburgh. This matter-of-fact, peasant-like approach to life and faith, with its roots in Rusyn folklore and homespun religious practice, produced a broad-based spiritual belief system that prioritized the individual's private and personal relationship with God, rather than a narrow, rule-defined dogma.

Gopnik repeats a remark by Father Sam Matarazzo, the prior of Saint Vincent Ferrer Roman Catholic Church, where Warhol visited two or three times a week to sit and pray "in the shadows," that Warhol's lifestyle was "absolutely irreconcilable" with the teachings of the Catholic Church. But he fails to mention the priest's humane, insightful speculation: "Warhol was bonding with a God and a Christ above and beyond the church."[253] Among Rusyn peasants and Rusyn American immigrants, the overall value of being "a good person," as indefinite as that might be, could trump ecclesiastical rules. Whether Andy Warhol met that bar is beyond the judgment of scholars and biographers.

Hospodi pomilui (Lord Have Mercy)

Nonetheless, one cannot disagree with those who point out that "Warhol certainly lived a less holy life, made more profane art and committed more mortal sins than should have been on the conscience of any devout Catholic, as defined in his era."[254] Did he question where he stood in terms of the Ten Commandments, the Seven Capital Sins, or the foreboding Four Sins that Cry to Heaven for Vengeance, listed in *Heavenly Manna*? (The second of which is "the sin of Sodom"). Throughout his life, Warhol certainly gave due consideration, even if only in his art, to the Four Last Things—death, judgment, hell, and heaven. But the most common prayer repeated in countless liturgical litanies and uttered often as a spontaneous exclamation by his mother, was *Hospodi pomilui* (Lord have mercy).

According to Andy's nephew, Donald Warhola, after Warhol's 1987 death, the family wanted him to be buried from Saint John Chrysostom, the family's church in *Ruska dolina*. But the priest there refused on the grounds that his parishioners objected to Warhol's lifestyle. "That still disturbs me," said Warhola. "Whether or not my uncle's life fitted into the nice, neat whole of Catholicism, whatever, he was a good person in his heart. He was very conflicted, he compartmentalized his life: he didn't talk the talk but he walked the walk."[255] Warhol's funeral service took place at John Warhola's parish church, Holy Ghost Byzantine Catholic Church on the North Side, where the pastor and officiant was Monsignor Peter Tay. Tay did not know Warhol personally, and even twenty-five years later when he told interviewers about his funeral homily, he did not seem to grasp the tenor of the artist's life.

> I talked about Andy Warhol, his origins. I said he created art that many people admired and others did not. In the sermon I said there was only one woman in his life, his mother. At the same time, I knew that his was not the ideal way of life. There are parts of his life to which I might have objections, such as films with the starlets and similar things that he made. This is part of the darker side of his life. I wasn't familiar with it in detail but I know that it existed just as it exists in each one of us.[256]

The part of the sermon that is cited most often by biographers was reported by a correspondent from the *New York Post*: "'It seems at times he wandered far away from his church,' said Msgr. Tay in one of the great understatements of our time, 'but we do not judge him, we do not condemn him.' . . . The priest also told a disturbing parable that left members of the Warhola family exchanging nervous glances as they sat on the hardwood pews. 'Jesus forgave the thief on his right. He did not forgive the thief on his left. . . . It means there is always hope but it also means nobody should take salvation for granted.'"[257]

This passage is not in the original text of Monsignor Tay's homily, which is reproduced in *Andy Warhol a Československo*.[258] Jerry Jumba, who served as cantor for Warhol's funeral, recalls Monsignor Tay's gravelly voice as he mentioned the two thieves in the funeral sermon and refused to judge Warhol.[259] As for the "disturbing parable," biographers and reporters seem to be unfamiliar with its import. In Luke 23:39–43, the thief on the left of Jesus mocks him and dares him to "save yourself and us." The thief on his right confesses, "We are receiving the due reward of our deeds" and entreats, "Remember me when you come into your kingdom." Jesus responds, "Truly, I say to you, today you will be with me in Paradise."[260] It is unknown how much of the parable Monsignor Tay included in his sermon, since it seems to have been an impromptu addition to his planned homily. But a quick look at scripture would show the error in Gopnik's comment that Jesus "managed to forgive" the sinning thief, as though the act of forgiveness was randomly and grudgingly bestowed. The moral message of the parable is the importance of repentance.

In his description of the distinctive character of the religiosity of Byzantine Catholic immigrants, Alexander Motyl writes, "The Rusyn . . . peasants who lived and worshiped in the Carpathians and in Pittsburgh knew that, despite Catholicism's moral strictures, the parish priest would also be ready to forgive their many lapses if the appropriate prayers were said and the appropriate sacraments were performed."[261] Bob Colacello's acquaintance with Andy Warhol was prompted by a review he wrote of the Warhol film *Trash*. "I wrote that it was a great Roman Catholic masterpiece in the tradition of Mary Magdalene—you know, everybody can be redeemed, we Catholics believe, including prostitutes and hustlers and junkies. And that's what I thought *Trash* was about—redemption. My introduction to Andy was the result of that review. I got a call from Paul Morrissey, who said, 'I work for Andy Warhol. We loved your review. No one ever got that Catholic thing before.'"[262]

Warhol may not have thought of forgiveness and redemption as a "Catholic thing"; it was a lesson he learned from his mother. In one of her taped narratives, Julia delivers a homily on the subject, based on a parable of her own creation. Speaking in Rusyn, Julia tells the story of a woman named Katrina who lived in luxury, defying church laws and conventional morality.[263] Julia's recorded narrative is a conscious performance of a folktale, with rhythmic prose, repetition, and rhyming refrains—*do tserkvi ne khodila, do posta ne postila* (to church she did not go, the fast she did not keep). When Katrina was young, she lived in sin, spurned marriage, and violated the commandments of God and the Church. As she grew older, Katrina became concerned about the fate of her immortal soul. Eventually Death came for her, personified in Rusyn folk style, as a powerful old woman armed with a scythe and a broom. But the wily Katrina managed to trick Death into coming back for her the following day.

As Julia tells the story, early the next morning she went "far, far away to a great forest," where holy monks lived among the deer and forest animals. Katrina confessed, repented, and renounced sin. However, her carnal sins were so egregious that God did not accept her soul. Saint Peter refused to open the gates of Heaven, and Jesus Christ denied the sinful woman entrance into the heavenly kingdom. Only when the All-pure Virgin Mother of God beseeched her son did Jesus forgive Katrina, and angels bore her soul into heaven. The story ends with Julia's exhortation: "If we are sinful, God will not accept our souls into his kingdom, but if we repent sincerely, he will have mercy." She follows the narrative with a repetitive chant of *Hospodi pomilui*, Lord have mercy.

Julia's message is the same as Monsignor Tay's. There is always hope, but salvation requires repentance. She undoubtedly shared such original homilies with her children. Whether or not he practiced it regularly, Andy Warhol claimed to believe in forgiveness and expected redemption. In his diary, he talks about trying to show kindness to someone he does not like "because God forgives so so should I."[264] In her article "Warhol's Confession: Love, Faith, and Aids," Jessica Beck describes Warhol's depiction of Christ in the *Last Supper* paintings. "The image of Christ offering his flesh in the Eucharist was a symbol of salvation during a time of suffering, an unusually personal and emotional image for Warhol. . . . The painting speaks of sex and of judgment. It is an allegorical triangulation of mourning, punishment, and fear."[265] She leaves out the factor that Julia Warhola considered most important—repentance. But it may not have been lost on Andy, who reiterated his mother's message in a stark silkscreen print that declared in cursive script "Repent," followed, in block letters, by "AND SIN NO MORE!"

Julia Warhola, Superstar

In a press conference covered in the November 11, 1966, issue of the *New York Times*, Warhol refers to a movie he made "yesterday afternoon."[266] "It starred my mother, who played an aging peroxide movie star with a lot of husbands. We're trying to bring back old people."[267] This was Andy's nonchalant announcement of Julia Warhola's screen debut in the film he called *The George Hamilton Story*, but is more often presented erroneously today as "Mrs. Warhol."[268]

This is not the place for a lengthy discussion of Warhol's cinematic art, but it is important to note the most significant features of a Warhol film—his disdain for plot, scripts, and technical matters. "I never liked the idea of picking out certain scenes and pieces of time and putting them together, because then it ends up being different from what really happened—it's just not like life."[269] Most of his films are improvisations vaguely organized around a sketchy narrative plotline, which is constantly transgressed when the actors respond to offscreen comments or play to the camera. Warhol insisted that "professional actors and actresses are all wrong for my movies."[270] Instead, he preferred amateur performers who were spontaneous and capricious. "What I like are things that are different every time. That's why I like amateur performers and bad performers—you can never tell what they'll do next."[271] His favorite amateurs had strong personalities: "Somehow, we attract people who can turn themselves on in front of the camera. In this sense, they're *really* superstars."[272] In 1966, Julia Warhola, who had honed her acting skills in Miková folk dramas, became a Warhol superstar.

The George Hamilton Story, which consists of two thirty-three-minute reels, was never screened publicly during Warhol's lifetime. Filmed in Julia's ground-floor apartment in Andy's Lexington Avenue town house, it features Julia with her costar Richard Rheem, Warhol's boyfriend at the time, who lived with him for about six weeks during the winter of 1966. Also present offscreen, and occasionally heard on the soundtrack, are Warhol's colleagues Paul Morrissey and Susan Pile. Pile described Julia as "gracious and nice, albeit unintelligible," and most reviewers of the film have commented on Julia's "almost unintelligible, heavy Czech accent."[273] However, for viewers familiar with Julia's speech style and knowledgeable about her Carpatho-Rusyn background, the cinematic portrait differs substantially from her standard description in film festival promos such as "Warhol's delightfully oddball mother."[274]

The opening shot is a close-up of the almost seventy-five-year-old Julia, wearing glasses, a pink flowered-print blouse and a black-and-white-checked dirndl skirt. Her permed gray/blonde hair is covered with a loose net that ties under her chin, an American version of the cap or kerchief worn by married Carpatho-Rusyn women in the Old Country. J. J. Murphy, an American scholar of Warhol's films, says, "She looks very much like an Eastern European peasant."[275] But the Slovak screenwriter and film theorist, Ivan Stadtrucker, who is undoubtedly more familiar with East European peasants, has a different opinion. "Based on this film, the viewer gets to know Mrs. Julia Warhola as a gentle, intelligent woman who, in her appearance and her psychology, is reminiscent of an elementary school teacher. Her personality differs from that of the primitive, rural woman described in [some] memoirs."[276] In fact, while Julia's language and mannerisms are typical of immigrant Rusyn peasant women, her animated personality and genteel appearance would set her apart markedly from her peers in Europe, as became clear when her sister visited from Miková the following summer.

Richard Rheem was a darkly handsome twenty-year-old in 1966. Julia affectionately calls him "Richik" (pronounced Reecheek, with a trilled *R*), "Richko," and in a double diminutive, "Richichko." The relationship between Julia and "Richik" is close and playful. She strokes his hair and touches his face, they tickle one another, and refer to secrets and shared activities, whispering with furtive smiles about shopping together for whiskey. The film opens with what seems to be an impromptu conversation between Julia and Rheem. On closer analysis, it is a vetted interview, in which Rheem asks pointed questions meant to elicit predetermined stories, activities, and linguistic peculiarities. In the opening shot, Julia nods to the camera and addresses Rheem: "What we gonna talk now, Rich?" Rheem responds, "Tell the story about the wedding," a favorite topic of Julia's

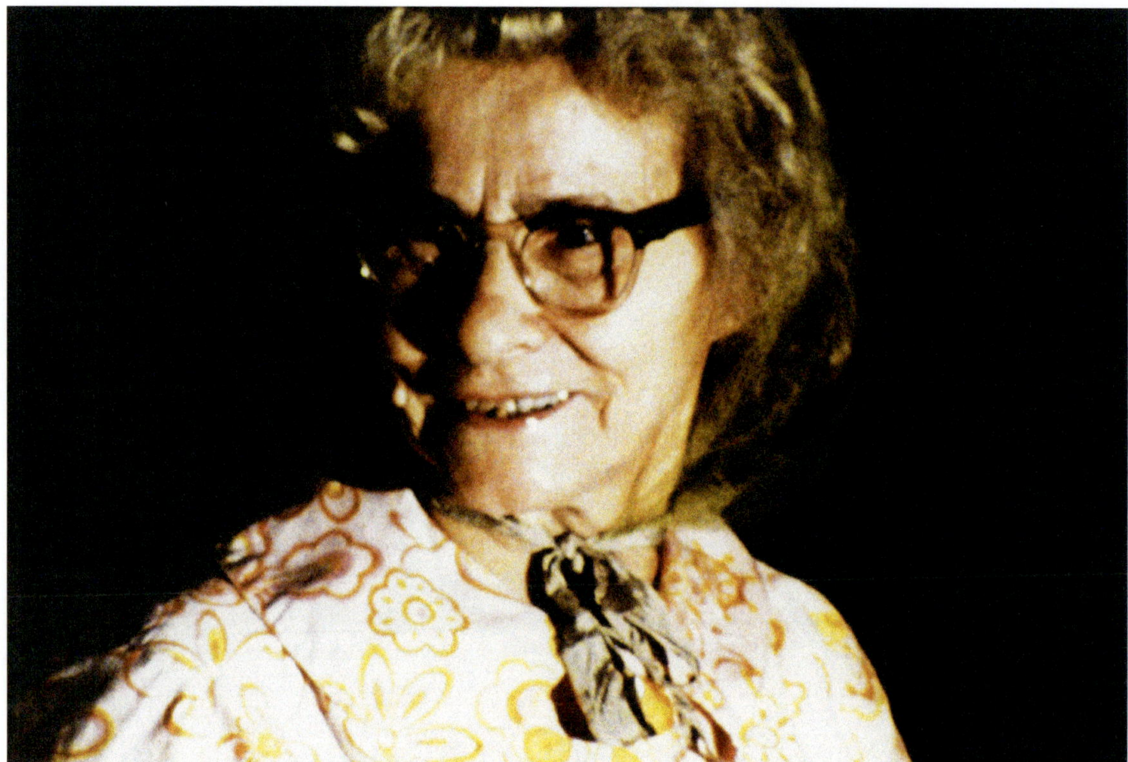

Figure 5.21. Film still of Julia Warhola, from Andy Warhol, *The George Hamilton Story*, 1966.

that Rheem would have known from the *Esquire* interview, which had been published just days earlier, and probably from previous conversations. But Julia resists, "Oh no, that not . . . I don't . . . when me was little girl, Rich . . . no, I gonna talk something else for you, Richik." Julia interrupts her planned narrative and, probably on cue, she redirects the conversation, asking Rheem how old he is. Rheem answers facetiously that he will be seventy-five on November 20. In fact, it is Julia who will turn seventy-five years old that day, which Rheem clearly knew.

Their ensuing conversation touches on food, language, the Greek Catholic priesthood, and Julia's childhood task of tending cows.[277] She talks about her cats— Hester ("She was really good, she was smart") and the "black bum," who keeps her up at night with his meow. The crew laughs at some of Julia's old-world word choices and nonstandard usages like *bum* and *bogeyman*, as well as her faulty pronunciation. Rheem toys with her as one would with a child, having her repeat *yogo* (her word for yogurt) and chuckling each time she says it, to Julia's amused perplexity. Mrs.

Warhola's unintelligibility and her innocent participation in the verbal buffoonery is a primary source of the film's humor. As they banter back and forth in teasing verbal play, Rheem scrambles to direct, and sometimes to keep up with, Julia's performance.

After another discussion of pussycats, Julia tries to introduce her own topic. Once again, she announces a performance narrative with "when me was little girl."

> JW: You know Richik, when me was little girl, I was stuck, hurting. [With emotion.] I go to . . . my post office was far away from farm, named Havaj [pronounced Havai]—this post office.
> RR: Hawaii? You went to Hawaii?

Struggling to make herself understood, Julia is delighted at what seems to be Rheem's grasp of her story, and she responds eagerly.

> JW: Yeah, Havaj . . . was Havaj name, this post office. You know this post office was named Havaj.

Viewers familiar with the Carpatho-Rusyn context would know that Havaj is a village near Miková that served as the postal center. Julia goes on, mixing Rusyn conjunctions into her English-language narrative.

> JW: And you know what? Next door living priest *i* [and] . . . wife, *i* four children. He always call me . . . Julia, go to the Havaj, bring me a letter, letter. You know letter? I don't know how say English.
> RR: Letter? [Picks up piece of paper.]
> JW: Yes, here this letter. You know what, Richik, I go. Was big woods. Maybe two mile. I no running, I flying. [With animation.] I come back, bring letter to for priest, he say, you no was not post office Havaj. I say yeah I was. I give you letter, you know, too many letter, you know for people. He give me . . . he say oh, how you flying. I'm flying, Richik. I was really hurting. I was, maybe I was thirteen years old. [Distressed, tearful.] Always I go help, priest children, you know, priest children.

The narrative goes no further, as Julia is sidetracked onto a discussion of married priests in the Greek Catholic Church.

The full import of Julia's narrative is not certain, since we do not have the statement in Rusyn. But it seems clear that she struggled to "fly" to please the priest, and she smarted at his distrust. At this point in the story, her distress is apparent, her voice reveals genuine agitation, and she is almost in tears. Today, the road from Miková to Havaj is 3.6 miles, although Julia would have taken a back way through the forest. In mountainous terrain—Miková is 1,362 feet and Havaj, 906 feet above sea level—before paved roads, in bad weather, one can imagine that the trip from Miková to Havaj was no easy task, and it seems she was called on to undertake it frequently, with no thanks from the priest. In the film shoot, Julia gets no sympathy from her interlocutor, her audience, or her son behind the camera, who surely had heard the story before and knew the facts. But Andy was more interested in the fortuitous semantic shift that placed his immigrant mother on a beach in Hawaii, a phenomenon he called transmutation.

> Something that I look for in an associate is a certain amount of misunderstanding of what I'm trying to do. Not a fundamental misunderstanding; just minor misunderstandings here and there. When someone doesn't quite completely understand what you want from them, or when they didn't quite hear what you told them to do, or when the tape is bad, or when their own fantasies start coming through, I often wind up liking what comes out of it all better than I liked my original idea. . . . If people never misunderstand you, and if they do everything exactly the way you tell them to, they're just transmitters of your ideas, and you get bored with that. But when you work with people who misunderstand you, instead of getting transmission you get transmutation, and that's much more interesting in the long run.[278]

In this respect, Julia is a perfect associate for Warhol, for try as she might, she cannot follow directions, and the misunderstandings she generates are creative and productive. In "Mrs. Warhol," she gets carried away not by fantasies, but by memories, which seep through the levels of artifice and rise to the surface in a moment of self-disclosure that reveals a personal, and painful, truth.

The irony and the art of this "Havaj" sequence is in the fact that Andy was the only one present—as well as the only one in most subsequent screenings—who "got" the joke. In her study of Warhol's home movies, Ara Osterweil notes that in "Mrs. Warhol," as in many of Warhol's films, "fiction dissolves into documentary." In fact, the opposite takes place in this sequence. If Warhol had filmed a documentary, the full story of Julia's travails that are just hinted at in this film might be told—taking the cows to pasture, surviving the war, and working for the priest's family. These were real aspects of her life, and today the lack of information in this potentially revealing firsthand narrative is regrettable. But for Warhol, it is not the factual, documentary details that matter, but the creative "psychodrama" that emerges when Julia's memory intrudes into present-day life. In the words of Richard Whitehall, "Warhol is a camera with the shutter open. He records, quite coldly, that moment when fantasy clashes with reality and out of the dissonance come glimpses of pain, loneliness, fear, too close to the soul to be simulated. When his actors, despite themselves, seem to stumble over truths they'd rather not face."[279] For Julia and Andy, the dissonance is multileveled: there is the fictional Hollywood screen star, the performer and real-life mother Julia Warhola, and the Carpatho-Rusyn peasant girl Ulia Zavacka, whose pain and fear come alive in the performance.

"*Chekai*, Dear Husband"

In the second reel of the film, Julia plays an aging Hollywood star who has poisoned her previous fifteen husbands and is now married to the young, attractive Rheem. Julia opens the scene by calling: "Richik, you ready? Come, I show you how I do for you. Eat scrambled eggs. Maybe I give it for you, for you girlfriend, Susie [Susan Pile]."

> RR: I don't have a girlfriend. You're my wife.
> JW: That's what everyone tell me.
> RR: What do I need a girlfriend for when I have a wife like you?
> JW: I'm too old for you, too old for you. You just keeping me for cook.
> RR: That's not true.
> JW: You need sweetheart . . . for date, for love. . . . If you be good husband, I always be making for you scrambled eggs. . . . Everyday. You be so big, you can't eat no more.

Julia makes scrambled eggs and coffee for the crew, while teasing Rheem and chatting continuously. As she focuses on feeding her guests, she forgets the role she is supposed to be playing and asks the offscreen observers if they want sugar, pepper, or coffee, and moves out of camera range to serve them. Rheem tries to bring her back to the premise of the plot by insisting that she is poisoning his food and making him her next victim. There is a good bit of playful banter, in which Julia gives as good as she gets, interspersing Rusyn words in her heavily accented English.

> JW: OK mister [*meester*], my dear husband. . . . *Chekai* [wait], I give you coffee. *Chekai, chekai,* dear husband, you such a big one, you very big one. . . . Husband, you too big. You leg too big.

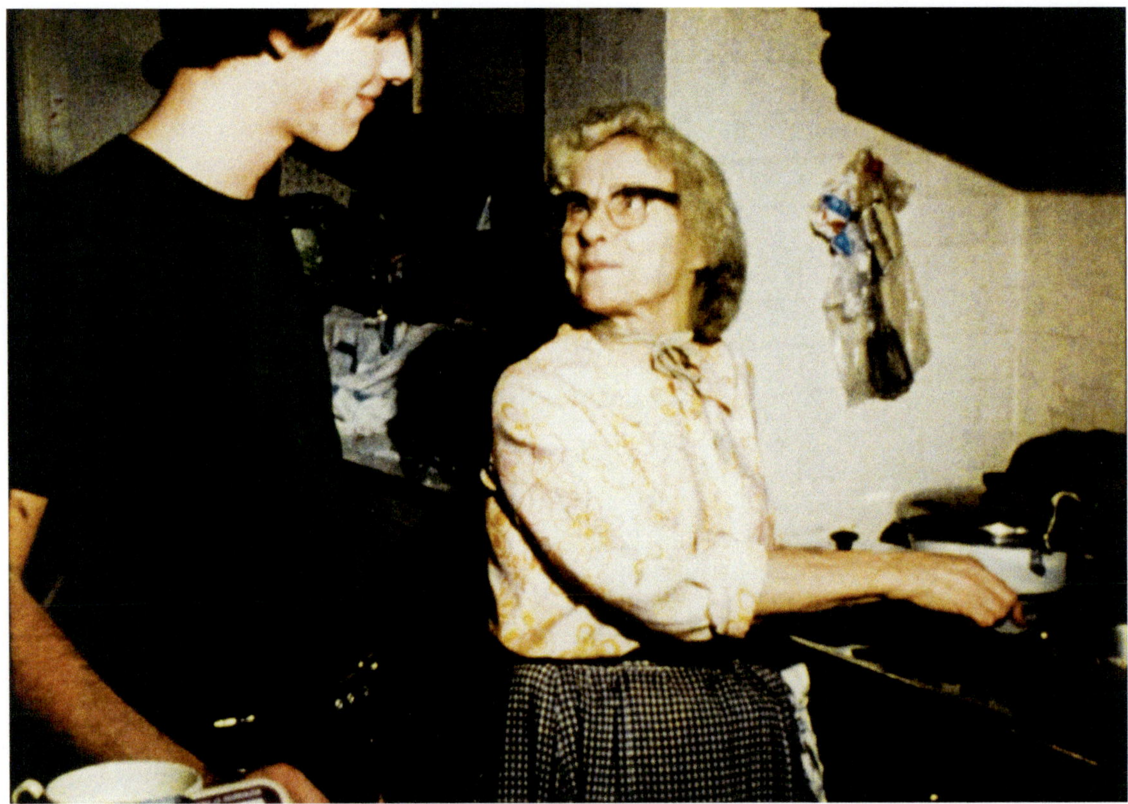

Figure 5.22. Film still of Julia Warhola and Richard Rheem, from Andy Warhol, *The George Hamilton Story,* **1966.**

RR: You don't like me now. I'm too big.

JW: I like you sometime, when you sleep.

RR: You're gonna get rid of me now, because I'm too big?

JW: I think so. I be looking for 'nother one. With one leg.

RR: With what?

JW: With one leg. So he can't beat me.

The offscreen observers laugh.

As the action proceeds, Julia becomes visibly tired of playacting and several times tries to tell her own story. In the process of "falling out" of her role, Julia Warhola emerges from the fictional construct of "Mrs. Warhol" into her own personal performance.

RR: For what movie did you win your academy award?

JW: Oh Richik, no movie. This time there was war. You know? You see, about war . . .

But before Julia can describe her wartime hardships, Rheem interrupts, dismissing her real-life story and returning to the fictitious Academy Award: "A war movie? . . . 'Combat'"? Rheem had fortuitously transmuted Havaj to Hawaii, but his effort now to place Julia in *Combat!*, a popular television series in 1966, fails. Disappointed at being rebuffed in her effort to tell her war story, Julia deflects his question, returning to her guests: "I put in pepper for Paul. *Chekai*, Paul—I talk to you, I talk to you Slovak." And she chuckles at her own vacillation between English and Rusyn, which contributes to the fluctuation between reality and illusion—at least for those who understand it.

Rheem continues to push the premise, and Julia follows along:

JW: I put poison in that black pepper. [Laughter.] I always poison with black pepper.

RR: Why don't we have a party and poison everybody with black pepper.

JW: I won't poison nobody, only old men.

RR: Just old men?

JW: Old men, who want marry me.

She tells Rheem she cannot remember how many husbands she has poisoned, but, "I'm gonna keep you for rest of you life." Richik responds with feeling, "You really like me." But to Rheem's gesture, she replies, "You want kiss, I no kiss you. [Shakes head.] No, I kiss nobody."

Finally, Julia looks directly into the camera, to her son, and says, "Already finished, no? Andy, nothing to do, put away." But Warhol does not relent, and the camera continues to roll. Then with determination in her voice, she again starts her own story, announcing a performance, for the third time, with, "When me was little girl," and she tells the story about "chopping" grass for cows, discussed earlier. "In Europe you want milk from cow, you have to get something for cow." Ignoring her interjection and bringing her back to the narrative line, Rheem asks: "How many husbands did you have in Czechoslovakia?" In a tone that expresses weariness and surrender, Julia answers, "I don't know, seven-eight-nine. I don't know." Then Rheem asks,

RR: Did you ever marry a cow?

JW: A cow? Cow?

And the reel ends just when the treatment of Julia begins to take what might be interpreted as a sadistic turn.[280]

Rather than Warhol's portrayal of his mother, most commentators have focused on the mother–son relationships revealed in the film. J. J. Murphy calls the film "a highly convoluted Oedipal fantasy."[281] In the first reel, when Julia finally runs out of conversation topics, she asks, "What else?" and takes a furtive look into the camera, at Andy. According to Susan Pile, Warhol was standing just out of frame, feeding his mother lines, topics, and directions. She responds to his direction, saying, "I be pressing already. C'mon, Richik. I iron you shirt," apparently a preplanned activity. After setting up an ironing board and fumbling energetically for an extension cord, she unexpectedly deviates from the plan and picks up some laundry. "I be pressing for you. Rich, you don't know pressing? Rich, c'mon, I be pressing for you underwear. Underwear is *gachi*, Rich. I be pressing for you *gachi*." Julia irons a pair of men's jockey briefs, then lifts and shakes them out, to the laughter of Rheem and the crew. The effect achieved by her unforeseen turn to *gachi* shows Julia's flare for comedy and is, as Warhol described transmutation, better than his original idea.

After folding underwear and socks in accordance with Julia's directions, Rheem returns to the script and asks her to iron his shirt, saying "I'll take it off." Julia objects: "No, no, no. Take jersey. Somebody see you . . . somebody see you in window." He takes off his long-sleeved green shirt, stands for a moment shirtless, smiling knowingly and seductively into the camera, and then puts on the black T-shirt that Julia gives him. Julia begins to teach him how to iron a shirt, chattering constantly, "I be your boss teacher . . . do it like this . . . do it nice straight . . . always pull more straight . . . you don't have to squeeze, take it easy . . . you good boy, Richik." The implicitly maternal role Julia has been playing in relation to Rheem becomes explicit.

> JW: I bet your mama no teach you.
>
> RR: No, she no teach me.
>
> JW: You be good boy, your mama no teach you. Be good for your wife if you know pressing. Richik, fix it nice, like this. Fix it like this.

Julia shows no awareness of her son's relationship with Rheem. Warhol's camera lingers lovingly on Richik's handsome face as he and Julia talk, joke, and tease one another playfully and flirtatiously. Julia picks hair from Rheem's shirt, they look closely into one another's eyes, and Julia pats his cheeks, as if he were a child.

Richard Rheem came from a prominent but emotionally cold, upper-class Los Angeles family. In letters to Andy, he described his own mother as depressing, and his stepmother as "wicked." "I have to shut [mother] out when she goes on & on about nothing. You may wonder why I visit her. She is more loving & enjoyable then Dad & stepmother."[282] Given this bleak relationship with his mother figures, it is no wonder that Rheem appreciated Julia Warhola's down-to-earth motherly warmth. Although, given his conversations with Julia, there is an amusing irony in his statement about "shutting out" his mother "when she goes on and on about nothing."

Another mother–son relationship is hinted at in Warhol's original title for the film, *The George Hamilton Story*. At a moment when the crew is busy eating scrambled eggs, the conversation flags, and offscreen whispers can be heard prompting, "George?" Paul Morrissey says, "I'll ask it." He then questions Julia, "Do you like that one that's marrying the president's daughter?" A confused exchange of overlapping voices follows, and the vague reference to George Hamilton goes no further. In 1966, Hamilton was in the news for his romantic relationship with Lynda Bird Johnson. But his relevance to Warhol's film is his close relationship with his mother, Anne Stevens, a glamorous socialite, who had four failed marriages and numerous affairs with high-profile movie stars. In Hollywood, Hamilton was viewed as a privileged, sensitive mama's boy. In his words, "My mother . . . was incredibly beautiful, a real charmer, the ultimate Southern belle, irresistible to men, and able to pull rabbits out of hats."[283] The film presents an ironic portrayal of the parallels between Hamilton and Warhol, their mothers, and their respective mother–son relationships. In terms of glamour, Andy was no George Hamilton, and Julia was no Anne Stevens.

For Rheem, as for many of Warhol's friends, Julia's down-home, childlike charm must have prevailed over her lack of traditional glamour. As Brigitte Weingart points out, "'Mrs. Warhol' demonstrates the error in the judgment that Julia lacked glamour."[284] Just as Warhol raises banal objects to the level of artistic fantasy in his art, his camera expands the spectrum of normative glamour to include Julia's simple charm, a foil to the screen glamour of Hollywood and the high-class allure of George Hamilton's mother. Warhol, like many children of Rusyn immigrants, may well have wished for a more sophisticated, fashionable mother, but in his film, he, perhaps unwittingly, transmutes and valorizes the unpretentious beauty of his simple, loving parent. Susan Pile commented about the relationship between Andy and Julia: "They were so sweet with one another—I recall her constantly speaking of 'my Andy.'"[285]

Rheem clearly revels in Julia's open affection and responds accordingly. In fact, his fondness for Julia must have outweighed his attachment to Andy. In the second week of December, when Warhol encountered Rheem on the street with another young Factory regular, he turned him out of the house and changed the locks. It is unknown whether Julia received an explanation for the disappearance of her dear "Richik," or how she reacted to losing her confidante and shopping partner. Rheem, however, did not forget her. In a blank envelope marked "To Andy Warhol's Mother," a note in Rheem's hand reads, "Dearest Julia, God Bless you and Andy. I love and pray for you both. Always, Richard Rheem. June 6, 1968." That was three days after Warhol was shot.

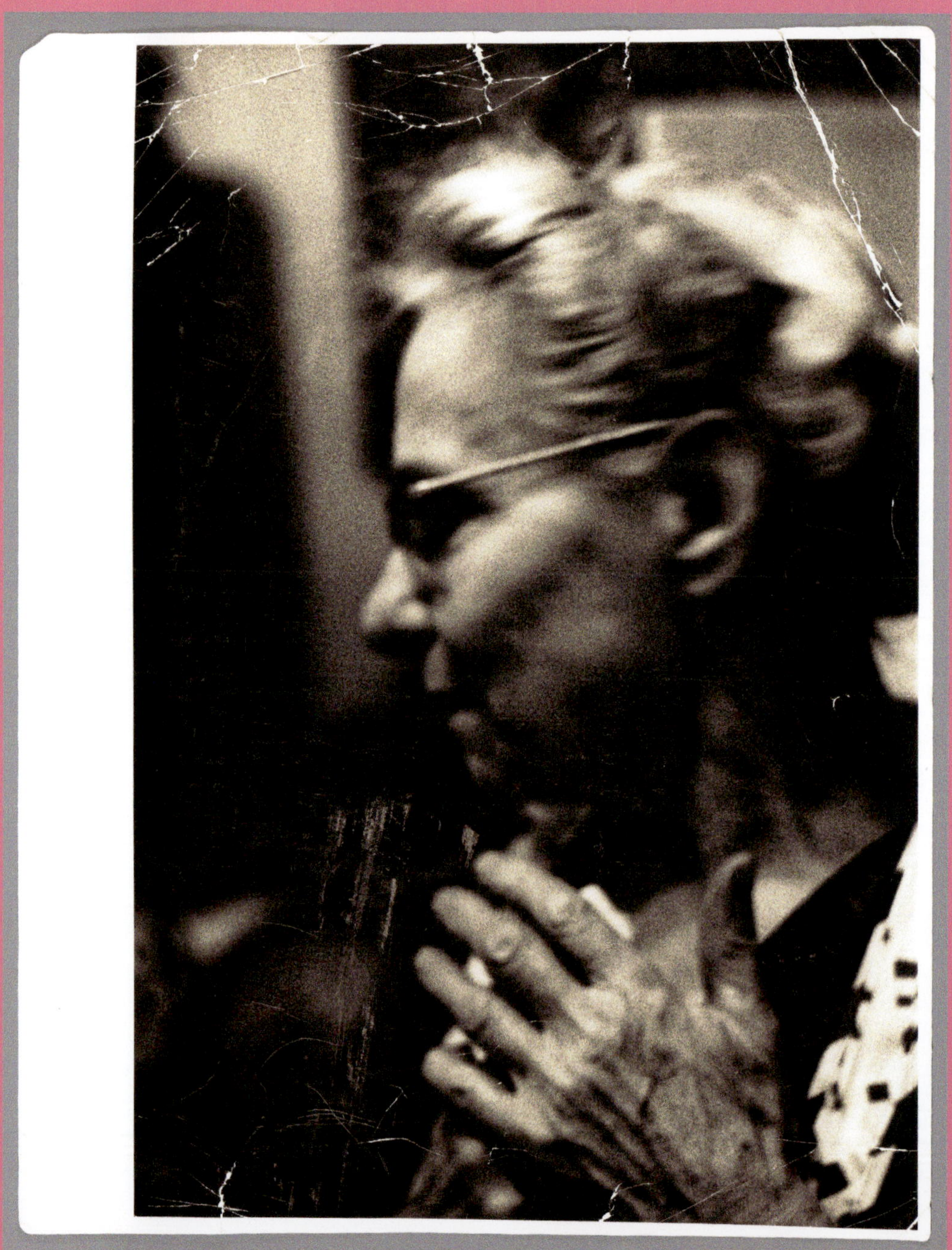

Figure 6.1. Julia Warhola at prayer.

6

"My Beloved Sister"

With few friends and limited English, when Julia could no longer contribute to her son's work, she was left to her own devices. Before her health began to deteriorate in the late 1960s, an ordinary day might have found her cooking, cleaning, and sewing. She shopped for groceries at Finast or Gristedes across the street and pasted S&H Green Stamps into books to redeem catalog products. She cooked dinner for Andy and his friends—roasts or "Czechoslovakian pancakes or something with various stuffings."[1] She watched television—*I Love Lucy*, Lawrence Welk, and Walter Cronkite. It didn't matter that she did not fully understand the dialogue. Music, dancing, and slapstick comedy entertained her. She carried on an extensive correspondence with her sisters in Europe and sent cards and gifts to grandchildren, who called her "Bubba," from the Rusyn word for "grandmother." She played with her cats and talked with her mynah bird, Echo. And she prayed.

Julia's grandson George described her morning routine: "Bubba would get up, comb her hair (she had long hair), sing in Rusyn, braid her hair, and then we would pray in front of the altar. Four children. We would kneel down, hands on the floor. . . . [Bubba] prayed very seriously, she prayed from the heart, on her knees with open arms. My Bubba. Then she would go and feed the cats." As she fed them, she sang.[2] After Andy had his fresh-squeezed orange juice, delivered to his bedroom by Julia or the grandchildren when they visited, "[Uncle Andy] would come downstairs, kneel, pray, and joke around with us."[3] Grandson Paul, the future priest, remembers, "She loved her private time in her little chapel area. At different times during the day, we would see her in her corner." Father Paul also described how Julia and Andy prayed together before he left for work or went out for a night on the town: "Before my uncle would leave the house, I can still hear his voice. 'Ma, ma, I'm goin' now.' She would come with her apron on, she'd come over to the stairwell, with her prayerbook. They'd say *Vo imia otsa* (In the name of the Father) and *Otche nash* (Our Father). It only took a minute or two, but I could see that Uncle Andy really needed that. We were right there. I thought it was wonderful."[4]

Paul and John visited New York several times a year with their families.[5] In down-home fashion, Andy's brother Paul and his six or seven children appeared without notice, and Warhol settled the kids in makeshift beds amid Campbell's soup cartons and stacks of Brillo boxes. "It looked like a grocery store," said Paul. One of his daughters appropriated a Campbell's carton. Paul remembered Andy's jocular response: "You did? Just for that you're not getting a wedding gift."[6] For children, the house at 1342 Lexington was an amusement park. Their uncle's antiques and collectibles were oddities—carved carousel horses, penny arcade machines, a Charlie McCarthy ventriloquist dummy, a crushed-car sculpture by the artist John Chamberlain, and a huge metal magnet salvaged by Paul from his junkyard. "I kept asking dad or Uncle Andy, 'Why do you have a wrecked car? Why is there a car in the house? What is it doing here?' And they told me, 'It's art, you know.'"[7] Punch, a six-foot painted, carved wooden cigar-store figure was a favorite. Julia called it "the bogeyman," a term, unrelated to race, used by Rusyn American immigrants to frighten children into good behavior. Punch did not intimidate the two youngest children, Madalen and Marty, who stuffed crayons into his mouth.[8]

Warhol put the older kids to work, stretching canvases and coloring drawings. Contrary to the blank, impersonal image he presented to the public, his nephews and nieces describe Uncle Andy as affectionate and engaging. "He wasn't hard to approach to talk to at all. He had a sense of humor for sure. He was not aloof. You could ask him anything anytime."[9] "We waited on the steps until he woke up at 10:00 or 11:00 and called us in to his bedroom. . . . When we brought orange juice or mail up to him in the morning . . . he welcomed us—we would just come right in and jump on the bed."[10] Andy urged them to play with the cats and told them about the famous people he had met the night before. It was often noted by his family, as well as by outsiders, that Andy liked kids. A nephew recalled, "He was such fun to be with. He'd go out and buy a birthday cake when it wasn't even my birthday. I asked him why, and he just said, 'It's a nice thing to do.'"[11]

Warhol's nephews and nieces remember that their uncle was always interested in them and asked about how things were going in school. But they were also aware that much of his life was concealed from them. "I remember there was this cowboy movie," Madalen said. Warhol was screening one of his films with a Western theme and sexual content, probably *Lonesome Cowboys*. "Every time Marty and I would peep around the corner, he'd shut the movie off."[12] As the boys got older, Andy teased and joked with them. "I can remember there was a stairway going up to the little area where he would do his drawings and he'd be real intent. I'd be sitting on the third or fourth step watching him, we'd be talking back and forth, and he'd ask me, 'Well, do you have a girlfriend, Pauly?' And I'd say, 'Gee, Uncle Andy, not really,' and he'd say, 'Oh come on, Pauly, what do you mean you don't have a girlfriend?'"[13] As a young adult, George made the most of visits to his New York uncle. "I went up with a lot of my friends. [Uncle Andy] would give me a key and we'd go out. He'd joke with us, 'Did you have a good time? Did you meet any Black girls or drag queens?' He treated us good."[14]

Julia was the quintessential Rusyn Bubba. She cooked old-world dishes. "It always tasted better when Bubba made it. She used to make a lot of steak, fried eggs, she used a lot of butter She'd get a lot of fancy things we wouldn't have, like from the bakery."[15] Greeting the children with hugs and kisses, she invented games to entertain them. Donald Warhola, John's son and the youngest of the grandchildren, played a coin-flipping game Bubba devised with his brothers. They all ended up with some change to keep for themselves. Julia Rusynized the boys' names to affectionate diminutives, Donnichik and Jeffreychik. When they misbehaved, she consoled them, "Dobry boysy" (good boys) in her mixed Rusyn-English.[16] Julia gave them coloring books. "We'll always remember how Bubba would slip a little money into each of them for us. That was sweet of her."[17] She took the girls shopping at Lerner's, clutching their hands tightly and warning, "I don't want the bogeyman to get you."[18] Andy worried about his mother. A Zavacky cousin recalled, "Andy was always afraid. . . . He always said, 'If you go anyplace, take a taxi home. Make him stop and wait until you get in the door.' He didn't trust people with his mama."[19] But according to grandson Paul, "Thanks to her strong faith in God, I don't think Julia was ever afraid of anything." Paul asked Julia once if it would be possible to get a tape recorder like Uncle Andy's. She didn't hesitate. "'Oh yes, we'll go out, we'll find it.' We checked some of the electronic stores and found the exact same tape recorder. She bought it for me. I know she was so happy I was in the seminary, that I wanted to be a priest, but she treated all the kids with regard."[20]

As Madalen Warhola Hoover said, "It was weird how a lot of people didn't know about us. He kept us apart from his business world and art world."[21] In fact, Andy shared little about his family with his associates. His business partner Vincent Fremont said he never mentioned them.[22] Others counter that Warhol enjoyed talking about his family.[23] Suzie Frankfurt remembers, "Andy was always very sweet to his family and he felt guilty about his brothers, saying 'I make more in two minutes than they make in a year.' . . . He loved them, he was never ashamed of them at all."[24] Awkward as it may have been, Warhol's relationship with his family was one that any successful child of immigrants can appreciate. After a visit from his brother John and John's wife, Warhol commented in his *Diaries* on the contradictions of family, where people so closely related can also be so distant. "And it's so odd, it's two people you don't really know who look so different from you and their ideas are so weird and it's one more thing to make you think what is this life all about."[25]

Family Things

Julia had grown accustomed to Andy's career, which she considered "just another job," and she accommodated herself to the house that was chockablock with offbeat art and eccentric friends. Although the family was supportive, "I don't think we understood it," said Warhol's nephew James. "When we were all together as a family, my mom would sometimes question Uncle Andy about his art. You know, 'What's that meant to be?' or even 'Why are you wasting your time on this?' And he would give as good as he got—not in a hostile way, but saying that this was his work, it had value and importance for him."[26] His celebrity was unknown to the family. Paul said, "I never even knew Andy was so famous until he was shot [in 1968] and got all those headlines and stories."[27] Julia wrote to her family in Slovakia that her son was a painter, but they did not know whether he painted pictures or houses.[28] In their correspondence, very few Pittsburgh friends or relatives mentioned seeing him on television or in magazines. The artist kept his two lives separate. "To us he's always the same old Andy. When we go there to see him, we talk about family things—our children and our mother. He's real modest and quiet. Just the same old Andy. You'd never know he was doing anything unusual."[29]

Julia visited her Pittsburgh family occasionally when she was in good health, traveling most often by Greyhound bus. John Zavacky remembers her attending Sunday liturgy at Saint John Chrysostom in *Ruska dolina* on one visit from New York, wearing a fur coat, a gift from Andy.[30] When she was ill, Paul and Ann, and later their daughter Eve, cared for Julia in New York. "Andy would call me and ask me to stay with her for a week or two until he got back. Otherwise we often talked on the telephone. Andy always said, 'Call me anytime, reverse the charges. Don't worry about the expense.' Andy was very generous. He was always worried about us, whether we had enough money, enough to pay the bills . . . and so on."[31] Andy accepted his brother John's collect calls every Sunday for thirty-eight years, as evidenced by letters and phone bills in the archives. "One Sunday John's wife asked John to skip a Sunday call and see if Andy noticed. The following Sunday, Andy's first question was, "You didn't call last Sunday. Is anything wrong?"[32]

The Time Capsules contain a voluminous correspondence that testifies to the closeness of the family and their mutual support. Letters from John to Julia and Andy began, "Slava Isusu Christu" (Glory to Jesus Christ), and ended with "I'll call on Sunday. God bless you both." The content of the letters—the weather, the garden vegetables, and the health of acquaintances—was less important than family connection. Grandchildren sent Valentines, Mother's Day, and birthday cards, and wrote about the minor events of their lives. Their mothers warned them not to write anything that would upset Bubba. "Dear Baba, how are you? I am sorry I didn't write sooner but I have been very busy at school. I got your Dollar and thanks for it. Mary Lou." "Our pigs are getting real big. Rover broke loose and he bit some kid. We got to go to bed now. Good-bye, Eve. P. S. Bring home 2 kittys." "Dear Buba and Uncle Andy, How are you feeling, I hope you are feeling well. We are coming up to your house for Easter. I am sick, Donny's eye is crossed, he went to the Doctor. . . . Sincerely yours, Jeffrey Warhola." His mother added, "Jeffrey prays for you every night. He prays that you live to 100 years." Younger children sent pictures they drew of a carefully detailed church building and their own portraits of Bubba and President Kennedy. Mary Lou Warhola Simpson recalled, "We would wait for Bubba to send us packages. This is how we learned to write thank you's. She'd have something wrapped in a napkin—marked for Eve, for Mary Lou—or a dollar or two for one of the kids she didn't have something wrapped up for. We didn't have a lot back then, so to get something from New York was special."[33] Phone calls were expensive. When the family reached their Pittsburgh home after a trip to New York, they called Bubba and let the phone ring twice before they hung up, to signal they had arrived safely.

Julia also kept in touch with old friends in Pittsburgh. The Girmans, parents of Andy's childhood friend, regularly sent Christmas cards. Cousins Mary and Peter Dudich, Andrii's cousin and supervisor at Eichleay, wrote regularly. Friends who had immigrated from Czechoslovakia to Pittsburgh or McKees Rocks responded to Julia in the self-addressed envelopes she sent them. A notebook from around 1967, preserved by John Warhola, lists, in handwriting that was not Julia's, the names and addresses of her nieces and the names and ages of their children. Nieces from Butler, daughters of her brothers Stephen and John, were faithful letter writers. In May 1965, Mary (Judy) Sobkouz, the daughter of Stephen Zavacky, began a letter, "I received your most welcomed Easter card and the dollars. I do want to thank you very much for it and my dad also wants me to thank you for his card and dollars." It is unlikely that Julia's niece or her brother needed a few dollars, but it was unthinkable for Rusyns to send a greeting card or make a visit without them. Julia encouraged her nieces to visit her in New York. She wrote to Mary (Sally) Zymboly, "How good it would be for you to come here, Mary. You wouldn't have to spend much in New York. I would give you the address and you could take a yellow cab. I would very much love to see you. I would pay the fare when it will be convenient for you to leave your home for a month, if you could be here with me, for I am more and more at home. Andy works at his studio and is very little at home."[34]

Family, friendship, and kinship networks were essential to immigrant women as a means to thwart isolation and strengthen family solidarity. Feminist scholars note that immigrant women sustained kinship celebrations across generational lines. "Even more than in the homeland, maintaining contact among kin—sometimes called 'kinship work'—became immigrant women's responsibility. . . . In this way, women in the immigrant working classes created a 'female world of cards and holidays' that functioned somewhat as the female world of 'love and ritual' did for middle-class women. Within their world, women enjoyed sociability beyond the nuclear family, while demonstrating their power and expertise to a sizeable social group."[35]

The correspondence between Julia and her American correspondents is a good example of the Rusyn-English pidgin language of immigrants and second-generation Rusyn Americans into the late 1950s. Lexical borrowings from English infiltrated the Rusyn language, especially for words or concepts unknown in the Old Country. Paul's wife Ann wrote to Julia about one of her daughters: *Doctor kazal ye mala mumps . . . Dal ye shot & dobre medicine.* (The doctor said she had the mumps . . . he gave her a shot and good medicine.) John apologized: *Ya ne mala času dostats present pre Mother's Day.* (I didn't have time to get a present for Mother's Day.) Phrases like *dobro house* (a good house), *rent platit* (pay the rent), *lem pyat minute ride* (just a five-minute ride), and *James dostal cara* (James got a car) were convenient mixed-language phrases that appear in Julia's correspondence and would be understood by bilingual speakers. English verbs were transformed by adding Rusyn endings: *Mam klinuvati apartment* (I have to clean the apartment), *Mr. Bogdansky mene spikčeruval* (Mr. Bogdansky took my picture), *vi ne feelujete dobri* (you do not feel well). The Rusyn-English hybrid was a common means of oral communication for immigrants navigating an alien culture in a new language, but the mix of alphabets, the inconsistent spelling and lack of grammar make their written communication abstruse.

However, the Warholas retained the Rusyn language longer than many Rusyn American families. Julia spoke Rusyn with her sons and relatives throughout her life. Paul and John spoke Rusyn somewhat fluently and were able to communicate with Rusyn relatives in Slovakia and even give radio interviews when they visited in the late 1980s. As we see in the video *Factory Diaries*, Andy understood his mother's language perfectly, although he preferred to answer in English. His active knowledge of Rusyn was limited to discrete lexical items. That is, he knew individual words for everyday use, but not how to link them in grammatically correct syntax. With family, he interspersed Rusyn words in English-language conversations. To his nephew George, he said, "*Pozri* [look], I'll give you everything you want. Stay with me and I'll look after you."[36] When Julia's sister visited from Miková in 1967, she reported that Andy rarely spoke with her and his mother, but he understood. And he prayed with them in Rusyn Church Slavonic.[37]

The Old Country

Julia had not seen her brother Yurko or her two youngest sisters, Elena and Eva, since she left Miková in 1921, and over the next forty-five years, momentous changes had taken place in the Old Country. In the Prešov Region, the most socially and economically underdeveloped area of Czechoslovakia, almost 90 percent of the peasants were still subsistence farmers even as late as 1939.[38] A bad harvest in the early 1930s was exacerbated by the worldwide economic crisis and American restrictions on immigration, which put an end to the supplemental income from abroad that had sustained peasants in the early years of the century. The resulting bankruptcies and foreclosures in villages sparked uprisings against the officials who enforced them. The largest insurrections took place in 1935 in the villages of Habura and Čertižne, just a few miles from Miková. Over two hundred gendarmes were brought in to put down the rebellions. In September 1938, the Munich Pact granted Hitler the Sudetenland, and a year later Nazis invaded Poland, setting off another world war in Central Europe. During the war, the Warhola/Zavacky homeland was ruled by a Slovak fascist nationalist regime that harshly repressed Carpatho-Rusyn educational, cultural, and religious institutions and enforced Nazi Germany's policy of liquidating the Jewish population.

The Carpathian region was once again caught between warring enemy forces. By 1944, the Soviet army had pushed the Germans into the northern foothills of the Carpathian Mountains, and for two months, the Dukla Pass was again a bloody battlefield. In Miková, partisans battled the German occupiers, as Nazi troops seized men from the village to dig trenches and bunkers. A mandatory evacuation forced the inhabitants from their homes. On their return, they found their villages in ruins. As the Germans retreated, they looted and destroyed the dwellings, confiscated food, crops, and domestic animals, and wrecked farming equipment. The First Czechoslovak Army Corps finally liberated Miková on November 26, 1944. Seventy villagers lost their lives in the fighting. This was the second war in which Julia's sisters experienced devastation and were forced to rebuild.

During the years immediately following the war, the Democratic and Communist Parties in Czechoslovakia vied for control. In the 1946 parliamentary elections, a communist was elected prime minister, and two years later, with the backing of the Soviet Union, the Czechoslovak Communist Party took over the government, which continued to operate under Soviet domination until 1989. Following the Soviet model, the party instituted radical political, economic, and social changes that revolutionized daily life. Alterations to language, religion, and national identity blighted traditional Rusyn culture.[39]

Beginning in 1949, the agricultural sector was collectivized. Individual small-scale farmers were compelled to give up their land, livestock, and farming tools to large, centralized collectives, which compensated them with small salaries. Carpatho-Rusyn peasant farmers resisted the change, and the process moved slowly. As early as March 1946, Julia had filed a document with the Czechoslovak Consulate in Pittsburgh that officially granted her sister Eva power of attorney to administer Andrii's property until Julia returned to the homeland. A year later, when prospects for democracy had dimmed and a communist takeover was imminent, Julia and her sons signed documents in which the possibility of her return was omitted, and the relinquishment of inheritance rights was termed "irrevocable."

According to Michal Bezek, Eva's son, the family refused to join the collective system, opting to turn over a quota of their produce to the state in exchange for maintaining their own property. "We had to give the state everything.... In years when the harvest wasn't good, we were left with just a third of our produce. Those were hard times.... The 1950's—that was the worst period."[40] However onerous the quotas, autonomy over their own lives, land, and work was preferable to life on a collective farm. The Bezeks' escape from collectivization would probably have been impossible without Andrii's land and the financial help provided by

Julia, dollar by dollar. Similarly, Edward Kasinec, the son of Rusyn immigrants in Yorkville, recalled, "Every Saturday, it was almost a ritual. My father would go to an agency—Union Tours—on Thirty-Sixth and Fifth Avenue, which would prepare relief packages to be sending to relatives in the homelands who were just devastated, of course, by the war and all of the circumstances in the late '40s and '50s."[41] In 1954, Julia wrote to her sister Anna in Pittsburgh, "Eva wrote me from Europe and told me to give you God's blessing. She can't write to you because it costs a lot to send a letter, and she doesn't have a cent. I sometimes send her a dollar in a letter to buy bread. The grain harvest was bad, and she has small children, so her life is very hard."[42] Julia's parcels of used clothing and housewares, which are often trivialized in the Warhol literature, were crucial to the survival of her family.

The Czechoslovak Communist Party followed the Soviet model in its attitude toward religion and the church, the pillar of traditional Rusyn culture and spiritual values. In 1950, the Greek Catholic Eparchy of Prešov, viewed by the Soviets as an arm of the Vatican, was liquidated. In a campaign known as "Action P" for *pravoslavny* (Orthodox), the communist government pressured believers to transfer to the Moscow-ruled Orthodox Church. Greek Catholic priests who refused to accept Orthodoxy were arrested or deported to the Czech lands with their families, where they were consigned to manual labor. Others went into hiding and offered liturgies and the sacraments clandestinely. But the communists underestimated the passionate religious convictions of Greek Catholics, who often stood up to their own subservient parish clergy and hurled stones at government agents. As of April 1950, only twelve villages and 30–40 percent of believers in the Prešov Region had converted to Orthodoxy.[43] The Greek Catholic church in Miková came under Orthodox control, but Julia's brother-in-law Vasyl Bezek insisted on walking fifteen or twenty kilometers, according to his son, to find services conducted by a Greek Catholic priest.[44]

In the United States, ecclesiastical authorities and the immigrant press kept the American faithful informed of events in the Old Country, fueling anticommunist passions. The Rusyn-language press followed the story of the disappearance and subsequent arrest and imprisonment of Pavel Goidych (Slovak: Pavel Gojdič), bishop of the Greek Catholic Eparchy of Prešov. Goidych had consistently upheld Rusyn national interests, and during the war, he helped save hundreds of Jews from deportation to death camps. In an article from June 15, 1950, the *Amerikansky Russky Viestnik* (*ARV*) cited a dispatch from Vienna:

> The persecution of Byzantine Rite Catholics in Eastern Slovakia, according to refugees, has become a veritable invasion of that region by the Moscow-ruled schismatic Orthodox

> church. The fate of [Bishop Goidych] has become a mystery, while practically all others in that region are virtual prisoners in their residences. . . . The black night of April 13–14, according to the Vatican Radio, is one that Catholics are not likely to forget. All through the night Catholic religious were arrested and rounded up by communist police and taken in jammed trucks to the "concentration monasteries," which are about the only ones that still exist. They have become prison camps surrounded by cordons of Red police.[45]

Churches were looted and desecrated, seminaries were closed. Byzantine-rite priests were arrested, tortured, and pressured to renounce the church. In February 1951 the *ARV* reported that Goidych was accused of high treason, military espionage, and other crimes. After torture, a forced confession, and a show trial, he was sentenced to life imprisonment. He died in 1960 in a political prison in Slovakia.[46]

While American Greek Catholics prayed for their coreligionists in the homeland, ecclesiastical newspapers fanned the flames of anticommunism. An issue of *Byzantine Catholic World* from August 15, 1965, found among Julia's possessions, contains an article from the Religious News Service headlined, "Vatican Daily Warns of Red Propaganda." Another article condemned the infiltration of American university faculty by "Reds." Fear of Soviet communism was also alive in Pittsburgh's *Ruska dolina*. A column in *ARV* warned, "You can bet your life that STALIN has a big X mark on his map for the Dolina and the Steel Mills in the Tri-State area."[47] Philip Pearlstein, the classmate with whom Warhol moved to New York, commented that Julia Warhola was a great fan of Senator Joseph McCarthy, infamous for his witch hunts of suspected communists in American government and culture in the early 1950s.[48] Julia's alleged admiration for McCarthy is often repeated in the literature, but without the context from which it emerged. The liquidation of the Greek Catholic Church in Slovakia and the "Red Scare" that surrounded American Rusyns, coming after decades of turmoil caused by the celibacy crisis and church schisms, had a chilling effect on the American-born generation. Andy Warhol's detachment from the Greek Catholic Church in the New York years and his turn to the more normalized American Roman Catholic Church was not atypical. Furthermore, Warhol may have had a visceral reaction to communism, generated by his mother. Bob Colacello describes an attempt to take a quick tour of East Berlin together in the early 1970s. "At Checkpoint Charlie the East German border police seized a copy of French *Vogue* . . . and Andy panicked. 'This is too scary,' he said. . . . 'It's too scary. It's too scary.'"[49]

In addition to ravaging the Carpatho-Rusyn agricultural and spiritual structure, communism deprived Rusyns of their national identity. The Czechoslovak

Communist Party followed guidelines that were set by the Comintern in 1924 and enforced by the Soviets in 1948 with a decree ordering that whatever they may have called themselves, the East Slavic inhabitants of the Prešov Region would be listed in official documents as Ukrainian. The term "Rusyn" was proscribed, and the Rusyn language disappeared from education and the press. The Ukrainian language was introduced into schools, and Ukrainian-leaning organizations promoted local theater and folk festivals as examples of "Ukrainian" culture. The common people defiantly responded to their classification as Ukrainian, which they found alien, by identifying themselves as Slovaks, the only available alternative, and sending their children to Slovak schools. This led, in the 1950s and 1960s, to the greatest degree of national assimilation that the Rusyns in Slovakia had ever experienced.[50]

These impositions of communism on the Carpatho-Rusyn people—collectivization, Ukrainianization and subsequent Slovakization, and the liquidation of the Greek Catholic Church—were toxic for traditional Rusyn culture. Paradoxically, even more detrimental for family structure were the socialist economic achievements that led to modernization and social mobility. Electrification of rural communities began in 1957, and transportation networks connected hinterland villages with provincial towns. Beginning in 1956, factories and mills were built throughout the region, attracting young people from rural farms to industrial towns and regions of Czechoslovakia where wages were higher.

Tuzex

Except for a few money transfers from Julia's first years in Pittsburgh, no correspondence between Julia and her old-country relatives has survived from the prewar decades, and almost none survives from the early Cold War era. But according to Julia's youngest sister's husband, Julia was already sending money in the 1920s, and we know that even during the Great Depression, Julia encouraged her sons to pitch in with their teenage earnings to help her sisters in the Old Country. It was illegal for Czechoslovak citizens to hold dollars, but there were ways around the laws. "[Eva] would give the Jews the dollars and they would change it for our money."[51]

In 1948, the communist Czechoslovak government adopted a system that existed in all Soviet bloc countries to procure the hard currency they needed for foreign trade on international markets. Amnesty was decreed for currency offenders, and a chain of Darex (after 1957, Tuzex) hard-currency stores was established.[52] Lucky citizens with dollars could trade them at any bank for vouchers to buy items at

Darex/Tuzex stores that were substantially more expensive on the open market, if available at all. According to a 1950 Associated Press article, a kilogram of rice that could be purchased at Darex for 30 crowns would cost 300 crowns on the open market, coffee was 120 crowns as against 800, and tea was 180 crowns at Darex and nine times as much on the free market.[53] By the summer of 1950, there were eleven Darex stores in Czechoslovakia selling fine western consumer goods and items of local manufacture made exclusively for hard currency sales. In addition to major cities and tourist locales where westerners were targeted, hard currency stores were disproportionately located in underdeveloped eastern Slovakia, because so many of its inhabitants had relatives who had emigrated to the United States in the early years of the century.[54] A Darex store, and later a Tuzex, were located in Prešov, about forty-five miles from Miková.

In the 1950s and 1960s, foodstuffs and textiles were the most popular items. By 1963, Americans could order food, clothing, and even luxury items through their local Tuzex agency to be delivered for free to their relatives in Czechoslovakia, with no duty charges. In Czechoslovakia, it was also possible, if legally hazardous, for citizens to exchange money and sell goods on the thriving black market. In 1959 the official exchange rate in Prague was 7 crowns to the US dollar, but over the next decade, one could get 30–40 crowns to the dollar illicitly, which would most likely be exchanged for Tuzex coupons. By the end of the 1960s, coupons traded on the street could bring five times their face value. Corruption was rife and a fact of life. As Paulina Bren puts it, "Bartering, hoarding, speculating, and smuggling had become an everyday reality for almost everyone," not to thrive, but to survive.[55] John Warhola recalled that without Julia's packages, her sisters would have had nothing to wear after the war, and with her packages, they had more than enough to share.[56] It is not inconceivable that Julia's family was making money on her gifts through the 1950s. In a letter from 1965, a niece tells Julia that they had not received anything from her in a long while. She frets that, although they have many relatives in America, only Julia sends parcels. "We have nothing [to pass on]. People leave us dissatisfied."[57]

In 1952, a receipt from American Express was issued in Pittsburgh to Julia Warhola for $20, to be transferred to the Darex gift account of Eva Bezek in Miková. An undated note from Julia to Eva reads, "Dear Sister and family, I'm sending you a few cents for the Easter holiday. When you receive them, use them to get something for yourself at Tuzex. May God give you everything good. God bless you."[58] Julia also sent parcels through the mail, although direct parcels cost the sender high postage rates and imposed duty charges on the recipient. She wrote to Eva: "I am sending you envelopes, a couple of stockings and a sweater for you, pink nylon. Do not give it to anyone. Wear it yourself while you are healthy. Write me how much you will pay for it. Maybe it is not worth it to send anything because you will have to pay a lot. So write me how much you will pay."[59] A "Reclamation Inquiry" from the post office submitted by Julia to the 34th Street Post Office in New York in November 1955 sought to locate a lost parcel that contained three cotton headscarves, a nylon print skirt, and four pairs of stockings, worth a total of $13.35. An undated customs declaration tag lists a parcel's contents in Julia's handwriting: peas, raisins, pepperoni, soup mix, candy, cheese, tea, coffee, prunes, margarine, and pepper. Another parcel contained plastic tablecloths, bedspreads, and "used clothing," valued at $12 and insured for $10.[60] The parcel weighed thirty pounds, and the international postage in 1967 must have been substantially more than the value of the contents. Eva's daughter remembered,

> As long as Aunt Julia lived, she sent us parcels. There were parcels and parcels: clothes, dressing gowns, nylon stockings, black with a seam. . . . Sometimes she sent food: flavored chewing gum, oranges, chocolate, or coffee. She sent the food in small boxes and the clothes in sewn jute sacks with an address glued on, written in her typical script. . . . Dad would go to the post office in Havaj to get the parcels. Sometimes there were two in a week. He would then come home to Miková at dusk by the back way through the forest. It was a shortcut, but it was also so no one in the village would see him. You know, people envied us.[61]

Purchasing and packaging the items and taking them to Overseas European Merchants, the Tuzex agent on East 74th Street in Yorkville, must have occupied much of Julia's time. She also sent small amounts of money through the mail, a risky venture under the corrupt socialist system. According to Eva's daughter, Julia and her mother had a coded language. "Is it cold again?" meant the money had been stolen again. According to a Bezek family story, Julia had planned to take fifteen-year-old Eva with her when she emigrated to America. "To the end of her life she regretted not having taken our mother with her to America. Mama would have been willing to sail then. Julia had passage paid for her, but somehow it didn't work out. That was why she helped her all her life; it was because in the end she hadn't taken her."[62]

"Bowing Letters" and Songs

The Time Capsules contain numerous letters from Julia's relatives in Europe. Eva was the most faithful correspondent, but there are also letters from her sister Elena

[Helena] and brother Yurko. Julia corresponded with, and sent parcels to, nieces she had never met. They responded with letters and snapshots of their children, which Julia carefully preserved. Unfortunately, Julia's weekly letters to Europe have not survived. After Eva died, one of her daughters burned them. "They were all in one sack," remembered Vasyl Bezek, "and everything was written down in those letters. She always remembered her native land."[63] In one preserved letter, a sister complimented Julia on her writing and commented that she had "such a good memory."[64] We can presume that Julia's letters were a memoir, as well as a diary, and their loss is regrettable.

The Bezek family preserved only a few of Julia's notes to Eva, mostly written on holiday greeting cards.[65] To get an idea of what Julia told her siblings about her life and her son in her numerous letters from New York, we need to read between the lines of the responses from Miková. But that is not easy. Most letters are not dated. Stamps and postmarks were removed. A few dated letters are from as early as 1951, but most of the correspondence is apparently from the early to mid-1960s. The mixed languages, phonetic spelling, lack of punctuation, and, in most cases, the sloppy penmanship of Julia's generation make their letters almost impossible to decipher, as even the Czech, Slovak, and Rusyn editors of *Andy Warhol a Československo* admit.[66] We are often left with tantalizing tidbits of information.

In the classic early work of sociology, *The Polish Peasant in Europe and America*, the authors William Isaac Thomas and Florian Znaniecki devote a good deal of attention to the concept of the "peasant letter," an appropriate framework within which to examine the Zavacky correspondence. It was typical of immigrant peasants and their families in the homeland to write many long letters. "This is particularly striking, since the business of writing or even of reading letters is at best very difficult for [them]. It requires a rather painful effort of reflection and sacrifice of time. Letter writing is for [them] a social duty of a ceremonial character, and the traditional fixed form of peasant letters is a sign of their social function."[67] Known as "bowing letters," they were formulaic, beginning with information that the writer, praise God, is in good health, and she wishes the same for the reader and her family. This is followed by greetings, or "bows" to all family members. "These elements remain in every letter, even when the function of the letter becomes more complicated; every letter, in other words, whatever else it may be, is a bowing letter, a manifestation of [family] solidarity." So, a 1966 letter to Julia from sister Elena begins, "Dear sister Ul'ka and your dear son Andriiko, from my family, from our children and Maria our daughter and her family, we all together wish you, dear sister Ul'ka and your dear son Andriiko, fervent, heartfelt blessings of the dear Lord, and we also greet your dear son

Paul and his sweet family and John and his family with all our heartfelt kind regards, dear sister Ul'ka, and we wish you good health from the dear Lord God."[68] Eva, who wrote more often, truncated the obligatory salutation, but included at least some version of the "bows" that bound the family together, even though they had been physically separated for almost half a century.

They exchanged photographs. From Slovakia, photos of growing children and grandchildren, family weddings and get-togethers, and a few photos of the aging Eva, Elena, and Yurko with their spouses filled in the blank decades since Julia had last seen her siblings in their teens and twenties.[69] Conscious of how much time had changed them, on the reverse side of the snapshots, everyone apologized for looking old. Julia sent Polaroid photos of herself, writing on the back, "Do not show this to anyone because I look really bad. I am not as old as I look in the picture." On another photo taken at the same time, she wrote, "This is me with my tomcat. We are both already old. . . . You will laugh, dear sister." Although she shows her age, there is nothing comical about the photos. Dressed in a cardigan, with what is probably a religious medal on a chain around her neck, Julia seems to have had her hair done in soft curls. Another snapshot shows her with her hand on her face. She wrote, "I was crying. I am sad that you are ill." Although there must have been more photos of children and grandchildren over the years, only one photograph of Andy was preserved and reproduced in Rudo Prekop and Michal Cihlář's *Andy Warhol a Československo*. Characteristically, Julia apologizes for its quality: "Here's a photo of my son Andy. The photo looks very dark. . . . He did not take a very nice picture." The oval photo shows an attractive Andy Warhol in his teens or twenties, wearing a jacket and tie.

Julia was remembered in Miková for her sweet singing voice. Community singing accompanied all aspects of Rusyn village life, and from an early age, uneducated peasants instinctively learned principles of harmony, pitch, and rhythm. There were songs for specific holidays and life events, all of which were learned by ear and memorized. Although there were regional and dialectical variants in the multiethnic region of northeastern Slovakia, the song repertoire was culturally specific, which became especially important in the immigration. Singing old village songs at Pittsburgh festivals promoted social cohesion among the immigrant community and bound it with the cultural traditions of their old-country parents and grandparents. It was a performance of Rusyn identity for the benefit of participants and onlookers.

In Thomas Bell's *Out of This Furnace*, the immigrant Bodnar laments that he and his compatriots cannot work together with their American colleagues to "make the world a better place for everybody." Their cooperation is not asked for. "We're only

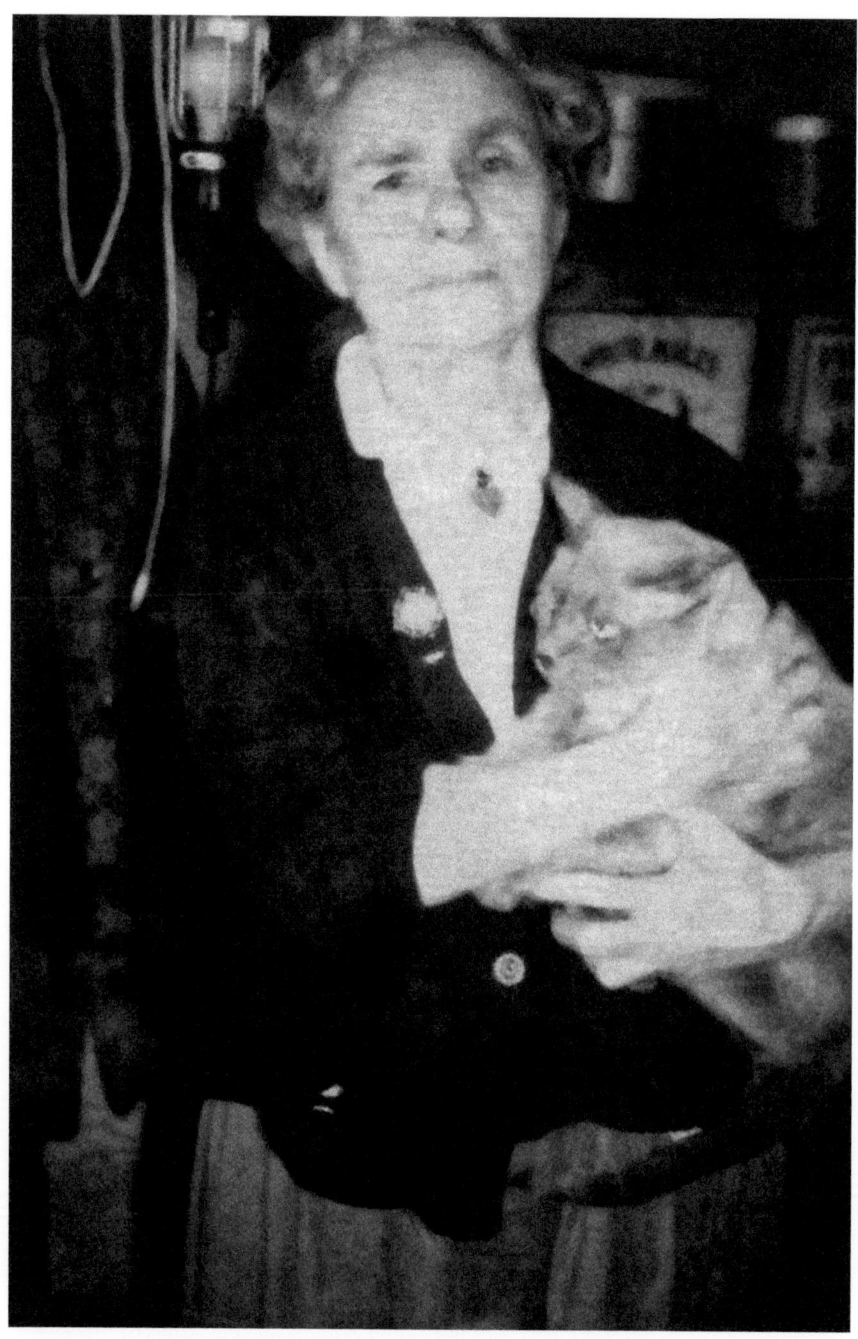

Figure 6.2. Julia Warhola with her tomcat.

Hunkies." "Once I had an idea, I thought to myself: If we were to sing some of our songs and explain what they were about—would it surprise them to learn that we sang about such things and had such feelings?"[70] Bodnar's dream was not fulfilled, but Rusyns in Slovakia and America kept on singing. In 2000, the ethnomusicologist Robert Metil noted:

> In comparison with a randomly selected group of non-Rusyns anywhere in Slovakia, for example, or an average assembly of people in the United States, Rusyns sing quite often, very well, and with a great deal of conviction and intensity.... Weeping is also common at singing events, and is usually considered socially acceptable, as are displays of reverie and even physical and psychic states that appear akin to trance.... Rusyns generally demonstrate above-average technical ability and control as singers, besides investing their performances with a great amount of feeling and range of emotions. Overall, their intensity, technical facility and smoothness, confidence and lack of inhibition, are characteristics of Rusyn singing culture.[71]

When Warhol procured a reel-to-reel tape recorder for his mother in 1957, Julia filled much of her time reproducing the Rusyn singing culture of Miková and Pittsburgh. She recorded her voice at the kitchen table, singing folk-art songs and religious chants, accompanied by meows from her cats.

Among Warhol's early assistants, Nathan Gluck and Joseph Giordano commented on Julia's recordings. "Somebody showed her how she could re-record .. . and sing along with herself! And so it sounds like a duet!"[72] Julia did more than "sing along with herself." She harmonized with her initial recording, as she had done instinctively in Miková and with her sister Mary in Pittsburgh. The result was rich and sonorous in the traditional musical style of Carpatho-Rusyn peasants. Giordano, many of whose assessments are questionable, described her voice as atonal. "You couldn't tell one song from the next. But she claimed that she was a great opera singer in Czechoslovakia ... and that she used to ride from town to town on horseback, singing."[73] Julia may indeed have ridden from village to village singing, although her boast of being a great opera singer, if Giordano got that right, was one of her tall tales. But unless he had a tin ear for folk music, Giordano's dismissal of her performance is another of his unsupported opinions. Julia's voice is warm, kind, and smooth, if sometimes thin, given her advanced age. According to the ethnomusicologist Jerry Jumba, "Her large repertoire includes songs of true love, infidelity, flirtation, unrequited love, cartoonish stories with whimsical and clever texts, community songs, and more. The melodies are rich and varied in tempo and

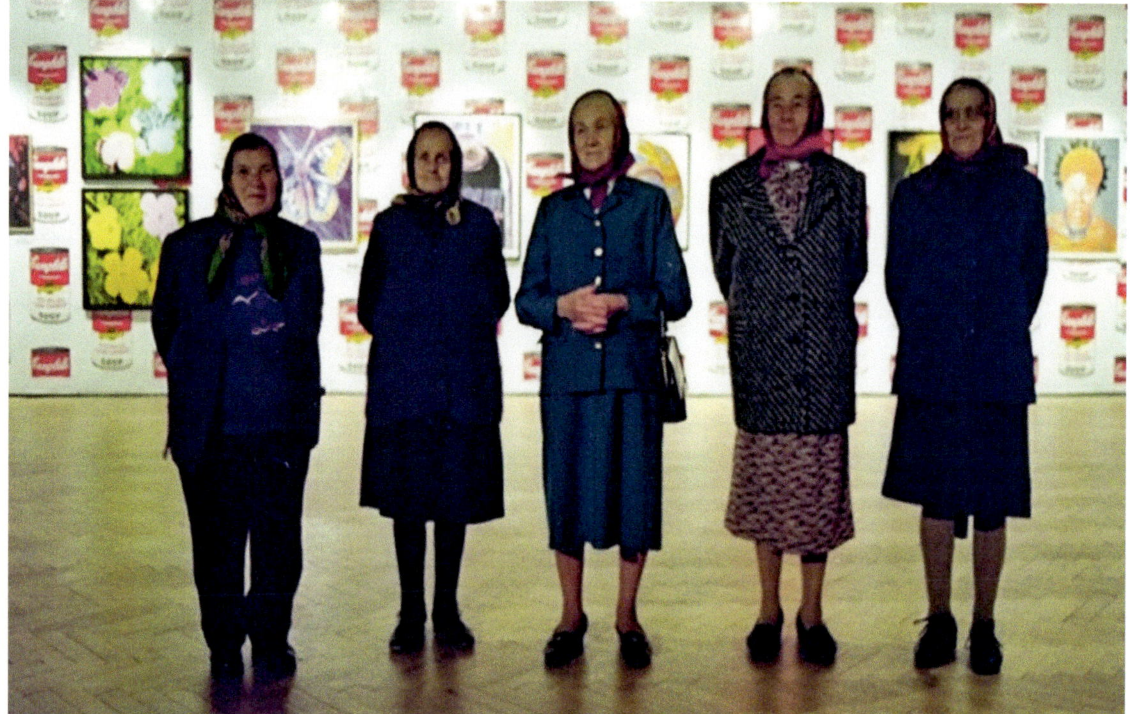

Figure 6.3. Film still from *I Am from Nowhere*, 2002. Women from Miková sing along with Julia Warhola's recording at the Andy Warhol Museum of Modern Art in Medzilaborce, Slovakia.

artistic temperament. The pitch, intonation, and rhythm are excellent. When you listen, you know she loved to sing and has an artistic flare that makes you smile."[74]

When she was still living on lower Lexington Avenue, Julia, perhaps with Andy's help, went to Sanders Recording Studio off Times Square and made a vinyl record of Rusyn folk songs and prayer recitations. She sent the record to her sister, writing on the sleeve, "Let's hope it doesn't get broken."[75] In Stanislaw Mucha's film *Absolut Warhola*, Michal Bycko, the curator of the Andy Warhol Museum of Modern Art in Medzilaborce, says that Julia sent the record to her sister in the 1960s, but since "nobody in Miková had a gramophone," it gathered dust until it was rescued for the museum. But according to a niece, the family listened to Julia's record at home in Miková. "We put the record on the gramophone and sang with it. I was sorry that Aunt was so far away in that foreign land. . . . So we were in tears, crying and singing."[76]

Conscious of the recital she was performing, Julia formally announces each title, "Teper zaspivam . . ." (Now I will sing . . .), as if she were a radio vocalist. Several of her recorded songs are sad—a hunter kills one of a pair of doves, leaving the female *holubka* to die of sorrow; a daughter moans to her mother, who married her off to a graybeard; a maiden rebukes the lover who took her virtue and married another. In "Chervena ruzha troiaka" (Red rose of three shades), an assertive woman leaves her abusive husband to save her own life. Other songs are cynically comic. An old *dido* drowned his wife in a brook, only to have her come to life as he returns from church with a young wife. He grumbles, "In my old age, how can I care for two wives?" A mother prevents her son from marrying a widow who promises to take care of him. "Vdova znaie charuvaty / vcharuvala muzha svoho / vcharuie t'a molodoho" (The widow casts spells / she charmed her husband / she'll bewitch you too, young man). In a song from the man's point of view, the lyrical persona pleads with a young maiden to marry him, promising that she will not have to work in his house, where the oven bakes the bread, the cat brings in wood, and the wind sweeps the floors. "Dobri bude tobi u mene" (You will have it good with me). But as the song is sung by women, the man's magical promises fall flat. Julia's songs were classics of Carpatho-Rusyn culture that stirred the hearts of her audience. There is an especially poignant moment in the 2002 documentary *I Am from Nowhere* when a Miková tour group of elderly women in babushkas stands before Warhol's soup cans in the Medzilaborce museum and sings along with Julia, with tears in their eyes.[77]

Old Women's Friendships

After singing mournfully with Julia about lost innocence, the Miková women joke among themselves about looking at the portraits of men at the museum, but express preference for "a real guy." In the course of the documentary, they break out in impromptu recitations of original poetry and harmonious song. Eva Prekstova, a distant cousin, tells the film crew, "You guys are a great bunch." This was Julia's cohort, the women's society she would have been part of had she remained in Miková—laden with troubles, oppressed by poverty, dazed by modernization, but lively and resilient.

Thomas and Znaniecki talk about "old women's friendships," which anticipates contemporary feminist studies of women's "kinship work."

> The women seek in each other a help against their respective families and comfort in domestic troubles, and, being of the same generation and the same social group, they agree perfectly with each other, particularly as there are no practical problems to divide them. The necessity of such a friendship is felt mostly in older age by

women who do not know how to adapt themselves to the young generation and who begin to feel solitary in their own families. . . . In their relation the old women manifest much mutual adulation, and this shows that their friendship has still another function; it is their only way of getting social recognition of the kind and degree they desire.[78]

With few friends of her own generation, social class, or ethnic background in New York, Julia found long-distance consolation in the correspondence with her sisters and nieces in Pittsburgh and Europe. Although the process of writing and posting them was difficult and often costly, the frequent letters were a comfort for Julia and her sisters. Eva's daughter recalled, "I never saw Aunt Julia but it's as if I knew her very well. After all, she used to write my mother a letter every week. And not just one page, often as many as eight pages. She always began, 'My beloved sister!' That would always make Mama cry. I feel like crying too, just remembering it now. They were real love letters."[79] A particularly emotional letter from Eva reads,

> My dear sister Ulia, we greet you and your dear son Andriiko with the dear Lord Jesus Christ. We want to write just a few words, dear sister Ulia. . . . My hands are shaking from grief. May God grant I live long enough to come to you. I shall tell you about everything. If only the dear Lord helps me. Dear sister, I'm so terribly aggrieved, I don't even know what could heal my heart. All I have now in the wide world is you. My most dear, good sister, kind sister Ulia. I'm not writing much. I am sick and my heart is breaking from my great grief. I'll finish now. I send you lovely greetings, stay healthy. If only you could come and see me, dear sister.

Eva's distress was caused by changes to family structure and traditional morality brought about by new social and economic developments and a difficult daughter-in-law. The details are unknown, but Julia could certainly commiserate with Eva about generational changes.

Reading the Bezeks' holiday messages from Julia, and reading between the lines of Julia's correspondents' responses to her letters, we can surmise that Julia freely expressed her own fears and grievances in the same effusive sentimental style, a kind of performative outpouring in writing. Judging from Eva's comment, "You write that it's hard to find pennies Ulia, don't worry when you don't have a dollar handy," Julia must have voiced financial worries. There are also frequent references to Julia's concerns about her son, apparently a frequent topic in her letters. In 1963, Julia's brother Yurko wrote that he felt sorry for her and worried about her being alone with only Andy for company. In 1965 a daughter of Eva Bezek wrote, "*Mila Tetko* [dear aunt], if only you had a daughter, maybe she would understand, maybe she would spend more time with you than your sons. I know your sons are great, but a daughter is better for a mother. But what can you do, dear aunt?" She goes on to sympathize and hope that Andriiko will be around more often to take care of her. In a note to a niece in Pittsburgh, Julia wrote, "I don't know, dear Mary, if I wrote you that I feel really sad here in New York. I don't have my family with me. My son Andy is at home very little. He works a lot and travels a lot on airplanes. He often goes to play music with the band. Now he has been in Detroit, Michigan at the college school. The band played for the kids."[80] Julia's description of Andy's activities with the Velvet Underground and the "Exploding Plastic Inevitable" rock-and-roll psychedelic extravaganza is a good indication of how distant she was from his life and how little she understood it. On the other hand, she knew that something was not right in her son's world. Eva responded to one of her complaints, "I'm sad that the people around Andriiko are not good to him."[81]

While Eva and Julia shared their problems and their faith in Jesus to deliver them from their troubles, Julia's sister Elena was more up to date and down to earth. Elena had left Miková for the more cosmopolitan town of Cheb (formerly Eger) on the border with Germany. To Julia's woeful grievances that Andy was not making enough money, Elena responded, "Your life is hard now. I think about you a lot . . . but no one anywhere gives something for nothing. Man must live, dear sister. We must bear it." Elena was astonished to hear that Julia was then paying two women a dollar an hour each to clean her house and provide care. By Elena's measure, that was a lot of money for easy work. Julia longed for the simple but long-gone old-world, family-centered life of Miková that she had left in the 1920s, and her upscale complaints did not resonate with her correspondents. On the back of a photo, one of Julia's sisters wrote, "Dear Sister Ulia, don't feel homesick. It's much better where you are than it is here."

Thomas and Znaniecki place this kind of immigrant letter in the context of the breakdown of old habits, the weakening relations between parents and children, and the evolution of the next generation's independence. In their study of the correspondence of immigrant women, they found that mothers' disappointment with children made them cling to sisters and old-country relatives, the only link with the old life. "This proves at the same time how much stronger the old sentimental habits are as compared with the new ones [adopted in America], and how much more difficult is the adaptation to new conditions for a woman than a man."[82]

A Strange Place to Live

Julia was surely lonely during the 1960s, when Andy had moved his work from the house to the Silver Factory, when he went out every night, and traveled often. Visits from her sons and grandchildren cheered her, and Julia, who was joyful and optimistic with family, cast the best light on the situation. But her everyday life must have been somewhat dark, and she may have found relief in fantasy. According to her niece Nora, "Aunt Julia claimed that she'd had a boyfriend in New York. She'd met him in the church, and apparently, he was terribly rich and had taken her on various trips. He would come in his big flashy car, and he loved hot-dogs, and he took Julia to the funfair park on Coney Island to watch the parachutists. I asked her where her boyfriend was now. She answered me in her lingo, 'Oh, I don't see him long time.' And a moment later she added calmly, 'He probably died.'"[83] While the story sounds fantastic, Joseph Giordano recalls a similar account. "And then, she had fallen in love with this man in Czechoslovakia, but somehow or other . . . they never got married. However, when she came to America and when they lived on 242 Lexington, this man used to come and pick her up. And in a chauffeur-driven limousine. . . . They used to go somewhere to have lunch." Giordano also expressed disbelief. "Now, I wouldn't be a bit surprised that Missy paid to have the limousine come and pick her up. I mean, she was exactly like Andy—she was a myth-maker."[84]

A rare objective view of Julia's daily life comes from Bernard Weinraub, the *Esquire* journalist who interviewed her in 1966. He describes her sitting in the "basement apartment," where the sofa and chairs were covered with sheets. On the wall were pictures of Christ, President Kennedy, and grandchildren. Due to Julia's heavy accent, Weinraub got some of the details wrong—he has her living alone until recently, when she visited Andy and collapsed, weeping, "I'm gonna die." Her account of being hospitalized for more than a month was factual, but his understanding that she was now temporarily recuperating at Andy's house was conjecture, based on her complaint, "I'm sick. I need sun. This near hospital."[85] What follows in the interview is the information about her courtship, wedding, her daughter's death, the war, her husband, and her sons.

According to Weinraub, when he knocked on the door and told Warhol he was there to interview his mother, Andy "sort of giggled."[86] "It was the middle of the afternoon and he just giggled, and I didn't know what the hell was going on." Weinraub had no further conversation with Warhol. He described the apartment as a large floor-through space, where "strange people" gathered in the far corner of the room, "an unending group of people coming and going." Julia was dressed in black, "peasant-like, in a simple way that you don't usually see," and Weinraub was surprised at the incongruity of Julia Warhola with her son's entourage. "I don't know if she knew where I was from, I don't think she knew *Esquire* magazine. I began asking questions, and I think it was very strange for her because nobody had talked to her. Who is this person asking me questions?"

Recognizing her limited English, Weinraub asked very basic questions. "She didn't really answer. She just began talking, then began crying. I didn't understand what was going on. . . . I didn't ask about her wedding, she brought it up." And in a kind of stream of consciousness, Julia launched into a natural, spontaneous performance, indulging in happy and sorrowful memories, probably glad to have a willing audience. The "strange people" in the room, most likely Warhol's Factory followers, remained in the background, and Weinraub sat alone with her. Andy showed no particular interest and did not listen in on their conversation. Recalling it as a difficult interview because of the communication problems and Julia's incomprehensible emotionalism, Weinraub meshed together her disjointed narrative. His overwhelming impression addressed the curiosity of Julia's presence among Warhol's crowd. "I remember this older lady in black sitting there, very emotional for reasons I didn't understand, and there's Andy walking around giggling. . . . What was so strange was all these weird people wandering around, and there was this very old lady in black sitting there. She was a total fish out of water. . . . It was a strange place for her to live."

A controversial topic in the biographical literature of Warhol and his mother is Julia's use of alcohol. The controversy may have started with Andy's interview with George Gruskin of the South African publication *Scope*. According to Kenneth Goldsmith, Gruskin "set out to prove Andy Warhol to be the fraud that they assumed him to be. However, Warhol magnificently deflects Gruskin's hostility."[87] Gruskin was particularly interested in Andy's mother, and Andy was loath to talk about her. Gruskin asks, "You used to live with your mother, didn't you?" In this interview, published in March 1973, Warhol answers, "Oh yes, she is around somewhere." In fact, Julia had returned to Pittsburgh in 1971 and died November 22, 1972. Gruskin asked if his mother would be shocked or embarrassed by his films. Warhol's answer is a complete non sequitur: "She likes to take to the bottle once in a while." In Jean Stein's book on Edie Sedgwick, which Warhol reviled, Emil DeAntonio, an independent filmmaker who knew Warhol in the late 1950s, says that Julia Warhola cleaned compulsively, a notion that contradicts most accounts, got up at 5:00 a.m. and started drinking.[88] To Patrick S. Smith, DeAntonio admitted, "Nobody ever got upstairs. Andy had his painting up there and his mother. And she was a fairly heavy drinker [and] cleaned the house for Andy [and] made sure that he went to church."[89]

Apparently, DeAntonio never got upstairs himself, and he offered no evidence for his claim.

After Warhol's death, biographers picked up the theme. According to Fred Lawrence Guiles, Julia had a drinking problem and Andy bought Cutty Sark by the case.[90] David Bourdon repeats DeAntonio's unsupported claim that Julia was "an assiduous housekeeper, arising before dawn to start her cleaning chores." He tempers the Cutty Sark allegation, saying, "Andy laughingly claimed that she went through a case of Cutty Sark scotch each week," and adds an imprecise assessment: "Friends occasionally did see her down a large glass of straight scotch, but she never appeared tipsy and when she answered the phone during the afternoon and evening hours she sounded as spry and alert as ever."[91] As stories often proliferated in the biographical literature after Warhol's death, Victor Bockris also repeats DeAntonio's account of early morning housecleaning and, based on Carlton Willers's portrayal from the early 1950s of a supposedly staggering, slightly drunk Julia, "giggling uncontrollably at some private thought," he concludes that she was "beginning to develop a drinking problem."[92] In the end, Julia's weekly case of Scotch, like her twenty-five cats, may be a story that's too good not to be true. Despite his claim about Julia's "drinking problem," Bockris admits that the "alcoholic mother" trope, which recalls Warhol's early fascination with Truman Capote's mother, was "a staple of Warhol's emerging legend which he took pains to embellish."[93] Gerard Malanga told me, "Julia liked her Scotch. No, I never saw her drink a drop, but maybe she did. I don't know. A little drop once in a while."[94]

The biographers' derogatory descriptions evoked sharp denials from the family. John Warhola said, "They wrote all kinds of things about mother. She never drank. That infuriated me."[95] When Bockris visited Pittsburgh to promote his Warhol biography in 1989, John refused to appear on television with him.[96] James Warhola objected to a *New York Times* reviewer who made the same claim: "My grandmother did not live in a basement with a few sticks of furniture and drink Scotch all day long. I guarantee you that she had a lovely garden apartment with beautiful furniture, and she did not drink!"[97]

The family's reaction to exaggerated descriptions of alcohol abuse is natural, but there are indications that Julia may have enjoyed a drink from time to time. Nathan Gluck wrote in 1971, "As for mrs. warhol, she's a sweet old lady, she is approaching her 80th year. her english is adequate and quaint. she's not an alcoholic—she has a heart condition and other infirmities for which the doctor once prescribed a shot of scotch now and then—so Andy buys his mother Chivas Regal!!"[98] Evidence of Chivas Regal in the house is the cover of Julia's prayer book, improvised from a Chivas Regal box. Her grandson Paul Warhola remembered a housekeeper named

Virginia, with whom Julia was friendly. "But one day [Julia] happened to look into her bag and noticed a couple of bottles of Scotch that my uncle used to buy by the case to give out to his friends. That was the end of Virginia."[99] Another grandson fondly recalled a family gathering in Julia's kitchen, when, as was common for Rusyns, a bottle of whiskey stood on the table. In Warhol's 1966 film, featuring his mother and his then boyfriend Richard Rheem, Julia refers to a shopping trip they made together, to which Rheem responds in a whisper, "To buy whiskey." Julia looks away in mild embarrassment. Bockris quotes her grandson George, "I remember that Bubba always used to like to take a drink. I'd be in the kitchen with her, she'd take a drink, wipe her mouth and go, 'Sshhhh.'" Julia would certainly not be the first lonely elderly woman, Rusyn or not, to take solace in a shot of Scotch.

1967: Miková Comes to New York

In *POPism*, Warhol reviewed life in New York in 1967. Miniskirts were in, modeled by "boyishly feminine" girls like Twiggy.[100] Big hats, high boots, and psychedelic prints—"Everything mod-mini-madcap that had been building up since '64 was full-blown." Men's fashions were changing, too, signaling "big social changes that went beyond fashion into the question of sex roles." Be-ins in Central Park attracted thousands to mobilize against the Vietnam War. The Beatles' *Sgt. Pepper's Lonely Hearts Club Band* provided theme music for the summer. The "Exploding Plastic Inevitable" played in the former Slovak Sokol athletic hall on East 71st Street.

Warhol's film *The Chelsea Girls*, which celebrated sex, drugs, and violence, had four hundred screenings in the city, bringing in $25,000 in the first six months of the year.[101] In May, Warhol traveled to the Cannes Film Festival with his entourage, where he dined with Brigitte Bardot, and then to Paris for an exhibition of his *Thirteen Most Wanted Men*. More than once in their travels, the "kids," as Warhol called his acolytes, were thrown out of hotels for their scandalous behavior. In the summer of 1967, Warhol met Candy Darling, a transgender actress, and a sadistic boyfriend who went by the name of Rod La Rod. Throughout the year, Warhol spent evenings at Max's Kansas City restaurant. The back room, a hangout for artists, actors, and celebrities of the counterculture, became known for conflict and sexual license.

In its best light, the atmosphere of 1967 was captured by Warhol and Pat Hackett in a description of the West Village: "There were lots of flower children tripping and lots of tourists watching them trip. 8th Street was a total carnival. Every store had purple trip books and psychedelic posters and plastic flowers and beads and incense and candles, and there were Spin-Art places where you squeezed paint onto a spinning wheel and made your own Op Art painting (which the kids loved to do on acid), and pizza parlors and ice cream stands—just like an amusement park."[102]

One event Warhol left out of his review of the year, an experience that sparked as much culture shock in his own life as any of the 1960s phenomena, was the visit of his aunt Eva, Julia's youngest sister, from Miková. Julia had repeatedly invited Eva, and Andy arranged to pay for the trip. Eva said she would rather have the dollars than spend them on airfare, but Julia told her, "I want to see you. There has always been money and there will always be money, but we will not always be."[103] Propelled by family difficulties that she yearned to share with Julia, Eva made a quick decision, writing in the margin of a letter, "I'm definitely coming. Just give the money for the passport to that agent." In an undated letter, Julia writes to an American cousin, "I am inviting my sister Eva here from Europe. I sent the affidavit a long time ago, but it goes very slowly with the passport. My son Andrew invites my sister here—$500 for the journey. I don't know when she will come."[104] In an "Affidavit of Support," dated February 23, 1967, Andy Warhol attested that it was his intention and desire to have his relative, Eva Bezekova, come to the United States for a temporary visit not to exceed six months. He stated his occupation as "advertising" at Andy Warhol Enterprises, Inc., and listed his average yearly earnings as $10,000.[105]

Eva traveled first to Prague, where her daughters helped her negotiate the embassies and airlines to acquire the necessary papers. No one was allowed to accompany her to America. Julia's niece and namesake said, "The communists would never have let me out of the country."[106] So, Eva traveled on Air India from Prague to New York on June 9, 1967, wearing a tag around her neck to identify her. A flight attendant took charge of her for the journey.[107] Eva said, "I was terrified when they took me to the plane. Such a small cylinder chamber that carries people inside. Phut! and up you go, faster than up a ladder. It smoked like a chimney and floated up and down."[108] She told her husband, "When I arrived in America and got out of the airplane there were families waiting for everyone, but I stood there all alone and nobody came up to me. But then an old lady [*babka*] in a headscarf approached me and asked, 'Have you seen Eva Bezeková?' 'But that's me, sister,' I answered."[109] Despite decades of exchanging letters and photos, each sister retained the image of the other as she had been in 1921. Coming face to face in old age was overwhelming for both.

Eva stayed with Julia and Andy at 1342 Lexington Avenue and then visited family in Pittsburgh. Julia's grandchildren remember *Teta* (Aunt) vaguely, as an elderly woman dressed in dark clothes, long skirts, and an ever-present headscarf. A granddaughter recalls, "She seemed to have it on all day and all night. I don't think she ever took it off. She was a bigger woman then Bubba. Bubba was a small slight lady and Teta was big."[110] Photographs point up the cultural differences between the sisters.

Eva Bezeková's comments about her trip to America were preserved in an interview with Michal Bycko. Twenty years after the trip and just a year before her death, she provided a radical outsider's view of Julia's life in New York. Not surprisingly, she was shocked and frightened by America.

> Once I was in the city in a car. I had never seen anything like it There were some seats like in a small bus. They looked like armchairs. From the outside, the windows were black. I was afraid. I'll suffocate in there. I won't even be able to see the light. But when I got in the car, the windows cleared, and it was easy to see everything. We were driven—me, Ulia, and Andriiko—by a fellow who was blacker than shoe polish. Only his eyes, his teeth, and his shoes were white. And when he laughed, his tongue was white. He looked like a chimneysweep or a devil, but he was kind.

Robert Zecker begins his article on Slavic immigrants and race: "Almost from the moment they got off the boat, immigrants have been telling stories, perhaps apocryphal, about their first bewildered encounters with the 'Negro.' The steerage passenger's first sighting of blacks has become a trope, representing newcomers' fear and amazement at this frightening place."[111] Eva's astonishment is understandable. Julia's familiarity and comfort with the driver and the chauffeured car was a measure of the distance between them. At the time, Julia also had an African American cleaning woman, probably the Scotch-thieving Virginia, whose kisses unnerved Eva.

Eva remembered shopping with a pretty young woman who came to visit Julia. "She had just one flaw, she smoked like a man and talked strangely. I was surprised that Ulia understood her."

> We went to a store. We don't have stores like that here. There was so much it will never be all bought up. Ulia bought me a sweater, a modern one, and I told her, "But Ulio, this is for a young woman, not for me! She just laughed. Apparently, that's what they wear there. Andriiko just watched and didn't say anything, but when Ulia said something to him, he would answer something like O-KOO. I didn't understand what that meant, but it was enough for Ulia. Ulia never asked the saleslady for an item, just pointed, and Andriiko

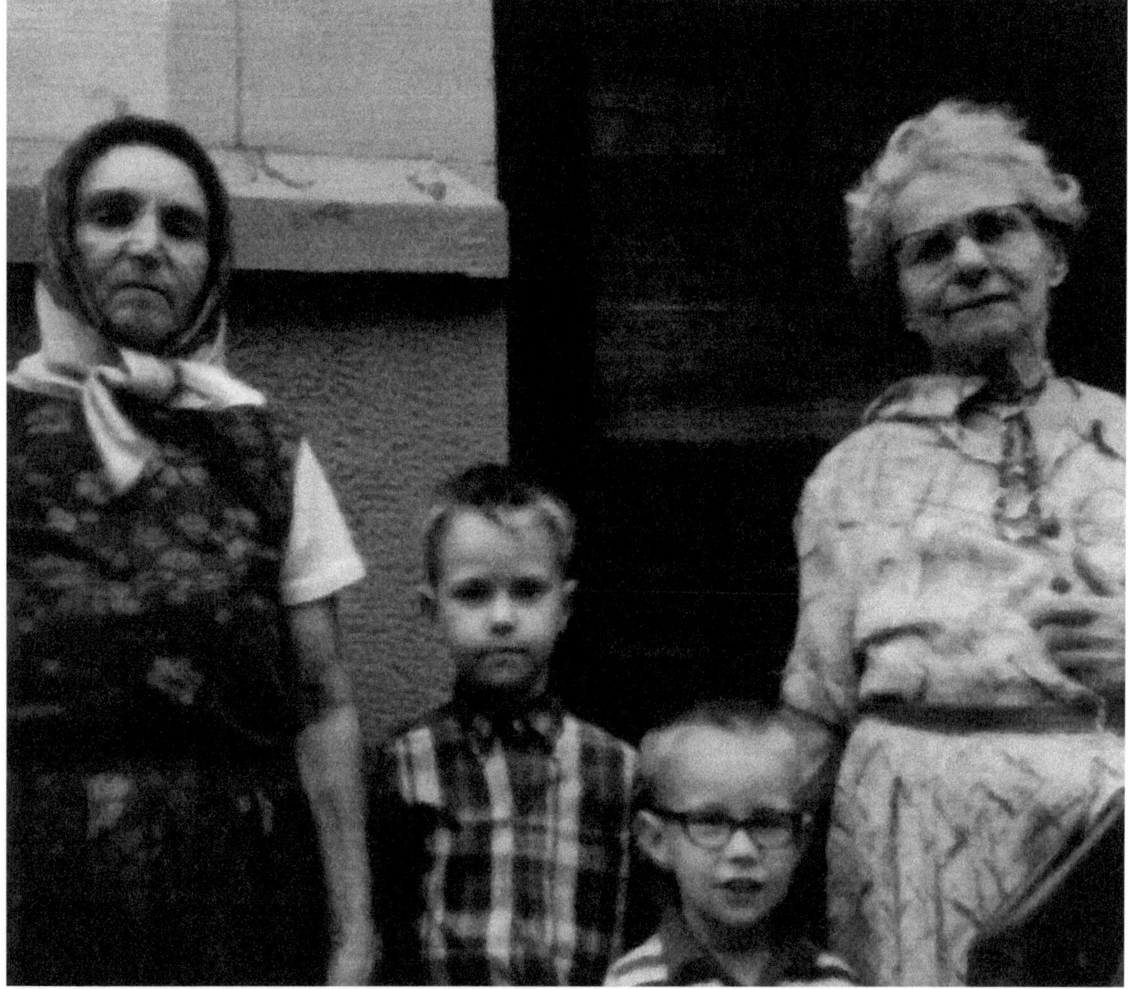

Figure 6.4. Eva Bezeková and Julia Warhola with Julia's grandsons Jeffrey and Donald Warhola, 1967.

would ask for it in American. Ulia bought a scarf for my old man, such an expensive one. He still has it. They always bought a lot, as if it were Christmas.

After decades of sending parcels, Julia now wanted to provide for her sister in person. She may also have desired to impress her, to tout her Americanness. While Andy's income was at a relatively low point at the time, picking out sweaters and scarves for purchase would have been no financial burden for him, and no longer uncommon for Julia. Eva's airline tickets show that while she departed Prague with suitcases weighing seven kilograms, she returned with twenty-five kilograms, paying an excess-weight charge of $22.40.[112] Eva could not understand the extravagance that, at one time, would have also discomfited Julia. She asked, why did Julia "waste kilos of oranges," squeezing out the juice for Andy every morning?

Eva's reaction to Warhol's house underscores just how primitive Miková was, even in 1967. "They build houses there as high as the sky. God will punish them for that! . . . Those buildings like the one Ulia lived in didn't even have a cold cellar. They put their food in a big steel box. (Now I know it was a refrigerator.) They didn't eat much there. They have a lot, but don't eat it. And when they do eat, for four days they eat from that iron box." Photographs of Eva with her American sisters, Julia, Mary, and Anna, depict the enormous chasm that existed between the modern cities of New York and Pittsburgh and old-fashioned Miková. But surprisingly, Eva's favorite activity in America was going to the harness races with Paul Warhola and his family at the Meadows Racetrack, where she placed a bet and won $50.

Eva attended church with Julia in New York and gathered with family in Pittsburgh and Lyndora. She met her brothers, Stephen, John, and Andrew, and her sisters, Mary and Anna, all of whom had emigrated to America before Eva was five years old. She was most comfortable in rural Lyndora. Andy's cousin Nora remembered, "She loved it here. She said she would come back to stay if her husband died. It was the first time she tasted Jell-O."[113] Asked by her Miková family about Carpatho-Rusyns in America, Eva responded, "There are a lot of them, as many as poppy seeds. They have it good, but they yearn for home, the Old Country. Every time Ulia began to speak about the homeland, she started to cry. She grieved for the child who died there."

Eva found most Americans "ungodly," making an exception for Julia and Andy, who, she said, were "God-fearing." The only positive thing she had to say about Andy was that he prayed together with her and his mother. "Everyone there is unwell. That Andy is so strange. He looks as though he's never seen the sun. He's never still. He's always doing something or he's on the phone. In his hand he carries a kind of little box that a human voice comes from. It's Satan's work! . . . The people around him were also odd. All of them were white with strange eyes, like my Vasyl when he's been drinking. They looked at you as though they didn't see you. I didn't like that America. There was nothing good there. Those people are different."

Although Eva had a six-month visa, she could endure America for barely two months, and she left for Prague on August 6. Eva noticed that Warhol was annoyed.

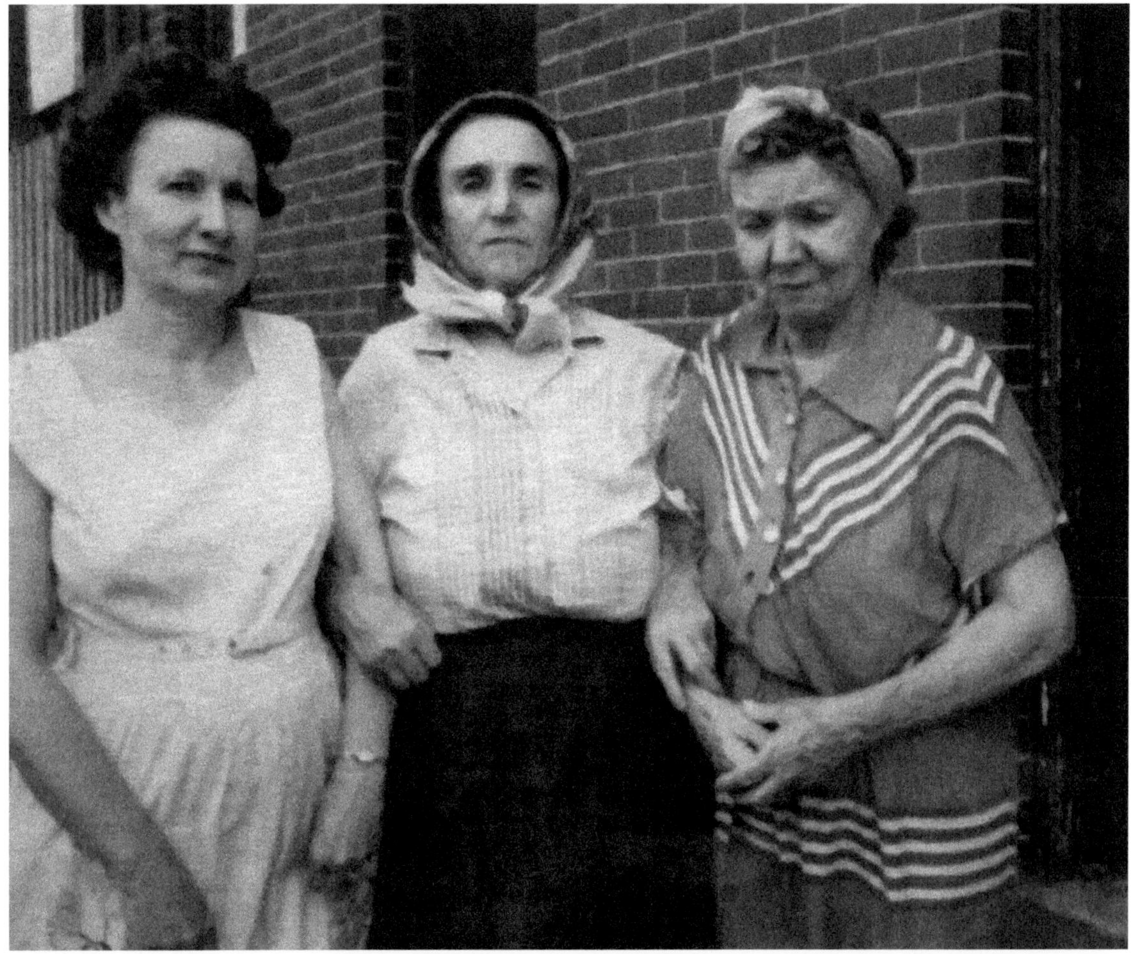

Figure 6.5. Julia's sisters. Left to right: Anna Zavacky Lasky, Eva Zavacky Bezekova, Mary Zavacky Preksta, 1967.

When I was leaving for home, Ulia, Andriiko, and that black fellow took me to the airplane. Ulia was crying, but I was happy to be going home. Andriiko was angry that I didn't want to stay and take care of Ulia. She was already ill. I said good-bye to Ulia at the airport. Andriiko didn't kiss me. I said to him, "Andriiko, my boy, let me at least kiss your hand for bringing me here." He just said that "O–KOO" and left. Ulia was crying. She cried a lot. I was crying too. It was the last time we saw one another. May God grant her eternal peace.

Forty-five years of separation and a hundred-year gap in culture and life experience could not be easily bridged, even for these tightly bonded sisters. While Warhol's friends and contacts saw Julia as peasant-like, by contrast with Eva, an authentic old-country *babka*, Julia had become American.

Pittsburgh Women

Women and the Trades, the first volume of the *Pittsburgh Survey*, investigated the conditions of labor for working women in the man's city of iron and steel. The author Elizabeth Beardsley Butler noted the paradox: "Pittsburgh as a workshop for women seems a contradiction in terms."[114] Her investigation in 1907 and 1908 took her into more than 400 factories employing over 22,000 women. Her findings showed, not surprisingly that women worked long hours in conditions that were injurious to health, at wages that were insufficient to sustain them. Upscale work in shops was available only to English speakers. Garment factories employed Jewish, German, and American girls, while east European women were more likely to work in tenement sweat shops that manufactured cheap cigars, known as stogies. Most of the processes involved in making stogies could be done by unskilled labor, and Slavic women did the least desirable job of stripping tobacco.[115] According to a manager of a stogy factory, "No girl can keep up her pace more than six years," and the sociologist Butler concluded that the stogy industry "is taking young, underdeveloped girls, lifting their speed to its highest pitch, and wearing them out."[116]

Like their male counterparts in the mills, Slavic women workers were recognized for their docility. A foreman told Butler, "They would work all night if I would give them the chance. We never have any trouble with them. We can't give them enough to do." Butler's interpretation of this backhanded compliment is disparaging: "For the most part, the Slavic women in Pittsburgh are limited by lack of training, trade indifference, and a stolid physical poise that cannot be speeded at the high pressure to which an American girl will respond. They accept factory positions that girls of other races regard as socially inferior. They consent to do the rough and unpleasant work, work that leads and can lead to nothing except coarsening of fibre and a final break in strength."[117] She was more complimentary of the "fair, light-handed, delicately built" Slavic girls who worked in canneries and cracker factories, and she was seemingly in dubious awe of the "rough-skinned stolid women" who worked in glass factories, lamp works, and the metal trades. But regardless of where they worked, Slavic women, like Slavic men, received little credit for their industriousness and willingness to take on backbreaking work. In the minds of the *Pittsburgh Survey* reformers, who held middle-class American cultural assumptions, their fate was decided: "Either through the barrier of language or in part through their own indifference, they are still used for the less desirable work in such occupations as in a measure they have made their own."[118] In other words, their lamentable situation was due to their own backwardness.

Eva Morawska exposed the divergence of perspectives held by the investigators and the immigrants they studied.

> In the minds of the immigrants, outward acceptance of [deplorable] conditions had a different meaning and a definite practical purpose. It reflected a combination of the cynical generalized pragmatism typical of members of the lowest socioeconomic class, who expect no favors from the ruling groups, whoever they might be, and a deliberate strategy of action in pursuit of the specific life goals that had brought them to America. . . . These hopes of achieving status and prosperity in the New World that had been denied them in the old country remained invisible to Survey investigators. The immigrants' apparently passive acceptance of exploitative work and abusive treatment masked a determined ambition to better themselves.[119]

As critics of the *Pittsburgh Survey* have pointed out, the Progressive reformers "did not acknowledge that working-class families might regard their labor, their fraternal and benevolent organizations, their churches and lodges, and their homes as worthwhile indicators of progress toward their own goals."[120] Slavic women, for whom the greatest old-country compliment was that they were good workers, were accustomed to spending long hours in the fields working alongside men. As immigrants, they accepted the most physically demanding jobs and occupied "socially inferior" positions with pride and dignity. With an eye toward the well-being of the family and the next generation, they violated rigid middle-class gender and workplace norms. For this they were belittled by American reformers and social workers, who had no conception of old-world visions of "status and prosperity." As indications of their progress in the New World, Carpatho-Rusyn immigrants proudly sent relatives in the Old Country photographs of themselves and their children dressed in modern American-style clothing.

By 1920, only 28 percent of Pittsburgh women were wage earners, well below the national average. Even fewer foreign-born women, only 4 percent, worked outside the home.[121] The Zavacky women contributed to household income by working at times with their husbands in the Standard Steel Car Company. Stephen

Zavacky's wife was hired to work as a janitor at the car company in 1928 when she was thirty-nine and had six children. Her sixteen-year-old daughter probably cared for her siblings.[122] Andrew Zavacky's wife took a job as a janitor at Standard Steel at age twenty-seven in 1920, when the oldest of her three children was eight and the youngest was three. She was laid off after two years but returned in 1924 to work as a "heater" in the construction department at 20¢ per hour. Stephen's wife was probably just contributing to family finances, but in 1920, Andrew Zavacky's wife was already sensing the unreliability of her husband, who would soon abandon her, and felt the need to support herself and her children.[123]

Most women who worked outside the home did housecleaning and laundry to bring in extra cash. Domestic workers, among whom were found most Slavic wage-earning women, were not included in Butler's survey of women's employment. "Female Help Wanted" ads in the *Pittsburgh Press* from the 1920s and 1930s demonstrate a specific demand for Carpatho-Rusyn women, known then as "Slavish": "Girl—Reliable. Polish or Slavish for general housework"; "Girl—For housework. Slavish or Hungarian"; "Girl—Foreign. Slavish preferred." The demand for "Slavish" housekeepers counters the criticism leveled by many social workers, who attributed deficiencies in hygiene and housekeeping to ethnicity, rather than poverty.[124] Even discounting language and educational issues, the hard physical labor required of housewives living in tenements with several children and no plumbing made work outside the home almost impossible. When the Warhola family lived on Beelen Street in the late 1920s, of their female neighbors, only one dayworker in housekeeping and one office cleaner reported an occupation. Even on Dawson Street, immigrant women were not wage earners. But the 1930 and 1940 federal censuses show many of their twenty-year-old daughters claiming white-collar occupations as stenographers, bookkeepers, and clerks.

"Somebody's Widow"

In 1941, the Greek Catholic Union (GCU) placed an ad for life insurance in the *Amerikansky Russky Viestnik*. It was addressed to immigrant men.

> The city newspapers are filled with advertisements under the caption "Situations Wanted." Many of these pathetic appeals for work are from somebody's widow. If your wife becomes a widow, will she have to resort to the "Situations Wanted" columns? Imagine her answering the questions of the Boss who will have none but efficient

employees. "Can you operate a typewriter?" "Do you know shorthand?" "Do you understand bookkeeping?" "Are you an accountant?" To all these she must answer: "No." Then, "Just what can you do?" "O, sir, I never have done anything but keep house and the babies." But there is no house to keep nor babies to tend in that business institution. Had you not best anticipate this tragic situation of YOUR WIDOW by leaving her a goodly amount of life insurance?

While Julia's life in immigrant America was difficult—losing her husband when she was fifty, raising teenagers on her own, coping with serious illness, cleaning houses for a dollar a day—her position was comparatively enviable. Andrii had left her $600 in GCU life insurance, money in the bank, a mortgage-free house, and funds for Andy's education. Two of her sons did well in the working-class economy, and one was destined for unimaginable heights. But immigrant Slavic women, even more than most working-class women of the time, were dependent on men for their well-being. When husbands died or proved unreliable, women faced difficult choices and bleak prospects.

Widows were most vulnerable, and widows were plentiful. Industrial accidents among immigrants left young and middle-aged widows with small children. In 1920, 15.5 percent of widows were foreign-born, while the corresponding figure among native-born American women was 10.2 percent. Moreover, immigrant women showed a higher percentage of widowhood in the relatively low age group of thirty-five to forty-four years of age.[125] In her study of Pittsburgh's working class, S. J. Kleinberg treats widows as a distinct subclass. "Widowhood left women bereft of mate, income, and place in society simultaneously; in a culture where daily life revolved around the man's coming and going, the husband's death deprived the woman of the linchpin of her existence. His death could be an incalculable emotional loss with drastic economic and social consequences, for even when the man carried insurance, it rarely paid for more than the funeral, with perhaps enough left over for several months' maintenance."[126]

Because Pittsburgh's economy offered so few opportunities for women, the city's philanthropic community focused attention on them. According to Kleinberg, "Few cities matched Pittsburgh's attention to impoverished widows."[127] Since the mid-nineteenth century, Pittsburgh society women had administered religious and social charities that targeted women and children for relief. But class and language barriers meant that few non-English-speaking immigrants sought or received help from mainstream charities. Carpatho-Rusyns and other Slavs turned to their own ethnic churches and fraternal organizations, which managed mortuary and trust funds for their needy compatriots. The Greek Catholic Union provided aid to injured and indigent members, "when financial conditions permit."[128] But since these ethnic organizations depended on contributions from fellow Rusyns who had little surplus to spare, financial conditions did not often permit. In 1918, the GCU opened an orphanage near Scranton to house and educate children who were orphaned or could not be cared for by widowed mothers who were forced to work.

A foreign-born widow had few options. With small children, she could not get a paying job, even if there was something she could qualify for.[129] With little or no English and no education, the only work she could hope to get was housecleaning or taking in laundry. Church communities sponsored raffles, collections, and contributions for new widows, but such support could not be sustained. In *Out of This Furnace*, a young widow is advised: "For a few days everybody is sorry for you; after that you're just another widow. And a widow—there are hundreds of widows. Widows are nothing."[130]

In the early years of Slavic immigration, men outnumbered women by vast margins. In ads under the "Matrimonial" rubric in the *Pittsburgh Press*, a man could reach out to women readers, presenting himself in the best light and setting specific requirements: "Slavish American, aged 28, would like acquaintance of girl or widow with high school education; object matrimony"; "Refined young man, Catholic, Slavish-American, would like acquaintance of girl or widow aged 25 to 32." Widowers invited women to raise their children: "Slavish widower, coal miner with 2 children, 5 and 9 years, having $1,400, desires to make acquaintance with Slavish or Bohemian or Polish-speaking lady of Catholic religion, aged 30 to 42"; "Slavish widower, aged 40, naturalized American, wishes acquaintance with a lady or widow, aged 30 to 40; no objection 2, 3 children, and weighing not over 150 pounds, not less 110 pounds." Of course, there are no such ads from women. Often a widow's only hope was to remarry as quickly as possible. Church and family networks may have immediately begun to search out eligible husbands, but too often a hasty decision landed a widow in an abusive marriage. Many found a solution in a malleable relationship that would provide support, even if it ran afoul of legal or moral conventions.

The picture of Slavic immigrants painted in most general surveys and enshrined in the imaginations of their descendants shows them to be religious, hardworking, frugal, family-oriented, and upright, their only likely fault being a penchant for drink. But the underside of family life—abuse, divorce, abandonment, and infidelity—has been less explored in quantitative studies of immigrants, in part because families concealed awkward facts and covered up for embarrassing relatives. No ethnic group is devoid of family stories about a grandmother who left an abusive husband, widows who lived with male "friends" to whom they were not technically married, and young women who "got into trouble." But evidence of broken marriages, unwanted pregnancies, illegitimate children, and sexual abuse is largely anecdotal, preserved more readily in works of historical fiction than in legal records. In Bell's *Out of This Furnace*, the flawed protagonist abandons his wife and lives with a seductive woman who takes his money and leaves him when his business fails. Another man grumbles about his wife: "I give her my whole pay, I drink only on paydays, I beat her no oftener than twice a week, and still she complains."[131] In *Turnip Blues*, Helen Campbell's award-winning novel from 1993 about family, guilt, shame, and forgiveness in the lives of Rusyn women in Pittsburgh, granddad comes home from work at the mill to beat his wife, who takes to the bottle in desperation.[132] The novel's psychologically complex figures suffer from a congenital lack of self-esteem even into the second and third generations. Sociologists of the Progressive movement referred vaguely to the "immorality" accompanying "the boarder problem" and other habits persisting from the old world or arising from grim conditions of the new, but for the most part, the embarrassing details were whispered only among family.

Commonly hushed-up facts can be found in the desperate notices published in Slavic-language newspapers under the rubric "Where is?"[133] A brother seeks his sister, who had been working as a servant for a gentleman in New York before she disappeared. A mother is looking for her sixteen-year-old daughter who ran off with the church cantor, who left a wife and family in the Old Country. Wandering husbands and wayward wives were sought in pitiful appeals. "I'll give $5.00 to whoever can tell me where to find my husband Hnat S., a native of Gorlice County. He is tall and thin; recently he was working in the sugar refinery in Jersey City. He left me last year on Easter Sunday." A husband asks, "Who knows where to find Tatiana L. and Nikolai R., who fled together from St. Louis. Tatiana left her husband, took $200, and went off to see the world with her lover." "My husband Ivan K. left me with four children and without a cent." "Where is Luka S., who was living in Butler, Pa. and left his pregnant wife Efrozina and a five-year-old son. She will be forced to put the children in an orphanage and find work to survive."

Some notices sound like modern-day soap-opera plots: "Fetso R., twenty-five years old, six feet tall, of powerful dark build, took off on August 2 with my wife from Ford City, Pa., probably headed for the New York area. He speaks only

Rusyn and doesn't know how to read or write. My wife Maria is of medium height, plain-looking, blonde, twenty-six years old. They took a substantial amount of my money. A reward is offered for information." This notice was posted by a priest:

> On February 3, 1912, Vasyl H. married Olena S. in Latrobe, Pennsylvania. A few weeks after the wedding he left his wife. It has been reported that he is going by the name Vasyl D. and that he has a wife in Europe. Anyone who knows this man's whereabouts should contact the undersigned. If Vasyl himself comes across this notice, he should write whether it is true that he is married in the Old Country. Olena should not be tormented. If she is certain that her marriage is invalid, she will marry someone else and at least partially forget this injustice.

Such heartbreaking messages were published over decades in Slavic American newspapers. The details of each incident are left to the imagination, but it is important to recognize that the rosy image of our sainted ancestors was rarely precise. The reality of difficult economic and social conditions, especially for women, provides context for the life stories of the Zavacky sisters.

Mary

In 1906, Mary Zavacka, two and a half years older than Julia, married Vasyl Preksta in Miková at age seventeen. Ten months after their wedding, her husband emigrated to Guernsey County, Ohio, the site of seventy-seven bituminous coal mines. Thousands of immigrants from eastern Europe, especially Slovaks and Rusyns, were attracted to the Cambridge Coal Field.[134] Ruins of an Orthodox church stand today in Belle Valley, and a Byzantine Catholic church, established in 1898, is still active in Pleasant City. The names of the towns stand in stark contrast to the dirt and coal dust of the breakers, the row houses of the coal patches, and the culm banks that peppered the landscape. In February 1910, Mary followed her husband to Ohio, accompanied by his adolescent sisters, Anna and Zuzanna. The Preksta family settled in Byesville, where Vasyl's brother and cousins lived with their large families. Today, Byesville is the site of a life-size bronze statue of a coal miner, a memorial to the more than four hundred men who lost their lives in southeastern Ohio in the heyday of coal mining.

According to census records, by the end of January 1920, Mary and Vasyl had four daughters and a newborn son named Andy. There is no further sign of Andy

Preksta in census records, which suggests his early death. Another son, William, was born September 18, 1920. He was named after his father, who, like many Rusyn men named Vasyl, went by William or Charles in official American documents. In less than a year, baby William died of cholera infantum, known commonly as "summer diarrhea," an often-fatal form of gastroenteritis occurring in infants. The Prekstas had two more children—a son John, born in 1922, and a daughter Josephine Justina, known as Tinka.

When Tinka was born on May 17, 1924, her father had already been dead a month. Vasyl (Charles) Preksta died on April 22, the result of an operation performed on April 6 for a mastoid infection caused by chronic otitis media. The doctor's notes refer to a brain abscess stemming from the operation, a common complication in the pre-antibiotic era. The economic difficulties and emotional trauma Mary faced during those months can only be imagined. On October 28, 1924, six months after her husband's death, she submitted a Petition for Naturalization to the Court of Common Appeals in Cambridge, perhaps prompted by the fact that many states required citizenship for a person to receive Mothers' Pension benefits and any other government aid that might have been available. In her application for citizenship, Mary listed the names of her six living children and admitted that she could not speak English, "just a few words."

Left in Ohio with her husband's family and six children under the age of thirteen, Mary probably longed to be with her own siblings in Pennsylvania. The *1930 US Federal Census* shows Mary Preksta living on Beelen Street in Pittsburgh, a few blocks from her sister Julia's family, where she rented a house for $15 monthly. She now claimed to speak English. Five children live with her. Her oldest daughter, Anna, was married, and Helen, her second oldest at sixteen years of age, worked in a beauty salon. Four others, ranging in age from five to thirteen, were in school. Mary likely received financial assistance and support from Julia and Andrii Warhola. Paul and John recalled weekly visits to her home on the North Side when they were children. Even in the late 1960s, Mary wrote Julia that John Warhola had brought her a gift of dried mushrooms. "He always comes to see me."

By 1940, Mary was living in a dodgy neighborhood on Henderson Street on Pittsburgh's North Side. But her homelife had stabilized and she must have enjoyed some measure of financial security. Her oldest daughter Anna and Anna's husband Michael Tarasovich lived with their two children in the same building with Mary. Her twenty-six-year-old daughter Helen had married a man from Boston and divorced him in short order, citing "utter desertion." By 1940, Helen was living with her mother and working as the manager of a business for a "private photographer," making an annual income of $900, about $16,000 in 2020 purchasing power. Her photography business was an outgrowth of the photo shop run by John Warhola in the converted root cellar on Dawson Street, when Johnny Preksta worked in the darkroom and his sisters were colorists and assistants.[135] In 1941, Helen married a son of Italian immigrants, not in her Greek Catholic home parish, but in Guardian Angels Roman Catholic Church, a Polish parish in the West End. Although Helen's divorce decree was submitted together with her marriage license, this Roman Catholic priest was either unaware of it or willing to bend the rules.

From New York, Julia followed developments in her Pittsburgh family and may have visited to attend weddings and funerals. Mary's oldest daughter Anna Tarasovich died in 1956, and her forty-year-old daughter Milanna Loy died in 1958. Photographs among Julia's possessions are captioned, "Sister Mary's daughter Milanna was so sick," and "This is sister Mary and sister Anna [in the photo]. We were so sad." Mary's son Johnny returned from World War II with a case of what today would be called post-traumatic stress disorder, which left him seriously disabled. In later years, John and Paul Warhola went out of their way to assist him.

Mary is later identified inconsistently in records as the widow of William Preksta or the spouse of Michael Guke (alternate spelling Gukl). No marriage records can be found, but city directories of the 1920s and 1930s show Mary living with Guke. In 1931, they had a son, George, who was identified as George Guke or George Preksta.[136] On Michael Guke's 1965 death certificate, his son George reported the Preksta-Guke marital status as "separated" but Michael Guke's obituary identifies Mary as his wife. However, the family's reports to medical authorities and newspapers do not match official records. At the time of Michael Guke's death, Mary had already been married for eleven years to Michael Lacko (alternate spelling Lasko). Court records show that on July 12, 1954, at age sixty-five, Mary Preksta and Michael Lacko, seventy-one, applied for a marriage license. In the application, she attests that she had been married only once before to Vasyl Preksta, making no mention of Guke. Mary and Michael Lacko were married on July 31, 1954, at Holy Ghost Byzantine Catholic Church. When she died in 1970, Mary's obituary identified her as the wife of Michael Lacko, mother of three living daughters and two sons (John Preksta and George Guke), grandmother of twenty, and great-grandmother of one.

The relationship between Mary Zavacky Preksta and Michael Guke seems to have been unofficial and malleable, but probably economically critical when she had small children to support in the 1930s. There is evidence that Guke had been married in 1905; it is uncertain whether he was officially divorced. In her study of immigrant women, Donna Gabaccia writes, "Immigrant men of peasant backgrounds, learning that common-law and civil marriages were legal in the U.S., sometimes concluded that Old World religious prohibitions against bigamy or cohabitation by the unmarried had no force in the United States, where 'people could do as they wanted' sexually."[137] There are numerous examples of pragmatic liaisons that disregarded legal issues in favor of economic advantage, especially for widows. They were quietly acknowledged within the family. But American society required a degree of decorum, especially when it came to the status of children, and information in some documents and obituaries could be "adjusted" to blur unwelcome truths.

Little is known about Michael Lacko, Mary's second husband. According to the *1920 US Federal Census*, he was born in Austria in 1882 and is identified as "Slavish." Working as a laborer in the "Bolt Works," he had already been widowed twice. From her late sixties until her death in 1970, Mary lived in Lacko's brick row house on the North Side with his two sons and their families. Julia addressed letters to Mary as "Mrs. Mary Lasko." No correspondence survives from earlier decades when Mary lived with Michael Guke. In a letter dated June 30, 1965, John Warhola drily tells his mother, "I heard Mike Juke [*sic*] died last week. I did not see him."[138]

Mary was Andy Warhol's "nice aunt." In his *Diaries*, he remembers "something that happened to me at her house once. She always gave me pennies for candy and so I used to like to visit her, she was good to me, she lived in a house on the North Side. And one day I remember she had a lady over who had no teeth and the lady was eating a bowl of soup and she didn't finish it and my aunt gave it to me and made me finish it. I guess because she had no money and didn't want to waste food."[139] Mary's youngest child, Tinka, was the closest in age to Andy of all his cousins. As children, they played while their mothers sang together and cried over letters from Europe.[140] It was to his Aunt Mary's house that Andy retreated during his father's wake. Mary appears in many family photos, usually with a somewhat melancholy expression.

In a letter to Julia that can be dated to late 1969, Mary thanked her sister for the two dollars she had sent and regretted that the sisters could not be together. She consoled Julia, "I would like to be with you, because I don't have long to live. We only have *Pani* Maria, the Blessed Virgin. She will help you." Mary then had less than a year to live, and Julia would live only two more years.

Anna

In 1917, the social worker Grace Abbott wondered why so many girls from Galicia and northern Hungary had the courage "to undertake this excursion into the unknown."

> A professor in the Polish University of Lemberg [L'viv], which Americans have learned since the war began is the capital of Galicia and the center of a large Polish and a larger Ruthenian population, told me that the first thing I needed to understand in any study of emigration from this region was that the peasants did not go because they needed work; there was plenty of work for them there; he knew landlords whose crops were rotting in the ground because the men and women of the neighborhood had all gone to America. It was a fever that was running through the entire peasantry, he explained. They went to the United States as he might go to the next street. It is much simpler to break entirely with the past, to abandon the picturesque costume, the little farm, the dependence on the landlord of the neighborhood, and to stake everything on possible success in America than to try to break down the century-old social barriers of the village. In other words, it was the fact that apparently nothing could change either for themselves or for their children, which sent many of these women from Austria and Hungary to America.[141]

In a study of emigration from Hungary, Julianna Puskás notes, "From what I learned about the beginning of emigration among the women, especially the young ones, it appears that, initially, the villagers spoke ill of any girl who would take such a step. . . . Generally speaking, the young women who left for overseas were those who had come into conflict with the community's value system in one way or another."[142] For adventurous young women, emigration sparked ambitious aspirations and opened unknown possibilities. But it also held dangers. If Mary's life was a sad drama, Anna's was a soap opera, with its share of tragedy, violence, and mystery.

Born on September 6, 1898, Anna was seven years younger than Julia. In America, whether purposefully or for lack of certainty, Anna often shaved two years off her age, citing a birth date of 1900. In the federal censuses of 1920 and 1930, Anna reported that she had arrived in the United States in 1910. That means she emigrated at about twelve years of age, which would be quite unusual, unless she traveled with family. Her sister Mary Preksta emigrated in 1910, but Anna's name is not found on the same passenger list. According to Raymond Herbenick, the author of *Andy Warhol's Religious and Ethnic Roots*, his mother was a classmate of Julia's sister Anna in Lyndora.[143] It is not inconceivable that Anna, who had an adventurous and impetuous spirit, might have wangled passage to her Zavacky relatives in Lyndora, where she may even have gone to school, but it cannot be verified. For better or worse, Anna was certainly the most "American" of the Zavacky sisters.

The first available documentary evidence is Anna's marriage license to Michael Dobriansky (later Dobransky). Dobransky, a Rusyn from Galicia, came to the United States in 1906 at age nine with his mother, joining his father in Pittsburgh. The oldest of ten children, he was working in a Cambria County coal mine at age seventeen. Michael enlisted in the Pennsylvania National Guard and served eight months before he was honorably discharged by a surgeon's certificate on November 27, 1917. On December 11, the *Pittsburgh Post-Gazette* reported the issuance of a marriage license to Michael Dobransky, age twenty-one, and Anna Zavacky, nineteen. Their son Paul was born six months later. The 1920 census shows Michael, Anna, and baby Paul living on Hansen Avenue in Lyndora with Michael's mother. A daughter, Josephine Justina, was born in 1920.

Dobransky's military service did not extend beyond his time in the national guard. When he applied for veteran's service compensation in 1920, his address was the State Sanitorium in Cresson. Located on land donated by Andrew Carnegie two thousand feet above sea level in the Allegheny Mountains, Cresson provided the most up-to-date treatment for tuberculosis—fresh air, diet, bed rest, and isolation. Long-term treatment was free of charge to all patients.[144] On February 2, 1922, a note in the *Altoona Tribune* reported, "Michael Dobransky, who has been ill for some time, is in a critical condition." He died on March 20 at age twenty-five of miliary tuberculosis, an especially lethal form of the disease.

Dobransky's death certificate indicates that the duration of the disease was three years and six months, that is, it went back at least to September 1918. During World War I, tuberculosis was the most common reason for discharge from military service. More than 22,000 cases were reported, 18,500 of them in United States training camps.[145] Public health officials debated whether the government was responsible for the care of sick draftees and trainees, or whether they should be released to their families, where they might spread tuberculosis in their communities. In May 1918, the Medical Department adopted a policy that "any soldier who shall have been accepted on his first physical examination . . . shall be considered to have contracted any subsequently determined physical disability in the line of duty."[146] It is unknown whether Dobransky, who probably contracted TB during his stint in the National Guard, was eligible for benefits. At the time of his death, his widow Anna was twenty-three years old with two children under four. Her four years of marriage must have been largely consumed by her husband's illness. She had little education, no occupation, and no marketable skills.

Just nine months after Michael's death, the *Butler Eagle* announced the issuance of a marriage license to Anna Dobransky and Peter Kozlowski.[147] Kozlowski, twenty-three years old, was a bricklayer living in Lyndora. Although records of an official name change could not be found, sometime soon after their marriage in 1923, Kozlowski started using an alternate surname, Lasky. He may have been born in 1900, 1901, or 1902, in Cleveland, as he claimed upon three admissions to the Allegheny County Workhouse. Or he may have been born in Poland, as suggested by his mother's immigration data, as he himself attested on his World War II draft registration card, and as indicated in his obituary. A notation on the marriage license indicates they were married in a Greek Catholic church, and Anna Zavacka Dobransky adopted the name she would use for most of her life, Anna Lasky.

We cannot know what attracted Anna to Lasky, other than the urgent needs of a widow. Unlike her sisters Mary and Julia, who had married before they left the Old Country, Anna came of age in America at the beginning of the Roaring Twenties. Her vivacious personality must have sought release from illness and childcare in the social and cultural shifts then taking place in Pittsburgh and the nation. The rise of consumerism and growing affluence tempted immigrants who felt oppressed in factory jobs and ethnic slums to change their lot in life by whatever means possible. Secularization and liberalization of norms, along with music, movies, and other new entertainments, promoted a permissive culture that began to alter traditional notions of morality. A great-nephew remembered Anna in her later years as a high-spirited dyed redhead who loved to dance. She may have seen the ambitious Lasky as a potential escape from the hardships of working-class immigrant life, but she could not have known how bumpy the road ahead would be.

On January 22, 1924, a year after their marriage, a son, Samuel, was born. Eight months later, Anna Lasky filed charges against her husband for nonsupport.[148] She testified that during the previous year Pete Lasky did "unlawfully fail to furnish and provide his wife and minor child with the necessaries of life, and that she is compelled to earn her own living by hard manual labor." Lasky was arrested in August and committed to the county jail. Court records do not indicate whether the case went to trial, but within a year Anna and her husband were in court again.

On May 22, 1925, Anna charged Lasky with felonious assault and battery with intent to murder, by striking her on the head and body with his fists. "And further, the said defendant did then and there point firearms and discharge the firearms with intent to kill." At a hearing, witnesses for Mrs. Lasky included Eva Dobransky, the mother of her first husband. Peter Lasky was returned to jail in default of $1,000 bail, and in June, he was indicted by a grand jury on three counts of assault and battery. He pleaded guilty to two counts, but court records do not indicate whether he served time.

By October, Lasky was in court again, this time charged by the Commonwealth with adultery.[149] A warrant was issued by a county detective, who testified that several times over the past year, Lasky had carnal knowledge of one Anna Peters, "not being the wife of the said Pete Lasky and the said Pete Lasky being a married man and having a lawful wife alive at the time." Peters testified at the trial, describing an incident that might today be designated rape. Peter Lasky, with a buddy, took her out driving. When they stopped by the side of the road, the accomplice left the scene and, "Pete Lasky . . . asked me to get in the back seat of the car, which I did, and Pete had intercourse with me."

Lasky pleaded guilty and was sentenced to a year in the Allegheny County Workhouse. His intake information describes him as twenty-four years old, five feet, ten inches tall, 175 pounds, with black hair and blue eyes. He gave his place of birth as Ohio, his religion as Roman Catholic, and his occupation as bricklayer. He had left school at age fourteen, and he admitted that he was "occasionally intemperate" in his drinking.[150] While he was incarcerated, Lasky's sister, Sophia Kozlowski, petitioned the court to release him to attend the funeral of his father. Lasky was released on $300 bond for five days in July, his sentence was commuted to eight months, and he was discharged in August 1926.

The Allegheny County Workhouse, located outside the town of Blawnox, ten miles northeast of Pittsburgh, maintained a prison population from 1869 until 1971. The inmates, most of whom were convicted of minor offenses, worked a one-thousand-acre farm. Inmates imprisoned with Lasky were charged with vagrancy and indecent exposure (each of these offenses carried sentences of thirty days), aggravated assault and child neglect (three months), rape (six months to one year), sodomy (one to two years), forgery (one year), and sale and possession of liquor (eight months to one year).

Lasky did not go home to a welcoming wife. To support herself and her children, Anna worked at the Spaide Shirt Factory in Butler, and in April 1926, she began work as a "heater" in the construction department of the Standard Steel Car Company at 20¢ per hour.[151] In July, she served Lasky with divorce papers at the workhouse. She charged that from April 13, 1923, that is, three months after their wedding, Lasky had committed adultery, endangered her life, and "rendered her condition intolerable and life burdensome." It would be another decade before the divorce was finalized.

From the religious perspective, divorce and remarriage was not an option for Carpatho-Rusyn Greek Catholics. In the Old Country, where marriage united not just two individuals but two families, divorce was unthinkable. However, cases of desertion and spousal abuse were common. Victimized women sought support from family and community, but in peasant culture. domestic violence was often tolerated. By contrast, in the United States, strong-willed women began to take a pragmatic approach and pursue legal action, even if it meant violating ecclesiastical laws. Ewa Morawska searched the divorce files in nearby Cambria County for east central European names. Between 1900 and the late 1930s, about two hundred such cases were filed in the county, a relatively low number of five or six per year. Before World War I, over 40 percent of cases were complaints of husbands deserted by wives. Of that number, almost half of the women were said to have run away with another man, and about one-fourth "ran back to mother." Another one-fourth were accused of open adultery. Women who filed for divorce, making up about 60 percent of divorces, most often charged their husbands with desertion or abuse.[152] Anecdotal evidence and accounts in immigrant newspapers confirm that while divorce, adultery, and "living in sin" were frowned upon by society and concealed by families, our immigrant ancestors were likely no more virtuous than their fellow American citizens.

Among the Zavacky immigrants, it was the women who availed themselves of the option of divorce. Anna Youshock Zavacky divorced Julia's brother Andrii for "cruel and barbarous treatment" and adultery in 1922. Five years later, Andrii remarried in Wellsburg, West Virginia, a "Gretna Green," where Pennsylvania residents transacted marriages to avoid restrictions imposed by their local jurisdiction. Anna Youshock Zavacky was able to support herself and raise three children at a time when divorced women faced social discrimination and economic adversity. In 1924, she was working as a "heater" at the Standard Steel Car Company. Later she was employed for fifty-seven years as a cook for the Phillips family of the Phillips Petroleum Company, in Butler, Pennsylvania, and Texas. She led an active life and did not remarry. A member of the Ladies Guild at her church and the Veterans of Foreign Wars Auxiliary, she was the oldest member of the Women of the Moose lodge when she died in Butler. Although Anna Youshock was from an immigrant family of Carpatho-Rusyn ethnic heritage, however, it is important to note that she was born in the United States, which undoubtedly made it easier for her to advance, independent of a husband. Women with little English and no American education had it much harder.

Prohibition and Petty Criminals

As shown in the earlier newspaper accounts of Rusyn life in Lyndora, middle-class propriety and the temperance movement associated alcohol with working-class immigrants. When Prohibition went into effect nationwide in January 1920, Slavic and other immigrants, whose cultures were more tolerant than Protestant America of imbibing alcohol, generally ignored the law. Many Rusyns, like Julia's brother John Zavacky in Lyndora, continued to produce and consume homemade wine and moonshine as they had in the homeland. Zavacky's daughter recalled that he had a winepress in the basement of his store, but shared his wine only with trusted friends.[153] Because the Volstead Act did not specifically outlaw the consumption of alcohol, there was little risk to those who limited its use to personal consumption and private gatherings. The enterprising Warhola cousin Peter Dudich, who bought a saloon in 1925, only to see it raided the next day, publicly swore off the profession of tavern keeper.[154] But for many low-paid industrial workers, bootlegging and illicit distilleries were attractive moneymaking endeavors.

Historians have noted that the temperance movement never had a chance in Pittsburgh, and stories of speakeasies, corruption, and crime during the 1920s and 1930s are legendary. In August 1920, the *Butler Eagle* newspaper editorialized, "The ease with which whiskey has been obtained at Pittsburgh and other Western Pennsylvania places and transported throughout the country has excited wonder for many months." Between 1926 and 1930, "Eighteen thousand people were arrested; about four million gallons of mash, moonshine, wine, beer and miscellaneous spirits were confiscated; and 3,000 distilleries were shut down. A *Pittsburgh Post* reporter estimated in 1930 that the region was still the 'wettest spot' in the United States."[155] Prohibition gave rise to organized crime and flashy "booze barons," but most of the lawbreakers were small-time offenders, like Lyndora's Pete Lasky.[156] However, violation of the liquor laws often led to more violent crime.

Lasky's first arrest for violation of prohibition in Butler was related to the adultery charge for which he was incarcerated. Two years later, on November 2, 1927, another liquor violation led to violence and spousal abuse. In a search of the apartment in a two-story brick building on Hansen Avenue on Red Row where Lasky was living with Anna and their three-year-old son, officers found one gallon and one pint of intoxicating liquor concealed in the kitchen and bedroom. At the scene, Anna gave evidence against Lasky, claiming that over the previous six weeks he had sold three gallons of liquor to various individuals. In reprisal, Lasky struck, choked, and threatened to kill her. He was charged with drunk and disorderly conduct, assault and battery, resisting arrest, and assault on a police officer. On December 17, he was headed back to the Allegheny County Workhouse. The only charge mentioned in his intake papers was violation of the liquor laws. Lasky served ten months in the workhouse laundry, and was released on October 16, 1928.

Despite all this, the 1930 census finds Anna and Peter Lasky living together at 33 Evergreen Avenue with their children Paul, age twelve, Josephine, ten, and Sam, six. Paul and Josephine Dobransky are listed as stepchildren of Peter Lasky. But Paul and Josephine are also claimed as residents by Eva Dobransky, their paternal grandmother, who lived next door. Records show that the Dobransky children lived off and on with their grandmother until they became adults. As a witness in the 1925 assault case, Mrs. Dobransky had stepped up to protect Anna from Lasky. But divorce was costly, and dealing with the legal system was difficult. At least one trial involved interpreters. Pennsylvania did not grant mothers' pensions to divorced women, unmarried mothers, or families in which fathers had deserted or were imprisoned, and there was a stigma against seeking outside aid. Like many victims of domestic violence, Anna very likely held out hope that her situation would improve and she was unwilling to give up whatever financial support she may have received from Lasky, legal or not. But Lasky drifted further into the criminal world, and Anna found herself in greater danger. In 1933 he pleaded guilty to carrying a concealed .45 caliber automatic pistol, "with the intent therewith unlawfully and maliciously, to do injury to Mrs. Pete Lasky and other persons." He spent another ten months at the workhouse.

Anna finally obtained a divorce from Peter Lasky in 1936. In her petition, she stated again that from the start of their marriage, Lasky had rendered her condition intolerable. In addition, she charged that since April 15, 1931, Lasky "hath willfully and maliciously deserted and absented himself . . . without reasonable cause." Records show that in June 1931, Lasky had attempted to cross from Buffalo, New York, to southern Ontario. With his traveling companion, a railroad worker from Butler, he was barred from entering Canada and was promptly sent back to Ohio, his stated residence. The purpose of his attempted flight to Canada and whatever ties he may have had in Ohio are unknown, but the travel record corroborates Anna's charge of desertion. Her divorce was granted on June 22, 1936.[157] But the timing of Anna's divorce petition was calculated—there was already another man in her life. On October 5, 1936, just four months after Anna's divorce, Butler County records show that one Roy Alven Swartz obtained a divorce from his wife of eleven years. On February 15, 1937, four months after they were both at liberty to marry, Anna Lasky, age thirty-eight, and Roy Swartz, thirty-four, were married by a minister in Wellsburg, West Virginia.

Most marriages among immigrant groups were endogamous, that is, between members of the same ethnic group. The church preached, "Happy marriages usually result when one marries one's own kind," and the first-generation Slavic immigrant community frowned upon exogamous marriages as "not socially appropriate."[158] According to Morawska's study of Johnstown, in the 1920s and 1930s the intermarriage rate between east central Europeans and native-born Americans or people of west European stock did not exceed 5–10 percent.[159] But, she notes, for some immigrant women, marrying a native-born American was the wished for "happy ending" of their American dream. Roy Alven Swartz was born in 1903 in Butler. His family's roots went back to the early nineteenth century in Middlesex, then a rural agricultural area of Butler, where Swartz's father owned a small farm. Swartz was of German and Scottish descent, Presbyterian and Methodist religion, and his grandfathers fought for the Union in the Civil War. To Anna, whose previous husbands were Rusyn immigrants, he might have seemed a "real American." But Swartz turned out to be another poor choice. Like Lasky, he had a record of petty crime—embezzlement of small funds from his employer and liquor law violations. In 1931 he spent thirty days in the Allegheny County Workhouse.

How Anna's life with Roy Swartz unfolded is unknown, but the marriage did not last long. In the 1940 census, Roy Swartz is a lodger in a house on Liberty Street. His marital status, "married," is crossed out, and in his 1942 draft registration, he is "separated," with no dependents. In the same 1940 census, Anna Swartz called herself a widow. She was living with her sixteen-year-old son Samuel and two women lodgers. In 1942, she was again using the name "Lasky" in city directories. Unfortunately, we do not have correspondence between the sisters earlier than the 1950s, so we cannot know to what extent Julia was aware of the twists and turns of Anna's life. The name "Swartz" does not appear in Julia's correspondence or anywhere in Anna's official records after the marriage license, although there is no evidence of divorce.[160]

When Julia wrote to Anna in 1954 about her difficult life with her son in the 242 Lexington Avenue house, she sent wishes to "dear Andrew and your sweet children." Andrew was Andrew Serensky, the most mysterious of Anna's partners. From the early 1950s, Anna's letters to Julia bear the return address of "A. Serensky," and Julia addressed holiday cards to Mr. and Mrs. Andrew Serensky. Although no record of a legal marriage has been found, in the 1951 Butler city directory, both Anna and Andrew cite 14 Thomas Avenue as their address, and they seem to have lived together until Anna's death in 1985. Sixteen years younger than Anna, Andrew Seredynsky (later Serensky) was born in Butler, the son of Rusyn immigrants from Galicia. Andrew's 1996 obituary identifies him as a veteran of World War II and a forty-year employee of ARMCO Forged Steel Wheel Company. No surviving children are mentioned in his obituary. Nor is Anna Zavacky Lasky Swartz, although they were still living (apparently together) on Thomas Street. They were buried from the same funeral home, and both were members of Saints Peter and Paul Ukrainian Orthodox Church. In Anna's obituary, headed "Mrs. Peter Lasky," her first two husbands are named, but there is no mention of Roy Swartz or Andrew Serensky.[161] Anna was buried with her son Paul Dobransky, and the name on her tombstone is Anna Lasky.

In late 1969, Mary Preksta Lacko wrote to Julia, "Sister Anna deeply grieves her dead son. He was very good to her and gave her money. He worked for the government and had good insurance—ten thousand dollars for his sister and his brother Samko and his mama." Anna's oldest son Paul Dobransky enlisted in the Army Air Force in 1939. In the 1940 census, he was at Langley Field in Virginia, and his occupation was "bombardier." His twenty-year-old sister Josephine was a live-in maid for the family of a Butler city government worker. By 1945, she was married, and Paul, who had lived most of his life with his paternal grandmother, listed her as next of kin in his draft registration, which suggests that he may have been estranged from his mother at the time. In August 1945, an item in the *Butler Eagle* noted that along with other enlisted men from Butler, Dobransky had received a commendation "for the part they played in the historic series of five low-level incendiary attacks on Japan during an all-out offensive." His grandmother, Eva Dobransky, is listed as his nearest relative. Master Sergeant Paul Dobransky was discharged from the 484th Bombardment Squadron in October 1945. After the war, he graduated from Carnegie Institute of Technology and was employed as a chemical engineer at the Bureau of Mines.[162] Dobransky died suddenly of a heart attack at age fifty-one on June 16, 1969.

Anna must have been equally proud of her third child, Samuel or "Samko," the son of Peter Lasky, the often-convicted adulterer, abuser, and violator of liquor laws, who spent so much time in the county jail and workhouse. Sam Lasky served as a radio operator in the Philippines during the war, returning home with five Bronze Stars and the Purple Heart. A testament to the social progress made by the second generation of Carpatho-Rusyns and opportunities open to them, Lasky chose a career path diametrically opposed to that of his father. He joined the Butler police force in 1948 and was named chief of police in 1965, a position he held until his retirement in 1973.[163]

Unfortunately, we have no information about Anna's family ties during the turbulent 1920s and 1930s. In 1930, Julia Warhola had three children under eight and, along with her sister Mary, was struggling to survive in the Beelen Street tenements. The brothers in Lyndora were raising large families and working to establish themselves. Whatever they knew about Anna's troubles, they probably kept to themselves. Julia's son John Warhola passed down a memory that Anna had married "a gangster," which must have been common knowledge in the family. He recalled an occasion when the gangster-husband was putting on an overcoat and a pistol fell out of his pocket.[164] Victor Bockris, who interviewed relatives in the 1980s for his Warhol biography, reported that Anna was known as the "black sheep" of the family.[165] Judging from their correspondence in the 1950s and 1960s, Julia was kindhearted and nonjudgmental. Today, nieces are reluctant to talk about Anna, saying only that she "did not live a good life."

Women's Kinship Networks

It was not easy for immigrant women of any ethnicity to "live a good life." The experience of Irish women, who immigrated by the hundreds of thousands beginning in the mid-nineteenth century, is well studied and documented. In *Erin's Daughters in America*, Hasia Diner argues that the persistence of Irish old-world cultural values allowed them to make greater economic and social progress in America than other immigrant women. The Irish-Catholic culture encouraged independence for women, and they married late or not at all. In contrast to Slavic peoples, among Irish migrants there was an excess of women over men. Live-in domestic service gave women a strong economic foothold and allowed them to make economic progress largely independent of men. And of course, most Irish immigrants had the advantage of speaking English. But even given these cultural advantages, the challenge of adaptation to America was substantial. Diner's study explores widowhood and desertion, domestic violence, mental illness, and the "dismal statistics on Irish female arrest records and the astounding figures on alcoholism," which she attributes to "the pathologies of Irish culture." She concludes that ethnicity and cultural values proved to be most significant in the acculturation of Irish women.[166]

Corinne Azen Krause comes to a similar conclusion in her comparative oral history of three generations of Jewish, Italian, and Slavic American women in Pittsburgh.[167] "Ethnic background is a deep and significant fact of life, often ignored, often unconscious, but psychologically important. . . . Female perceptions, the way women carry out their roles at different life stages, the values they hold concerning family, home, education, work, and sexual morality are in part shaped by their ethnic heritage."[168] Among the three ethnic groups she studied, Krause found that Slavic women were most likely to attend a nationality church and to live in an ethnic neighborhood, and they were more likely than Italian women to participate in social activities with others of their own ethnic background.[169] They were less likely than Jewish or Italian women to say their ethnic identity was very important to them, but this was likely the result of the confusion of ethnic identity among many Slavs. Similarly, it is not surprising that they were least likely to feel a bond to their European country of origin, given the lack of a stable national homeland. For lack of a nation state, Slavic women were more committed to their ethnic church than were Italian women.

Traditional culture defined a distinctive system of values that Carpatho-Rusyn women brought with them to the New World to help them stand up to the disorganizing forces they encountered in industrial Pittsburgh, but old-world patterns of social control and family support were disrupted. Modern American culture exerted a seductive and deleterious attraction. Instead of relating exclusively with people and family who were known to one another, individuals were now exposed to unfamiliar ways of being. Women, more than men, missed the security of the structures of the Old World. Years of poverty in Pittsburgh slums and Lyndora factories, widowhood, desertion, and domestic violence tested the strength of even the hardiest of women. They could now avail themselves of legal protection, but they had lost the warmth and intimacy of peasant communities.

In response, Julia and her sisters developed a women's kinship network that stretched from Lyndora to New York to Miková and provided mutual support, both practical and emotional. In their letters, they celebrated family and shared their deep religious faith. They sponsored liturgies for one another and their children.[170] Julia's dollar contributions to Eva kept the Bezek family afloat. Their hopes for a better life for themselves may not have been realized, but that was secondary to their hopes for their children. The next generation included professional women, war heroes, a police chief, a world-famous artist, and numerous thriving Rusyn American families. While the sisters' lives in the immigration were full of tears and troubles, they held on to old-world ideals, but one can hardly blame them for longing for the simplicity of old-world Miková.

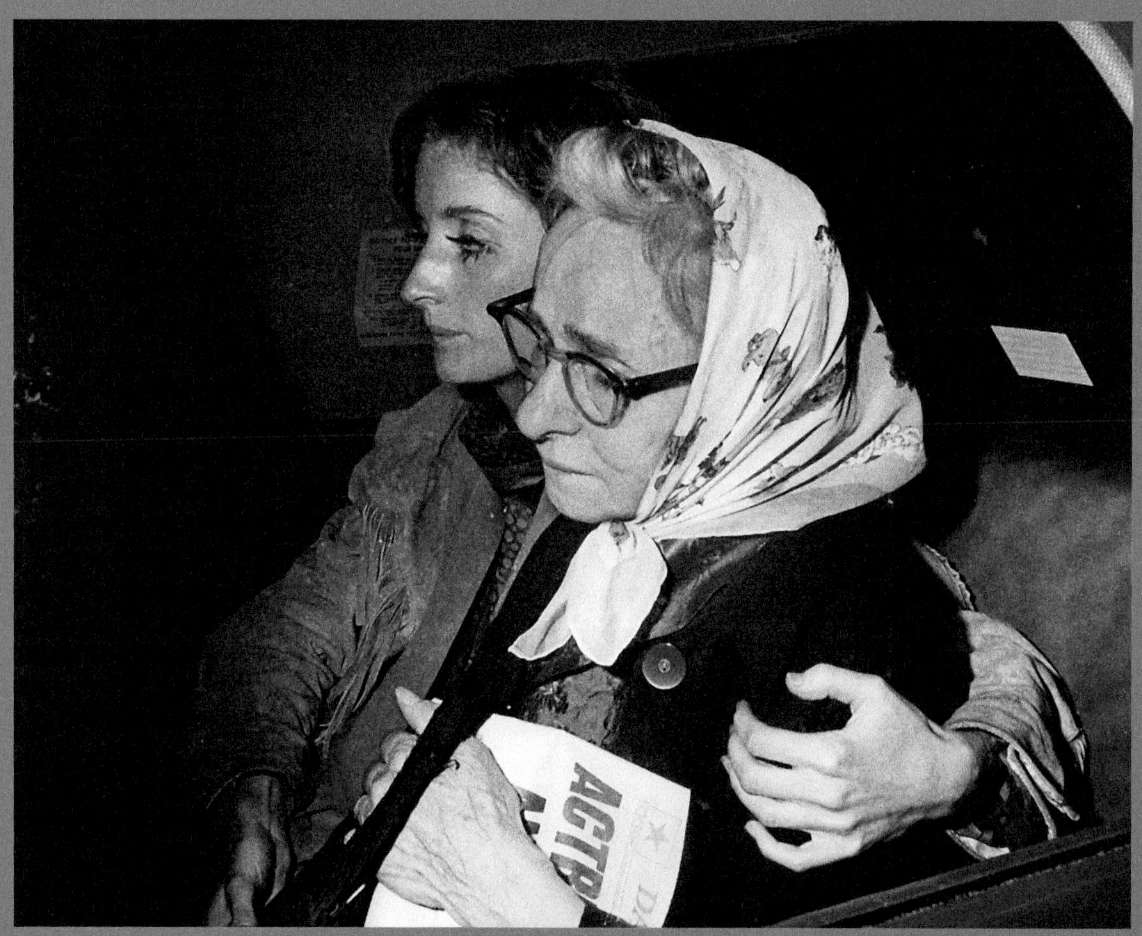

Figure 7.1. Viva Hoffman escorts Julia Warhola from the hospital after her son's shooting.

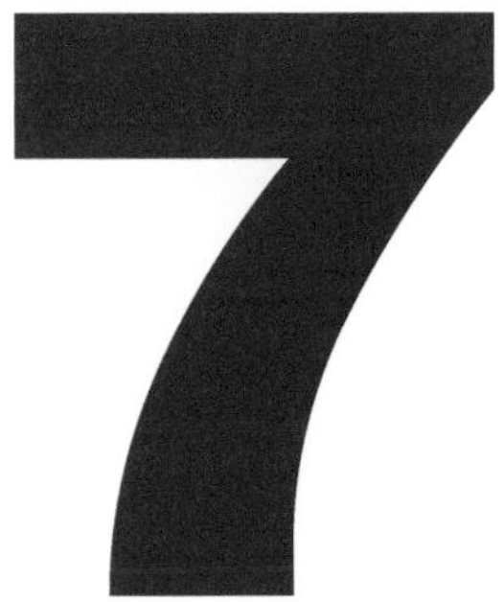

"Your Life Hangs by a Thread"

On the afternoon of Monday, June 3, 1968, Julia opened the door of Warhol's Lexington Avenue town house to find Gerard Malanga on the doorstep. He had been on the outs with Warhol for more than a year and had just recently returned from Europe, but Julia immediately recognized him. Malanga recalled, "Just as she opened the door . . . the phone rang and I said to her 'Let me get that.' I ran up the stairs. . . . Luckily I got to the phone in time. It was a friend of Julia's from Brooklyn calling her, because it was already on the news that Andy was shot. I introduced myself to the woman on the phone and said 'I'm a friend of Julia's. I'm going to take her to the hospital. Everything's okay, thanks for calling. Good-bye.'"[1] Malanga told Julia "a noble lie"—Andy had hurt himself in the stomach and was on his way to the hospital. He told her to get dressed—she was in her housedress—and he would take her to the hospital. She took about fifteen minutes downstairs and then negotiated the spiral staircase to the foyer.

Malanga had just come from Warhol's Union Square studio, where he went to pick up a check Andy had promised him. When the elevator opened on the sixth floor, he found "total pandemonium." Andy was lying in a pool of blood, screaming in pain. Mario Amaya, a museum director, there for a meeting with Warhol, emerged from a rear room where he had taken refuge, the back of his shirt bloodied by a gunshot wound. Warhol's associates were blotting up blood with paper towels and calling for help. Friends were crying, comforting Andy, and holding his hand. After some twenty minutes of chaos, an unconscious Andy Warhol was loaded into an ambulance.[2]

Warhol had been gunned down by Valerie Solanas, a mentally disturbed would-be actress and writer, whose radical feminist views, coupled with paranoid delusions, targeted her angry aggression on Warhol. "He had too much control of my life," she told police.[3] Valerie's bullet pierced Warhol's chest and crossed through his body, damaging his diaphragm, liver, spleen, and colon, and severing his esophagus from his stomach.[4] When he reached the hospital, his pulse was faint, his blood pressure scarcely registered, and he was pronounced clinically dead. Cardiac massage resuscitated him, and for over five hours, surgeons struggled to keep him alive and repair the damage. After the operation, the doctors gave him only a fifty-fifty chance of survival.[5]

"The first thing I thought of," recalled Malanga, "was to get Julia." Paul Morrisey gave him "a bunch of bills" to pay for a cab to Warhol's house. "No way I could get there in time by taxi, so I took the subway and got there faster. And I had the taxi money to cover the cab going down to the hospital." In the cab with Malanga, Julia was calm. "Everything was okay. She was with me, not a stranger. Luckily, she didn't have all the facts in front of her at that moment."[6] At Columbus Hospital, they found a throng of press, gawkers, and Factory regulars crowding the small lobby. For *Newsday* correspondents, the crowd in the hospital waiting room in their "tattered-mod costumes" conjured up a casting call for a Warhol film. "One exception to the motif was Warhol's mother, a little old woman whose babushka and square clothing made her look like a peasant woman."[7] When the actress Viva saw Malanga arrive with Andy's mother "in her trademark babushka," she thought bringing her to the hospital was "not one of Gerard's better ideas."[8] Viva thought Julia looked like "an old peasant woman, stooped over and grey, wearing a threadbare black coat, black stockings with runs in them, and a babushka." She was crying, "Me Andy! Me Andy!"[9]

The media described the rare public appearance of Andy Warhol's mother with little regard for her distress or her privacy. Howard Smith of the *Village Voice* reported, "Warhol's mother, a tiny old woman wearing a babushka, was brought weeping out of a back room. . . . A flock of photographers struggled for front photographs, almost trampling the old woman in the process."[10] According to the *Daily News*, Warhol's "babushka-wearing mother" wept and talked to herself in a Slavic language.[11] The superstar Ultra Violet flaunted her purported close acquaintance with Julia. Twenty years later, she described Julia's anxiety by "quoting" her Slovak speech, which was supposedly communicated and translated in the hurly-burly waiting room environment by "someone who knew the [language]." The Slovak transcription in Ultra Violet's memoir, *Famous for 15 Minutes*, translates to: "My child is dead. They've killed my baby. Oh my God, you fools, my baby is dead. My love is dead, my beloved son is gone, he was the best, my Andy, my dear." Of course, Julia would have spoken Rusyn, not standard Slovak as presented here, and there is no indication that Ultra Violet knew either language. It is more likely that these were Ultra Violet's thoughts, but they are cited in subsequent accounts as Julia's direct speech. And, just in case no one had noticed, Ultra Violet adds, "She was wearing a babushka."[12]

Repeating newspaper accounts, Ultra Violet expands:

> Photographers fight for front positions and in the process almost trample Julia's wheelchair [which had been brought by hospital assistants]. She bends her head low to escape the photographers. She does not want her picture taken. For many in the entourage, this is their first view of Andy's mother. They crane to get a look at the Old World peasant, transplanted to New York, who has been concealed inside his brownstone all these years, shielded from the unorthodox life of the Factory. Now Viva is comforting her. Andy's mother is muttering to herself in English: "My boy good boy. He go one o'clock mass St. Paul every Sunday. Good religious boy. They kill him, my Andy . . ."

Blake Gopnik sums up the belittling firsthand portraits of Julia and adds a dollop of snark: "Old lady Warhola starred as a babushka, *in* a babushka, weeping and wailing and praying for her 'good, religious boy.'" Julia surely did not say, at this time, that Andy was a good religious boy who went to one o'clock mass at Saint Paul's every Sunday. The entire phrase comes from Julia's 1966 interview in *Esquire* and has no relation to the 1968 shooting.[13] When Ultra Violet describes a later visit to Mrs. Warhola, Julia's "quoted" conversation is lifted, with minor alterations, from David Bailey's faked documentary—"stupid" was Warhol's word for it—where an actress impersonated his mother.[14]

Thankfully, hospital attendants were concerned for the distraught old woman caught in the motley crowd of hipsters and newshounds. They brought a wheelchair, took her to a private room, and gave her a sedative. A hospital spokesman told reporters there was nothing seriously wrong with Mrs. Warhola, but they wanted her "away from the excitement of Andy's friends." The hospital's publicist asked Viva to talk to the reporters. "After I agreed, with the condition that they allow us to leave unmolested, he asked me to lean more heavily on Gerard and try to look more devastated. I arranged my expression accordingly and they snapped some photos before we jumped into a cab."[15] Ultra Violet wrote, "[Julia] is the only one not interested in publicity. Shamelessly, the rest of us vie for position in front of the cameras. Viva and I make the paper the next day."[16] In one photo, a spuriously upset Viva has her arm around a sincerely disconsolate Julia, who clutches a copy of the early edition of the June 4 issue of the *New York Daily News*, its front-page headline blaring, "Actress Shoots Andy Warhol." A sidebar comment purports to come from an interview with Julia. "Mrs. Julia Warhol, the artist's Czechoslovakian-born mother: 'Andy always took care of me.'"

Falsities, distortions, and clichés are piled one upon another in the account of Andy Warhol's mother's appearance at the hospital. While Julia's distress is certain, there is no reliable description of her words or behavior the day of the shooting. Portrayals in the media and in subsequent histories—with the obligatory reference to her "babushka," a term that Julia would not have used—are condescending and demeaning. It is hardly surprising that Warhol shielded his mother throughout her time in New York, introducing her only to trusted friends: "If you got to meet Andy's mother, then you knew that Andy liked you very much"; "It was an honor to meet his mother, a mark of his trust."[17] Warhol, who was always keen to control the image, could not have been happy with the exploitation of his mother by his associates and the media.

Andy Will Be "All Right"

Word got to the Warhola family quickly. "Mother called us and we rushed right up," said Paul.[18] They were soon to learn the meaning of the adage they had heard frequently from their mother: "Your life hangs by a thread."[19] Andy's nephew Donald, who was about six years old at the time, remembers coming home from school to his mother's admonition, "You have to behave. Uncle Andy was hurt. Dad had to go to New York."[20] Paul and John were able to see Andy in the recovery room at the hospital, where they were shocked: "His head was as big as a watermelon." But by the time they arrived at Warhol's house, Julia was composed and tranquil, and she set about comforting her sons. Paul recalled, "She knew he was going to pull through. All she did was pray for hours and hours and hours in front of her altar."[21]

Just a week later, the director of Columbus Hospital announced that although Warhol was still in critical condition, he was "much better and on his way to complete recovery." He had been conscious and able to talk since the day after the shooting, and his mother and brothers were allowed to visit him in the intensive care unit.[22] Julia was buoyed by her faith, just as she had been when diagnosed with colon cancer. She knelt and prayed by the hospital bed, and told her sons not to worry, Andy would be "all right."[23] Later, Warhol recalled hearing snippets about the shooting and death of Robert Kennedy on June 5. "It was all so strange to me, this background of another shooting and a funeral—I couldn't distinguish between life and death yet."[24] He asked his brother Paul, "Why didn't I die?"[25]

During the eight weeks that Warhol was in the hospital, out-of-town relatives cared for Julia, whose declining health was worsened by the stressful events. Warhol's nephew Pauly, who was on summer break from his graduate studies at Catholic University, took charge of the household. As Andy began to recover, he was eager to get caught up on gossip and back to work. Pauly went to the hospital daily to deliver his mail, and at Andy's request, he retrieved the checkbooks for four or five different accounts. "Once a week somebody from the office would come to Andy and say, 'Mr. Warhol, we need some money.'" There was confusion about Warhol's insurance policy, which turned out to cover much less than Andy expected.[26] The bills racked up quickly. "But he was getting really good care at Columbus Hospital," said Pauly, who took Julia to visit her son.

> We would always take the bus from 89th and Lex. It was a pretty good distance. My uncle told us to take a cab. He was definitely happy to see her. We would sit there, she would ask questions [in Rusyn] about how he felt, then she would put her hands on his forehead and say a little prayer, a little blessing. We didn't stay real long. I know he didn't want her to feel uncomfortable. When he developed infections, he was in a lot of pain. They had to take him down, open him up, clean him out. It was tremendously painful, and hard for Julia to see.[27]

"I realized he wanted me there with him all the time and got upset when I missed a day—so I didn't miss too many days," Pauly told David Bourdon.[28]

Columbus was a Catholic hospital, founded to meet the needs of Italian immigrants. When Warhol was moved to a private room, a crucifix hung over his bed. When he was recovering at home, his nephew asked if he would like to confess and receive communion. "My uncle didn't think twice," said Pauly, who arranged for a Byzantine Catholic priest to visit him.[29] In his first press interview after his recovery, Warhol was asked whether the shooting left him feeling fearful. "I wasn't afraid before. And having been dead once, I shouldn't feel fear. But I am afraid. I don't understand why. I am afraid of God alone, and I wasn't before."[30]

Eight years later, in his *Philosophy*, Warhol quipped, "If you value your privacy, don't ever get shot, because your private life turns into an open house very quickly."

> Paulie [*sic*] stayed on with my mother after the other relatives left, because she didn't
> speak much English and was sort of batty by then. She couldn't be left alone, certainly,
> since she had a habit of letting anybody into the house who rang the bell and said they
> knew me. Any reporter could have gone right up there to talk to her and, if nobody was
> there to stop her, she'd take them on a complete tour, play my tapes for them, arrange a
> marriage with me if it was a girl, or with one of my nieces if it was a man—I mean, any
> embarrassing thing could happen if my mother became a hostess.[31]

There are no accounts of such intrusions. The "batty" Julia Andy described did not
differ substantially from the mother he had lived with for the past twenty years,
who regularly played hostess to friends of her son and grandchildren, regaling
them with stories and advice. Viva and the superstar Brigid Berlin visited Julia
while Warhol was in the hospital and were taken aback by the rosary beads hanging
from doorknobs and "the Blessed Virgin statues all around the living room." Viva
recalled, "I took to visiting the devastated Mrs. Warhola nearly every day. Her
peasant-influenced common sense was an antidote to my feelings of unreality. She
spent the time complaining that my skirts were too short, fingering the materials,
asking me how much they cost and insisting that it was a waste of money to spend
so much on so little. She was worried that Andy couldn't possibly pay me enough.
Her accent was heavy, her English broken. . . . Nevertheless Julia herself was articulate enough to beg me each time I visited her to 'marry me Andy.'"[32] Viva wrote to
Andy in the hospital: "Your mother just told me the history of: A–the 3 men who
wanted to marry her, B–Her 3 pregnancies (only the boys)."[33] Julia's religious faith
and her "peasant-influenced common sense" sustained her, propped up her sons,
and, except for her hope that Viva would marry Andy, injected a dose of reality into
the surreal world of Warhol's New York devotees.

"The Soviets Tank into Czechoslovakia"

On July 29, the *Pittsburgh Post-Gazette* published an Associated Press story:
"Pop artist and underground filmmaker Andy Warhol, a Pittsburgh native, left
Columbus Hospital today, almost two months after he was shot in his office." In
Carpatho-Rusyn families, caring for sick members was a family affair, and many
of Warhol's Pittsburgh relatives pitched in to help. His nephew brought the frail
Warhol home from the hospital. Pauly, a strapping young man, propped up his
uncle to tackle the long staircases, stopping for breath every few steps. "He needed
plenty of rest to regain his strength because the whole ordeal of fighting for his

life to begin with and then fighting the onslaught of infection had really taken its toll—mentally, emotionally, spiritually and, needless to say, physically."[34] Andy's brother John bathed his wounds and applied clean bandages "because his mother was too upset with all the stress," said John's wife.[35] Later, a Warhola family friends looked in on him to drain the wounds and change the dressings.

Nephew Pauly noted that after a few days at home, his uncle seemed to relax. As he recovered, Warhol spent August working on small-scale projects and watching the news on television. "I watched the Soviets tank into Czechoslovakia," he wrote in *POPism*.[36] The Soviet-led Warsaw Pact invasion of Czechoslovakia on August 20–21, 1968, halted the democratizing reforms of Alexander Dubček's "Prague Spring." Cinema played a leading role in the cultural relaxation in Czechoslovakia, as filmmakers subtly undermined oppressive government censorship. In the previous summer of 1967, Warhol had attended the Lincoln Center film festival, which featured Czech New Wave films. Noted for their rejection of conventional film forms, their mix of documentary and fiction, their nonprofessional actors and improvised dialogue, the avant-garde Czech films would naturally have attracted Warhol's attention. He socialized with a visiting delegation of Czech directors at an organized get-together, and the Czechs attended a party at Warhol's studio.[37]

The relaxation of authoritarian government ended when, just before midnight on August 20, the armies of the Soviet Union, Poland, Hungary, and Bulgaria converged on Czechoslovakia from the north, east, and south. Focused on transportation and communications networks in the cities, the invading troops passed through the hinterland home of the Rusyns. Villagers badgered the soldiers, a two-year-old child was killed by a military vehicle forty miles from Miková, and the city of Košice, about sixty-five miles away, reported more casualties and injuries than any other city in Slovakia.[38] The next day, tanks of invading troops occupied the streets of Prague and other major cities.[39] Over one hundred civilians were killed and more than five hundred were injured.

Given his confused sense of ethnicity, Warhol may have felt some connection to the events in Czechoslovakia. He may even have been aware that his childhood idol, Shirley Temple, was an eyewitness to the violence in Prague. Shirley Temple Black, representing the International Federation of Multiple Sclerosis Societies, had a meeting scheduled with Dubček the very day of the invasion. An AP report in the *New York Daily News* on August 21 told America that Black was in Prague and could not be contacted. On August 23, a follow-up article reported that she had crossed the border from occupied Czechoslovakia to West Germany through Soviet barriers and checkpoints in a cavalcade of embassy vehicles.[40] When Shirley

Temple Black was named ambassador to Czechoslovakia in 1989, she reminisced about her experience as eyewitness to history. "I saw a Czech middle-aged woman shaking her fist at the soldiers. She was shot in the stomach and went down. That was a bad sight."[41]

The Carpatho-Rusyns of northeastern Slovakia did not endure the street fighting that took place in Prague, but they felt the crackdown of authoritarianism that succeeded it. Dubček's eight-month period of liberalization had opened the door to progress for the Rusyns of Czechoslovakia in the religious and cultural spheres. During the Prague Spring, hierarchs of the Greek Catholic Church, which had been officially abolished in 1950 and silenced for eighteen years, rallied for its reinstatement. Greek Catholic and Orthodox believers fought over parishes and church property, often in violent clashes. Alarmed, local authorities appealed to the government for "an expedited handling of this problem."[42] Accordingly, the communist government officially reinstated the Greek Catholic Church on June 13, 1968, and its rehabilitation was one of the few lasting achievements of the short-lived experiment in political liberalization. As a result of plebiscites, 206 of the 241 parishes that had existed in 1948 returned to the Eastern Rite of the Catholic Church.[43] The term "Rusyn" had made a reappearance under Dubček, as activist journalists protested the artificial imposition of Ukrainian identity, and efforts were made to introduce the Rusyn vernacular into publications. These progressive moves were halted by the invasion and the Soviet-style policy of "normalization" that followed. The communist government's official nationality policy of Ukrainianization was reinstated, and Carpatho-Rusyns were once again threatened with the loss of their identity.

Sociopolitical and economic changes had altered traditional society and culture in northeastern Slovakia since the war. By 1970, only about 50 percent of the population was engaged in agriculture, forestry, and related activities, while 27 percent worked in industry and 10 percent, in the building trades.[44] The average income of Carpatho-Rusyns in 1968 was almost 40 percent below the Czechoslovak average, and Rusyns left their villages for large Slovak cities or Czech regions where wages were higher. Julia's sister Elena left Miková for Bohemia. Her brother Yurko and sister Eva remained in their native village, but many members of the younger generation moved on to greener pastures—in strictly figurative terms. The photographs they sent Julia during the 1960s depict modern consumer culture—fashionable western-style clothing and hairdos on girls in studio portraits, brides in long white gowns and veils, young people on motorbikes, and even a Škoda sedan. Rusyn culture survived primarily in the religion and the language, which the younger generation spoke only at home, and Carpatho-Rusyn identity seemed to be evaporating.

By then a household name in the United States and western Europe, Andy Warhol was unknown to the broad public of communist Czechoslovakia, where bourgeois American culture was broadly reviled. Even after Eva visited New York, saw with her own eyes Andriiko's "door-sized pictures," and met some of his Factory friends, none of the family in Miková knew of his fame. Letters to Julia from European relatives reveal that she had told them about the shooting. The family's response was predictably rooted in religious faith. A niece wrote that she was praying daily for Andriiko's recovery. Julia's sister Mary in Pittsburgh expressed faith in the power of Julia's prayers for her son, and Anna pronounced Valerie Solanas "a devil from hell" with evil eyes, saying, "An angel was with Andriiko and protected him."[45]

After the shooting, Warhol became convinced that he was being targeted. When he received gifts of food or candy, he had his nephews or brothers sample them first. Julia insisted that Andy had been tracked by unknown enemies who were envious of his success. She told Paul and John, "Somebody's jealous and they're going to kill him."[46] She was voicing the superstition of the Evil Eye, pervasive among Slovaks and Rusyns, a reference to nefarious "others" who, in the peasant world of "limited goods," are jealous of what one has.[47] Julia's superstitious belief was part of her jaundiced worldview. In a *Factory Diaries* video from early fall 1970, she admonished her son, who was then planning a European trip. "Will you lock up the house? They would steal everything from you, *synok* [little son]. If somebody would find out that Andy Warhola is not here, you would have nothing to come back to."[48]

"When You Feel Unhappy"

As Andy recovered, Julia's health declined. She had been suffering bouts of illness since the early 1960s, which can be traced through correspondence and sporadic medical reports. According to a letter from Ted Carey's mother, in December 1964, Julia was hospitalized and "quite ill," but she was released in time for the holidays. On January 9, 1965, Warhol's cousin Mary (Sally) Zymboly wrote to Andy, inquiring about what must have been the same episode.[49] "Just recently I heard that your mother wasn't feeling well and we are worried about her. Maybe you could write and tell us about her illness. . . . We all love your mom. She is a wonderful person, so full of affection and such a good sense of humor. Let us know, Andy." Two months later, Zymboly followed up: "My mother, who herself is not well, is very anxious to know how [Julia] is and keeps asking if I heard from you. . . . We are all praying for her, and waiting for your reply." Julia herself responded to Zymboly in December: "You know, dear Mary, I am only now beginning to be able to talk. For a month I lay in bed very sick. I couldn't eat anything. I thought I would die, but my savior Jesus Christ gave me life, and now I am a bit better. I can walk a little but only around the house. I can't do anything. I have two women who work around the house, one day one, the next day the other." She went on to defend her son for his failure to respond to his cousins' entreaties: "You write me that Andy should sometime write you a letter. You know, Mary, Andy is very busy with his work. I seldom see him. He comes home to sleep a little, in daytime he goes quickly to work and has no time to talk with me. So Andy cannot write letters to anyone."[50] Julia's Rusyn-language explanation is unclear, but she excuses her son from writing letters, because "it is not good for his head," which is presumably consumed by his work.

By summer, it was clear to all that Julia had been suffering from tuberculosis. Twenty years later, in his *Diaries*, Warhol downplayed his mother's illness. "My mother had [TB] after she came to New York, and you just have to take a lot of antibiotics. She never coughed or anything . . . Doc Cox found out she had it and she got over it in a month."[51] A letter from Doctor Denton S. Cox in November 1965 informed Julia that a preliminary test of her last sputum specimen showed no bacteria, and her October chest X-ray indicated "healing bilateral moderately-advanced pulmonary tuberculosis." Julia did not "get over it in a month." Two years later, in March 1967, she wrote to her niece Mary Zymboly, "I have been ill with a cold. I'm feeling better now and can move around the house. I'm still coughing, but that's my old age. It won't get any better."[52] Records show that Julia was still being treated for tuberculosis in 1968. At some point in the mid-1960s, her grandchildren were thought to be at risk. Paul's children were all tested; only Georgie tested positive.[53]

Other illnesses can be surmised from correspondence and medical receipts. On December 10, 1965, Julia wrote a note to remind herself, "Monday I have to go to lady doctor Werden." Virginia Werden was a New York obstetrician and gynecologist. She had completed her residency at Elizabeth Steele Magee Hospital in Pittsburgh, which specialized in women's diseases and where Julia had surgery in 1940. Whatever "female problems" had prompted the surgery may have lingered, as Julia continued to see Dr. Werden at least through 1967. In December 1965, she closed a letter to her niece, saying, "Greetings from Aunt Julia to all my family. I am not able to write to them, I am very old. Be well with God."[54] She refers to another episode of illness in the 1966 *Esquire* interview, describing what happened "one night several months ago." She was preparing a sandwich for Andy, when she suddenly felt faint, and blood began dripping from her nose. "I'm gonna die, Andy, I'm gonna die," she moaned.[55] Julia's performative streak may have kicked in. An invoice from an annual visit with Dr. Cox in October 1966 indicates no unusual tests or concerns, and Julia's performance in *The George Hamilton Story* in November shows fewer limitations than might be expected from a seventy-five-year-old woman. But by summer 1967 when Julia's sister Eva visited, Warhol was concerned about his mother's health issues. He wanted Eva to stay in New York to take care of Julia, who was, according to Eva, already ill.

A letter to Julia from Dr. Cox on May 3, 1968, references an office visit on April 17, when he had prescribed several medications: isoniazid, an antibiotic for the treatment of active tuberculosis, which had the potential side effect of serious liver damage; pyridoxine hydrochloride, a treatment for liver disease and the vitamin B deficiency and neuropathy that were side effects of isoniazid; and Aldactone for high blood pressure and edema caused by heart failure. Julia was on a merry-go-round of medications, side effects, and drug interactions that she could not understand. Dr. Cox expressed concern that Mrs. Warhola "had been off [her] medication for so long." It had been barely three weeks since he sent her home with prescriptions, but Julia may not have been taking her medication regularly even before that. He told her to bring sputum and stool specimens to her next office visit, scheduled for July 1968. Her son's shooting on June 3, his hospitalization until July 29, his recuperation at home for several more weeks, and a follow-up surgery in March 1969 to remove a bullet fragment surely interfered with Julia's medical treatment.

On New Year's Eve 1968–1969, Julia was admitted to New York Hospital. For the first two weeks of January, she submitted to numerous bacteriology and cytology tests, X-rays, and an electrocardiogram. She had a consultation with Dr. Thomas Killip, a cardiologist with a reputation for advanced cardiac care, but he did not alter her treatment. Released on January 17, she was sent home with seven prescription drugs. Through 1969, between hospital visits she was treated at home by visiting nurses. Paul Carroll describes an interview with Warhol in summer 1969, when Warhol apologized for being late because he had been visiting his mother in the hospital. According to Carroll, Warhol wore a black bullskin coat and a tall olive fedora with the brim turned down, which looked like "a tall Pilgrim hat." "Throughout the visit, Warhol keeps clutching a shopping bag, which, combined with fur coat and hat, suggest the appearance of an aging European woman. It's as if he were trying to keep his mother well by emulating her."[56]

When nephew Pauly returned to his studies in Washington, DC, in fall 1968, Jed Johnson stepped up to care for Andy and his mother. Johnson was nineteen years old when he and his twin brother began sweeping floors at the Union Square studio the previous year. As Andy recovered and Julia declined, Jed began to stop in at the Warhol home to help manage the house. "Andy was a pack rat—he'd saved everything, every bit of junk mail, every empty box and tin can. I sorted things out, put paintings with paintings and cans with cans. I ended up being there all the time so I just stayed."[57] About eight weeks after Warhol's return from the hospital, he moved in, and for the next twelve years, he was Warhol's live-in boyfriend. Jed described his role in Warhol's life to David Bourdon as "housekeeper." He tried to introduce order into the chaotic household, painting the walls and arranging the furniture.[58]

In the months after the shooting, Jed took Warhol's mother to doctors' appointments, and he looked after her as she sank into dementia. "She got really senile and she would just go out and leave the door open, forget where she went. We were just afraid that she would get lost. Once, the police came."[59] Marge Warhola, John's wife, got a phone call in Pittsburgh from New York police, who had found Julia wandering on the street. Information on a pill bottle in her purse led them to Warhol's house, where they found John's phone number next to the phone. According to Jed, "She really needed full-time attention and Andy couldn't do that." Neither could he bring himself to consign her to institutional care.

Jed Johnson is described as tireless and sweet-tempered, soft-spoken, mild-mannered, and painfully shy, but his description of the enfeebled Julia demonstrates more exasperation than compassion.[60]

> [Warhol's] mother spent a lot of time in bed. . . . I used to have to take her to the doctor once a week. . . . She was really difficult. She needed medication which she didn't remember to take, and then she made a lot of demands but she didn't know what she was doing. I mean, she was like a bag lady. She had things stuffed in shopping bags and her whole bed was surrounded by shopping bags and she had things safety-pinned to her clothing. It was unbelievable. Little notes, money and lost buttons. And she didn't sleep, she'd be up and she had a hard time walking around the house. She didn't make sense. Sometimes she'd get emotional but you didn't really know what she wanted. It was hard.[61]

Julia had Jed move her bed away from an exposed-brick wall because she thought the New York Fertility Center next door had buried babies there, and she imagined she could sense the odor of their decomposition. In the paranoia of dementia, she accused Jed of trying to poison her.[62] Johnson was in favor of sending her "some place," but "Andy didn't want her to go." Suzie Frankfurt said, "Andy didn't really do a hell of a lot for her. I'm sure she hated Jed."[63] The Warhola family resented him.

"Mother didn't care too much for Jed," said Paul, in an understatement. "Jed sort of moved in there and Mother used to tell me a lot of incidents. . . . Mother didn't like him because it seemed like that was her house and she didn't want nobody to take over."[64] John's son Donald remembers that even as a child, he got "a negative vibe" from Jed. "He never impressed me as a warm, friendly, kind person."[65] The family suspected that Jed was behind Warhol's ultimate decision to send Julia back to Pittsburgh.

In early 1970, Julia was admitted to Doctors Hospital in the Yorkville area, probably for a stroke. There are records of ten follow-up office visits with Dr. Cox between February and October, with repeated tests for kidney, liver, and thyroid function, as well as heart disease. Visiting nurses called regularly through the summer, and cousin Nancy Zupancic provided in-home assistance for his mother. Andy and Julia grudgingly accepted Nancy's help. Neither of them wanted outsiders in their home, but Rusyn-speaking Nancy was somewhat more acceptable. Julia, who had assisted her son in his early work, cooked and cleaned for him, starred in one of his films, and socialized with his friends, was now resigned to weakness, inactivity, and uselessness. Dr. Cox prescribed Dexamyl, an amphetamine stimulant combined with a barbiturate depressant. Cox's instructions on the label were, "Take half a tablet when you feel unhappy."[66]

"Nobody Understand"

Even as her illness worsened, Julia did what she could to assist her son. Before Warhol began to document the goings-on at his studio on tapes known as *Factory Diaries*, he performed test runs with his mother as subject. Three videos were shot in Mrs. Warhola's apartment on the lower level of Andy's town house and are labeled by the Andy Warhol Museum "Julia Warhola in bed, talking," "Julia Warhola in T-shirt, sick," and "Julia Warhola in bed, talking, sleeping."[67] It is uncertain exactly when Warhol acquired his camera, but internal evidence dates the tapes to early autumn, 1970. The videos document Julia's depression, confusion, and irritability, but they also reveal her attachment to her son and the nuanced mother–son relationship.

In *Julia Warhola in Bed, Talking*, Andy has settled his mother in the camera frame, lying in bed on her right side against the brick wall. While Andy fiddles with the camera, Julia talks—and talks—in Rusyn.[68] Her monologue is at times rambling and sometimes confused, but she is articulate and mostly coherent. She speaks to her forty-two-year-old son as to a child, in affectionate diminutives. *Tvoia koshul'ka tu brudna Andik,* shir*ka brudna* (Your shirt is dirty here, Andik), using a childish diminutive for the Rusyn word, *koshulia,* and then adding a diminutive Rusyn ending (*-ka*) to the English translation, "shirt." Her speech is laced generously with pet names and terms of endearment—Andik (pronounced Andeek), Andriiko, *synok* (little son), *synochko* (a more tender version of "little son"), *syne mi zlaty* (my golden son). However, she also uses diminutives in reproaches about his indifference and neglect. As he prepares for a trip to Europe, she complains, her voice full of fear and distrust, "*Hospodi* (Lord), who will be here with me, *synok?* . . . During the day is one thing, but at night I'm afraid to sleep here by myself. *Understand* [English], Andy?" Then sarcastically, she scolds in Rusyn, "But why would you care about that?" Andy reassures his mother that her granddaughter Eve will be there to care for her. Julia agrees, "My Eve is *nice girl, very good girl*" [English]. She asks who will come with Eve, and Andy answers in Rusyn with a single word, "*Sama*" (alone). Julia worries about Eve's airplane trip, which she finds "frightening." And two years after her son's shooting, she is apprehensive about his activities: "Andy, why would you go to Europe? I'm afraid there are not good people there. I don't want you to get hurt."

For the most part, Warhol is silent behind the camera. We first hear his voice when Julia complains that her side hurts and she tries to get up, moving out of the camera frame. "Lay down, lay down, mom, lay down," he repeats, even as she responds in discomfort, "Yoi, Andik." At one point, the phone rings and Warhol carries on a conversation in another room, while Julia obediently remains in place. After another attempt to get up, protesting, "My hip hurts, my side is hurting when I breathe," countered by the same "Lay down, mom," she asks, like an eager-to-please child, "So how is it, Andy? How I'm laying down? Is it all right?" Even to this, there is no verbal response. Finally, after a long pause, during which Julia seems silently distressed, Andy addresses her in a tender voice with the classic Slavic expression of affection—an offer of food: "You want something to eat, mom? eat? *ïsty?* What *ïsty* you want?" In English, Andy offers "a good sandwich," tea, and potatoes, but Julia refuses, answering in Rusyn, "I don't want to eat. Leave it, give me peace, Andy." Mournfully, she sighs, "If only I didn't have stomach problems, if only I could get over this somehow. But I don't think I will be around very long, because my breath gets stuck here." But before the tape runs out, she regains her spirit, and with animation, she tells the story of the "old devil" who permed her hair and "boiled" her scalp.[69]

For Julia, aging was harder and more dispiriting than attending her son through his childhood illness or battling colon cancer. After she moved to New York, she found her purpose in looking after her adult son, assisting with his work, and supporting his career, but she found herself oppressively sad and bereft of her former optimistic dynamism. Now at age seventy-eight, she was still assisting her son, submissively posing for his camera, even as she bemoaned the pain it caused. The woman who had survived poverty, loss, hardship, war, illness, and widowhood wanted and deserved to be looked after, but dependence bred helplessness and resentment. Julia's overweening love for Andy is unmistakable, but her subservience to him is disturbing. Andy's impassivity in face of her pain and reproach suggests that his mother's indulgence is a long-standing pattern of behavior that he accepts as his due. Julia responds with emotional ambivalence, as her affectionate diminutives give way to a sarcastic riposte: "But why would you care?" The uncomfortable mother–son dynamic is a noted cultural pattern. In his ethnography of Slovaks and Rusyns in McKeesport, Howard Stein says, "The elderly . . . often bitterly feel that they have given enough (while feeling they must continue to give), and that it is time for them to be taken care of (while wishing to avoid being dependent, and mistrustful of the 'good' intentions of those who care for them). It becomes a problem for the caring and the cared for."[70]

The video *Julia Warhola in T-Shirt, Sick* highlights the challenges for caregivers. Julia sits on her bed, again posing for her son's camera. Claiming her status as Warhol's official assistant, she flaunts her familiarity with the procedure, snapping in Rusyn, "Don't touch anything, Nancy. He wants to do something with me." She scolds, "You'll break it. What do you know about it? . . . I don't want you here. Go to the kitchen." Nancy is heard telling Andy, "She doesn't understand." When the nurse tries to give Julia her pills, she resists, concealing them in her hand. Nancy warns, "No, no, you're going to lose them that way." Julia responds irritably (in Rusyn), "Don't worry, do you think I've lost my mind? You think I'm stupid? I'm not crazy. Just go away. I'll give them to Andy."

Distrustful of nurse Nancy, Julia turns to Andy, and her tone shifts markedly. "Andrii, *synok, syne mi zlaty*, I can't eat now. I'll just have coffee." Warhol patiently doles out her pills. "All these, Andy?" she asks tremulously, and swallows the pills slowly, with great difficulty. "It won't go down. For all the world, it doesn't want to go down, Andy. The pills are stuck in my throat . . . on an empty stomach . . . I still have four more big white ones." After crossing herself three times and saying a prayer, she manages to swallow the pills and the lunch Andy brings her. "I don't know what kind of pills they're mixing for me. Look, *synok*, they want to make sure nothing will happen to me." According to Paul Warhola, Julia took fifteen pills three times a day.[71]

Warhol is solicitous of his mother, patiently encouraging her to swallow the pills and eat lunch, and later running to the store to buy carrots for soup. But when they have finally completed the difficult task of giving and taking the pills, he goes back to work behind the camera and directs his mother to call for another caregiver to participate in the scene he is taping. This is followed by the conversation about Andy's childhood confrontation with African American neighbors, for which his brother Paul was penalized. Again, Julia emerges from her listless mood and becomes animated when she enters performance mode, telling the story from Andy's childhood artfully, in a spirited narrative style.

Julia Warhola in Bed, Talking, Sleeping is the only one of the "Julia videos" occasionally shown in public at museums or film festivals. It seems to portray a peacefully sleeping Julia, but for the first time in these test runs, she participates unwillingly. "Andy, don't bother with me, I sleep." Her mixed Rusyn-English monologue is disjointed and querulous. Again, she has trouble eating: "Maybe I'll choke, Andy." She laments that she does not have a daughter, and complains about "Jed *paskudnyi*" (disgusting Jed), who seems to be burning something in the kitchen. "What's there, Andy? He understand, Andy? Nobody understand. I not happy, Andy." Dr. Cox's pills were not working. Finally, Julia tells Andy she is not up to performing for him. "If I could only take some pills so I could sleep. My head is burning, my eyes too, that's how much I want to sleep." Mercifully, she falls asleep, in her glasses and kerchief, and she sleeps until the tape runs out.

John Richardson, Warhol's eulogist, described Julia as "the source of tenacity and gentleness and down-to-earth resilience" for her son. "Narrow and uneducated she may have been, but Julia struck those who met her as humorous, mischievous, and shrewd—like her son."[72] According to Victor Bockris, "Underneath her naïve peasant exterior, Julia was the only person in Andy's life who was as complex, manipulative, and powerful as he."[73] In these firsthand, unmediated video films, Julia and Andy jockey for control of the relationship. Julia treats her adult son gently, addressing him in tender, but patronizing, diminutives. She manipulates her nurse and contrives to have Andy administer her pills, shifting from warm endearments to caustic reprimands. Her over-giving self-sacrifice contends with a need for appreciation that could not be met. Andy, "a grand master of passive aggression," responds in like manner.[74] "He could be generous and he could be withholding, and you never knew which he would choose—the classic technique of the passive-aggressive."[75] In the Factory, he was known as Drella, for the two sides of his personality, Dracula and Cinderella. Bob Colacello described him as "impossible, so demanding and so ungiving, so needy of the loyalty and love he was incapable of returning. . . . Andy

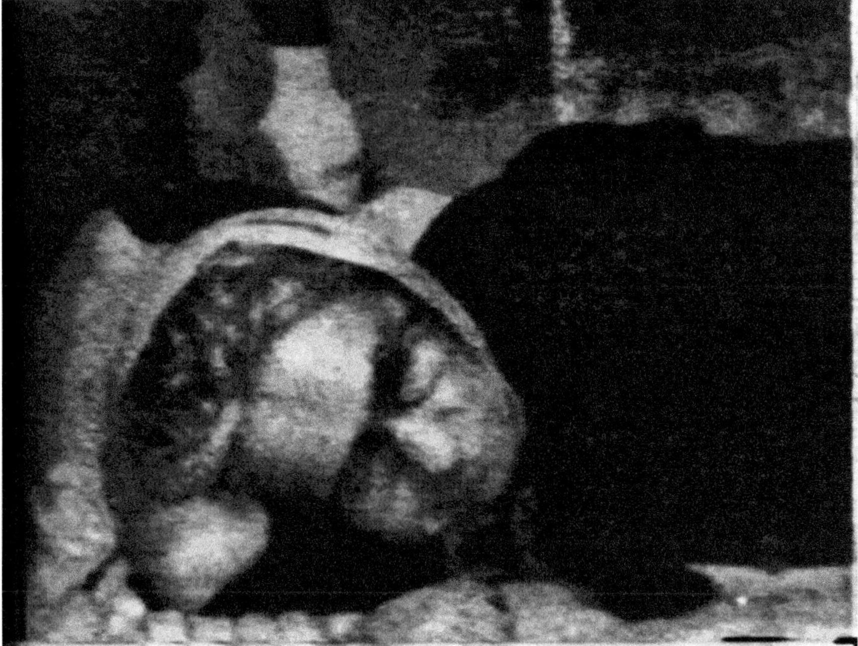

Figure 7.2. Film still of Julia Warhola from *Factory Diary: Julia Warhola in Bed, Talking, Sleeping*, ca. 1970–71.

knew how to push my buttons to get the desired dramatic results, as he did with all of us who were closest to him."[76] In this respect, Warhol and his mother were a matched set.

Intergenerational tensions are amplified in immigrant families, where children frequently feel a complex mélange of admiration, affection, gratitude, embarrassment, irritation, and obligation toward their "foreign" parents. In Carpatho-Rusyn culture, children understood from an early age that they were expected to care for their parents in their old age. At the same time, immigrant life demanded self-sacrifice from parents for the sake of the child. The result was a parent–child relationship of codependency, where each was responsible for the other, each needed the other, and each needed to be needed. In this dysfunctional dynamic, feelings of resentment and entitlement simmered beneath the surface of mutual love. In these intimate, private videos, Julia is simultaneously protective and critical. Andy is both caring and indifferent. Each seems to feed on the insecurity of the other in an emotionally desperate effort to control the relationship, at the cost of mutual trust, understanding, and comfort.

"Get Me out of Here"

"If Andy ever wants you to take me to Pittsburgh, don't do it," Julia told John's wife Marge, "because I want to stay here and some day Andy's going to come home and he'll find me and I'll just fall asleep and die in my sleep. This is the way I want to die."[77] Unfortunately, Julia did not get her wish. According to Bockris, in February 1971, she had a stroke and was hospitalized in New York.[78] Marge Warhola said she had pneumonia, "a black mark on her lung." Julia insisted there was nothing wrong and adamantly rejected surgery.

There was almost no greater cause of family discord among the children of Slavic immigrants than the care of their elderly. It is a rare second-generation Carpatho-Rusyn family that has not experienced such conflict, which often generated family rifts and long-lasting acrimony. In the most common pattern, one child, usually a daughter, assumed the primary responsibility of caring for the elderly parent. Julia felt the absence of a daughter in her life, as she lamented in one of the videos. However, a female caregiver would not have prevented problems, and she had two attentive daughters-in-law. The role of "parent-keeper," whether a man or a woman, was accompanied by strain and tension for the children, who were all expected to contribute to parental support. It is an understatement among sociologists that "such arrangements among siblings were not, of course, always negotiated smoothly."[79]

Problems were compounded by the ethnic mindset. In Corinne Azen Krause's study of Italian, Jewish, and Slavic women in Pittsburgh, every one of the first-generation Slavic women lived in her own home or in a separate apartment in a family-owned house. Stability and home ownership, which represented a level of independence, were particularly important for Slavic women, even into the third generation.[80] John Warhola understood, "Well, the worst thing to do is take an older person like that from the environment that she knew."[81] However, accustomed as Julia may have been to Andy's house, New York City was not a congenial environment for an elderly woman with limited English, who was developing dementia. In 1970 and 1971, Warhol was constantly traveling to the West Coast and Europe, and acceptable caregivers were scarce. Finally, the family had to face reality. "Andy wanted her to come to Pittsburgh because she was getting pretty bad." John and Marge took her in. "She started to get up at night. I guess she was getting senile but she wanted to leave the house and we just couldn't watch her," said John. Paul's place "out in the country" seemed more appropriate, and in spring 1971, Julia went to the Paul Warhola home. Paul remembered, "She'd get up every morning. 'Hey!

I'm going back to New York!' And she had her bags packed and all. I said, 'The bus ain't gonna be here today. It's not running,' and we got her back in."[82]

On May 14, 1971, Paul's daughter Eve, who had taken care of Julia in fall 1970, wrote to her Uncle Andy, "Hey, I heard the good news about Buba [*sic*] staying at our house. I think it's a good change for her and who knows maybe after a while she won't even want to go back to N.Y. My mother wrote and said that she's eating real good and that she's not having any problems with her. I guess you were right about the whole idea about getting her back to Pgh. I'm sure she will be much happier. There's people around so she won't have to feel lonely."[83]

In June 1971, Julia had another stroke and was admitted to Mercy Hospital in a coma. There are no records of her treatment, except for Ann Warhola's implausible comment: "While she was in the coma I used to pour whisky and ginger ale down her throat every morning."[84] After about a month, the doctor told Paul, "We can't do much for her, you'll have to take her. I advise you to take her home.'" But by now, Julia's needs exceeded what anyone could provide at home, even with help. On July 27, 1971, Ann Warhola signed an admission agreement for Julia Warhola at Wightman Manor, a nursing home and rehabilitation center in the Squirrel Hill neighborhood of Pittsburgh, and Julia was transported by ambulance the same day from Mercy Hospital to Wightman for extended care. Monthly invoices detail the particulars of palliative care—colostomy bags, diapers, gowns, and prescription medicines—that were added to the monthly charge of $660.[85]

A nursing home was the option of last resort. Krause's study of ethnic women in Pittsburgh ends with the implications of ethnicity for mental health: "Home— their own home—is especially important to Slavic grandmothers. When they can no longer take care of their house, when they must live in a nursing home or home for the elderly, this will present a traumatic and heartbreaking experience. Every effort should be made to ease this very difficult transition."[86] Immigrant elders, with minimal levels of English, were unfit to fend for themselves with doctors and caregivers, unable to socialize with residents outside their own class and ethnic group, and uncomfortable in alien institutional settings. Moving parents to an institution was no less difficult for ethnic adult children, for whom it carried an onerous stigma. They lived with the burden of guilt and felt compelled to offer justifications: "She could have fallen down the steps"; "She was wandering too much"; "Her mind was gone"; "But we took good care of her." True as they may have been, such justifications reflected the blame they felt, which often grew into recriminations. John reproached Paul and Ann for consigning Julia to a home against Andy's wishes. Paul protested that he did not "shut her up in the home." Andy, who loved family gossip even from

Bob Colacello about his Brooklyn grandmother—"She moved out of your aunt's house? Gee!"—paid the Wightman bills, but was otherwise oddly detached.[87]

Wightman Manor advertised itself as "Pittsburgh's prestige nursing home." Help Wanted ads sought licensed nurses at $3.20 per hour (about $20 in 2020) plus benefits, with slogans like: "If you truly care, if you are a 'cut above,' we need you." A 165-bed facility in 1972, Wightman catered to the upscale Squirrel Hill population.[88] Obituaries of patients from 1971 and 1972, when Julia was resident there, describe Anglo-Saxon Protestants, doctors and their widows, bank officers, teachers, and prominent members of various Ladies' Auxiliaries. There were likely few, if any, Rusyn speakers, and there would have been little community for Julia. A niece wrote to Warhol about a male resident who had a strong resemblance to "Uncle Andy," probably referring to Julia's brother Andrew. "Your mother really believes it is him. She keeps talking to him in our language and gets so sad when he yells at her."[89] The same niece reported compassionate treatment from the staff. "The nurses . . . all just love her. They kiss and hug her all the time."[90] Other relatives left withering reviews. Paul Warhola described the place, "nice as it was," as very depressing, with an unpleasant odor.[91] Paul's son, Pauly, was more negative. "Wightman Manor wasn't the best. . . . They tied her into her chair, cut her braids off. . . . I'd have to give them a grade of C. It was sort of a warehouse. I'm sure there would have been better places. I don't know why they went there. My dad and uncle . . . anything they did would have been fine with Uncle Andy."[92] Julia's niece Nora reflected, "I used to visit her at the nursing home, and I was angry then, a little bit angry. Andy was rich, he should have sent her to a better place. Several times she was caught walking down the sidewalk in her nightgown and slippers. It smelled of pee."[93] The reviews of inexperienced nieces and grandchildren are generalizations that might apply to even the best nursing homes, but there is no doubt about Julia's unhappiness. Her grandson George recalled, "It was sad when she was up in Wightman Manor. . . . She'd say, 'Georgie, come on, get me out of here.'"[94]

Wightman Manor was Julia's home for the last sixteen months of her life. Perhaps it was fortunate that for much of the time, she returned in her mind to Miková. Ann told a reporter, "Andy phones her every day, and she looks forward to that. But she lives in the past a good bit, too."[95] Julia asked her son John if he had milked the cows. She mistook Paul for her husband, asked if he had come up with the horse and cart, and if he would take her back home with him.[96] However, her niece Mary Zymboly described a visit with Julia in August 1972, just three months before her death, which reveals an alert and active mind. "We had such a nice visit. I taught her a little prayer my father [Julia's brother John] taught me as a child and she repeated it over and over again. She was so sincere when she prayed it, looking up and folding her hands in prayer. . . . We walked the hall and your mom said such humorous things I laughed and laughed. Like her roommate, a woman who continually talks to herself and argues with imaginary people and your mother said, '*tota baba shalena yak kurka*'—this lady is like a crazy chicken."[97] Two months before her death, Julia told the same niece the story about the birth and death of her baby girl, a tragedy that had not been generally shared with the younger generation.[98] Letters like these pricked Warhol's conscience. John Warhola told Zymboly that one of her letters had made Andy "feel bad." "I'm sorry, Andy, but I just wanted to convey to you my observations about my dear Aunt Julia, your mother," Zymboly wrote. It is uncertain whether Andy ever responded, although on October 7, 1972, Sally thanked him for sending her photographs. "I just started a new album and you can be sure your photos will have the first page."

The stress of dealing with aging parents often resurrects long-standing family conflicts. Paul and John argued about who was doing more for their mother and who visited her more often. But, except in an oblique thirdhand reference, there is little mention of their having urged Andy to visit his mother. Whether they assumed he was doing his part by paying the bills, or they excused him because of the distance and his busy lifestyle, there is little evidence of any exhortations. A month before Julia's death, only Ann Warhola hinted at Warhol's alleged indifference. Defending Andy to a reporter, she said that he had never been completely well since the 1968 shooting and he "lives in fear a good bit of the time." "Listen, we know that Andy's in a world of his own. He's something else, something special." Andy's greatest critic, Ann voiced the stress that Julia's care caused the Pittsburgh family and the apparent indifference of her New York son. "As far as I know, he never thinks of us or our children, but then he's involved in that kind of life and with those people who are so different. He's just got another way of life and it's not like ours."[99] When John wondered aloud to Julia whether Andy would stay in touch after her death, she "snapped out of her trance" and replied, "You keep it going."[100] Paul reported that her final words to him were, "Promise me you'll take care of Andy. I want you to look after him because sometimes I wonder if he don't have a childish mind."[101]

No records of letters or phone calls from Warhol to his mother exist, but one page from an unidentified magazine found in a Time Capsule, may have been a tender tribute from him to his mother. A photograph of Andy and Julia taken by Duane Michals was used to illustrate an article that referenced Warhol's latest publicity stunt—his announced intention to change his name to John Doe. In the photo, tagged "John Doe & his mother Mrs. Warhola," Julia is in sharp focus in the

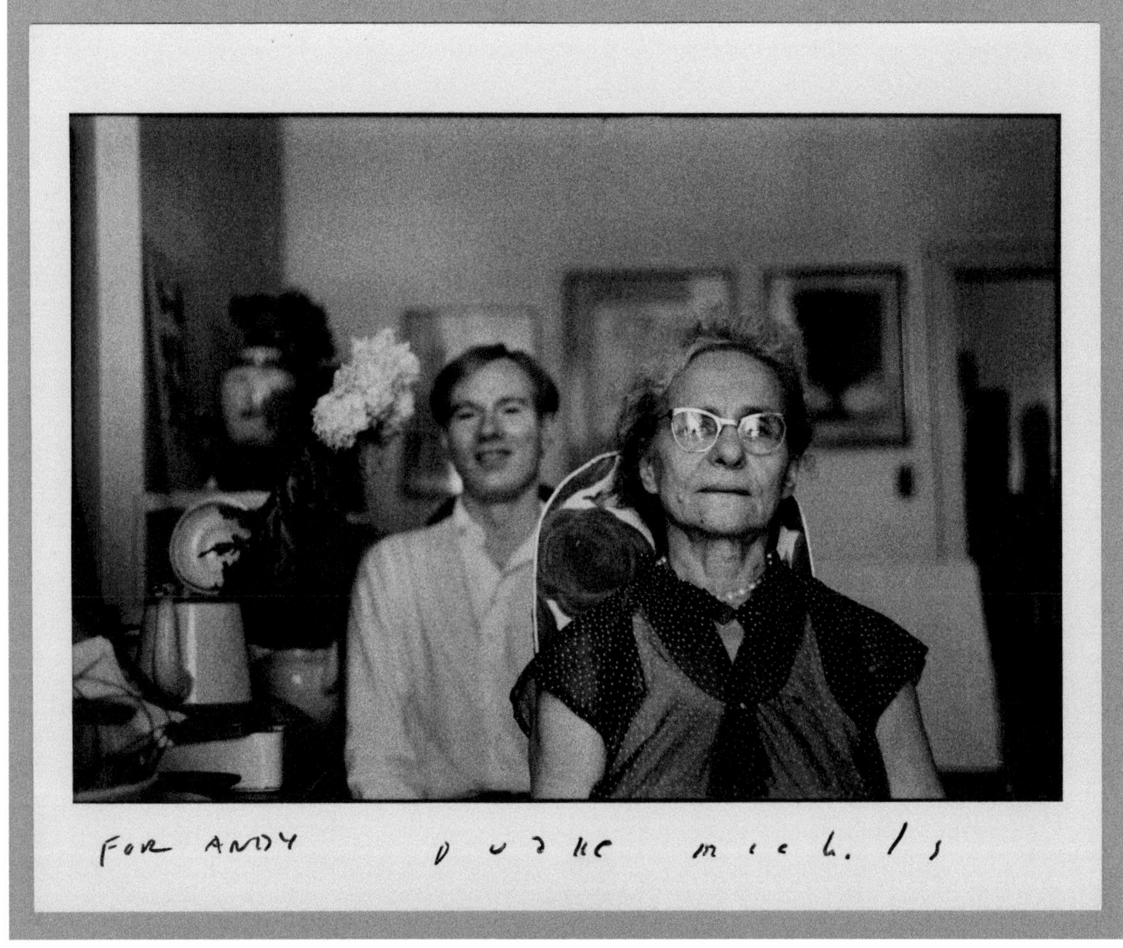

Figure 7.3. Duane Michals, *Andy Warhol and Julia Warhola*, 1958.

foreground, while her son's face in the background is blurred. Internal evidence dates the clipping to midsummer 1971, when Julia was already in Pittsburgh. Andy had circled the photograph and, as if excited to share it, he wrote in the margin, "Mum, picture of you. Andy."[102] It was probably never sent.

Sons Paul and John, grandchildren and nieces visited Julia, demonstrating the tight family bonds that were earlier shown in cards and letters. But Julia desperately wanted to see her youngest son. When John Zavacky visited, Julia called him by the Rusyn diminutive she had used for him as a child, pointed out the window and said, "Look, Andy's coming home."[103] But that was wishful thinking. Andy never visited his mother during her time at Wightman Manor. His brothers made excuses. Paul said, "I covered up for him a lot," and John told the biographer Fred Lawrence Guiles what was likely a face-saving fib, that Andy visited his mother "once or twice" without telling anyone.[104] The strongest and most direct reproach came from Andy's plainspoken cousin Mary Zymboly, two months before Julia's death.

> Dear Cousin Andy, Yesterday I had the privilege of visiting my dear Aunt Julia, your mother, again and I hope you don't mind [my] giving you this report. . . . Andy, in my estimation, I don't think your mother will be in this world too much longer. She is steadily weakening and I think she's clinging desperately to live in order that she may see you again. Her subconscious mind is filled with thoughts of you and I don't think God is pleased with your staying away. . . . I saw her three times this summer and I have yet to see her smile. And that's not like your mother. I remember her laughter of days gone by. It was pitiful for me to see her walk down the hall and inquire at every door if anyone has seen you, because she told them in our language that she is ready to leave to go to Butler with me and doesn't want to leave you alone. In fact she once tried to move a heavy wardrobe in her room because she said that you are bashful and are hiding behind it. She even got up on a chair to try to look over the top of it. So you see Andy? Her last days are filled with desire to see you. Please come. I'm telling you your conscience will bother you terribly someday and you'll wish you would have heeded your brother John's and my advice, but it will be too late.[105]

Thirteen years later, Warhol commented to his diary, "At Christmas time, I really think about my mother and if I did the right thing sending her back to Pittsburgh. I still feel so guilty."[106]

"I Hope I Don't Die in Winter"

Julia Warhola died of a stroke at Wightman Manor on Tuesday, November 28, 1972, at 8:00 a.m., six days after her eighty-first birthday.[107] The same morning, John called Andy with the news. According to Gopnik's interpretation of the recorded phone call, Warhol's reaction was "strangely cold," as "he answered his brother's sobs in quick, clipped tones."[108] Gopnik muses, "Maybe his reserve came from shock." Andy could hardly have been shocked, given the many warnings he had received of his mother's imminent death. A few days before, he had skipped an important meeting, "apparently because he'd had news of his mother's decline." "But," Gopnik continues, "on her death day itself he was perfectly normal and busy. He had three servings of lasagna for dinner."[109]

An alternate interpretation of Andy's response to his brother might be that his tone is composed, restrained, and even mildly compassionate. The brothers' conversation is lengthy, not curt or brusque, as they discussed how to handle their mother's death. On the day his mother died, Warhol went about his usual business, which is no less than might be expected from the artist, for whom work meant satisfaction, diversion, and control. As Bob Colacello, who worked closely with him in the 1970s, described it, "Andy had a very peculiar attitude toward 'work.' He wanted to make money, and to keep it, but he also couldn't relax, hated vacations, dreaded having time on his hands to think about 'problems,' by which he almost always meant something to do with love. . . . [He] wanted to have people around to make work 'fun.' But the minute it really became fun, he turned it back into work, to keep control."[110] In this case, work might have helped him to control his emotions.

Although Warhol was occupied after his call with his brother, his thoughts were on death. Ron Tavel, Warhol's screenwriter, was suing him for money he believed Andy owed him, and Warhol spent the afternoon of November 28 in a lawyer's office. "Ronnie was being deputized [*sic*] and interrogated and a woman was taking shorthand and it was so scarey [*sic*], hearing about my early past and he would talk about every star in every movie and everyone he mentioned is dead now—the person in *Suicide* is dead, Edie in *Vinyl* is dead, Marie Menken in *Life of Juanita Castro* is dead, Philip Fagen [*sic*] in Screen Test is dead."[111] Without a pause, he added, "Came to the office and did some office work." Although he did not mention them specifically, the thoughts about death that were prompted by Tavel's memories began in the morning with his mother.

That evening, Warhol went to a society dinner, which to him, was another kind of "work." Colacello, the editor of Warhol's *Interview* magazine and his sales agent for commissioned portraits, said, "Working with Andy was fun, but having fun with Andy was work. And going out with Andy was 'getting ideas,' 'getting portraits,' 'selling ads,' 'finding new people for *Interview*,' bringing home the bacon."[112] The dinner that night was at the home of Adriana Jackson, an art collector who had helped Colacello snag his first portrait commission earlier that year and who continued to bring Warhol and Colacello into contact with potential clients at social occasions.[113] Warhol reported events of the evening to his diarist Pat Hackett. After listing the dinner guests, he added an aside: "A lot of lasagna was served and I had three helpings." He then immediately moved on to further gossip. The full context of the evening might challenge Gopnik's description of a self-satisfied lasagna feast.

The following day, Wednesday, November 29, Warhol had lunch with Lee Radziwill and they spent the afternoon shopping. In summer 1972, Radziwill, a socialite and the sister of Jackie Kennedy Onassis, rented the main cottage on the compound in Montauk, Long Island, that Warhol had purchased in fall 1971. Jackie Kennedy and her children, Caroline and John John, stayed at the house with Radziwill and her children. The underground film master and mentor Jonas Mekas, one of the guests at the compound, recalled that summer as "one of happiness and continuous celebrations of life and friendships."[114] Radziwill recalled, "We spent long lazy afternoons on the beach, talking and burying each other in the sand. At times like this, Andy wasn't as strange as he initially seemed, but revealed himself as a keen, subtle observer of everything around him."[115] Gopnik dismisses the friendship between Warhol and Radziwill. "Warhol might have had his head turned by his fancy new friends, but he was no fool. He knew perfectly well that he was in their world on sufferance, so long as they found him useful or amusing."[116] Indeed, by 1979, Warhol was disavowing the friendship in diary comments. But in 1972 he appears together in photographs with Radziwill and for several years, he maintained an amiable, personal relationship with her.

On the day after his mother's death, Warhol took Polaroid photos of Radziwill, and in 1973 he did a portrait from one of the photos, not as a commission, according to Gopnik, but for his own pleasure. "He kept the studio's standard forty-by-forty-inch canvas just for himself. He still owned it when he died."[117] It was unusual for Warhol to do a portrait without being paid for it, which suggests a special bond with Radziwill. When he set out for his afternoon with her, Warhol uncharacteristically, but deliberately, failed to turn on his ever-present tape recorder, with which he recorded most of his social gatherings. Pat Hackett's elliptical transcribed text from Warhol's telephone report of the afternoon reads, "Didn't tape because I was afraid to (too much personal stuff)."[118] Warhol gave Hackett the details of their lunch, a museum visit, and a tour through the museum's basement, but entirely left out the conversation about the "personal stuff," which he was "afraid" to commit to tape. Death, and especially the death of his mother, was something too personal to express publicly, but the unspecified and unrecorded personal conversation with Radziwill one day after Julia's death is intriguing. Perhaps it occurred to Warhol that while he had been playing with the upper-class set on the beach, his mother was pining for him at Wightman Manor.

Three years later, Warhol expressed his thoughts on death explicitly, or as explicitly as he ever was on the subject, in his *Philosophy*: "I don't believe in it, because you're not around to know that it's happened. I can't say anything about it because I'm not prepared for it."[119] Speaking here about his own death, he exposes a posture that goes back to his father's death thirty years earlier and applies as well to the death of his mother: Don't prepare for it, ignore it, hide from it when it happens. This was the tone of his response to his brother John. Although their temperaments differ—John is emotional, while Andy is reserved—the brothers are patient and understanding with one another in the phone call. Andy told John that he would not attend the funeral because it would make him too nervous. He insisted that John and Paul should keep his mother's death "as secret as possible" and give her "the cheapest funeral," because that's what Julia would have wanted. Gopnik attributes this notion to Warhol's "avant-garde" perspective, which, he says, may have been shared by Julia.[120] But in the Warholas' religious and cultural context, there was no place for an "avant-garde" funeral, whatever that might mean. Carpatho-Rusyn tradition and the sympathies of family and clergy ensured that Julia would be laid to rest in a traditional, reverential ceremony.

The funeral took place at Saint John Chrysostom church in *Ruska dolina* on Friday, December 1. It was concelebrated by Julia's grandson Father Paul, and three hierarchs of the Pittsburgh Byzantine Catholic clergy: Monsignor Daniel Maczkov, the pastor of the Nativity of the Blessed Virgin Mary in Squirrel Hill, Monsignor Michael Hrebin, the pastor of Paul Warhola's family church in Clairton, and Monsignor John Bilock, the rector of the Byzantine Catholic cathedral of Saint John the Baptist.[121] Bilock, who had been Julia's pastor in 1949–1950 at Saint John Chrysostom was elevated the year after her funeral to Auxiliary Bishop of the Byzantine Catholic Archeparchy of Pittsburgh. Monsignor Hrebin was mentor to Father Paul Warhola, and Julia attended liturgy at his church when she lived with Paul's family in Clairton. Monsignor Maczkov ministered to her at Wightman Manor. Concelebrating her funeral liturgy was a sign of respect and affection, a personal tribute to Julia Warhola. Unfortunately, there are no memories of the homily.

It is uncommon for anyone less prominent than a respected clergyman or politician to have three shining lights of the Pittsburgh clergy (plus a clerical grandchild) celebrate their funeral liturgy. The commemoration of Julia's life in the Office of Christian Burial would have been solemn, triumphant, and traditional, the very opposite of "avant-garde." The priests sang, "O God of spirits and of all flesh, You trampled Death and broke the power of Satan, and granted life to Your world. Now grant rest, O Lord, to the soul of your departed servant in a place of light, joy, and peace, where there is no pain, sorrow, or mourning. . . . In blessed repose, grant, O Lord, eternal rest to the soul of Your servant, and remember her forever." The congregation chanted the response, exultant in concept, lugubrious in tone: "*Vichnaia pamiat*. Eternal memory. Blessed repose and eternal memory."[122]

Julia's funeral was handled by the John N. Elachko funeral home. Elachko was the American-born son of the Warholas' duplex neighbors, Alexander and Katrena Elachko, Carpatho-Rusyns from villages near Miková. Elachko began operating a funeral parlor out of his Dawson Street house in 1943. After the war, he opened a facility a few blocks from the Warhola home.[123] Elachko had tender memories of Julia from their early days on Dawson Street: "She was soft on everyone. She wouldn't hurt a fly and just felt sorry for everyone."[124] Well in advance of her death, Julia had given some thought to her funeral. Many times over the years, she told John Zavacky, "I hope I don't die in winter when it's cold. I'd be worried about the people who would be in my funeral."[125] Julia's preconceived solicitude was to no avail. On the day when she was laid to rest next to her husband in Saint John the Baptist cemetery, the high temperature was thirty-two degrees Fahrenheit, the low was twenty-six. Three inches of new snow lay on the ground.[126] Zavacky, along with the other pallbearers, including Michael and Joseph Warhola, sons of Andrii's brother, and John Girman, a family friend from Dawson Street, carried her casket up the slope, struggling to maintain their footing on the icy planks around the grave. Because of the weather, the funeral lunch was served in the church social hall before, instead of after, the burial.

Andy, who was paying the expenses, told his brothers to get "the cheapest funeral." Elachko's invoice does not demonstrate any particular parsimony. No limousines were ordered, and the "casket and services," at $1,650, were probably not top of the line. But clothing and hairdresser services were purchased, along with a "flower car." The total cost of the funeral was just under $2,000, about $12,000 in 2020 dollars.[127] There would have been two evenings of visitation at the funeral home, at which a priest and cantor offered the traditional *parastas* memorial service. Prayer cards with gold-backed images of saints in the style of traditional Byzantine icons were distributed to visitors to mark the date of Julia's death. She was predeceased by her American brothers, Stephen, John, and Andrew and her sister Mary. Andrii's brother Joseph had died four months earlier in July, which left only Julia's sister Anna from the Zavacky-Warhola immigrant generation. Julia's younger sisters Elena and Eva and her brother Yurko outlived her in Europe. The funeral guestbook was signed by numerous nieces, nephews, grandchildren, and friends, including Ilona Kalinyak, Julia's travel companion on her voyage to America. But her son Andy was conspicuously absent. His brother Paul covered for him: "I covered up for him a lot. I told relatives he happened to be out of the country. Andy didn't want to see nobody dead."[128]

"She's Gone to Bloomingdale's"

One of Andy's proscriptions that the brothers observed was to keep their mother's death as secret as possible. The line on Elachko's invoice denoting "Newspaper notices" is blank, and no published obituary of Julia Warhola has been found. But word circulated among the family and in the churches where Julia worshipped, ensuring a substantial turnout. Andy's motive for secrecy surrounding his mother's death was not unreasonable. By 1972, he had a national reputation. Any public mention of his mother, and certainly his own presence at her funeral, might have attracted the same kind of attention from press and gawkers that attended his shooting, turning a solemn event into a circus. He was already being importuned by annoying solicitations. In response to the *Pittsburgh Press* article, in which Ann Warhola said Andy called his mother every day, a Sister Teresa, who had no connection to Warhol or the family, wrote to compliment Andy on the "concern and care for your dear old Mother."[129] But her letter, which reached Andy just a few days after his mother's death, included a request for money. "Since your story gave me the feeling that you love people and are concerned about them, I wondered if you might be interested in helping us out with a community money raising project." This tone-deaf appeal was probably one of many such solicitations Warhol received. It is not surprising that he would be unwilling to make public expressions of grief that could potentially exploit his own celebrity and the memory of his mother.

Despite what some have called his "strangely cold" response to his brother's news, family members remember Andy's private grief at his mother's death. A Butler relative took a photo of Julia in her coffin and sent it to him, a macabre but common custom among older Carpatho-Rusyns. Jed Johnson told George Warhola, "Your uncle was very upset about that."[130] George, who spent a month with his uncle after Julia's death, said Andy was tired of everyone calling to bother him. "He was real nervous for like a week and a half. It was like he was tired of all this crap and just wanted to escape it all. I remember my uncle used to always keep that handkerchief of hers. He didn't want anybody to see him but he'd take off his wig and put the handkerchief on his head." Andy later told Marge Warhola, "It's always on my mind. I should never have sent her to Pittsburgh. I feel so guilty."[131] When he helped to serve an Easter meal at the Church of the Heavenly Rest fourteen years later, he still saw his mother. "A lot of the ladies looked like my mother."[132]

To New York friends and associates, however, Andy said nothing. His business manager Fred Hughes found out about Julia's death only when he happened to answer a phone call from John Warhola. Vincent Fremont, the manager of Warhol's studio, learned of it a few years after the fact. Bob Colacello's sister worked at an Yves Saint Laurent boutique, where Warhol bought a knit sweater ensemble for his mother. "He picked out a peach shell with a ribbed, narrow sweater. It was tiny. I was thinking to myself, 'Is this going to fit his mother?' I wrapped it up for her." This was in 1974, two years after Julia's death, when Barbara Colaciello worked at the boutique.[133] When Brigid Berlin asked Andy about his mother, he said, "I switch to another channel in my mind, like on TV. I say, 'She's gone to Bloomingdale's.'"[134] When friends asked about his mother, "Warhol said, 'Oh, she's great. But she doesn't get out of bed much.'"[135] It was only in 1979 when Warhol attended a gala at the Heinz Galleries in Pittsburgh that a local reporter forced an admission from him. "Some time ago, *People* reported that when someone asked you how your mother was, you said she was fine but quieter now, when in fact she had died at Wightman Manor here. Is that true?" Perhaps enough time had passed, or perhaps because he felt more responsible to the truth in Pittsburgh, Warhol equivocated: "No, I said my mother had died. Oh, but they printed it the way you say. Magazines do that."[136]

In his ethnographic analysis of Slovak and Rusyn cultural patterns, Howard Stein found that "a virtual denial of remorse at the death of a close relative" was a common reaction. As a result of the ambivalent codependent relationship between generations endemic in Slavic immigrant culture, "one almost defiantly refuses to be saddened." "It is a way of demonstrating one's independence from "a cultural ethos that demands the lifelong dependence of the individual upon the mother, family, Church, neighborhood, employer, and finally God . . . one gives an air of detachment, of matter-of-factness, often invoking theological explanation as a means of denying to oneself and to others the closeness of attachment and the depth of feeling evoked by loss and final separation. Bereavement often takes the form of a denial of mourning, a masked depression, wherein the individual doggedly recommits himself to the tasks of the workaday world."[137] From this perspective, Warhol's response to Julia's death demonstrates an excess of feeling, rather than its absence, and an inability to deal with it. As an adolescent, he could not process the death of his father, and for the rest of his life, he distanced himself from his father's memory. He dealt with the death of his cat, the "darling Hester," and his mother's mynah bird in the same way: "She went to pussy heaven . . . I don't want to think about it"; "It went to bird heaven, but I really can't think about that . . . it just took a walk."[138] A 1985 mailing from his mother's church evoked a comment in his *Diaries*: "I guess they don't know that my mother's gone to heaven."[139] But for public consumption, she had just "gone to Bloomingdale's." According to associates, Warhol was terrified of death, and rarely attended funerals. "He didn't verbalize the dark side of himself."[140] Instead, he incorporated the inevitability of death in his art, with images of car crashes, cans of poisoned tuna, the electric chair, the atomic bomb, guns, and skulls, all of which illustrated one of his mother's favorite sayings: "Remember, your life hangs by a thread."[141] In his final years, Warhol integrated his mother's message in his screenprint, *Heaven and Hell Are Just One Breath Away!* A month after his mother's death, he bought himself a Christmas present, a dachshund puppy he named Archie. Colacello describes Warhol carrying Archie around at the office party, whispering into his ear, "Talk, Archie, talk. Oh, Archie if you would only talk. I wouldn't have to work another day in my life. Talk, Archie, talk." Colacello comments, "The funny thing is, I think he was really serious."[142] Archie was a beloved companion, but a poor substitute for Julia.

"She's Fine"

Repressing thoughts of his mother's death and urged on by art-dealer friends who were impatient for his return to painting after his preoccupation with film, Warhol turned to "the tasks of the workaday world."[143] His first major project since 1964 was a series of portraits of Mao Zedong. After President Richard Nixon's weeklong visit to the People's Republic of China in February 1972, Chinese was "in fashion," and Warhol resolved to profit from it. "I could make a lot of money. Mao would be really nutty . . . not to believe in it—it'd just be fashion."[144] In 1972 and 1973, Warhol produced 199 canvases of Mao's image, precipitating a serious turn to portraiture in a new, more "painterly" style that appealed to the "beautiful people" of high society.[145] In contrast to his minimalist portraits of the 1960s with their flat surfaces and bright, monochrome, poster-like color blocks, in the 1970s, modulated hues, thickly layered paint, rough, fluid brushstrokes, and finger-painted scribbles embellished the mechanical effect of the silkscreen process. "When I do the portraits, I sort of half paint them just to give it a style. It's more fun—and it's faster to do. It's faster to be sloppy than it is to be neat."[146] Portraits that appeared "hand-painted" appealed to Warhol's international clientele of art dealers, show-business personalities, athletes, politicians, and heads of state, who paid $25,000 for a single forty-inch-square painting, and $5,000 for each additional panel of the same image. "I really would still rather do just a silkscreen of the face without all the rest, but people expect just a little bit more. That's why I put in all the drawing."[147] For the next decade, Warhol focused on what he called "business art," giving his clients what they wanted. Patrons and customers swarmed to the celebrity artist, and flattering portraits became Warhol's primary source of income. By 1981, his art was bringing in $1.7 million annually.[148]

While painting society portraits, socializing with the jet set, and traveling internationally to secure commissions, Warhol did not forget his mother. In September 1974 he painted nine portraits of Julia Warhola.[149] What prompted Warhol to paint his mother's portrait two years after her death is unknown. According to Neil Printz and Georg Frei, "Warhol rarely, if ever, undertook a new group of paintings or a series . . . without an exhibition, a commission, or an occasion in mind."[150] Warhol was still concealing his mother's death from his closest friends. David Bourdon helped Warhol select four of the "Julia portraits" for the January 1975 cover of *Art in America*. Warhol never told him she had died.[151] He was open only with his family, to whom he repeated, "It's always on my mind."

Warhol based the portrait of his mother on a photograph taken by Edward Wallowitch at Warhol's Lexington Avenue town house.[152] Warhol and Wallowitch, an up-and-coming young photographer, became lovers in 1956, and the photographer took numerous sensitive photos of Andy and a few portrait photos of Andy's mother.[153] For his portrait of Julia, Warhol chose a straightforward photograph, in which Julia sits upright, dressed in a dark dress and a ruffled apron before an elaborate screen topped by a 1950s-style starburst wall hanging. For the portrait, Warhol cut out the background and flipped the image.

The general consensus of critics and scholars on Warhol as portraitist is that he "made little attempt to portray people in character."

> His silkscreened faces are essentially stylized, cosmetic, skin-deep treatments of surfaces rather than a probing of the individual's personality. Instead of illuminating character, he presented faces as glossy masks. Only art historians with extremely sharp perception—or vivid imaginations—could detect the artist's probes into the mental states of his subjects. Robert Rosenblum, for instance, asserted that Warhol "captured an incredible range of psychological insights among his sitters," and Charles Stuckey declared that the artist displayed "a remarkable sensitivity to his subject's personalities." . . . Despite these claims, it remains questionable what importance Warhol placed on knowing his subjects in order to make his portraits.[154]

Warhol's nine completed portraits of his mother differ substantially from his society portraits, which usually consisted of a single or double panel of objective, "skin-deep" images. Obviously, he knew his mother more thoroughly than he knew any of his sitters, and he was extraordinarily sensitive to her personality and psychology. To a greater degree than his other portraits, Warhol's images of his mother are subjective, humanized, and emotionally charged. Our knowledge of the relationship between the artist and his subject, to a large extent based on his own words in interviews and private videos, cannot help but affect the way we interpret the artwork. And whether the artist intended it consciously or not, for the viewer who knows the biography of Julia Warhola, Warhol's portraits of his mother paint a visual narrative of her life.[155]

Of the nine portraits of Julia Warhola, the one that has been most often exhibited and reproduced is a full-face depiction of the elderly woman in glasses, with a pleasant, kindly expression. Two zones of color shade the face, dividing it into light and dark. Light blue-violet hues on one side blend subtly into orange and pink tones on the other. Her red dress, with hand-painted squiggles around the neckline, stands out against the deep ultramarine blue background. The sitter's expression, posture, and the blended colors evoke a sense of calm, which produces a portrayal of Bubba Julia, the mother who cooked and cleaned for her son, sent presents to her grandchildren, and prayed for all the family. Two other canvases, predominantly in blue tones, display a more distinct contrast in the face, as though light were illuminating the kindly expression of the eyes and mouth. Hand-painted scribbles blur the contours of the head and body, as the figure melts serenely into a dark purple background.

Frei and Printz noted, "In a sense, when Warhol painted his mother's portraits in 1974, 'Andy Warhol's Mother' was an established persona as much as a subject."[156] Known as her son's calligrapher and assistant, author of *Holy Cats* and folksy angels, she was often described as naive and childlike. Bourdon noted that Warhol's expressionistic finger painting is particularly noticeable in the portraits of his mother.[157] Frei and Printz expanded the point: "Finger painting not only embellished upon the unsophisticated and child-like characteristic for which Julia Warhola was known among her family, friends, and Warhol's circle, it allowed Warhol to channel her influence animistically, as it were, by adopting the mannerisms of painting like a child—i.e., scribbling into wet paint with the tips of his fingers and smudging color."[158] In one canvas, Warhol uses contrasting green and orange hues, with frenetic squiggles in gray and bright blue that evoke the playful cat lover, whimsical calligrapher, and comic actress. In another, where Julia's face and glasses are less distinct, a splash of color near the mouth suggests lip paint. In the vibrant and sloppy brushstrokes, a knowledgeable viewer may see a younger, carefree Julia Warhola, who painted cottages and tended cows.

A seemingly overexposed image depicts a blurry, shadowy form, a ghostly figure in muddy pinks and oranges that emerges from, or perhaps fades into, a deep ultramarine blue ground. In this otherworldly portrait, Julia's glasses and facial features

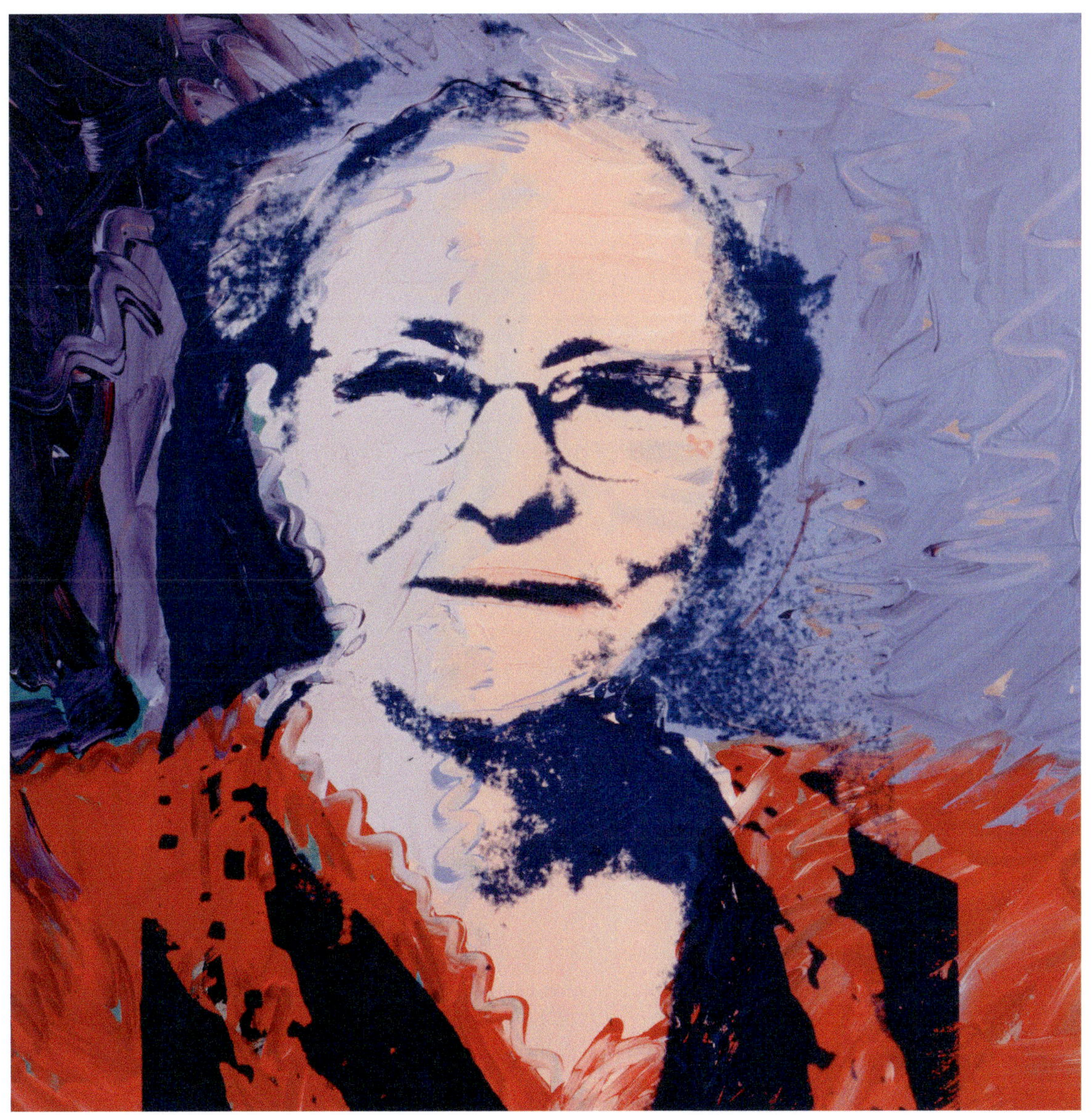

Figure 7.4. Andy Warhol, *Julia Warhola*, 1974. Acrylic and silkscreen ink on linen, 40" × 40".

are scarcely discernible, and she projects an enigmatic, spiritual presence. As Frei and Printz describe it, "Julia Warhola's features seem to materialize from or dissolve into blurs of light, like the developing states of photographic film. It is as if Warhol were not painting his mother so much as conjuring her absence."[159] Like the pussycats who play with angels in *Holy Cats*, Julia's image seems to float in the air, where she consorted with the saints in her prayer books and icons. In a deeper-toned version of the image, with hues of dark red and orange and a decorative purple squiggle in the dress, an enigmatic figure stands out against a deep purple background. Her facial features are vague, but two tones of orange seem to suggest an expression of defiance, calling to mind the feisty Julia Warhola and the conclusion of *Holy Cats*, where a gently mocking puss is captioned, "And once in a while one of them goes to the devil."

Two of Warhol's portraits of his mother, which have rarely been exhibited, present a marked contrast to the pleasant expressions and ethereal state of being suggested in most of them. Against a background of orange and red, a dark figure looms grimly, her face divided in masks of red and dark sienna. Her eyes, nose, and mouth are muddy gray smears, leaving her expressionless. Aggressive zigzags line the contours of her head, face, and clothing. In Warhol's most expressive and emotionally charged portrait of his mother, bright, contrasting colors enliven a fragmented figure. In the same frenetic fashion, the artist splashes paint even more vigorously. The division between the pink and purple halves of Julia's face is marked with a textured squiggle. One of her eyes, as well as her nose and her mouth, seem almost to be bloodied in red paint. The complex zigzag contours around her head stand out against a brilliant yellow background, and the edges of her dress rise in contrasting bright blue waves. In Gopnik's words, "Julia Warhola's face, so much like her son's in life, is sometimes close to buried under the frantic strokes of Warhol's childlike finger painting. In some of the canvases, that can feel like signs of a scared child's frantic caresses. In others, Warhol's scribbles come very close to being a petulant crossing-out."[160] One can sense the artist's conflicted feelings of love and embarrassment, his frustration and silence in response to her constant chatter, and his own overweening guilt. Still, the colors of this canvas, which stand out from the muted palette of the rest of the series, express a sense of exuberance.

If, as is often asserted, Warhol's portraits of celebrities and the Beautiful People are "sheer surface," that does not describe the portraits of Julia Warhola. As Robert Rosenblum expressed it:

> For beneath these virtuoso variations, there presides in both clear focus and ghostly fade-outs a photographic image of a bespectacled old lady, the artist's mother, a

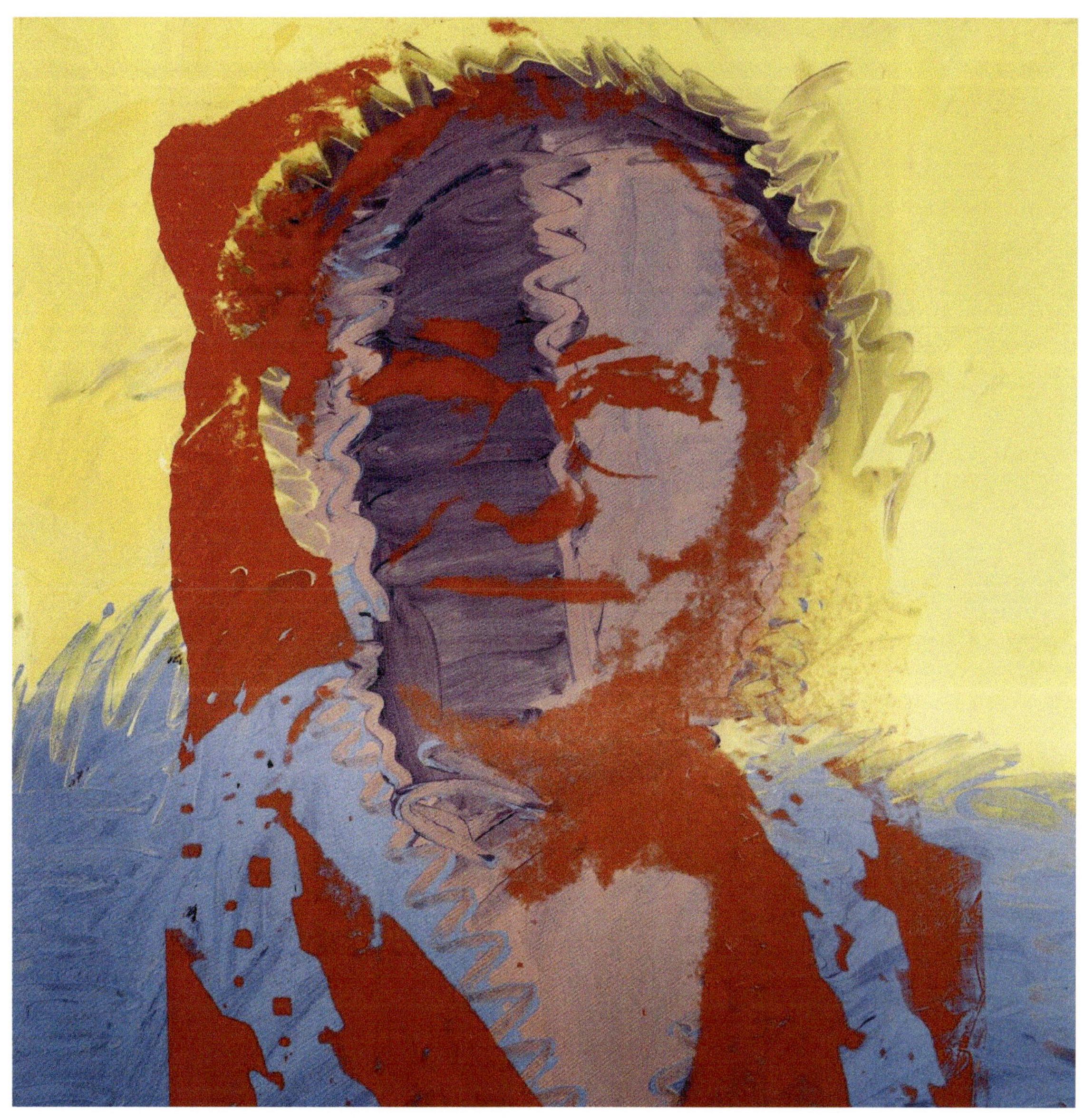

Figure 7.5. Andy Warhol, *Julia Warhola*, 1974. Acrylic and silkscreen ink on linen, 40'' × 40''.

haunting memory at once close and distant. In the midst of this racy and ephemeral company of *Women's Wear Daily* and *Interview*, her glamourless countenance is all the more heart-tugging, an enduring and poignant remembrance of family things past. She reminds us of the last thing we expected to think about in Warhol's fashionable Hall of 1970s Fame, that art and life, that personal and public history may overlap but, in the end, are very different things.[161]

Rosenblum's words come from his introduction to the catalogue of Warhol's *Portraits of the 70s*, an exhibition of 112 commissioned portraits of 56 subjects—each was shown in a pair of portraits—which opened at the Whitney Museum in November 1979. Wealthy collectors and their wives, film stars, fashion icons, and jet-setters looked down from the walls of the museum. The only exceptions to the double-portrait format were made for Chairman Mao, who appeared in three giant canvases in the middle of the floor, and Julia Warhola, whose eight-portrait series was installed in a small room off the main gallery. "Warhol must have sensed the uniqueness of this series, given that he installed the pictures in their own isolated room. . . . Julia didn't fit with the rich and powerful in death any better than she had in life."[162]

Warhol's portraits of his mother brought her to life not only for viewers, who reacted to them as enthusiastically as Warhol's friends had responded to Julia herself, but also for her artist son. For Andy, who immortalized her for future generations, Julia was an enduring presence. Bob Colacello described her portraits as "unexpected icons from another world," in all their "haunting, nervous, almost abstract splendor." "Several guests told me that they found these portraits more interesting than anything else in the show, though whenever anyone asked Andy about them, he gave them the same old line, murmured like a prayer, 'She's fine. She's fine.'"[163]

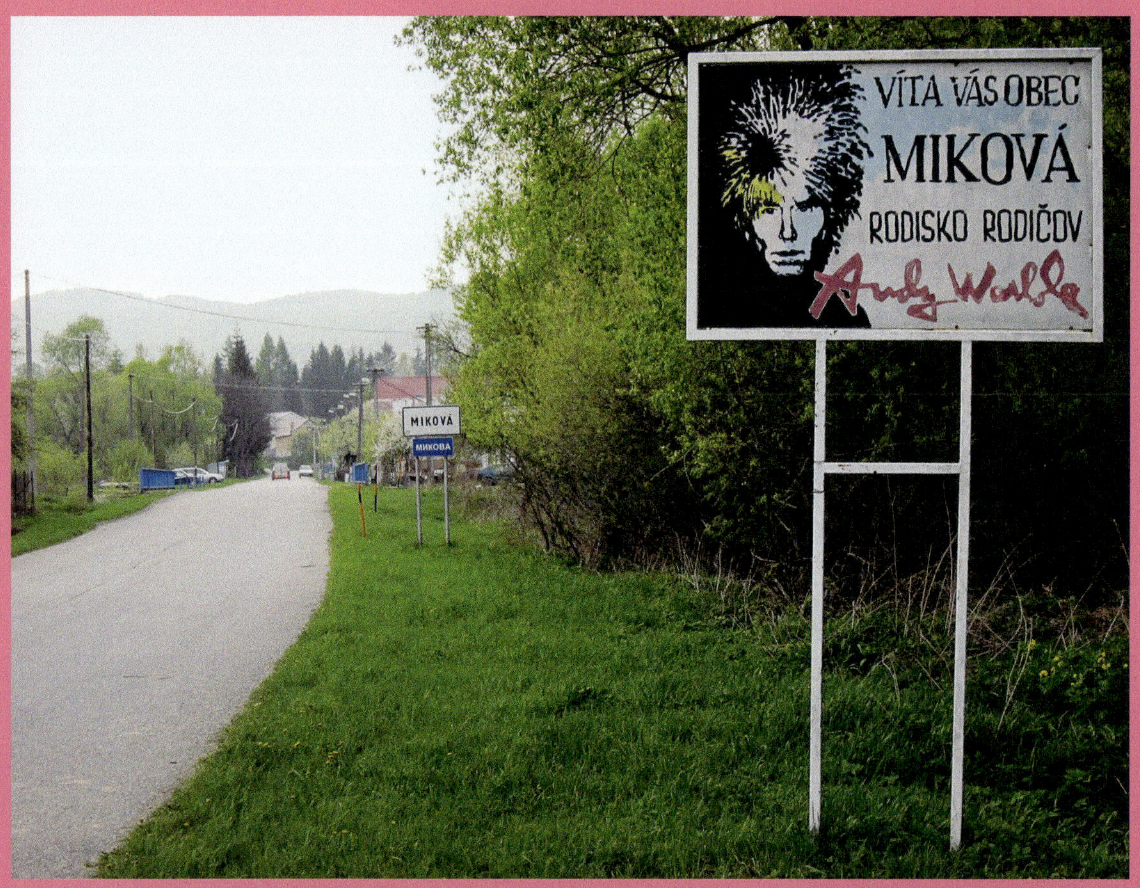

Figure 8.1. *Welcome to Miková, home of Andy Warhol's parents.* Sign at the entrance to the village.

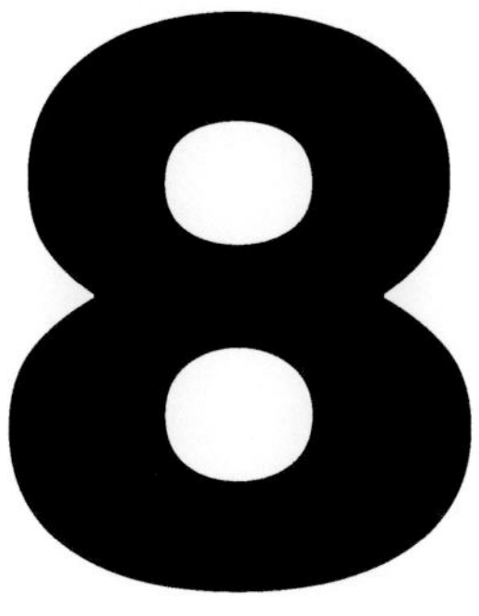

"A Simple Rusyn Woman"

The fall of communism in East Central Europe in 1989 followed shortly upon the unexpected death of Andy Warhol in 1987 at age fifty-eight after routine gallbladder surgery.[1] Under communism, which viewed avant-garde Western art as decadent rubbish, Warhol was unknown in Eastern Europe. Given the limited access to information and restrictions on communication across borders, the existence of an international superstar who had connections to a small village in northeastern Slovakia easily went unnoticed. It was only after Warhol's death that he was discovered by the Carpatho-Rusyns of Slovakia, who were then just embarking on their own quest for identity and self-determination.

After the peaceful Velvet Revolution in 1989, Czechoslovakia rejected totalitarianism in favor of democracy. Censorship was lifted, borders were opened, private businesses were legitimized, and land held in collective farms was returned to former owners. The same year saw the beginning of the European recognition of Warhol's Carpatho-Rusyn roots. In 1990 the Andy Warhol Society (Spoločnosť' Andyho Warhola) was founded in eastern Slovakia, and soon after the recognition of the Rusyn Warhol came the official emergence of the movement for Carpatho-Rusyn identity and recognition. In Slovakia, the Rusyn Renaissance

Society (Rusynska obroda), was established to promote the recognition of Carpatho-Rusyns as a distinct nationality, to codify the Rusyn vernacular language, and to foster the development of Rusyn culture. The first issue of the society's journal, *Rusyn*, bore on its cover the ghostly image of a purple Andy Warhol in his fright wig, a self-portrait created just a year before his death, and the term "Rusyn" became indissolubly linked with "Warhol."

As incongruous as the match may seem, artists and activists of the Rusyn movement embraced Warhol as their own and made the most of their link to world celebrity. In a process of subjective projection, they reconstructed the image of Andy Warhol to suit local tastes, enhancing congenial attributes and altering or diminishing embarrassing features. In a reciprocal process, as a Rusyn icon, Warhol had a significant impact on the Rusyn movement and the recognition of Carpatho-Rusyns worldwide. Warhol, the enigmatic artist, filmmaker, author, and collector, who said of himself "I am from nowhere," became an emblem of the people who can equally be said to be "from nowhere"—or at least from no easily identifiable cultural space.[2] Andy Warhol never visited his parents' homeland during his lifetime, but posthumously, he became a favorite son.

Given Warhol's evasiveness about his background and the public's unfamiliarity with Carpatho-Rusyns, it was up to the Rusyns themselves to establish Warhol's identity. The first published statement to this effect was Paul Robert Magocsi's article in a scholarly newsletter, the *Carpatho-Rusyn American* (*C-RA*), in 1980.[3] At a time when false information proliferated even in respected reference books, Magocsi established the facts by consulting with the Warhola family. In 1977, Magocsi sent Warhol a copy of his phrasebook *Let's Speak Rusyn*, based on the Prešov dialect spoken by the Warholas.[4] The letter went unanswered, but it was found, along with the book, preserved in one of Warhol's Time Capsules.

The *C-RA* article, however, did reach Michal Bycko, a young Rusyn high-school art teacher in Medzilaborce. Unofficially and covertly, Bycko began to gather information about Warhol's roots. Eventually, he set out to Miková, where he found Eva Bezeková, Julia's youngest sister. Bycko could hardly believe his eyes when Warhol's relatives brought out a box of letters and cards from Julia, family photos, sketches, and an official document by which Andy and his brothers relinquished the rights to their father's property in Miková. Eva told Bycko, "Take it home and look through it. We don't know what's there."[5] It would later become known that over the years, Warhol's relatives in Miková had received care packages from Julia containing drawings by her son. "We didn't think much of them," said Andy's cousin in *Absolut Warhola*. "We put some in the attic and used the rest to make paper trumpets for the kids. . . . After a flood, we cleaned out the attic and threw them all away. Nobody knew they were so valuable."[6]

Just before his death in 1987, Andy learned that his brother John was planning a trip to Miková. Reportedly, Warhol was pleased and told John to take "lots of photos."[7] Six months after Andy's death, John visited relatives in Slovakia for the first time and he also met Michal Bycko. John Warhola was then vice president of the Andy Warhol Foundation for the Visual Arts, established in accordance with Warhol's will as a philanthropic organization dedicated to the advancement of the arts. Bycko asked him if it might be possible to acquire a few of Warhol's works for a gallery in Slovakia. Warhola advised him to arrange with a local museum to negotiate with the foundation for the donation of a painting or two by Warhol. But in the days of communist rule, this was not the gift it might seem to be. Of the invited institutions, not a single one had any interest in what they described as the "bourgeois pseudo-artist Warhol and that dull pop art."[8] Bycko recounts a 1987 conversation with a gallery director who told him, "Let them send the paintings and we'll decide if they're worth anything."[9] But he persisted until he received support from the municipal authorities of Medzilaborce for a museum that would carry the name of Andy Warhol.

The story of the museum's establishment is replete with absurdities that Warhol would have enjoyed.[10] Socialist town planners had deliberately situated a massive Palace of Culture, constructed in what has been called the style of "socialist megalomania," opposite the Orthodox Church, as a sign of the victory of communism over religion and the past. In a twist no one could have predicted, it became instead the showcase for Warhol's avant-garde celebration of Western capitalism. The plaza in front of the cultural center was redesigned around a statue of Warhol, and the street name was changed from "Lenin Street" to "Andy Warhol Street." Michal Cihlář, a well-known Czech artist, and Rudo Prekop, a Slovak photographer, designed the interior of the building in an effort to "transform the inflated socialist house of culture into an American museum."[11] The grand opening of the Warhola Family Museum of Modern Art took place on October 5, 1991, with an exhibit titled *Andy Warhol in the Land of His Parents*. The grand opening received broad press coverage and was televised on Czechoslovak national television, giving Rusyn Slovakia its moment in the sun. The arrival of Warhol was a local demonstration of the optimistic social and cultural changes that were then invigorating all Eastern Europe. Along with a Velvet Underground Revival band from Prague, a Carpatho-Rusyn dance troupe from Pittsburgh performed at the ceremony, bringing traditional Rusyn culture full-circle.

The museum opened with thirteen original Warhol works donated for an indefinite period by the Andy Warhol Foundation for the Visual Arts. Exhibits included paintings by Andy's brother Paul, who had taken up art in retirement, and drawings by his nephew James, a professional illustrator and graphic artist. The foundation supported the Medzilaborce museum in the first decades of its existence with grants of $10,000 to $20,000 annually, and $5,000 went to the historic preservation of Miková's eighteenth-century church.[12] Known today as the Andy Warhol Museum of Modern Art, the museum displays hundreds of original prints and drawings, most of which were donated or lent by the Warhola family, the Warhol Foundation, private collectors, and corporations such as US Steel, which has a factory in eastern Slovakia.

After Slovakia joined the European Union in 2004, the town applied for funds to transform Medzilaborce into "Warhol City." Bus shelters were designed in the shape of Campbell's soup cans and building façades were embellished in the style of pop art, in an effort to "bring a little bit of pop into the town's soul." Pop entered the town's educational system when in 2009 the Vocational High School in Medzilaborce changed its name to Stredna Odborna Škola Andyho Warhola (Andy Warhol Polytechnic Secondary Vocational School). The school's website proudly asserts that it is the only educational institution in the world to carry the name of the king of Pop art.[13] For better or worse, it is difficult to imagine a school board in the United States eager to make the same claim.

The Medzilaborce museum is the second largest Warhol collection worldwide after Pittsburgh's Andy Warhol Museum, which was established three years later. The story of the establishment of the Pittsburgh museum is almost as complex as that of the museum in Medzilaborce and awash with the same kinds of problems—difficulty acquiring space and public funding, internecine bickering, and unmet deadlines.[14] The arguments for and against both museums were remarkably similar. Like the Medzilaborce museum, the Pittsburgh institution, one of four Carnegie museums, was not promoted on the basis of Warhol's artistic merit. "Fearing the criticisms of Warhol's lifestyle and personality that might arise from too much exposure to his work," activists sold the museum "on the strength of its economic drawing power as a tourist attraction."[15] But while both museums honor Warhol the artist, the Medzilaborce museum has always had a larger mission. "We did not want to 'prove' to the Americans that we can do something American-like here, in this region of the republic," said Bycko. "All we wanted was to render homage to people who gave birth to the man who has influenced the world of the 20th century. Those people were Julia and Andrii

Warhola from Miková."[16] And he advised foreign tourists, "If you want to know Andy Warhol the superstar, go to Pittsburgh. But if you want to know him as a person and what he was like before he became famous, you need to come to Medzilaborce."[17]

When Warhol said that in the future everyone would be world famous for fifteen minutes, (if he actually said it), even he could not have believed the statement would apply to the people of his mother's village of Miková, who have now enjoyed, or perhaps endured, much more than their fifteen minutes.[18] After the death of Warhol and the opening of national borders, television crews and journalists descended on the village of 150 residents. Ján Zavacky, the son of Julia's brother Yurko and onetime mayor of Miková, said, "If I had known in 1969, when I started to build this house, that so much filming would take place here, I would have made the rooms much bigger, so that all the lights and cameras and the whole film crew would fit in."[19] Villagers began to refer to themselves as "actors," and Warhol look-alikes appeared on the streets. Jozef Keselica, a young English teacher and passionate Warhol fan, made a film called *15 minút slávy Andy Warhol* (15 minutes of fame for Andy Warhol), which was awarded a bronze medal at the International Union of Cinemas. Keselica is better known for the starring role he plays in two films about Warhol—the Danish ethnographer Tom Trier's *The Warhol Nation* (1997) and a documentary by the Austrian director Georg Misch, *I Am from Nowhere* (2002). Both films focus on the people of Miková, 35 percent of whom then claimed to be related to Warhol. Misch described his film as the archetypal tale of the "rich American uncle." "For the people of Miková Warhol has assumed almost messianic proportions in that he delivers them from provincial obscurity, spreading hope among them all."[20]

Keselica is conspicuous by his absence in Stanislaw Mucha's *Absolut Warhola* (2001), the best known of the Miková documentaries.[21] The film concentrates on interviews—most often over a glass of vodka—with elderly Miková residents who present an uninformed, skewed image of the artist. While on one level, the Miková films display the villagers' boorish awkwardness, on another level, they are stars, their gnarled faces revealing lively and feisty folk wisdom, not unlike Julia's videotaped performances. Julia's adorable cousin Eva Prekstová, ninety-three years old in 2002, steals the show. Like Julia, Prekstová enjoys socializing with young people, the "great bunch of guys" in the film crew, and she proposes, "Let's have a drink and we'll feel better." Together, they raise a toast to Warhol. At the conclusion of *I Am from Nowhere*, the Mikováns gather around the sign at the entrance to the village, which will soon display the image of their famous son, poignantly singing "Vichnaia pamiat'" (Eternal memory), for their American superstar-countryman.

Immediately after communism fell in Slovakia, Keselica established the Andy Warhol Club. Addressed primarily to young Rusyns, the club showed films, held concerts, and sponsored small-scale exhibits, popularizing not only Warhol, but contemporary art and music in general. Together with another Warhol cousin, Michal Zavacky, in 1992 Keselica enlivened sleepy Miková with a "Festival of Rusyn Culture in Honor of Andy Warhol." Over the next thirty years, the annual celebration grew in size and concept. For three days every summer around Warhol's August 6 birthday, Rusyn folk ensembles, local rock groups, and European pop artists performed before a background of Warhol photos and neon lights.[22] The festivities concluded with a requiem service for the soul of the artist in the village church where his parents were married.

Images of girls in folk costume dancing before a backdrop-portrait of a silver-wigged Warhol demonstrate what the Rusyn American journalist Brian Požun called "cultural schizophrenia." When forced Ukrainianization ended in 1989, it was necessary to reclaim old Carpatho-Rusyn traditions. "Therefore, Rusyn culture started out the 1990s looking backward to try to preserve folk, religious and village traditions. . . . An anachronistic situation emerged—the Rusyns are living in the 21st century with a 19th century culture." That is, with one exception—Andy Warhol. Požun notes the paradox:

> Throwing Warhol's works into the mix of Rusyn culture is a bit misleading, since he officially considered himself to be from "nowhere," and never once made his Rusyn roots public knowledge. However, the fact that the Rusyn movement has focused on him so intensely guarantees his place in Rusyn culture, whether he likes it or not. Ever since the rebirth of the Rusyn cause in 1989, Andy Warhol has been the patron saint—or celebrity if nothing else—of the movement, thanks to his fame and international prominence. These were seen as beneficial to the national cause, even if Warhol himself had nothing to do with Rusyn culture as such.[23]

Magocsi, the preeminent historian of Carpathian-Rus', concedes that "Warhol himself never contributed anything to Rusyn culture," but his fame as an international celebrity has raised awareness worldwide about Carpatho-Rusyns.[24]

Thanks to the internet, social networking, and the spread of English among the younger generation, the twenty-first century has seen a boom of pop culture among

Rusyns in Europe, and Warhol is no longer an embarrassing cultural paradox. Young journalists of Ruska Bursa, the cultural center of the Lemko-Rusyn community in Poland, cooperate with Carpatho-Rusyn organizations and media worldwide to disseminate political, educational, and cultural information, with the goal of reinforcing ethnic identity and resisting assimilation. Toward this aim, Warhol still plays an important role.[25]

While Warhol is now a Rusyn icon, his mother is a veritable Rusyn saint. In fact, the Rusyn adulation of Andy often seems but a pretext for the exaltation of his mother, "a simple Rusyn woman," who had no education, but "the wonderful, common-sense philosophy of a simple village person."[26] Rusyn commentators dissolve whatever doubts they have about Warhol's sexuality and lifestyle in a celebration of his bond with his mother. In a kind of mystical genetics, Rusyn critics attribute Warhol's talent almost entirely to his mother, tracing her influence to his childhood, when Julia kept him entertained in his sickbed with drawings and magazine cutouts. Vasyl' Khoma [Choma] writes: "It is not a straight, direct influence of mother on son. Here we have something more delicate, a spiritual exchange of creative potential, grounded in maternal feelings and her own life experiences. The young, attentive Andy assimilated this spiritual process to his own inner world, which was forming in different circumstances from those in which his mother was raised and shaped."[27] That is, according to Carpatho-Rusyn scholars, the American Andy Warhol was informed by Rusyn Miková.

For many visitors to the Medzilaborce museum, the most popular exhibits are Warhola family photographs and artifacts—the christening gown in which Andy and his brothers were baptized, letters from Julia to her Miková relatives, her address book, a family tree, and the recording of folk songs and prayers she sent to her sister. In 1999, the museum planned a fanciful project to ship bottles of Miková water to America along the route of her emigration, with concerts, lectures, and other "happenings" along the way, but the project was canceled for lack of funds.[28] In the Andy Warhol Museum of Modern Art, the chandelier that lights the main staircase is designed from Julia's drawing of an angel in flight holding aloft a cross.

After decades of confusion about Warhol's origins, the first exhibitions in Europe highlighted his family background. In 2010, an exhibition titled "Andy Warhol and Julia" opened in Košice, the largest city in eastern Slovakia. The following year, a major exhibit in Prague's Dvorak Sec Contemporary Gallery focused on Warhol's ties to the land of his forebears. Organized with financial support from the Slovak Ministry of Culture, it included Julia's drawings, recordings, and a clip from *The George Hamilton Story.* The Central Gallery in Prague houses a permanent exhibition of the three world famous artists who have links to Czechoslovakia—Alphonse Mucha, Salvador Dalí, and Andy Warhol. The *Warhol/Warhola* display tells the story of "how Andrew Warhola became Andy Warhol," with a focus on his mother. Warhol's nephew James is quoted in the exhibit brochure: "She was a connection to the old world, and Andy was the bloom of something new—the fruit of her energy."[29]

In addition to her contribution to art through her own drawings and her influence on her son, Julia is remembered today for her music. The recording of folk songs and prayers that she sent to her sister has inspired contemporary artists to adapt Rusyn folk culture to modern musical forms. The opera singer Igor Kucer reworked Julia's recorded songs in a fresh fusion of opera, jazz, rock, pop, and swing, releasing a compact disc in 2015 called *Andy Warhol: Piesne mojej matki Júlie* (Andy Warhol: Songs of my mother Julia). On his CD and in live performance, we hear Julia announce her songs: "Teper vam zaspivam 'Chervena ruzha troiaka'" (Now I will sing for you, "A Red Rose in Three Shades"). In a somber tone, Julia sings without accompaniment: "Chervena ruzha troiaka, chervena ruzha troiaka, mala ia muzha, muzha ia mala, mala ia muzha pyiaka" (A red rose in three shades, a red rose in three shades, I had a husband, a husband I had, I had a husband, a drunken man). At the end of the introduction to this well-known Rusyn song, the tremulous voice of the elderly woman fades, and the deep tenor of Igor Kucer, backed by his five-piece ensemble, picks up the lyrics and melody. On stage, against a kaleidoscopic backdrop of projected photographs and artwork by Warhol and his mother, Kucer sings eight of Julia's songs, in styles ranging from upbeat jazz to classical opera and lyrical romance.[30]

"Our ambition from the beginning," said Kucer, "was to convey the charm of these songs in a new non-traditional, more contemporary style that is closer to the young audience, diverging from the traditional notion of folklore. Reworking the songs, we searched for forms that would best capture the texts, emotions and melodies of Julia Warhola's *a cappella* interpretation." Of the fusion of jazz, pop, rock, and Rusyn folk music, he says, "It can't be described. It has to be experienced."[31]

Tołhaje ("thieves" in Hungarian), a band from Warsaw, draws its inspiration from the ethnic musical traditions of the Carpathian Mountains, particularly the Lemko-Rusyn region that straddles the Carpathian arc between Poland and Slovakia. Using traditional instruments—violin, lyre, pipe, hurdy-gurdy, and hammered dulcimer—Tołhaje mixes traditional folk melodies with rock and electronic styling. In 2018, the group released the album *Mama Warhola*, based on the recording that Julia made in New York. The artists did archival research to verify accurate linguistic and melodic sources and texts. The songs resonated with the group's vocalist, whose family had roots in the Prešov Region: "Julia sounded exactly like my grandmother. Every sound—syllables, soft consonants and diphthongs, she uttered like my grandmother."[32]

In Tołhaje's folk-rock reworkings of Julia's songs, her voice is integrated into the melodic line in a musical dialogue between tradition and modernity. In distinction from Julia's somber styling, the group's version of "Chervena ruzha troiaka" is upbeat, but undertones of Julia's sorrowful vocalization add texture and authenticity. The Polish music critic Jarek Szubrycht was captivated by *Mama Warhola*'s evocation of "the indomitable woman who carried a snippet of her cultural identity across the ocean, cherished it for decades, and then passed on. . . . In the end, I felt that the real heroine of the album is not Julia, not the mother of the eccentric Andy, but the Song she preserved, which, although banished, muffled, and distorted, survived all these years to come back to life outside of time and place. Tołhaje managed to find this spark and fan it into a flame, making it even warmer and brighter."[33]

Julia's songs have been celebrated in Carpatho-Rusyn events at Pittsburgh's Andy Warhol Museum, but in American music, her most prominent appearance is in *Songs for Drella*, written by Lou Reed and John Cale, both formally of the Velvet Underground.[34] In "Open House," they sing, "It's a Czechoslovakian custom my mother passed on to me / The way to make friends Andy, is invite them up for tea." The representation of Andy Warhol's mother in American films is less flattering. She appears momentarily in *I Shot Andy Warhol*, played by the actress Faith Greer as an aged woman in the obligatory "babushka," holding a rosary and repeating Ultra Violet's imagined chatter, "He go to Mass . . . a good religious boy." In *Factory Girl*, a biopic of Edie Sedgwick that skewers Warhol, Beth Grant portrays Julia as a manic and nasty harridan. In a totally implausible scene, she serves a formal dinner to Edie and Andy in an upper-class dining room. The director adds a layer of crassness to Julia's Czech-language harangue goading Andy to marry by having her perform a vulgar gesture indicating masturbation. Warhol repeatedly brushes her aside or responds with one word—in Czech, not Rusyn—"dost'" (enough).[35] The 2022 Netflix documentary series *The Andy Warhol Diaries* includes two short clips of Julia from the Factory Diary videotapes. Taken out of context, they are misleading and unflattering.[36]

Julia Warhola has her own page on the Internet Movie Database (IMDb). It references her role as "actress" playing herself in "Mrs. Warhol" (*The George Hamilton Story*), but also her "role" in David Bailey's 1973 documentary *Warhol*, thereby perpetuating the false identification of Julia Warhola with the impersonator in the

Bailey film. For better or worse, Julia has a place in almost every reconstruction of her famous son's life, on stage and in film, but American pop culture does her an injustice. The complex, Carpatho-Rusyn immigrant, who lived a meaningful life, is reduced to a cliché and exploited to suit the agenda of the director.

As curators have begun to emphasize Warhol the man along with Warhol the artist, they have included his mother's artwork and artifacts that bear witness to her life in exhibitions of her son's work. In 2004, the Andy Warhol Museum collaborated with the Museum für Moderne Kunst in Frankfurt, Germany, to present *Andy Warhol's Time Capsules*, which displayed fifteen boxes containing some three thousand items. A highlight of the German exhibition was the reconstruction of a "bedroom" containing Julia's personal items. Described by one reviewer as "spooky," it was located in the entrance "because it represented Andy's own beginning."[37] A large wardrobe held Julia's dresses, hats, skirts, and headscarves. The bedside table was covered with drawings, letters, and greeting cards from her grandchildren. The bed was covered with a makeshift "quilt" patterned from Christmas cards Warhol had designed, interspersed with samples of Julia's distinctive script. In 2013, her drawings in Warhol's artist books and her own *Holy Cats* from the 1950s are featured in the exhibition *Reading Andy Warhol*, organized by Germany's Museum Brandhorst, later shown in an expanded form as *Warhol by the Book* at the Williams College Museum of Art and the Andy Warhol Museum. In *Andy Warhol: Revelation*, which opened at the Andy Warhol Museum in 2019 and closed at the Brooklyn Museum in 2022, a gallery is devoted to Julia's drawings of cats and angels, along with her prayer books and photographs. She is included among the women who played important roles in Warhol's world in *Femme Touch* (2020). The Warhol retrospective at the Tate Modern (2020) sought to "take [Warhol] out of the hype" and look at the artist through three important lenses—the immigrant story, queer identity, and the idea of death and religion. One of the first items on display was part of the ship's passenger list that recorded Julia Warhola's arrival at Ellis Island in 1921. It brought "a lump to the throat" of at least one reviewer.[38]

After Warhol's death, his portrait of Julia was proposed for a postage stamp in Czechoslovakia. Another tribute was the proposal for a Julia Warhola Chair of Carpathian Studies to promote the study of Carpatho-Rusyn history, art, and culture in the United States.[39] But neither a governmental authorization nor an honorary professorship seemed an appropriate memorial to the talented primitivist artist. A more fitting popular commemoration is the computer font "FF Pepe," created by graphic designer Pepe Gimeno and inspired by Julia Warhola's famous handwriting. "The design of this typeface shows certain nonchalant allure, freshness and vitality. It seems as if every single letter was made with a caress."[40]

From Miková to Pittsburgh and New York, fascination surrounded Julia Warhola during her lifetime and persists to the present day. Naive but shrewd, traditional but eccentric, tender but manipulative, she survived peasant primitivism and New York sophistication. Both spiritual and superstitious, starry-eyed and cynical, she was an enigma to those who know her superficially as "Andy Warhol's Mother," but a dominant force in the formation of her son. Contextualizing her story in the Carpatho-Rusyn immigrant experience clarifies the subjective worldview and ethnic culture that she internalized and her artist-son unconsciously absorbed and manifested. Would we know Julia today if not for Andy Warhol? Probably not. But like many immigrant women, she has her own story to tell—a tale of family, war, loss, poverty, and humiliation, which she survived through her own creativity, determination, and religious faith. This raises a second question: Would her son have become the Andy Warhol we know today without her?

Acknowledgments

While this book recounts the Carpatho-Rusyn immigrant experience through the life of Julia Warhola, it also reflects the collaborative and amicable Carpatho-Rusyn scholarly experience. I am indebted to old friends, new acquaintances, academic colleagues, and Warhola/Zavacky family members for making it possible.

In the early days of research, Mary Huzinec helped me to envision the overall project and conceptualize the subject. Her professional background in writing, as well as her advice and enthusiasm, buoyed its progress through what were occasionally troubled waters, and supported it to the conclusion. Another early Julia Warhola enthusiast who freely offered her time and expertise was Diane Beley, whose ancestors were from Miková, and her grandfather, like Andrii Warhola, was an Eichleay house mover. Diane's familiarity with Pittsburgh Carpatho-Rusyn church communities and neighborhoods, not to mention her ease in navigating the courthouses and prothonotary offices of Pittsburgh and Butler, greatly facilitated my research.

Carpatho-Rusyn friends contributed more than I can say. Darina Protivnak spent hours with me observing and translating videos of Julia Warhola. She was aways ready to comment on the validity of a translation or to put me in touch with a Zavacky relative. Bogdan Horbal, the curator for Slavic and East European Collections at the New York Public Library, along with Richard Custer, a scholar of Rusyn immigration, helped tremendously with translations and church records. Bogdan and Rich also searched for images, researched sources, and explicated various aspects of Rusyn culture. Ethnomusicologist Jerry Jumba, a friend of the Warhola family and cantor at Andy Warhol's funeral, shared his tapes of Julia Warhola's songs, as well as his memories and knowledge of Carpatho-Rusyn traditional culture. I am grateful to Jerry for allowing me to listen to Julia's recordings with him, and for countless illuminating conversations.

Paul Robert Magocsi reviewed my preliminary texts on Warhol's genealogy and ethnicity. David Felix and Diane Beley assisted with genealogy, Michele Parvensky contributed photographs from her travels through Carpatho-Rusyn Slovakia, and

Mary Gido, an expert on Rusyn textile arts, provided information on traditional spinning, weaving, and lace making. Mary Anne Mistick shared photographs of her beautiful handmade pysanky. I cannot thank Rob Wanenchak enough for preparing the images that add a valuable dimension to the story of Julia Warhola. Mark Wansa and Ron Matviak, World War I buffs, and Martin Drobňák, historian and cofounder of the Beskydy Military History Club in Slovakia, weighed in on the Carpathian war and assisted with military terminology. From Poland, Natalia Małecka-Nowak supplied the image of a traditional Lemko/Rusyn wedding, which could not be found in the United States. In Slovakia, genealogist Michal Razus aided my research into the Warhola-Zavacky family background. Before his untimely death in 2018, Jozef Keselica, a Rusyn Warhol enthusiast, provided me with material published in Eastern Europe. Keselica also put me in touch with Anna Knežova, who generously took the time to visit Miková, take photographs, and interview Julia Warhola's nephew, Ján Zavacky.

The large number of images that illustrate Julia Warhola's story were made possible by the generous financial support of the John and Helen Timo Foundation of Pittsburgh. Thanks also to the officers of the foundation, Maria and Cathy Silvestri, for their friendship, encouragement, and moral support. The late Carl Fischer took the photograph of Julia Warhola that accompanied the 1966 *Esquire* magazine interview. Special thanks go to Ken Fischer, who gave me permission to use his father's photo on the book cover.

During my years of work on this book, I've come to love Pittsburgh and its environs—if not the Pennsylvania Turnpike. There must be few cities that preserve and celebrate their history as well as Pittsburgh, thus facilitating local research. I have been assisted by the staff at the Thomas & Katherine Detre Library and Archives at the Senator John Heinz History Center, especially the records of the Eichleay House Moving company. The Historic Pittsburgh website, hosted by the University of Pittsburgh Library System, aided me in the use of their online historic resources. Sara Dickensheets at the Butler Historical Society and Margaret Hewitt, the archivist and special collections librarian at the Butler Area Public Library, assisted me in finding images and family employment records. The Special Collections Research Center at the library of the University of Kentucky searched out a photograph of the Zavacky family that had somehow made its way to the *Kentucky Magazine*. I am also indebted to the staff at my own university library, the Albin O. Kuhn Library and Gallery at the University of Maryland, Baltimore County, especially personnel in the interlibrary loan department and the special collections reading room. My colleagues and friends, Steven Young in linguistics, Michael J. Conlon, attorney at law, and Ling Yan, MD, kindly enlightened me on matters of language, real estate law, and medicine.

In Pittsburgh I was fortunate to meet with Reverend Father Thomas Schaefer, pastor of Saint John Chrysostom Greek Catholic Church, the Warhola family's parish, and with Kevin Beres, cantor and church historian. Maria Silvestri, John Righetti, James Warhola, Diane Beley, and Joanne Tedder took me on tours of the neighborhoods where the Warholas lived. I am especially grateful to James Warhola for a day spent in the Warhola home on Dawson Street.

Author Thomas Kiedrowski guided me through Andy Warhol's New York. At the time of my visit, the townhouse where Julia Warhola lived with her son for almost twenty years was for sale. A kindly real estate agent invited us in and allowed us to explore the premises. Native New Yorkers Edward Kasinec and Joanne Medvecky shared their knowledge of Carpatho-Rusyn churches and the life of the city's Rusyns. Aleksey Gibson, grandson of Father Alexis Vislocky, former pastor of Saint Mary's Greek Catholic Church, provided me with archival material and family memories, which he shared in many engaging conversations. Brian Požun, editor of the blog *Slavs of New York*, alerted me to several little-known aspects of Carpatho-Rusyn life in the city.

From the Warhol scholarly community, I am grateful to Reva Wolf, who invited me to participate in the 2022 Translating Warhol symposium and assisted with creative and editorial advice. The meticulous chronicle of Warhol's life by Gary Comenas at his blog Warholstars.org, as well as his astute advice and guidance, has been extremely helpful. Warhol biographer Blake Gopnik readily answered questions and shared his sources. Thanks go to other interviewers of Warhol and his mother, as well as colleagues and followers who imparted their experiences. They are identified in the text and endnotes.

I am most indebted to Julia Warhola's nieces and grandchildren, who spoke enthusiastically with me about "Aunt Julie" or "Bubba Julia." Julia's niece Christina Zavacky Soley, her daughter Tina, and her sister Nora Zavacky invited me and Mary Huzinec to their Butler home, where they told stories, shared family photos, and showed off drawings given to them by "cousin Andy." On the Warhola side of the family, John Warhola's son Donald has been extremely helpful in moving the project forward. Active in the education department of the Warhol Museum and liaison with the Warhol Foundation, he arranged presentations to the museum staff, the Carnegie Institute, and the Warhol Foundation board. Donald also provided me with documents, letters, and photographs from his father's archives, as well as personal memories. Paul Warhola's children, Mary Lou Warhola Simpson,

George Warhola, James Warhola, and Paul Constantine Warhola, kindly made time to meet with me and speak for hours by phone. I am especially grateful to Father Paul (Constantine), who died in early 2023, for his sincere and openhearted testimony, his enthusiasm for the book, and his prayers. John Zavacky, a cousin of Andrii Warhola's and a pallbearer for Julia Warhola, shared his memories of her and Andrii. Mary Zavacky Preksta's grandson George Guke Jr. filled in some blanks in the family history with his memories and photos, and Gregory Zymboly passed on letters to his mother from her Aunt Julia. All the Warholas and Zavackys reflect the kindness, humor, and unpretentious sincerity that must have characterized their uncle, their parents, and their grandparents.

Over the years I have made several research visits to the Andy Warhol Museum, in Pittsburgh, where I had access to Warhol's Time Capsules and the treasures they contain, as well as the expertise and guidance of the staff. I was fortunate to spend time with the late Matt Wrbican, who shared his vast knowledge of Andy Warhol and his family. I am also indebted to the archivists Erin Byrne and Matt Gray, the director of film and video Greg Pierce, the director of publications, clearances and photographic services Pat Seymour, and others on the museum staff for their assistance in conducting research and their patient responses to my interminable questions and requests. I extend my gratitude to the team at the University of Pittsburgh Press for their interest in my topic and their expertise in carrying it through to completion.

Finally, I could not have completed this project without the help, support, and patience of my family. My brother Bill read several drafts of the manuscript and recognized the parallels with our own family, which led to interesting discussions. Moreover, he turned out to be an excellent copyeditor. My daughter Julia saved me from many computer crises and taught me new tricks in the digital domain. My son Ben exercised his research skills to track down copyright holders and procure permissions. My husband, Stuart Rothenberg, made more trips to Pittsburgh, visits to Warhol exhibitions and Carpatho-Rusyn events than any political analyst should have to endure. Then he kept the house running through the months of COVID, when I rarely left my desk. Through it all, our pandemic puppy Pepper kept us smiling. Many thanks to all.

Notes

A Note on Names, Dates, and Sources

1. The term "Rusyn" was historically applied also to Ukrainians and Belarusians. When used here for convenience, it refers specifically to Carpatho-Rusyns.

2. These figures are based on informed estimates by Paul R. Magocsi in *With Their Backs to the Mountains*, 1. For an explanation of the problems of statistics in official census counts of Rusyns, see Magocsi, *Our People*, 14–15.

3. "Slovakia Church and Synagogue Books, 1592–1935," Database with images, FamilySearch, https://FamilySearch.org, Odbor Archivnictva [Department of Archives], Slovakia.

Chapter 1: "My Town—Miková, Czechoslovakia"

1. Julia Warhola, in Weinraub, "Andy Warhol's Mother," 101. Julia's comments on her wedding presented here are from this interview.

2. In all Slavic cultures, the peasant wedding was established by tradition as "a collective rite intended to bind the couple and the new household to the patriarchal culture of the village and the Church." Orlando Figes, *Natasha's Dance: A Cultural History of Russia* (New York: Metropolitan Books, 2002), 246. In Carpatho-Rusyn culture, the text of the wedding varied in detail according to village and region, but everywhere it observed the order of scenes and conventions that were rooted in its initial magical function. Although Julia provided only a sketchy description of her wedding, laced with some exaggeration, we can reasonably envisage the ritual that was followed based on ethnographic study of the customs of Rusyns of the Prešov Region of eastern Slovakia.

3. I have drawn my description of Carpatho-Rusyn wedding customs primarily from Chyzhmar, *Narodne vesilia rusyniv*. I have also used Jumba, "Carpatho-Rusyn Wedding"; Mušynka, "Folk Customs of Carpatho-Rusyns"; and Nedziel'skii, *Ugro-Russkii teatr*. The narrative presented here is abbreviated. A full account of the typical Carpatho-Rusyn wedding ritual would include many more songs, customs, superstitions, and ritual acts. A short dramatized Rusyn-language version of the wedding ritual in eastern Slovakia is available on YouTube: "Carpatho-Rusyn Wedding in Makovitsa," https://www.youtube.com/watch?v=CukiHFnyK2o.

4. According to birth records, Andrii was twenty-two at the time of the wedding. Emigration records show that he spent two or three years in America between 1905 and 1908.

5. Rendering spoken language in written form, especially nonstandard dialects, may seem to imply inferiority or a negative stereotype. Julia's speech, as presented by Bernard Weinraub was so perceived by her Pittsburgh-based sons. Here and throughout, I intend no pejorative attitude in my presentation of Julia's oral performance in her own voice.

6. Typically, Rusyn weddings began with invitations on Saturday and continued with the church ceremony and wedding festivities on Sunday and Monday. The Zavacka-Varchola wedding is dated in the civil register as May 22, 1909, a Saturday, and in the church register as May 24, 1909, a Monday. "Slovakia Church and Synagogue Books, 1592–1935."

7. This was the standard greeting among Carpatho-Rusyns, equivalent to "Hello" or "Good

day." The standard response was "Glory forever!" Here and throughout, translations of the ritual speeches and songs are my own, unless otherwise indicated.

8. The *Esquire* interview includes: "Very big veil." Since veils were not part of the traditional Carpatho-Rusyn wedding costume, this might have been Julia's easy reference to the bridal headdress, which had long, streaming ribbons. The "veil" might have been an insertion by the interviewer, a miscommunication, or an embellishment on Julia's part.

9. The translation of songs throughout is literal, omitting the rhythm and rhyme of the original. Traditionally, the *svashki* also sang parodic, erotic verses in the capping ceremony. This will be covered later in this chapter.

10. Mary Lou Warhola Simpson, interview by author, August 14, 2019.

11. Nora Zavacky, interview by author, August 25, 2017.

12. A note, penned probably by John Warhola, on David Bourdon's draft description of Julia's wedding reads, "Beware—Esquire article was a bit exaggerated. Julia enjoyed telling stories, stretching them a little." David Bourdon Papers, Archives of American Art, Smithsonian Institution.

13. Bernard Weinraub, interview by author, February 25, 2020.

14. George C. Rosenwald and Richard L. Ochberg, "Introduction," in *Storied Lives: The Cultural Politics of Self-Understanding* (New Haven, CT: Yale University Press, 1992), 3–4.

15. Kristin Langellier, "Personal Narrative, Performance, Performativity: Two or Three Things I Know for Sure," *Text and Performance Quarterly* 19, no. 2 (1999): 127.

16. Angell, *Something Secret*, 4.

17. Weinraub, interview by author, February 25, 2020.

18. Henry Bial and Sara Brady, "Ritual," in *The Performance Studies Reader*, 3rd ed. (London: Routledge, 2016), 95.

19. Nedziel'skii, *Ugro-Russkii teatr*, 7.

20. Patricia Caulfield protested Warhol's "borrowing" of her photograph, which became the basis for his *Flowers* series. Other works that were appropriated by Warhol and challenged by their originators include the Brillo box, the *Race Riots* series, and the *Jackie* prints (Scherman and Dalton, *Pop*, 237–38). Pat Hackett said she authored most of *The Philosophy of Andy Warhol* (Warhol, *Diaries*, xv). Bob Colacello chafed at ghostwriting the text in *Andy Warhol's Exposures*, where he claims to have told his own stories as Andy's: "It was a form of lying, of course, but there was no other way to write an Andy Warhol book, no more Warhol way" (*Holy Terror*, 557–58). In 1967, Warhol sent an imposter to take his place on a speaking tour of four western colleges. The story of the hoax and its unearthing at the University of Utah is told in Hill, "Artist Is Not Present."

21. Koch, *Stargazer*, 17; Cresap, *Pop Trickster Fool*, 23; and Scherman and Dalton, *Pop*, 1.

22. Gopnik, *Warhol*, 469.

23. Warhol and Hackett, *POPism*, 313.

24. Giordano, in Smith, *Warhol*, 128.

25. Peter Wollen, "Raiding the Icebox," in O'Pray, *Andy Warhol*, 17. The "theatricalization of experience" was also part of the camp sensibility, as described by Susan Sontag in "Notes on Camp," *Partisan Review* 31, no. 4 (1964): 515–30.

26. Nedziel'skii, *Ugro-russkii teatr*, 6.

27. The most comprehensive history of the Carpatho-Rusyns, from which I draw much of my historical, geographical, and statistical information, is Magocsi, *With Their Backs to the Mountains*.

28. Hackett, "Introduction" to Warhol, *Diaries*, xii; and Colacello, *Holy Terror*, 219.

29. The number of years a person had attended school was included in the *1940 United States Federal Census*. Andrii's younger brother Joseph reported that he had attended school for only two years. Julia's brother Stephen indicated that he had completed eighth grade; her brother John and her sister Mary said they had finished sixth grade. Anna, Julia's younger sister told the census taker she had finished four years of school. Some of these facts may have been inflated, and in this context, Julia's response to the question—that she and her husband had completed one year of high school—was certainly exaggerated.

30. Information on military conscription is drawn from Rita J. Simon and Mohamed Alaa Abdel-Moneim, *A Handbook of Military Conscription and Composition the World Over* (Lanham, MD: Lexington Books, 2011), 106–8.

31. Mary Lou Warhola Simpson, Julia's granddaughter and Andy's niece, sang the hymn for me, which she had learned as a child. Interview by author, August 14, 2019. It is certain that her father Paul and his brothers, John and Andy, also knew and sang the Rusyn anthem in Pittsburgh.

32. Aleksander [Oleksandr] Dukhnovych, "Vruchanie" [Dedication, 1851], in *Tvory* (Bratislava, 1977), 1:248. Translation is my own.

33. On this point, see Magocsi, *With Their Backs to the Mountains*, 177–78, 193.

34. According to the historian Paul R. Magocsi, if a self-identified "Czechoslovak" was not Jewish, then he or she was most likely Carpatho-Rusyn. Email communication with author, June 3, 2020.

35. Warhol, in "Ira von Fürstenberg," *Interview*, October 1978, 27.

36. Although this statement is often quoted in the literature, I have not been able to find a primary source. It most likely stems from the inexplicit observation made by Warhol's associate Bob Colacello: "'I come from nowhere,' Andy once said." *Holy Terror*, 14.

37. "Carnegie Institute of Technology, Supplementary Information," the John Warhola Family Private Collection, courtesy Donald Warhola.

38. William Jovanovich, *The Temper of the West: A Memoir* (Columbia: University of South Carolina Press, 2003), 75.

39. John Warhola, in Steinmetz, "Slovaks Desperately Searching for Famous Countrymen."

40. Paul told Bourdon, and repeated to me in 2010, "A Harvard professor who was a specialist historian [Paul Robert Magocsi] told us we were Rusyns." David Bourdon Papers, Archives of American Art, Smithsonian Institution.

41. Bockris, *Warhol*, 106, 115; Bourdon, *Warhol*, 274; Scherman and Dalton, *Pop*, 408; and Watson, *Factory Made*, 5.

42. Julia Warhola's brother John is an example of an early immigrant who had an explicit identity as Carpatho-Rusyn. This issue will be explored in chapter 3.

43. Mucha, *Absolut Warhola*; see also Misch, *I Am from Nowhere*.

44. Scherman and Dalton, *Pop*, 1–2.

45. Phillimore, *In the Carpathians*, 108–9.

46. Phillimore, *In the Carpathians*, 83.

47. Browning, *Girl's Wanderings*, 314.

48. Balch, *Our Slavic Fellow Citizens*, 214.

49. Browning, *Girl's Wanderings*, 112, 311.

50. See Rusinko, *Straddling Borders*, 124–27, 249–62.

51. "Rodyna" [Homeland], in *Poety Zakarpattia: Antolohiia zakarpatouraïns'koï poeziï (XVI St.–1945 r.)* [Poets of Transcarpathia: Anthology of Transcarpathian poetry (16th c.–1945)], (Bratislava, 1965), 261–62.

52. Ievhenii Fentsyk, "Karpaty," cited in Rusinko, *Straddling Borders*, 261.

53. Magocsi, *With Their Backs to the Mountains*, 145.

54. Allan Tong, "Andy Varchola's 15 Minutes," *Globe and Mail* (Toronto), August 17, 1991. Lexis Nexis Universe: General News Topics. Online.

55. Nora Zavacky, interview by author, August 25, 2017.

56. Historical and geographical information on Miková and the Zavacky and Warhola families is drawn from Choma, *Miková*; Miroslav Kropilák, *Vlastivedný slovník obcí na Slovensku* [A national lexicon of Slovakian villages] (Bratislava, 1977); *Obec Miková* [The village of Miková], https://www.mikova.sk/sk/; and Prekop and Cihlář, *Andy Warhol a Československo*, 28–36. An abridged English-language version, *Andy Warhol and Czechoslovakia*, was published in 2012. My citations are from the original Slovak-language edition.

57. Olbracht, *Nikola the Outlaw*, 16–17.

58. Magocsi, *With Their Backs to the Mountains*, 258.

59. Morawska, "Replica of the 'Old-Country' Relationship," 34. See also Magocsi, *With Their Backs to the Mountains*, 257–63.

60. Morawska, "Replica of the 'Old-Country' Relationship," 39.

61. Bennard B. Perlman, "Andy Warhol: The Pittsburgh Years, 1928–1949" (typescript, 2007), Bennard B. Perlman Papers, Andy Warhol Museum Archives (AWMA), cited in Gopnik, *Warhol*, 928.

62. Dukhnovych, *Virtue Is More Important*.

63. Phillimore, *In the Carpathians*, 97.

64. Robert A. Rothstein, "Jews in Slavic Eyes: The Paremiological Evidence," *Proceedings of the World Congress of Jewish Studies*, Jerusalem, 1986, D, 2:186, https://www.jstor.org/stable/23529354.

65. Morawska, "Replica of the 'Old-Country' Relationship," 42.

66. Rothstein, "Jews in Slavic Eyes," 184.

67. Bogatyrev, *Vampires in the Carpathians*, 53. This superstition was carried by Rusyn immigrants to the New World. This author's father, a ruddy dark-haired man, was paid by neighbors in his immigrant community to be the first to visit their home on holidays.

68. John Warhola, oral history, AWMA.

69. Colacello, *Holy Terror*, 21.

70. Nora Zavacky, interview by author, August 25, 2017. Zavacky's thought is erroneously given the opposite meaning in her interview with Rudo Prekop and Michal Cihlář in *Andy Warhol a Československo*, 84. The Prekop and Cihlář version is repeated in Gopnik, *Warhol*, 11. Zavacky claimed to have been misquoted and mistranslated more than once in the Prekop and Cihlář book.

71. Colacello, *Holy Terror*, 591. Colacello's assertion that Julia Warhola's grandmother was Jewish (16) has been disproved. See Rusinko, "Andy Warhol's Ancestry."

72. Gopnik, "Andy Warhol's Jewish Question."

73. Milena Hübschmannová, "Economic Stratification and Interaction: Roma and Ethnic Jati in East Slovakia," in *Gypsies: An Interdisciplinary Reader*, ed. Diane Tong (New York: Garland, 1988), 253.

74. Giordano, in Smith, *Warhol*, 127. Giordano claimed that Julia was his source for this information, but he admits that he did not know whether her story was myth or reality.

75. Hübschmannová, "Economic Stratification," 235.

76. David Z. Scheffel, "Belonging and Domesticated Ethnicity in Vel'ky Šariš, Slovakia," *Romani Studies* 25, no. 2 (2015): 118.

77. Urbarium of 1767, https://archives.hungaricana.hu/en/urberi/view/zemplen-mikova.

78. Information about the Urbarial Census is based on Joe Palma, "Great-Great-Great-Granpap Was a Serf," and the work of Martin Votruba, partially presented here: http://thehungaryexchange.blogspot.com/2015/09/urbarium-census-of-1767.html.

79. Information on land, farming, and the Rusyn homestead is drawn from Choma, *Miková*; Magocsi, *With Their Backs to the Mountains*; and Myroslav Sopolyga, "Tradytsiini sil's'ki budivli hospodars'koho pryznachennia Ukraïntsiv skhidnoï Slovachchyny" [Traditional village household structures of the Ukrainians of eastern Slovakia], *Naukovyi zbirnyk muzeiu Ukraïnskoï kul'tury u Svydnyku* 15 (1990): 257–67.

80. Fényes Elek, *Magyarország geographiai szótára* [Geographical dictionary of Hungary], vol. 2, 89, https://rusynsociety.com/wp-content/uploads/2021/10/fenyes_mgsz_1.pdf.

81. Interview with Ján Zavacky by Anna Knežova, November 20, 2021. Later, the Miková sandstone was used to make cemetery monuments for wealthy families.

82. Ján Zavacky refers to a "Matthias Zavacky," but records show that the surname of the Matthias from Poland was Mrocsko. He was Julia's maternal grandfather. See Rusinko, "Andy Warhol's Ancestry."

83. John Warhola, oral history.

84. Giordano, in Smith, *Warhol*, 128.

85. For a detailed genealogy of the Warholas and Zavackys with family trees and documentation from parish records, see Rusinko, "Andy Warhol's Ancestry." Birth, death, and marriage dates are from FamilySearch, "Slovakia Church and Synagogue Books, 1592–1935," in the possession of the author, as are reproductions of census materials. Immigration records are from "Immigration and Emigration Records," Ancestry.com.

86. In 1930, Joseph told a census taker that he immigrated in 1910. Ancestry.com, *1930 United States Federal Census*. More reliable is the date of arrival

given on his naturalization documents—October 20, 1909. Ancestry.com. Pennsylvania, U.S., Federal Naturalization Records, 1795–1931.

87. Prekop and Cihlář, *Andy Warhol a Československo*, 34.

88. This uncommon name in Rusyn-inhabited lands south of the Carpathians is alternately spelled Mrocska, Mroczko, Mrotsko, and Mrocsek in Hungarian transliteration, and Mrochko in English transliteration from Cyrillic.

89. Inconsistencies in the records suggest that another woman, Zuzana Hoshak, perhaps a first wife to Mathias, may have been Julia's biological grandmother. Hoshak's identity and ethnicity is probably Slovak. For details, see Rusinko, "Andy Warhol's Ancestry."

90. Weinraub, "Andy Warhol's Mother," 158.

91. Nora Zavacky, interview by author, August 25, 2017.

92. Connie Schaber, "Divided We Stand: The Family in the 1980s," *Kentucky Monthly*, December 1980, 47–50.

93. Steve Vest, the publisher of *Kentucky Monthly*, email communication to the author, September 11, 2017.

94. The late Matt Wrbican, the former curator of the Andy Warhol Museum, recalled that Charles Lisanby, a boyfriend of Warhol's in the 1950s, was from Princeton, Kentucky. Warhol was known to prank Lisanby in his ads for I. Miller shoes (Smith, *Andy Warhol's Art and Films*, 369) and in a mock newspaper page, *The Princeton Leader* (De Salvo, *Andy Warhol*, 170). This use of the Zavacky family photo may seem to be a payback prank, but I have been unable to uncover any connection between Lisanby and *Kentucky Monthly*.

95. Archyp Danyljuk, "A Village Museum and the Problems of Lemko Culture in Contemporary Poland," *Carpatho-Rusyn American* 10, no. 2 (1987), 9. Further information on housing is drawn from Myroslav Sopolyga, "Narodne budivnytstvo Ukraïntsiv skhidnoï Slovachchyny" [Folk-style construction of the Ukrainians of eastern Slovakia], *Naukovyi zbirnyk muzeiu Ukraïnskoï kul'tury u Svydnyku* 7 (1976): 387–403.

96. "Lyst yz staroho kraia" [Letter from the old country], *ARV*, July 27, 1911.

97. Warhol, *Diaries*, 109, 120.

98. Paul Warhola, in Prekop and Cihlář, *Andy Warhol a Československo*, 64.

99. Fedash, *Blossoms on a Rooftop*, 5–7.

100. Morawska, *For Bread with Butter*, 42.

101. Choma, *Miková*, 100–101.

102. Ján Zavacky, interviewed by Anna Knežova, November 20, 2021.

103. Morawska, *For Bread with Butter*, 58.

104. Ján Zavacky, Julia's nephew, told the interviewer Anna Knežova, "They were on a higher level."

105. Morawska, *For Bread with Butter*, 322–23, n85.

106. Eva Bezekova, interview with Michal Bycko, in Bycko, *Nočné dialógy*, 82.

107. Gopnik, *Warhol*, 13.

108. Baycura, "Introduction," *Lyndora Chronicles*, 45.

109. "Lemkovskŷ prypovidkŷ" [Lemko proverbs], in *Nasha knyzhka*, 159.

110. Gabaccia, *From the Other Side*, 17.

111. Worobec, "Temptress or Virgin?" 228, https://doi.org/10.2307/2499482.

112. *Vesil'nŷ, sval'bianŷ spivankŷ z erotichnŷm motivom* [Wedding songs with erotic themes], supplement to Chyzhmar, *Narodne vesilia*.

113. Aleksandr V. Gura, "Coitus in the Symbolic Language of Slavic Culture," *Electronic Journal of Folklore* 30 (2005): 145–54, https://doi.org/10.7592/FEJF2005.30.gura.

114. Nadiia Varkhol, "Erotychni motyvy v paremiiakh Rusyniv-Ukraïntsev Chekho-Slovachchyny" [Erotic motifs in oral folk literature of the Rusyn-Ukrainians of Czechoslovakia], *Naukovyi zbirnyk muzeiu Ukraïns'koï kul'tury u Svydnyku* 16 (1990): 292–95.

115. "Lemkovskŷ prypovidkŷ," 159.

116. A great many collections of Carpatho-Rusyn folk songs have been published in Slovakia since the "Rusyn renaissance" of 1989. There are several ethnomusicological studies, but few interpretive analyses, and almost nothing in English. For specific examples, I have chosen to

concentrate on an accessible source: Mačoškova, Servicka, and Sikorjakova, *Three Stars—Three Generations*. Lyrics in the liner notes were translated by Zuzana Zvirinská, Paul Robert Magocsi, and Steven Chepa. I have adapted the translations for clarity and style. Additional examples and general comments on Carpatho-Rusyn folk music are drawn from the following: Ľuboslav Kraiňák, *Úvod do štúdia hudobného folklóru Rusínov na Slovensku* [Introduction to the musical folklore of the Rusyns of Slovakia] (Prešov, 2002); *Švit' mišačku* [Shine on, moon] (Prešov, 1992); Helena Slyvkova, *Niet pomoči našomu narodu? Spivankŷ zo Staškivskoj i Mykivskoj dolynŷ* [Is there no help for our people? Songs from the Staškovce and Miková valley] (Staškovce, 2008); and *Spivankŷ Annŷ Matsibobovoi* [Songs of Anna Matsibobova], introduction and afterword by Mykhail Hyriak (Prešov, 1993).

117. A full examination of this topic would include a comparison with men's folk-song performances. Specific to men are historical and war songs, songs of shepherds, and comic songs. In regard to romantic relationships, a theme that stands out is the man's resistance to marriage. "I won't marry / I'll just wander / Through the mountains / After other women // Other women are the kind / That bring you whiskey / Whiskey and wine / Drink, boys, drink all day." Perhaps the most popular male voice in the songs of Carpatho-Rusyn immigrants, sung with special vigor at festivals and gatherings, was the Lemko-Rusyn song "Ia parobok z Kapušany" [I'm a bachelor from Kapušany], in which a young man bemoans the material demands of a wife. "Why do I need a wife / I have enough trouble on my own." *Lemkovskŷi narodnŷ spivankŷ*, 31.

118. Suzie Frankfurt, in Bockris, *Warhol*, 130.

119. Viva Hoffman to Andy Warhol, AWMA, cited in Gopnik, *Warhol*, 644.

120. Rosenwald and Ochberg, "Introduction," 7.

121. Helena Chomová, in Prekop and Cihlář, *Andy Warhol a Československo*, 161.

122. Arthur C. Danto, *Andy Warhol* (New Haven, CT: Yale University Press, 2009), 12.

123. Makovskii, *Narodnoe iskusstvo*, 40, 29.

124. Makovskii, *Narodnoe iskusstvo*, 36.

125. Information on *pysanky* is drawn from Markovyč, *Rusyn Easter Eggs*, 125–26.

126. Markovyč, *Rusyn Easter Eggs*, 55.

127. Glenn O'Brien, "Interview: Andy Warhol," in Goldsmith, *I'll Be Your Mirror*, 254.

128. See Mickens, "Warholas at Work."

129. Samuel Hazzard Cross and Olgerd Sherbowitz-Wetzor, eds. *The Russian Primary Chronicle, Laurentian Text*, https://www.mgh-biblio thek.de/dokumente/a/a011458.pdf, 111.

130. O'Brien, "Interview," 258.

131. The artist's nephew Donald Warhola noted that the liturgy's performative, theatrical nature is somewhat reminiscent of his uncle's raucous "Exploding Plastic Inevitable" multimedia shows of the 1960s. Barbara Klein, "A Pop Icon's Iconic Beginning," *Carnegie Magazine*, Fall 2019, https:// carnegiemuseums.org/carnegie-magazine/fall-2019 /a-pop-icons-iconic-beginning/.

132. Eva Bezekova, interview with Michal Bycko, in Bycko, *Nočné dialógy*, 82–83; and Vasyl Bezek, in Prekop and Cihlář, *Andy Warhol a Československo*, 147.

133. Julia's acquaintance with the painters of the Miková church will be explored further in chapter 4.

134. Mušynka, "Folk Customs of the Carpatho-Rusyns," 4.

135. Dillenberger, *Religious Art*; and Gopnik, *Warhol*, 16. The issue of Warhol's religion will be discussed further in chapter 5.

136. Ethnographic information is drawn from Bogatyrev, *Vampires in the Carpathians*; Chori, *Vid rodu do rodu*; and Iosif Varkhol, "Divochi vorozhin-nia v chasi zymovoho sontsestoiannia" [Girls' fortune-telling at the winter solstice], *Naukovyi zbirnyk muzeiu Ukraïns'koï kul'tury u Svydnyku* 15 (1988): 163–71. See also the following articles by Mykola Mušynka in *Carpatho-Rusyn American*: "Folk Customs of the Carpatho-Rusyns," "Pentecost/Rusalja," "St. George's Day," and "Harvest Festival."

137. Blessed bread, distinct from the consecrated Eucharist, is distributed in Byzantine Catholic churches after holiday liturgies. Crumbs

of this bread are found preserved in Julia Warhola's church envelopes in Warhol's Time Capsules.

138. Barbara Alpern Engel, "Peasant Morality and Pre-Marital Relations in Late 19th Century Russia," *Journal of Social History* 23, no. 4 (1990): 700.

139. Bogatyrev, *Vampires in the Carpathians*, 76–77.

140. Paul Morrissey, in Prekop and Cihlář, *Andy Warhol a Československo*, 135.

141. Richardson, "Warhol at Home," in Richardson, *Sacred Monsters, Sacred Masters*, 248.

142. Perry, "Introduction" to Perry and Brownley, *Mothering the Mind*, 3–10.

143. Ivan Karp, quoted in Scherman and Dalton, *Pop*, 327.

144. Gerard Malanga, quoted in Scherman and Dalton, *Pop*, 327

145. John Warhola, quoted in Burns, *Andy Warhol*.

146. Karp, quoted in Wilcock, *Autobiography and Sex Life*, 98–99; and Bourdon, *Warhol*, 232.

147. Bohumil Hrabal, *Total Fears: Letters to Dubenka*, trans. James Naughton (Prague: Twisted Spoon Press, 2014), 74.

148. Koestenbaum, *Andy Warhol*, 112.

149. Richardson, "The Secret Warhol," in Richardson, *Sacred Monsters, Sacred Masters*, 124.

150. Warhol, *Diaries*, 641, 558, 654, 678, 590, 643.

Chapter 2: "Then Everything Bad"

1. Information on folk practices concerning childbirth are taken from Mušynka, "Folk Customs of Carpatho-Rusyns: Birth and Baptism," and Iosyf Varkhol, "Z rodyl'noï obriadovosti Snynshchyny" [Customs connected with childbirth in the Snina region], *Naukovyi zbirnyk muzeiu ukraïns'koï kul'tury u Svydnyku* 21 (1998): 171–200.

2. Mary Lou Warhola Simpson, interview by author, August 14, 2019.

3. Bogatyrev, *Vampires in the Carpathians*, 97.

4. Warhol biographers have put forth various names for the child. Victor Bockris and Wayne Koestenbaum call her "Justina." Bockris, *Warhol*, 16; and Koestenbaum, *Andy Warhol*, 20. David Bourdon dubs her "Josephine." Bourdon, *Warhol*,

16. Rudo Prekop and Michal Cihlář more tentatively christen her "Jozefina (or Julia)." *Andy Warhol a Československo*, 37. Even the Warhol Museum of Modern Art in Medzilaborce erroneously refers to her as Josephine. Julia Zavacky herself is often represented in the literature as "Julia Justina." Church records clarify the confusion. Julia's name at birth was Julianna. Justina was her mother, and Josephine was her maternal grandmother. Her daughter was Maria.

5. Weinraub, "Andy Warhol's Mother," 158.

6. Vasyl Bezek, in Prekop and Chilář, *Andy Warhol a Československo*, 147.

7. Weinraub, "Andy Warhol's Mother," 158. This must have been a communication error. As indicated by Bezek, Julia took care of Andrii's mother and perhaps other elderly Varchola relatives. Andrii's father had died in 1896.

8. Information and facts about emigration are drawn from Balch, *Our Slavic Fellow Citizens*, 104–47; Puskás, *Hungary to the United States*, 27–115; and Rácz, "Attempts to Curb Hungarian Emigration."

9. Magocsi, *Our People*, 14. Hungarian scholars calculate that one-quarter of all emigrants from Hungary left illegally. Rácz, "Attempts to Curb Hungarian Emigration," 18.

10. Choma, *Miková*, 92.

11. Facts on wages and return immigration are drawn from Puskás, *Hungary to the United States*, 55–84; Morawska, *For Bread with Butter*, 64–75; Rácz, "Attempts to Curb Hungarian Emigration," 10; and Baines, *Emigration from Europe*.

12. "Pod'me khloptsi pod'me do toi Amerychky" [Let's go, boys, to that America], https://www.youtube.com/watch?v=_hLXEsjELgM.

13. Rácz, "Attempts to Curb Hungarian Emigration," 14.

14. Vasyl Khoma [Choma], "Fenomen Endi Varhol," 39.

15. Puskás, *Hungary to the United States*, 99; and Rácz, "Attempts to Curb Hungarian Emigration," 28–29. According to Baedeker's 1905 *Austria-Hungary Handbook for Travelers*, the exchange rate was $1 to 4.8 crowns (https://www.geshergalicia.org/about-galicia/historical-austro

-hungarian-empire-exchange-rates/). According to MeasuringWorth.com calculations, $37.50 in 1912 is equal to upward of $1,000 in 2020.

16. Monika Glettler, *Pittsburg—Wien—Budapest: Programm und Praxis der Nationalitätenpolitik bei der Auswanderung der ungarischen Slowaken nach Amerika um 1900* (Vienna: Verlag der Österreichischen Akademie der Wissenschaften, 1980), 25, cited in Wyman, *Round-Trip to America*, 33.

17. Morawska, *For Bread with Butter*, 40.

18. Aleksander Pavlovych, "Chestnyi Rusnak s Makovytsy rozdumue v Amerytsy" [Reflections of an honest Rusnak from Makovytsia in America], *Izbrannye sochineniia* [Selected works] (Uzhhorod: Unio, 1942), 251–52.

19. *Misiatsoslov na 1900 god* (Uzhhorod, 1900), 65–72. For a more complete analysis, see Rusinko, "Going to America," in Custer, *Rusyn-American Almanac*, 115–17.

20. Puskás, *Hungary to the United States*, 86–87.

21. See Rusinko, "From the *Starŷi krai*."

22. Commons and Leiserson, "Wage-Earners of Pittsburgh," 113.

23. Fitch, *Steel Workers*, 4.

24. Roberts, "Immigrant Wage-Earners," in Commons and Leiserson, *Wage-Earning Pittsburgh*, 33. This article was first published as "The New Pittsburghers: Slavs and Kindred Immigrants in Pittsburgh," in *Charities and the Commons: A Weekly Journal of Philanthropy and Social Advance*, no. 2 (January 1909): 533–51.

25. Roberts, "Immigrant Wage-Earners," 38.

26. Roberts, "Immigrant Wage-Earners," 39.

27. Roberts, "Immigrant Wage-Earners," 41.

28. Roberts, "Immigrant Wage-Earners," 54. The postal savings system was inaugurated in 1911 to provide saving facilities for underserved populations. The comparison is probably misleading, since western European immigrants and native-born Americans had options other than postal banks to deposit their savings.

29. Information on wages is drawn from Roberts, "Immigrant Wage-Earners," 55.

30. Commons and Leiserson, "Wage-Earners of Pittsburgh," 179.

31. John Warhola, oral history.

32. On this passenger list, Stephen reports that he had been in Butler from 1904 to 1908. The confusion in remembering exact dates of previous journeys is an indication of how routine they had become.

33. R. L. Polk & Co., *Butler Directory 1913–1914*, preface, n.p.

34. Cited in Ralph Goldinger and Audrey Fetters, *Butler County: The Second Hundred Years* (self-published, 1994), 52.

35. *Butler Eagle*, July 21, 1902, in Baycura, *Lyndora Chronicles*, 48; and *Butler Eagle*, November 12, 1902, in Baycura, *Lyndora Chronicles*, 49–50. Subsequent references to articles in the *Butler Eagle* will be indicated in the text with the date of their original publication. They are reproduced in Baycura, *Lyndora Chronicles*.

36. Quoted in Goldinger and Fetters, *Butler County*, 52.

37. Prekop and Chilář, *Andy Warhol a Československo*, 46.

38. Warhol, *Diaries*, 57, 789; see also 286, 297, 420.

39. Roberts, "New Pittsburghers," 60.

40. Kleinberg, "Seeking the Meaning of Life," in Greenwald and Anderson, *Pittsburgh Surveyed*, 100.

41. Handlin, *Uprooted*, 144.

42. Handlin, *Uprooted*, 168–69.

43. Greene, "Polish-American Worker," 63.

44. Bodnar, "Immigration and Modernization," 53.

45. Ancestry.com, U.S., World War I Draft Registration Cards, 1917–1918.

46. Divorce petition, Court of Common Pleas, Butler County, December 1922, Book 41, 182.

47. Eva Prekstová, in Prekop and Cihlář, *Andy Warhol a Československo*, 160.

48. Christina Zavacky Soley, interview by author, August 25, 2017.

49. By 1913, Frank Lobert had married, moved out of the Zavacky apartment, and opened his own meat market on nearby Kohler Avenue. In December 1913, his wife committed suicide by drinking carbolic acid, leaving behind a two-year-old child.

No apparent cause for the suicide could be found. *Butler Citizen*, December 24, 1913. Three months later, Lobert was shot in his market by a customer in a dispute over a minor price disagreement. The full story behind these incidents is unknown, but they speak to the turbulent nature of the Zavackys' environment.

50. Bodnar, *Transplanted*, 131–34.

51. Tina Soley, interview by author, February 29, 2024.

52. *Butler Citizen*, January 1, 1918, March 21, 1918, February 8, 1919. Among the 142 Buick buyers listed in the ad, Zavacky is the only obviously Slavic name.

53. Handlin, *Truth in History*, cited in David Nasaw, Introduction to "AHR Roundtable: Historians and Biography," *American Historical Review* 114, no. 3 (June 2009), https://doi.org/10.1086/ahr.114.3.573.

54. "Hey, chorna Ameryka" [Hey, America is a dark place], trans. Richard Custer, in Custer, *Rusyn-American Almanac*, 180.

55. *Butler Times*, October 10, 1907, in *Lyndora Chronicles*, 123.

56. "Four Dead and Score Is Injured," *Pittsburgh Post-Gazette*, October 7, 1907; updated in Amy Brunner, "Pullman Standard," *Butler County Historical*, http://butlerhistorical.org/items/show/29. Subsequent descriptions are from this article.

57. "Company Is Exonerated," *Pittsburgh Post-Gazette*, October 30, 1907.

58. In addition to the three disasters in the Pittsburgh region, December 1907 saw mine catastrophes in Alabama and New Mexico. In all, over seven hundred coal miners were killed in thirty-one days.

59. Information on the Darr mine disaster is drawn from the following sources: John R. Ball, "Mutilation of Bodies Testifies to Force of Explosion," *Pittsburgh Daily Post*, December 20, 1907; "Explosion Is Feared: Eleven Bodies Recovered," *Pittsburgh Daily Post*, December 21, 1907; "Perished Miners Finally Located in Small Group," *Pittsburgh Daily Post*, December 23, 1907; John Thomas, "Prompt Measures Necessary to Quell Disorder Which Follows Mine Horrors," *Pittsburgh Daily Post*, December 20, 1907; "Darr Mine Disaster Historical Marker," https://explorepahistory.com/hmarker.php?markerId=1-A-2C7; "Mine Explosion Entombs 250 Men," *New York Times*, December 20, 1907, https://timesmachine.nytimes.com/timesmachine/1907/12/20/101732038.pdf; "Centennial of the Miracle of St. Nicholas," https://www.stnicholascenter.org/pages/centennial/; and Nicholas P. Ciotola, "The Darkest Month: Coal Mining Disasters of December 1907," *Western Pennsylvania History* 90, no. 4 (2007–8): 24–33, https://journals.psu.edu/wph/article/view/7793/7566.

60. Excerpts from the *1907 Report of the Department of Mines* and *The United Mine Workers Journal*, in "Mine Disasters in the United States," https://usminedisasters.miningquiz.com/saxsewell/darr.htm.

61. Jackson, *Dreadful Month*, 102.

62. *Pittsburgh Dispatch*, December 19, 1907, cited in "Uzhasnaia katastrofa" [A Terrible Catastrophe], *Amerikansky Russky Viestnik*, December 26, 1907.

63. *Amerikansky Russky Viestnik*, published in Rusyn between 1892 and 1952, was the official organ of the Greek Catholic Union, the first fraternal society established specifically for Carpatho-Rusyns. Until 1926 it was published in both a Cyrillic- and a Roman-alphabet edition. Translations are my own.

64. *ARV*, January 23, 1908.

65. *Annual Report of the Department of Mines*, in "Mine Disasters in the United States," https://usminedisasters.miningquiz.com/saxsewell/darr.htm.

66. Eastman, *Work-Accidents*, 11–13.

67. Commons and Leiserson, "Wage-Earners of Pittsburgh," 118.

68. Shergold, "Wage Rates in Pittsburgh." Statistics cited here are taken from Shergold.

69. *New York Times*, November 21, 1907, and November 22, 1907, cited in Shergold, "Wage Rates in Pittsburgh," 184.

70. "Get-Away of Foreign Workmen Continues," *Butler Times*, March 6, 1908, in Baycura, *Lyndora Chronicles*, 129.

71. "Monthly Steerage Flow from Voyage Database," cited in Keeling, *Business of Transatlantic Migration*, 202.

72. *Commercial and Financial Chronicle*, 86

(March 21, 1908), cited in Shergold, "Wage Rates in Pittsburgh," 183.

73. "V Amerytsi dobri" [In America it's good], trans. Richard Custer, in Custer, *Rusyn-American Almanac*, 179. See video at https://www.youtube.com/watch?v=UQwxpltJPtU&t=131s.

74. According to Julianna Puskás, typically, a returning emigrant to villages in Zemplyn purchased two to five acres of land. *From Hungary to the United States*, 80. Morawska gives a figure of 1.2–3 hectares (3–7 acres) as the typical land purchase. *For Bread with Butter*, 75.

75. Reproduced in Prekop and Cihlář, *Andy Warhol a Československo*, 150–51.

76. See Rusinko, "From the *Starŷi krai*," 279.

77. Varžaly, Stefan, *Selska svad'ba: veseloihra iz žizni podkarpato-russkaho naroda* [A village wedding: A comedy from the life of the Carpatho-Rusyn people], cited in Rusinko, "From the *Starŷi krai*," 279.

78. Slepcov, "K problematike I. svetovej vojny," 56.

79. Weinraub, "Andy Warhol's Mother," 158.

80. Rácz, "Attempts to Curb Hungarian Emigration," 24.

81. See Abbott, *Immigrant and the Community*, 4.

82. Whelpley, *Problem of the Immigrant*, 245–48.

83. Dirk Hoerder, "The Traffic of Emigration via Bremen/Bremerhaven: Merchants' Interests, Protective Legislation, and Migrants' Experiences," *Journal of American Ethnic History* 13, no. 1 (Fall 1993): 88.

84. For a detailed study of the competing interests between state and private business and the system of migration control that resulted, see Kvale, "Emigrant Trains." I have drawn information on the overland trek of the Miková emigrants from Kvale.

85. Although some migrants were able to travel through Germany privately, most came through the more affordable emigrant system operated by the shipping companies. In 1909, 64,500 persons arrived in Bremen on 284 emigrant trains, 56,000 in emigrant cars attached to regular trains, and only 24,000 in regular train cars. Cited in Hoerder, "Traffic of Emigration," 91.

86. Quote from the *Berliner Illustrierte Zeitung* 39, 1900, 612–13, cited in Kvale, "Emigrant Trains," 155.

87. Hoerder, "Traffic of Emigration," 94. In 1913 only twelve cases of complaints had to be taken up by authorities.

88. Steiner, *On the Trail of the Immigrant*.

89. Reports of the United States Immigration Commission, "Steerage Conditions," https://archive.org/stream/cu31924021182500/cu31924021182500_djvu.txt.

90. *New York Herald*, "The Aristocracy of the Steerage," September 12, 1909, quoted in Keeling, *Business of Transatlantic Migration*, 230.

91. "Atlantic Crossing in Winter," https://lindagartz.com/atlantic-crossing-in-winter/.

92. Tunstall, *Blood on the Snow*, 7–8.

93. Sources provide varying data. My information is drawn from the following: Hronský, "Priebeh bojov na území Slovenska"; and "The First World War: The Fights in the Carpathian Mountains in 1914–1915," Exhibit, Slovak National Museum, Museum of Ukrainian Culture, Svidník, February 18, 2015–March 18, 2015, https://www.snm.sk/?current-exhibitions-11&clanok=the-first-world-war-the-fights-in-the-carpathian-mountains-in-1914-1915.

94. "1. Svetová vojna: Boje na Slovensku boli tak krvavé ako na západnom fronte" [World War I: Battles in Slovakia were just as bloody as those on the western front]," July 28, 2014, https://www.topky.sk/cl/10/1413489/1.

95. Colonel Georg Veith, "Carpathian War Sidebar: Eyewitness to Agony," HistoryNet, May 13, 2014, https://www.historynet.com/carpathian-war-sidebar-eyewitness-to-agony.htm.

96. Accurate war losses, direct and indirect, are almost impossible to calculate. An extensively sourced analysis is offered by Anatol Schmied-Kowarzik, "War Losses (Austria-Hungary)," *1914–1918 Online International Encyclopedia of the First World War*, doi: 10.15463/IE1418.10964.

97. Bockris, *Warhol*, 27.

98. "Pervaia pochta yz staroho kraia" [First mail from the old country], *ARV*, September 10, 1914; and "Starokraevaia pochta" [Old-world letters], *ARV*,

October 1, 1914. Subsequent citations will be noted in the text by date. Translations of letters are my own. In some cases, I have condensed and slightly adapted the text for clarity and cohesion.

99. The letter writers used the term "cannon" loosely to refer to artillery pieces for which they would not have known the technical terminology. They could be describing howitzers, rifled guns, or trench mortars. I have chosen to use "cannon" in the text to capture the writers' sense and connotation.

100. Slepcov, "K problematike I. svetovej vojny," 58. Zborov is about thirty miles from Miková.

101. "Bullets" (*kuli*) might be projectiles from rifles or machine guns. "Hot bullets" (*goriachie kuli*) refer to artillery fire. In some cases, they seem to refer to airburst shrapnel shells, antipersonnel artillery shells loaded with shrapnel, timed to explode as airbursts over troops on the ground. Some letter writers describe such shrapnel as "hot-stone-hail" (*goriachii-kamenets-grad*).

102. Bezek, in Prekop and Cihlář, *Andy Warhol a Československo*, 147. Julia was taking care of two sisters and her mother, and possibly also her mother-in-law.

103. Francesco Frizzera, "Refugees (Austria-Hungary)," *1914–1918 Online International Encyclopedia of the First World War*, DOI: 10.15463/ IE1418.11171.

104. J. F. Archibald, "Fighting in the Carpathians as Seen with the Austrian Army," *Scribner's Magazine*, April 1915, http://jfredmacdonald.com/ worldwarone1914-1918/austria-15fighting-carpat hians.html.

105. Hannes Leidinger, "War against the Local Population," *The World of the Habsburgs*, https:// ww1.habsburger.net/en/chapters/war-against -local-population.

106. Slepcov, "K problematike I. svetovej vojny," 61–62.

107. Magocsi, *With Their Backs to the Mountains*, 173. Magocsi notes that in some eastern regions of Subcarpathia and Maramureş, the Russians were, in fact, welcomed as liberators from Magyar oppression.

108. Jaroslav Hašek, *The Good Soldier Švejk and His Fortunes in the World War* (London: Heinemann, 1973), 573–74.

109. *ARV*, March 18, 1915.

110. "O našej obci" [About our village], *Miková*, http://www.mikova.sk/sk/ukazka-strany-2/.

111. Prekop and and Chilář, *Andy Warhol a Československo*, 36.

112. Howard Phillips, "Influenza Pandemic," *1914–1918 Online International Encyclopedia of the First World War*, 2014, DOI: 10.15463/ IE1418.10148.

113. John Warhola, quoted in "Andy Warhol," *Literárny týždennik: časopis Zväzu slovenských spiso-vatelov* [Literary Weekly: Organ of the Society of Writers of Slovakia], June 8, 1990, 9.

114. Rado Turik, "Vojnové cintoríny z prvej svetovej vojny v obci Miková" [World War I cemeteries in Miková], *Klub vojenskej histórie Beskydy*, http://www.kvhbeskydy.sk/vojnove-cintoriny -z-prvej-svetovej-vojny-v-obci-mikova/.

115. See Maureen Healy et al., "Social Conflict and Control," *1914–1918 Online International Encyclopedia of the First World War*, 2014, DOI: 0.15463/ IE1418.10541; Matteo Ermacora, "Rural Society," *1914–1918 Online International Encyclopedia of the First World War*, 2014, DOI: 10.15463/IE1418.10530; and Pastor, "Hungary in World War I."

116. Warhol, "Julia Warhola in T-Shirt Sick."

Chapter 3: Pittsburgh, Pennsylvania

1. Bockris, *Warhol*, 28. By saying Julia went "to look for" her husband, Bockris seems to imply some doubt about their relationship. John Richardson ascribes this comment about "looking for" her husband to Andy. "Secret Warhol," 125. Bockris also adds the phrase "or so he claimed" to the statement that Andrii sent the fare five times, adding, "We don't know whether he had tried to send her the fare previously in the seven years since he left." As demonstrated, Andrii sent Julia wire transfers of funds before and during the war. The delay in the couple's reunion was due to the war and Julia's family responsibilities. There is no suggestion that Andrii did not want Julia to join him in Pittsburgh.

2. Bourdon, *Warhol*, 16.

3. Weinraub, "Andy Warhol's Mother," 158.

4. This story was recounted to me by Ann War-hola in 2010 and confirmed by her daughter Mary

Lou Warhola Simpson on August 15, 2019. In addition to the brief accounts in Bockris and Bourdon, a more complete version of the story is included in Prekop and Cihlář, *Andy Warhol a Československo*, 78.

5. Juraj Čisarik, *Genealogy of Eastern Slovakia*, "Mini-Schematizmus: Index of All Byzantine Church Reverends in Slovakia in the period 1674–1948," https://www.cisarik.com/MINISCHE MATIZMUS-abc.htm.

6. Elena Chomová, in Prekop and Cihlář, *Andy Warhol a Československo*, 161.

7. Jacob Horak, "Effects of the War upon Emigration from Czechoslovakia," *Social Service Review* 2, no. 1 (March 1928): 78–79.

8. Keeling, *Business of Transatlantic Migration*, 261–62.

9. Julia's passport was found in Time Capsule 522, along with copies of her birth, marriage, and naturalization certificates, in a large manila envelope from Chase Manhattan Bank. The envelope also contained a letter from the bank to Andy Warhol, referencing a safe-deposit box he had opened in 1958 and for which he had ceased paying rent. The bank's letter informed Warhol that the box had been forcibly opened in November 1980. If not claimed, the bank would dispose of the contents after the expiration of two years, that is, in November 1982. Another letter, dated June 10, 1982, reminded him of the upcoming deadline. Apparently, Warhol claimed the box with his mother's documents just months or weeks before the papers would have been destroyed. Then, ten years after Julia's death, he consigned her valuable documents to a Time Capsule.

10. Dirk Hoerder, "The Traffic via Bremen/Bremerhaven: Merchants' Interests, Protective Legislation, and Migrants' Experience," *Journal of American Ethnic History* 13, no. 1 (1993): 68–101.

11. The first German liner to carry passengers to America after the war did not sail until late September 1921. "First German Liner Since the War Sails for U.S.," *New York Daily Herald*, September 18, 1921.

12. Keeling, *Business of Transatlantic Migration*, 262.

13. They are included on a list of outbound passengers from the United Kingdom as transmigrants, that is, "alien passengers (other than first-class passengers) who arrived in the United Kingdom, having in their possession Prepaid Through Tickets, and in respect of whom security has been given that they will proceed to places outside the United Kingdom." UK and Ireland, Outward Passenger Lists, 1890–1960, available at Ancestry.com. Julia's name was misspelled by the indexer as "Julia Vashold."

14. Martyn Pring, *Boat Trains: The English Channel & Ocean Liner Specials: History, Development and Operation*. Pen & Sword Books. Kindle Edition, loc. 294.

15. "The Famous Big Four of the New York-Liverpool Service"; "White Star Line Fleet, History, and Services," *GG Archives*, https://www.gjenvick.com. Subsequent comments on the *Celtic* come from this brochure.

16. "RMS *Celtic* Dinner Menu Card, 6 July 1919," *GG Archives*, https://www.gjenvick.com.

17. Information about the voyage is drawn from the following newspaper articles, all from June 21, 1921: "200 Irish Girls Land Here to Be Movie Stars, Not Servants," *New York Herald*; "Housework Has No Appeal for 140 Girl Immigrants," *New York Tribune*; and "Irish Girls Seek Careers," *New York Times*.

18. However, on her Zemplyn County documents, Julia signed her surname as "Warhola," the American spelling that Andrii had already adopted.

19. Marian L. Smith, "A Guide to Interpreting Passenger List Annotations," https://www.jewish gen.org/infofiles/manifests/.

20. "Housework Has No Appeal for 140 Girl Immigrants," *New York Tribune*, June 21, 1921. On Julia's manifest, the anticipated arrival date, June 20, is crossed out, and replaced with June 21.

21. Information on Julia's railroad journey to Pittsburgh is drawn from the following sources: "AnTide," *Bulletin* 15, no. 11 (July 16, 1887), Historic Pittsburgh, https://www.historicpitts burgh.org; and *Official Guide of the Railways and Steam Navigation Lines* (June 1921), 326, http://cprr.org/Museum/Books/I_ACCEPT

_the_User_Agreement/Official_Rail_Guide _1921.pdf

22. Walko, *Eternal Memory*, 164.

23. Steve Mellon, *Pittsburgh: The Dark Years*, https://newsinteractive.post-gazette.com/prohibition/.

24. Oseroff, "Survey of Workingmen's Homes," 8, 11. An extract from his thesis was published as "Soho Hillside," Appendix II in Commons and Leisersing, *Wage-Earning Pittsburgh*, 406–10. An appendix to his thesis, available at the University of Pittsburgh Library, was a statistical survey of the homes and families in the district.

25. Oseroff, "Survey of Workingmen's Homes," 11–12.

26. Dinwiddie and Crowell, "Housing of Pittsburgh's Workers," 100–101.

27. A "star border" was "a highly favored and privileged lodger," who may have had a sexual relationship with the landlady. See Andrew Vázsonyi, "The Cicisbeo and the Magnificent Cuckold: Boardinghouse Life and Lore in Immigrant Communities," *Journal of American Folklore* 91, no. 360 (April–June, 1978): 641–56, http://www.jstor.com/stable/538918.

28. *1910 United States Federal Census*, Pennsylvania, Allegheny County, Pittsburgh ward 4, enumeration district 317. The American census taker mangled the spelling of Rusyn names, and misidentified their place of birth as Austria and their nationality as Slovenian.

29. Lubove, *Twentieth-Century Pittsburgh*, 64.

30. *Historic Pittsburgh*, "Real estate plat-book of the city of Pittsburgh: Wards 1–6 and 9," https://historicpittsburgh.org/maps-hopkins/1923-volume-1-plat-book-pittsburgh.

31. The Lithuanian Hall later housed the Sahara Temple and, most recently, a substance abuse recovery group. The building was destroyed in a three-alarm fire in 2005.

32. Bell, *Out of This Furnace*, 122.

33. Bell, *Out of This Furnace*, 16.

34. Bell, *Out of This Furnace*, 19.

35. *Pamietniki Emigrantow: Stany Zjednoczone*, ed. Marian M. Drozdowski (Warsaw: Kasiaska i Wiedza, 1977), 2:431, quoted in Morawska, "Immigrants Pictured and Unpictured," 231.

36. Bell, *Out of This Furnace*, 18.

37. Mary Miroka Laver, oral history, November 23, 1976, in Krause, *Grandmothers, Mothers and Daughters*, 150.

38. Morawska, "Immigrants Pictured and Unpictured," 229, 232.

39. "Dobri w Ameryci" [It's good in America], https://www.youtube.com/watch?v=UQwxpltJPtU.

40. Skrabec, *World's Richest Neighborhood*, 7.

41. Paul Warhola, in Colacello, *Holy Terror*, 15.

42. Ethnic descriptions in the census are unreliable. Zabolotny, and certainly his wife from Czechoslovakia, may have been Rusyn.

43. Paul Warhola, in Bockris, *Warhol*, 22.

44. "Insanitary Conditions in Soho Complained Of," *Pittsburgh Press*, June 24, 1921; "Jealous Man Shoots Widow and Kills Self," *Pittsburgh Post-Gazette*, November 14, 1921; "Held for Attempted Murder," *Pittsburgh Daily Post*, November 15, 1921; "Given Life Sentence: Negro Who Slew Beelen St. Man Is Sentenced," *Pittsburgh Press*, April 27, 1926; "Orr Street Place Raided," *Pittsburgh Post-Gazette*, January 13, 1924; "One Man Killed, Three Injured in Fifth Avenue Auto Smash-Up," *Pittsburgh Daily Post*, June 15, 1927; "Hold-up of Gulf Oil Company Station," *Pittsburgh Press*, July 3, 1933; and "Distilleries Raided," *Pittsburgh Post-Gazette*, October 10, 1930.

45. Robert A. Woods and Albert J. Kennedy, *Handbook of Settlements* (New York: Charities Publication Committee, 1911), 282–83. See also the following in the *Pittsburgh Post-Gazette*, "Soho's New Dental Clinic," June 29, 1913; "Neighborhood Workers Open Busy Season in Soho District," December 4, 1910; and "One Settlement Does Much Good," November 2, 1911.

46. Anna Katsur Firda, unpublished oral history, interviewed by Diane Beley.

47. Bockris, *Warhol*, 19.

48. Bailey, *Andy Warhol*.

49. Bockris, *Warhol*, 20.

50. Maria Patton Knox, "Report on a Questionnaire Submitted to the Principals of the Pittsburgh

Public Schools by the Survey Commission," March 31, 1917. Email, courtesy of Diane Beley.

51. Bockris, *Warhol*, 30.

52. Warhol, *Julia Warhola in T-Shirt Sick*.

53. Bell, *Out of This Furnace*, 330. Bell's characters use the explicit uncensored term.

54. Robert M. Zecker, *Race and America's Immigrant Press: How the Slovaks Were Taught to Think Like White People* (London: Bloomsbury Academic, 2011), http://dx.doi.org/10.5040/9781 628928273.ch-001.

55. See Blake Gopnik, "Warhol: A Yuletide Tale," virtual lecture at Poetry and Prose, Washington, DC, November 30, 2020, https://www .youtube.com/watch?v=S1fA5iuKF-M.

56. Eli Zaretsky, Introduction to Thomas and Znaniecki, *Polish Peasant*, 42.

57. Howard Wilson, *Mary McDowell, Neighbor* (Chicago, 1928), 69–80, cited in Zaretsky, Introduction, 42.

58. Van'o Hunianka, "Leshko Mŷrna," in *Nasha knyzhka* (Yonkers, NY: Lemko-Soiuz), 105.

59. Bennard Perlman, a college classmate of Warhol's, claims that Andrii was employed at Jones and Laughlin. Perlman, "Education of Andy Warhol," 147. I have found no evidence of such employment. According to John Warhola's oral history interview, Andrii would have preferred an indoor mill job, but could not get one.

60. "50 Persons Driven from Homes," *Pittsburgh Post-Gazette*, February 17, 1920; and "Saloon Raided Twice in Four Hours," *Pittsburgh Post-Gazette*, August 7, 1925. A certain John Zavacky, who was in charge of Dudich's bar, was arrested in the raid. This was probably the Warhola cousin who emigrated to Pittsburgh with Andrii Warhola and Maria Dudich, not Julia's brother.

61. "Grants' Hill: Removal of the 'Hump,'" http://www.brooklineconnection.com/history/ Facts/Hump.html; and "On the Frick Building, at the Corner of Fifth Avenue and Grant Street Is a Sign Stating 'Street Grade Prior to 1912,'" *Pittsburgh City Paper*, March 24, 2005, https://tinyurl.com/da3vsy7h.

62. Information on the John Eichleay Jr. Company, later reorganized as the Eichleay Engineering Corporation, is drawn from Eichleay, *House Movers*; the Eichleay website, https://www .eichleay.com/heritage; and Eichleay Engineering Corporation Records and Photographs, 1889– 1989, in the Thomas and Katherine Detre Library and Archives at the Senator John Heinz History Center in Pittsburgh. The story of the pachyderm is told in "House-Movers Use Engine to Bury Gusky," *Pittsburgh Press*, May 18, 1926.

63. Eichleay, *House Movers*, 5.

64. John Warhola, oral history. Andrii's draft registration from 1942, just a month before his death at age fifty-five, describes him as five feet, six inches and 185 pounds.

65. Eichleay, *House Movers*, 29. In 1926, the 30,000-ton Haugh Hotel in Indianapolis was moved by the Kress-Oravetz House Moving Company of Pittsburgh. Founded by the Slovak Michael Oravetz, the company employed mostly Rusyns and Slovaks, including, at times, Andrii Warhola. A video of the moving process of the Haugh Hotel is available at www.tinyurl.com/53huex8r.

66. The *Indiana Telephone News*, 12. The article consists of several subsections with different titles. Authorial attribution is "By the Editor, with plenty of help from the engineering department." Accessed at the Detre Library and Archives.

67. "Building Moving Hoover-Indiana Bell," 1930–1931, box 6, folder 7, Detre Library and Archives.

68. Eichleay, *House Movers*, 29.

69. On this point, see Kevin Kirkland, "A Moving Bond," *Pittsburgh Post-Gazette*, August 18, 2001, 15, 17.

70. John Zavacky, interview by author, July 29, 2020.

71. Craig Smith, "Preservationists Praise Rehab Plan for Old Morgue," *Pittsburgh Tribune-Review*, March 11, 2011, https://phlf.org/2011 /03/11/preservationists-praise-rehab-plan-for -old-morgue/. For details and photographs, see "The Curious Move of the Allegheny County Morgue," *Third Stop on the Right*, July 9, 2021, https://www.thirdstopontheright.com/allegheny -county-morgue/.

72. "This Used to Be Here—Pittsburgh's Shantytown," *Point of Pittsburgh* http://www.the

pointofpittsburgh.com/this-used-to-be-here-pitts
burghs-shantytown/.

73. Bodnar, "Immigration and Modernization," 49–50.

74. Bodnar, Simon, and Weber, *Lives of Their
Own*, 159.

75. Warhol, quoted in Brian Wallis, "Absolute
Warhol," *Art in America* 77, no. 3 (1989), 25.

76. "Big Downtown Projects Made Realty
Activity in 1926," *Pittsburgh Post-Gazette*, January
1, 1927.

77. The same block of homes had been sold
in 1920 by Ida R. Stein to an "out-of-town investor." "Bouquet Street Transfer," *Pittsburgh Press*,
December 17, 1920.

78. *Pittsburgh Post-Gazette*, November 14,
1931; and *Pittsburgh Press*, November 11, 1933.

79. Allegheny County Pennsylvania Deed
Book 2498:554, April 30, 1934. See also "Aronson
Company Sells Oakland Home," *Pittsburgh Press*,
May 20, 1934, where it is stated that the house was
sold "for a private consideration."

80. Allegheny County Pennsylvania Deed
Book 2504:90, August 16, 1934. It has been suggested that the $1.00 sales price might "signal some
sort of tax dodge—the kind of thing that Warhol
was not above trying later"(Gopnik, *Warhol*, 12).
The $1.00 sales price, a legal fiction to keep the
sales price out of the record, was standard for the
block of homes on Dawson Street. There are any
number of reasons why sellers and buyers might
have wanted to keep the sales price private. Sellers
may have wanted to conceal profits and losses, and
Carpatho-Rusyn buyers had a propensity to mask
their assets, a learned behavior that Andy Warhol
later exhibited in New York: "He didn't want people
to see how rich he was." Colacello, *Holy Terror*, 323.

81. John Warhola, oral history.

82. Property Valuation of Dawson Street, Pittsburgh, PA, http://www.city-data.com/allegheny
-county-properties/D/Dawson-Street-5.html.

83. Jared Jenkins, "Remo Bufano: Our Forgotten Ancestor," student paper, University of
Connecticut, 1997, quoted in Gary Comenas,
"From Nowhere to Up There," https://warholstars
.org/nowhere/andy_warhol_p4.html.

84. John Warhola, oral history.

85. Bockris, *Warhol*, 31.

86. I was able to tour the Warholas' Dawson
Street house on August 2, 2021. Many original features of the house remain unchanged.

87. The entry for the Andrii Warhola family in
the 1940 census is not entirely legible and is probably in error. Codes indicate that it was Julia who
gave the information to the census taker. In the
column indicating whether the home is owned or
rented, the symbol is unclear, but appears to be an
R, that is, "rented." Under "value of home or rent,"
the number given is $35. This must have been a
communication error, referring to the rent paid by
the lodgers, rather than the value of the house. The
value of similar neighboring homes was $2,100 to
$2,400.

88. The cold cellar in the basement was converted as a photographic darkroom in the 1930s,
and only later, probably in the 1940s, a toilet was
installed.

89. John Warhola, oral history.

90. Bockris, *Warhol*, 33. Paul Warhola's
memories of the good old days may have been
rose-colored. His brother John recalled being
bullied by "tough Irish kids." John Warhola, oral
history.

91. Gopnik, *Warhol*, 12n118.

92. H. L. Mencken, "The Libido for the Ugly,"
in *Prejudices: Sixth Series* (New York: Knopf, 1927),
187.

93. John F. Bauman, *Before Renaissance: Planning in Pittsburgh 1889–1943* (Pittsburgh, PA:
University of Pittsburgh Press, 2006), 42.

94. Bell, *Out of This Furnace*, 40.

95. Motyl, "Was Andy Warhol Ukrainian?" 549.
Gilda Williams calls the Warhola neighborhood
"an impoverished eastern-European ghetto in Pittsburgh." "On Andy Warhol's Mother," in *Tate, Etc.*,
no. 10 (Summer 2007), http://www.tate.org.uk
/context-comment/articles/warhol-stumbled
-across-real-america-pantry-woman-who-never
-adapted-american. Bob Colacello and the art
critic Dave Hickey refer to a "Slavic ghetto" and a
neighborhood that "felt like, looked like, and acted
like a central European ghetto, a great distance

from America," in Burns, *Andy Warhol*. These descriptions may apply to the Warholas' first slum residences, but not to Andy Warhol's formative years on Dawson Street.

96. Bockris, *Warhol*, 31.

97. Morawska, *For Bread with Butter*, 247.

98. Weinraub, "Andy Warhol's Mother," 158.

99. John Warhola, oral history.

100. Bockris, *Warhol*, 34. Elachko's comment echoes the reputation of the Varchola family in Miková, "They were on a higher level."

101. John Warhola, oral history.

102. Sophonisba P. Breckinridge, *New Homes for Old* (1921), 111–13, https://www.gutenberg .org/ebooks/41291.

103. Ann Elachko, in Bockris, *Warhol*, 34.

104. Ann Elachko, in Colacello, *Holy Terror*, 21–22.

105. Albert Ziontz, in Colacello, *Holy Terror*, 21.

106. Prekop and Cihlář, *Andy Warhol a Československo*, 53. Paul Warhola's comment is probably exaggerated, perhaps by the translators. In Pittsburgh, where there was a large Orthodox and Eastern Catholic population, schools would have made accommodations.

107. Warhol, *Diaries*, 568.

108. In *Amerikansky Russky Viestnik* and other Rusyn-language writings, Subcarpathian Rusyns like the Warholas and Zavackys referred to themselves as Rusyns or Uhro-Rusyns, that is, Rusyns from Hungary.

109. *Opportunity Realized*, 10. Rusin is an alternate transliteration from the Cyrillic alphabet.

110. For more on the Rusyn–Ukrainian dispute, see Elaine Rusinko, "Was Andy Warhol Ukrainian? Carpatho-Rusyns and 'Ukrainianism' in Pittsburgh." https://www.academia.edu/81496524/Was_ Andy_Warhol_Ukrainian_Carpatho_Rusyns _and_Ukrainianism_in_Pittsburgh.

111. Morawska, *For Bread with Butter*, 173.

112. Greene, "For God and Country," 455–56.

113. Richard Custer, email communication with the author.

114. Paul C. Warhola (1943–2023), the son of Andy's brother Paul, was ordained a Greek Catholic priest in 1969 at the Cathedral of Saint John the Baptist in Munhall, Pennsylvania. In 1974, he left the Eparchy of Pittsburgh to open a Byzantine Catholic church in Denver, under the patronage of the bishop of Parma. By 1977, he had decided to leave the Catholic Church. He was married in 1978. Paul C. Warhola, interview by author, February 20, 2020.

115. Paul C. Warhola, interview by author, July 23, 2020.

116. "Parish History," in *St. John's Greek Catholic Church, Lyndora, Pa., 40th Jubilee Book 1912–1952* (no city, no pub.), 1952.

117. The justification for this decision can be traced to decrees of the Communist Party in Subcarpathia in the early 1920s. In 1926, the Transcarpathian Branch of the Czechoslovak Communist Party adopted a resolution to "rid ourselves of the name *Rusyn*" and assume a Ukrainian identity. For details, see Magocsi, *With Their Backs to the Mountains*, 312–14.

118. Wall text for "Andy Warhol: His Roots," by Alexander J. Motyl. *Andy Warhol: Endangered Species*, October 7, 2018–February 7, 2019, Ukrainian Museum, New York, http://www.ukrainianmu seum.org/ex_181006warhol.html.

119. Paul Robert Magocsi, "Andy Warhol: His Art and Ethnic Roots," lecture at the Ukrainian Museum, New York, February 15, 2019, https://www .c-rrc.org/andy-warhol-his-art-and-ethnic-roots/. For more on church schisms and the disputes over Warhol's ethnicity, see Elaine Rusinko, "Was Andy Warhol Ukrainian?" academia.edu, https://www.academia.edu/43283109/Was_Andy _Warhol_Ukrainian_Carpatho_Rusyns_and_ Ukrainianism_in_Pittsburgh.

120. John Zavacky, "Letter to the Editor," *ARV*, April 20, 1911.

121. *Opportunity Realized*, 45–46.

122. Warhol, *Diaries*. Page numbers are noted in the text.

123. Gopnik, *Warhol*, 11.

124. Warhol's godfather was Stephen Kalinyak from Miková, the husband of Julia's 1921 travel companion. His godmother, Maria Shack, had also been godmother to his sister in Miková in 1912. He was baptized and confirmed by Reverend Stephen Kozak.

125. "Greeks Hurry $100,000 Church to Aid Jobless," *Pittsburgh Press*, March 12, 1932; and "Art Work Finished for Greek Church," *Pittsburgh Press*, September 8, 1934. Accounts of the cost of the new church range from $80,000 to $100,000.

126. Magocsi, *Our People*, 66.

127. Morawska, *For Bread with Butter*, 254.

128. *ARV*, March 17, 1938.

129. *ARV*, April 21, 1938.

130. *ARV*, March 31, 1938. "Carpatho-Russian" here should be read as "Carpatho-Rusyn."

131. For a bilingual edition of the play, see Dukhnovych, *Virtue Is More Important*.

132. "Uspišnoe predstavlenije v Frankstown-Pittsburgh, Pa." [A successful presentation in Frankstown-Pittsburgh], *ARV*, February 15, 1934; and "Uspišnoe predstavlenije v Forward Ave., Pittsburgh, Pa." [A successful presentation on Forward Avenue, Pittsburgh, PA], *ARV*, May 14, 1931. "Forward Avenue" was the former name of Saline Street, the current street address of Saint John Chrysostom. The Greenfield area of Pittsburgh where *Ruska dolina* is located was formerly known as Frankstown.

133. See Bicha, "Hunkies." The term and the stereotype persisted long after 1920. I was confronted by it in an insult as late as the mid-1980s.

134. Information on the traditions surrounding Christmas are drawn from the following: Bogatyrev, *Vampires in the Carpathians*, 37–58; Ivan Kalyniak and Liuboslav Kalyniak, *Vifleemskŷi vechur* [Bethlehem play] (Prešov: Rusynska obroda, 2002); and Jerry Jumba, "The Bethlehem Play," unpublished manuscript, 1990.

135. Paul Warhola in supplement to Vecchiet, *Vies et morts d'Andy Warhol*.

136. Nedziel'skii, *Ugro-russkii teatr*, 25–29.

137. Walko, *Eternal Memory*, 24.

138. Weinraub, "Andy Warhol's Mother," 99.

139. Bogatyrev, *Vampires in the Carpathians*, 71.

140. Warhol, *Diaries*, 120.

141. Greene, "Polish American Worker," 64–65, 77.

Chapter 4: "I Raise My Children Okay"

1. Weinraub, "Mothers," 96–101, 156–58.

2. The *Esquire* article caused consternation in the Warhola family. According to Julia's son John, "Andy asked [*Esquire* magazine] not to quote the way she spoke, not to copy down her broken English. They promised they wouldn't. They had done an interview with one football player and his mother, and had presented what she said very nicely, in perfect English. But when it came to Andy's mother, it looked as though she was completely mentally deficient." John said Andy was so angry that he later deliberately gave inaccurate responses to questions about his date and place of birth. Prekop and Cihlář, *Andy Warhol a Československo*, 48. Warhola's explanation is dubious, and its exposition in *Andy Warhol a Československo* is unreliable. According to Weinraub, he had no conversation with Warhol, and there was no request to standardize Julia's English. Bernard Weinraub, interview by author, February 25, 2020. Each woman's speech was rendered in her regional accent and personal style. Furthermore, there is no indication that Julia's interview brought any embarrassment to Warhol. It is more likely that Andy had tried to appease his brother's discomfiture at the exposure of their mother's "broken English" by attributing it to a journalist's manipulation. For more on this topic, see Rusinko, "Andy and Julia in Rusyn."

3. Eli Zaretsky, Introduction to Thomas and Znaniecki, *Polish Peasant*, 6. The study pertains also to Carpatho-Rusyn immigrant adaptation.

4. Thomas and Znaniecki, *Polish Peasant*, 240. Emphasis in the original.

5. Kathleen Neils Conzen, "Thomas and Znaniecki and the Historiography of American Immigration," *Journal of American Ethnic History* 16, no. 1 (1996): 18.

6. Zaretsky, Introduction to Thomas and Znaniecki, *Polish Peasant*, 15.

7. James Warhola, in Prekop and Cihlář, *Andy Warhol a Československo*, 17.

8. "A Taste of Paradis: Diana Ross in Conversation with Andy Warhol," *Interview Magazine*, September, 1975, https://www.interviewmagazine.com/culture/a-taste-of-paradis-diana-ross-in-conversation-with-andy-warhol.

9. Paul and John Warhola in Bockris, *Warhol*, 23.

10. Donald Warhola, interview by author, August 24, 2017.

11. Paul Warhola, in Bockris, *Warhol*, 23.

12. Thomas and Znaniecki, *Polish Peasant*, 71.

13. John Warhola, oral history. Unless otherwise indicated, comments from John here regarding his father are from the same interview. See also Bockris, *Warhol*, 23.

14. Bodnar, "Immigration and Modernization," 57.

15. Duda, "At Home in Pittsburgh."

16. Mary Preksta, in Colacello, *Holy Terror*, 22.

17. Bockris, *Warhol*, 32.

18. See "Palko Rostoka," in Emilij Kubek, *Narodny povisti i stikhi* [Folk stories and verse], vol. 1 (Scranton: Obrana, 1922), 7–85.

19. Thomas and Znaniecki, *Polish Peasant*, 72.

20. Information on the Warhola children's money-making is drawn from Bockris, *Warhol*; Colacello, *Holy Terror*; John Warhola's oral history; and Bennard B. Perlman, "Andy Warhol: The Pittsburgh Years, 1928–1949" (typescript, 2007), cited in Gopnik, *Warhol*, 21.

21. At an exhibition game, John was lucky enough to get Babe Ruth's autograph. Paul witnessed the final three home runs of Ruth's career on May 25, 1935. Robert Dvorchak, "Ruth Had Final Hurrah at Forbes 75 Years Ago," *Pittsburgh Post-Gazette*, May 25, 2010, https://www.post-gazette.com/sports/pirates/2010/05/25/Ruth-had-final-hurrah-at-Forbes-75-years-ago/stories/201005250264.

22. Mickens, "Warholas at Work."

23. "Scalpers Trimmed, Give Tickets Away," *Pittsburgh Press*, September 26, 1943, 2.

24. Bockris, *Warhol*, 45.

25. Nora Zavacky, interview by author, August 25, 2017.

26. See "T is for Tooth Fairy," in Matt Wrbican, *A Is for Archive: Warhol's World from A to Z* (Pittsburgh: Andy Warhol Museum, 2019), 230–36.

27. Prekop and Cihlář, *Andy Warhol a Československo*, 53.

28. John Warhola, oral history.

29. *Boys Life*, November 1930, 50, https://books.google.com. The Kodatoy projector, produced from 1930 to 1934, was a 16 mm movie projector, intended for use by children. A motor-driven model was available for $18.50, motor sold separately at $6.50. "The Kodak Collector's Page," http://www.nwmangum.com/Kodak/Kodatoy-1.html. The Keystone "Universal" AC-DC 9.5 mm motorized model, which sold for $8.98, better fits Warhola's description. "Grahame N's Web Pages," http://www.pathefilm.uk/95gear/95gearkeystone/95gearkeystone.htm.

30. "Nova cerkov budujetsja v 'Russkom Sel'i Pittsburgha, na Forward Ave" [A new church is being built in Pittsburgh's "Rusyn valley"], *ARV*, February 9, 1933.

31. Prekop and Cihlář, *Andy Warhol a Československo*, 68.

32. Paul Warhola, in Bockris, *Warhol*, 24. In 1985, when Andy Warhol's boyfriend Jon Gould broke up with him, Warhol sometimes sent him small amounts of cash in the mail—"like your mother would do," his friend Benjamin Liu told him. Liu in Colacello, *Holy Terror*, 630.

33. Marge Warhola, in Bockris, *Warhol*, 32.

34. Prekop and Cihlář, *Andy Warhol a Československo*, 66.

35. Andrii Warhola letters, the John Warhola Family Private Collection, Andy Warhol Museum Archives (AWMA).

36. The hotel was built in 1896 and underwent several changes in ownership, but I can find no Slavic connections in the hotel's management.

37. Translations here are my own, with help from Darina Protivnak. Unfortunately, there are phrases and sentences in the letter that remain unclear.

38. United States Bureau of Labor Statistics, *Handbook of Labor Statistics*, 2:312 (Washington, DC: Government Printing Office, 1941), DOI: https://hdl.handle.net/2027uiug.30112018120003.

39. Courtesy of Donald Warhola.

40. Bockris, *Warhol*, 42.

41. Giordano and Gluck, in Smith, *Warhol*, 76, 130.

42. Warhol, *Philosophy*, 21.

43. "My Favorite Superstar: Notes on my Epic, *Chelsea Girls*," interview of Andy Warhol by Gerard

Malanga, 1967, in Goldsmith, *I'll Be Your Mirror*, 130.

44. Bockris, *Warhol*, 46.

45. Koestenbaum, *Andy Warhol*, 26.

46. Cresap, *Pop Trickster Fool*, 95.

47. Warhol, *Philosophy*, 154; and "Andy Warhol's Life, Loves, Art and Wavemaking," interview by Bess Winakor, *Chicago Sun-Times*, 1975, in Goldsmith, *I'll Be Your Mirror*, 227.

48. Shore, in Scherman and Dalton, *Pop*, 414; and Makos, *Warhol*, 74.

49. Warhol, *Philosophy*, 100, 102.

50. Pat Hackett, *Hand-Held Warhol: An Exhibit of Photographs by Pat Hackett of Andy et al. 1971–76 & 1985–87*, Ogunquit Museum of American Art, Ogunquit, Maine, July 14–September 1, 2013.

51. Warhol, *Diaries*, 460.

52. Morrison, in Prekop and Cihlář, *Andy Warhol a Československo*, 345; and Warhol, *Philosophy*, 178.

53. Warhol, *Diaries*, 647.

54. Colacello, *Holy Terror*, 158; Warhol, in Lana Jokel, *Andy Warhol*, documentary, 1972, cited in Gopnik, *Warhol*, 701.

55. Warhol, *Andy Warhol's Exposures*, 143.

56. John Reinhold, in O'Connor and Liu, *Unseen Warhol*, 141.

57. Warhol, in Colacello, *Holy Terror*, 460.

58. John Warhola, in Bockris, *Warhol*, 97.

59. Warhol, *Philosophy*, 94.

60. John W. Smith, "Andy Warhol's Art of Collecting," in *Possession Obsession: Andy Warhol and Collecting*, ed. John W. Smith (Pittsburgh: Andy Warhol Museum, 2002), 14.

61. Colacello, *Holy Terror*, 321. Gopnik confirms the price of the town house and notes that according to Warhol's business partner Fred Hughes, it was a bargain because of the recent market crash. *Warhol*, 784.

62. Warhol, in Lana Jokel, *Andy Warhol*, quoted in Gopnik, *Warhol*, 701.

63. Giordano, in Smith, *Warhol*, 129.

64. Colacello, *Holy Terror*, 461.

65. Jane Holzer, "A 'Superstar' Recalls Her Factory Years," in O'Connor and Liu, *Unseen Warhol*, 48.

66. Carlton Willers, in Smith, *Warhol*, 144.

67. An unnamed acquaintance in Bockris, *Warhol*, 104.

68. Suzie Frankfurt, "A Friendship," in *The Andy Warhol Collection*, vol. 3: *Jewelry and Watches* (New York: Sotheby's, 1988), n.p.

69. Gopnik, *Warhol*, 112.

70. Frankfurt, in Bockris, *Warhol*, 132.

71. Warhol, unpublished diary entry for November 1, 1972, cited in Gopnik, *Warhol*, 702.

72. Bockris, *Warhol*, 44.

73. Morawska, *For Bread with Butter*, 245.

74. Bodnar, Simon, and Weber, *Lives of Their Own*, 36.

75. See Rusinko, "From the *Starŷi krai*."

76. Walko, *Eternal Memory*, 146. I recall receiving the same reprimand as a child.

77. Marion Brownfield, "The Child Who Reads Too Much," *Svit ditej*, February 15, 1925.

78. Bodnar, "Immigration and Modernization," 55.

79. Bockris, *Warhol: The Biography*, 42.

80. Patricia Lowry, "Warhol's Big Brother," *Pittsburgh Press*, March 5, 1990, 17.

81. At some point, John aspired to more schooling and solicited help from his younger brother Andy, who had outstripped John's income. In an undated letter, he writes to his mother, "Tell Andy he could send me a check for $48 for school if he has it. Next month I will need $32 because my tuition $77.50 will be all paid. I hope I can finish this school O.K," AWMA.

82. Richard Leiby, "Their Brother's Keepers," *Washington Post*, May 15, 1994, https://www.washingtonpost.com/archive/lifestyle/style/1994/05/15/their-brothers-keepers/aba29970-b2c2-4a2f-af88-220ad7cb4f2c/.

83. John Warhola, interview by Michal Bycko, "Čo povedali bratia o Andy" [What the brothers said about Andy], in *Nočné dialógy*, 80.

84. Bockris, *Warhol*, 77. Gopnik repeats and dismisses the cautionary comment about Bogdański, 80, 84.

85. "Moe kresy. Dobromil, cz. 1," https://nto.pl/moje-kresy-dobromil-cz-1/ar/4600775.

86. Maria Przedżdziecka, "Dzieje rodu Bogdań-

skich, malarzy cerkiewnych po obu stronach Karpat" [History of the Bogdański family, church painters on both sides of the Carpathians], *Naukovyi zbirnyk muzeiu Ukraïnskoï kul'tury u Svydnyku* 1 (1965): 110, 112.

87. Muzeum Budownictwa Ludowego–Sanok, http://travelmat.com.pl/podkarpacie-w-pigu-ce .html.

88. Pehotsky, *Slavic Immigrant Woman*, 39.

89. Bradley Buell, "The Immigrant in the Community," quoted in Mink, *Wages of Motherhood*, 28.

90. Pehotsky, *Slavic Immigrant Woman*, 40.

91. Mink, *Wages of Motherhood*, 3.

92. John F. McClymer, "Gender and the 'American Way of Life': Women in the Americanization Movement," *Journal of American Ethnic History* 10, no. 3 (1991): 12–13.

93. Krause, "Urbanization without Breakdown," 292. Based on "Women, Ethnicity, and Mental Health," an oral history study of three generations of Italian, Jewish, and Slavic women in the Pittsburgh area, directed by Corinne Azen Krause.

94. Breckinridge, *New Homes for Old*, 124.

95. Paul Warhola, in Prekop and Cihlář, *Andy Warhol a Československo*, 52.

96. AWMA. On May 22, 1942, a duplicate of Andy's baptismal certificate was issued by the pastor of Saint John Chrysostom Church, which affirmed his birth on August 6, 1928, and his baptism on August 28. The need for this certificate was probably connected to administrative affairs connected with his father's death, which took place a week before the certificate was released. Further documentation was required when Warhol applied to college. A notarized affidavit filed May 2, 1945, by Julia Warhola and witnessed by her neighbor Katrena Elachko, officially attested to Andy's birth date.

97. Colacello, *Holy Terror*, 20.

98. John Warhola and Justine Preksta, in Bockris, *Warhol*, 35. Ann and John Elachko, in Colacello, *Holy Terror*, 21.

99. Nora Zavacky, interview by author, August 25, 2017.

100. Colacello, *Holy Terror*, 21.

101. John Warhola, in Gangewere, "Ten Years Later?"

102. Paul C. Warhola, interview by author, February 20, 2020.

103. Nora Zavacky, interview by author, August 25, 2017.

104. Julia Warhola's recipe for homemade chicken soup was included in the brochure for the Andy Warhol Museum's sixth annual Carpatho-Rusyn event in 2003.

105. Jennifer Wolff, "The Literate Gourmet," *Best Life* 5, no. 3 (April 2008): 54.

106. Gopnik relates a story that Warhol prepared pheasant under glass for a 1950s friend. Gopnik, *Warhol*, 122.

107. Hackett, *Hand-Held Warhol*, 12; and Warhol, *Diaries*, 373.

108. Gopnik, *Warhol*, 7.

109. Beverly Russell, "Andy Warhol on Food, from Ketchup to Caviar," *House & Garden*, July 1974. Gopnik notes that the story of ketchup soup was popular among penniless Abstract Expressionists, and Warhol may have stolen it from them. *Warhol*, 5n17. John Warhola has denied that the family ever ate such soup. Interview by Andrei Kritenko, *Forbes Ukraine*.

110. Nora Zavacky, in Prekop and Cihlář, *Andy Warhol a Československo*, 64. In *Warhol's Working Class*, Anthony E. Grudin argues that before World War II, brand-based advertising was aimed at elites, and later in the 1960s, possession of the "proper commodities" promised status to the broad masses. In the 1930s, of course, there was no question of "social status" through brand names, which were beyond the immigrants' pocketbooks. From my own experience in the 1950s, there was a sense among second- and third-generation Americans, for whom a noonday meal was not complete without soup, that homemade soups were immigrant fare, and Campbell's was what "real Americans" ate.

111. Paul Warhola, in Prekop and Cihlář, *Andy Warhol a Československo*, 61.

112. Mary Lou Warhola Simpson, interview by author, August 15, 2019.

113. Lillian "Kiki" Lachester, in Bockris, *Warhol*, 34.

114. Julia Bezeková-Běláčová, in Prekop and Cihlář, *Andy Warhol a Československo*, 165.

115. In 1970 when he was shooting *L'Amour* in Paris, Andy was taught to crochet by a member of the cast. He had learned to do needlepoint in the hospital after being shot. Gopnik, *Warhol*, 721.

116. Perlman, "Education of Andy Warhol," 162.

117. Jerry Saltz, "This Too Is Andy Warhol: Living Room, 1948," *New York Magazine*, November 12, 2018, https://www.vulture.com/2018/11/andy-warhol-whitney-retrospective.html.

118. Bourdon, *Warhol*, 18.

119. Lizabeth A. Cohen, "Embellishing a Life of Labor: An Interpretation of the Material Culture of American Working-Class Homes, 1885–1915," *Journal of American Culture* 3, no. 4 (1980): 752–75.

120. James Warhola, note to David Bourdon in David Bourdan papers, Archives of American Art, Smithsonian Institution.

121. Paul Warhola, in Colacello, *Holy Terror*, 26. Bennard Perlman says that Warhol left out "family photographs and trinkets that normally decorated the mantlepiece" so as not to give away his authorship ("Education of Andy Warhol," 163). Warhol also flipped the image to misrepresent his home. In reality, if one is facing the fireplace, the windows are to the right. He also added a door opposite the fireplace.

122. Michael J. Golec, *The Brillo Box Archive: Aesthetics, Design, and Art* (Hanover, NH: University Press of New England, 2008), 95.

123. Ruth Benedict, "Child Rearing in Certain European Countries," *American Journal of Orthopsychiatry* 19 (1949): 342–50.

124. Stein, "Ethno-Historic Study." Stein conducted research on Slovaks and Rusyns in 1970–1971 in McKeesport, a mill town near Pittsburgh, to investigate the relationship between Slovak/Rusyn culture and the American experience. The framework of his ethnohistorical analysis is psychoanalytical anthropology, a school that uses Freudian ego psychology to illuminate the anthropological understanding of culture. In his study, Stein separates the ethnographic data from the psychodynamic issues. To this reader, Stein's empirical data are convincing, and his observations ring true. I will not address the psychoanalytic theory that may, or may not, explain them.

125. Benedict focused on Polish child-rearing. Slovak and Carpatho-Rusyn attitudes and values are virtually identical with those formulated by Benedict for the Poles.

126. Benedict, "Child Rearing," 345.

127. Scherman and Dalton, *Pop*, 281–82. See also Gary Indiana, *Andy Warhol and the Can That Sold the World* (New York: Basic Books), 50–51.

128. Bockris, *Warhol*, 43, 204.

129. Stein, *An Ethno-Historic Study*, 418.

130. Bockris, "Dinner with Andy and Bill, February 1980," in Goldsmith, ed., *I'll Be Your Mirror*, 280.

131. *Warhol*, 53–63.

132. Stein, "Ethno-Historic Study," 289–90, 317.

133. Monica McGolddrick et al., "Overview," in *Ethnicity and Family Therapy* (New York: Guilford Press, 2005), 2. For specific examples of the generalities suggested here, see the oral histories in Stein, "Ethno-Historic Study," 289–436.

134. Paul Warhola, in Bockris, *Warhol*, 34.

135. Nora Zavacky, interview by author, August 25, 2017. Nora was six years younger, and her brother John was two years older, than Andy. Stephen Zavacky's five other children were five to sixteen years older. Most of the ten children of John Zavacky were also considerably senior to Andy. His playmate in the family was Lillian "Kiki" Lachester, the daughter of his oldest first cousin, Helena Zavacky. Julia's younger sister Anna also lived in Lyndora with her three children, born in the 1920s. Her sister Mary Preksta, who had been a neighbor on Beelen Street, later lived on the North Side of Pittsburgh with her six children, all of whom were older than Andy. Justine, known as Tinka, four years older than Andy, was closest to him in age.

136. Mary (Sally) Zymboly to Andy Warhol, October 9, 1972, AWMA.

137. Eva Bezeková, interview by Bycko, in *Nočné dialógy*, 84.

138. A member of Holy Spirit Greek Catholic Church in Oakland, Zeedick was active in the 1930s celibacy movement in cooperation with the cantor and parishioners of Saint John Chrysostom. In 1938 he traveled to Europe with the president of the Greek Catholic Union (GCU) and the GCU's legal adviser to protest the *Cum Data Fuerit* decree

of the Vatican, which imposed celibacy on all future Eastern Catholic priests. The group met with ecclesiastical and governmental officials in Czechoslovakia. On their return trip, they had an audience with Pope Pius XI at the summer palace at Gondolfu. *ARV*, October 20, 1938.

139. *Opportunity Realized*, 94.

140. Christine Soley, interview by author, August 25, 2017.

141. John Zavacky, interview by author, July 20, 2020.

142. *ARV*, July 30, 1931, 3.

143. Paul Warhola, in Bockris, *Warhol*, 43.

144. Paul C. Warhola, interview by author, February 20, 2020.

145. Nora Zavacky, interview by author, August 25, 2017.

146. *Pittsburgh Press*, October 18, 1935; *Pittsburgh Post-Gazette*, October 18, 1935.

147. Stein, "Ethno-Historic Study," 386.

148. Warhol, *Philosophy*, 53.

149. Rusinko, *Straddling Borders*, 42.

150. John Warhola, oral history; and Gopnik, *Warhol*, 21.

151. John Warhola, oral history.

152. Shannon George, "Let's Learn About: The Heinz Pickle Pin," *Pittsburgh Post-Gazette*, September 24, 2009; and Nathan Gluck in Smith, *Warhol*, 67–68. For more on *Thirteen Most Wanted Men*, see Gopnik, *Warhol*, 375–80.

153. Breckinridge, *New Homes for Old*, 123–24, 184.

154. Paul Warhola's memories about Julia's door-to-door sales of tin-can flowers are found in Mickens, "Warholas at Work" and Leiby, "Their Brother's Keepers." A description of the process Julia used to make the flowers, with descriptive sketches by John and Paul Warhola, are in Prekop and Cihlář, *Andy Warhol a Československo*, 64.

155. Weinraub, "Andy Warhol's Mother," 101.

156. Fiona Russell Powell, "The *Face* Interview," *The Face*, March 1985, 50, cited in Gary Comenas, "The Origin of Andy Warhol's Soup Cans or The Synthesis of Nothingness," https://warhol stars.org/andy_warhol_soup_can.html. In the Warhol literature (Bockris, Warhol, 31; and Grudin,

Warhol's Working Class, 37), this quotation is often conflated with Warhol's comment in an interview with the German magazine *Stern*. Eva Windmöller, "Ich Liebe Ates Geld," *Stern*, October 8, 1981, 198. Asked whether his mother understood art, he responded, "More than that. She did a lot for me. She was a really good artist, in the primitivist style" [Mehr als das. Sie hat viel für mich gemacht, sie war eine richtig gute Zeichnerin, im Stil der Primitive]. There was no mention of his mother's tin-can flowers in the *Stern* interview, and no reference to her primitivist style in the 1985 *Face* interview.

157. Gopnik, *Warhol*, 22.

158. Prekop and Cihlář, *Andy Warhol a Československo*, 46.

159. Warhol, *Philosophy*, 21. Andy also inaccurately identifies his hometown here as McKeesport.

160. John Warhola, interview by Kritenko.

161. Bernard Weinraub, interview by author, February 25, 2020.

162. Nathan Gluck, letter to Andreas Brown, May 16, 1971, AWMA; and Nathan Gluck, in "A Conversation with Nathan Gluck," interview by Mark Allen, http://markallencam.com/nathan-gluck.html.

163. "Julia had her shortcomings as a mother. . . . Her refusal to learn English kept her at a considerable distance from the reality of being a hunkie [sic] child in the Pittsburgh ghettoes. . . . She was largely out of touch with the reality of their lives outside the home and refused to learn English." Bockris, *Warhol*, 22, 29. The *Factory Diary* video in which Julia tells the story of Andy's confrontation with African American neighbors challenges this assessment.

164. John Warhola, oral history.

165. Bockris, *Warhol*, 17.

166. Nora Zavacky, interview by author, August 25, 2015.

167. Paul C. Warhola, interview by author, February 20, 2020.

168. Nathan Gluck, in Allen, "Conversation with Nathan Gluck." See also Giordano in Smith, *Warhol*, 127.

169. *Selections from Julia's Tapes: Carpatho-Rusyn Songs, Chants, Prayers and Stories*, A program created

for the 9th Annual Carpatho-Rusyn Event at the Andy Warhol Museum, July 2006, brochure notes.

170. Jerry Jumba's catalog of the tapes lists sixty-two folk songs, mostly Carpatho-Rusyn with a few East Slovak songs, one Czech, and one Hungarian song; seventeen Carpatho-Rusyn liturgical chants and feast-day hymns; fourteen prayer recitations in Rusyn Church Slavonic; one three-part Rusyn-language moral parable; and one twenty-five-minute original story in English.

171. Rendering spoken language in written form, especially nonstandard dialects, may seem to imply inferiority or a negative stereotype. Julia's speech, as presented by Bernard Weinraub in the *Esquire* article, was so perceived by her Pittsburgh-based sons. Here and throughout, I intend no pejorative attitude in my presentation of Julia's oral performance in her own voice. Rather, I consider Julia's accent and nonstandard vernacular language to be integral elements of her verbal art.

172. The digitized version starts in medias res, and the introduction of the hobo and Homestead are missing. Jumba, who has heard the original reel-to-reel version, supplied that information.

173. The expression "take it easy" was popularized in ads for Coca-Cola, Kellogg's, Gimbels, and numerous department stores. According to Newspapers.com, in a selected number of Pittsburgh newspapers from the 1940s, the phrase appeared in 3,531 articles and images—in the Joe Palooka comic strip, in descriptions of wartime bombing runs and patriotic army shows, on the sports pages, in advice columns, and as the official 1946 Pittsburgh traffic slogan.

174. Paul C. Warhola, interview by author, February 20, 2020.

175. *Heavenly Manna*, 1941, 1.

176. Krause, "Ethnic Culture," 303–4.

177. Paul Warhola, in Prekop and Cihlář, *Andy Warhol a Československo*, 351.

178. "Huge Communion Served at 5th Anniversary Session," *Pittsburgh Sun-Telegraph*, August 17, 1953.

179. Paul C. Warhola, interview by author, February 2, 2020.

180. Mary (Sally) Zymboly to Andy Warhol, May 25, 1977, AWMA.

181. Warhol, in *Diaries*, 449, 500.

182. John Warhola, in Bockris, *Warhol*, 17.

183. Dufresne, *Famous for 15 Minutes*, 147. In the photograph used on her naturalization certificate, a safety pin is visible beneath the sheer fabric of Julia's dress.

184. Motyl, "Was Andy Warhol Ukrainian?" 551.

185. The *ARV* published numerous ads for pseudoscientific treatments and patent medicines: Gold Medal Haarlem Oil for the kidneys, bladder, and liver; a "Pain expeller" for neuralgia and back pain; and Lydia E. Pinkham's vegetable compound for women's monthly pain—"over 100 million bottles sold." Testimonials were published from elderly women who suffered rheumatism for more than twenty years, but now walk like young girls after drinking Rheumolek tea. Various roots and serums, supposedly from the Old Country, promised cures for almost every ailment.

186. Glenn O'Brien, "Interview: Andy Warhol," 1977, in Goldsmith, *I'll Be Your Mirror*, 260. In 1966 Warhol shot a film called *Velvet Underground Tarot Cards*. In the same year, the Andy Warhol Museum integrated Warhol's personal tarot cards in an exhibit on contemporary magic. https://www.warhol.org/exhibition/contemporary-magic-a-tarot-deck-art-project/.

187. "How the World Thanks You for Doing Good," Hyriak, *In the Seventy-Seventh Kingdom*, 61–77.

188. Warhol, *Julia Warhola in Bed, Talking, Sleeping*.

189. Jed Johnson, in the David Bourdon papers, Archives of American Art, Smithsonian Institution.

190. Italicized words indicate utterances that Julia Warhola spoke using English. In his biography of Warhol, Gopnik referred to this passage, citing me and Darina Protivnak as translators. *Warhol*, 739. However, Gopnik changed "old devil'" to "old bitch," replacing the mild insult, a relatively inoffensive expression of frustration, with a word that, in Rusyn, conveys malice and vulgarity. My translation with Protivnak, a native speaker of Rusyn from a village near Miková, was done with Julia Warhola's sociocultural orientation in mind.

191. Prekop and Cihlář, *Andy Warhol a Československo*, 77. Paul told this, or another version of the story to Bockris. *Warhol*, 37.

192. Paul C. Warhola, email communication with author, February 6, 2018.

193. Daniel R. Baldwin, "An Interview with Paul Warhola," *Slovo: A Publication of the National Czech & Slovak Museum & Library* 2, no.1 (Summer 2001): 7–8. The name of the building is erroneously designated here as Volkiene Bread. Jerry Jumba heard the same story directly from Paul Warhola. Interview by author, March 3, 2020.

194. Colacello, *Holy Terror*, 23.

195. Bockris, *Warhol*, 35.

196. Colacello, *Holy Terror*, 20.

197. Amy Zavacky Passarelli, in "E! True Hollywood Story: Andy Warhol," television broadcast, March 1998, cited in Gopnik, *Warhol*, 22.

198. Bockris, *Warhol*, 24.

199. Mary (Sally) Zymboly, letter to Andy Warhol, January 9, 1965, AWMA.

200. It is uncertain precisely to whom this threat was directed. The pronoun is the formal "you," which Carpatho-Rusyn children in traditional families used to address a parent. It could also be a plural "you." The context here seems to suggest that the threat was addressed to the entire family audience.

201. Warhol, *Philosophy*, 147.

202. Warhol in Warhol and Hackett, *POPism*, 108.

203. Bockris, *Warhol*, 41.

204. Warhol, *Philosophy*, 21.

205. Information on rheumatic fever and chorea was drawn from the following sources: A. E Bennett and Foster E. Bennett, "Acute Infectious Chorea: Medical Management and Treatment," *American Journal of Nursing* 47, no. 11 (1947): 5–7, www.jstor.org/stable/3456747; Arild E. Hansen, "Rheumatic Fever," *American Journal of Nursing* 53, no. 2 (1953): 168–71, www.jstor.org/stable/3459895; and Irving R. Roth, "On Rheumatic Fever," *American Journal of Nursing* 30, no. 2 (1930): 131–35, www. jstor.org/stable/3409965.

206. Gopnik notes that Warhol also mentioned three attacks in a private medical history, given to his doctor. *Warhol*, 23n32.

207. Bockris, *Warhol*, 38.

208. Bennett and Bennett, "Acute Infectious Chorea," 5.

209. PANDAS—Questions and Answers," https://www.nimh.nih.gov/health/publications/pandas/index.shtml, cited in Gopnik, *Warhol*, 23. The PANDAS hypothesis is controversial. See S. Orlovska et al., "Association of Streptococcal Throat Infection with Mental Disorders: Testing Key Aspects of the PANDAS Hypothesis in a Nationwide Study," *JAMA Psychiatry*, May 24, 2017, http://dx.doi.org/10.1001/jamapsychiatry.2017.0995.

210. Bockris, *Warhol*, 38–39.

211. Gopnik, *Warhol*, 23n35.

212. Hansen, "Rheumatic Fever," 170.

213. Hansen, "Rheumatic Fever," 171.

214. Roth, "On Rheumatic Fever," 135.

215. Weinraub, "Andy Warhol's Mother," 158.

216. Warhol, *Philosophy*, 21–22.

217. Hickey, in Ric Burns, *Andy Warhol*.

218. Koestenbaum, in Ric Burns, *Andy Warhol*.

219. Perry, "Introduction" to Perry and Brownley, *Mothering the Mind*, 4.

220. Weinraub, "Andy Warhol's Mother," 158.

221. Perry, "Introduction" to Perry and Brownley, *Mothering the Mind*, 12.

222. Wilson, in Smith, *Warhol*, 8; and Wylie, in Craig Lambert, "Fifteen Percent of Immortality," *Harvard Magazine*, July–August 2010, https://harvardmagazine.com/2010/07/fifteen-percent-of-immortality?page=all.

223. Perlman, "Education of Andy Warhol," 156.

224. John Warhola, in Bockris, *Warhol*, 39.

225. Paul and John Warhola, in Bockris, *Warhol*, 40.

226. Roth, "On Rheumatic Fever," 135.

227. Warhol, *Philosophy*, 117.

228. Dufresne, *Famous for 15 Minutes*, 45.

229. Pennsylvania, US Federal Naturalization Records, 1795–1931, Ancestry.com.

230. Paul Warhola, in Bockris, *Warhol*, 42.

231. *Polk's Pittsburgh City Directory*, 1938.

232. John Warhola, oral interview.

233. Cited in Gopnik, *Warhol*, 928.

234. Julia Warhola, in Weinraub, "Mothers," 158.

235. John Warhola, in Bockris, *Warhol*, 42.

236. "United Will Relocate Two Big Hangars," *Hartford Courant*, March 8, 1941; "1000-Tons Hangar Is Being Moved to New Site on Rentschler Field," *Hartford Courant*, April 4, 1941; and P. M. Barnes, "Moving a 2,500-ton Hangar Building," *Engineering News Record*, September 11, 1941. It was for this job that John Warhola remembered his father was away for six months.

237. Paul Warhola, in Bockris, *Warhol*, 42.

238. John Warhola, oral history.

239. Prekop and Cihlář, *Andy Warhol a Československo*, 66. Paul here contradicts what he told Bockris about his father's gallbladder surgery. The English translation of *Andy Warhol a Československo* erroneously states that Andrii was ill for six *weeks*, rather than six months.

240. P. Dineen, W. Homan, and W. Grafe, "Tuberculous Peritonitis: 43 Years' Experience in Diagnosis and Treatment," *Annals of Surgery*, December 1976: 717–22. DOI: 10.1097/00000658-197612000–00010.

241. Eichleay Engineering Corporation Records and Photographs, 1889–1989, MSS 960, Thomas and Katherine Detre Library and Archives, Senator John Heinz History Center, box 15, folder 63.

242. John Zavacky, interview by author, July 20, 2020.

243. Paul Warhola, in Bockris, *Warhol*, 44.

244. World War II Selective Service Draft Cards: Fourth Registration, 1942, National Archives and Records Administration, https://www.archives.gov/files/research/military/ww2/draft-cards-fourth-registration.pdf.

245. *Pittsburgh Post-Gazette*, April 28, 1942, 13.

246. On Andrii's death and funeral and Andy's reaction, see Bockris, *Warhol*, 44–45.

247. Bockris, *Warhol*, 45.

248. Mykola Mušynka, "Folk Customs of Carpatho-Rusyns: The Funeral," *Carpatho-Rusyn American* 9, no. 3 (Fall 1986): 5.

249. Weinraub, "Andy Warhol's Mother," 158.

250. Julia Warhola to Mary (Sally) Zymboly, December 21, 1965. Courtesy Gregory Zymboly.

251. Records of the Russian Brotherhood Organization of the USA, courtesy Richard Custer.

252. "Stephen Fechosko of Westwood," *Pittsburgh Post-Gazette*, February 13, 1985. Fechosko's father, Kondrat Feciaszko, immigrated to Carnegie, Pennsylvania, in 1884. Stephen was born around 1893.

253. John Warhola Family Papers, AWMA.

254. John Warhola, oral history.

255. Julia's comment in the *Esquire* interview that Andrii had left her $11,000 in the bank probably includes the value of the house, of which Julia was joint owner.

256. Allan Tong, "Andy Varchola's 15 Minutes," *Globe and Mail* (Toronto) August 17, 1991, *Lexis Nexis Universe: General News Topics*. Online. www.nexis.com.

257. Gilbert Love, "New Security Act Changes Provide 'Free' Insurance," *Pittsburgh Press*, December 26, 1939.

258. Gopnik, *Warhol*, 37n223.

259. "Naturalization Record Broken," *Pittsburgh Press*, April 19, 1939.

260. Her documents were preserved in Andy Warhol's safe deposit box. Certificate of Naturalization and Voter Registration Certificate, AWMA.

261. Information on Pittsburgh's contribution to the war effort is drawn from Anthony Letizia, "Pittsburgh and World War II: We Can Do It!" November 23, 2015, https://geekfrontiers.com/heinz-history-center/pittsburgh-and-world-war-ii-we-can-do-it/.

262. For a summary of Strank's life and heritage with photographs, see Richard Custer, "Sgt. Michael Strank: A Carpatho-Rusyn Pennsylvanian," *Carpatho-Rusyns of Pennsylvania*, June 23, 2016, http://rusynsofpa.blogspot.com/2016/06/sgt-michael-strank-carpatho-rusyn.html#more.

263. The Sergeant Michael Strank Memorial Bridge carries PA-271 over the Conemaugh River and connects Franklin Borough to East Conemaugh Borough.

264. Information concerning the nationality booths is taken from the following sources: "Plan Initiated Here May Help to Sell Bonds," *Pittsburgh Press*, October 3, 1942; "Nationality Bond Plan Catching On," *Pittsburgh Sun-Telegraph*, October 3, 1942; Mary Hallam, "Women in

Nationality Groups Sell War Bonds by Thousands," *Pittsburgh Sun-Telegraph*, December 6, 1942; Frances C. Walker, "Hard Working Head of Nationality Groups Spurs Bond Sales," *Pittsburgh Post-Gazette*, December 15, 1943; "Carpatho-Russian Booth to be Dedicated in Pittsburgh on November 14," *ARV*, November 12, 1942; and "Greko Kaft. Sojedinenije kupilo bondy na $100,00 podčas posvjačenija Karpato-Russkoj chižiny v Pittsburgh, Nov. 14," [The GCU bought $100,000 of bonds at the dedication of the Carpatho-Russian booth in Pittsburgh, Nov. 14], November 19, 1942.

265. Despite biographical references to the Merchant Marine, Paul Warhola's Veteran Compensation Application files indicate that he served in the US Navy, as does his obituary. "Obituary: Paul Warhola," *Pittsburgh Post-Gazette*, February 2, 2014; and Pennsylvania, Veteran Compensation Application Files, WWII, 1950–1966, Ancestry.com.

266. Kate Giammarise, "Obituary: Anna Warhola / One of Pittsburgh's First Woman Trolley Operators," *Pittsburgh Post-Gazette*, November 17, 2016.

267. Bell, *Out of This Furnace*, 14.

268. John Warhola, in Bockris, *Warhol*, 46.

269. Drawn from the chronology in Historic Pittsburgh, http://exhibit.library.pitt.edu/chronology.

270. Peter Ebson, "Inflation Nears 1920 Levels and Heads Up and Up," *Pittsburgh Press*, September 28, 1946.

271. John Warhola, oral history.

272. John Warhola, in Bockris, *Warhol*, 47–48.

273. Gopnik, *Warhol*, 37n226.

274. Mary Lou Simpson, interview by author, August 15, 2019. Subsequent comments from Simpson on Julia's colostomy are from this interview.

275. Paul Warhola, in Bockris, *Warhol*, 48.

276. T. E. Jones and R. W. Kehm, "Management of the Permanent Colostomy," *Cleveland Clinic Quarterly* 13, no. 4 (1946): 198.

277. Guiles, *Loner at the Ball*, 26.

278. Weinraub, "Andy Warhol's Mother," 158.

279. John Zavacky, interview by author, July 25, 2020; and Gopnik, *Warhol*, 47.

280. Perlman, "Education of Andy Warhol," 148. For a complete account of Warhol's art education, see Bockris, *Warhol*, 49–77, and Gopnik, *Warhol*, 41–81.

281. Dufresne, *Famous for 15 Minutes*, 41.

282. Mary Adeline McKibbin, cited in Gopnik, *Warhol*, 34.

283. Bockris, *Warhol*, 69.

284. Carnegie Institute of Technology, "Certificate of Secondary School Courses for Admission to Day Courses," July 25, 1945, AWMA.

285. Weinraub, "Andy Warhol's Mother," 158.

286. For details on Warhol's college experience, see Perlman, "Education of Andy Warhol"; Bockris, *Warhol*, 59–77; Gopnik, *Warhol*, 42–109; and "Andy Warhol: The College Years," Andy Warhol Museum, https://www.warhol.org/exhibition/andy-warhol-the-college-years/.

287. Gopnik, *Warhol*, 39.

288. Bockris, *Warhol*, 59.

289. See Gopnik, *Warhol*, 39n241.

290. Bockris, *Warhol*, 62–63.

291. Suzanne Martinson, "Wholesale Produce Moves with Friendly Finesse in Strip's Wee Hours," *Pittsburgh Press*, August 29, 1990.

292. Paul C. Warhola, interview by author, July 23, 2020.

293. John Warhola, oral history.

294. Andy would later dismiss the significance of the award, telling an interviewer, "I did get some prizes in school. It wasn't my best work. One time after summer vacation I did some fruit truck pictures. I won five dollars." O'Brien, "Interview," in Goldsmith, *I'll Be Your Mirror*, 236.

295. Gopnik, *Warhol*, 49.

296. For details on gay sexuality in Pittsburgh, see Gopnik, *Warhol*, 53–63.

297. Bockris, *Warhol*, 71, 74.

298. George Arnold, in Marylynne Pitz, "Andy Warhol Had Early Start as Horne's Window-Dresser," *Pittsburgh Post-Gazette*, July 19, 2015.

299. Bockris, *Warhol*, 73.

300. Michael Sean Snow, "Dreams Realized and Dreams Deferred: Social Movements and Public Policy in Pittsburgh, 1960–1980," PhD

diss., University of Pittsburgh, 2005, 59, cited in Gopnik, *Warhol*, 58n220.

301. Philip Pearlstein, in Rainer Crone, "Das Bildnerische Werk Andy Warhols," PhD diss., Frei Universitat, 1976, 263, quoted in Gopnik, *Warhol*, 37n219.

302. Julia's reaction to Warhol's homosexuality will be discussed in chapter 5.

303. Perlman, "Andy Warhol: The Pittsburgh Years," cited in Gopnik, *Warhol*, 53n154.

304. Bernard Weinraub, interview by author, February 25, 2020.

305. John and Paul Warhola, in Bockris, *Warhol*, 77.

306. Philip Pearlstein, "My Warhol(a) Experience, 1947–1950 and a Little Beyond" (typescript draft, 2014), cited in Gopnik, *Warhol*, 80.

Chapter 5: "To Live with My Andy"

1. Warhol and Hackett, *POPism*, 5.

2. Weinraub, "Andy Warhol's Mother," 101.

3. Colacello, *Holy Terror*, 27. See also Gopnik, *Warhol*, 84.

4. Paul Warhola to David Bourdon, August 10, 1987, David Bourdon papers, Archives of American Art, Smithsonian Institution.

5. Bockris, *Warhol*, 96.

6. Giordano, in Smith, *Warhol*, 127.

7. Bockris, *Warhol*, 48.

8. The postcard is addressed to Mr. Andrew Warhol (minus the final a), indicating that Julia recognized and accepted the artist's newly adopted identity. Based on this note, Gopnik states that Warhol could read Rusyn, but this mix of English and Rusyn words spelled phonetically in the Latin alphabet is far from standard Rusyn. At best, Warhol understood, and as an adult spoke, rarely, a Rusyn-English pidgin language. For more on this point, see Rusinko, "Andy and Julia in Rusyn."

9. Clairton was dominated by the Clairton Coke Works. It was nominally the hometown of characters in the movie *The Deerhunter*, although none of the film was shot there. In his diary entry from November 29, 1978, Warhol noted that the opening scene of the film took place in Clairton, Pennsylvania, "where all my cousins are from." Warhol, *Diaries*, 185.

10. Paul Warhola in Bockris, *Warhol*, 96; Prekop and Cihlář, *Andy Warhol a Československo*, 70; and Julia Warhola in Bockris, *Warhol*, 98.

11. Bockris, *Warhol*, 96. Paul and his family mention an early summer move, but it is likely that Julia's move to New York was a gradual transfer that stretched over a period of months. By March 1, 1952, she already had a bank account registered to her New York address. Gopnik, *Warhol*, 121n131. But in May, she was still sending money to her sister in Miková from Dawson Street, according to an American Express receipt. Andy Warhol Museum Archives (AWMA).

12. Nora Zavacky, interview by author, August 25, 2017.

13. Vecchiet, *Vie et morts d'Andy Warhol.*

14. Giuliano, "Gerard Malanga on Andy Warhol's Mother."

15. Warhol, postcards to Julia Warhola, 1956, reproduced in Wrbican and Huxley, *Andy Warhol Treasures*, supplement.

16. Allegheny County Pennsylvania Deed Book 3883:317, December 3, 1960. In Julia's address book, she noted the names of the purchasers under the ungrammatical and mixed-language heading: "Sto may Howz kupili" (Who bought my house).

17. Paul Warhola, letter to David Bourdon, in David Bourdon papers, Archives of American Art, Smithsonian Institution.

18. Gopnik, *Warhol*, 48.

19. Cited in Gopnik, *Warhol*, 87.

20. John Warhola, interview by Andrei Kritenko.

21. Groell, in Smith, *Warhol*, 30.

22. Gopnik, *Warhol*, 106.

23. "Upcoming Artist: Andy Warhol," *Art Director & Studio News* 2, no. 12 (April 1951): 20, cited in Gopnik, *Warhol*, 107n155.

24. Bockris, *Warhol*, 101. A variant of this story, or perhaps an account of another pitiful Thanksgiving, has John Warhola making sure that they had a turkey. "Obituary: John Warhola," *Pittsburgh Post-Gazette*, December 25, 2010.

25. Diane Beley, email communication, November 2, 2019.

26. Rizek, Rizek, and Medvecky, *Financial District's Lost Neighborhood*, 106. Much of my information on Carpatho-Rusyn immigrants in the city is drawn from this book of photographs, which covers Rusyn immigrant life in New York in the first half of the twentieth century.

27. Rizek, Rizek, and Medvecky, *Financial District's Lost Neighborhood*, 13.

28. Joseph Kindya, in Medvecky, *Legacy of Faith*.

29. Rizek, Rizek, and Medvecky, *Financial District's Lost Neighborhood*, 47–49. In 1947, Slezak's restaurant moved to a new location, where it remained in business until 1971, when it was forced to give way to the World Trade Center.

30. John Petrick, in Medvecky, *Legacy of Faith*.

31. Rizek, Rizek, and Medvecky, *Financial District's Lost Neighborhood*, 7.

32. "The Reminiscences of Edward Kasinec," Harriman Institute Oral History Project, Columbia University, 2016, Session 1–2, https://oralhistoryportal.library.columbia.edu/document.php?id=ldpd_13878147.

33. The term "Czech" as used to characterize the language of Yorkville was probably shorthand to refer to the multiple mutually intelligible Slavic languages that were spoken in the neighborhood.

34. Kiedrowski, *Andy Warhol's New York City*, 36; Brian Požun, Slavs of New York!, "Slavs at the 1939 World's Fair in Queens," http://nycslav.blogspot.com/2008/11/other-week-slavs-of-new-york-was-lucky.html, November 27, 2008.

35. Barbara Crossette, "In Search of the Czechoslovak East Side," *New York Times*, September 10, 1976. In *POPism*, Warhol noted, "One night as I was walking home from the art supply store with some brushes, past the little old German ladies in Yorkville sweeping their sidewalks, I realized I'd forgotten to get my mother her Czech newspaper." Warhol and Hackett, *POPism*, 38. Warhol (and his ghostwriters) referred to Julia's language as Czech. She may have read Slovak, but it is unlikely that she could read newspaper-style Czech. The Lemko-Rusyn newspaper *Karpatska Rus'* (Carpathian Rus'), published from 1939 to 1999 in Yonkers, may have been available in Yorkville.

36. *75th Anniversary Book*, Saint Mary's Byzantine Catholic Church, New York City, December 18, 1988. Information on the history of Saint Mary's is drawn from this booklet.

37. *ARV*, February 27, 1941.

38. Calculated at MeasuringWorth.com.

39. *ARV*, March 30, 1950.

40. Pearlstein, in Patricia Lowry, "CMU Forum Analyzes Warhol Myth, Reality," *Pittsburgh Press*, May 5, 1988.

41. Robert Pipta, "History of the Byzantine Catholic Seminary of Saints Cyril and Methodius," *Gathered Fragments* 27, no. 1 (January 1, 2017), https://dsc.duq.edu/gf/vol27/iss1/9. Eventually, in 1950, the Byzantine Seminary of Saints Cyril and Methodius was founded in Pittsburgh to train men exclusively in the Byzantine Catholic tradition, meeting the exacting liturgical, spiritual, and linguistic needs of the church. Warhol's nephew, Paul Constantine Warhola, was a seminarian there in the 1960s.

42. "First Eastern Rite Benedictine Prior," *ARV*, September 28, 1950.

43. "Renovated Church Rededicated Here," *New York Times*, December 1, 1952.

44. Giuliano, "Gerard Malanga on Andy Warhol's Mother." In 1960, Warhol's income was $70,000, equivalent to $621,000 in 2020 dollars. Julia's contributions to the church for 1961, including her donation to the building fund, were $1,129.30, around $10,000 in 2020. Her contributions of $68.30 in 1962 and $41.00 in 1966 were more typical of her annual giving.

45. See the photo essay by Haytham ad-Din, "St. Mary's Byzantine Catholic Church," https://medium.com/the-photographic-muslim/st-marys-byzantine-catholic-church-a127e93b95de.

46. Weinraub, "Andy Warhol's Mother," 101.

47. Haytham ad-Din, "St. Mary's Byzantine Catholic Church."

48. John Warhola, interview by Andrei Kritenko; and Paul C. Warhola, interview by author, February 20, 2020.

49. Cited in Gopnik, *Warhol*, 140.

50. Adolf Benca, in Prekop and Cihlář, *Andy Warhol a Československo*, 229.

51. Julia converses with Warhol's friend Richard

Rheem about what she called the "junk house" in Warhol's 1966 film, *The George Hamilton Story*.

52. Vito Giallo, in Bockris, *Warhol*, 113–14.

53. Mary Lou Warhola Simpson, interview by author, August 25, 2019.

54. Julia Warhola to Anna Lasky, January 3, 1954, AWMA. Gopnik notes that the rent Julia cites is about right, but he misunderstands Julia's comment that the apartment is "very high," which he translates as "very costly." *Warhol*, 135n59, 60. Julia is speaking not of the cost, but of the fact that the apartment is literally high, up four flights of stairs. Julia writes in pidgin Rusyn-English without punctuation. I have modified the translation slightly for easier comprehension.

55. "A Conversation with Nathan Gluck," http://www.markallencam.com/nathangluck.html.

56. Giallo, in Bockris, *Warhol*, 114.

57. Warhol, *Diaries*, 691. When he made this statement on November 3, 1985, Andy had only fourteen months to live.

58. G. R. Swenson, "What Is Pop Art?" 1963, in Goldsmith, *I'll Be Your Mirror*, 15.

59. Bourdon, *Warhol*, 33.

60. Bockris, *Warhol*, 127. Julia's name (also spelled "Warhol") is on the minutes of the first meeting of the corporation on July 2, 1957. Gopnik, *Warhol*, 177n75. Although Julia may have instinctively distrusted the accountant, she would not have had the capacity to serve as secretary of any corporation, and the signatures were surely entered by her son.

61. In Warhol's 1966 film *The George Hamilton Story*, Julia tells her costar, "Andy had two floor, two apartment. Second floor, he pay three hundred dollar, and top five floor he pay $200. *Na* [per, Rusyn] month he pay 500 dollar." The rent may have increased since 1957, when, according to Gopnik, the lease for the upstairs apartment was less than $100, or Julia's account, expressed with incredulity, may be a performative exaggeration.

62. For details, see Gopnik, *Warhol*, 179.

63. Robert Fleisher, in Smith, *Warhol*, 114; Warhol, *Philosophy*, 23; Amy Vanderbilt, in an undated clipping of Martha MacGregor, "The Week in Books," *New York Post*, ca.1966, cited in Gopnik, *Warhol*, 120.

64. Giallo, in Smith, *Warhol*, 53.

65. Paul Warhola, in Bockris, *Warhol*, 127; and Ann Warhola, in Bourdon, *Warhol*, 40.

66. Carey, in Smith, *Warhol*, 86; and Bockris, *Warhol*, 102.

67. Carey, in Smith, *Warhol*, 86.

68. For a detailed description of the process, see Gopnik, *Warhol*, 70–71, and "Andy Warhol's Blotted Line," Andy Warhol Museum, https://www.warhol.org/lessons/andy-warhols-blotted-line.

69. Gopnik, *Warhol*, 70.

70. Bourdon, *Warhol*, 43–44.

71. Ellen Lupton and J. Abbott Miller, "Line Art: Andy Warhol and the Commercial Art World of the 1950s," in De Salvo, "Learning the Ropes," 32.

72. Gluck, in Bourdon, *Warhol*, 43–44.

73. Rossi-Wilcox, "Social Satire,"158.

74. Schleif, "Clever Frivolity," 133n90.

75. Rossi-Wilcox, "Social Satire," 158.

76. Mickens, "Warholas at Work."

77. See Schleif, "Clever Frivolity," 78–134.

78. Matthew Gray, Manager of Archives, Andy Warhol Museum, email, May 20, 2022.

79. For more detail, see Bourdon, *Warhol*, 44.

80. Mary Lou Warhola Simpson, interview by author, August 25, 2019.

81. Charles Lisanby, Television Academy Interviews, October 22, 2017, https://interviews.televisionacademy.com/interviews/charles-lisanby.

82. Bourdon, *Warhol*, 58; and Gopnik, *Warhol*, 149.

83. Schleif, "Clever Frivolity," 106.

84. See Wrbican, "Meeooaaww-AW-AWW," 265.

85. However, the trope may have been familiar to her from Rusyn women's suggestive folk songs: "If only I knew / where my boyfriend is mowing / I would bring him / Something from under my apron." Warhol was known to draw cats as far back as his Carnegie Tech days. A classmate remembered that "he would walk around and, if he liked you, he'd say, 'Do you want to see my kittens?' and he'd reach for the book." Guiles, *Loner at the Ball*, 28.

86. However, her son contributed to the finished product. According to Warhol's assistant Nathan Gluck, "[Julia] stayed up all night trying to do it. Her writing would go uphill and got progressively smaller. Instead of covering the whole space, she would write the whole text in two inches . . . . They finally convinced her to write it all out and Andy . . . cut it up and spread it out over the whole space." David Bourdon Papers, Archives of American Art, Smithsonian Institution.

87. Julia's script is also credited, along with Andy's typography, on a Thelonious Monk album cover (*Monk*, Prestige, 1958). She won another prize in 1959 for her work on Warhol's letterhead.

88. Jon Davies, "Sell Your Parents: Marketing the Handwriting of Julia Warhola and Phung Vo," *Master Drawings* 58 no. 3 (September 2020): 369.

89. Gopnik, "Warhol Outside-in," in *Adman: Warhol before Pop*," ed. Nicholas Chambers (Pittsburgh: Andy Warhol Museum, 2017), 31–32.

90. Schleif, "Carefully Unplanned," 20.

91. Stephen Bruce, typed notes by David Bourdon, in David Bourdon papers.

92. Ellen Lupton, "Mother Tongue: The Script of Julia Warhola," in Chambers, *Adman, Warhol before Pop*, 74.

93. James Warhola, *Uncle Andy's Cats*, unpaginated.

94. In his illustrated book for children, James Warhola repeats Andy's fanciful story that Hester was a gift from "a fabulous movie star called Gloria." His father Paul claimed that she came from Gloria Swanson's housekeeper. Prekop and Cihlář, *Andy Warhol a Československo*, 61. The most complete history of the Warhola cats is told by Blake Gopnik in *Warhol*, 136–37. For Warhol's relationship with animals, see Wrbican, "Meeooaaww-AW-AWW"; and Grudin, "Warhol's Animal Life."

95. Giallo, in O'Connor and Liu, *Unseen Warhol*, 20; and Giallo, in Johnson, *Thank You Andy Warhol*, 25.

96. Prekop and Cihlář, *Andy Warhol a Československo*, 61.

97. Smith, *Andy Warhol's Art and Films*, 70.

98. Bourdon, *Warhol*, 33. Willers, interview by David Bourdon, quoted in Gopnik, *Warhol*, 136.

99. Wayne Koestenbaum suggests that Hester was named after Hester Prynne, "who wears the scarlet A, Andy's own, in *The Scarlet Letter*." Koestenbaum, *Andy Warhol*, 36. Julia was surely not familiar with Hester Prynne.

100. Gopnik, *Warhol*, 136. Warhol's brother John dismisses the idea that Andy and his mother ever had more than two or three cats. John Warhola, oral history. James Warhola said there may have been just fifteen, who were never all in the same place at the same time. Mickens, "Warholas at Work." The journalist Bernard Weinraub, who interviewed Julia Warhola in 1966 in Warhol's town house noticed no sign of cats. Weinraub, interview by author, February 25, 2020. But Warhol's associate who accompanied Julia home from the hospital when Andy was shot in 1968, describes "an oilcloth covered table puddled with urine from the seven or eight cats she owned." Hoffman, "Warhol Superstar Viva."

101. Madalen Warhola Hoover, in Prekop and Cihlář, *Andy Warhol a Československo*, 395.

102. Mary Lou Warhola Simpson, interview by author, August 25, 2019.

103. Giallo in Johnson, *Thank You Andy Warhol*, 25.

104. Andy Warhol, interview with Lee Radziwill, *Interview*, March 1975.

105. According to Gillian Jagger, Julia was killing Hester's kittens in the 1950s. Interview by Gopnik, *Warhol*, 137n93.

106. Warhol, *Diaries*, 536; see also 683–84.

107. Rhoda Marshall, cited in Gopnik, *Warhol*, 137n92.

108. Grudin, "Warhol's Animal Life," 604, 618n59.

109. Lisanby, Television Academy Interviews. Lisanby had earlier told Patrick S. Smith another version: "It was so funny. There is no text. The text is the title, and I wrote the title, which was, I don't know, an amusing thing. He said, 'What should I call it?' I just said that. So, he wrote that down, which I think is funny." Smith, *Warhol*, 135.

110. Warhol worked from photographic images of cats in two books of photographs, *All Kinds of Cats* (New York: Knopf, 1952) by the photographer

Walter Chandoha, and *Sam*, text by John Crawford, photographs by Edward Quigley (New York: Stackpole Sons, 1937). The latter may have been the source for the name of the Warhola Sams. See Wrbican, "Meeooaaww-AW-AWW," 265.

111. In an intriguing article, "One Blue Pussy," Lucy Mulroney proposes an alternate interpretation. In her reading, the code shared by the artist and his targeted audience is "the language of camp," characterized by double entendre and self-parody. The context is not the literal world of Sams and Hester, but the social scene of gay men, which was at once public and invisible. Mulroney cites Neil Printz's reading of Warhol in relation to the blue pussy: "Loser or loner, Warhol was historically cast—a hapless child in an adult world, a hopeless femme among the butches, the blue pussy" (quoted in Mulroney, "One Blue Pussy," 35n62). She concludes, "I am not suggesting that only gay male readers could access or participate in the social space facilitated by Warhol's books. Rather, Warhol's books reveal how meaning is tied to one's position as a reader" (33n36). I accept the ambiguity of Warhol's early work and do not dispute Mulroney's compelling argument. But for my purposes I adhere to Julia Warhola's position as artist, writer, and reader.

112. *Merriam-Webster.com Dictionary*, "holy cats," https://www.merriam-webster.com/dictionary/holy%20cats.

113. Andy Warhol, *Holy Cats by Andy Warhol's Mother*, unpaginated.

114. Gopnik, *Warhol*, 137n90.

115. Giordano claimed that while he was working with Warhol, "There wasn't a meal I had alone." Smith, *Warhol*, 129.

116. "Nativity of Our Lord God and Savior, Jesus Christ," in *Divine Liturgy*, 111, 166–68.

117. *Heavenly Manna*, 24, 58. Several editions of this prayer book were found among Andy Warhol's and Julia Warhola's possessions.

118. David Bourdon papers.

119. In Eva Windmöller, "Ich liebe altes Geld Und Neue Schecks: Interview with Andy Warhol," *Stern*, October 8, 1981.

120. These images recall the primitive style of traditional icons of the Carpathian region, productions of local handicraft, "which allowed [Carpatho-Rusyns] to keep their ethnic identity." Grešlík and Šukajlová, *Ikony Šarišského múzea*, 10. Painters from villages and workshops of poor monasteries "often invented different forms of expression which, in certain archaisms, in naïve simplicity, and . . . folkloristic adaptations, make even the observers of today forget their weaker artistic merits." Skrobucha, *Icons in Czechoslovakia*, vii. See also Kłosińska, *Icons from Poland*. By the nineteenth century, the distinct folk style had given way to Western influence, and traditional Rusyn icons were replaced by devotional pictures. Julia may have instinctively expressed the same naive simplicity that characterized early Rusyn icon painters, but it is unlikely that she consciously imitated them.

121. Colin Rhodes, *Outsider Art: Spontaneous Alternatives* (New York: Thames and Hudson, 2000), 8, 24. See also Charles Russell, *Self-Taught Art: The Culture and Aesthetics of American Vernacular Art* (Jackson: University Press of Mississippi), 2001.

122. Gary Alan Fine, "Crafting Authenticity: The Validation of Identity in Self-Taught Art," *Theory and Society* 32, no. 2 (April 2003): 175–76.

123. Chris Bentley, "'Outsider' Art Is Going Mainstream. But In Chicago, It's Always Been In," *WBUR Here and Now*, April 11, 2019, https://www.wbur.org/hereandnow/2019/04/11/outsider-art-chicago.

124. Blake Gopnik, *Warhol Outside-in*, in Chambers, *Adman*, 27, 31.

125. Bourdon, *Warhol*, 58.

126. Frankfurt, quoted in Bockris, *Warhol*, 130.

127. Frankfurt, Preface to Warhol and Frankfurt, *Wild Raspberries*, unpaginated.

128. Giordano, in Smith, *Warhol*, 127. It is hard to believe that the entire discussion between Julia and Andy would have taken place in English. Frankfurt may be referring to the same incident in a self-serving comment about Julia's absence and return. "The house was totally a nightmare because they were so disorganized. . . . It was much nicer

when [Julia] wasn't around, because I could do it much better than she could." Frankfurt, quoted in Bockris, *Warhol*, 133.

129. Giordano, in Smith, *Warhol*, 129.

130. Giordano, in Smith, *Warhol*, 127.

131. Colacello, in Guy Trebay and Ruth La Ferla, "Tales from the Warhol Factory," *New York Times*, November 12, 2018, https://www.nytimes.com/2018/11/12/style/andy-warhol-factory-history.html?searchResultPosition=2.

132. Giordano, in Smith, *Warhol*, 127. Julia also allegedly told Giordano that "Warhola" meant "Valhalla," a word that Julia would not have known. It is more probable that he misunderstood an explanation of the Rusyn name "Varkhola." There may have been other miscommunications in his accounts.

133. Gerard Malanga, interview by author, March 10, 2016.

134. Howard F. Stein, "Envy and the Evil Eye among Slovak-Americans: An Essay in the Psychological Ontogeny of Belief and Ritual," *Ethos* 2, no. 1 (1974): 26.

135. Thomas and Znaniecki, *Polish Peasant*, 73.

136. Ara Osterweil, "Sons, Mothers, and Lovers: Ara Osterweil on Andy Warhol's and Rainer Werner Fassbinder's Queer Home Movies," *Artforum* 55, no. 9 (May 2017), https://www.artforum.com/print/201705/ara-osterweil-on-andy-warhol-s-and-rainer-werner-fassbinder-s-queer-home-movies-67936.

137. Frankfurt, quoted in Bockris, *Warhol*, 130.

138. Wood, in Smith, *Warhol*, 43.

139. Gluck, in Smith, *Warhol*, 76; and Bockris, *Warhol*, 98.

140. Lisanby, in Smith, *Warhol*, 138; and David Mann, quoted in Bourdon, *Warhol*, 32.

141. Bailey, *Andy Warhol*.

142. Bailey, *Andy Warhol*.

143. Bourdon, *Warhol*, 310; Cresap, *Pop Trickster Fool*, 106n33; and Dufresne, *Famous for 15 Minutes*, 174.

144. Bailey, *Andy Warhol*.

145. Warhol, *Diaries*, 313.

146. Carey, in Smith, *Andy Warhol's Art and Films*, 252–53.

147. Carey, in Smith, *Warhol*, 94.

148. Giallo, quoted in Bockris, *Warhol*, 114. Julia sent Warhol's sample shoes to her relatives in Slovakia. Since he was given a single shoe rather than a pair, Julia sent shoes that were mismatched. In *Absolut Warhola*, a cousin laughingly recalls, "I had loads of high heels. Three suitcases full. . . . They didn't wear out easily. It was real leather. They had lovely colors: red, maroon, yellow, green. I loved to wear one red shoe and one green one."

149. Nickels, "Andy Warhol's First Boyfriend."

150. Ultra Violet, in O'Connor and Liu, *Unseen Warhol*, 251.

151. Tavel, *Andy Warhol's Ridiculous Screenplays*, 14–15.

152. Gluck, in O'Connor and Liu, *Unseen Warhol*, 32; and Malanga, in Giuliano, "Gerard Malanga on Andy Warhol's Mother."

153. Kessler, in Gopnik, *Warhol*, 135; and Bockris, *Warhol*, 103.

154. Malanga, interview by author, March 10, 2016.

155. Malanga, in Giuliano, "Gerard Malanga on Andy Warhol's Mother." According to Malanga, "Andy was thrilled by the whole thing."

156. Malanga, in Giuliano, "Gerard Malanga on Andy Warhol's Mother." Asked if there were communication problems between Malanga's Italian immigrant mother and Carpatho-Rusyn Julia Warhola, Malanga said, "I don't think so. Julia certainly had a distinct accent, but her English was okay." Malanga noted that both he and Andy had parents who were older than the parents of their peers. Malanga, *Archiving Warhol*, 61. But it is worth noting that Julia was fourteen years older than Mrs. Malanga.

157. Prekop and Cihlář, *Andy Warhol a Československo*, 309.

158. Weinraub, "Andy Warhol's Mother," 101.

159. Prekop and Cihlář, *Andy Warhol a Československo*, 292.

160. Letter from Jeanne Milié Shaffer to Julia; apron and note from Mrs. Milié, AWMA. For more on Milié, see "William Milie Dies, Dancer, Choreographer," *Pittsburgh Post-Gazette*, September 5, 1987.

161. Warhol and Hackett, *POPism*, 84. Herko's grandparents were immigrants from Kamienka, a village about seventy-five miles from Miková. As a third-generation American, he might have been far enough removed from the ethnic influence that it would not have been noticed by Warhol. In 1964, dancing naked while high on speed, Herko threw himself through a fifth-floor window to his death at age twenty-eight. For more on Herko, see Warholstars.org.

162. Paul C. Warhola, interview by author, July 23, 2020.

163. David Bourdon papers. This dynamic is captured in Warhol's film *The George Hamilton Story* to be discussed later in this chapter.

164. My account of the house is based on a description offered by Nathan Gluck in a letter to Andreas Brown, May 16, 1971, AWMA, and a Brown Harris Stevens real estate sales brochure. When the house was on the market in 2008, I was able to wander the premises. It had been renovated since Andy and Julia lived there, but the structure remained the same.

165. Scherman and Dalton, *Pop*, 153.

166. Emile de Antonio, in Stein and Plimpton, *Edie*, 189.

167. David Bourdon, in Wilcock, *Autobiography and Sex Life*, 43.

168. See Robert Fleisher and Buddy Radish, in Smith, *Warhol*, 114, 119. Bockris's informants painted a gloomy picture of Julia's confinement in a "dark, dank subterranean room" (*Warhol*, 146), a fiction that has been repeated by other commentators and disputed by Andy's nephew, who described her flat as "a lovely garden apartment." James Warhola, "Letter to the Editor," *New York Times*, June 8, 2003.

169. Scherman and Dalton, *Pop*, 72.

170. Hopps, in "When Walter Hopps Met Andy Warhol," *New Yorker*, June 5, 2017. The account presented here is based on Hopps's most recent telling of the story.

171. Hopps, in Stein and Plimpton, *Edie*, 192.

172. Malanga, interview by author, March 10, 2016.

173. Scherman and Dalton, *Pop*, 62.

174. Williams, "Warhol Stumbled."

175. David Bourdon and Taylor Mead, in Wilcock, *Autobiography and Sex Life*, 43, 137; and Bockris, *Warhol*, 104.

176. Giuliano, "Gerard Malanga on Andy Warhol's Mother."

177. Leo Castelli, in Prekop and Cihlář, *Andy Warhol a Československo*, 304; Giallo, in O'Connor and Liu, *Unseen Warhol*, 20; and Giallo, in Bockris, *Warhol*, 114.

178. Frankfurt, in Bockris, *Warhol*, 130.

179. Giordano, in Smith, *Warhol*, 129.

180. James Warhola in *Today's Zaman* (Istanbul), May 8, 2014 (site unavailable); Paul C. Warhola, interview by author, February 20, 2020; and George Warhola, in Vecchiet, *Vie et morts d'Andy Warhol*.

181. Giallo, in Smith, *Warhol*, 53.

182. Williams, "Warhol Stumbled."

183. Warhol, *Julia Warhola in Bed, Talking, Sleeping*."

184. Herbert Muschamp, "How I Got That Interview," *New York Times*, December 5, 2004, https://www.nytimes.com/2004/12/05/maga-zine/how-i-got-that-interview.html.

185. Nickels, "Andy Warhol's First Boyfriend."

186. Giordano, in Smith, *Warhol*, 128.

187. Weinraub, interview by author, February 25, 2020.

188. Krause, *Grandmothers, Mothers and Daughters*, 130.

189. Artspace editors, "Photographer Stephen Shore on How Andy Warhol Taught Him to Be an Interesting Artist," Artspace, http://www.artspace.com/magazine/interviews_features/stephen-shore-andy-warhol.

190. Malanga, interview by author, March 10, 2016.

191. Carey, in Smith, *Warhol*, 83.

192. Carey, in Smith, *Andy Warhol's Art and Films*, 254.

193. Bockris refers to the "first and last time [Julia] appeared at one of his public events," placing it in June 1952 at the opening of *Andy Warhol: Fifteen Drawings Based on the Writings of Truman Capote*. "Julia came to the opening and hovered in the background in her cloth coat and babushka,

making Andy even more nervous." Bockris, *Warhol*, 99. Carey's account is more plausible.

194. Bockris, *Warhol*, 398

195. Bockris, *Warhol*, 97; and Bycko, *Nočné dialógy*, 87.

196. Photograph by Duane Michals, in Leo Lerman, "The Village Idea," *Mademoiselle*, June 1962, 70.

197. Gopnik, *Warhol*, 205. For details of the boom in art in the 1960s, see 205–7.

198. Robert Rosenblum, "Saint Andrew," *Newsweek*, December 7, 1964, 100–104.

199. Andy Warhol and Edie Sedgwick Interview, *Merv Griffin Show*, 1965, https://www .youtube.com/watch?v=qYLiw5blnlE&t=518s.

200. John Warhola, interview by Michal Bycko, September 15, 1987, in *Nočné dialógy*, 90.

201. Gopnik, *Warhol*, 477.

202. Willers, in Nickels, "Andy Warhol's First Boyfriend."

203. Scherman and Dalton, *Pop*, 179.

204. Gluck, in O'Connor and Liu, *Unseen Warhol*, 34.

205. Willers, in Nickels, "Andy Warhol's First Boyfriend."

206. *Absolut Warhola*, quoted in Scherman and Dalton, *Pop*, 2.

207. Russia Beyond, https://www.rbth.com/ history/332399-no-sex-in-ussr-phrase-history.

208. Williams Institute, "Public Attitudes towards Homosexuality across Time and Countries," https://williamsinstitute.law.ucla.edu/ publications/public-attitudes-intl-gay-rights/; see also Aleksandar Štulhofer and Theo Sandfort, *Sexuality and Gender in Postcommunist Eastern Europe and Russia* (New York: Hayworth Press, 2005).

209. Semyonova Tian-Shanskaia and Ransel, *Village Life*, 25–27.

210. Thomas and Znaniecki, *Polish Peasant*, 195.

211. Willers, in Nickels, "Andy Warhol's First Boyfriend."

212. Gluck, in Smith, *Warhol*, 62–63.

213. "Gerard Malanga: Andy's Mother," in Heather Robinson, *A Walk Into the Sea: Danny Williams and the Warhol Factory*, DVD, 2007.

214. Malanga, interview by author, March 10, 2016.

215. Lisanby, in "E! True Hollywood Story: Andy Warhol," television broadcast, March 1998, quoted in Gopnik, *Warhol*, 121n140. On Warhol's relationship with Lisanby, see Gopnik, *Warhol*, 173.

216. Ruth Heimbuecher, "Stanley Kauffmann Analyzes Movies," *Pittsburgh Press*, May 21, 1968, 27.

217. George Thomas, "Pitt Hears Warhol, Or Lean-In," *Pittsburgh Press*, March 27, 1968. See also "Andy Warhol's Pittsburgh," *Carnegie Magazine*, https://carnegiemuseums.org/carnegie-magazine/ fall-2019/andy-warhols-pittsburgh/.

218. Paul C. Warhola, email communication with author, October 27, 2020. Warhol expressed his friction with Paul's mother Ann several times in his *Diaries*, 179, 499, 500, 574.

219. Julia Warhola, in Bockris, *Warhol*, 258.

220. John Zavacky, interview by author, March 7, 2021. Zavacky disputes Gopnik's statement, attributed to him, that Julia wrote to a female cousin asking why her Andy was "different." He also contradicts Gopnik's claim that the letter survives in his (Zavacky's) collection. Gopnik, *Warhol*, 121n138. Zavacky remembers the letter because he had used it as a bookmark, but he later gave it away, along with all of his father's correspondence with Julia. A few letters from Zavacky's father to Julia are found in the Time Capsules.

221. Nora Zavacky, Prekop and Cihlář, *Andy Warhol a Československo*, 84. Nora challenged the accuracy of her interview as published by Prekop and Cihlář. In an interview with the author, August 25, 2017, she vented her persistent belief that Andy "never made love with boys."

222. Weinraub, "Andy Warhol's Mother," 101.

223. Pat Hackett, Introduction to Warhol, *Diaries*, xi.

224. John Warhola, in Jumba, "In Memoriam," 3; and Gopnik, *Warhol*, 16.

225. José Carlos Diaz, ed., *Andy Warhol: Revelation* (Pittsburgh: Andy Warhol Museum, 2019), 44; and John Warhola, in Vecchiet, *Vie et morts d'Andy Warhol*.

226. "In the process of seeking out imagery for his Last Supper series, Warhol seemed to go out

of his way to find humble or 'low-brow' sources." Miranda Lash, "Kitsch You Can Believe In: Warhol's Incessant *Last Supper*," in Diaz, *Andy Warhol*, 19.

227. For a detailed explanation, see Rusinko, "Was Andy Warhol Ukrainian?"

228. Bockris, *Warhol*, 22, 36. Gopnik cites Jumba, "In Memoriam," but I can find no mention of the Warholas' alleged childhood study of Church Slavonic in Jumba's obituary of Warhol.

229. Magocsi, *With Their Backs to the Mountains*, 244; and Girman, in Prekop and Cihlář, *Andy Warhol a Československo*, 103. John Warhola affirmed that the children were taught Rusyn, their native language, in religious school, not Old Slavonic. John Warhola, interview by Andrei Kritenko. I attended the same kind of religious classes some twenty-five years later at what was known as "Greek school," for the Greek Catholic Church it was associated with. We were taught to recite prayers in Rusyn Church Slavonic, to read a bit of Cyrillic, and speak elementary Rusyn.

230. Prekop and Cihlář, *Andy Warhol a Československo*, 69–70.

231. For a brief summary, see Rusinko, "We Are All Warhol's Children," 44–48. Relevant studies include Benjamin Bennett-Carpenter, "The Divine Simulacrum of Andy Warhol: Baudrillard's Light on the Pope of Pop's 'Religious Art,'" *Journal for Cultural and Religious Theory* 1, no. 3 (2000): 1–36; Zan Schuweiler Daab, "For Heaven's Sake: Warhol's Art as Religious Allegory," *Religion and the Arts* 1, no. 1 (1996): 15–31; Dillenberger, *Religious Art of Andy Warhol*; Robert Pincus-Witten, "Pre-entry: Margins of Error. Saint Andy's Devotions," *Arts Magazine* 63, no. 10 (1989): 58–59; and John Richardson, "Warhol at Home," in *Sacred Monsters*, 247–59.

232. Julianne McShane, "Exhibit Explores Profound Role Religion Played in Andy Warhol's Life and Art," NBC News, https://www.nbcnews .com/news/exhibit-explores-profound-role -religion-played-andy-warhols-life-art-rcna7777.

233. Karen Rosenberg, "For Andy Warhol, Faith and Sexuality Intertwined," *New York Times*, December 2, 2021.

234. Makos, *Warhol*, 53; and Viva, in Stein and Plimpton, *Edie*, 226.

235. Andy Warhol and Bianca Jagger, "New Again: Sting," August 21, 2013, https://www.inter viewmagazine.com/music/new-again-sting#.

236. Benjamin Secher, "Is Andy Warhol's Secret Catholicism the Key to His Art?" *Daily Telegraph*, March 7, 2020, https://www.telegraph .co.uk/art/what-to-see/andy-warhols-secret -catholicism-key-art/#comment.

237. Warhol, in "Sylvia Sidney: Better Pugs than Diamonds," interview by Andy Warhol and Catherine Guiness, *Interview Magazine*, April 1978, unpaginated.

238. "A Taste of Paradis: Jodie Foster, in Conversation with Andy Warhol," *Interview Magazine*, April 10, 1980, https://www.interviewmagazine .com/culture/a-taste-of-paradis-jodie-foster-in -conversation-with-andy-warhol.

239. As someone who grew up in the Byzantine Ruthenian Catholic Church but was educated in a Roman Catholic school with the "nuns, mass, priests, and sense of guilt" that Makos refers to, my interpretation is partly based on my own experience of the two rites in the 1950s. My characterizations do not necessarily hold true today.

240. Jane Holzer, in the transcript included with David Bailey, *Bailey on Andy Warhol*, DVD (London: Network, 2006), cited in Gopnik, *Warhol*, 17n163; and Colacello, *Holy Terror*, 160.

241. Weinraub, "Mothers," 99.

242. Paul C. Warhola, interview by author, February 2, 2020.

243. Dillenberger, *Religious Art*, 33; and Richardson, "Warhol at Home," 249. Four worn editions of *Heavenly Manna* were found among Warhol's possessions after his death. According to John Warhola, one was buried with him. Bradford R. Collins, "Dick Tracy and the Case of Warhol's Closet: A Psychoanalytic Detective Story," *American Art* 15, no. 3 (Autumn 2001): 72n20.

244. Warhol, in Glenn O'Brien, "Interview: Andy Warhol" (1977), in Goldsmith, *I'll Be Your Mirror*, 253.

245. Cutrone, in O'Connor and Liu, *Unseen Warhol*, 69–70.

246. Gopnik, *Warhol*, 17.

247. David Bailey, *Andy Warhol: Transcript*; and Warhol, *Diaries*, 313.

248. Gopnik, *Warhol*, 17.

249. Warhol, in O'Brien, "Interview: Andy Warhol" (1977), 253; and Warhol, quoted by Christopher Makos in "extras" to Vecchiet, *Vie et morts d'Andy Warhol*.

250. *Life After Life and Reflections on Life After Life* was included in a sampling of books from Warhol's library in the exhibit *Warhol by the Book*, Andy Warhol Museum, Pittsburgh, October 10, 2015–January 10, 2016.

251. Warhol, *Diaries*, 643.

252. Gopnik, *Warhol*, 16.

253. Father Sam Matarazzo, as quoted in Jane Daggett Dillenberger, "The Religious Art of Andy Warhol," in *Andy Warhol by Andy Warhol*, ed. Gunnar B. Kvaran (Milan: Skira, 2008), 50, partially cited in Gopnik, *Warhol*, 17–18n163. The full quotation appeared first in Dillenberger's 2001 book, *Religious Art*, 33.

254. Gopnik, *Warhol*, 17.

255. Rev. Thomas G. Shaefer and Kevin Beres, interview by author, April 15, 2016; and Donald Warhola, in Secher, "Is Andy Warhol's Secret Catholicism the Key?"

256. Peter Tay, in Prekop and Cihlář, *Andy Warhol a Československo*, 382.

257. Doug Freiden, "Andy's Home At Last," *New York Post*, February 27, 1987, 13. Significantly, none of the coverage of Warhol's funeral in the Pittsburgh papers included this quotation from Monsignor Tay. Edward Hayes, the New York lawyer who managed the settlement of Warhol's estate, remembered the following statement from Tay's graveside comments: "Andy had a deep loving trust in God. This man will reach to the steps of the very throne of God." Edward Hayes, with Susan Lehman, *Mouthpiece: A Life In—And Sometimes Just Outside—The Law* (New York: Broadway Books, 2010), 167.

258. Prekop and Cihlář, *Andy Warhol a Československo*, 384.

259. Jerry Jumba, interview by author, May 7, 2020.

260. The Holy Bible, RSV-CE.

261. Motyl, "Was Andy Warhol Ukrainian?" 551.

262. Colacello, in O'Connor and Liu, *Unseen Warhol*, 80.

263. Julia gives Katrina a specific surname. It is uncertain whether she is relating a fictional tale, or an account based on reality.

264. Warhol, *Diaries*, 559.

265. Jessica Beck, "Warhol's Confession: Love, Faith, and AIDS," 90, https://www.warhol.org/warhols-confession-love-faith-and-aids/.

266. Parts of this section were previously published in Elaine Rusinko, "Andy and Julia in Rusyn: Warhol's Translation of His Mother in Film and Video," *Journal of Art Historiography* 26 (June 2022), https://arthistoriography.wordpress.com/wp-content/uploads/2022/05/6-rusinko.pdf.

267. "The Painting on the Dress Said 'Fragile,'" *New York Times*, November 11, 1966. The reporter comments that Warhol made the remark about old people "a little sadly."

268. Greg Pierce, director of film and video at the Andy Warhol Museum, devised a standardized titling system for Warhol's films, in which titles given by Warhol are indicated by italics, and films titled according to information found on the box or reel are denoted in quotation marks. Hence, *The George Hamilton Story* and "Mrs. Warhol." I offer a more thorough analysis of this film in "Andy and Julia in Rusyn."

269. Warhol and Hackett, *POPism*, 110.

270. David Bourdon, "Warhol as Filmmaker," *Art in America* 3 (1971): 51.

271. Warhol, *Philosophy*, 82.

272. "Andy Warhol Movieman: 'It's Hard to Be Your Own Script,'" in Goldsmith, *I'll Be Your Mirror*, 187.

273. E-mail from Susan Pile, July 25, 2015. Douglas Crimp remarks that the film narrative is comprehensible only from Richard Rheem's part of the dialogue. *Our Kind of Movie* (Cambridge, MA: MIT Press, 2012), 123.

274. "Four of Andy's Most Beautiful Women," Harvard Film Archive, Film Series, February 8, 2004, https://harvardfilmarchive.org/calendar/four-of-andy-warhols-most-beautiful-women-2004-02.

275. Murphy, *Black Hole*, 147.

276. Ivan Stadtrucker, "Andy Warhol a Júlia," *Líterárny týždenník* 23, no. 39–40, November 18, 2010, 16.

277. The film is the source for many of Julia's statements and memories that have already been raised in this study.

278. Warhol, *Philosophy*, 99.

279. Richard Whitehall, "Andiflix II: The Home Movie as Art Form," *Coast FM and Fine Arts*, September 1969, 24, https://warholfilmads.files.wordpress.com/2015/02/war-coast-12.jpg.

280. Warhol film scholars have debated whether in his movies cruel manipulation occurs in what may seem to be objective, documentary-like treatments. Warhol often focused on vulnerable individuals, exploiting their weaknesses to create dramatic tension for the ultimate amusement of the audience. See Murphy, *Black Hole*, 58, 96–129.

281. Murphy, *Black Hole*, 151, 146.

282. Richard Rheem to Andy Warhol, September 4, 1966, AWMA.

283. George Hamilton, *Don't Mind If I Do* (New York: Touchstone, 2009), 17.

284. Brigitte Weingart, "Carrots/carats: Die doppelte Erscheinung der 'Mother of Pop Art' in Mrs. Warhol," lecture, German Film Institute and Museum, Frankfurt, January 16, 2014, https://www.youtube.com/watch?v=tKMUO1KF8ao.

285. Email from Susan Pile, July 25, 2015.

Chapter 6: "My Beloved Sister"

1. Lisanby, in Smith, *Warhol*, 138.

2. George Warhola, in Prekop and Cihlář, *Andy Warhol a Československo*, 92; and George Warhola, interview by author, August 15, 2019.

3. Madalen Warhola Hoover, in Prekop and Cihlář, *Andy Warhol a Československo*, 97.

4. Paul C. Warhola, interview by author, February 20, 2020.

5. James Warhola describes a 1962 visit in his illustrated children's book, *Uncle Andy's*.

6. Paul Warhola, in Markus, "Two Years after His Death," 68.

7. Martin Warhola, in Prekop and Cihlář, *Andy Warhol a Československo*, 100.

8. Madalen Warhola Hoover, in Prekop and Cihlář, *Andy Warhol a Československo*, 92, 98–99. According to George Warhola, Andy promised the statue to Madalen, but it was sold at the auction of Warhol's estate for over $60,000. Purchased by Joseph A. Hardy III, the founder of the 84 Lumber Company, it now stands in the cigar bar of Hardy's Nemacolin Woodlands Resort in the Laurel Highlands of Pennsylvania, about seventy miles from Pittsburgh.

9. James Warhola, in Thomas, "Relatives Recall Visits."

10. Madalen Warhola Hoover, in Prekop and Cihlář, *Andy Warhol a Československo*, 97.

11. Rupert Cornwell, "The Famous Deny Andy 15 Minutes of Their Time," *Independent* (London), May 16, 1994, *Lexis Nexis Universe: General News Topics*, www.nexis.com.

12. Madalen Warhola Hoover, in Thomas, "Relatives Recall Visits."

13. Paul C. Warhola, interview by author, February 20, 2020.

14. George Warhola, interview by author, August 19, 2019.

15. George Warhola, interview by author, August 19, 2019.

16. Donald Warhola, interview by author, August 24, 2017.

17. Martin Warhola, in Prekop and Cihlář, *Andy Warhol a Československo*, 100.

18. Mary Lou Warhola Simpson, interview by author, August 25, 2019.

19. Nora Zavacky, interview by author, August 25, 2017.

20. Paul C. Warhola, interview by author, February 20, 2020.

21. Madalen Warhola Hoover, in Thomas, "Relatives Recall Visits."

22. Bockris, *Warhol*, 362.

23. Dufresne [Ultra Violet], *Famous for 15 Minutes*, 37.

24. Bockris, *Warhol*, 132.

25. Warhol, *Diaries*, 729.

26. James Warhola, in Stephen Smith, "He Loved Weightlifting and Buying Jewels: Andy Warhol's Friends Reveal All. *Guardian*, August 14, 2015, https://www.theguardian.com/artanddesign/2015/aug/14/andy-warhol-friends-reveal-all.

27. Carlin, "Andy Warhol," 248.

28. Ján Závacký, in Mucha, *Absolut Warhola.*

29. Carlin, "Andy Warhol," 248.

30. John Zavacky, interview by author, July 29, 2020. Carlton Willers told David Bourdon that Andy bought his mother a $5,000 fur coat at Bergdorf's, but "she thought it was too expensive, so she exchanged it for one at Klein's, which, rumor says, she wore only to the A&P." Typed notes, David Bourdon Papers, Archives of American Art, Smithsonian Institution. The matching fur hat makes an appearance in Warhol's film *The George Hamilton Story.*

31. Paul Warhola, in Prekop and Cihlář, *Andy Warhol a Československo,* 72.

32. Gangewere, "Two Andys from Pittsburgh," 51.

33. Mary Lou Warhola Simpson, interview by author, August 19, 2019.

34. Julia Warhola to Mary [Sally] Zymboly, December 21, 1965, courtesy of Gregory Zymboly.

35. Gabaccia, *From the Other Side,* 63–64.

36. George Warhola, in Prekop and Cihlář, *Andy Warhol a Československo,* 94.

37. Vasil′ (Vasyl) Bezek, in Prekop and Cihlář, *Andy Warhol a Československo,* 163.

38. On the 1930s and World War II in Czechoslovakia, see Magocsi, *With Their Backs to the Mountains,* 224–30, 283–84; Magocsi, *Carpathian Rus′,* 58–61; and "Miková—Oficiálne stránky obce Miková."

39. On this topic, see Magocsi, *With Their Backs to the Mountains,* 321–29.

40. Michal Bezek, in Prekop and Cihlář, *Andy Warhol a Československo,* 164.

41. "The Reminiscences of Edward Kasinec," Harriman Institute Oral History Project, Columbia University, 2016, Session 1–2, https://oralhistoryportal.library.columbia.edu/document.php?id=ldpd_13878147.

42. Julia Warhola to Anna Lasky, January 3, 1954, AWMA.

43. Marty Manor Mullins, "A Remarkable Reversal: Communist Czechoslovakia's Reinstatement of Eastern Rite Catholicism during the Prague Spring," *Journal of Church and State* 58, no. 2 (2016): 340.

44. Michal Bezek, in Prekop and Cihlář, *Andy Warhol a Československo,* 163.

45. "Kommunisty presl′idujut Greko Kaftolikov v Prjaševskoj Diocezii v Slovakii" [Communists persecute Greek Catholics in the Prešov Diocese of Slovakia], *ARV,* June 15, 1950.

46. "Goidych, Pavel," in Magocsi and Pop, *Encyclopedia of Rusyn History,* 140–41. Goidych was beatified by Pope John Paul II in 2001 and recognized as Righteous among the Nations by Yad Vashem in 2007.

47. Johnny Lane, "Russka Dolina Tick Talk," *ARV,* February 1, 1951.

48. Pearlstein, in Vecchiet, *Vies et morts d'Andy Warhol;* and Pearlstein, in Guiles, *Loner at the Ball,* 77.

49. Colacello, *Holy Terror,* 67.

50. Accordingly, members of the American Warhola family sometimes identified themselves as Slovak, but never as Ukrainian. See Rusinko, "Was Andy Warhol Ukrainian?"

51. Vasil′ (Vasyl) Bezek, in Prekop and Cihlář, *Andy Warhol a Československo,* 147.

52. Adam Havlík, "Místo jedněmi zbožňované, jinými zatracované: Podnik zahraničního obchodu Tuzex a jeho působení v socialistickém Československu" [A place adored by some, damned by others: Tuzex foreign trade company and its activities in socialist Czechoslovakia], Academia.edu/40253513, 202.

53. Information on the Czech hard-currency stores is drawn from the following syndicated articles found on Newspapers.com: "Prague Finds U.S. Dollars Mighty Handy," *Cedar Rapids Gazette,* November 27, 1950; Ed Koterba, "Assignment: Washington," *Times Record* (Troy, NY), December 11, 1959; "Czechs Using New Coupons to Benefit from U.S. Cash," *Fort Worth Star-Telegram,* January 2, 1961; and Lucia Lucas, "Czechs behind Iron Curtain Hanker for American Letters and Presents," *Herald Statesman* (Yonkers, NY), March 4, 1963.

54. Bren and Neuburger, "Tuzex and the Hustler," 30.

55. Bren and Neuburger, "Tuzex and the Hustler," 40.

56. John Warhola, oral history, November 24, 2004.

57. Anna Lipčaková, letter to Julia Warhola, Andy Warhol Museum Archives (AWMA).

58. Prekop and Cihlář, *Andy Warhol a Československo*, 125.

59. Prekop and Cihlář, *Andy Warhol a Československo*, 129.

60. Prekop and Cihlář, *Andy Warhol a Československo*, 166.

61. Julia Bezeková-Běláčová, in Prekop and Cihlář, *Andy Warhol a Československo*, 165.

62. Maria Bezeková-Šmatláková, in Prekop and Cihlář, *Andy Warhol a Československo*, 145.

63. Vasil' (Vasyl) Bezek, in Prekop and Cihlář, *Andy Warhol a Československo*, 147.

64. Helena Šviderová, letter to Julia Warhola, February 20, 1966, AWMA.

65. Reproduced with translations in Prekop and Cihlář, *Andy Warhol and Czechoslovakia*, 24–29.

66. Prekop and Cihlář, *Andy Warhol a Československo*, 124. The Andy Warhol Museum of Pittsburgh has recently initiated a project with the Andy Warhol Museum of Modern Art in Medzilaborce, Slovakia, to translate the Rusyn-language correspondence between Julia and her relatives.

67. Thomas and Znaniecki, *Polish Peasant*, 98.

68. Unless otherwise stated, the letters from Julia's family are from AWMA, in my translation.

69. Photographs from relatives in Slovakia are in AWMA. Photos sent by Julia to Slovakia are reproduced in Prekop and Cihlář, *Andy Warhol a Československo*, 121, 136, 138.

70. Bell, *Out of This Furnace*, 196.

71. Metil, "Post-Velvet Revolutionary Cultural Activism," 121, 125, 133.

72. Allen, "A Conversation with Nathan Gluck." Multitracking was developed in the mid-1950s by the guitarist Les Paul and his wife, Mary Ford.

73. Giordano, in Smith, *Warhol*, 127.

74. Jumba, "Julia Warhola Recordings," 27–28.

75. Prekop and Cihlář, *Andy Warhol a Československo*, 142.

76. Prekop and Cihlář, *Andy Warhol a Československo*, 142. Although Bycko insists that his record is one of a kind, at least one other such vinyl record is in the possession of Donald Warhola. The note on the label is addressed by Julia to her sister Eva, but apparently the record was never sent. Interview with Donald Warhola by author, August 24, 2017.

77. Misch, *I Am from Nowhere*.

78. Thomas and Znaniecki, *Polish Peasant*, 115.

79. Prekop and Cihlář, *Andy Warhol a Československo*, 165.

80. Prekop and Cihlář, *Andy Warhol a Československo*, 126. Based on its content, Blake Gopnik rightly dates the note to 1966, when Warhol was on tour with the Velvet Underground. But he confuses the letter to Mary with another on the same page, written to Anna in 1962. Gopnik, *Warhol*, 514n62.

81. Prekop and Cihlář, *Andy Warhol a Československo*, 157.

82. Thomas and Znaniecki, *Polish Peasant*, 154.

83. Prekop and Cihlář, *Andy Warhol a Československo*, 84.

84. Giordano, in Smith, *Warhol*, 127–28.

85. Weinraub, "Andy Warhol's Mother," 101.

86. Weinraub, interview by author, February 25, 2020.

87. Kenneth Goldsmith, introduction to George Gruskin, "Who Is This Man Andy Warhol?" in Goldsmith, *I'll Be Your Mirror*, 200. Gruskin's interview is on pages 201–20.

88. Stein and Plimpton, *Edie*, 189.

89. De Antonio, in Smith, *Warhol*, 188.

90. Guiles, *Loner at the Ball*, 124.

91. Bourdon, *Warhol*, 68,

92. Bockris, *Warhol*, 107.

93. Bockris, *Warhol*, 146. According to Gopnik, in the early 1960s, Warhol told a teenage friend that his mother drank a bottle of whiskey a day. *Warhol*, 124n172.

94. Malanga, interview by author, March 10, 2016.

95. John Warhola, Interview by Andrei Kritenko.

96. Donald Miller, "'Warhol' an Odd Tale Told Well," *Pittsburgh Post-Gazette*, December 4, 1989, 11.

97. James Warhola, Letter to the Editor, *New York Times*, June 8, 2003.

98. Nathan Gluck, letter to Andreas Brown, May 16, 1971, AWMA.

99. Paul C. Warhola, interview by author, February 20, 2020.

100. Warhol and Hackett, *POPism*, 201–52.

101. Gopnik, *Warhol*, 559.

102. Warhol and Hackett, *POPism*, 224–25.

103. Vasil' (Vasyl) Bezek, in Prekop and Cihlář, *Andy Warhol a Československo*, 147.

104. Prekop and Cihlář, *Andy Warhol a Československo*, 126. The cost of the trip as written by Julia ($5), is an error. The fare on the Air India airline ticket was $526.30.

105. Warhol's income as specified in the affidavit was close to accurate. In purchasing power, $10,000 was about $77,500 in 2020 dollars. As listed on his tax forms, his income was $59,000 in 1959 and $70,000 in 1960 ($612,000 in 2020 purchasing power). Scherman and Dalton, *Pop*, 48; and https.www.Measuringworth.com. It dropped through the 1960s, when he turned from commercial art to fine art. In 1966, he took in just over $38,000 from fine art sales and about $5,000 in movie rentals and screenings, while he claimed $32,000 ($250,000) in business expenses. That year he was able to pay himself just $7,000 ($56,000) in salary. Gopnik, *Warhol*, 500. It was not until he started doing commissioned portraits in the 1970s that Warhol began making money again. Gopnik provides details on Warhol's income throughout his career.

106. Julia Bezeková-Beláčová, in Prekop and Cihlář, *Andy Warhol a Československo*, 166. Travel restrictions were much more stringent on young people who might defect than on elderly travelers.

107. According to Eva's daughters, there was a stopover in France, and the flight attendant took Eva to a hotel.

108. Eva Bezeková, interviewed by Michal Bycko, in *Nočné dialógy*, 82–85. Excerpts from this interview, translated into English for the first time, are from this source.

109. Prekop and Cihlář, *Andy Warhol a Československo*, 148.

110. Madalen Warhola Hoover, in Prekop and Cihlář, *Andy Warhol a Československo*, 99.

111. Robert Zecker, "Let Each Reader Judge: Lynching, Race, and Immigrant Newspapers," *Journal of American Ethnic History* 29, no. 1 (2009): 31–32.

112. Prekop and Cihlář, *Andy Warhol a Československo*, 144.

113. Nora Zavacky, interview by author, August 25, 2017.

114. Butler, *Women and the Trades*, 17, 27.

115. Selavan, "Jewish Wage Earners," 274–75; and Butler, *Women and the Trades*, 24.

116. Butler, *Women and the Trades*, 96.

117. Butler, *Women and the Trades*, 24.

118. Butler, *Women and the Trades*, 25.

119. Morawska, "Immigrants Pictured and Unpictured," 228–29.

120. S. J. Kleinberg, "Seeking the Meaning of Life: The Pittsburgh Survey and the Family," in Greenwald and Anderson, *Pittsburgh Surveyed*, 101.

121. Joseph A. Hill, *Women in Gainful Occupations, 1870 to 1920*, Census Monograph IX, cited in Krause, "Italian, Jewish, and Slavic Grandmothers in Pittsburgh," 18.

122. Mrs. Stephen Zavacky worked at Standard Steel Car Company until 1930, when the company had a reduction in force. In 1927, Stephen was working at the car company as a fitter in the construction department, for 36¢ per hour.

123. Standard Steel Car Company employment records. Courtesy of the Butler County Historical Society and the Butler Area Public Library. The records are not complete, so they do not represent the full employment data of the Zavacky family.

124. See Bicha, "Hunkies," 23–24.

125. Niles Carpenter, *Immigrants and Their Children 1920* (New York: Arno Press and the New York Times, 1969), 215.

126. Kleinberg, *Shadow of the Mills*, xxiv, 241–42.

127. Kleinberg, *Widows and Orphans First*, 79.

128. *Opportunity Realized*, 10–11.

129. In 1913, Pennsylvania was among the first states to adopt "widows' pensions" or "mothers' aid" legislation, a state-level cash-transfer program designed for families that were deprived

of a father's support. Grants were small and carried intrusive restrictions. It is unknown whether Carpatho-Rusyns, who generally spurned government aid, would have been willing or able to avail themselves of such aid. See Kleinberg, *Widows and Orphans First.*

130. Bell, *Out of This Furnace,* 214.

131. Bell, *Out of This Furnace,* 33.

132. Campbell, *Turnip Blues.* See Elaine Rusinko, "Review of *Turnip Blues*," *New Rusyn Times* 12, no. 5 (2005): 2.

133. The "In search of" notices here were published in *Svoboda,* the organ of the Rusyn National Union in Olyphant, Pennsylvania, between 1900 and 1912. The original columns were compiled, translated, and reproduced by Richard Custer at https://www.facebook.com/hashtag/WheresThat-Lemko?_gid_=1610930395808309. I have slightly modified the translation and deleted the surnames.

134. Dan Davis, "A Century of Coal Mining in Guernsey County," *Daily Jeffersonian,* February 28, 2017, https://www.daily-jeff.com /business/20170228/century-of-coal-mining-in -guernsey-county.

135. Helen Preksta Cirocco went on to become a successful photographer. Her 2002 obituary describes her as a "pioneer photographer" at the North Side Market House and Three Rivers Stadium, where she worked for over sixteen years.

136. In the 1958 obituary for Mary's daughter Milanna, George is listed as "George Preksta."

137. Gabaccia, *From the Other Side,* 65.

138. Guke died on June 19, 1965.

139. Warhol, *Diaries,* 496.

140. Bockris, *Warhol,* 35.

141. Abbot, *Immigrant and the Community,* 60.

142. Julianna Puskás, "Some Results of My Research on the Transatlantic Emigration from Hungary on the Basis of Macro- and Micro-Analysis," in *Overseas Migration from East-Central and Southeastern Europe 1880–1940,* ed. Julianna Puskás (Budapest: Akadémiai Kiadó, 1990), 55.

143. Raymond Herbenick, *Andy Warhol's Religious and Ethnic Roots: The Carpatho-Rusyn Influence on His Art* (Lewiston, ME: Edwin Mellen Press, 1997), vi.

144. The fictional Mary Dobrejcak in the novel *Out of This Furnace,* spent more than a year at Cresson with her children.

145. C. R. Byerly, *"Good Tuberculosis Men": The Army Medical Department's Struggle with Tuberculosis* (Fort Sam Houston, TX: Office of the Surgeon General, 2013), 122.

146. Byerly, *"Good Tuberculosis Men,"* 114–15.

147. *Butler Eagle,* January 23, 1923, 3. In Peter Lasky's obituary, his parents' names are given as Samuel and Josephine Kozlowsky Lasky. *Butler Eagle,* June 14, 1956.

148. Unless otherwise noted, marriage, divorce, and court records were acquired at the Office of the Prothonotary, Butler County, Commonwealth of Pennsylvania.

149. Until the mid-twentieth century, most states had laws against adultery and fornication, although they were not consistently enforced. Pennsylvania abolished its adultery laws in 1973.

150. Information on incarceration at the workhouse is from Ancestry.com. *Pennsylvania, U.S., Prison, Reformatory, and Workhouse Records, 1829–1971,* 2016.

151. On her Standard Steel Car Company employee record card, Anna gives her husband's address as the Allegheny County Workhouse.

152. Morawska, *For Bread with Butter,* 342–43n76.

153. Christine Soley, interview by author, August 25, 2017.

154. The story of Dudich's saloon is told in chapter 3 of this book.

155. Alex J. Weidenhof, "Prohibition Rather Quiet from County Standpoint," *Butler Eagle,* January 18, 2020, http://www.butlereagle.com/ article/20200118/NEWS01/701189911.

156. For a comprehensive summary of newspaper reports on raids and arrests in Pittsburgh, see Pittsburgh Old Newspaper Project Updates, http://sites.rootsweb.com/~paallent/page15/ page15.html.

157. In 1940 and 1942, Lasky was living on Bessemer Avenue in Lyndora and working at the Standard Steel Car Company. On his 1942 draft registration, under "Name of person who will

always know your address," he notes "Josephine Lasky," presumably Anna's daughter Josephine Dobransky. Peter Lasky died of a heart attack in Chicago in 1956. His body was brought to Lyndora for burial in Calvary Cemetery. There is no mention in his obituary of his wife or his incarceration. *Butler Eagle*, June 14, 1956.

158. "Raising Children Properly," *ARV*, January 12, 1950.

159. Morawska, *For Bread with Butter*, 171.

160. In 1942–1943, Swartz, a truck driver, served eleven months at the Army's Transportation Corps at Fort Slocum, New York. He died in 1965 at the Soldiers' and Sailors' Home in Erie, Pennsylvania.

161. "Mrs. Peter Lasky," *Butler Eagle*, March 28, 1985; and "Andrew Serensky," *Butler Eagle*, November 24, 1996.

162. "Six Butlerites Commended by Commanding General," *Butler Eagle*, August 10, 1945; "Paul Dobransky," *Butler Eagle*, June 17, 1969; and US, Headstone Applications for Military Veterans, 1925–1970.

163. Jill Cueni-Cohen, "Former Police Chief Disciplined, but Kind," *Pittsburgh Post-Gazette*, December 11, 2002, 89. Samuel Lasky is mentioned in his father's obituary as "a city policeman in Butler." *Butler Eagle*, June 14, 1956.

164. John Warhola conveyed this anecdote to his daughter-in-law, Jarmila Warhola.

165. Bockris, *Warhol*, 107.

166. Diner, *Erin's Daughters*, 43–69, 106–19, 153.

167. Krause, *Grandmothers, Mothers, and Daughters*. The Slavic group included women of "Slovak" (many of whom were probably Rusyn), Polish, Croatian, Serbian, Slovenian, Russian, and Bulgarian descent. Ethnopsychiatrists understand these east central Europeans to share cultural patterns that are remarkably similar in personality and family dynamics. Howard F. Stein, "A Dialectical Model of Health and Illness Attitudes and Behavior among Slovak-Americans," *International Journal of Mental Health* 5, no. 2 (1976): 125.

168. Krause, *Grandmothers, Mothers, and Daughters*, 5, 7.

169. Krause, *Grandmothers, Mothers, and Daughters*, 28, 32, 34.

170. Church records show that Anna offered a liturgy for the special intention of her nephew Andy Warhol in 1960.

Chapter 7: "Your Life Hangs by a Thread"

1. Gerard Malanga, interview by author, March 16, 2016. See also Giuliano, "Gerard Malanga on Andy Warhol's Mother."

2. For a detailed description of the shooting and its aftermath, see Bockris, *Warhol*, 296–312; and Gopnik, *Warhol*, 616–21.

3. Frank Faso, Martin McLaughlin, and Richard Henry, "Actress Shoots Andy Warhol," *New York Daily News*, June 4, 1968, https://www.nydailynews.com/new-york/nyc-crime/andy-warhol-shot-valerie-solanas-1968-article-1.2235937. Solanas was charged with attempted murder, assault, and illegal possession of a firearm. Receiving a diagnosis of paranoid schizophrenia, she was sentenced to three years in prison, part of which included treatment in a psychiatric hospital. Released in 1971, she continued to pursue Warhol with threatening phone calls. She was arrested and institutionalized several times before her death in 1988.

4. For a detailed description of Wathol's injuries and the surgery that saved him, see Gopnik, *Warhol*, 1–3.

5. Richard F. Shephard, "Warhol Gravely Wounded in Studio; Actress Is Held," *New York Times*, June 4, 1968.

6. Malanga, interview by author, March 16, 2016.

7. Viva Hoffman, quoted in David Behrens and Jack Mann, "Andy Warhol Is Shot by Actress," *Newsday*, June 4, 1968.

8. Hoffman, "Warhol Superstar Viva." When Malanga later visited Warhol in the hospital, Andy gave him the $50 check he had come for on June 3. Malanga thought this was partly in appreciation for the concern he had shown Julia. Malanga, interview by author, March 10, 2016.

9. Hoffman, in Bockris, *Warhol*, 302.

10. Howard Smith, "The Shot That Shattered the Velvet Underground," *Village Voice*, June 6, 1968,

https://www.villagevoice.com/2018/11/12/andy
-land-3-the-shot-heard-round-the-demimonde/.

11. Faso, McLaughlin, and Henry, "Actress Shoots Andy Warhol."

12. Dufresne [Ultra Violet], *Famous for 15 Minutes*, 172.

13. For Julia's epithet "good religious boy," Gopnik cites Raymond Herbenick's quotation of Ultra Violet's borrowing from Bernard Weinraub's *Esquire* interview ("Andy Warhol's Mother"), which was published two years before the shooting.

14. Dufresne, *Famous for 15 Minutes*, 175–76; Bailey, *Andy Warhol*; and Warhol, *Diaries*, 313.

15. Hoffman, "Warhol Superstar Viva."

16. Dufresne, *Famous for 15 Minutes*, 173.

17. Ted Carey, in Smith, *Andy Warhol's Art and Films*, 252–53; and Taylor Mead, in Prekop and Cihlář, *Andy Warhol a Československo*, 309.

18. Paul Warhola, in Markus, "Two Years after His Death," 67. Since Julia did not know of the shooting before she left her home in the afternoon, it is more likely that Malanga or another of Warhol's associates made the call.

19. Donald Warhola, interview by author, August 24, 2017.

20. Donald Warhola, interview by author, August 24, 2017.

21. Bockris, *Warhol*, 304.

22. "Warhol's Condition Is Much Improved," *New York Times*, June 11, 1989, 43.

23. John Warhola, in Gangewere, "Ten Years Later."

24. Warhol and Hackett, *POPism*, 274.

25. Paul C. Warhola, interview by author, July 23, 2020.

26. Paul C. Warhola, interview by author, July 23, 2020. According to John Warhola, Warhol's insurance agent had embezzled his premiums, and he could not afford to pay his substantial hospital bills. Bills from the surgeon who saved his life went unpaid, and the check Warhol finally sent to him bounced. Without the doctor's agreement, Warhol sent him paintings in lieu of payment. See Bockris, *Warhol*, 314; and Gopnik, *Warhol*, 654–56.

27. Paul C. Warhola, interview by author, February 20, 2020.

28. David Bourdon Papers, Archives of American Art, Smithsonian Institution.

29. Paul C. Warhola, interview by author, July 23, 2020. The visit by the Byzantine Catholic priest Father Papp is described in chapter 5.

30. Leticia Kent, "Andy Warhol: Alive and Well," *Village Voice*, September 12, 1968, https://www.villagevoice.com/2020/10/14/andy-warhol-alive-well/.

31. Warhol and Hackett, *POPism*, 275–76.

32. Hoffman, "Warhol Superstar Viva"; Brigid Berlin [Polk], in Paul Carroll, "What's a Warhol?" (1969), in Pratt, *Critical Response*, 55.

33. Viva to Warhol, 1968, Andy Warhol Museum Archives (AWMA). According to Bockris, Julia also told Viva about the death of her daughter. Bockris, *Warhol*, 306.

34. Paul C. Warhola, letter to David Bourdon, the David Bourdon Papers, Archives of American Art, Smithsonian Institution.

35. Bockris, *Warhol*, 310.

36. Warhol, in Warhol and Hackett, *POPism*, 284.

37. Jaromil Jireš, in Prekop and Cihlář, *Andy Warhol a Československo*, 215.

38. Marty Manor Mullins, "Prague Spring on the Periphery: Eastern Slovak Steelworkers React to Reform and Invasion in 1968," *Kosmos: Czechoslovak and Central European Journal* 1, no. 2 (Winter 2018): 64; "Oběty okupace 1968" [Victims of the 1968 occupation], https://obetio kupace.dejepis21.cz/; and https://web.archive.org/web/20110718191818/http://www.ustrcr.cz/en/august-1968-victims-of-the-occupation#esr. Among the victims of "Slovak nationality" were citizens of Rusyn ethnicity.

39. "Invasion of Czechoslovakia," 1968, https://i.redd.it/72kzqy3d7oa51.jpg.

40. Russ Braley, "100 Yankees Reach Safety," *New York Daily News*, August 23, 1968, 4.

41. Craig R. Whitney, "Prague Journal: Shirley Temple Black Unpacks a Bag of Memories," *New York Times*, September 11, 1989. For more on her perilous navigation of roadblocks, checkpoints, and low-flying planes from Prague to the West German border, see Norman Eisen, *The Last*

Palace: Europe's Extraordinary Century through Five Lives and One House in Prague (New York: Crown, 2018), 259–82.

42. Quoted in Marty Manor Mullins, "A Remarkable Reversal: Communist Czechoslovakia's Reinstatement of Eastern Rite Catholicism during the Prague Spring," *Journal of Church and State* 58, no. 2 (2016): 349.

43. Jaroslav Coranič, "Legalization of Greek Catholic Church in Czechoslovakia in 1968," *E-Theologos* 1, no. 2 (2010): 199.

44. See Magocsi, *With Their Backs to the Mountains*, 329–34.

45. Undated letters from Mary Lacko and Anna Serensky to Julia Warhola, AWMA.

46. Bockris, *Warhol*, 308.

47. Howard F. Stein, "Envy and the Evil Eye among Slovak-Americans: An Essay in the Psychological Ontogeny of Belief and Ritual," *Ethos* 2, no. 1 (Spring, 1974): 15–46.

48. *Julia Warhola in Bed, Talking*, VR.00.0025, AWMA.

49. Mary Zavacky Zymboly was the daughter of Jullia's brother John. She used the nickname Sally to distinguish herself from other cousins named Mary. I will refer to her here as Mary Zymboly, as her aunt Julia did.

50. Julia Warhola to Mary Zymboly, December 21, 1965, AWMA.

51. Warhol, *Diaries*, 708. Denton Sayer Cox, MD, had been Andy Warhol's doctor and friend since 1960. An internist specializing in comprehensive preventative care and anti-aging medicine, he treated many high-profile patients. He was said to have "a warm bedside manner," but when Warhol referred Bob Colacello to him, his recommendation was, "He's a great doctor, Bob. He has a big Rolls-Royce." Colacello, *Holy Terror*, 326.

52. Julia Warhola to Mary Zymboly, March 28, 1967. Courtesy of Gregory Zymboly.

53. George Warhola, interview by author, August 15, 2019.

54. Julia Warhola to Mary Zymboly, December 21, 1965.

55. Weinraub, "Andy Warhol's Mother," 101.

56. Carroll, "What's a Warhol?" 47–48.

57. Johnson, in Bockris, *Warhol*, 310.

58. David Bourdon Papers, Archives of American Art, Smithsonian Institution.

59. The most complete story of Julia's decline, based on information from relatives who experienced it, is in Bockris, *Warhol*, 350–53. My summary here is drawn from Bockris, unless otherwise stated.

60. Bockris, *Warhol*, 351; Bourdon, *Warhol*, 308; and Alan Weizenberg, in Gopnik, *Warhol*, 645.

61. Bockris, *Warhol*, 310, 352. Johnson does not make the obvious link between Julia's bag-lady persona and Warhol's pack-rat habits.

62. David Bourdon Papers, Archives of American Art, Smithsonian Institution.

63. Bockris, *Warhol*, 352.

64. Bockris, *Warhol*, 310, 351.

65. Donald Warhola, interview by author, August 24, 2017.

66. Introduced in 1950, Dexamyl was marketed as a drug to curb appetite and elevate mood. Long-term usage of Dexamyl had potential for dependency and abuse. It was discontinued in 1982, when new antidepressants became available. Nicholas Rasmussen, "America's First Amphetamine Epidemic 1929–1971," *American Journal of Public Health* 98, no. 6 (June 2008): 974–85.

67. *Julia Warhola in Bed, Talking*"; *Julia Warhola in T-Shirt, Sick*; and *Julia Warhola in Bed, Talking, Sleeping*. *Julia Warhola Watching Television* is less than a minute of footage at the beginning of Warhol's "Whitney Museum Retrospective," VE.30.0004, AWMA. Details from Warhol's childhood revealed in *Julia Warhola in T-Shirt Sick* were discussed in chapter 3.

68. Parts of this section were first published in "Andy and Julia in Rusyn: Warhol's Translation of His Mother in Film and Video," *Journal of Art Historiography*, no. 26 (June 2022), https://arthistoriography.files.wordpress.com/2022/05/6-rusinko.pdf.

69. This performance is discussed in chapter 4.

70. Howard F. Stein, "A Dialectical Model of Health and Illness Attitudes and Behavior among Slovak-Americans," *International Journal of Mental Health* 5, no 2 (Summer 1976): 133.

71. Bockris, *Warhol*, 350. In a letter from March 31, 1965, John tells his mother that she could get her medication by injection. "Ask Andy if those pills are too hard to swallow if you should have the shot." AWMA.

72. Richardson, "Secret Warhol," 125.

73. Bockris, *Warhol*, 98.

74. Gopnik, *Warhol*, 455.

75. Louis Menand, "Did Andy Warhol Change Everything?" *New Yorker*, January 11, 2010, https://www.newyorker.com/magazine/2010/01/11/top-of-the-pops.

76. Colacello, *Holy Terror*, 557, 626, xix.

77. Bockris, *Warhol*, 351.

78. Bockris, *Warhol*, 352. No records of a 1971 hospitalization in New York have come to light.

79. David I. Kertzer and Peter Laslett, eds., *Aging in the Past: Demography, Society, and Old Age* (Berkeley: University of California Press, 1995), 292–96.

80. Krause, *Grandmothers, Mothers, and Daughters*, 134.

81. Bockris, *Warhol*, 352.

82. John and Paul Warhola, in Bockris, *Warhol*, 352.

83. Eve Warhola to Andy Warhol, May 14, 1971, AWMA.

84. Bockris, *Warhol*, 353.

85. "Admission agreement for extended care (Medicare) patients," AWMA. When the Medicare subsidy was exhausted on August 21, the monthly bills for 1971 ran to about $750. Wightman Manor statements, AWMA.

86. Krause, *Grandmothers, Mothers, and Daughters*, 171.

87. Colacello, *Holy Terror*, 59.

88. *Pittsburgh Press*, May 11, 1973; July 2, 1974; August 19, 1973; and July 15, 1974.

89. Mary Zymboly, letter to Andy Warhol, October 9, 1972, AWMA. Zymboly mentions that one of the nurses was from *Ruska dolina* and could speak to Julia in her language.

90. Mary Zymboly, letter to Andy Warhol, September 15, 1972, AWMA.

91. Bockris, *Warhol*, 353.

92. Paul C. Warhola, interview by author, July 23, 2020.

93. Nora Zavacky, interview by author, August 25, 2017.

94. George Warhola, interview by author, August 15, 2019.

95. Carlin, "Andy Warhol."

96. Bockris, *Warhol*, 353.

97. Mary Zymboly, letter to Andy Warhol, August 1, 1972, AWMA.

98. Mary Zymboly, letter to Andy Warhol, September 15, 1972, AWMA.

99. Carlin, "Andy Warhol."

100. Bockris, *Warhol*, 361.

101. Paul Warhola, in Bockris, *Warhol*, 361.

102. A pair of photographs by Michals of mother and son in the same pose, one that focuses on Julia and another where the focus is on Andy, were taken in 1958. The photo discussed here was reproduced first in the catalog for a Warhol exhibit at the Gotham Book Mart in 1971. For more on the Michals photographs, see Printz, "Other Voices, Other Rooms," 82–87.

103. John Zavacky, interview by author, July 29, 2020.

104. Bockris, *Warhol*, 362; and Guiles, *Loner at the Ball*, 328.

105. Mary Zymboly to Andy Warhol, September 15, 1972, AWMA. Zymboly later said she had sent Andy "about twenty letters about Julia when she was at Wightman Manor." Quoted in Donald Miller, "Avant-garde Warhol Given Traditional Farewell," *Pittsburgh Post-Gazette*, February 27, 1987.

106. Warhol, *Diaries*, 704.

107. Commonwealth of Pennsylvania Department of Health, death certificate for Julia Warhola.

The date of birth on her death certificate, November 17, 1899, is incorrect. She was born on November 22, 1891. The informant, John Warhola, could not provide Julia's father's name or her mother's maiden name.

108. Tape of recorded telephone call with John Warhola, November 28, 1972, AWMA.

109. Warhol, unpublished diary entry for November 28, 1972, AWMA. (In Gopnik's *Warhol*, 741n25, it is dated 1973, a typographical error.)

110. Colacello, *Holy Terror*, 225.

111. Warhol, unpublished diary entry for

November 28, 1972, AWMA. Warhol probably meant to say that Ronnie was being deposed. Tavel had worked with Warhol on the film *Suicide* in 1965; Edie Sedgwick, who starred in Warhol's *Vinyl* (1965) died in 1971; Marie Menken died in 1970; and Philip Fagan, an early boyfriend of Warhol's, had appeared in several Warhol films and a screen test in 1964 and 1965.

112. Colacello, *Holy Terror*, 225.

113. Colacello, *Holy Terror*, 153–54, 595.

114. Jonas Mekas, in Frank F., "A Look at Jackie Kennedy and Warhol's Friendship," *Grunge*, October 4, 2021, https://www.grunge.com/623399/a-look-at-jackie-kennedy-and-andy-warhols-friendship/?utm_campaign=clip.

115. Lee Radziwill, in Frank F., "A Look at Jackie Kennedy and Warhol's Friendship."

116. Gopnik, *Warhol*, 715.

117. Frei and Printz, *Paintings and Sculpture*, 161, cited in Gopnik, *Warhol*, 735.

118. Warhol, unpublished diary entry for November 29, 1972, AWMA.

119. Warhol, *Philosophy*, 123.

120. Gopnik, *Warhol*, 741.

121. Information on Julia's funeral is from the funeral program and guestbook, "Dedicated to the Memory of Julia Warhola." Courtesy of Donald Warhola.

122. *The Divine Liturgy*, 33–36.

123. John N. Elachko Funeral Home, "About us," https://www.elachko.com/about/about-us.

124. Bockris, *Warhol*, 40.

125. John Zavacky, interview by author, July 29, 2020.

126. "Weather Forecast," *Pittsburgh Press*, December 1, 1972, 51.

127. John N. Elachko Funeral Home invoice, AWMA. The cemetery plot had already been paid for. Honoraria for clergymen and the funeral lunch were not included in the invoice.

128. Bockris, *Warhol*, 362.

129. Sister Teresa, letter to Andy Warhol, November 27, 1972, AWMA.

130. Jed's statement that he did not learn of Julia's death until the summer of 1975 contradicts George Warhola's memory that Jed had seen the photograph of Julia in her coffin. According to Colacello, Jed knew about Julia's death, but was under strict orders from Warhol to keep it quiet. *Holy Terror*, 356.

131. Bockris, *Warhol*, 362, 363.

132. Warhol, *Diaries*, 722.

133. Barbara Colaciello, telephone interview by Mary Huzinec, April 6, 2019. Barbara Colaciello retained the original spelling of the family surname.

134. Bockris, *Warhol*, 362.

135. Bourdon, *Warhol*, 322.

136. Donald Miller, "Words with Warhol: Artist at Gallery Gala," *Pittsburgh Post-Gazette*, October 1, 1979.

137. Howard F. Stein, "Aging and Death among Slovak-Americans: A Study in the Thematic Unity of the Life Cycle," *Journal of Psychological Anthropology* 1, no. 3 (1978): 314–15.

138. Warhol, *Diaries*, 325; and Warhol, "On My Mind," 165.

139. Warhol, *Diaries*, 704.

140. Ronnie Cutrone, in Vecchiet, *Vies et morts d'Andy Warhol*.

141. Julia Warhola, quoted by Donald Warhola, interview by author, August 24, 2017.

142. Colacello, *Holy Terror*, 194–95.

143. Leo Castelli and Peter Brant, cited in Gopnik, *Warhol*, 742.

144. Warhol to David Bourdon, Bourdon, *Warhol*, 317.

145. Frei and Printz, *Paintings and Sculpture*, 167.

146. Warhol, in Phyllis Tuchman, "Pop!" *ArtNews*, May 1974, 26. For detailed descriptions of Warhol's artistic technique in these portraits, see Bourdon, *Warhol*, 327, 337–40; Colacello, *Holy Terror*, 236–37; and Gopnik, *Warhol*, 745–46.

147. Warhol, in Barry Blinderman, "Modern Myths: An Interview with Andy Warhol," in Goldsmith, *I'll Be Your Mirror*, 294.

148. Gopnik, *Warhol*, 866.

149. A tenth portrait remained unfinished. Frei and Printz, *Paintings and Sculpture*, appendix 9, 530.

150. Frei and Printz, *Paintings and Sculpture*, 420.

151. Bourdon, *Warhol*, 322–23.

152. In his 2000 PhD dissertation, "Other Voices, Other Rooms," Neil Printz writes that the portraits were based on a Duane Michals

photograph from 1958, but Michals denied he photographed the source portrait. Frei and Printz, *Paintings and Sculpture*, 524n50. Donald Warhola has identified it as a Wallowitch photograph, taken in the Lexington Avenue town house.

153. On the Warhol–Wallowitch relationship, see Gopnik, *Warhol*, 183–84. Julia also attempted a portrait of Wallowitch. One of her scribbled drawings of a male torso with curly hair is labeled "Ed Volovch."

154. Bourdon, *Warhol*, 340.

155. Warhol's portraits of his mother are numbers 2799–2807 in Frei and Printz, *Paintings and Sculpture*, 506–10.

156. Frei and Printz, *Paintings and Sculpture*, 420.

157. Bourdon, *Warhol*, 330.

158. Frei and Printz, *Paintings and Sculpture*, 419.

159. Frei and Printz, *Paintings and Sculpture*, 420. Andy gave this portrait to his brother John.

160. Gopnik, *Warhol*, 775–76.

161. Robert Rosenblum, "Andy Warhol: Court Painter to the 70s," in *Andy Warhol: Portraits of the 70s* (New York: Whitney Museum of Art, 1979), 20.

162. Gilda Williams, "Warhol Stumbled."

163. Colacello, *Holy Terror*, 575.

Chapter 8: "A Simple Rusyn Woman"

1. Portions of this chapter were previously published in Rusinko, "We Are All Warhol's Children."

2. Although this statement is quoted frequently in the literature on Warhol, I have not been able to find a primary source. It most likely stems from the inexplicit observation made by Bob Colacello: "'I come from nowhere,' Andy once said." *Holy Terror*, 11. Magocsi used the phrase for the title of his illustrated history of Carpatho-Rusyns, *The People from Nowhere* (New York: Carpatho-Rusyn Research Center, 2006). A picture of Warhol is prominently featured on the book's cover.

3. Paul R. Magocsi, "Andy Warhol," *Carpatho-Rusyn American* 3, no. 2 (1980): 3.

4. Paul R. Magocsi, *Let's Speak Rusyn: Prešov Region Edition* (Englewood, NJ: Transworld, 1976).

5. Bycko, *Nočné dialógy*, 13.

6. Mucha, *Absolut Warhola*.

7. Michal Bycko, *Andy Warhol v kraji sovjich rodičov* [Andy Warhol in the land of his parents] (Medzilaborce: Múzeum moderného umenia rodiny Warholovcov, 1991), n.p.

8. Jozef Keselica, "The Warhol Story in Czechoslovakia," *Carpatho-Rusyn American* 14, no. 4 (1991): 8.

9. Bycko, *Nočné dialógy*, 96.

10. For the complete story of the establishment of the museum, see Rusinko, "We Are All Warhol's Children," 21–37.

11. Prekop and Cihlář, *Andy Warhol a Československo*, 184.

12. The Andy Warhol Foundation for the Visual Arts, *20-Year Report, 1987–2007*, vol. 2, Grants and Exhibitions, https://warholfoundation.org/pdf/volume2.pdf.

13. "Spojená škola v Medzilaborciach" [United School in Medzilaborce], https://www.sosaw.sk/.

14. Avis Berman, "The Right Place: The Founding of the Andy Warhol Museum," in *The Andy Warhol Museum* (Pittsburgh: Andy Warhol Museum, 1994), 33.

15. Berman, "Right Place," 27.

16. Ruth Ellen Gruber, "Warhol Pops Up in Carpathia," *New York Times*, February 21, 1993.

17. James Geary and Jan Stojaspal, "The Rusyns, Slovakia," *Time Europe*, August 29, 2005.

18. On Warhol's famous saying, see Blake Gopnik, *Warholiana*, https://warholiana.com/post/81689862604/in-the-future-everyone-will-be-world-famous-for.

19. Misch, *I Am from Nowhere*. Ján Zavacky refers to a total of eight films that were made about Miková, https://presov.korzar.sme.sk/c/4578061/bratranec-andyho-warhola-jan-zavacky-sa-objavil-vo-viacerych-dokumentoch.html. Today Zavacky's house stands on the land of the family's homestead, where Julia Zavacka grew up.

20. "Director's statements," on official website of *I Am from Nowhere*, http://www.iamfromnowhere.com/index_flash.html, accessed August 7, 2011 (site discontinued). A more somber depiction of present-day Miková is presented by Jakub Mejer in "Exploring Andy Warhol's Ancestral Home," *Pittsburgh Quarterly*, October 25, 2019, https://pittsburghquarterly.com/articles/exploring-andy-warhol-s-ancestral-home/.

21. *Absolut Warhola* was awarded the 2001 German Film Critics Prize for Best Documentary Film and the Audience Prize at the 2001 Mannheim-Heidelberg Film Festival.

22. "Festival," Miková, https://www.mikova.sk/sk/festival/; https://www.mikova.sk/sk/category/festival-2/; and https://www.facebook.com/mikovafestival/. See also "Festival Miková" on YouTube.

23. Brian Požun, "Cultural Schizophrenia: Creating a Rusyn Pop Culture," *Outpost Dispatch* 1, no. 1 (October 2003), https://www.outpostdispatch.xyz/archive/volume-1-issue-1-october-2003/cultural-schizophrenia-creating-a-rusyn-pop-culture-part-1.

24. Paul Robert Magocsi, "Andy Warhol," in Magocsi and Pop, *Encyclopedia of Rusyn History and Culture* (2005), 539.

25. See https://www.lem.fm/. A search for "Warhol" brings up news of Warhol exhibits around the world, new publications, and sales of his works.

26. Bycko, "Pohliad na Endi Varhola," 29.

27. Vasyl' Khoma [Choma], "Fenomen Endi Varhol i eho genealogiia" [The phenomenon of Andy Warhol and his genealogy], *Rusyn'skŷi literaturnŷi almanakh na 2005-yi rik* (Prešov: Spolok rusyn'skŷkh pysateliv Sloven'ska, 2006), 42.

28. Anna Plishkova, "Labirskŷi muzei v konteksti svitovoho umenia" [The Medzilaborce museum in the context of world art], *Rusyn*, no. 5/6 (1999): 37.

29. Gallery of Art, Prague, *Warhol/Warhola*, https://goout.net/en/warhol-warhola/sznpdhf/.

30. A concert from 2013 can be seen on YouTube: "Back to the Roots," https://www.youtube.com/watch?v=0bLSU8pHsHs&t=155s. Both the CD and the concert begin with Julia's reading of a few lines from her English-language story, "The Hobo and the Magic Pocketbook," and end with her recitation of the Lord's Prayer in Rusyn Church Slavonic. This concert, which took place in the Christmas season, ends with a Carpatho-Rusyn Christmas hymn.

31. Robert Kotian, "Andyho Warhola poznajú všetci: A jeho mamu?" [Everyone knows Andy Warhol: But who knows his mother?], June 20, 2019, https://kultura.sme.sk/c/22149421/andyho-warhola-poznaju-vsetci-a-jeho-mamu.html. Kucer has toured Europe with his show, and in 2016 he performed in New York City at the Bohemian National Hall.

32. Jarek Szubrycht, "Julia Warhola—mama i muza Andy'ego: Jak to się stało, że zaśpiewała na nowej płycie bieszczadzkiej supergrupy Tołhaje? [Julia Warhola was Andy's mama and muse: How did it happen that she sang on the new album by the supergroup Tołhaje from the Beskyd Mountains?], April 25, 2018, https://wyborcza.pl/7,113768,23319033,julia-warhola-mama-i-muza-andy-ego-jak-to-sie-stalo-ze-zaspiewala.html.

33. Szubrycht, "Julia Warhola—mama i muza Andy'ego."

34. *Songs for Drella* (1990), a concept album dedicated to the memory of Warhol by Reed and Cale, formerly of the Velvet Underground. "Drella," a combination of Dracula and Cinderella, was a nickname Warhol's followers used for him.

35. *I Shot Andy Warhol*, directed by Mary Harron, 1996; and *Factory Girl*, directed by George Hickenlooper, 2006.

36. Andy Rossi, dir., *The Andy Warhol Diaries*, TV mini-series, Netflix, 2022, https://www.netflix.com/title/81026142.

37. Williams, "Warhol Stumbled"; and Lynne Margolis, "Out of the BOX," *Carnegie Online*, September/October 2004, https://carnegiemuseums.org/magazine-archive/2004/sepoct/feature1.html.

38. "Andy Warhol, Exhibition Guide," https://www.tate.org.uk/whats-on/tate-modern/exhibition/andy-warhol/exhibition-guide; Laura Cumming, "Andy Warhol Review: Hurrying through the Masterworks," *Guardian*, March 15, 2020, https://www.theguardian.com/artanddesign/2020/mar/15/andy-warhol-tate-modern-review; and Gilda Williams, "Not Another Warhol Show," *Frieze*, March 13, 2020, https://www.frieze.com/article/not-another-warhol-show-review-tate-modern.

39. On the postage stamp, see Prekop and Cihlář, *Andy Warhol and Czechoslovakia*, 325; and *Andy Warhol a Československo*, 411. In 1988, Paul R. Magocsi proposed the Julia Warhola Chair of Carpathian Studies to John Warhola as a project for the Andy Warhol Foundation. Magocsi, personal correspondence.

40. "Andy Warhol from A to Z," *Genealogy of Style*, https://thegenealogyofstyle.wordpress.com/2013/09/01/andy-warhol-from-a-to-z/.

Selected Bibliography

The research for this book involved many sources, ranging across numerous disciplines in several languages. In the bibliography, I have included the most relevant and valuable resources from which I have cited heavily and which are most easily accessible to general readers. The selected bibliography emphasizes English-language materials, although some important studies in less common languages are also noted. Facts of publication for more specialized scholarly sources not included in the bibliography can be found in the endnotes.

Online Archives

Below is a list of the most significant online archives I have accessed through Ancestry.com.

1910, 1920, 1930,1940, 1950 *US Federal Census*

Baltimore, Passenger Lists, 1820–1964

New York, Passenger and Crew Lists (including Castle Garden and Ellis Island), 1820–1957

Ohio, Death Records, 1908–1932, 1938–2007

Pennsylvania, Birth Certificates, 1906–1911

Pennsylvania, Death Certificates, 1906–1966

Pennsylvania, Federal Naturalization Records, 1795–1931

Pennsylvania, Marriages, 1852–1968

Pennsylvania, Prison, Reformatory, and Workhouse Records, 1829–1971

Pennsylvania, Veteran Compensation Application Files, World War II, 1950–1966

Pennsylvania, Veterans Burial Cards, 1777–2012

Pennsylvania, Wills and Probate Records, 1683–1993

Slovakia, Church and Synagogue Books, 1592–1935

US City Directories, 1822–1995

US Social Security Applications and Claims Index, 1936–2007

US World War I Draft Registration Cards, 1917–1918

US World War II Army Enlistment Records, 1938–1946

US World War II Draft Cards Young Men, 1940–1947

US World War II Draft Registration Cards, 1942

West Virginia, Marriages Index, 1785–1971

Newspapers

Newspapers consulted through Newspapers.com are included in endnotes.

Primary and Secondary Sources

Abbott, Grace. *The Immigrant and the Community.* The American Immigration Library. 1917. Reprint, New York: Jerome S. Ozer, 1971.

ad-Din, Haytham. "St. Mary's Byzantine Catholic Church: A Photo-Essay on Carpatho-Rusyns between East & West." Medium, February 2, 2020. https://medium.com/the-photographic-muslim/st-marys-byzantine-catholic-church-a127e93b95de.

Allen, Mark. "A Conversation with Nathan Gluck." http://www.markallencam.com/nathangluck.html.

Angell, Callie. *Something Secret: Portraiture in Warhol's Films.* Sydney: Museum of Contemporary Art, 1994.

Bailey, David. *Andy Warhol: Transcript of David Bailey's ATV Documentary.* London: Bailey Litchfield/Matthews Miller Dunbar, 1972.

Baines, Dudley. *Emigration from Europe, 1815–1930.* Cambridge: Cambridge University Press, 1995.

Balch, Emily Greene. *Our Slavic Fellow Citizens.* New York: Charities Publication Committee, 1910.

Baycura, Peter. *Lyndora Chronicles: The Legendary Decades, 1902–1921.* Butler, PA: John Baycura, 1998.

Bell, Thomas. *Out of This Furnace.* Pittsburgh, PA: University of Pittsburgh Press, 1976.

Benedict, Ruth. *Patterns of Culture.* Boston: Houghton Mifflin, 2005.

Bezeková, Eva. "Záznam autentického rozhovoru s Evou Bezekovou" [Transcript of an authentic conversation with Eva Bezekova]. In Bycko, *Nočné dialógy s Andym,* 82–85.

Bicha, Karel D. "Hunkies: Stereotyping the Slavic Immigrants, 1890–1920." *Journal of American Ethnic History* 2, no. 1 (1982): 16–38.

Bockris, Victor. *Warhol: The Biography.* New York: Da Capo Press, 2003.

Bodnar, John. "Immigration and Modernization: The Case of Slavic Peasants in Industrial America." *Journal of Social History* 10, no. 1 (1976): 44–71.

Bodnar, John E. *The Transplanted: A History of Immigrants in Urban America.* Bloomington: Indiana University Press, 1998.

Bodnar, John E., Roger D. Simon, and Michael P. Weber. *Lives of Their Own: Blacks, Italians, and Poles in Pittsburgh, 1900–1960.* Urbana: University of Illinois Press, 1983.

Bogatyrev, Petr. *Vampires in the Carpathians: Magical Acts, Rites, and Beliefs in Subcarpathian Rus'.* Translated by Stephen Reynolds and Patricia Ann Krafcik. New York: East European Monographs. Dist. Columbia University Press, 1998.

Bourdon, David. *Warhol.* New York: Abradale Press, 1991.

Breckinridge, Sophonisba P. *New Homes for Old.* 1921. New York: Harper, 1921. https://www.gutenberg.org/ebooks/41291.

Bren, Paulina, and Mary Neuburger, eds. "Tuzex and the Hustler: Living It Up in Czechoslovakia." In *Communism Unwrapped: Consumption in Cold War Eastern Europe,* 21–48. New York: Oxford University Press, 2012.

Browning, H. Ellen. *A Girl's Wanderings in Hungary.* London: Longmans, Green and Co., 1896. https://books.google.com/books/about/A_Girl_s_Wanderings_in_Hungary.html?id=yFhrzhWqPPAC.

Burns, Ric. *Andy Warhol: A Documentary Film.* DVD. PBS Paramount, 2006.

Butler, Elizabeth Beardsley. *Women and the Trades: Pittsburgh 1907–1908.* New York: Charities Publication Committee, 1911.

Bycko, Michal. *Nočné dialógy s Andym* [Nocturnal dialogues with Andy]. Prešov: Cuper, 1996.

Bycko, Michal. "Pohliad na Endi Varhola zo sotsialnoho boku" [A view of Andy Warhol from the social aspect]. *Rusyn,* no. 3–4 (1997): 28–29.

Bycko, Michal. "Ulin syn Andriiko" [Julia's son Andriiko]. *Rusyn,* no. 1 (1991): 16–17.

Campbell, Helen. *Turnip Blues.* Duluth, MN: Spinsters Ink, 1998.

Carlin, Margie. "Andy Warhol . . . Is He for Real." *Pittsburgh Press,* October 22, 1972.

Choma [Khoma], Vasil'. *Miková: Rusínska obec v premenách siedmich storočí* [Miková: Seven centuries of a Rusyn village]. N.p.: Published by the author and the municipality of Miková, 2010.

Chori, Iurii. *Vid rodu do rodu: Zvychaievo-obriadovi tradyciï Zakarpattia* [From generation to generation: Customs, rituals, and traditions of Subcarpathia]. Uzhhorod: V. Padiak, 2001.

Chyzhmar, Ivan. *Narodne vesilia Rusyniv vykhodnoi Slovakii* [The folk wedding of the Rusyns of eastern Slovakia]. Svidník: Self-published, 2006.

Colacello, Bob. *Holy Terror: Andy Warhol Close Up*. New York: Vintage Books, 2014.

Commons, James R., and William M. Leiserson. "Wage-Earners of Pittsburgh." In *Wage-Earning Pittsburgh*. Vol. 6, *The Pittsburgh Survey*, 113–88. New York: Russell Sage 1914.

Cresap, Kelly M. *Pop Trickster Fool: Warhol Performs Naivete*. Urbana: University of Illinois Press, 2004.

Custer, Richard D., ed. *Rusyn-American Almanac of the Carpatho-Rusyn Society*. Pittsburgh, PA: Carpatho-Rusyn Society, 2005.

DeSalvo, Donna. *Andy Warhol: From A to B and Back Again*. New York: Whitney Museum of American Art, 2018.

DeSalvo, Donna M. "Learning the Ropes." In *Success Is a Job in New York: The Early Art and Business of Andy Warhol*, 1–25. New York: Grey Art Gallery and Study Center New York University, 1989.

Dillenberger, Jane. *The Religious Art of Andy Warhol*. New York: Continuum, 1998.

Diner, Hasia R. *Erin's Daughters in America: Irish Immigrant Women in the Nineteenth Century*. Baltimore: Johns Hopkins University Press, 1986.

Dinwiddie, Emily Wayland, and F. Elizabeth Crowell. "The Housing of Pittsburgh's Workers." In *The Pittsburgh District: Civic Frontage*. Vol. 5, *The Pittsburgh Survey*, 87–123. New York: Russell Sage, 1914.

The Divine Liturgy: A Book of Prayer. Compiled and adapted by Rev. William Levkulic. Pittsburgh, PA: n.p., n.d.

Duda, Katherine M. "At Home in Pittsburgh: Andy Warhol's Youth." *Carnegie Magazine*, August 1996. https://carnegiemuseums.org/magazine-archive/1996/julaug/feat2.htm.

Dufresne, Isabelle Collin [Ultra Violet]. *Famous for 15 Minutes: My Years with Andy Warhol*. New York: Harcourt, Brace, Jovanovich, 1988.

Dukhnovych, Aleksander. *Virtue Is More Important Than Riches: A Play in Three Acts*. Translated by Elaine Rusinko. Fairview, NJ: Carpatho-Rusyn Research Center. Dist. Columbia University Press, 1994.

Eastman, Crystal. *Work-Accidents and the Law*. Vol. 2, *The Pittsburgh Survey*. New York: Russell Sage Foundation, 1910.

Eichleay, John W. Jr. *The House Movers*. Pittsburgh, PA: Eichleay, 2010.

Fedash, Luba Czerhoniak. *Blossoms on a Rooftop*. Pittsburgh, PA: Dorrance, 2006.

Fitch, John A. *The Steel Workers*. Vol. 3, *The Pittsburgh Survey*,1910. Reprint, Pittsburgh, PA: University of Pittsburgh Press, 1989.

Frei, Georg, and Neil Printz. *Paintings and Sculpture 1970–1974: Warhol 03—The Andy Warhol Catalogue Raisonné*. New York: Phaidon, 2010.

Gabaccia, Donna R. *From the Other Side: Women, Gender, and Immigrant Life in the U.S., 1820–1990*. Bloomington: Indiana University Press, 1994.

Gangeware, R. Jay. "Ten Years Later—What Would Andy Say?" *Carnegie Magazine*, 1977. https://carnegiemuseums.org/magazine-archive/1997/mayjun/feat4.htm.

Gangewere, R. Jay. "Two Andys from Pittsburgh." *Carnegie Magazine*, June 1994, 20–25, 50–54.

Giuliano, Charles. "Gerard Malanga on Andy Warhol's Mother Julia—Berkshire Fine Arts." http://www.berkshirefinearts.com/06-04-2015_gerard-malanga-on-andy-warhol-s-mother-julia.htm.

Giuliano, Charles. "Tina Olsen Talks about Warhol at Williams—Berkshire Fine Arts." http://www.berkshirefinearts.com/06-01-2015_tina-olsen-talks-about-warhol-at-williams.htm.

Goldsmith, Kenneth, ed. *I'll Be Your Mirror: The Selected Andy Warhol Interviews*. New York: Carroll & Graf, 2004.

Gopnik, Blake. "Andy Warhol's Jewish Question." *Artnet News*, November 22, 2016. https://news.artnet.com/opinion/andy-warhol-before-and-after-757139.

Gopnik, Blake. *Warhol*. New York: Ecco, 2020.

Greene, Victor. "For God and Country: The Origins of Slavic Catholic Self-Consciousness in America." *Church History* 35, no. 4 (1966): 446–61.

Greene, Victor. "The Polish-American Worker to 1930: The 'Hunky' Image in Transition." *Polish Review* 21, no. 3 (1976): 63–78.

Greenwald, Maurine Weiner, and Margo J. Anderson, eds. *Pittsburgh Surveyed: Social Science and Social Reform in the Early Twentieth Century*. Pittsburgh, PA: University of Pittsburgh Press, 1996.

Grešlík, Vladislav, and Margita Šukajlová, eds. *Ikony Šarišského múzea v Bardejove* [Icons of the Šariš Museum at Bardejov]. Bratislava: Ars Monument, 1994.

Grudin, Anthony E. "Warhol's Animal Life." *Criticism* 56, no. 3 (2014): 593–622.

Grudin, Anthony E. *Warhol's Working Class: Pop Art and Egalitarianism*. Chicago: University of Chicago Press, 2017.

Guiles, Fred Lawrence. *Loner at the Ball: The Life of Andy Warhol*. London: Bantam Press, 1989.

Handlin, Oscar. *Truth in History*. Cambridge, MA. Harvard University Press, 1981.

Handlin, Oscar. *The Uprooted*. 2nd ed. Boston: Little, Brown, 1990.

Hašek, Jaroslav. *The Good Soldier Švejk: and His Fortunes in the World War*. Translated by Cecil Parrott. London: Heinemann, 1973.

Heavenly Manna: A Practical Prayer Book of Devotions for Greek Rite Catholics. Uniontown, PA: n.p., 1960.

Hill, Scotti. "The Artist Is Not Present: Andy Warhol's 1967 Utah 'Hoax' as Performance and Self-Portraiture." Master's thesis, University of Utah, 2011.

Hoffman, Viva. "Warhol Superstar Viva Remembers Andy, His Mother and the Artist's Early Brush with Death." I love Warhol, March 23, 2015. https://ilovewarhol.com/warhol-superstar-viva-remembers-andy-his-mother-the-artists-early-brush-with-death/.

Horbal, Bogdan. "Communism." In *Encyclopedia of Rusyn History and Culture*, edited by Paul Robert Magocsi and Ivan Pop, revised and expanded ed. Toronto: University of Toronto Press, 2005.

Hronský, Marián. "Priebeh bojov na uzemí Slovenska a Slováci v Rakúsko-Uhorskej armáde za prvej svetovej vojny" [Battles on the territory of Slovakia and Slovaks in the Austro-Hungarian Army in the First World War"]. https://velkavojna.sk/downloads.php?cat_id=3&download_id=2.

Hyriak, Mikhail, ed. *In the Seventy-Seventh Kingdom*. Translated by Patricia Krafcik. New York: Carpatho-Rusyn Research Center, 2015.

Jackson, Carlton. *The Dreadful Month*. Bowling Green, OH: Bowling Green University Popular Press, 1982.

Johnson, Catherine. *Thank You Andy Warhol*. New York: Glitterati, 2012.

Jumba, Jerry. "The Carpatho-Rusyn Wedding." *Carpatho-Rusyn American* 1, no. 3 (1978): 6.

Jumba, Jerry. "In Memoriam: Andy Warhol (1928–1987)." *Carpatho-Rusyn American* 10, no. 1 (1987): 4.

Jumba, Jerry. "The Julia Warhola Recordings Archive Work Proposal." Unpublished manuscript, 2016.

Keeling, Drew. *The Business of Transatlantic Migration between Europe and the United States, 1900–1914*. Zurich: Chronos, 2012.

Kennedy, Albert J. *Handbook of Settlements*. Edited by Robert A. Woods. New York: Russell Sage Foundation, 1911.

Khoma [Choma], Vasyl'. "Fenomen Endi Varhol i eho genealogiia" [The phenomenon of Andy Warhol and his genealogy]." *Rusyn'skŷi literaturnŷi almanakh na 2005-yi rik*, 34–47. Prešov: Spolok rusyn'skŷkh pysateliv Sloven'ska, 2006.

Kiedrowski, Thomas. *Andy Warhol's New York City: Four Walks Uptown to Downtown*. New York: Little Bookroom, 2011.

Kleinberg, S. J. *The Shadow of the Mills: Working-Class Families in Pittsburgh, 1870–1907*. Pittsburgh, PA: University of Pittsburgh Press, 1989.

Kleinberg, S. J. *Widows and Orphans First: The Family Economy and Social Welfare Policy, 1880–1939*. Urbana: University of Illinois Press, 2006.

Kłosińska, Janina. *Icons from Poland*. Warsaw: Arkady, 1989.

Koch, Stephen. *Stargazer: The Life, World, and Films of Andy Warhol*. 3rd rev. ed. New York: M. Boyars, 1991.

Koehler, Robert. "Absolut Warhola." *Variety*, June 25, 2002. https://variety.com/2002/film/reviews/absolut-warhola-1200547631/.

Koestenbaum, Wayne. *Andy Warhol*. New York: Viking, 2001.

Krasovs'kyi, Ivan. "Traditional Lemko Women's Clothing." *Carpatho-Rusyn American* 10, no. 3 (1987): 6–7.

Krause, Corinne Azen. "Ethnic Culture, Religion, and the Mental Health of Slavic-American Women." *Journal of Religion and Health* 18, no. 4 (1979): 298–307.

Krause, Corinne Azen. *Grandmothers, Mothers, and Daughters: Oral Histories of Three Generations of Ethnic American Women*. Boston: Twayne, 1991.

Krause, Corinne Azen. "Italian, Jewish and Slavic Grandmothers in Pittsburgh: Their Economic Roles." *Frontiers: A Journal of Women Studies* 2, no. 2 (1977): 18–28.

Krause, Corinne Azen. "Urbanization without Breakdown: Italian, Jewish, and Slavic Immigrant Women, 1900 to 1945." *Journal of American Urban History* 4, no. 3 (1978): 291–305.

Kvale, Nicole Ingrid. "Emigrant Trains: Migratory Transportation Networks through Germany and the United States, 1847–1914." PhD diss., University of Wisconsin-Madison, 2009.

Leiby, Richard. "Their Brother's Keepers." *Washington Post*, May 15, 1994. https://www.washingtonpost.com/archive/lifestyle/style/1994/05/15/their-brothers-keepers/aba29970-b2c2-4a2f-af88-220ad7cb4f2c/.

Lemkovskŷi narodnŷ spivankŷ [Lemko folk songs]. "Ja Parobok z Kapushan." Lemko-soiuz, 1935. https://nashe.com.ua/song/11973.

Lubove, Roy. *Twentieth-Century Pittsburgh*. Vol. 1. Pittsburgh, PA: University of Pittsburgh Press, 1996.

Mačoškova, Maria, Anna Servicka, and Andrea Sikorjakova. *Three Stars—Three Generations: Live in Concert at the 7th World Congress of Rusyns*. Compact disc. Nordstone Financial Corporation, 2003.

Magocsi, Paul R. *Carpathian Rus': A Historical Atlas*. Toronto: University of Toronto Press, 2017.

Magocsi, Paul R. *Our People: Carpatho-Rusyns and Their Descendants in North America*. 5th rev. ed. New York: Carpatho-Rusyn Research Center, 2023.

Magocsi, Paul R. *With Their Backs to the Mountains: A History of Carpathian Rus' and Carpatho-Rusyns*. Budapest: Central European University Press, 2015.

Magocsi, Paul R., and I. I. Pop, eds. *Encyclopedia of Rusyn History and Culture*. Toronto: University of Toronto Press, 2002 (rev. and exp. ed., 2005).

Makos, Christopher. *Warhol: A Personal Photographic Memoir*. New York: New American Library, 1989.

Makovskii, Sergei. *Narodnoe iskusstvo Podkarpatskoi Rusi* [The folk art of Subcarpathian Rus']. Prague: Plamia, 1925.

Malanga, Gerard. *Archiving Warhol: An Illustrated History*. London: Creation, 2002.

Markovyč, Pavlo. *Rusyn Easter Eggs from Eastern Slovakia*. Vienna: Braumüller, 1987.

Markus, Julia. "Two Years after His Death, the Curtain Rises on Andy Warhol." *Smithsonian Magazine* 19 (1989).

Medvecky, Joanne. *Legacy of Faith*. DVD. Highland Products, 2003.

Metil, Robert. "Post-Velvet Revolutionary Cultural Activism and Rusyn Song in the Prešov Region of Eastern Slovakia, 1989–2000." PhD diss., University of Pittsburgh, 2000.

Mickens, Julie. "Warholas at Work." *Pittsburgh City Paper*, August 21, 2003. https://www.pghcitypaper.com/pittsburgh/warholas-at-work/Content?oid=1335573.

"Miková—Oficiálne stránky obce Miková" [The official site of the village Mikova]. https://www.mikova.sk/sk/.

Mink, Gwendolyn. *The Wages of Motherhood: Inequality in the Welfare State, 1917–1942*. Ithaca, NY: Cornell University Press, 1995.

Misch, Georg. *I Am from Nowhere*. Navigator Films, 2002. https://dafilms.com/film/7097-i-am-from-nowhere.

Moore, Patrick, José Carlos Díaz, and Miranda Isabel Lash, eds. *Andy Warhol: Revelation*. Pittsburgh, PA: Andy Warhol Museum, 2019.

Morawska, Ewa. *For Bread with Butter: The Life-Worlds of East Central Europeans in Johnstown, Pennsylvania, 1890–1940*. New York: Cambridge University Press, 1985.

Morawska, Ewa. "The Immigrants Pictured and Unpictured in the *Pittsburgh Survey*." In *Pittsburgh Surveyed*, 221–41. Pittsburgh, PA: University of Pittsburgh Press, 1996.

Morawska, Ewa. "A Replica of the 'Old-Country' Relationship in the Ethnic Niche: East European Jews and Gentiles in Small-Town Western Pennsylvania, 1880s–1930s." *American Jewish History* 77, no. 1 (1987): 27–86.

Motyl, Alexander. "Was Andy Warhol Ukrainian?" *Harvard Ukrainian Studies* 32–33, Part 2 (2011–2014): 549–55.

Mucha, Stanislaw. *Absolut Warhola*. DVD. TLA Releasing, 2004.

Mulroney, Lucy. "One Blue Pussy." *Criticism* 56, no. 3 (2014): 559–92.

Murphy, J. J. *The Black Hole of the Camera: The Films of Andy Warhol*. Berkeley: University of California Press, 2012.

Mušynka, Mykola. "Folk Customs of the Carpatho-Rusyns." *Carpatho-Rusyn American* 6, no. 2 (1983): 4–5.

Mušynka, Mykola. "Folk Customs of Carpatho-Rusyns: Birth and Baptism." *Carpatho-Rusyn American* 8, no. 2 (1985): 4–6.

Mušynka, Mykola. "Folk Customs of Carpatho-Rusyns: The Wedding." *Carpatho-Rusyn American* 8, no. 3, 4 (1985), and 9, no. 1 (1986).

Mušynka, Mykola. "The Harvest Festival and St. Andrew's Day." *Carpatho-Rusyn American* 8, no. 1 (1985): 6–7.

Mušynka, Mykola. "Pentecost/Rusalja." *Carpatho-Rusyn American* 7, no. 2 (1984): 5–6.

Mušynka, Mykola. "St. George's Day." *Carpatho-Rusyn American* 7, no. 3 (1984): 9–10.

Nasha knyzhka [Our book]. Yonkers, NY: Lemko-Soiuz, 1945.

Nedziel'skii, Evgenii. *Ugro-Russkii teatr* [Uhro-Rusyn theater]. Uzhhorod: Lemko-Soiuz, 1941.

Nickels, Thom. "Andy Warhol's First Boyfriend." From the Field (blog), February 22, 2016. https://thomnickels.blogspot.com/2016/02/andy-warhols-first-boyfriend.html.

O'Connor, John T., and Benjamin Liu, eds. *Unseen Warhol*. New York: Rizzoli, 1996.

Olbracht, Ivan. *Nikola the Outlaw*. Evanston, IL: Northwestern University Press, 2001.

Opportunity Realized: The Greek Catholic Union's First One Hundred Years, 1892–1992. Beaver, PA: Greek Catholic Union of the U.S.A, 1994.

O'Pray, Michael. *Andy Warhol: Film Factory*. London: BFI, 1989.

Oseroff, Abraham. "A Soho Hillside: The Persistence of Sanitary Neglect in Central Pittsburgh." In Commons and Leiserson, *Wage-Earning Pittsburgh*, 406–10.

Oseroff, Abraham. "Survey of Workingmen's Homes in the Soho District of Pittsburgh: A Study of Civic Neglect in the Heart of a Great City." Master's thesis, University of Pittsburgh, 1914. http://www.info-ren.org/projects/btul/exhibit/sohofta.html.

Palma, Joe. "Great-Great-Great-Granpap Was a Serf: Researching Your Rusyn Ancestors through Urbarial Census Records." *New Rusyn Times* 9 no. 4 (2002), 8–9.

Pastor, Peter. "Hungary in World War I: The End of Historic Hungary." *Hungarian Studies Review* 28, no, 1–2 (2001): 163–84.

Pehotsky, Bessie Olga. *The Slavic Immigrant Woman*. 1925. Reprint. San Francisco: R and E Research Associates, 1970.

Perlman, Bennard. "The Education of Andy Warhol." In *The Andy Warhol Museum*, 147–65 Pittsburgh, PA: Andy Warhol Museum, 1994.

Perry, Ruth, and Martine Watson Brownley, eds. *Mothering the Mind: Twelve Studies of Writers and Their Silent Partners*. New York: Holmes & Meier, 1984.

Phillimore, Lion. *In the Carpathians*. New York, 1912. https://www.google.com/books/edition/In_the_Carpathians/IeJKAQAAIAAJ?hl=en&gbpv=1&dq=lion+phillimore&printsec=frontcover.

Phillips, Howard. "Influenza Pandemic." *1914–1918-Online International Encyclopedia of the First World War*, 2014. https://doi.org/10.15463/IE1418.10148.

Pratt, Alan R., ed. *The Critical Response to Andy Warhol*. Westport, CT: Greenwood Press, 1997.

Prekop, Rudo, and Michal Cihlář. *Andy Warhol a Československo* [Andy Warhol and Czechoslovakia]. 1st Czech/Slovak-language ed. Řevnice: Arbor Vitae, 2011.

Prekop, Rudo, and Michal Cihlář. *Andy Warhol and Czechoslovakia*. Abridged English-language ed. Revnice: Arbor Vitae, 2012.

Printz, Neil. "Other Voices, Other Rooms: Between Andy Warhol and Truman Capote, 1948–1961." PhD diss., City University of New York, 2000. ProQuest (9969720).

Puskás, Julianna. *From Hungary to the United States (1880–1914)*. Budapest: Akadémiai Kiadó, 1982.

Rácz, István. "Attempts to Curb Hungarian Emigration to the United States before 1914." *Angol Filológiai Tanulmányok/Hungarian Studies in English* 7 (1973): 5–33.

Richardson, John. *Sacred Monsters, Sacred Masters: Beaton, Capote, Dalí, Picasso, Freud, Warhol, and More*. New York: Random House, 2001.

Richardson, John. "The Secret Warhol: At Home with the Silver Shadow." *Vanity Fair*, July 1987. https://archive.vanityfair.com/article/1987/7/the-secret-warhol-at-home-with-the-silver-shadow.

Rizek, Barbara, Martin Rizek, and Joanne Medvecky. *The Financial District's Lost Neighborhood 1900–1970*. Portsmouth, NH: Arcadia, 2012.

Rossi-Wilcox, Susan. "Social Satire in the Guise of a Cookbook: Warhol's Wild Raspberries." In *Reading Andy Warhol: Author, Illustrator, Publisher*, ed. Nina Schleif, 156–65. Ostfildern: Hatje Cantz, 2013.

Rusinko, Elaine. "Andy and Julia in Rusyn: Warhol's Translation of His Mother in Film and Video." *Journal of Art Historiography* no. 26 (June 2022). https://arthistoriography.wordpress.com/wp-content/uploads/2022/05/6-rusinko.pdf.

Rusinko, Elaine. "Andy Warhol's Ancestry: Facts, Myths, and Mysteries." Academia. edu. https://www.academia.edu/38098098/Andy_Warhols_Ancestry_Facts_Myths_and_Mysteries.

Rusinko, Elaine. *Committing Community: Carpatho-Rusyn Studies as an Emerging Scholarly Discipline*. New York: Columbia University Press, 2009.

Rusinko, Elaine. "From the *Starŷi Krai* to the New World: Rusyn-American Literature." In *Committing Community: Carpatho-Rusyn Studies as an Emerging Scholarly Discipline*, 273–91. New York: Carpatho-Rusyn Research Center, 2009.

Rusinko, Elaine. "Was Andy Warhol Ukrainian? Carpatho-Rusyns and 'Ukrainianism' in Pittsburgh."

Accessed May 17, 2024. https://www.academia.edu/81496524/Was_Andy_Warhol_Ukrainian _Carpatho_Rusyns_and_Ukrainianism_in_Pittsburgh.

Rusinko, Elaine. "We Are All Warhol's Children: Andy and the Rusyns." *Carl Beck Papers in Russian and East European Studies* (2012): 16. http://carlbeckpapers.pitt.edu/ojs/index.php/cbp/article/ view/190.

Rusinko, Elaine. *Straddling Borders: Literature and Identity in Subcarpathian Rus'.* Toronto: University of Toronto Press, 2003.

Saint Mary's Byzantine Catholic Church (East Village). "Slavs of New York!" https://slavsofnewyork. tumblr.com/post/17111805681/st-marys-byzantine-catholic-church-east.

Saint Mary's Catholic Church of the Byzantine Rite." https://www.stmarybccnyc.org/home.html.

Scherman, Tony, and David Dalton. *Pop: The Genius of Andy Warhol.* New York: Harper Collins, 2009.

Schleif, Nina. "Carefully Unplanned: Books in Andy Warhol's Oeuvre." In Schleif, *Reading Andy Warhol,* 10–78.

Schleif, Nina. "Clever Frivolity in Excelsis: Warhol's Promotional Books." In Schleif, *Reading Andy Warhol,* 78–133.

Schleif, Nina, ed. *Reading Andy Warhol: Author, Illustrator, Publisher.* Ostfildern: Hatje Cantz, 2013.

Selavan, Ida Cohen. "Jewish Wage Earners in Pittsburgh, 1890–1930." *American Jewish Historical Quarterly* 65, no. 3 (1976): 272–85.

Semyonova Tian-Shanskaia, Olga, and David L. Ransel. *Village Life in Late Tsarist Russia.* Bloomington: Indiana University Press, 1993.

Shergold, Peter R. "Wage Rates in Pittsburgh during the Depression of 1908." *Journal of American Studies* 9, no. 2 (1975): 163–88.

Skrabec, Quentin R. *The World's Richest Neighborhood: How Pittsburgh's East Enders Forged American Industry.* New York: Algora, 2010.

Skrobucha, Heinz. *Icons in Czechoslovakia.* London: Hamlyn, 1971.

Slepcov, Igor. "K problematike I. svetovej vojny na východnom Slovensku v rokoch 1914–1915" [The First World War in Eastern Slovakia in 1914–1915]. *Historie a vojenství* 3 (1993): 55–78.

Smith, Patrick S. *Andy Warhol's Art and Films.* Ann Arbor, MI: UMI Research Press, 1986.

Smith, Patrick S., ed. *Warhol: Conversations about the Artist.* Ann Arbor, MI: UMI Research Press, 1988.

Stein, Howard F. "An Ethno-Historic Study of Slovak-American Identity." PhD diss., University of Pittsburgh, 1972.

Stein, Jean, and George Plimpton. *Edie: American Girl.* New York: Grove Press, 1994.

Steiner, Edward Alfred. *On the Trail of the Immigrant.* New York: Fleming H. Revell, 1906. https://www. gutenberg.org/files/40887/40887-h/40887-h.htm#page_213.

Steinmetz, Greg. "Slovaks Desperately Searching for Famous Countrymen." *Globe and Mail,* April 27, 1996. LexisNexis Universe: General News Topics.

Tavel, Ronald. *Andy Warhol's Ridiculous Screenplays.* Silverton, OR: Fast Books, 2015.

Thomas, Mary Ann. "Relatives Recall Visits to Uncle Andy's Home, His Early Art." *TribLive,* September 23, 2011. https://archive.triblive.com/news/relatives-recall-visits-to-uncle-andys-home-his-early- art/ .

Thomas, William Isaac, and Florian Znaniecki. *The Polish Peasant in Europe and America.* Edited and abridged by Eli Zaretsky. Urbana: University of Illinois Press, 1984.

Tunstall, Graydon A. *Blood on the Snow: The Carpathian Winter War of 1915.* Lawrence: University Press of Kansas, 2010.

Vecchiet, Jean-Michel. *Vies et morts d'Andy Warhol.* DVD. Eva Productions, 2005.

Walko, Ann. *Eternal Memory.* Pittsburgh, PA: Sterling House, 1999.

Warhol, Andy. *Andy and Sam Green on Phone Talk about Food Shopping.* CD. Audio Companion to the Andy Warhol Museum. Pittsburgh: Andy Warhol Museum, 1994.

Warhol, Andy. *Andy Warhol's Exposures.* Edited by Bob Colacello. New York: Arrow Books, 1980.

Warhol, Andy. *Holy Cats by Andy Warhol's Mother.* New York: Random House, 1987.

Warhol, Andy. *Julia Warhola in Bed, Talking.* VR.00.0025. *Factory Diaries,* ca. 1970. Andy Warhol Museum Archives (AWMA).

Warhol, Andy. *Julia Warhola in Bed, Talking, Sleeping.* VR.30.0015. *Factory Diaries,* ca. 1970. AWMA.

Warhol, Andy. *Julia Warhola in T-Shirt Sick.* VR.30.0024. *Factory Diaries,* 1970. AWMA.

Warhol, Andy. *The Andy Warhol Diaries.* Edited by Pat Hackett. New York: Warner Books, 1991.

Warhol, Andy. "On My Mind." *Vogue* 161, no. 2 (1973): 164–65.

Warhol, Andy. *The Philosophy of Andy Warhol (From A to B and Back Again).* Orlando, FL: Harcourt, 2006.

Warhol, Andy, and Suzie Frankfurt. *Wild Raspberries.* Boston: Bulfinch Press, 1997.

Warhol, Andy, and Pat Hackett. *POPism: The Warhol Sixties.* Orlando, FL: Harcourt, 2006.

Warhola, James. *Uncle Andy's: A Faabbbulous Visit with Andy Warhol.* New York: G. P. Putnam's, 2003.

Warhola, James. *Uncle Andy's Cats.* New York: G. P. Putnam's, 2009.

Warhola, John. "Čo povedali bratia o Andym" [What the brothers said about Andy]. In Bycko. *Nočné dialógy s Andym,* 78–81.

Warhola, John. Interview by Andrei Kritenko. *Forbes Ukraine* 7, July 1, 2014. forbes.net.ua.

Warhola, John. Oral history. Interview by Matt Wrbican. Tape recording, November 24, 2004. AWMA.

Watson, Steven. *Factory Made: Warhol and the Sixties.* New York: Pantheon Books, 2003.

Weinraub, Bernard. "Mothers." *Esquire,* November 1966, 96–101, 155–58. "Andy Warhol's Mother," 99, 101, 158.

Whelpley, James Davenport. *The Problem of the Immigrant.* New York: E. P. Dutton 1905.

Wilcock, John. *The Autobiography and Sex Life of Andy Warhol.* New York: Trela, 2010.

Williams, Gilda. "Warhol Stumbled across the Real America." Tate Etc. https://www.tate.org.uk/art/artists/andy-warhol-2121/andy-warhols-mother.

Worobec, Christine D. "Temptress or Virgin? The Precarious Sexual Position of Women in Postemancipation Ukrainian Peasant Society." *Slavic Review* 49, no. 2 (1990): 227–38.

Wrbican, Matt. "Meeooaaww-AW-AWW." In *Andy Warhol, Ai Weiwei,* ed. Max Delaney and Eric Shiner, 257–80. New Haven, CT: Yale University Press, 2016.

Wrbican, Matt, and Geralyn Huxley. *Andy Warhol Treasures.* London: Goodman, 2009.

Wyman, Mark. *Round-Trip to America: The Immigrants Return to Europe, 1880–1930.* Ithaca, NY: Cornell University Press, 1996.

Zaretsky, Eli. "Editor's Introduction." In Thomas and Znaniecki, *The Polish Peasant in Europe and America,* 1–53.

Illustration Credits

<table>
<tr><td>1.1</td><td>Reprinted from Zapomniane obrazy: Łemkowszczyzna w fotografiach Johna Masleya z lat 1923 i 1938 [The forgotten images: Lemkovyna in photographs of John Masley from the years 1923 and 1938], ed. Jerzy Starzyński (Legnica: Łemkowski Zespół Pieśni i Tańca Kyczera, Wydawnictwo Edytor, 2018), 160.</td></tr>
<tr><td>1.2</td><td>"Carpathian Rus,' 1919–1938." With Their Backs to the Mountains (Budapest: Central European University Press, 2015), 168. Reprinted with permission of the author Paul Robert Magocsi.</td></tr>
<tr><td>1.3</td><td>Frontispiece to the literary almanac, Greetings to the Rusyns for the Year 1851, compiled and published by Aleksander Dukhnovych. Photo courtesy of Paul R. Magocsi.</td></tr>
<tr><td>1.4</td><td>Photograph of the Zavacky family, published in Kentucky Monthly, December 1980, 2, no. 2, pp. 46–47, as part of story by Connie Schaber, "Divided We Stand: The Family in the 1980's." Courtesy Stephen M. Vest, President and Publisher of Kentucky Monthly.</td></tr>
<tr><td>1.5</td><td>Photograph by Robert Wanenchak Jr.</td></tr>
<tr><td>1.6</td><td>The Andy Warhol Museum, Pittsburgh; Founding Collection, Contribution The Andy Warhol Foundation for the Visual Arts, Inc.</td></tr>
<tr><td>1.7</td><td>Photo courtesy of Mary Anne Mistick.</td></tr>
<tr><td>1.8</td><td>Andy Warhol, Cow, 1966. © 2024 The Andy Warhol Foundation for the Visual Arts, Inc. / Licensed by Artists Rights Society (ARS), New York.</td></tr>
<tr><td>2.1</td><td>Red Row, photo courtesy the Butler County Historical Society.</td></tr>
<tr><td>2.2–2.3</td><td>Photograph of John Zavacky, his wife, and daughters, published in Peter Baycura, Lyndora Chronicles: The Legendary Decades, 1902–1921 (Butler, PA: John Baycura, 1998), 176.</td></tr>
<tr><td>2.4</td><td>"World War I in the Carpathians." With Their Backs to the Mountains (Budapest: Central European University Press, 2015), 192. Reprinted with permission of the author Paul Robert Magocsi.</td></tr>
<tr><td>3.1</td><td>Andy Warhol, Envelope (to Paul Warhola [Konstantin] from Mr. Andy Warhola, (not posted). Addressed by Julia Warhola, 1960s. The Andy Warhol Museum, Pittsburgh; Founding Collection, Contribution The Andy Warhol Foundation for the Visual Arts, Inc.</td></tr>
<tr><td>3.2</td><td>Passport (Julia Warhola), 1920. The Andy Warhol Museum, Pittsburgh; Founding Collection, Contribution The Andy Warhol Foundation for the Visual Arts, Inc.</td></tr>
<tr><td>3.3</td><td>Wing of the Largest Tenement in the District. Abraham Oseroff, "A Soho Hillside," Appendix II in Commons and Leisersing, Wage-Earning Pittsburgh, 1914, 407. Edward L. Bafford Photography Book Collection. Special Collections University of Maryland, Baltimore County.</td></tr>
<tr><td>3.4</td><td>A Hillside Battery of Disease. Abraham Oseroff, "A Soho Hillside," Appendix II in Commons and Leisersing, Wage-Earning Pittsburgh, 1914, 408. Edward L. Bafford Photography Book Collection. Special Collections University of Maryland, Baltimore County.</td></tr>
<tr><td>3.5</td><td>Tustin Street. Pittsburgh city photographer, October 13, 1921. Pittsburgh City Photographer Collection, Contribution University of Pittsburgh.</td></tr>
</table>

3.6   *Indiana Bell Building during Moving Process, 1930*. Bass Photo Co Collection, Indiana Historical Society.

3.7   *Newsletter (Indiana Telephone News, November 1930), 1930*. The John Warhola Family Collection.

3.8   Russian Brotherhood Organization of the USA (Collection 3035), The Historical Society of Pennsylvania. Photograph courtesy of Richard Custer.

3.9–3.11   Reprinted from *Golden Anniversary and Solemn Re-dedication of Newly Decorated St. John Chrysostom Greek Catholic Church, Nov. 26, 1960*. Unpaginated.

4.1–4.2   The Andy Warhol Museum, Pittsburgh; Founding Collection, Contribution The Andy Warhol Foundation for the Visual Arts, Inc.

4.3   Andy Warhol, *Living Room*, 1949. Courtesy of James Warhola. The Andy Warhol Foundation for the Visual Arts, Inc. / Licensed by Artists Rights Society (ARS), New York

4.4   Photograph by Elaine Rusinko.

4.5   Photo courtesy of James Warhola.

4.6–4.8   The Andy Warhol Museum, Pittsburgh; Founding Collection, Contribution The Andy Warhol Foundation for the Visual Arts, Inc.

4.9   Photograph courtesy of James Warhola.

5.1–5.2   Photographs by Haytham ad-Din.

5.3   The Andy Warhol Foundation for the Visual Arts, Inc. / Licensed by Artists Rights Society (ARS), New York

5.4   The Andy Warhol Museum, Pittsburgh; Founding Collection, Contribution The Andy Warhol Foundation for the Visual Arts, Inc.

5.5–5.6   The Andy Warhol Foundation for the Visual Arts, Inc. / Licensed by Artists Rights Society (ARS), New York

5.7–5.8   The Andy Warhol Museum, Pittsburgh; Founding Collection, Contribution The Andy Warhol Foundation for the Visual Arts, Inc.

5.9   Courtesy of James Warhola.

5.10–5.15 The Andy Warhol Museum, Pittsburgh; Founding Collection, Contribution The Andy Warhol Foundation for the Visual Arts, Inc.

5.16–5.19 Courtesy of James Warhola.

5.20   Andy Warhol, *Jesus Statue*, painted between 1938 and 1941. Courtesy of Jeffrey Warhola.

5.21–5.22 Andy Warhol, *The George Hamilton Story*, 1966, 16 mm. film, color, sound, 67 minutes. © The Andy Warhol Museum, Pittsburgh, PA, a museum of Carnegie Institute. All rights reserved. Video still courtesy of The Andy Warhol Museum.

6.1   Julia Warhola. Photo by Edward Wallowitch. ©2024 Wallowitch. All rights reserved.

6.2   Bezek family collection. Reprinted from Rudo Prekop and Michal Cihlář, *Andy Warhol a Československo*, 121.

6.3   Film still from *I Am from Nowhere*, dir. Georg Misch.

6.4–6.5   Bezek family collection. Reprinted from Rudo Prekop and Michal Cihlář, *Andy Warhol a Československo*, 145, 164.

7.1   Photograph by Stan Wolfson/Newsday LLC via Getty Images.

7.2   © Duane Michals. Courtesy of DC Moore Gallery. New York.

7.4–7.5   © 2024 The Andy Warhol Foundation for the Visual Arts, Inc./ Licensed by Artists Rights Society (ARS), New York.

8.2   Photograph by UA-Lora, Creative Commons, licensed under CC BY-SA 4.0.

Index